Oxford Studies in Social History
General Editor: Keith Thomas

On the Parish?

On the Parish?

The Micro-Politics of Poor Relief in Rural England c.1550–1750

STEVE HINDLE

CLARENDON PRESS · OXFORD

OXFORD
UNIVERSITY PRESS

Great Clarendon Street, Oxford OX2 6DP

Oxford University Press is a department of the University of Oxford.
It furthers the University's objective of excellence in research, scholarship,
and education by publishing worldwide in

Oxford New York

Auckland Bangkok Buenos Aires Cape Town Chennai
Dar es Salaam Delhi Hong Kong Istanbul Karachi Kolkata
Kuala Lumpur Madrid Melbourne Mexico City Mumbai Nairobi
São Paulo Shanghai Taipei Tokyo Toronto

Oxford is a registered trade mark of Oxford University Press
in the UK and in certain other countries

Published in the United States
by Oxford University Press Inc., New York

First published 2004

British Library Cataloguing in Publication Data
Data available

Library of Congress Cataloging in Publication Data
Data applied for

ISBN 0–19–927132–1

1 3 5 7 9 10 8 6 4 2

Typeset by Regent Typesetting, London
Printed in Great Britain
on acid-free paper by
Biddles Ltd,
King's Lynn, Norfolk

For Louise

ACKNOWLEDGEMENTS

On the Parish? was first planned in November 1994 when, in framing an application for a Warwick Research Fellowship in the Department of History at the University of Warwick, I was forced to think about how I might use the luxury of the six (yes, *six*!) years of research time that the job offered. Little did I suspect at that stage that I would actually have the chance to write the book, and I am immensely grateful to Patrick Collinson, John Walter, and Keith Wrightson, each of whom wrote so warmly on my behalf in support of that application; and to my colleagues at Warwick, especially Bernard Capp, Robin Clifton, Peter Marshall, Sarah Richardson, and Penny Roberts for making me feel so welcome after I was appointed. As it turned out, even six years was not enough to carry out the research for, let alone produce a draft of, a project of this size and ambition. Indeed, it was only in 2002–3, when I was awarded a term's leave under the Arts and Humanities Research Board Research Leave Scheme, to supplement the term for which I was eligible (rather than entitled!) from the University of Warwick, that I finally got the chance to hammer out a typescript. I am grateful both to the AHRB and to the university for the opportunity to do so. The final version does, however, incorporate the findings, in many respects radically reworked, of a number of 'trailer articles', published in *Past and Present*, the *Historical Journal*, *Rural History*, the *Transactions of the Royal Historical Society*, and *Cultural and Social History*.

My research has been conducted in a number of record repositories throughout England, and I am grateful for the kindness and patience of the staff of the National Archives (formerly the Public Record Office) at Kew; of the county record offices in Aylesbury, Bedford, Beverley, Carlisle, Chelmsford, Hertford, Lewes, Lincoln, Northampton, Norwich, Preston, Taunton, Trowbridge, Truro, Warwick, and Worcester; of the Shakespeare Birthplace Trust in Stratford-upon-Avon; and of the British Library, the Bodleian Library, Cambridge University Library, and Warwick University Library.

Numerous friends and colleagues have read drafts of parts of this book. Tom Arkell, Patrick Collinson, Heather Falvey, Adam Fox, Colin Jones, and John Walter all offered detailed and unfailingly constructive criticism on drafts of Chapters 1–3 and 5–6, each of which has been sharpened by their scrutiny. Keith Snell was kind enough not only to read Chapter 1 but also suggested the cover illustration. David Feldman made some very perceptive comments on Chapter 5 which helped clarify my reading of settlement just before the book went to press. Naomi Tadmor encouraged me to think again at a late stage about just how much my sources were telling me about what the rise of parish relief might have meant for family life and kinship relations. Two anonymous readers for Oxford University Press and (in his capacity as general editor of Oxford Studies in Social History) Sir Keith Thomas offered invaluable suggestions and encouragement at a time when I was beginning to think that completion of the project was beyond me. Ruth Parr has proved to be a very efficient and enthusiastic editor. Once again, however, I am beholden above all to Keith Wrightson. His role in helping frame the questions to which this book seeks answers will be apparent to all my readers. I am grateful for his willingness to read and comment on the whole typescript and, especially, to take a long hard look at Chapter 4 at the last minute.

All this is to say nothing of the numerous other friends who have been so generous over the years with references, suggestions, and criticisms. In this respect, this would be a much weaker book but for the kindness of John Broad, Christopher Brooks, Bernard Capp, Richard Connors, Mark Goldie, David Hayton, Joanna Innes, Peter King, Peter Marshall, John Morrill, Dave Rollison, Pamela Sharpe, Alex Shepard, Paul Slack, Richard Smith, Alannah Tomkins, Andy Wood, and Michael Zell. Some of these colleagues, and others too numerous to mention, have been in the audience at seminars and conferences—in Cambridge, Durham, Exeter, Hull, Manchester, Northampton, Oxford, Perth, Reading, Toronto, and Warwick—where versions of parts of several chapters were first rehearsed. I am sure that they will recognize the way their responses have shaped the argument in its final form.

Louise Hindle has lived with this book almost as long as she has lived with me. Without her enthusiasm, encouragement, and patience, *On the Parish?* would have been several years longer in the making. It is with love and gratitude, not least for keeping Thomas and Joseph from toddling into my study (and, sometimes—always the *right* times—for encouraging them just to barge their way in) in the long hot summer of 2003, that this book is dedicated to her.

S.H.

Kenilworth, October 2003

CONTENTS

ABBREVIATIONS

APC	*Acts of the Privy Council of England*, ed. J. R. Dasent, 32 vols. (London, 1890–1907)
BL	British Library, London
Bodl.	Bodleian Library, Oxford
CBS	Centre for Buckinghamshire Studies, Aylesbury
CRO	Cumbria Record Office, Carlisle
CUL	Cambridge University Library
ERO	Essex Record Office, Chelmsford
HALS	Hertfordshire Archives and Local Studies, Hertford
HMC	Historical Manuscripts Commission
LA	Lincolnshire Archives, Lincoln
LRO	Lancashire Record Office, Preston
NA	National Archives (formerly the Public Record Office), London
NRO	Northamptonshire Record Office, Northampton
RO	Record Office
SARS	Somerset Archives and Research Service, Taunton
SBTRO	Shakespeare Birthplace Trust Record Office, Stratford-upon-Avon
Slack, *Poverty and Policy*	Paul Slack, *Poverty and Policy in Tudor and Stuart England* (London and New York, 1988)
'The Book of Orders'	*Orders and Directions, Together With a Commission for the Better Administration of Justice and More Perfect Information of His Majestie* (London, 1630)
WCRO	Warwickshire County Record Office, Warwick
VCH	*Victoria County Histories*

Introduction: Poverty Beyond Public Policy

Those generally are to be deemed poore which cannot live without reliefe of the statute.

An Ease for Overseers of the Poore (1601)[1]

LIKE most monographs, this book stands in the shadow of a great one, in this case Paul Slack's seminal *Poverty and Policy in Tudor and Stuart England*, published in 1988. Slack was part of that generation of historians who, in the late 1960s, 1970s, and 1980s, effectively transformed the historiography of early modern poverty. The scholarly tradition that Slack and his contemporaries inherited was preoccupied with the study of statutory provision for the poor, and had only just begun to scratch the surface in analysing the implementation of national policy by local authorities.[2] Slack and others—including Peter Clark, Keith Wrightson, David Levine, John Walter, Lee Beier, and Tim Wales—were, however, the first historians to set early modern social policy in a more richly realized socio-economic context.[3] The findings of this phase of historiography, not only

[1] *An Ease for Overseers of the Poore: Abstracted from the Statutes* (Cambridge, 1601), 22. The statute referred to was, of course, 43 Elizabeth c. 2 (1601).

[2] E. M. Leonard, *The Early History of English Poor Relief* (Cambridge, 1900); S. and B. Webb, *English Local Government*, vol. vii: *English Poor Law History Part I: The Old Poor Law* (London, 1927); E. M. Hampson, *The Treatment of Poverty in Cambridgeshire, 1597–1834* (Cambridge, 1934). For a detailed rehearsal of the subsequent historiography of parish relief, see P. Fideler, 'Symposium: The Study of the Early Modern Poor and Poverty Relief. Introduction: Impressions of a Century of Historiography', *Albion*, 32 (2000), 381–407.

[3] P. Slack, 'Poverty and Politics in Salisbury, 1597–1666', and P. Clark, 'The Migrant in Kentish Towns, 1580–1640', both in P. Clark and P. Slack (eds.), *Crisis and Order in English Towns, 1500–1700: Essays in Urban History* (London, 1972), 164–203, 117–63; P. Clark, 'Migration in England during the Late Seventeenth and Early Eighteenth Centuries', repr. in P. Clark and D. Souden (eds.), *Migration and Society in Early Modern England* (London, 1987), 213–52; K. Wrightson and D. Levine, *Poverty and Piety in an English Village: Terling, 1525–1700* (1979; 2nd edn., Oxford, 1995); K. Wrightson, 'Two Concepts of Order: Justices, Constables and Jurymen in Seventeenth-Century England', and J. Walter, 'Grain Riots and Popular Attitudes to the Law: Maldon and the Crisis of 1629', both in J. Brewer and J. Styles (eds.), *An Ungovernable People: The English and their Law in the Seventeenth and Eighteenth Centuries* (London, 1980), 21–46, 47–84; T. Wales, 'Poverty, Poor Relief and the Life-Cycle: Some Evidence from Seventeenth-Century

the first to be influenced by the Thompsonian paradigm of 'history from below' but also the first to take advantage of the findings of historical demography, were creatively synthesized in *Poverty and Policy*. Slack's formidable achievement was to demonstrate the impact of sixteenth-century economic change—demographic increase, price inflation, the growth of a wage-earning sector in the economy, economic differentiation, social polarization—on both elite and popular perceptions of poverty. The traditional distinction between the *deserving* and the *undeserving* poor, originally fashioned in Scripture and refined by medieval theologians and Tudor humanists to the point where it attained the status of a moral orthodoxy, was shattered by the discovery of a third group of poor people whose predicament could not be explained by either their physical incapacity or their unwillingness to work.[4] In the great urban censuses of the late sixteenth century, local elites discovered the existence of the *labouring* poor, a sector of the population who were either unable to find work at all or too poorly paid for what little regular employment they could secure, to support themselves and their families.[5] This change in perception of the *nature and causes* of poverty was compounded in years of political crisis and/or harvest failure (1569–72, 1586–7, and, above all, 1594–7) by a growing awareness of its increasing *scale*, as even those who had once been charitable to their neighbours found themselves in need of relief.[6] It was, from this perspective, hardly surprising that the crisis of the 1590s, with its associated anxieties about vagrancy, theft, and insurrection, finally drove the last Elizabethan parliament into codifying that long series of sixteenth-century statutes, which had cumulatively sought to ameliorate the condition of the deserving poor and to punish the idle, to form a comprehensive programme of legislation that catered not only for the traditional categories of the poor (the impotent and the idle) but also for the under- and unemployed.[7]

The guiding principles of this legislation are a subject to which we will return, but it is important for the moment to recognize that *Poverty and Policy* was emphatically not simply an economic history of the causes of indigence in early modern England. Slack's sophisticated discussion of the timing of legislative initiatives was almost overshadowed by his brilliant analysis of the institutional and intellectual context from which they emerged. The roles of Christian humanism and of Protestant conceptions of charity, of projectors seeking political patronage and of Puritan MPs salving their godly consciences, took their place in Slack's

Norfolk', in R. M. Smith (ed.), *Land, Kinship and Life-Cycle* (Cambridge, 1984), 351–404; A. L. Beier, *Masterless Men, the Vagrancy Problem in England, 1560–1640* (London, 1985).

[4] Slack, *Poverty and Policy*, 17–36.

[5] Ibid. 73–9.

[6] Ibid. 48–53.

[7] Ibid. 122–37.

vision alongside the increasing desire of the Elizabethan regime to vindicate its paternalistic credentials at a time when the social order was perceived to be especially fragile.[8] From this perspective, Slack's account of policy formation disclosed the vibrancy of the political culture from which it emerged and demonstrated that the poor laws were above all a *political* achievement, providing a framework on which the social policy of the English state was based from 1598 to 1834.

If the strongest dimensions of *Poverty and Policy* were its analyses of the nature and timing of the Elizabethan poor laws, it also took very seriously the problems experienced by central and local government in securing compliance with the legislative programme in the provinces. Indeed, it was part of Slack's agenda to demonstrate that local experiment had often provided the model on which the legislation itself was designed, and it was therefore little surprise to him that local elites should modify and adapt those parts of the social policy agenda which suited their requirements and discard those which did not.[9] He was, therefore, able to reconstruct, on the one hand, the 'growth of welfare' as statutory provision for the poor gradually became the norm across Stuart England; and, on the other, the problems associated with 'controlling the machine' as the costs of providing relief spiralled in the closing years of the seventeenth century.[10] Although Slack was sceptical that, without the secular trend of economic growth that enabled substantial transfers of wealth from large numbers of respectable householders to the poor, the poor laws could, in and of themselves, have ameliorated the condition of the poor as a class, he nonetheless conceded that the welfare machine alleviated poverty for a substantial proportion of the population.[11]

Poverty and Policy is a book with which several generations of students of poverty have now become familiar but one whose putative status as a textbook has arguably prevented it from receiving the recognition it deserves as a highly original piece of scholarship.[12] In fact, Slack's own research interests gave *Poverty and Policy* a very distinctive shape. As its title indicated, one of Slack's principal concerns (and one of his major achievements) was to reconstruct the political and intellectual archaeology of national poor law policy, an agenda to which he subsequently returned in analysing the discourses that gave rise to both 'policy and projects'.[13] Less obvious, however, was the fact that Slack's long-standing

[8] Ibid. 114–22.

[9] Ibid. 148–61.

[10] Ibid. 162–87, 188–204.

[11] Ibid. 207–8.

[12] K. Wrightson, *English Society, 1580–1680* (London, 1982), arguably fits into the same influential category for similar reasons.

[13] P. Slack, *From Reformation to Improvement: Public Welfare in Early Modern England* (1999). Cf. Slack, *Poverty and Policy*, 138–61.

interest in the history of towns meant that, although he was determined to reveal the speed and spread with which the Elizabethan statutes were implemented in the provinces, the local dimensions of *Poverty and Policy* were notably urban in focus.[14] To be sure, the prominence of major towns in Slack's account arguably reflects both the experiences of those urban communities in which the relief system was pioneered and where it is usually thought to have been implemented most effectively and (in turn) the biases of the documentary record. But it left three avenues of the history of the old poor law unexplored, each of which this book sets out to investigate.

In the first place, as the question mark in its title indicates, *On the Parish?* is written in the recognition that *poor relief* and *parish relief* were not necessarily synonymous. It takes very seriously the implications of the finding that those 'in need', the 'conjunctural poor', constituted a much larger proportion of the population (perhaps 20 per cent on average) than those on relief, the 'structural poor' (as few as 5 per cent in most parishes).[15] It accordingly emphasizes the difficult and often desperate plight of that 'penumbral' sector of parish populations whose indigence was not rewarded by receipt of a parish pension, or 'collection' as it was more commonly called.[16] It pays very considerable attention to the other resources, both human and environmental, on which the needy perforce drew as they struggled to make ends meet. In turn, it recognizes that, until almost the end of the seventeenth century (and arguably even thereafter), parish provision for that tiny minority who were fortunate enough to be on regular relief was in and of itself insufficient to support the needs of an indigent family. It therefore seeks to reconstruct the networks of informal support with which collection was necessarily supplemented, in turn raising questions about the place of parish relief in the 'hierarchy of resort' of which survival strategies were composed.

Second, as its subtitle indicates, *On the Parish?* is conceived as a book about the *micro-politics* of poor relief, and proceeds on the assumption that

[14] Cf. Slack, 'Poverty and Politics in Salisbury'; *Poverty in Early Stuart Salisbury*, ed. P. Slack (Wiltshire Record Society 31, Devizes, 1975); P. Slack, 'Great and Good Towns, 1540–1700', in P. Clark (ed.), *The Cambridge Urban History of Britain*, vol. ii: *1540–1840* (Cambridge, 2000), 347–76.

[15] Slack, *Poverty and Policy*, 39–41, 65–6. Cf. A. L. Beier, 'Poverty and Progress in Early Modern England', in A. L. Beier *et al.* (eds.), *The First Modern Society: Essays in English History in Honour of Lawrence Stone* (Cambridge, 1989), 207.

[16] M. J. Braddick and J. Walter, 'Introduction: Grids of Power: Order, Hierarchy and Subordination in Early Modern Society', in eid. (eds.), *Negotiating Power in Early Modern Society: Order, Hierarchy and Subordination in Britain and Ireland* (Cambridge, 2001), 33. This group almost certainly corresponds to those who were exempt from the hearth taxes of the 1660s and 1670s, excepting those who were actually on relief. Cf. Ch. 4.4 below.

statutory prescription was not invariably reflected in, and indeed was frequently modified by, social practice. Although it is by definition based to a significant degree on institutional archives and is intimately concerned with institutional culture, it does not directly engage with institutions themselves. It is, rather, concerned with the impact of various practices of poor relief upon the quality of social relations both within and, to a lesser extent, between parishes. Because this book has been written against the background of the exhaustive and illuminating research (carried out by Slack in particular, but also by many others across a century of historiographical development from E. M. Leonard to Joanna Innes) on legislation and conciliar policy, it is freed both to focus on the decision-making process transacted in those 'micro-sociologies of power' which permeated the lower rungs of the administrative hierarchy and to enhance scholarly understanding of the negotiations to which poor relief gave rise in the 'politics of the parish'.[17]

Third, as its subtitle also announces, *On the Parish?* is primarily concerned with rural communities (though also to a lesser extent with small market towns), in which the overwhelming majority of the population still lived even at the end of our period. This study is intended to redress the balance of a scholarly literature which, partly due to Slack's own reluctance to emphasize the extent of his urban focus, has tended to privilege the experience of towns.[18]

To an extent, therefore, the account of *parish* relief offered here builds upon, rather than contests, Slack's contribution. To be sure, some of its findings (on the chronology of the assessment and collection of parish rates, for instance, and on the effectiveness of the 1697 badging statute) significantly revise, and in some respects challenge outright, Slack's conclusions.[19] At the same time, moreover, it recognizes the significance of several provisions of the Elizabethan poor laws (the kinship obligation clause, for example, and the requirement that overseers should bind out as apprentices the children of poor labouring parents who were thought

[17] Leonard, *Early History of English Poor Relief*; J. Innes, 'Parliament and the Shaping of Eighteenth-Century English Social Policy', *Transactions of the Royal Historical Society*, 5th ser., 40 (1990), 63–92; Innes, 'The State and the Poor: Eighteenth-Century England in European Perspective', in J. Brewer and E. Hellmuth (eds.), *Rethinking Leviathan: The Eighteenth-Century State in Britain and Germany* (Oxford, 1999), 225–80. Cf. Braddick and Walter, 'Introduction: Grids of Power', 39; K. Wrightson, 'The Politics of the Parish in Early Modern England', in P. Griffiths *et al.* (eds.), *The Experience of Authority in Early Modern England* (London and New York, 1996), 22.

[18] E. A. Wrigley, 'Urban Growth and Agricultural Change: England and the Continent in the Early Modern Period', repr. in id., *People, Cities and Wealth: The Transformation of Traditional Society* (Oxford, 1987), 163 (table 7.2), estimates that even in 1750 only 21% of the population lived in towns of more than 5,000 inhabitants.

[19] See Chs. 4.1 and 5.5 below.

unable to support them) that are almost invisible in *Poverty and Policy*.[20] This is to say nothing of the extensive treatment offered here, for which there is no equivalent in Slack's work, of the worlds of informal and semi-formal relief, the survival strategies of those who were made, or preferred, to remain independent of the parish. *On the Parish?* is therefore in some respects a companion volume to *Poverty and Policy*: the earlier book liberates this one from the obligation to be fully comprehensive, enabling it to focus on areas which are not strongly represented in the existing historiography. From one perspective, this is a strength, but it is also a weakness, for the reader unfamiliar with that historiography, especially as it stood when Slack crystallized it in 1988, will be at a disadvantage in reading this book.

So much then for the extent to which *On the Parish?* is much less than a general survey of the implementation of social policy. There are a number of ways, however, in which it seeks, at the same time, to be much more. The analytical imperative of this book is that the micro-politics of poor relief, the local negotiations that took place over the allocation of resources between the prosperous and the needy, have not received anything like comprehensive treatment in the historiography of poverty. This omission is all the more remarkable given that the principal issue on which micro-politics of this kind turned—the obligations and responsibilities which existed not only between rich and poor but also between neighbours—must be regarded as fundamental to an understanding of the nature and quality of social relations in this period. More specifically, one of the central themes of this book is the interplay between, on the one hand, the enduring notion that householders had a social and religious duty to exercise charity towards the poor, and, on the other, the developing sense that the indigent had a *right* to expect relief of this kind. In exploring the 'popular acculturation of entitlement', the social process through which the poor came to believe that they had a moral, perhaps even a legal, claim on the charity of their betters and (in time) of the parish, the discussion will extend beyond the analysis of the minutiae of poor law administration into the reconstruction of conflicting discourses over the responsibilities and obligations which existed between the propertied and the propertyless as they were rehearsed across thousands of local communities.

Analysis of this kind raises questions of both prescription and practice, examining not only the forms of provision for the poor made by kin, by neighbours, by charity trustees, and by parish officers (and the interest groups—ratepayers, settled parishioners—they represented) but also the

[20] See Chs. 1.3 and 3.2 below.

official directives and quasi-official exhortations by which such forms were determined and which they occasionally subverted or even resisted. This approach has been shaped by the conviction that analysis of provision for the poor might help answer a number of those fundamental questions with which historians of English social relations are currently preoccupied: changing attitudes to riches, idleness, and poverty; the extent of popular use of the law; the social and political role of the 'middling sort'; the nature of the relationship between governors and governed; and the extent of social solidarity in the local community. *On the Parish?* is intended to stimulate fresh thinking on this range of questions by exploring relatively new and distinctive fields of enquiry, especially the relationships between informal, semi-formal, and formal networks of care, and by approaching the subject in a way that is both geographically broad and thematically inclusive. It seeks to demonstrate not only that the nature and scale of provision for the poor is a useful index of social and cultural change, but that a persistent concern with the parameters of eligibility for, and entitlement to, various forms of relief did a very great deal to fashion the distinctive shape of rural social relations. In turn, its suggests that the analysis of parish relief helps us to identify the processes of inclusion and exclusion through which local communities were constructed, sustained, and ultimately absorbed into a national political culture.[21]

The source materials for this study are, of necessity, diverse, eclectic, and both regionally and locally uneven. They include parish records (overseers', churchwardens', and charity trustees' accounts, and vestry minutes) in a large number of counties (but most intensively in Buckinghamshire, Essex, Hertfordshire, Lincolnshire, Somerset, and Warwickshire); printed treatises and sermons; official injunctions, articles, and visitations, with their attendant court records; statutes and proclamations; the records of central government, of assize circuits, and of quarter sessions (especially for Cumberland and Lancashire, in addition to the printed calendars for numerous other counties); and gentry papers (estate archives and administrative records). Although the book is, therefore, intended as a national survey, it is perforce attuned to the issues of regional particularity and economic and cultural difference. Indeed, one of its principal arguments is that the fundamental strength of the welfare system that spread across rural England in the early seventeenth century lay in its paradoxical ability to reconcile the statutory requirements of national policies on assessment, disbursement, and audit with

[21] Cf. P. Collinson, '*De Republica Anglorum*: Or History with the Politics Put Back', in id., *Elizabethan Essays* (London, 1994), 26–7.

the widely divergent practices of exhortation, collection, and charity that pre-existed across 9,000-odd parishes. Local ecologies of relief were ultimately, sometimes painfully, subsumed within a national administrative system.

The structure of *On the Parish?*, as seems appropriate for a study seeking to characterize the nature and quality of social relations, is thematic. It nonetheless employs an overarching narrative scheme, which is itself governed by the spread of formal welfare provision. Parish relief, and especially the provision of cash pensions for the impotent poor, was the developing backdrop against which the discourses and practices of charity discussed in the other chapters must be understood. The institutionalization of relief also accounts for the broad chronological parameters of the book, which loosely stretch from the first mid-sixteenth-century attempts to appoint officers ('collectors') who would be responsible for the relief of the poor in each parish to the early eighteenth-century initiatives to restrict the scale of out-relief under the terms of the workhouse test. Indeed, one of the many paradoxes of the parish relief system is that although its limited resources ensured that it could never be anything like central to the survival strategies of the overwhelming majority of the indigent, its archives contain by far the most significant evidence available to those historians who seek to penetrate the obscure world of informal relief. This is most obviously true of those formal petitions for pensions which, when read against the grain, disclose the ways—the exploitation of the perquisites of field, forest, and fen; the accumulation and forgiveness of debt; the kindness of kin and neighbours—in which prospective recipients of relief had struggled to survive until they could no longer avoid the shame of a public request for aid.[22] It is also, however, true of the more laconic testimony of overseers' accounts themselves, in which both the tiny number of regular recipients and the relatively small (though gradually increasing) sums they were paid indicate that the significance of parish relief can be understood only in the context of an enduring reliance on informal and semi-formal networks of support.[23]

Other than to introduce briefly the terms of the Elizabethan statutes, therefore, it would make little sense to begin the analysis of the micro-politics of relief with the significance of 'collection'. Indeed, the running theme of the book, that receipt of a parish pension was only the final (and by no means the inevitable) stage in a protracted process of negotiation between prospective pensioners (or 'collectioners', as they came to be called) and parish officers, is itself reflected in a series of chapters whose

[22] Cf. Chs. 1 and 6 below. For the significance of the much less commonly surviving petitions to charity trustees, see Ch. 2.6 below.

[23] See Ch. 4.3 below.

sequence seeks to mirror the experience of indigence, moving gradually (and by stages) from the world of informal support into the poor relief system. Each chapter therefore offers a specific narrative of social, political, and legal change. As the scope of the project is much wider than a consideration of the evolution of, and immediate reactions to, public policy, it eschews an unproblematic linear approach for one that allows the development and elaboration of a number of thematic narratives. The book therefore begins by analysing the significance of reliance on the casual support provided by kin and neighbours; continues by discussing the development of habits of dependence among those who drew upon semi-formal doles and endowed charity; and culminates in an exploration of the experience of labour discipline under the governance of the civil parish.

Accordingly, the first chapter, 'Shift', rehearses the historiography of informal relief strategies in the early modern period, emphasizing the significant impact on the scholarship of Keith Thomas's allusion to the 'tradition of mutual help' and, perhaps more significantly, of Olwen Hufton's concept of the 'economy of makeshifts', first developed in her seminal *The Poor of Eighteenth-Century France* (Oxford, 1974). It discusses the relative and enduring significance of four specific aspects of informal relief in the parishes of rural England: the exploitation of common right; the support of kin; the kindness of neighbours; and the resort to 'crimes of necessity'. It suggests that, even though parish relief eventually did spread across rural England during the course of the early modern period, there was no inevitable transition from informal to formal care, and that even at the end of the period those in receipt of parish pensions perforce supplemented their collection with a wide range of income generated from other sources, especially the informal and quasi-formal networks of charity. The second chapter, 'Dole', reconstructs the texture and significance of semi-formal relief in rural parishes by analysing the contribution of alms, doles, and endowments to the relief of the poor. It emphasizes the resilience of private charitable initiatives, which were never entirely 'crowded out' by formal relief; discusses the influence of the frequently restrictive criteria of eligibility for charity on the demeanour of would-be recipients; and analyses the strategies of those who sought to gain access to the perquisites of endowments.

The third chapter, 'Work', recognizes the often neglected emphasis on labour and employment schemes in the Elizabethan relief statutes; explains the problems which led to the abandonment of experiments to set the poor on work in rural parishes; suggests that the imperative to labour discipline enshrined in the legislation was rather more successfully met by apprenticing the children of the labouring poor than by setting their parents on work; and reconstructs the attitudes of children, parents, parish officers, magistrates, and employers to this often controversial project. The fourth chapter, 'Collection', measures the spread of formal parish relief across rural England, emphasizing geographical variation, and reconstructing in particular the differential patterns of provision both between regions and between parishes within regions. It assesses the relative contributions of permanent and casual relief, and the motives for, and significance of, the giving of relief in kind, especially in the form of medical care, rent, fuel, and clothing.

The fifth chapter, 'Exclusion', explores the thresholds of belonging set by ratepayers and parish officers in deciding how eligibility for relief should be decided, and reconstructs the techniques they deployed in ridding themselves of prospective burdens. It emphasizes the tensions between the Elizabethan poor laws and the 1589 statute regulating the accommodation of inmates and lodgers; discusses the significance of marriage as a process through which poor strangers might be identified and excluded; and reconstructs the variables that might explain why some poor migrants were assimilated to, and others marginalized from, the community of the parish. The sixth chapter, 'Negotiation', recognizes that parish pensioners were only ever a tiny proportion of those who considered themselves indigent, and explores the predicament of the penumbral poor who were in need and not on relief. It reconstructs in detail the strategies of prospective pensioners in seeking relief from parish officers and appealing against those decisions that went against them. It concludes with an analysis of the implementation of the policy of shaming the poor of the parish under the statute of 1697, emphasizing the changing and ambiguous semiotics of badging pensioners, even (perhaps especially) those who were thought to be deserving.

As will be apparent from this brief rehearsal of the structure of the book, *On the Parish?* is intimately concerned with the provisions of the Elizabethan poor laws, and it is therefore fitting that a brief reiteration of those provisions and of the evidence they generated should draw this introduction to a close. The corpus of legislation with which all the following chapters are, to a greater or lesser extent, concerned was formulated over the course of the sixteenth century, but it received its decisive expression in three stages.[24] An act of 1572 represented a

[24] The best summary is Slack, *Poverty and Policy*, 122–31, esp. 124–6. The following discussion artificially ignores the treatment of vagrancy, for which see C. S. L. Davies, 'Slavery and Protector Somerset: The Vagrancy Act of 1547', *Economic History Review*, 2nd ser., 19 (1966), 533–49; Beier, *Masterless Men*, 146–70.

significant break with the pre-existing tradition of voluntary collections by introducing the principle of compulsion in the assessment and collection of rates.[25] In each of the divisions in the counties where they were in commission, justices of the peace were required to survey the poor and then to 'tax and assess' all inhabitants to provide for them. In turn overseers, who were to conduct monthly inspections to exclude strangers from the dole, were to be appointed in each parish. The statute had some significant structural weaknesses. The division of responsibility between magistrates and overseers was ambiguous, and the hierarchy of authority, and especially of accountability, was confused. Magistrates inevitably found it difficult to survey the poor and institute rates in the numerous parishes of which their divisions were composed, with the result that provision remained haphazard.

It was not until the statute of 1598 that these ambiguities were resolved.[26] This act placed responsibility for the administration of relief firmly on the shoulders of churchwardens and overseers of the poor in every parish. They were to assess and collect rates 'by taxation of every inhabitant and every occupier of lands'. Begging was prohibited, unless licensed by the parish officers, and the assumption appears to have been that such licences would be granted rarely and reluctantly. The statute required overseers to provide outdoor relief for the 'impotent' poor, but it should be emphasized that pensions in cash or in kind were considered a last resort, to be distributed only in genuine cases of impotence, and only after the family circumstances of the indigent had been inspected. If lineal kin (parents, children, or grandparents) were in a position to contribute to the maintenance of their relatives, then parish relief would be denied. Even where such family support was unforthcoming, however, the act was careful to define 'impotence' in terms not of age or sickness but of the incapacity to contribute to one's own living through labour. In other words, the statute assumed that the first call on the stock raised by parish rates would be working materials on which the deserving poor, even the elderly and the sick, might be set on work. In addition, although it is often assumed that one of the fundamental principles of the statute was the provision of work for the under- and unemployed, it should be noted that overseers were first required to reduce the burden of expenditure among poor labouring families by binding out their children apprentice. Only in those cases where children had been exported to more prosperous households, or where they were too young to be apprenticed,

[25] 14 Elizabeth I, c. 5 (1572).

[26] 39 Elizabeth, c. 3 (1598). The statute is most conveniently available in *Tudor Economic Documents*, ed. R. H. Tawney and E. Power, 3 vols. (London, 1924), ii. 346–54.

would work or relief be provided for those who were considered to be overburdened with children. The role of magistrates, who had been the workhorses of relief under the terms of the 1572 statute, was drastically reduced, their responsibilities being confined to those of audit, supervision, and arbitration. Responsibility for the administration of relief therefore devolved upon men of more humble status, though doubtless those chosen overseers were the 'better sort' of the inhabitants of the parish, as contemporaries understood that term. The legislation finally reached its definitive form in 1601 in a statute which enshrined all the key provisions of the 1598 act but quietly (so quietly, in fact, that many contemporaries entirely failed to notice) closed the loophole through which begging might be permitted.[27]

This, then, was the legal code that governed parish relief over the following two centuries or so. The hierarchy of provision envisaged by the MPs who had drafted the legislation was clear—in descending order of significance: kin support, working materials, parish apprenticeship, weekly collection. This is not, of course, to say that this order of priority was necessarily reflected in the preferences of those who administered relief on the ground. Indeed, the presiding narrative of parish relief is one in which the most expensive option, the provision of cash pensions, gradually came to the fore across the seventeenth century. It is also true that the relatively clear parameters of provision dictated by those who drafted the statutes were policed by more technical clauses in the legislation: on the identification of those children who were most suitable to be bound apprentice; on the length of residence which might render an indigent person eligible for relief; on the procedure through which a claimant for relief might make his or her needs known. These technicalities will be introduced in detail in those later chapters where they are immediately relevant to the discussion at hand, a decision which, it is hoped, will make even more sense when it becomes clear that the controversies generated by these ambiguous clauses necessitated intervention by the judiciary.[28] Indeed, the significance of the role of the judiciary in interpreting the poor laws should be emphasized at the outset. Although it might seem surprising that the poor laws went in all essentials unreformed throughout the seventeenth century, the absence of any very significant parliamentary amendment is at least partly to be explained by the fact that the judges, both on circuit and in King's Bench, were so regularly called upon to interpret the statutes. As in so many other aspects

[27] 43 Elizabeth I, c. 2 (1601).

[28] See, respectively, Chs. 3.2, 5.1, and 6.4 below.

of English governance, the judiciary played a decisive role not only in administering but also effectively in remaking poor law policy.[29]

It has become conventional in recent discussion of poor relief to emphasize the historical problem of defining and identifying the poor, difficulties which are thrown into even greater relief by the apparent ease with which sixteenth- and seventeenth-century policy-makers, using a process of 'progressive binary division', sorted them into approved categories: impotent and idle, deserving and undeserving, settled and vagrant.[30] It is, as we have seen, clear that a far greater proportion of the population were in need than were ever on relief, and, furthermore, that indigence was itself, to some extent at least, a life-cyclical problem.[31] There are, accordingly, profound problems in deploying the label 'the poor' to describe in any meaningful sense a constituency whose composition was shifting both in reality and in perception. This difficulty is compounded by the migration of meaning of the noun 'pauper', a term which is conventionally used by historians to refer to those in receipt of parish relief, but which in fact only acquired that meaning in the late eighteenth century. In the sixteenth century, a 'pauper' was a person destitute of property or means of livelihood; one who had no means, or who was dependent upon the charity of others; a beggar. This position might well shade into, but was certainly not synonymous with, that of the 'pensioner' or 'collectioner' who was in regular receipt of parish relief.[32] *On the Parish?* is emphatically not concerned only with those on relief (or 'in collection', as the overseers' accounts of the period have it). It assumes that the poor law 'reached beyond the relatively small numbers of the poor actually in receipt of pensions and affected the much larger groups immediately above them in the social hierarchy who were potentially dependent on poor relief', in other words that it influenced the economic and moral conduct not only of *collectioners* but also of *paupers*.[33] 'The poor', then, were not simply 'those which cannot live without reliefe of the statute', whatever the anonymous author of *An Ease for Overseers of the Poore* might argue, or at least not in the narrow sense of those who were actually relieved by the parish.[34] If anything, 'the poor' were, to use a particularly resonant and ambiguous seventeenth-century term, those 'likely to become chargeable': in other words all those families who

29 See Chs. 3.2(*b*) and 6.4(*b*) below.

30 Slack, *Poverty and Policy*, 2–5; P. Collinson, 'Puritanism and the Poor', in R. Horrox and S. Rees-Jones (eds.), *Pragmatic Utopias: Ideals and Communities, 1200–1630* (Cambridge, 2001), 244.

31 Wales, 'Poverty, Poor Relief and the Life-Cycle', 360–9.

32 *OED*, sub 'pauper'.

33 Braddick and Walter, 'Introduction: Grids of Power', 33.

34 *An Ease for Overseers of the Poore*, 22.

supported themselves by their labour, whom early eighteenth-century commentators would christen the 'labouring poor'. They, and their ambiguous relationships with the parish relief system, are the principal subjects of this book.

It is, finally, almost *de rigueur* in an introduction of this kind to emphasize the blind spots of the project. *On the Parish?* certainly has them. Although begging is one of its central concerns, it has little or nothing to say about vagrancy, and concerns itself mainly with mendicancy amongst the known neighbourhood poor.[35] Its treatment of other items on the social policy agenda is highly selective: the absence of any discussion of houses of correction, for example, is thrown into greater relief by the analysis of the impact of parish workhouses on the scale of out-relief in the early eighteenth-century parish.[36] Similarly, although it reconstructs the fit between certain planks of policy (co-ordinated almsgiving and parish relief, for instance, or the licensing of cottages and the provision of habitation for the poor), it accepts that the regulation of the grain markets, which arguably remained far more significant than the 'transfer payments' made under the poor law at least until the 1630s, has been so well rehearsed in the recent scholarship that it requires no further discussion here.[37] Most obviously, no explicit narrative of economic change is offered here, partly for reasons of space, and partly because the changing intensity of the birth pangs of market culture has been so recently and so powerfully evoked in Keith Wrightson's *Earthly Necessities*, an economic history of early modern Britain which gives the reader pause to wonder how those who supported themselves by wages ever managed to put food on the table or pay the rent. In their own terms, these men and women 'lived by the providence of God: the employment they found was so precarious and uncertain they could not give it a name'.[38] Whenever they did attempt such a description, however, their preferred idiom was to explain that they made 'shift'.

[35] Cf. P. Slack, 'Vagrants and Vagrancy in England, 1598–1664', repr. in Clark and Souden (eds.), *Migration and Society*, 49–76; Beier, *Masterless Men*; J. R. Kent, 'Population Mobility and Alms: Poor Migrants in the Midlands during the Early Seventeenth Century', *Local Population Studies*, 27 (1981), 35–51.

[36] J. Innes, 'Prisons for the Poor: English Bridewells, 1555–1800', in F. Snyder and D. Hay (eds.), *Labour, Law and Crime: An Historical Perspective* (London, 1987), 42–122. Cf. Ch. 3.1 below.

[37] See Chs. 2.2 and 4.1 below; and cf. P. Slack, 'Books of Orders: The Making of English Social Policy, 1577–1631', *Transactions of the Royal Historical Society*, 5th ser., 30 (1980), 1–22; Slack, *Poverty and Policy*, 138–48; Slack, 'Dearth and Social Policy in Early Modern England', *Social History of Medicine*, 5 (1992), 1–17; Slack, *From Reformation to Improvement*, 61–5.

[38] K. Wrightson, *Earthly Necessities: Economic Lives in Early Modern Britain* (New Haven, 2000), 313.

I
Shift

Whereas Right honourable and Worshipful we Combers have petition'd unto Mr Smyth's Worship last fryday for worke & he told us that our townsmen had p[ro]missed him that we should have worke but it proufe noe such matter for I have asked both the towns-men & the Overseers & and they regard not my complaint & [I] have not had half worke Enough sinc[e] Witsentide & my Charg[e] is soe great that I can make shift noe longer for I have 5 Cheldren to keep & I had much adoue to keep them when I had worke Enough & I have made all the Shift that I can. For my owne parte I have never chargd the towne for a penny, not soe I desire now but Crave work of them to mayntaine my Charg[e]. I never took noe lewed course for to rong any man nor yet Rune about the Country as others have done as it is well knowne that some went for Corne to the sea sid[e] & tooke it by violen[ce]. Some again ran up to London beagging. I never stand [?idle] but kept my worke & it is nothing els which now I crave to maintain my Charg[e] that I may not take noe unlawfull co[u]rse for it is hard to starve Job saieth, since for skin & all that a man hath he will give for his life.

Petition of Richard Hammond of Bocking (Essex), *c.*1636–7[1]

LIKE so many of his contemporaries across rural England, Richard Hammond was wage-dependent yet found it difficult to maintain his family even when he was fully employed. Without regular work, more-over, he found it impossible even to improvise a living. He was, nonethe-less, as reluctant in 1637 as he had been throughout his life to ask for parish relief and in his direst need sought employment rather than charity from the overseers of the town. He had never, he insisted, succumbed to the temptations of riot, theft, or begging and claimed that he would starve rather than break the law.

[1] ERO, D/DEb/7/4, cited in J. Walter, *Understanding Popular Violence in the English Revolution: The Colchester Plunderers* (Cambridge, 1999), 237. The biblical allusion is to Job 2: 4–5: 'Skin for skin, Satan replied, a man will give you all he has for his own life. But stretch out your hand and strike his flesh and bones and he will surely curse you to your face'.

Exactly how Richard Hammond and thousands like him kept body and soul together in such straitened circumstances without either falling upon the parish or turning to crime is the central theme of this chapter.[2] Hammond himself offers few clues as to how this question might be answered, for his own characterization of the strategies which had enabled him to survive a career of under-employment, let alone one critically punctuated by a period altogether without work, is couched in terms so vague as to be almost euphemistic. He had, he argued, 'made all the shift' he could but now could 'make shift noe longer'. While Hammond was clear that, for him at least, 'shift' did not include begging, theft, or riot, he remains silent as to the nature of the resourcefulness that shift might imply. So what exactly was 'shift' and what did it mean to make it?[3] In answering these questions, however, other related problems will be raised which will be running themes throughout this book, not the least of which are the vexed issues of why men like Hammond should have been so reluctant to claim parish relief, how they survived for so long without it, and how they might react if it was denied them.

There has been a distinguished tradition within the historiography of English welfare practices, dating back to Leonard, the Webbs, and Hampson, which sought to analyse the administration of parish relief.[4] The exploration of the informal relief strategies implied by 'making shift' is, however, of rather more recent provenance. In part, the reluctance of the first generation of historians of welfare to engage with the other systems of support available to the poor arose from their uncertainty about how such casual networks might be researched and analysed. The general, but unspoken, assumption that there was a hidden world of informal expedients which would for ever lie beyond historical reconstruction was crystallized in Keith Thomas's allusive but characteristically suggestive recognition of the central role in the maintenance of the elderly and infirm played by the neighbourly 'tradition of mutual

[2] Cf. P. Clark, 'The Migrant in Kentish Towns, 1580–1640', in P. Clark and P. Slack (eds.), *Crisis and Order in English Towns, 1500–1700: Essays in Urban History* (London, 1972), 144 ('few honest poor can have survived').

[3] The *OED* suggests significant changes in the sense of the verb 'to shift' across the 16th and 17th centuries: its original meaning, 'to make a living by one's own devices' or 'to shift for oneself', can be traced in the 1510s and 1520s. By 1673, however, it had come to mean managing 'with something inferior or without something desirable'. Somewhere between these two dates, it also began to connote evasion: the practising or use of indirect methods, including fraud or other temporary expedients.

[4] E. M. Leonard, *The Early History of English Poor Relief* (Cambridge, 1900); S. and B. Webb, *English Local Government*, vol. vii: *English Poor Law History Part I: The Old Poor Law* (London, 1927); E. M. Hampson, *The Treatment of Poverty in Cambridgeshire, 1597–1834* (Cambridge, 1934).

help'—involving small loans, casual labour and the provision of food and drink.[5]

It was not until 1974, however, with the publication of Olwen Hufton's *The Poor of Eighteenth-Century France*, that informal relief received its first systematic historical analysis. Indeed, it to Hufton that the historiographies of poverty, charity, and welfare owe the evocative phrase 'the economy of makeshifts' as a characterisation of the innumerable expedients from which strategies of survival were constructed in early modern society.[6] Hufton first applied this terminology in the context of late eighteenth-century France where millions of poor households lived uncomfortably close to the knife-edge of subsistence, scratching out an insecure livelihood on miserable plots of land which yielded meagre and often insufficient crops. Making ends meet depended on supplementing agricultural production with a very wide range of other activities, from the spinning of wool to the repairing of tools and the growing of grapes. Hufton, however, identified the two central planks upon which the precarious platform of makeshifts was erected: long-distance seasonal migration and localized begging. Each was perforce adopted in recognition of the 'impossibility of making a living at home'.[7]

Every year, millions of French peasants would tramp hundreds of miles as migrant labourers, not only seeking the casual or seasonal employment which might earn vital income for their families but also, by virtue of their very absence, diminishing the principal burden of expenditure on those same households. Physical mobility on this scale not only promised additional earnings, it also actually meant one less mouth to feed and (in turn) an enhanced claim on the charity of neighbours and local institutions.[8] Those remaining at home engaged in systematic begging, effectively apprenticing their children in the customary practices of pleading for alms and exploiting (whether by gleaning, by scrumping, or by pilfering) the natural resources of field, forest, and coastline. Women begged both with their dependent children and well into old age, seeking relief in cash or kind to supplement the paltry wages they might earn from service or casual labour. As a last resort, their menfolk might beg too, piecemeal in the first instance perhaps, ultimately joining the straggling bands of vagabonds whose desperate circuits orbited the poles of hospitality—cathedrals, monasteries, and other charitable founda-

[5] K. Thomas, *Religion and the Decline of Magic: Studies in Popular Beliefs in Sixteenth- and Seventeenth-Century England* (London, 1971), 555, 562–4.

[6] O. Hufton, *The Poor of Eighteenth-Century France, 1750–1789* (Oxford, 1974), 69–127.

[7] Ibid. 70.

[8] Ibid. 69–106.

tions—from which relief might be expected.[9] It required only the happenstance of misfortune, which, after all, was entirely characteristic of a 'catastrophic' environment where the provision of food, clothing, and shelter could be dislocated by sudden calamity, to unbalance this equilibrium, leaving the peasant and his family vulnerable not only to indigence but to debt and destitution.[10] 'Life-chances' then depended on a number of even less attractive options, with starvation staved off only by other, unlawful, expedients, perhaps including theft and prostitution. Even then, outcomes were often wretched, involving many thousands of cases of child abandonment and infanticide, and eventuating in immiseration and a death whose onset had been accelerated by periodic bouts of epidemic disease and harvest failure.[11]

Students of women's work immediately identified the heroines of Hufton's account as the peasant girls who laboured long to amass a dowry and the resourceful mothers who scrimped hard to keep food on the table. Indeed, when discussed in the English context, the 'economy of makeshifts' has generally been applied rather to the working experience of womanhood in particular than to the strategy of mitigating hardship in general.[12] Historians of poverty in early modern England were initially hesitant to register the significance of Hufton's insights, but gradually came to realize that they were significant not only in the period *before* the Elizabethan poor laws, but also *long after* the introduction of formal welfare provision in the parishes. Indeed, it has recently become clear that the pattern of enforcement of the poor laws was neither rapid nor uniform across England. The most recent authority on the spread of welfare provision, for instance, is not confident that the majority of rural parishes were collecting rates before the mid-seventeenth century, although, as we shall see, there remains considerable room for debate (and greater still for further research) upon this subject.[13] Even where overseers were appointed, rates assessed, and collections distributed, moreover, it is now clear that the parish pension was never all-encompassing: few collec-

[9] O. Hufton, *The Poor of Eighteenth-Century France*, 107–27.

[10] Cf. D. E. C. Eversley, 'The Home Market and Economic Growth in England, 1740–1780', in E. L. Jones and G. E. Mingay (eds.), *Land, Labour and Population in the Industrial Revolution* (London, 1967), 255.

[11] Hufton, *The Poor of Eighteenth-Century France*, 245–84, 306–17.

[12] See e.g. M. Roberts, '"Words They Are Women, and Deeds They Are Men": Images of Work and Gender in Early Modern England', in L. Charles and L. Duffin (eds.), *Women and Work in Pre-Industrial England* (London, 1985), 141; S. Mendelson and P. Crawford, *Women in Early Modern England, 1550–1720* (Oxford, 1998), 256–300 (ch. 5: 'The Makeshift Economy of Poor Women').

[13] P. Slack, *From Reformation to Improvement: Public Welfare in Early Modern England* (Oxford, 1999), 66 n. 55. Cf. Ch. 4.1 below.

tioners were other than aged, and fewer still other than widows. Even for the tiny minority lucky enough to be in receipt of regular relief, moreover, 'collection' was not, in and of itself, sufficient to support the needs of a pensioner, especially in the first half of the century. Although it is 'at least highly likely that an individual living alone could survive on 1s a week' by 1700, 'it seems unlikely that a pauper could survive solely on 6d. a week in the early seventeenth century'.[14] The logical conclusion, argued Tim Wales, was that the significance of statutory social welfare provision could be measured only in the context of a widespread and enduring reliance on informal relief strategies (which he characterized explicitly in Hufton's terms), emphasizing in particular the diverse economic opportunities—casual labour in industry or agriculture; midwifery; household service—available to those who either wished, or were forced, to remain at least partly independent of parish support.[15] To his credit, Wales was also sensitive to a theme, almost invisible in Hufton's magisterial account, which has since become particularly prominent in the historiography of care: the role of kin in supporting the indigent, especially the elderly.[16]

Wales's groundbreaking insight encouraged a trend in the English historiography which has since come to construe 'informal relief' in very broad terms, expanding its definition considerably beyond the original remit of Thomas's 'tradition of mutual help' or Hufton's 'economy of makeshifts'. Indeed, the accounts of survival strategies currently offered by students of poverty and welfare in England differ very considerably from the French models.[17] This divergence is in part a function of context. Although it is clear that there was significant population turnover both *within* and *between* local communities as young men and women travelled to neighbouring parishes in search of working opportunities or marriage partners, large-scale seasonal migration seems to have been generally insignificant as far as the English labouring poor were concerned. The tramping poor travelling long distances, the vagrants whose

[14] T. Wales, 'Poverty, Poor Relief and the Life-Cycle: Some Evidence from Seventeenth-Century Norfolk', in. R. M. Smith (ed.), *Land, Kinship and Life-Cycle* (Cambridge, 1984), 356.

[15] Ibid. 353, 381–2.

[16] Ibid. 382–4. Cf. the discussion of 'informal relief' in Hufton, *The Poor of Eighteenth-Century France*, 194–216. For the further development of this theme, see the essays in M. Daunton (ed.), *Charity, Self-Interest and Welfare in the English Past* (London, 1996), and in P. Horden and R. Smith (eds.), *The Locus of Care: Families, Communities and Institutions and the Provision of Welfare Since Antiquity* (London, 1998); and the discussion in Ch. 1.3 below.

[17] The historiography of informal relief in France has itself, of course, moved on since 1974 and has gradually begun to explore the survival strategies of the poor in the early modern period. Among the most sophisticated recent work is M. Dinges, 'Self Help and Reciprocity in Parish Assistance: Bordeaux in the Sixteenth and Seventeenth Centuries', in Horden and Smith (eds.), *The Locus of Care*, 111–25.

journeys might have taken them forty, perhaps even a hundred, miles, accounted for only a relatively small proportion of the migrant population.[18] The high degree of toleration of begging, especially by the known neighbourhood poor, in France stands, furthermore, in contradistinction to practices of mendicancy in England, which were, in statute if not in practice, subject initially to regulation and ultimately to prohibition.[19]

The wave of studies of English informal relief practices which has broken since the late 1980s has, moreover, revealed numerous other informal channels of charitable activity along which even the settled poor might travel in the short and median terms, especially when threatened with destitution or starvation, long after the putatively decisive legislation of the 1590s. Students of charity and welfare are now very familiar with the informal marketing practices that insulated the poor against harvest failure;[20] with the monastic, clerical, and gentlemanly traditions of largesse that provided hospitality for poor tenants and parishioners, especially at Christmas;[21] with the extension of neighbourly credit that tided poor households over in times of under- or unemployment;[22] with the spontaneous gifts of food and shelter that were offered to neighbours and even to the migrant poor;[23] and with the customs of congregational fasting and almsgiving that were co-ordinated across the country at times of natural disaster.[24]

These important contributions notwithstanding, there has been no systematic attempt by historians of the early modern period to reconstruct in detail the relationship between these informal and semi-formal

[18] P. Slack, 'Vagrants and Vagrancy in England, 1598–1664', P. Clark, 'Migration in England during the Late Seventeenth and Early Eighteenth Centuries', and D. Souden '"East, West—Home's Best"? Regional Patterns in Migration in Early Modern England', all in P. Clark and D. Souden (eds.), *Migration and Society in Early Modern England* (London, 1987), 49–76, 213–52, 292–332; Beier, *Masterless Men*, 69–85.

[19] Beier, *Masterless Men*, 109–22.

[20] J. Walter, 'The Social Economy of Dearth in Early Modern England', in J. Walter and R. Schofied (eds.), *Famine Disease and the Social Order in Early Modern Society* (Cambridge, 1989), esp. 96–116.

[21] F. Heal, *Hospitality in Early Modern England* (Oxford, 1990), esp. 23–90, 141–91, 223–99; N. S. Rushton, 'Monastic Charitable Provision in Tudor England: Quantifying and Qualifying Poor Relief in the Early Sixteenth Century', *Continuity and Change*, 16 (2001), 9–44.

[22] C. Muldrew, *The Economy of Obligation: The Culture of Credit and Social Relations in Early Modern England* (London and New York, 1998), esp. 303–12.

[23] I. K. Ben-Amos, '"Good Works" and Social Ties: Helping the Migrant Poor in Early Modern England', in M. C. McClendon *et al.* (eds.), *Protestant Identities: Religion, Society and Self-Fashioning in Post-Reformation England* (Stanford, 1999), 125–40; Ben-Amos, 'Gifts and Favors: Informal Support in Early Modern England', *Journal of Modern History*, 72 (2000), 295–338.

[24] S. Hindle, 'Dearth, Fasting and Alms: The Campaign for General Hospitality in Late Elizabethan England', *Past and Present*, 172 (2001), 44–86.

practices and the introduction of formal relief, an omission which is rendered even more striking by the fact that the most subtle of the attempts to do so for the eighteenth century, Joanna Innes's conceptualization of the 'mixed economy of welfare', is focused on the overlaps and interstices between the various *institutions* which might cater for the differing interests of well-defined groups among the indigent.[25] Perhaps most surprisingly, moreover, the analysis of casual theft (so central to Hufton's original conception of 'making shift') has, in the English context, generally been undertaken from the 'interactionist' perspective of criminal justice history rather than by students of poverty interested in pursuing the possibility of a 'real' correlation between high prices and property crime.[26]

The following discussion takes very seriously the significance of those recent contributions that have recognized the breadth of the 'economy of makeshifts' in the English case while, at the same time, seeking to locate them in both the more general context of the survival strategies which were available to poor households and the more specific frame of reference of their relationship with public welfare provision. By definition, some survival strategies were regarded by contemporaries as illegitimate, sometimes even illegal. Indeed, the overarching argument of the following discussion is that the plethora of activities in which the poor might engage to protect themselves from indigence were subject at least to official regulation, if not outright prohibition, during the course of the seventeenth century. By the end of our period, the range of practices in which poor households might legitimately participate as part of the effort to make shift had significantly contracted, leaving the indigent vulnerable to parish relief on the one hand and the insecurities of an overstocked labour market on the other. Cumulatively, therefore, this chapter analyses the struggles of the labouring poor to avoid declension into dependency.

[25] J. Innes, 'The "Mixed Economy of Welfare" in Early Modern England: Assessments of the Options from Hale to Malthus (*c*.1683–1803)', in Daunton (ed.), *Charity, Self-Interest and Welfare*, 139–80. Slack, *From Reformation to Improvement*, esp. 150–66 (ch. 7: 'Civil Societies') adopts a very similar approach. For a fine, though impressionistic, study of popular initiatives to make shift in this later period, see R. W. Malcolmson, 'Ways of Getting a Living in Eighteenth-Century England', in R. E. Pahl (ed.), *On Work: Historical, Comparative and Theoretical Approaches* (Oxford, 1988), 48–60. Although they obviously take their lead from Hufton, the vast majority of the contributions to S. King and A. Tomkins (eds.), *The Poor in England, 1700–1850: An Economy of Makeshifts* (Manchester, 2003), are concerned with the period after 1700.

[26] C. B. Herrup, 'New Shoes and Mutton Pies: Investigative Responses to Theft in Seventeenth-Century East Sussex', *Historical Journal*, 27 (1984), 811–30. Cf. P. G. Lawson, 'Property Crime and Hard Times in England, 1559–1624', *Law and History Review*, 4 (1986), 95–127. For a review of this historiography, see S. Hindle, *The State and Social Change in Early Modern England, c.1550–1640* (London and New York, 2000), 121–5.

It begins with a brief characterization of the working lives of labouring people, emphasizing, on the one hand, the significance of the waged work by which most of them survived and, on the other, the sheer difficulty of getting a living and sustaining a household even they could obtain regular employment. It then unfolds as a narrative of the various shifts made by the poor in order to get by before they ultimately asked relief of the parish. By analysing, in turn, the opportunities afforded by customary rights, by kin support, by neighbourly credit, and by theft, it seeks to explain how and why 'the obligation to stay alive' not only transcended any system of social ethics, but ultimately drove the indigent into negotiations with charity trustees and parish officers.[27] At stake here was the ability of the labouring poor of seventeenth-century England to counter the threat of destitution, perhaps even of starvation, without succumbing to the shame of dependency and the fracturing of family relationships implied by falling 'on the parish'.

1. LIVES OF LABOUR

The countryside of late sixteenth- and early seventeenth-century England, it has recently been argued, 'witnessed the emergence of a larger and more wholly wage-dependent labouring population', which probably constituted at least half the English people by the mid-seventeenth century'.[28] It was, nonetheless, a paradox of the experience of labour that so much time was spent idle. This was particularly true of the agricultural sector where even the largest of farms supplied their demand for labour by employing resident servants.[29] Agricultural work for the cottager or labourer entailed not regular employment at fixed wages but a scattering of casual tasks, such as harvesting, sowing, or harrowing, whose rhythms were distinctly seasonal and which might be remunerated at different rates, sometimes in cash, sometimes in kind, often in arrears.[30] Paid farm work was not, therefore, a living in itself, but simply a vital cash supplement to a subsistence based on the cultivation of cottage gardens and the exploitation of common rights. But the labouring poor of rural areas also

[27] Cf. Hufton, *The Poor of Eighteenth-Century France*, 387.

[28] K. Wrightson, *Earthly Necessities: Economic Lives in Early Modern Britain* (New Haven, 2000), 197.

[29] A. Kussmaul, *Servants in Husbandry in Early Modern England* (Cambridge, 1981). Cf. D. Woodward, 'Early Modern Servants in Husbandry Revisited', *Agricultural History Review*, 48 (1999), 141–50.

[30] A. Everitt, 'Farm Labourers', in J. Thirsk (ed.), *The Agrarian History of England and Wales*, vol. iv: *1500–1640* (Cambridge, 1967), 396–465.

had other working opportunities, not least because manufacturing employment had penetrated so deeply into the countryside.[31] By the mid-sixteenth century, perhaps one in six adult males and one in three children and adult women drew their livelihoods from textile production in the cradles of rural industry.[32] Areas of industrial wage-dependence were particularly vulnerable to dislocation of the cloth trade, and it is tempting to dismiss the litany of complaints, so frequently voiced in the 1620s, about the multitude, misery, and despair of poor cloth-workers and their families as the product of the peculiar circumstances of a decade disfigured by war and dearth.[33] It is nonetheless true that the payment of poverty wages was endemic in the cloth industry, and that even a weaver who notionally worked all year round cannot have earned more than £10 a year, which was nowhere near enough to maintain his family, pay his rent, and buy his fuel. For the most part, of course, work in textiles was much more intermittent.[34]

Work was, therefore, often seasonal or highly insecure, and the growth of a pool of surplus labour down to the mid-seventeenth century entailed lower wages and widespread under-employment, a trend which was not significantly reversed even by the end of our period. Under-employment was not, then, simply a function of the unpredictability of opportunities to earn but also of the poor levels of remuneration even for those who were fortunate enough to work regularly.[35] It is nonetheless true that work in textiles was actually preferable to the even less attractive living that might be made as a farm-worker, for it is unlikely that the annual income of even the most fully employed agricultural labourer amounted to more than £9.[36] Little wonder that students of economic history have found it difficult to understand how the agricultural labourer and his family got through the year in seventeenth-century England.[37]

[31] J. Thirsk, 'Industries in the Countryside', in F. J. Fisher (ed.), *Essays in the Economic and Social History of Tudor and Stuart England in Honour of R. H. Tawney* (Cambridge, 1961), 70–88.

[32] M. Zell, *Industry in the Countryside: Wealden Society in the Sixteenth Century* (Cambridge, 1994), 113–52.

[33] B. Supple, *Commercial Crisis and Change in England, 1600–1642: A Study in the Instability of a Mercantile Economy* (Cambridge, 1959), 52–72, 102–19.

[34] J. Walter, 'Grain Riots and Popular Attitudes to the Law: Maldon and the Crisis of 1629', in J. Brewer and J. Styles (eds.), *An Ungovernable People: The English and their Law in the Seventeenth and Eighteenth Centuries* (London, 1980), 54–6, 64–5; Walter, *Understanding Popular Violence*, 237–84.

[35] Cf. C. Muldrew and S. King, 'Cash, Wages and the Economy of Makeshifts in England, 1650–1800', in P. Scholliers and L. Schwarz (eds.), *Experiencing Wages: Social and Cultural Aspects of Wage Forms in Europe Since 1500* (New York, 2003), 155–80.

[36] P. Bowden, 'Agricultural Prices, Farm Profits and Rents', in Thirsk (ed.), *Agrarian History*, iv. 598–601.

[37] J. A. Sharpe, *Crime in Seventeenth-Century England: A County Study* (Cambridge, 1983), 180.

That real wages fell across the sixteenth century in particular is now an established historiographical orthodoxy, although caution has recently been advised about the dangers of exaggerating either the extent or the consequences of the decline.[38] Even so, the closing decades of the century really were hard times, when even cheaper grains were often beyond the purchasing power of the artificer and poor labouring man.[39] These pressures brought into even greater prominence the plight of 'poore labouring people', who worked but whose domestic economies were based on improvisation and expedience and vulnerable to dislocation in the event of harvest failure, industrial slump, or personal misfortune. Usually, the labouring poor scraped by, less visible in the historical record than the tiny minority whose destitution, impotence, or sickness brought them under the case of the parish officers, but they constituted a large and growing presence, especially in those rural communities in which wage-dependence was common.[40] In agricultural parishes, the predicament of those 'poore foulkes' who were forced to 'beg their bread in miserie from door to door' could not escape their attention of even the most optimistic of social commentators.[41] For a growing proportion of the population, the diminishing capacity of earnings to meet their household needs meant that periodic hardship was inevitable. By the turn of the sixteenth century, therefore, poverty had become structural.[42] But it was also experienced with varying degrees of intensity across the life-cycle, for too many mouths to feed or the withdrawal of a family member from productive labour through age and/or sickness inevitably meant straitened circumstances.[43]

The distinctive life-cycle of the labouring poor rendered imperative the participation of all family members in the productive endeavours of the household economy. Work began in childhood and never really ended. Although most children of labouring families were spectators rather than participants in the labour market until they reached the age of 7, usually entertaining themselves in close proximity to their parents while they worked, after that age they invariably became engaged in some kind of economic activity.[44] At this stage their employment opportunities

38 Wrightson, *Earthly Necessities*, 146.

39 J.A. Sharpe, 'Social Strain and Social Dislocation, 1585–1603', in J. Guy (ed.), *The Reign of Elizabeth I: Court and Culture in the Last Decade* (Cambridge, 1995), 192–211.

40 Slack, *Poverty and Policy*, 27–32.

41 W. Harrison, *The Description of England*, ed. G. Edelen (Ithaca, 1968), 217.

42 Slack, *Poverty and Policy*, 39.

43 Wales, 'Poverty, Poor Relief and the Life Cycle'.

44 H. Cunningham, 'The Employment and Unemployment of Children in England, *c*.1680–1851', *Past and Present*, 126 (1990), 115–50.

were influenced less by their gender than by their physical strength and their possession of appropriate skills, which might allow them to help cut wood, brew ale, or fetch water, perhaps even to tend livestock or reap corn. While some boys and girls busied their hands in spinning and carding wool, others found seasonal agricultural work—weeding, stone-gathering, or bird-scaring, perhaps even gleaning—often alongside their mothers. In rural industrial areas, they might work lace or spin yarn, through which they might at least contribute to their keep if not earn it in full.[45] If they managed to avoid being apprenticed out by the parish officers at the age of 8 or 9, their full engagement with the labour market would be delayed until they reached 14 when the boys might be the subject of indentures to husbandry and girls sent into domestic service.[46] For the more fortunate among them, the mid-teens might bring a formal apprenticeship to a local tradesman.[47] The late teens and early twenties might see young men hire themselves out as agricultural labourers, and the beginning of precarious, though often protracted, careers of wage-dependence which were vulnerable to the impact of increased family expenditure, especially in rearing the children who were usually born in the immediate wake of marriage.

If the timing of entry to the labour market was predictable and in some respects regulated by the statutes of 1563 and 1601, the timing of retirement from it was altogether less certain, if indeed it occurred at all. Lives of labour were just that, cycles of work in which employment chances and earning capacities became ever more restricted under the pressure of deteriorating health, strength, and sight.[48] Even so, only those who were entirely incapacitated could expect to give up work altogether, and even then they might be expected to supplement their parish pensions with doorstep charity solicited on daily perambulations of the parish. The rest literally worked themselves to death.

The working lives of women were also characterized by a developmental cycle.[49] Most single women were employed either as domestics or as servants in husbandry, in which they were more frequently expected to

[45] D. Levine, 'Production, Reproduction, and the Proletarian Family in England, 1500–1851', in D. Levine (ed.), *Proletarianization and Family History* (London, 1984), 87–127.

[46] Kussmaul, *Servants in Husbandry*, 70–96; B. Capp, *When Gossips Meet: Women, Family and Neighbourhood in Early Modern England* (Oxford, 2003), 127–85. Cf. Ch. 3.2 below.

[47] M. G. Davies, *The Enforcement of English Apprenticeship, 1563–1642: A Study in Applied Mercantilism* (Cambridge, Mass., 1956); I. K. Ben-Amos, *Adolescence and Youth in Early Modern England* (New Haven, 1994), 69–83.

[48] P. Thane, *Old Age in English History: Past Experiences, Present Issues* (Oxford, 2000), 89–118.

[49] A. Froide, 'Old Maids: The Life-Cycle of Single Women in Early Modern England', in L. Botelho and P. Thane (eds.), *Women and Ageing in British Society Since 1500* (London, 1991), 89–110.

participate in dairying—milking, butter-churning—than in heavy field work. Married women were invariably besieged by the demands of their children, and were therefore dependent primarily on their husbands' earnings, which for the labouring poor were usually insufficient to meet household needs. The imperative to supplement family income both encouraged women to practise self-provisioning on the basis of common wastes and tiny holdings associated with their cottages and drove them into the shadowy world of casual, intermittent, and badly paid wage labour. They might earn a few pence here and there for sewing and washing the goods of their neighbours, charring and cleaning their households, or nursing the sick and aged.[50] At certain times of the year, especially in harvest time, they might be rewarded in cash or kind for performing seasonal agricultural tasks. More regular income could be derived from the putting-out industries in which a woman might earn two or three pence (half a day-labourer's usual wage) for a day's work spinning wool.[51] Widowhood brought the chance to re-enter domestic service, but more characteristically might drive the single mother into paid employment that could be carried out in the home and might be practised well into old age—the carding of wool, the plaiting of straw, the making of lace—until fading eyes and arthritic fingers rendered them incapable of any work at all.[52]

Widows were those most likely, in the end, to fall into desperate need and were characteristically regarded by almsgivers and overseers alike as deserving objects of pity.[53] Their well-documented careers as parish pensioners were, however, only the most conspicuous indicators of the economic vulnerability of the labouring poor. Most of the indigent, after all, attempted to support themselves by their labour and many did so for as long as they were able, yet the nature and incidence of that very labour provided the context that put them at risk of falling into poverty. The labouring poor, therefore, sought to shift for themselves and their families by supplementing their paid work with other resources.

[50] S. Wright, '"Churmaids, Huswyfes and Hucksters": The Employment of Women in Tudor and Stuart Salisbury', in Charles and Duffin (eds.), *Women and Work*, 100–21; M. Pelling, *The Common Lot: Sickness, Medical Occupations and the Urban Poor in Early Modern England* (London and New York, 1998), 79–102, 155–75, 179–202.

[51] Zell, *Industry in the Countryside*, 166–8.

[52] P. Sharpe, 'Literally Spinsters: A New Interpretation of Local Economy and Demography in Colyton in the Seventeenth and Eighteenth Centuries', *Economic History Review*, 2nd ser., 44 (1991), 46–65; S. Ottaway, 'The Old Woman's Home in Eighteenth Century England', in Botelho and Thane (eds.), *Women and Ageing*, 111–38.

[53] L. Botelho, 'Aged and Impotent: Parish Relief of the Aged Poor in Early Modern Suffolk', in Daunton (ed.), *Charity, Self-Interest and Welfare*, 91–112.

2. THE EXPLOITATION OF COMMON RIGHTS

These resources were not, in the first instance, human, but natural. Any genuine historical grasp of the processes of making shift would require both empathy with popular attitudes towards the landscape and awareness of the multifarious use of natural resources. The natural world was both accessible to, and psychologically significant for, the rural poor of seventeenth- and early eighteenth-century England to a far greater extent that would be the case for their descendants, and historians who fail to engage with the material and emotional value of the nuanced landscapes of which rural society was composed are guilty of a conspicuous failure of historical imagination. The recent literature on the economy of makeshifts, much of it written from a social scientific perspective, has largely been preoccupied with social behaviour and the attitudes which informed it at the expense of a sense of the place of these relationships within the natural world. What follows tries to steer a course between those studies of survival strategies that are principally concerned with landscapes and their exploitation, and those that are exclusively concerned with social relations. As we shall see, landscapes were both living environments dotted with buildings of stone or cob, their chimneys smoking with fires of wood or peat, and working environments teeming with people—reaping and raking, stone-picking and stick-gathering, dairying and ditching.

The poor themselves were vociferous in asserting the extent to which the customary right to exploit the resources of pasture, forest, and fen might insulate them from not only dependency but even indigence. Such claims were, of course, most strident when commoners felt that their customary practices were about to be abrogated by enclosure or encroachment. The law courts of the period resonated with the complaints of the poorer sort that they would be 'utterly undone and have small or no means to relieve themselves' or 'utterly overthrown in the best means of their livelihood' if their common rights were extinguished.[54] 'The pore people' of Cawston (Norfolk) claimed in 1601 that they had their 'cheipest lyving and maintenances by graving of flages and cutting of lynges'. A by-law of 1574, however, had sought to restrict common rights to dwellings that had remained undivided for the previous forty years, to define poor migrants as 'unlawful commoners', and to exclude cottagers from taking any fuel at all. Without these rights, customarily exercised on the commons between Lady Day and Lammas, the indigent alleged that 'some of them might [be forced to] begg ther

[54] Everitt, 'Farm Labourers', 406–7.

bred'.[55] Their better-off neighbours were equally convinced of this argument, and their defence of the fuel-gathering rights of the poor was motivated only partly out of magnanimity: they also had a vested interest in preventing the inflation of welfare costs which would inevitably result if these rights were abrogated or undermined.[56]

Any discussion of the value of common rights is indebted to Jeanette Neeson's remarkable study of 'the uses of waste' in the forest and fenland villages of Northamptonshire, and of the richness of the economic equilibrium to which they contributed.[57] The forest commons in particular offered not only pasture for cattle and swine but also reserves of fuel, herbs, nuts, berries, honey, birds, and game. 'Almost every living thing', enthused Alan Everitt, 'could be turned to some good use by the frugal peasant labourer or his wife.'[58] The exercise of customary right did not, moreover, guarantee access to fuel merely for domestic use: wood, peat, turf, dried dung, gorse, and heather might just as likely be traded for grain or other produce as be used to warm the cottages of those who collected it. Even if nominal payments were sometimes required to retain them (in 1601 only a penny a year earned each tenant of Cawston unlimited rights to gather fuel), customary perquisites such as these entailed significant exchange entitlements for the poor.[59]

Of all common rights, however, the pasturage of cattle on the common wastes was of most value to the poor. Cows, the milking of which was part of the domestic duties expected of a housewife, produced milk, cream, butter, and cheese that might be consumed at home, and any surplus (sizeable only if more than one cow was involved) might be marketed. Although the sale of these dairy products might help meet the financial demands of landlords and the budgetary necessities of clothing and fuel, it was a household strategy that left the poorer commoners who had only one animal with little nourishing food.[60] Contemporaries were

[55] Wales, 'Poverty, Poor Relief and the Life-Cycle', 370; Norfolk RO, MC254/1/3.

[56] The decisive law suits over access to common rights in Cawston are discussed in S. Amussen, *An Ordered Society: Gender and Class in Early Modern England* (Oxford, 1988), 18–20. The attitude of these more prosperous tenants is analogous to those in the Hertfordshire communities of Caddington and Berkhamsted in the 1620s and 1630s. Cf. S. Hindle, 'Persuasion and Protest in the Caddington Common Enclosure Dispute, 1635–39', *Past and Present*, 158 (1998), 37–78; H. Falvey, 'Crown Policy and Local Economic Context in the Berkhamsted Common Enclosure Dispute, 1618–42', *Rural History*, 12 (2001), 123–58.

[57] J. M. Neeson, *Commoners: Common Right, Enclosure and Social Change in England, 1700–1820* (Cambridge, 1993), 158–84.

[58] Everitt, 'Farm Labourers', 405.

[59] Amussen, *An Ordered Society*, 19.

[60] Cf. C. Shammas, *The Pre-industrial Consumer in England and America* (Oxford, 1990), 33–4; D. Levine and K. Wrightson, *The Making of an Industrial Society: Whickham, 1560–1765* (Oxford, 1991), 264–5.

entirely familiar with the idea that a cow and the right to pasture it might insulate the poor from indigence on the one hand and dependency on the other. Not for nothing did the early seventeenth-century surveyor of Cawston, George Sawer, divide the seventy-seven households in the parish that were too poor to pay the poor rate (but not receiving regular relief) into twenty (26 per cent) who had a cow and a cottage and fifty-seven (74 per cent) who did not.[61] As painstaking correlation of this listing with the records of overseers' payments has shown, this distinction was emphatically not purely notional, since the minority who could mobilize rights of pasture were significantly less likely to burden the parish.[62] This finding is all the more striking in the light of estimates of the proportion of cottagers who possessed cattle, which varied from about 55 per cent in the west of England, to 60 per cent in the Midlands, 70 per cent in the east, and 75 per cent in the north. Even so, the ownership of cattle did not necessarily bring security, for the vast majority of those whose inventories included cattle possessed no more than one or two beasts.[63]

Although it was widely recognized that rights of pasture carried with them at least the potential for independence, apologists and defendants of the customary economy might read that independence very differently. The commoners of Nassington (Northamptonshire) were, it was argued in 1551, 'able to live in such idleness upon their stock of cattle that they will bend themselves to no kind of labour'. Adam Moore argued in 1653 that the exploitation of common wastes enabled the poor to subsist even in their idleness, encouraging them in their 'stratagems to avoid work'.[64] It was but a short step from here to argue that idle commoners should not be supported, even in their old age. Why, argued the overseers of Coton (Cambridgeshire) in 1663, should they pay a pension to an inhabitant who had a cow and a calf, even if he was very elderly? Similar scepticism was voiced by the parish officers of Middle Claydon (Buckinghamshire), who, having been pressured by the parish clergyman into conceding a pension of 2*s.* 6*d.* to a woman who had perforce sold 'her hog and three sheep', reduced it to 1*s.* 6*d.* on the grounds that she still had a cow which would help towards her maintenance. To the poor themselves, however, independence was a matter not only of household survival but also of pride, an attitude rehearsed in 1738 when Robert Nicholson told the Cumberland bench that 'a house with some right of common ground or

61 Amussen, *An Ordered Society*, 17. The survey is conveniently reproduced in Wales, 'Poverty, Poor Relief and the Life-Cycle', 389–94.

62 Wales, 'Poverty, Poor Relief and the Life-Cycle', 370–8.

63 Everitt, 'Farm Labourers', 414.

64 A. Moore, *Bread for the Poor* (London, 1653), 6.

pasture at Rickerby' had long prevented his family from falling upon the parish until he was forced to sell it to raise cash.[65] The most potent threat to the independent lifestyle of poor commoners, however, came from enclosure. The elimination of common rights at Long Newton (County Durham) in the 1660s, for instance, meant that those poor commoners who had 'kept beasts and swine and so maintained themselves and families' were 'like to be wholly burdensome to the towne'.[66]

Historians have also long recognized the profound significance of customary rights to the household economies of the labouring poor in fenland, moorland, woodland, and open-field communities.[67] Despite some fascinating experiments, however, they have found it no easier than contemporaries to put a realistic financial value on common rights during the seventeenth century. Historians of later periods, however, are rather better served by the evidence, and they have estimated that the produce of a single cow kept on common land in the late eighteenth century could produce dairy products worth between £7 and £10 per annum, a sum which represents perhaps as much as 40 per cent of an agricultural labourer's annual income. The fact that most common-right cottages entailed rights to two cows suggests that this proportion might be doubled, with the implication that pasture rights might even grant virtual independence from wage labour.[68] The value of forest rights is more difficult to calculate, partly because of the extraordinarily diverse resources available in a woodland economy. It has nonetheless been estimated that fuel rights in the late eighteenth century could have been worth between £2 and £5 per annum or between 10 and 20 per cent of the earnings of an agricultural labourer.[69]

All of which brings us to the vexed question of who actually was *entitled* to common right. Historians are increasingly confident that within those families that enjoyed common rights (whether legally or not), the actual gathering and exploitation of resources was largely carried out by

[65] Everitt, 'Farm Labourers', 404; Bodl., MS Rawlinson, C948, fo. 95; J. Broad, 'Parish Economies of Welfare, 1650–1834', *Historical Journal*, 42 (1999), 995; CRO, Q/11/1/189/23.

[66] P. Rushton, 'The Poor Law, the Parish and the Community in North-East England, 1600–1800', *Northern History*, 25 (1989), 145.

[67] Everitt, 'Farm Labourers', 403–6; E. Thompson, 'The Grid of Inheritance: A Comment', in J. Goody *et al.* (eds.), *Family and Inheritance: Rural Society in Western Europe, 1200–1800* (Cambridge, 1976), 328–60; Thompson, *Customs in Common* (London, 1991), 97–184.

[68] J. Humphries, 'Enclosures, Common Rights, and Women: The Proletarianisation of Families in the Late Eighteenth and Early Nineteenth Centuries', *Journal of Economic History*, 50 (1990), 23–31; L. Shaw-Taylor, 'Labourers, Cows, Common Rights and Parliamentary Enclosure: The Evidence of Contemporary Comment, *c.*1760–1810', *Past and Present*, 171 (2001), 96.

[69] Humphries, 'Enclosures, Common Rights, and Women', 53; Neeson, *Commoners*, 165.

women. Common right, accordingly, looms large in recent discussions of women's work and the family wage.[70] The social-structural distribution of access to customary rights, however, remains controversial.[71] Jeanette Neeson argues that the effective regulation of commons preserved the customary use rights even, and perhaps even especially, of the poorest members of the community. She criticizes what she regards as historically uninformed models of the inevitable 'tragedy of the commons', in which ineffective management led inexorably to the exhaustion of natural resources, and emphasizes the fair and effective administration of common lands by manorial courts.[72] This interpretation has recently been bolstered by more general surveys of the political control of communal assets. Donald Woodward, for instance, cites very widespread evidence of seventeenth-century by-laws identifying those who had the right to share in natural resources; stipulating the amounts which each individual could carry away and whether such material could be sold to outsiders; and determining the seasonality of the legitimate collection of materials. 'Without such regulations,' he insists, 'many of the commons and wastes of early modern England would have been quickly denuded.'[73]

The effect of these regulations, however, remains ambiguous. On the one hand, Neeson suggests that communal regulation favoured poorer rather than more affluent commoners. The management of waste arguably fostered a fundamental social cohesion based on the ideology of custom, in which, she insists, 'the defence of common rights required the protection of lesser rights as well as greater'.[74] On the other, the highly legalistic reading of manorial court activity by Leigh Shaw-Taylor interprets regulation as an act of exclusion which by definition prevented

[70] Humphries, 'Enclosures, Common Rights, and Women'; S. Horrell and J. Humphries, 'Old Questions, New Data, and Alternative Perspectives: Families' Living Standards in the Industrial Revolution', *Journal of Economic History*, 52 (1992), 849–80.

[71] For a useful summary of the debate see L. Shaw-Taylor, 'The Management of Common Land in the Lowlands of Southern England *circa* 1500 to *circa* 1850', in M. de Moor *et al.* (eds.), *The Management of Common Land in North-West Europe, c.1500–1850* (Turnhout, 2002), 59–81.

[72] Neeson, *Commoners*, 55–80. Cf. G. Hardin. 'The Tragedy of the Commons', *Science*, 162 (1968), 1243–8. For an interesting theoretical critique, see B. J. McCay and J. M. Acheson, 'Human Ecology of the Commons', in B. J. McCay and J. M. Acheson (eds.), *The Question of the Commons: The Culture and Ecology of Communal Resources* (Tucson, 1987), 1–34.

[73] D. Woodward, 'Straw, Bracken and the Wicklow Whale: The Exploitation of Natural Resources in England Since 1500', *Past and Present*, 159 (1998), 54–5.

[74] J. M. Neeson, 'The Opponents of Enclosure in Eighteenth-Century Northamptonshire', *Past and Present*, 105 (1985), 138. Cf. the analyses of the social and cultural significance of custom in Thompson, *Customs in Common*, 1–15, 97–184; and in R. W. Bushaway, 'Rite, Legitimation and Community in Southern England, 1700–1850: The Ideology of Custom', in B. Stapleton (ed.), *Conflict and Community in Southern England: Essays in the History of Rural and Urban Labour From Medieval to Modern Times* (Gloucester, 1992), 110–34.

not only outsiders but also, more significantly, the occupants of non-commonable cottages from enjoying the uses of waste.[75] It is, however, overwhelmingly probable that virtually all residents sought to exploit common right in practice, irrespective of whether they had any legal claim. As the author of a seventeenth-century proposal for the enclosure of the commons of Clitheroe (Lancashire) put it, 'those who have the greatest right get the least shares, and those that have the least right or none at all, get the most'.[76] It is therefore unsurprising that the tenants of the ancient commonable cottages resented the poor migrants who claimed customary right simply on the basis of residence: they 'have no means to relieve themselves, there being little work to set them on, but by flocks go roving up and down the forest, parks and inclosed grounds near unto them to the great hindrance of all who have cattle and woods'.[77] For the poor migrant to the forest, therefore, custom came to be regarded not as *cohesive* but rather as a *restrictive* ideology, one of the structural constraints within, and around, which survival tactics were perforce developed.

Common rights, it seems, had always been managed, though the effectiveness with which regulations were enforced undoubtedly varied from community to community. What was distinctive about the sixteenth and seventeenth centuries, however, was the transition from the regulation to the restriction, and ultimately to the extinction, of popular rights of access to communal resources. This was only partly a matter of enclosure, the chronological progress of which remains, in any case, a matter of scholarly controversy.[78] Much more significant, however, was encroachment and the consequent recognition that the customary equilibrium of the wood-pasture economies had to be defended against the waves of shiftless migrants who were settling wherever land remained unappropriated. Since squatters were simply residents rather than ancient tenants they had no legal rights to the customary perquisites of forest,

[75] Shaw-Taylor, 'Labourers, Cows, Common Rights and Parliamentary Enclosure', 118–26. Cf. S. Hindle, 'A Sense of Place? Becoming and Belonging in the Rural Parish, 1550–1650', in A. Shepard and P. Withington (eds.), *Communities in Early Modern England* (Manchester, 2000), 103–5.

[76] H. R. French, 'Urban Common Rights, Enclosure and the Market: Clitheroe Town Moors, 1764–1802', *Agricultural History Review*, 51 (2003), 68 n. 102.

[77] NA, C3/332/42 (Band *vs.* Dale, *c.*1621–5).

[78] J. R. Wordie, 'The Chronology of English Enclosure, 1500–1914', *Economic History Review*, 2nd ser., 36 (1983), 483–505. Cf. J. Chapman, 'The Chronology of English Enclosure', *Economic History Review*, 2nd ser., 37 (1984), 557–9; J. Thirsk, 'Introduction', in id. (ed.), *Chapters from the Agrarian History of England and Wales, 1500–1750*, vol. iii: *Agricultural Change, Policy and Practice 1500–1750* (Cambridge, 1990), 2; R. C. Allen, *Enclosure and the Yeoman: The Agricultural Development of the South Midlands, 1450–1850* (Oxford, 1992), 32–6.

moor, and fen, but one of the numerous attractions of these environments was the very fact that they were not generally overshadowed by either the manor house or the parish church and were therefore somewhat ineffectively regulated. While enclosure might crystallize a solidarity of interest between the middling and poorer sort as they sought to defend the traditional allocation of resources against the innovations of their landlords, encroachment drove a wedge between them as the long-settled 'inhabitants' sought to protect their own interests against the depredations of foreigners, strangers, and off-comers.[79]

The identification of commonable properties therefore become a matter of acute importance and it is unsurprising that both landlords and chief inhabitants should seek to compile lists of those who were legally entitled to common right and those who were not. In the early seventeenth century, for instance, the manorial court of Brigstock (Northamptonshire) recorded that, of perhaps 170 households, fifty-three were 'suit-houses', the tenants of which were allowed *housebote* (the right to take specified quantities of timber for house repairs), two were half-suit-houses, and a further nine quarter-suit-houses. These rights cumulatively amounted to the taking of about fifty trees every year, and were supplemented by an annual allowance of sixty-two loads of suit-thorns at concessional rates out of the ridings of Geddington Chase. Similar provisions applied in the neighbouring parishes of Stanion and Geddington, though in these communities the ratio of 'suit-houses' to all residents is rather more difficult to calculate, at least until the early eighteenth century. The papers concerning a proposed enclosure in 1720, moreover, reveal dramatic variations in the proportion of common-right cottages between even these three adjacent communities which intercommoned together. The proportion of legally commonable cottages to all forest dwellings ranged from as high as 84 per cent in Stanion, to as low as 36 per cent in Brigstock and even 34 per cent in Geddington. Overall, therefore, only 43 per cent of the 351 households in these three communities formally enjoyed common right in Geddington Chase.[80]

The delicate social and economic balance of these wood-pasture communities is revealed in a fragmentary series of manorial orders which survive for Geddington in the 1730s.[81] At first sight, the presentment and fining of five individuals in 1730 for 'unlawful encroachment on the commons' implies that resources were being tightly regulated. However,

[79] For a local study of these mutable social alignments, see Hindle, 'Persuasion and Protest'.

[80] NRO, MS Montagu (B), x350 ('An Estimate of the Chase'); cf. Neeson, *Commoners*, 62 n. 23.

[81] The following analysis is based upon NRO, MS Montagu (B), x7523 (Geddington manorial court rolls, 1730, unfol.; 1731, fos. 6–7; 1732, fo. 6; 1734, fo. 5; 1735, fo. 5; 1738, fo. 29).

the fact that these same five, three of them widows and all of them in receipt of parish charity, were presented and fined again for the same offence in 1731, 1732, 1734, 1735, and 1738 suggests that these were not marginal individuals whose presence in the community was merely tolerated, but that they were the ancient poor of the parish whose precarious exploitation of the waste was reluctantly condoned, the fines amounting to little more than rents. The trouble, of course, was that, over several generations, the forest economy had come to absorb countless settlers of this kind. Squatters and other migrants were, in this sense, agents in the fabrication of their own economy of makeshifts: inventing traditions where there were none, claiming rights by virtue only of residence, manipulating custom in their own interest. Settlement at the margins of a forest economy was not, therefore, a survival *strategy* legitimately played out in the context of widely recognized ethical rules, but a survival *tactic* which ingeniously exploited the 'unstopped cracks in the wainscoting of power'.[82]

The result was the piecemeal process of stinting out, whereby access to communal resources was ever more tightly restricted in the interests of the tenants of ancient commonable cottages. Doubtless the pattern of regulation differed from community to community. In some areas, access to common waste or woodland was granted by the 'goodness and good favour' of a paternalistic landlord, as was reported by the inhabitants of Duffield Frith (Derbyshire) in 1587. Elsewhere it might be matter of political convenience, as in Staffordshire in 1644, when all the poor persons of the county were given permission to cut firewood on the lands of delinquent royalists.[83] The cottagers of Colyton (Devon), by contrast, had largely lost the right of free access by the mid-seventeenth century.[84] By 1738 Thomas Andrews felt able to argue that many of the 'meaner sort of people' had already been stinted out of their pasture rights: 'the poor are, in so many unenclosed commons, excluded by stints whereby their antient privileges are taken away and given to the rich'.[85] Little wonder that, where this process of stinting out can be traced in the history of a single local community, as in Caddington (Hertfordshire) in the late sixteenth and the seventeenth centuries, it often culminated in an explo-

[82] K. Wrightson, 'The Politics of the Parish in Early Modern England', in P. Griffiths *et al.* (eds.), *The Experience of Authority in Early Modern England* (London and New York, 1996), 35.

[83] F. Strutt and C. J. Cox, 'Duffield Forest in the Sixteenth Century', *Derbyshire Archaeological Journal*, 25 (1903), 210; *The Committee at Stafford, 1643–1645: The 'Order Book' of the Staffordshire County Committee*, ed. D. H. Pennington and Ivan Roots (Manchester, 1957), 29, 169.

[84] P. Sharpe, *Population and Society in an East Devon Parish: Reproducing Colyton, 1540–1840* (Exeter, 2002), 147.

[85] Shaw-Taylor, 'Labourers, Cows, Common Rights and Parliamentary Enclosure', 126.

sion of hostility towards landlords and their agents.[86] Similar tensions were also associated with two other practices that the poor claimed on the basis of customary usage: gleaning and fuel-gathering.

(*a*) Gleaning

Gleaning was a highly ritualized and ancient harvesting custom that provided perquisites of considerable value to the fragile household economies of the labouring poor.[87] Harvest, indeed, was not only a time of relatively high earnings because of the concentrated demand for labour at a time of intense agricultural activity; it was also the centrepiece of a complex mesh of responsibilities and obligations which the poor sought to maintain. Perpetuation of the custom of gleaning depended upon the exploitation of the tension between the priorities of farmers, for whom the harvest was property, and those of harvesters, whose claim to gleaning implied that rights in property were not absolute.[88] The successful negotiation of these conflicting interests arose out of customary notions of charity and paternalism that were fundamentally local, regulated by manorial courts. Blackstone wrote in 1772 that 'the poor are allowed to enter and glean upon another's ground after the harvest without being guilty of trespass'. Despite his confidence that this practice was guaranteed by 'the common law and custom of England', there had never in fact been any such thing as a common law *right* to glean. The manorial by-laws that regulated gleaning throughout the medieval period and into the sixteenth century emphasize that gleaners were only ever admitted by consent of the landholder and on his terms. Even so, the customary restriction of permission to glean to 'the young, the old, the decrepit and those unable to work' belies recent scepticism that there had never been a peculiar association between harvesting customs and the poor. After all, as victims of the life-cycle, these four categories collectively constituted the deserving poor. In sum, the antiquity, certainty, rationality, and continuance of the custom fostered a sufficiently powerful attachment to gleaning to render the contrast between Blackstone's legal right and the Thompsonian notion of custom a distinction without a difference, except

[86] Hindle, 'Persuasion and Protest'.

[87] For harvesting customs in general, see R. Hutton, *The Stations of the Sun: A History of the Ritual Year in Britain* (Oxford, 1996), 332–47. The historiography of gleaning in early modern, as opposed to medieval or 18th-century, England is fragmentary. For a very brief introduction, J. A. Sharpe, 'Enforcing the Law in the Seventeenth-Century English Village', in V. A. C. Gatrell *et al.* (eds.), *Crime and the Law: The Social History of Crime in Western Europe Since 1500* (London, 1980), 105–7.

[88] R. W. Bushaway, *By Rite: Custom, Ceremony and Community in England, 1700–1800* (London, 1982), 138.

in so far as the common law judges were asked to adjudicate, as they were in 1788.[89]

The value of gleaning in the early modern period is difficult to reconstruct, although some contemporary comment was optimistic. The Leicestershire justices reported that, even in a dearth year such as 1630–1, the poor only began to complain 'so soone as they had spent the corne which they had gathered by gleaning in the harveste', which, they estimated, 'was about Allhallowtide'. Some observers went even further in suggesting that aprons full of stubble might actually protect the poor altogether from the pressure of high prices. Even in the aftermath of the dearth of the late 1640s, John Cook was confident that 'the poor by help of their gleanings have not been much hunger-bitten'.[90] Some contemporaries thought a gleaner could earn almost as much in a day as a reaper.[91] Estimates provided by historians of later periods are, however, instructive. Even after the 'right' to glean had (as we shall see) been successfully challenged in the courts, the practice continued into the nineteenth century. Indeed, it has been suggested that gleaning might have accounted for as much as much as one-eighth of the annual earnings of a poor family, and an even greater proportion in those households headed by women.[92] This was, moreover, primarily women's work, customarily carried out with their children. In 1601, the Hertfordshire bench stipulated penalties specific to women and children (a whipping rather than a spell in the stocks) if they were convicted for the illicit gathering of corn.[93] Henry Best noted in 1642 that they customarily allowed 'the wives and children of those that work with us to gleane so long as we are shearinge [reaping] and on the landes with them'. Well into the eighteenth century, polemicists robustly publicized gleaning as one of the many unheroic female tasks upon which the maintenance of the household economies of the labouring poor depended.[94]

[89] W. Blackstone, *Commentaries on the Laws of England* (4th edn., 4 vols., London, 1770), iii. 212; W. O. Ault, *Open-Field Farming in Medieval England* (London, 1972), 31; CUL, Ee I.1, fo. 223v [1282]; Thompson, 'The Grid of Inheritance', 340 n. 29; R. M. Smith, 'Some Issues Concerning Families and their Property in Rural England, 1250–1800', in id. (ed.), *Land, Kinship and Life-Cycle*, 74; Wales, 'Poverty, Poor Relief and the Life-Cycle', 84.

[90] NA, SP16/193/89; J. Cook, *Unum Necessarium: or, The Poor Man's Case* (London, 1648), 28.

[91] Ault, *Open-Field Farming*, 30 n. 74.

[92] P. King, 'Gleaners, Farmers and the Failure of Legal Sanctions in England 1750–1850', *Past and Present*, 125 (1989), esp. 116, 145–50; King, 'Customary Rights and Women's Earnings: The Importance of Gleaning to the Rural Labouring Poor, 1750–1850', *Economic History Review*, 2nd ser., 44 (1991), 462–6, 474.

[93] Humphries, 'Enclosures, Common Rights, and Women'; *Hertford County Records*, ed. W. Le Hardy (9 vols., Hertford, 1905–39), i. 32–3.

[94] *The Farming and Memorandum Books of Henry Best of Elmswell, 1642*, ed. D. Woodward (Records

Attention has generally focused on the evaporation of the 'right' to glean under the pressure of agrarian capitalism and the elaboration of absolute definitions of property during the eighteenth century. In particular, the ambiguous significance of a 1788 judgment in Common Pleas, arising from contested practices by the 'poor', 'necessitous', and 'indigent' parishioners and inhabitants of Timworth (Suffolk) has been emphasized. While Steel *vs.* Houghton did not generally end the practice of gleaning, it did extinguish the claim of poor villagers to glean as of right.[95] Gleaning had, however, been regulated whenever and wherever it had been practised. As became apparent in 1788, the activity had always been derived not from a general right at common law but from local customary practice, which had in the medieval period generally recognized the right to glean only by specified groups, especially those too old or too young to reap, at specified times of day, and only after the interests of the farmers of the wheat had been accommodated.[96] Piecemeal regulation of the activity of gleaners on this model doubtless occurred well into the sixteenth century, as it did in the Shropshire manor of Cound, where tenants and their servants were prevented from gleaning altogether in 1579. Following the poor harvest of 1598, the manorial court of Weekley (Northamptonshire) placed restrictions on the gleaning of peas and subsequently fined five cottagers for doing so. In late sixteenth-century Barham (Cambridgeshire), permission to glean was restricted exclusively to the landless poor who had 'no corn growing'. In 1623, the manorial court of Keevil (Wiltshire) threatened those caught gathering bean stubs after harvest with a spell in the stocks. As late as 1632, the villagers of Burton Agnes in the East Riding of Yorkshire granted preferential gleaning rights to 'children and aged people'. The inhabitants of Elmswell reported in 1642 that they 'neaver suffere[ed] any such to gleane as [they] find able and unwilling to worke' and reserved the use of the drag rake to gather scattered corn to those that they found 'most unfitte for other labour'.[97] Official regulation along these lines did not, of course, deter

of Social and Economic History, NS 8, Oxford, 1984), 45. See the discussion of Mary Collier's rebuttal of Stephen Duck's *Thresher's Labour* in the 1730s in Roberts, '"Words They Are Women"', 146–7.

[95] P. King, 'Legal Change, Customary Right, and Social Conflict in Late Eighteenth-Century England: The Origins of the Great Gleaning Case of 1788', *Law and History Review*, 10 (1992), 1–31. Cf. Thompson, 'The Grid of Inheritance', 340; Bushaway, *By Rite*, 139–41; Thompson, *Customs in Common*, 138–44, 169–70.

[96] W. O. Ault, 'By-Laws of Gleaning and the Problem of Harvest', *Economic History Review*, 2nd ser., 14 (1961), 210–17; Ault, *Open-Field Farming*, 27–38.

[97] Shropshire RO, 5460/1/1; NRO, MS Montagu (B), x340/5–6; King, 'Customary Rights and Women's Earnings', 470; M. Ingram, *Church Courts, Sex and Marriage in England, 1570–1640*

more popular initiatives of the kind which took place in the Norfolk village of Thorpe Market in 1664, when four women apparently 'beat Matlaske's wife of Roughton gleaning in Thorpe where Thorpe had refused'; or in the Cambridgeshire parish of Chesterton the same year, when three inhabitants assaulted Elizabeth Walker oblivious to the fact that she 'had leave from the owner to gleane'. One yeoman of Ingworth (Norfolk) assaulted a woman who attempted to glean in his field and sarcastically 'bid her go to the justice to complain'.[98]

Even so, the pervasive fear that gleaning was carried out illicitly led in the late sixteenth century to closer parliamentary scrutiny of offences committed through stealth. The outcome was a statute of 1601 penalizing the 'sundry misdemeanours' committed by 'lewd and idle' persons, which were now made subject to the ever-increasing summary jurisdiction of magistrates out of sessions. Among them was the 'unlawful cutting or taking away of any corn and grain growing', a formula that effectively redefined unauthorized gleaning as the illegitimate theft of corn.[99] Although the absence of magistrates' notebooks renders it difficult to know how widely gleaning and other related misdemeanours were policed under the summary provisions of the statute, it is clear that assize judges, county benches, and parish vestries sought to restrict eligibility for this most valuable of customary perquisites throughout the seventeenth century. The Hertford bench complied with the 1601 act almost immediately, ordering that any poor inhabitants of Ashwell found gathering 'haume' (stubble) should be placed in the stocks. Even so, evidence suggests that the 1601 statute may generally have lain dormant for most of the century only to be revived after the Restoration. Prosecutions for unlawful gleaning in Essex, for example, cluster in the

(Cambridge, 1987), 82 n. 38; M. Turner and D. Woodward, 'Theft from the Common Man: The Loss of "Common" Use Rights in England', in T. Brotherstone and G. Pilling (eds.), *History, Economic History and Marxism: Essays in Memory of Tom Kemp* (London, 1996), 53; *Henry Best of Elmswell*, 46. Agrarian practice in Weekley is analysed in J. Ingram, 'The Conscience of the Community: Clerical Critiques of Wealth and Power in Early Modern England' (University of Warwick Ph.D., in progress 2004), ch. 5.

[98] *The Notebook of Robert Doughty, 1662–1665*, ed. J. M. Rosenheim (Norfolk Record Society 54, Norwich, 1989), 41; Bodl., MS Rawlinson, C948, fo. 75.

[99] 43 Elizabeth I, c. 7 (1601), sects. i and ii. The significance of this statute is briefly noticed by Sharpe, *Crime in Seventeenth-Century England*, 170–1; A. Fletcher, *Reform in the Provinces: The Government of Stuart England* (New Haven, 1986), 82; Slack, *Poverty and Policy*, 101. A bill of 1597–8 'for the repressing of offences that are of the nature of stealth' only narrowly failed to become law. The measure, debated extensively in the aftermath of the dearth of 1594–7, imposed summary corporal punishment on those convicted of grain theft, pilfering from orchards and gardens, hedge-breaking, and wood stealing, all offences characteristically committed by 'base and meane persons'. D. M. Dean, *Law-Making and Society in Late Elizabethan England: The Parliament of England, 1584–1601* (Cambridge, 1996), 189–95.

late 1660s, with harvesters reporting on the conduct of their poor neighbours in illicitly gathering armfuls of barley or corn from the shocks and tithe heaps due to local yeomen.[100] The pattern of prosecution for the theft of a 'bottle of hay' (i.e. as much as could be carried in one's arms) suggests that it was growing increasingly difficult throughout the century to distinguish between gleaning and the theft of corn.[101] Warwickshire quarter sessions indictments include numerous examples of individuals convicted of either theft of crops or trespass and removing crops, both of which probably imply transgressions of the ill-defined boundary between legitimate gleaning and theft.[102] Even where they did not result in prosecution, allegations of theft under colour of gleaning were ubiquitous, sometimes (as they were in the Leicestershire village of Sileby) surfacing in a discourse of credit and reputation which vilified the unlawful taking of corn as an offence not only against property but also against charity.[103]

It was in this light that the magistrates of Caroline Dorset took the initiative to police gleaning more closely in 1635.[104] Their depiction of the tricks and deceits of the labouring poor at harvest time vividly evokes the tactics the indigent might use to escape the shackles of custom. It was not unusual, they alleged, for gleaning to begin before the winter corn was 'mowed together' in the barn and the summer corn was made into ricks. Then there was outright theft, with gleaning becoming part of the 'saturnalia of power', men and women walking 'abroad in the night' carrying sheets to conceal the corn they stole and threatening the constables with actions at law if they interfered. More striking still, however, was the magistrates' assessment that, because gleaning was so

[100] *Hertford County Records*, i. 32–3; Sharpe, *Crime in Seventeenth-Century England*, 170–71; ERO, Q/SR417/23, 421/119.

[101] See Ch. 1.5 below. For 'bottle' meaning a 'bundle [of hay or straw]', see *Henry Best of Elmswell*, 288.

[102] *Warwick County Records*, ed. S. C. Ratcliff *et al.* (9 vols., Warwick, 1935–64), vi. 75, 77, 82, 118, 120, 125, 139, 160, 161, 196 (theft of crops); 27, 40, 47, 149, 150, 156, 161, 188 (trespass and removing crops and fruit). Sharpe, *Crime in Seventeenth-Century England*, 99, argues that many of the 217 prosecutions for theft of grain in mid-17th-century Essex were committed by harvest workers and suggest that tensions over gleaning lay behind these episodes. Some of the circumstances which gave rise to prosecutions of this kind are revealed in the informations and examinations in *Quarter Sessions Records of the County of Somerset*, ed. E. H. Bates-Harbin (4 vols., Somerset Record Society, 23, 24, 28, 34, Taunton, 1907–19), iii. 288, 292, 296, 301, 304, 306, 308, 309, 330, 332, 334, 335, 338, 340, 358, 359, 360, 361.

[103] B. Capp, 'Life, Love and Litigation: Sileby in the 1630s', *Past and Present*, 104 (2004), 71.

[104] Except where noted the following discussion is based on G. E. Fussell and K. R. Fussell, *The English Countryman: His Life and Work from Tudor Times to the Victorian Age* (London, 1981 edn.), 57.

profitable and provided a viable alternative to being hired as a reaper for wages, harvest labour was difficult to find. This assessment was shared by the farmers of Ashwell (Hertfordshire), who complained in 1649 that persons of 'loose carriage' were refusing harvest work except at 'excessive wages' and had determined 'to inrich themselves under colour of gleaning'. The Norfolk magistrate Robert Doughty was convinced that the difficulties in enforcing the labour laws owed much to the conviction, popular among 'wenches', that they could make far better earnings by 'gleaning & stealing in harvest' than they could in service in husbandry. Similar anxieties doubtless underlay the numerous warrants issued in the early 1660s by the Cambridgeshire JP Sir Thomas Sclatter 'for not working in harvest time and going up and down stealing corn'.[105] Even those Dorset labourers who did take harvest work by the piece conspired with their families and friends to glean after them, sometimes accepting bribes in return for leaving the harvested corn ungathered.[106] Indeed, it was 'unclean reaping' of this kind which so outraged the Northumbrian landlord Sir Thomas Haggerston, who recounted in 1665 that when he reproved his harvest workers for leaving corn ungathered, they 'retorted what shall we leave for the poor ones?' It was therefore little surprise to Haggerston that 'when he leads his corn many do come to glean in the field at the same time, so that those who should reap for hire do turn gleaners, to his great damage.'[107]

The response of the Dorset magistrates was to seek to enforce the terms of the 1601 statute to the letter: gleaning was to be restricted to the aged, the weak, and the infirm; constables were to police the fields during the harvest to ensure that the division of labour between reapers and gleaners was rigorously enforced; the idle must accept harvest work at the standard rates upon pain of a night in the stocks; anyone found in the harvest fields at night was to be arrested and bound to their good behaviour.[108] Elsewhere, it seems, regulation devolved upon the parish officers. In 1634, an assize order by the judges of the Norfolk circuit, surviving in the parish archive of North Elmham, effectively stipulated a system of licensed gleaning. The minister and parish officers were to draw up a list of all 'such aged impotent and other true poor persons' whom they thought 'fitt to suffer to gleane' within the parish at harvest time and

[105] *Hertford County Records*, v. 395; Norfolk RO, Norwich, AYL304 (and cf. Ch. 3.2(*d*) below); Bodl., MS Rawlinson, C948, fos. 4, 7. For the 'saturnalia of power' see J. C. Scott, *Domination and the Arts of Resistance: Hidden Transcripts* (New Haven, 1990), 202–7.

[106] Fussell and Fussell, *The English Countryman*, 57. Cf. Ault, *Open-Field Farming*, 30.

[107] *A Cavalier's Notebook*, ed. T. E. Gibson (London, 1880), 136.

[108] Fussell and Fussell, *The English Countryman*, 57.

to make a public declaration from the pulpit that 'none presume to gleane but such soe intitled or allowed'.[109] This order seems to have set something of a precedent, for when complaints of abuses (especially gleaning before corn was carried and the pulling of wheat from sheaves) arose in the Norfolk villages of Feltwell and in Swaffham Market in the 1650s, similar restrictions were adopted. The timing and technology of gleaning activity were regulated: gleaners were permitted to gather only for three days; only with their hands rather than rakes; and only after the farmers of the tithe had taken what was due to them.[110] Even so, fears that gleaning was illicitly carried out proved enduring. Hearing that 'poor people draw home to them their children and others to glean', the Norfolk bench stipulated further regulations in 1659: gleaning was to be practised only under licence from the minister and the parish officers; only after all the corn had been tithed and collected; and only for three days.[111] By the eighteenth century, the regulation of gleaning had become a monopoly of the chief inhabitants, usually administered on their behalf by the parish officers. When 'articles of agreement' for the regulation of the rights of gleaners in the common fields of Great Cheverell (Wiltshire) were drawn up in 1762, they were subscribed by the 'principal inhabitants' and recorded not by the manorial jury but by the overseers of the poor.[112]

The definition of those who were permitted to glean—sometimes referring only to the young, the aged, and the impotent, sometimes encompassing all the labouring landless poor—therefore shifted over time. Indeed, the stringency of the regulations imposed in the 1590s and 1630s, noticeably more sweeping than those of the 1650s, suggests that regulation almost certainly oscillated with the quality of the harvest, with more restrictive attitudes prevailing in years of dearth.[113] These variations also reflected the tensions that underpinned the scriptural justifications for leaving gleanings to the needy.[114] As the foregoing discussion sug-

[109] Norfolk RO, PD209/210. Cf. the practice on the manor of Basingstoke (Hants.) in the late 14th century, where only those impotent persons who 'passed by view of the bailiff and constable with the assent of two or three of the tenants' were permitted to glean. Ault, *Open-Field Farming*, 31.

[110] *Norfolk Quarter Sessions Order Book 1650–57*, ed. D. E. H. James (Norfolk Record Society, 26, Norwich, 1955), 48, 61, 90.

[111] Amussen, *An Ordered Society*, 94, 156–7.

[112] Wiltshire and Swindon RO, Trowbridge, PR/Great Cheverell St Peter/207/37.

[113] Walter, 'Social Economy of Dearth', 126–7; King, 'Customary Rights and Women's Earnings', 471 n. 33.

[114] Thompson, *Customs in Common*, 140; King, 'Gleaners', 141–2. The differing implications of the relevant passages in Leviticus (19: 9, which implied the poor in general) and Deuteronomy (24: 19, which specified 'the stranger, the fatherless and the widow', an interpretation also bolstered by Ruth 2: 6–8) are nicely brought out in L. Vardi, 'Construing the Harvest: Gleaners,

gests, moreover, the very close attention paid to the regulation of gleaning in Norfolk confirms the suspicion that gleaning 'played a larger role in the strategies of the poor in arable areas'. This should not necessarily lead us to believe, however, that gleaning was regionally specific, still less that it was confined to the south and east. After all, there were significant areas of arable in the predominantly pastoral north and west, and the dismissal of gleaning as almost wholly irrelevant in these areas is an argument from a silence which is probably better interpreted as the white noise that typically tends to fill those geographical vacuums where no research has been conducted.[115] Even so, the continuity of gleaning was most obviously vulnerable to the impact of enclosure and conversion to pasture. As Robert Powell wrote in 1636, 'the poore labourer' who 'was wont in harvest time to glean and lease up so much corne as would thriftily maintaine him a good part of the winter is now for want of tillage, destituted of that benefit'.[116]

Perhaps because the right to glean was unrecognized in certain areas, those who were suspected of the 'theft' of grain protested otherwise, as did the poor women of one Oxfordshire parish in the 1630s, who claimed that they were only gathering mustard. A blacksmith from Crewkerne (Somerset) explained that the barley found in his house in the autumn of 1656 'was gathered by his children in the latter end of harvest' and was not fetched from the fields of one of his neighbours.[117] Elsewhere, of course, the traditional defence of those who felt their entitlements to be threatened was to appeal to custom. One woman from Essex complained to the Essex bench in 1652 that a local farmer had beaten her up while she gleaned 'according to the custome in harvest tyme'. Others demonstrated their acute sensitivity to the customary nature of their rights. When the wife of a Hertfordshire labourer was first challenged and then subsequently assaulted by a farmer in Hitchin cornfield in 1603, her numerous female supporters explained that she was there 'to gleane graine as is usual for all the pore to doe'.[118]

Farmers and Officials in Early Modern France', *American Historical Review*, 98 (1993), 1436–9 and n. 60.

[115] Cf. Walter, 'Social Economy of Dearth', 91–2; King, 'Customary Rights and Women's Earnings', 467–9.

[116] R. Powell, *Depopulation Arraigned, Convicted and Condemned* (London, 1636), 67. For the relationship between the loss of gleaning rights at enclosure and prosecutions for the theft of corn in the 1740s, see P. Lane, 'Work on the Margins: Poor Women and the Informal Economy of Eighteenth- and Early Nineteenth-Century Leicestershire', *Midland History*, 22 (1997), 90.

[117] Mendelson and Crawford, *Women in Early Modern England*, 293; *Quarter Sessions Records of the County of Somerset*, iii. 186.

[118] ERO, Q/SBa2/81; *Hertford County Records*, i. 35–6.

(*b*) Fuel-Gathering

The poor were similarly tenacious in defending their custom of gathering wood for fuel. The literary stereotype of the forest dweller was that of a lawless squatter, his stubbornness and incivility matched only by his poverty, a view summed up by John Norden's characterization of *c.*1610: woods and forests, he argued, were 'the verye nurseryes of Idlenes Atheisme Beggerie perfidiousnes and meere disobedience to godes and the lawes of the kingdom'. 'For poverties sake, havinge noe other meanes', the inhabitants of forest villages had 'thruste themselves into theis obscure places (as they thincke) out of the view of god or men whoe become *Rudes et Refractorij*, Lyvinge most baselie, prophanelie and by thefte, A peste in a Comonwealth'.[119] There was, of course, a grain of truth here: woodlands were attractive precisely because they were generally less well regulated by manorial courts and might often be filled with hovels built by poor migrants who came in search of space and work yet who subsisted on the theft of timber and game.[120] Here too there was considerable legal ambiguity about the nature and origins of the 'right' to gather. In all Crown woodland, for instance, the gathering of wood for fuel was supposedly carried out only under licence from the forest officers, and it is likely that the ancient settled poor of the parish were the principal beneficiaries of such discretion. Thus, in Rockingham Forest, 'such only and so many of the poor persons as the verderers and woodward think meet' were be 'admitted to gather sticks on Mondays and Thursdays only in every week'.[121] This practice was evidently observed in the Northamptonshire parishes of Geddington and Newton, where Exchequer depositions of 1608 refer to the custom that 'divers poor' usually took 'thorns and bushes to burn'.[122] Licensed wood collection was, however, one thing, illicit 'gathering [of] sets and breaking of hedges' quite another. Hedge-breaking was a matter of acute concern on Geddington Chase from as early as 1577, when more stringent restric-

[119] Hatfield House, Herts., MS Cecil, 132/145. For commentary on the stereotype, see J. Thirsk, 'The Farming Regions of England', in Thirsk (ed.), *Agrarian History*, iv. 111–12; K. Thomas, *Man and the Natural World: Changing Attitudes in England, 1500–1800* (London, 1983), 193–5.

[120] P. A. J. Pettit, *The Royal Forests of Northamptonshire: A Study in their Economy, 1558–1714* (Northamptonshire Record Society, 23, Gateshead, 1968), 141–82; B. Sharp, *In Contempt of All Authority: Rural Artisans and Riot in the West of England, 1586–1660* (Berkeley, 1980), 156–74.

[121] Pettit, *Royal Forests of Northamptonshire*, 162, 193 (appendix III, clause 10).

[122] NRO, MS Montagu (B), x350 ('Brand Depositions'). For the context, see S. Hindle, '"Not by Bread Only"? Common Right, Parish Relief and Endowed Charity in a Forest Economy, *c.*1600–1800', in King and Tomkins (eds.), *The Poor in England*, 39–75.

tions on the admission of poor stick-gatherers were proposed. The late Elizabethan court records of Rockingham Forest reveal an annual average of fifty-six prosecutions for cutting greenwood or breaking hedges in the three parishes of Brigstock, Geddington and Stanion.[123] The very fact of poverty therefore ensured that 'there was a very fine line between the exercise of legitimate use rights and theft', especially in years of harvest failure. The dearth years of the 1590, for example, saw an epidemic of hedge-breaking at Ashford and New Romney in Kent where the indigent ransacked their neighbours' hedges and fences for firewood and building materials.[124]

The casual pilfering of wood for fuel had, moreover, long been subject to regulation in manorial courts, most often in those areas where small acreages of common woodland could not sustain the demands of the local community, especially where the population was swollen by unregulated immigration, or where rights of access were restricted to specific groups of residents such as the tenants of arable land. In these circumstances, the desperate demands of migrants, squatters, and under-tenants fell foul of the desire of the settled inhabitants to protect their own interests in the woods.[125] Like gleaning, this was an activity overwhelmingly carried out by poor women and their children, a tendency which encouraged its association in the popular mind with the beggary of migrant or squatter populations. This sense that hedge-breaking was *by definition* an offence committed by the disorderly poor occasionally found explicit recognition. In Much Hadham (Hertfordshire) in 1579, for instance, 'hedgebreakers or woodcaryers out of or in any grounde other than their own' were to be fined 6*d.* for each offence, masters or parents being liable for the infractions of their children or servants. Offenders who 'have any reliefe out of the poore mans boxe' were to forfeit one month's allowance after a first offence, two months' after a second, and all eligibility for relief after a third. Similar by-laws against hedge-breaking were introduced in Hatfieldbury (Essex) in 1579. In 1592, hedge-breaking

[123] Pettit, *Royal Forests of Northamptonshire*, 162.

[124] Woodward, 'Straw, Bracken and the Wicklow Whale', 55; P. Clark, *English Provincial Society from the Reformation to the Revolution: Religion, Politics and Society in Kent, 1500–1640* (Hassocks, 1977), 236.

[125] M. K. McIntosh, *Controlling Misbehaviour in England, 1370–1600* (Cambridge, 1998), 84–8 (esp. 84 n. 94 for the important distinction between the breaking of hedges to gather firewood and the often ritualized destruction of quicksets in opposition to enclosure). For the policing of hedge-breaking in the manorial courts of the Tudor north, see A. J. L. Winchester, *The Harvest of the Hills: Rural Life in Northern England and the Scottish Borders, 1400–1700* (Edinburgh, 2000), 125.

by 'the children of poor people' had become so sensitive that the assembly of Henley (Oxfordshire) threatened all idle children with gaol unless they agreed to be employed in stocking-frame knitting.[126]

Because the traditional manorial punishments of fines or amercements were inappropriate for those very poor people who illicitly gathered wood in this way, other sanctions, including physical punishment and eviction, were frequently adopted. The scepticism that very poor offenders might successfully be brought to book by manorial courts is tacitly expressed in the resolution of the chief inhabitants of Swallowfield (Wiltshire) in 1596 that all the company 'shall do their best' to suppress 'pilferers', 'hedge breakers', and other 'myscheveous persons', although the informal sanctions implied here remained unspecified.[127] The presentment of hedge-breaking seems nonetheless to have been an increasingly characteristic feature of manorial court activity across the sixteenth century, and had by 1600 become especially associated with the taking of under-tenants and inmates whose only access to fuel was by making illicit holes in the quicksets of their neighbours. An anonymous petition in the wake of the Midland Rising of 1607 complained of 'the settinge up of houses without 4 acres at the least to the same & at extreame rentes, whereby the tenants spoile other mens woodes for fyre, and maketh soe manie poore people that the townes cannot mainetaine them'. Little surprise then that the landlords who tacitly encouraged these practices should find themselves presented and fined, as they did at Wethersfield Hall (Essex) in 1561 or Norton Hall (Suffolk) in 1574.[128]

By the late sixteenth century, illicit fuel-gathering had become a matter of national concern, and both 'breaking of hedges, pales or other fences' and 'cutting or spoiling of woods or underwoods' fell, like unauthorized gleaning, under the summary jurisdiction of magistrates as a result of the 1601 statute against misdemeanours committed by 'lewd and idle' persons.[129] Although there is sporadic evidence of magistrates' activity in enforcing this statute, they were generally lenient even after convictions were secured, often ordering only that the perpetrators recompense their victims, and even excusing some offenders altogether on account of their

[126] L. L. Rickman, 'Brief Studies in the Manorial and Economic History of Much Hadham', *East Hertfordshire Archaeological Society Transactions*, 9 (1928–33), 290–1; ERO, D/DU/603/13; McIntosh, *Controlling Misbehaviour*, 87 n. 100. For the significance of the 'poor mans box', see Ch. 4.1 below.

[127] S. Hindle, 'Hierarchy and Community in the Elizabethan Parish: The Swallowfield Articles of 1596', *Historical Journal*, 42 (1999), 850 (article 18).

[128] NA, SP16/307/2; McIntosh, *Controlling Misbehaviour*, 86–7.

[129] 43 Elizabeth I, c. 7. Cf. Ch. 1.2(*a*) above.

poverty.[130] Justices of the peace seem to have been happy to delegate responsibility for policing and punishing the illicit gathering of fuel to parish officers. In a manner reminiscent not only of the minute of the Swallowfield town meeting prohibiting hedge-breaking, but also of manorial by-laws, a vestry order at Great Easton (Essex) as early as 1603 suspended poor relief for those guilty of 'breaking of hedges, pulling up of stiles, breaking of gates, and carting away either rails or bars'. A 'charge to the overseers of every town', probably issued by the magistrates of north-east Norfolk, in 1623 empowered overseers and constables to search the households of suspected persons for 'wood hedgstuff or other thinges wch they may be justlie suspected to have stolen' so that they may be forced to give magistrates 'an accompt wher they had the sayd wood or other thinges suspected to have ben unlawfully come by'. Those guilty of pilfering wood were to have their relief withheld and the sum forfeited was to be given as reward to those who informed the parish officers about 'any hedgstuff, pales, gates, or any other thing whatsoever stolen or unlawfully taken by any of the sayd Laborers or others'. Hedge-breaking was still being semi-formally policed in this way over a century later, for in 1697, and again in 1710, the overseers of Linton (Cambridgeshire) threatened hedge-breakers with being 'put off the collection'.[131] All this is to say nothing of the informal regulation of wood theft: one manorial steward in Gillingham (Kent) told the recipients of his master's charitable dole in 1700 that those who abused the trees on the estate could not expect to receive his bounty in the future.[132]

Magisterial interest in the protection of timber seems to have been reinvigorated by post-Restoration legislation. 'Having underwood and being unable to account for it' could bring summary conviction by a

[130] This relatively relaxed attitude certainly characterizes the activity of the Surrey justice Bostock Fuller, who recorded only four cases of hedge-breaking in the period 1608–22. 'Notebook of a Surrey Justice', ed. G. Leveson-Gower, *Surrey Archaeological Collections*, 9 (1885–8), 174, 202, 206, 207, 217.

[131] F. G. Emmison, 'The Care of the Poor in Elizabethan Essex: Recently Discovered Records', *Essex Review*, 62 (1953), 21; Bodl., MS Tanner 73, fo. 390; Hampson, *Treatment of Poverty in Cambridgeshire*, 184–5. The significance of the slightly damaged manuscript of the 1623 charge was first recognized by Leonard, *Early History of English Poor Relief*, 180–1, and was located in its Norfolk context by Wales, 'Poverty, Poor Relief and the Life-Cycle', 368, presumably because the ambiguous names of the townships listed at its head imply either Northrepps or Southrepps.

[132] D. R. Hainsworth, *Stewards, Lords and People: The Estate Steward and his World in Later Stuart England* (Cambridge, 1992), 208. For 17th-century charitable trusts in Buckinghamshire and Northamptonshire which excluded hedge-breakers from the perquisites of endowed charity, see Ch. 2.5(*c*) below. Even the statutes of some almshouses specifically excluded hedge-breakers, as they did at Duffield (Derby.) from 1612. C. Kerry, 'Anthony Bradshaw of Duffield and the Almshouses Founded by him at that Place', *The Reliquary*, 23 (1882–3), 140.

single magistrate under the terms of a statute of 1664.[133] Robert Doughty, for instance, issued a warrant in 1665 against eight 'poor boys and men' of Cromer 'for cutting stealing and spoiling the woods' on the estate at Uffords (Norfolk). By the 1740s, summary convictions for wood theft were common in Wiltshire, their tenor being poignantly captured by the case of a widow who was whipped for receiving stolen wood after she had sent her two young sons out to collect fuel. Even so, the Wiltshire magistrate William Hunt usually treated the offenders leniently, pardoning three poor women brought before him for wood-stealing in Urchfont in 1746 'in regard of their great poverty and their promises of not offending in the like again'. The seasonality of these offences, concentrated as they were in the winter months when the demand for fuel was greatest, is nonetheless instructive: Hunt dealt with ten cases of wood theft by shivering cottagers in December 1746 alone.[134] Doubtless these 'offenders' not only pleaded necessity but appealed to custom, as did Elinor Slade who, when accused of stealing wood from an orchard in Nettlecombe (Somerset) in 1656, explained that 'some of the poorer sort of the town did use to take the chips there', a customary right that had never been challenged by previous owners.[135]

It is, therefore, tempting to include common right in the 'economy of makeshifts'. In some respects, however, to regard the exploitation of common right as a 'makeshift' strategy is to misunderstand the nature of the highly diversified economies of those parts of England which failed to conform to the arable regime of sheep-corn country which has become the standard point of reference in most discussions of poverty. The drawing of one's livelihood from many different natural sources was far from 'precarious and uncertain', whatever the estate stewards of the period might have argued to the contrary, and had considerable merits, many of which might (in certain economic conditions) be far superior to wage labour, let alone to the parish pension.[136] From this perspective, the exploitation of common right is perhaps better described as part of an

[133] 15 Charles II, c. 2; J. M. Beattie, 'The Pattern of Crime in England, 1660–1800', *Past and Present*, 62 (1974), 79; R. W. Bushaway, 'From Custom to Crime: Wood Gathering in Eighteenth- and Early Nineteenth-Century England: A Focus for Conflict in Hampshire, Wiltshire and the South', in J. G. Rule (ed.), *Outside the Law: Studies in Crime and Order, 1650–1850* (Exeter, 1982), 65–101. Cf. the discussion in Bushaway, *By Rite*, 207–37.

[134] *Notebook of Robert Doughty*, 51; Beattie, 'The Pattern of Crime in England', 79; *The Justicing Notebook of William Hunt, 1744–1749*, ed. E. Crittall (Wiltshire Record Society, 37, Devizes, 1982), 15, 50, 55–6.

[135] *Quarter Sessions Records of the County of Somerset*, iii. 286. For other defences against allegations of wood theft, see *Quarter Sessions Records of the County of Somerset*, iii. 293, 380.

[136] Cf. Woodward, 'Straw, Bracken and the Wicklow Whale'.

'economy of diversified resources' rather than one of makeshifts: an economy whose products arrived just as regularly and seasonally, if less visibly in the historical record, as corn, sheep, and cattle.[137]

3. THE SUPPORT OF KIN

The resources available to the labouring poor were not, however, simply natural or environmental; they were also personal and familial. In times of hardship, whether caused by the short-term dislocation of the local and regional economy or by the more enduring problems associated with life-cycle poverty, the first recourse of the indigent was the informal domestic care that might be provided by near kin, who tended to be co-resident at certain stages of the life-cycle and who could even, as we shall see, be encouraged to cohabit in various circumstances. As might be expected, the best evidence of kin support tends to be generated in the circumstances of its exhaustion. Indeed, the disclosure of 'the "caring" family' only 'at its moments of failure' has provoked concern that its limitations may have received 'unnatural prominence'.[138] In the English context, moreover, the weakness of kin support has been regarded as predictable, the inevitable consequence of a demographic regime in which late marriage and widespread celibacy not only encouraged a significant cultural preference for nuclear family households but also created the likelihood of 'nuclear family hardship'. The death, illness, or loss of earning power of an adult member of such a household would by definition threaten its self-sufficiency, causing a serious, if not critical, rupture of its productive capacity.[139] Cogs shorn from the gears of the household economy in this way were particularly dangerous in a society where the structural characteristic of population turnover ensured that, for all its flexibility and permissiveness, the kinship system was relatively 'loose' and kin recognition was 'narrow and shallow'.[140] The unforth-

[137] For a classic example, which demonstrates the enduring capacity of such a lifestyle to support individuals and families, see E. H. Whetham, 'The Waygoing', in id., *The Agrarian History of England and Wales*, vol. viii: *1914–39* (Cambridge, 1978), 321–2.

[138] P. Horden, 'Household Care and Informal Networks: Comparisons and Continuities from Antiquity to the Present', in Horden and Smith (eds.), *The Locus of Care*, 29.

[139] P. Laslett, 'Mean Household Size in England Since the Sixteenth Century', in P. Laslett and R. Wall (eds.), *Household and Family in Past Time* (Cambridge, 1972), 125–58; Laslett, 'The Family and the Collectivity', *Sociology and Social Research*, 63 (1979), 432–42; Laslett, 'Family, Kinship and Collectivity as Systems of Support in Pre-Industrial Europe: A Consideration of the "Nuclear-Hardship" Hypothesis', *Continuity and Change*, 3 (1988), 153–75.

[140] K. Wrightson and D. Levine, *Poverty and Piety in an English Village: Terling, 1525–1700* (2nd edn., Oxford, 1995), 73–109, 187–97; K. Wrightson, 'Household and Kinship in Sixteenth-Century England', *History Workshop Journal*, 12 (1981), 151–8; Wrightson, 'Kinship in an English

coming character of kin support in the English context left the indigent family to the mercy of the 'collectivity', a term which implies informal and semi-informal networks of friendship, neighbourliness, and charity, but which has been commonly understood to imply formal bureaucratized support by 'the parish'.[141] Recent research has, however, questioned the determinism of this model, in which a bleak vision of nuclear families falling into dependency in north-western Europe, and especially in England, is implicitly contrasted with a rosier view of south-eastern Europe, where extended 'peasant' family households were sufficiently resourceful and supportive to obviate the need for external welfare agencies.[142] In societies across Europe, it has recently been argued, 'the household or resident family does not, at least since late medieval times, seem to have functioned as miniature welfare republic, caring adequately and unstintingly in proportion to its size'.[143]

These debates notwithstanding, it remains the case that, in theory at least, kin were *expected* to provide for needy family members in early modern England. The relief system created by the Elizabethan poor laws was by no means structured exclusively on the principle of public provision. Indeed, the importance of kinship care was absolutely central to the statutes.[144] Prospective pensioners who wished to emphasize their eligibility for relief were fully conscious that they had to circumvent the clause of the 1601 act, generally ignored in the historiography of welfare until the 1980s, that placed a clear obligation not only on parents to provide for their children and grandparents their grandchildren, but also on children to maintain their own parents. The 1697 act for the badging of the poor also, it should be noticed, emphasized the importance of kin obligations, exempting sons and daughters from wearing the badge if they contributed to the maintenance of their parents. To be sure, the range of kin who were required to prove their inability to contribute to the support of their relatives before the parish officers would grant a pension

Village: Terling, Essex 1500–1700', in Smith (ed.), *Land, Kinship and Life-Cycle*, 318–24. Cf. M. Chaytor, 'Household and Kinship: Ryton in the Late Sixteenth and Early Seventeenth Centuries', *History Workshop Journal*, 10 (1980), 25–60; D. Cressy, 'Kinship and Kin Interaction in Early Modern England', *Past and Present*, 113 (1986), 38–69; N. Tadmor, *Family and Friends in Eighteenth-Century England: Household, Kinship and Patronage* (Cambridge, 2001).

141 Laslett, 'Family, Kinship and Collectivity'.

142 This is the resounding conclusion of the essays collected in Horden and Smith (eds.), *The Locus of Care*.

143 Horden, 'Household Care and Informal Networks', 31.

144 Tadmor, *Family and Friends*, 109–10. In this, of course, the statutes were echoing 16th-century clerical exhortation for children to 'honour their parents, to labour for them, to see unto their necessities, to provide necessaries for them' if 'their parents be aged and fallen into poverty'. T. Becon, *Works* (Cambridge, 1844), 358.

was relatively restricted. No mention was made of siblings, cousins, or other lateral kin. The addition of grandparents to the list of those on whom the indigent had a prior claim was, moreover, almost an afterthought. And there was, finally, no reciprocal obligation on grandchildren to maintain their elderly grandparents. The obligation of kin to relieve did not, therefore, extend beyond descending and first-generation ascending relationships in the lineal line, and was, as we shall see, further diluted by considerations of geographical mobility, of ability, and of will.[145] Even so, both the earliest magistrates' orders enforcing the 1598 statute and the handbook for overseers used throughout the century placed heavy emphasis on kin obligations as a preferable alternative to parish relief, though *An Ease for Overseers of the Poore* was pessimistic about the potential for spontaneous kin support: 'miserable is that age that must be compelled by penalty of lawe to doe that it should extend by instinct of nature'.[146]

Surviving censuses of the poor nonetheless indicate that poor families often made, or were 'encouraged' into, quite complex residential arrangements to ensure the provision of care, especially for the elderly. Thus, of the sixty-four older widows recorded in the Norwich census of the poor (1570) who did not live alone, about half lived with a daughter, or with a daughter and her dependants, or even with the daughter's dependants only. Co-residence with sons was rather less common. Only eight women in this small sample lived with a married son and his family, although there were also three others who lived just with a son and a fourth who lived with a son and a daughter.[147] Such patterns were emphatically not

[145] 43 Elizabeth I, c. 2, sect. vii. Grandparents had, significantly, been omitted from the related clause in the 1598 act. 39 Elizabeth I, c. 3, sect. vii. The significance of this clause is belatedly receiving the recognition it deserves, partly in reaction to Thomson's suggestion that it was rarely enforced: D. Thomson, '"I Am Not My Father's Keeper": Families and the Elderly in Nineteenth-Century England', *Law and History Review*, 2 (1984), 265–6; Thomson, 'The Welfare of the Elderly in the Past: A Family or Community Responsibility?', in M. Pelling and R. M. Smith (eds.), *Life, Death and the Elderly: Historical Perspectives* (London, 1991), 196–9. Cf. Smith, 'Families and their Property', 74; Wales, 'Poverty, Poor Relief and the Life-Cycle', 383; W. Newman-Brown, 'The Receipt of Poor Relief and Family Situation: Aldenham, Hertfordshire 1630–90', in Smith (ed.), *Land, Kinship and Life-Cycle*, 406; Slack, *Poverty and Policy*, 84; R. M. Smith, 'Charity, Self-Interest and Welfare: Reflections from Demographic and Family History', and P. Thane, 'Old People and their Families in the English Past', both in Daunton (ed.), *Charity, Self-Interest and Welfare*, 34–5, 117; R. M. Smith, 'Ageing and Well-Being in Early Modern England: Pension Trends and Gender Preferences under the English Old Poor Law, *c.*1650–1800', in P. Johnson and P. Thane (eds.), *Old Age from Antiquity to Post-Modernity* (London, 1998), 64. For the 1697 act to badge the poor, see Ch. 6.5 below.

[146] *Tudor Economic Documents*, ed. R. H. Tawney and E. Power (3 vols., London, 1924), ii. 364; *An Ease for Overseers of the Poor Abstracted From the Statutes* (Cambridge, 1601), 23.

[147] Pelling, *The Common Lot*, 165, 166.

confined to the urban context. The censuses of such rural communities as Ardleigh (Essex), Chilvers Coton (Warwickshire), Corfe Castle (Dorset), Ealing (Middlesex), and Stoke-on-Trent (Staffordshire) disclose a relatively high proportion of elderly people—37 per cent of all widowers, 48 per cent of all widows—'lodging' in the households of their offspring (whether married or not), a tendency which probably reflects parish subsidies for the residential care of poorer relatives. Even so, it seems that elderly persons who were either single or widowed were 'as likely to be living with others as lodgers as with their kin'.[148]

In turning from the evidence of censuses to that of quarter sessions petitions for relief, the historian may hear vivid tales of ongoing filial duty and sacrifice, many of them, it should be noticed, involving relatives well beyond the narrow range of lineal kin stipulated in welfare legislation. The exceptionally rich archive of petitions for the county of Cumberland, for example, contains some 465 applications for poor relief in the period 1689–1749. When these petitions are read against the grain, it is possible to identify an otherwise invisible network of kin solidarity through which informal support was provided. That an elderly spinster like Jane Coulthard of Kirkoswald (Cumberland) might care for her mother, who was almost 100 years old and required a guide to help her walk, is (in the light of what we know from censuses) unsurprising. Rather less predictable are the experiences of Margaret Parke, an orphan of Tallentire who had left work to care for her brother 'stricken with the King's Evil and full of running sores'; or of bedridden Elizabeth Birkett of Crosthwaite, who 'would have starved by now if her sister Susan had not helped her'.[149] That kin support might not simply be a matter of residential care is, moreover, implied by the policy adopted by the vestry of Cumwhinton in 1706, where relief was refused to an 85-year-old widow on the grounds that her daughter could beg round the parish for her.[150] Most often, however, the nature of the support provided by kin, and indeed even the nature of the family relationship between donor and recipient, went unspecified. This tendency was especially clear in those

[148] P. Laslett, *Family Life and Illicit Love in Earlier Generations: Essays in Historical Sociology* (Cambridge, 1977), 204–5; Smith, 'Families and their Property', 79.

[149] CRO, Q11/1/5/27, 91/26, 97/10. Cf. the situation in the West End of London in the early 18th century, where 45 (51%) of the 89 relatives recorded as helping paupers lay beyond the narrow range of grandparent, parent, and children specified in the 1601 act. J. Boulton, '"It Is Extreme Necessity That Makes Me Do This": Some "Survival Strategies" of Pauper Households in London's West End During the Early Eighteenth Century', in L. Fontaine and J. Schlumbohm (eds.), *Household Strategies for Survival, 1600–2000: Fission, Faction and Cooperation* [*International Review of Social History Supplement* 8] (2000), 63.

[150] CRO, Q11/1/81/18.

cases where petitioners employed the idiom of 'friendship' to describe kin support. One widow of Bruton (Somerset) told the trustees of a parish charity that she would have perished during the recent winter 'had it not been for some well disposed charitable friends'. Yet another, destitute and burdened with four children, survived only through her labour and the 'smale assistance of friends'. Robert Coles's needs had similarly been met not only by the fruits of his labour, but also 'by Gods assistance and comfort of friends'.[151] Even so, it seems overwhelmingly likely that lodging was the most common form of support afforded to the poor by their kin. When Mary Wright of King's Lynn was abandoned by her husband in 1651 she migrated 'in want' to stay with 'kinred and friends' in Hilborough. Co-residence of this kind may also, of course, have involved reciprocal benefits, especially for young parents who might expect grandparents or other relatives to provide childcare while they went out to work.[152]

Even though there is unequivocal evidence—from Clayworth (Nottinghamshire), Hedenham (Norfolk), Aldenham (Hertfordshire), Cratfield (Suffolk), Whitchurch (Oxfordshire), and the Kent parishes of Cranbrook, Maidstone, and Tonbridge, for example—that the elderly were paid parish pensions even when their adult offspring *were* resident (and perhaps even paying rates) within the parish, Cumbrian petitioners for relief were frequently at pains to argue that they were bereft of kin support: Blanche Bell was 'old, blind and now friendless'; Widow Joyce had 'no means, friends or relations to support her two infants'; Richard Walton, a crippled orphan, had 'no relations to help' him; John White, evicted and destitute, had 'no friends or belongings'. These assertions were not merely strategic attempts to circumvent legal stipulations, for similar claims—that they had 'no father or mother or any friend to rely on'; that they had only 'the smale assistance of friends'—were also characteristic of those who pleaded for support from endowed charities.[153]

Where they did have kin, moreover, the indigent frequently explained

[151] SARS, DD\SE/45/1/64, 2/10, 1/28.

[152] *Norfolk Sessions Order Book*, 31; Boulton, '"Extreme Necessity"', 59

[153] CRO, Q11/1/56/27, 91/35, 99/18, 116/23; SARS, DD\SE/45/1/7, 2/10. Cf. Laslett, *Family Life and Illicit Love*, 59–60; Wales, 'Poverty, Poor Relief and Life-Cycle', 384–5; Newman-Brown, 'Poor Relief and Family Situation', 414; Botelho, 'Aged and Impotent', 102–3; Smith, 'Ageing and Well-Being', 79–80, 83; Boulton, '"Extreme Necessity"', 57–58; M. Barker-Read, 'The Treatment of the Aged Poor in Five Selected West Kent Parishes from Settlement to Speenhamland, 1662–1797' (unpublished Ph.D. thesis, Open University, 1988), 60–1. For the ambiguous kin connotations of the term 'friends', sometimes implying cousinage, sometimes neighbours, see Tadmor, *Family and Friends*, 167–98.

that their family members were no longer able to care for them. Ninety-year-old Elizabeth Robinson of Cockermouth had long been looked after by her daughter Ann, but by 1692 she was aged 60 and 'too old and feeble to support her'. Florence Scott of Bolton could pay no rent during her illness, though her daughter did what she could to help her out of her earnings from service. Ann Sharp similarly claimed that, although her husband had 'starved for want of relief', her son 'does what he can'. Mabel Wilson, a poor blind woman who had lived all her life in Skelton being cared for only by her mother, reported in 1697 that her mother's death three months previously meant that she was now destitute. Janet Thompson of Cumrew had been blind since she was nine months old, and had been kept by her brother Thomas, but his decision to sell up and leave the country had left her without support. Failing sight meant that Bridget Hodgson of Penrith could no longer earn her living as a book-binder and although her son had been 'a great support to her' he had recently been press-ganged. Janet Jackson had looked after her 4-year-old brother James in Kirklinton parish but was 'only a poor servant' and could no longer afford his care.[154]

Grandparents were, by definition, particularly vulnerable to the exhaustion of health, energy, and resources, and experienced similar pressures. Thomas Hewitson of Westward (Cumberland) explained that he was happy to care for one of his five orphaned grandchildren but could not afford to maintain the other four. An inhabitant of Sutton Coldfield (Warwickshire) pleaded that he was unable to maintain his widowed daughter-in-law and her child because he was already providing for two other grandchildren.[155] George and Sybill Latimer had cared for their retarded granddaughter for fourteen years after she lost her parents, but both were now in their eighties and could no longer 'look to the poor Ideot as they used to do'.[156] Some paupers even claimed that their family members had always been too poor to help them, some of them implying that their poverty was actually inherited. Margaret Parker explained that she had been born in Cockermouth of 'very poor parents' and had since the age of 20 been forced to 'go to several places to work as a servant, till old age, blindness and lameness overtook her'. Now 77 years old, she

154 CRO, Q11/1/20/26, 33/1, 42/12, 47/10, 47/25 49/14, 105/17.

155 CRO, Q11/1/49/26; *Warwick County Records*, ii. 243.

156 CRO, Q11/1/91/34. Cases of this kind are put in context by A. Fessler, 'The Official Attitude Toward the Sick Poor in Seventeenth-Century Lancashire', *Transactions of the Historic Society of Lancashire and Cheshire*, 102 (1951), 97–8; P. Rushton, 'Lunatics and Idiots: Mental Disorder, the Community and the Poor Law in North East England, 1600–1800', *Medical History*, 32 (1988), 34–50. Cf. the case of George Monk in G. C. Edmonds, 'Accounts of Eighteenth-Century Overseers of the Poor of Chalfont St Peter', *Records of Buckinghamshire*, 18 (1966), 14–16.

subsisted only on her neighbours' pity.[157] Agnes Churchill explained that her 'father and mother are poor and not able to supply what may be wanting'; Jane Parker simply stated that her family was as poor as she was; Robert Scott that his family had been plunged into hardship with him; Thomas Whiteside that his parents were 'low' too.[158]

There were, even so, occasional cases where the elderly were maintained by their children. Margaret Worsted of Runton (Norfolk), it was reported in 1665, 'hath lately been sick and her work is so little but when she was able she did help to relieve her mother'. Indeed, parish relief was sometimes refused to the elderly on the grounds that their kin *were* able to support them. William Sibson, the parish officers of Bridekirk argued, was perfectly able to relieve his mother but had obtained a relief order on her behalf simply 'to evade his duty'. Although the parish officers of Combe St Nicholas (Somerset) had been relieving Richard and Ursula Stockman for three years, they decided that their pension should cease in 1612 because their children might be compelled to relieve them. The overseers of Tottenhill (Norfolk) successfully persuaded Henry Gill to dwell with his mother in 1641 and he did so until she died, nursing her through her last illness for eleven weeks 'when she was not able to help herself'.[159] These instances are, however, the exception that proves the rule. Most assistance mentioned by paupers in their examinations by, and petitions to, the authorities 'seems to have flowed *down* or across family relationships rather than *upwards*, within a fairly narrow circle of close kin'.[160] The very small number—only two instances in Staffordshire between 1660 and 1666, for example, and as little as *three* instances in Warwickshire between 1625 and 1696—of quarter sessions orders which required children to maintain their elderly parents nonetheless presents considerable problems of interpretation.[161] On the one hand, they might be taken to imply that the 'kin obligation' clause, buried as it was in a lengthy statute whose numerous other provisions cumulatively implied that the guiding principle of public policy was to be parochial support, was ignored by children, overseers, and magistrates alike, thereby

[157] CRO, Q11/1/102/18. Cf. B. Stapleton, 'Inherited Poverty and Life-Cycle Poverty: Odiham, Hampshire, 1650–1850', *Social History*, 18 (1993), 339–55.

[158] SARS, DD\SE/45/1/30; CRO, Q11/1/23/16, 37/7, 67/19.

[159] *Notebook of Robert Doughty*, 52; CRO, Q11/1/8/16; *Quarter Sessions Records for the County of Somerset*, i. 73; Wales, 'Poverty, Poor Relief and the Life-Cycle', 386. For equally rare examples from 18th-century Cranbrook (Kent), see Barker-Read, 'Treatment of the Aged Poor', 61.

[160] Boulton, '"Extreme Necessity"', 62.

[161] J. Kent and S. King, 'Changing Patterns of Poor Relief in Some English Rural Parishes, *circa* 1650–1750', *Rural History*, 14 (2003), 156 n. 142; *Warwick County Records*, v. 198–9; vii. 44; viii. 235.

cementing the cultural prejudice that to maintain, or even to be expected to maintain, one's own parents was 'unEnglish'.[162] On the other, they might testify to the sensitivity and local knowledge of parish officers who recognized that the children of elderly paupers were rarely well placed to offer maintenance, perhaps because they too were overburdened with children.[163] They also plausibly reflect 'the flawed capacity' of the early modern demographic system, in which perhaps 40 to 50 per cent of elderly persons might be without a son or a daughter and 30 to 40 per cent may even have lacked both, to provide kin-based assistance to the aged.[164] These complexities were, inevitably, compounded by kin dispersal. Although it was more difficult to force children who had moved away to contribute to the relief of their parents, this did not stop parish officers from doing so on occasion, as they did in Warwickshire in 1673 when the overseers of Harbury sought to recover the *2s. 6d.* they were spending every week on the aged father of Sarah Shaw from his daughter, even though she had long lived some six miles away in Wolfhamcote.[165]

The elderly themselves, however, were rather more frequently required to contribute towards the maintenance of their grandchildren. When the parish officers of Catcott (Somerset) sought to divest themselves of the burden of Clement Gover in the late 1640s, they did so on the basis that his grandfather was earning enough to maintain him: 'If a man can earn 12d a day in harvest time and 8d a day the rest of the year, besides being a single man; is he not obliged, by the laws of God and man to maintain or contribute towards the relief of his grandson, who is unable to maintain himself?'[166] Occasionally, as might be expected, requirements of this kind were made where the children had been orphaned.[167] Even so, the comparative rarity of these cases, a consequence of the fact that orphans were invariably regarded as legitimate 'objects of pity' and were therefore usually treated by parish officers as unproblematic exempla of deserving poverty, is thrown into stark relief by the far larger number of instances where grandparental relief was expected for children who had lost only *one* parent, through either

[162] Thomson, 'The Welfare of the Elderly in the Past', 199.

[163] Smith, 'Charity, Self-Interest and Welfare', 35. The problems of securing intergenerational support in the context of life-cycle poverty are modelled in Smith, 'Families and their Property', 68–85.

[164] Smith, 'Ageing and Well-Being', 68.

[165] *Warwick County Records*, v. 198–9.

[166] SARS, Q\SPET/1/26.

[167] For grandparents required to help maintain orphans, see *Quarter Sessions Order Book, 1642–1649*, ed. B. C. Redwood (Sussex Record Society, 54, 1954), 165, 183; *Warwick County Records*, ii. 41; iv. 284; viii. 12.

bereavement or abandonment.[168] Indeed, cases of kin being required to care for children where the family had through 'kinship crisis' become 'sub-nuclear' are more frequent than more orthodox cases of 'nuclear family hardship'.[169] Grandparents were, furthermore, occasionally forced to contribute to their grandchildren's maintenance where *both* parents were alive, usually because they were ill, or overburdened with the demands of their offspring.[170] In such cases, relief was more likely to be given as a cash contribution to the overseers than in the form of co-residence, though at least one kinsman thought better of the arrangements he had originally made with parish officers and actually took his son, daughter-in-law, and their two children into his home in Whitacre (Warwickshire) rather than pay a shilling a week to the parish officers of neighbouring Aston towards their maintenance.[171] The almost complete absence of relief orders which stipulated that care was to be provided by any relatives other than lineal kin is, finally, explained by the simple fact that no such support was sanctioned by the law.[172]

Conversely, both manorial and parish authorities were devising policies which actively discouraged complex co-residential arrangements amongst the poor. Restrictions on offering house room to inmates and sojourners often extended to the prosecution of harbouring, an offence of which even close kin could be convicted in either manorial or ecclesiastical courts. In 1632, for instance, the court of Burton Agnes in the East Riding prohibited the admission of lodgers. The way the homage described the only exception to this blanket prohibition is, however, instructive: the 'father or mother' might be accommodated, provided that they were 'aged and unmarried and of good and honest behaviour by the order or judgement of the rest of the township'. In 1631, one young mother and her four children were ejected from her brother's house in Sprowston (Norfolk) as unlawful inmates. These policies extended even to grandparents who accommodated their children's offspring. Goodwife Martin of Stevenage (Hertfordshire) was threatened with the cancellation of her pension in 1677 if she failed to send her grandchildren home, presumably to their parents' household, from where they would be

[168] *Norfolk Sessions Order Book*, 52; [*Sussex*] *Quarter Sessions Order Book*, 3, 4, 93; *Warwick County Records*, i. 148, 201, 215; ii. 16, 21, 52, 111, 210, 243, 259; iii. 58, 221; vii. 112; viii. 235, 261, 271; ix. 86, 122, 127.

[169] Horden, 'Household Care and Informal Networks', 49.

[170] [*Sussex*] *Quarter Sessions Order Book*, 149–50; *Warwick County Records*, i. 47, 132; iii. 72; iv. 54–5.

[171] *Warwick County Records*, iv. 54–5, 78.

[172] For rare exceptions, see *Warwick County Records*, i. 19 (for four sisters and another, unspecified, kinsman in 1625), 116 (for a sister-in-law in 1631).

apprenticed.[173] These policies should also be seen in the context of the powers of parish officers to fracture and reconstitute the households of the poor, either by boarding their children out with their neighbours or forcing them into apprenticeship.[174] In this sense, there was a very clear tension between the principle of parish support on the one hand and the idea of kin solidarity on the other, a tension which was not only reflected in the relatively small size of poor households but which must have been exacerbated after the settlement laws of 1662 crystallized notions of belonging to the community of the parish which overrode more traditional ties of kinship.[175]

The decision to live independently of one's kin was, even so, probably less a matter of institutional control than of cultural preference reinforced by the relentless pressure of life-cycle poverty. By and large, it seems, the poor, and especially the aged poor, either lived in their own households or lodged with others: in a sample of early modern rural censuses, the proportions of the widowed who lodged with other residents of the local community to whom they were not related were as high as 48 per cent for males and 34 per cent for females, with a further 14 and 19 per cent respectively living alone.[176] Although there were undoubtedly significant local variations in patterns of inter-generational care, the poor therefore almost invariably drew their support less often from their kin or offspring than they did from their neighbours.

Overall, it seems, although the limited legal obligation for kin support was enforced only patchily by parish officers, a much broader range of practices of kinship solidarity proved enduring among the poor themselves. The overriding impression is that conditions of poverty were of critical importance to the maintenance of family life in early modern society. The policies of overseer and magistrate alike might tear apart the households of the poor only to reconstitute them forcibly on principles of labour discipline, and might even, as we shall see, prevent them from being formed at all.[177] Both marriage and the exercise of the responsibilities of parenthood were privileges to be granted to, rather than rights to be exercised by, the poor, whose claim to family life was rendered little

[173] Turner and Woodward, 'Theft from the Common Man', 53: NA, SP16/272/44; HALS, D/P105/8/2, fo. 5.

[174] For boarding, see Ch. 1.4 below; for apprenticeship, see Chs. 3.2 and 6.2(*e*) below.

[175] T. Sokoll, 'The Pauper Household Small and Simple? The Evidence from Listings and Inhabitants and Pauper Lists of Early Modern England Reassessed', *Ethnologia Europaea*, 17 (1987), 25–42; P. Styles, 'The Evolution of the Laws of Settlement', repr. in Styles, *Studies in Seventeenth-Century West Midlands History* (Kineton, 1978), 175–204.

[176] Laslett, *Family Life and Illicit Love*, 204–5.

[177] See Chs. 3 and 5 below.

more than conditional under the terms of the Elizabethan relief statutes. The attempts of the poor to maintain themselves independently of the parish were, therefore, less a matter of pride in their independence than a desperate and painful policy to keep their families intact.

4. THE KINDNESS OF NEIGHBOURS

The casual help offered by their neighbours to the resident poor is also, almost by definition, an elusive historical quarry. It is generally most visible when the community as a whole was exhorted to come together to relieve the indigent, not only in the festive customs associated with particular dates in the ritual year but also in ad hoc ales in which food and drink were sold to raise funds for specific cases of hardship. Thus it was conventional well into the Elizabethan period for the churchwardens of Hexton (Hertfordshire) to contribute funds raised during the annual hocktide festivities to the relief of the poor: 'after they had eaton, then the hockers did gather money of everie one what they pleased to give, part of it then given to the poore'. As late as 1635, the churchwardens of Shipstone on Stour (Worcestershire) donated £4 raised by a 'May game gathering' to the relief of the poor.[178] Bishop Piers's notorious defence of Somerset church ales during the controversy over the Book of Sports (1633) turned in part on his assertion that they were 'feasts of charity for relief of the poor, the richer sort then keeping open house'.[179] It is likely that, in some communities at least, formal assessments for the poor were introduced only when older traditions of corporate festivity were abrogated and parishes forced to gather rates, as they were when the church ales of the parishes of north Dorset were suppressed in the early seventeenth century.[180]

The expression of the charitable impulse through conviviality also took the form of ales for specific purposes.[181] Throughout the medieval period, the raising of funds for honest neighbours who had fallen on hard times was often organized through a 'help-ale' or 'bid-ale' in which the recipient retained his dignity, the donors avoided embarrassment, and the

[178] BL, MS Additional, 6223, fo. 13; WCRO, DR446/21, unfol.

[179] NA, SP16/250/20. For the context, see T. G. Barnes, 'County Politics and a Puritan Cause Cèlèbre: Somerset Churchales, 1633', *Transactions of the Royal Historical Society*, 5th ser., 9 (1959), 103–22.

[180] D. Underdown, *Revel, Riot and Rebellion: Popular Politics and Culture in England, 1603–1660* (Oxford, 1985), 60–1, 82–3, 97–8. Cf. Ch. 4.4 below.

[181] J. Bennett, 'Conviviality and Charity in Medieval and Early Modern England', *Past and Present*, 134 (1992), 19–41.

social solidarity of the neighbourhood was arguably reaffirmed.[182] The extent to which these 'drinkings' can realistically be described as gatherings at which the poor looked for, and often found, charity and support rather from each other than from their more prosperous neighbours remains controversial, not least because the manorial rolls in which fines for unlawful ale-selling are recorded are so generally uninformative about the social status of those who brewed and on whose behalf they did so.[183] It is nonetheless clear that occasional ale-selling by a large number of poor households could constitute 'a system of circulating aid in which economic activity, neighbourly assistance and festivity were subtly blended'.[184] Help-ales of this kind seem to have been extremely common in the fifteenth and sixteenth centuries, and there is some evidence that, in the north-west of England at least, they persisted even into the late seventeenth century: the Lancashire apprentice Roger Lowe, for instance, recorded his attendance at two 'ales' of this kind in Ashton-in-Makerfield in the years 1663 and 1664.[185] The fact that the hosts of such gatherings should, by the 1650s, increasingly fall foul of prosecution suggests that the same kinds of pressures that curtailed drinking, dancing, and sport at church ales were also operative on more ad hoc festivities.[186] If church ales for the relief of the poor of the community gradually gave way to formal assessments for the poor of the parish, help-ales were similarly supplanted by the more regularized practice of securing a charity brief, in which a distressed person would have their circumstances rehearsed from the pulpit in order that formal collections could be made on their behalf.[187]

Although the tradition of raising charitable funds through communal conviviality gradually died out, the fragmented sociability of the alehouse

[182] For some scepticism on this latter point in particular, see M. Moisa, 'Conviviality and Charity in Medieval and Early Modern England', *Past and Present*, 154 (1997), 221–34.

[183] Cf. Bennett, 'Conviviality and Charity', 20.

[184] K. Wrightson, 'Alehouses, Order and Reformation in Rural England, 1590–1660', in E. and S. Yeo (eds.), *Popular Culture and Class Conflict, 1590–1914: Explorations in the History of Labour and Leisure* (Hassocks, 1981), 5.

[185] *The Diary of Roger Lowe*, ed. W. L. Sachse (London, 1938), 45, 72.

[186] Wrightson, 'Alehouses, Order and Reformation', 5. On the wider pattern of regulating communal sociability, see Underdown, *Revel, Riot and Rebellion*, 44–72; Fletcher, *Reform in the Provinces*, 262–81; R. Hutton, *The Rise and Fall of Merry England: The Ritual Year, 1400–1700* (Oxford, 1994), 153–99; S. Hindle, 'Custom, Festival and Protest in Early Modern England: The Little Budworth Wakes, St Peter's Day, 1596', *Rural History*, 6 (1995), 155–78.

[187] Despite the pioneering work of W. A. Bewes, *Church Briefs* (London, 1896), charity briefs remain an under-researched subject. See, however, T. L. Auffenberg, 'Organised English Benevolence: Charity Briefs, 1625–1705' (unpublished Ph.D. thesis, Vanderbilt University, 1973); and the interesting discussion in M. Harris, '"Inky Blots and Rotten Parchment Bonds": London, Charity Briefs and the Guildhall Library', *Historical Research*, 66 (1993), 98–110.

might nonetheless continue to serve the interests of the indigent. Given the long-standing significance of brewing to the household economies of the poor, and especially to those of widows, it is hardly surprising that magistrates, overseers, and ratepayers alike should recognize that alewives would likely fall on the parish if prevented from selling ale.[188] It was accordingly common well into the seventeenth century to license women, and especially widows, to sell ale rather than support them through formal parish relief. To this extent, ale-selling itself became a species of out-relief, albeit one subject to stipulations of honesty and respectability.[189] Thus the inhabitants of the Huntingdonshire parish of Pidley-cum-Fenton petitioned on behalf of their neighbour Goody Michell, 'an honest poor woman of godly life and conversation having three children to nourish & living on her hand and nothing wherewith to help & succour them but what she earneth and getteth with her painfull and honest labour'. Because the ratepayers were already overcharged, they requested that she be licensed to keep an alehouse: 'this poor widow and neighbour of ours being one who has always been brought up with the practice of brewing' and has 'laboured thereby without any ryot or disturbance being used'.[190] This is to say nothing of those numerous occasions when neighbours turned a blind eye to those who sold ale *without* a licence who would, if prosecuted, become a parish charge. It was estimated in 1638 that there were at least 500 inhabitants of the West Riding who 'brew without license', most of them 'poor people that thereby maneteyne theire wyves and children, which otherwise would fall upon the parish for releefe'. Even so, there were a further 2,000 authorized alehouses in the county, many of which had probably secured a licence by mobilizing connections of patronage amongst parish officers and ratepayers.[191] Thus the 'pore inhabitants of Blickling' urged the Norfolk JPs at the turn of the sixteenth century to license Richard Smith's alehouse without which they and their families 'would have perished', especially since Smith had 'trusted' them, selling them beer and bread to

[188] J.M. Bennett, *Ale, Beer and Brewsters in England: Women's Work in a Changing World, 1300–1600* (Oxford, 1996); Fletcher, *Reform in the Provinces*, 233–4.

[189] Wrightson, 'Alehouses, Order and Reformation', 2; Sharpe, *Crime in Seventeenth-Century England*, 55.

[190] BL, MS Additional, 34401, fo. 232. For similar examples, see Wrightson and Levine, *Poverty and Piety*, 138; Sharpe, *Crime in Seventeenth-Century England*, 55. The majority of petitions concerning alehouses, of course, including (for example) the twenty-four presented to Essex quarter sessions between 1600 and 1650, argued the other way, requesting action against particular disorderly houses or a general reduction of provision to the necessary minimum. Wrightson, 'Alehouses, Order and Reformation', 19.

[191] NA, SP16/390/66.

them on credit.[192] Although the selling of ale by the poor, even to their poor neighbours, had long been a customary way of alleviating poverty, it sat, in its regulated form at least, quite comfortably alongside the provisions of the Elizabethan poor laws.

We have thus far been concerned with collective or semi-formal manifestations of neighbourly and communal support for the poor. It is, however, very occasionally possible to catch glimpses of neighbours making more spontaneous gestures of relief. Richard Gough recorded for posterity the sad case of Goodwife Hodgkins of Myddle (Shropshire) who, having been reduced by her husband's excessive drinking to living in a lodge on Harmer Heath, 'had nothing to maintaine herselfe but what neighbours sent'. Mabel Porter of Carlisle told the Cumberland justices that she had out of pity provided for two children of Dalston parish 'they having no one else to care for them'. A poor widow evicted from her lodgings in Kirkoswald had, she said, been saved from exposure and starvation only by the voluntary alms brought by a household servant of a local 'worthy family', the Aglionbys of Nunnery.[193]

Aid of this kind was most likely to be described and recorded either where it was habitual or where it was exhausted. Well into the late seventeenth century, claimants for parochial relief frequently made reference to those informal networks of aid within the local community that had enabled them to survive, often for many years, without calling upon the parish. They had always depended, they argued, 'on the charity of good neighbours', on 'their neighbours pity', on 'local charity', or on what 'well dispos'd Christians' gave them.[194] Richard Clough, a 60-year-old collier of Manchester (Lancashire), for instance, described in 1698 how illness, unemployment, and destitution had forced him 'to live in a barne in certain old rags that neighbours out of pity threw upon him' and how he had 'no relief but what his neighbours gave him out of Christian pity'.[195] Katherine Jackson of Kirklinton (Cumberland) proudly declared that 'all her honest neighbours' had 'come to see' her during her illness. James

[192] Norfolk RO, MS COL, 13/40.

[193] R. Gough, *History of Myddle*, ed. D. Hey (Harmondsworth, 1981), 191–2; CRO, Q11/1/47/4, 99/28.

[194] CRO, Q/11/1/88/14, 102/18, 117/7, 120/20. Such petitions are also, of course, symptomatic of the pathology of neighbourhood support, since they also argued that neighbours 'now say that the rest of the parish must pay their share' or that they 'growe weary of extending their charitable reliefe'. CRO, Q11/1/59/27, 74/4. Cf. Boulton, '"Extreme Necessity"', 65. For the rhetorical trope that charity was grown cold, see Ch. 6.4 below.

[195] LRO, QSP/820/1. For other Lancashire examples of the charity of neighbours, see LRO, QSP/818/14; 823/41, 53; 826/34. But here too, rhetoric of this kind often implied compassion fatigue, as it did in Tyldesley, where the charity of neighbours had begun to 'slacken'. LRO, QSP/823/53.

Little of Hayton-in-Gilsland, who needed four men to lift him in a blanket when they made his bed every fortnight, claimed that his neighbours were always 'willing to come when required'.[196] Mary Atkinson and her son would have had to sleep on the streets of Caldewgate had not a kindly neighbour taken them in. Mary Brown had been lodged by a neighbour in Newtown who proved 'very loving and tender over her'. Ann Bowman lamented that since the parish officers had accommodated her 'without the cry of her neighbours', she could no longer get relief in her hunger.[197] Claimants occasionally even counterposed the generosity of informal support with the stinginess of parish relief. Mary Davis testily told the Cumberland bench in 1716 that she had hitherto 'only her neighbours charity, nothing from the parish'. Neighbourly support did, however, depend on maintaining a reputation for honesty in the local community which might be officially reflected in, and in turn reflective of, the policies of the parish officers, as is suggested by the sad experience of Janet Nicholson of Greystoke, whose requests for alms were spurned in 1700. Since the parish officers denied her relief, she lamented, her neighbours withheld their charity.[198]

Such cases are a valuable reminder of the dangers of presenting an excessively rosy picture of mutual aid in the English local community. Although recent commentators have justifiably been sceptical of older models of the 'decline of neighbourliness', it would be naive to ignore the culture of suspicion and hostility that was sometimes bred even in situations of familiarity, a culture that was arguably fostered by the social and political dynamics of formal welfare provision.[199] Put-upon neighbours might not only live in indifference to or suspicion of one another, they might be drawn into tactics of harassment and even of ostracism when confronted with those who crossed the thresholds of charity. The poor themselves, of course, were expected to participate in the networks of surveillance and social discipline created to catch those idlers and pilferers who literally took the perquisites of the community for granted. The tensions revealed in cases where the accommodation of the indigent might create, or their offspring breed up, a charge on the parish are only the most drastic examples of the neighbourhood closing its ranks rather than opening its arms.[200]

[196] CRO, Q/11/1/96/8, 197/35.

[197] CRO, Q/11/1/196/25, 197/41, 212/17.

[198] CRO, Q11/1/57/14, 128/14.

[199] For the older tradition, see Thomas, *Religion and the Decline of Magic*, 553–7, 561–7, 582; A. Macfarlane, *Witchcraft in Tudor and Stuart England: A Regional and Comparative Study* (London, 1970), 168–77, 205–6. Cf. the suggestive remarks in Wrightson, 'The Politics of the Parish', 18–22.

[200] See Chs. 5.2, 5.3, and 6.2 below.

Neighbourly support for the indigent is therefore, like the giving of alms, most visible in the historical record either when it was exhausted or when it was encouraged or co-ordinated by the parish. The overseers' accounts of the period—from Aldenham (Hertfordshire) in 1628, from Great Malton (Norfolk) in 1639–40, from Pluckley (Kent) in the 1640s and 1650s, from Cratfield (Suffolk) in the 1660s, from Cowden (Kent) in the 1680s—are replete with examples of payments made to neighbours, themselves frequently poor, for keeping and/or nursing orphaned, disabled, or aged paupers, or for helping them out when sick.[201] 'Tending' was almost invariably described as woman's work, though even care of this kind did not invariably grant women privileged rights of access to the circuits of charity or welfare. In the late 1630s the overseers of several south Warwickshire parishes were making payments of this type: Margaret Bankes of Brailes 'for keeping of a child of one William Somertons at 16d the weeke'; Katherine Machin of Brailes, 6*d.* 'for washing John Coles' linnen'; Mrs Dabory of Bishop's Tachbrook, 4*s.* a week for maintaining 'William Hogges his three children'; Wife Hinkley of Tanworth, £2. 7*s.* 0*d.* 'for keeping of a child that a woman rane from'; Goodwife Harrod of Warmington, £1. 8*s.* 0*d.* 'for keeping a bastard child'.[202] At least they got the public recognition that they deserved, unlike the anonymous 'woman to attende [Thomas Harris] in the time of his sickness' to whom the overseers of Ilmington paid 4*s.* in 1639.[203] Women's 'right of entry to sheltered accommodation', it seems, was often made conditional on their providing caring services and 'a similar *quid pro quo* was extensively used by the poor law system'.[204]

Of the more generally co-ordinated practices of neighbourhood support, however, two in particular stand out: general hospitality, to which we will return in Chapter 2, and boarding. The practice of billeting the poor on their wealthier neighbours appears to have been widely encouraged in the late sixteenth century. In early 1597, the strategy of identifying and appointing 'to every man the person or persons wch he shall daylye relieve' had been suggested by Edward Hext in the second, and less well known, of his letters to Lord Treasurer Burghley.[205] Orders

[201] Newman-Brown, 'Poor Relief and Family Situation', 416–17; Wales, 'Poverty, Poor Relief and the Life-Cycle', 385 n. 66; N. Davie, 'Custom and Conflict in a Wealden Village: Pluckley, 1550–1700' (unpublished D.Phil. thesis, Oxford, 1988), 239; Botelho, 'Aged and Impotent', 102–3; Smith, 'Ageing and Well-Being', 82.

[202] SBTRO, DR37/85/6/3, 38, 39, 43.

[203] SBTRO, DR37/85/6/21.

[204] Pelling, 'Older Women', 174. For the increasing reliance on poor women to care for their neighbours in the later 18th century, see Sharpe, *Population and Society*, 244–6.

[205] BL, MS Lansdowne, 83, fo. 49^{v} (Hext to Burghley, 21 Feb. 1597).

issued by the Devon bench in 1597 included the requirement that each householder was to provide daily meals for up to three poor people. The mayor and council of Bristol made a similar order for the daily provision of meals to specified numbers of poor (varying between two and eight) by all the householders of the city.[206] As might be expected, boarding out seems to have been a tactic used especially for the elderly and for the young, those groups who might be considered a 'burdensome surplus' which might conveniently be exported to another household.[207] Once again, it is clear that the very fact of economic need rendered the families of the poor vulnerable to the intervention of the authorities. In some parishes, indeed, the boarding out of children might well have been a preliminary, perhaps elsewhere an alternative, to parish apprenticeship, under the terms of which children could be removed from their parents care for much longer periods. Among the most well-documented communities which placed considerable faith in boarding both adults and children is Hadleigh (Suffolk), where sixty-three paupers, two-thirds of them children, were billeted on their neighbours in the period 1579–96. Where adults, especially the elderly, were concerned, boarding seems to have been a temporary arrangement lasting a month or two during a period of illness or injury. Children, by contrast, were house-guests over a much longer term, averaging perhaps a year or two, and tended to fall into two groups: orphans (or those who had lost their mothers) who were boarded between the ages of 2 and 4; and those from large families overburdened with children, who were lodged in other households between the ages of 5 and 9, often in preparation for apprenticeship.[208]

Compliance with billeting also appears to have been particularly common in the south-west, where the policy was sometimes preferred to the provision of pensions. It was practised in the Devon parish of Farway from 1564, where two paupers were fed and lodged by specified neighbours on specific days of the week.[209] In Constantine (Cornwall), the practice was well entrenched by the mid-1590s. In May 1596 the vestry approved a list of some fifty householders who were between them to lodge sixty paupers, most of them children (though some of them were adults with children of their own). The 'lawmakers' or vestrymen of the parish themselves were not exempted, some of them being required to

[206] A. H. A. Hamilton, *Quarter Sessions Records from Queen Elizabeth to Queen Anne* (London, 1878), 16–17; Leonard, *Early History of English Poor Relief*, 123.

[207] Horden, 'Household Care and Informal Networks', 29.

[208] M. K. McIntosh, 'Networks of Care in Elizabethan English Towns: The Example of Hadleigh, Suffolk', in Horden and Smith (eds.), *The Locus of Care*, 78–80, 84.

[209] Devon RO, Exeter, 67A/PW1, unfol.

give house room to as many as four poor neighbours. Hosts were generally expected to provide meat, drink, and clothes for the parish child until they reached the age of 24. That some of the hosts were themselves needy is indicated by the caveat that children whose hosts were 'old and not able to get anything' were to be given clothing by the parish. That this was part of an ongoing commitment to billeting is suggested by the introduction, in June 1598, of fines of a shilling a week for any householder who refused or neglected to maintain 'any poor [person] committed' to him.[210] That there was elsewhere an overlap between billeting and formal relief is apparent in the Somerset parish of Staplegrove in 1598–9, where one of the two paupers billeted out was also in receipt of a cash payments totalling 12*s*.[211]

Boarding out was still widely practised in the 1630s in Devon, where the 'poore children of such as by their labour are not able to support their charge' were billeted upon 'those able to give relief', and in Somerset, where overseers made regular 'allowances' for 'parishioners who succoureth poor people and their families'. Boarding remained the principal means of relief in Cowden (Kent) into the 1640s.[212] It was equally common in Lancashire, where in 1636 the vestry of Prescot approved expenses not only for the for the 'tabling' of three children by their neighbours but also, in a decision which reveals the curious intersection of contractual and kin-based notions of family obligation, to subsidize the keeping of two children by their own parents. Elsewhere, it seems, boarding was a short-term arrangement, as it was in Radway (Warwickshire), where William Hyarne was paid 7*s*. 'for tabling Elizabeth Heynes 9 weeks' in 1639.[213] The justices of the Lancashire districts of Furness and Cartmell reported in 1638 that, of the 464 paupers for whom relief orders had been made, 176 (38 per cent) were relieved not by

[210] Cornwall RO, Truro, DD/P39/8/1, unfol. (resolutions of 7 May 1596, 8 June 1598). Population estimates for late 16th-century Constantine are difficult to come by. That 141 households were, however, assessed for the hearth tax in 1664 suggests that the population was approximately 1,000 in the 1660s and plausibly about 750–800 (perhaps divided amongst 170 households) in the 1590s. Well over half of all the households in the parish were, therefore, involved, either as hosts or as guests, in the 1596 scheme. *Cornwall Hearth and Poll Taxes 1660–1664: Direct Taxation in Cornwall in the Reign of Charles II*, ed. T. L. Stoate (Bristol, 1981), 115–16. I am grateful to Tom Arkell for providing these estimates.

[211] BL, MS Additional, 30278, printed in Leonard, *Early History of English Poor Relief*, appendix VI, esp. 327, 329.

[212] NA, SP16/189/5; SARS, D/P/b.my.13/2/1, unfol.; E. Turner, 'Ancient Parochial Account Book of Cowden', *Sussex Archaeological Collections*, 20 (1882), 107.

[213] *Prescot Churchwardens' Accounts, 1635–1663*, ed. T. Steel (Record Society of Lancashire and Cheshire, 137, 2002), 11 (these latter payments were made to two separate parishioners 'for and towards the keeping of [their] poore children'); SBTRO, DR37/85/6/34.

pensions but by being freely lodged and fed by named inhabitants. While some parishes preferred a mixture of pensions and billeting, others relied exclusively on compulsory residential relief in kind. Thus, in the hamlet of Allythwaite, thirty-nine poor residents were given house room by their neighbours.[214] The policy evidently had an afterlife well into the mid-seventeenth century in Constantine, where it was ordered in 1650 not only that any single mother who was chargeable to the parish was 'to be forced to service if she be able', but also (in a decision whose emotional consequences can only be imagined) that her children of weanable age 'shall be taken' from her and placed with their neighbours. Since these children were too young to be apprenticed, it is likely that they were boarded out in more prosperous households.[215] Board and lodging was therefore freely, if not always voluntarily, offered by householders as a means of avoiding a poor rate assessment. Even when householders were offered nominal payments of a penny or two a week to lodge adult paupers, as they were in Littleport (Cambridgeshire) in 1624, they were almost certainly out of pocket by the time they had fed them. This was all the more true where infants were concerned, since babies in early seventeenth-century Wisbech were boarded out at the weekly rate of 6*d.* or 8*d.*, dropping to 20*s.* annually when the child was able to participate in the household economy. By the time a child reached the age of 8 or 9, and might prove useful in craftwork or agriculture, payments were usually dropped altogether, leaving host and guest in a relationship analogous to that between master and servant.[216] Relief in kind on these models undoubtedly had attractions in an economy in which cash was not always in abundant supply.[217]

The most casual of all the relationships between the poor and their richer neighbours was the donation of gifts of alms, usually, though not invariably solicited through begging. Our concern here is not with the experience of vagrancy, and its associated careers of desperation, migration, petty crime, corporal punishment, and incarceration.[218] Our focus, rather, is on the 'depressing peregrinations from door to door' of resident poor people who could easily be located in the matrices of mutuality and obligation from which neighbourhoods and communities were con-

[214] NA, SP16/330/99.

[215] Cornwall RO, DD P39/8/1, unfol. (resolution of 20 Oct. 1650).

[216] Hampson, *Treatment of Poverty in Cambridgeshire*, 40, 46; McIntosh, 'Networks of Care', 84. See Ch. 3.2 below.

[217] C. Muldrew, '"Hard Food for Midas": Cash and its Social Value in Early Modern England', *Past and Present*, 170 (2001), 78–120.

[218] Slack, 'Vagrants and Vagrancy'; Beier, *Masterless Men*.

structed.[219] Begging was arguably the most long-standing of the survival strategies of the poor, its connotations of humility and dependence having deep roots in European culture. That begging enjoyed a long customary half-life was primarily due to its ancient sanctification in the traditions of Christian charity. Indeed, the outstretched hand and the pleading demeanour were among the most powerful of all gestures of piety, both symbolizing the supplicatory relationship between man and God and articulating a vision of spiritually impoverished humanity dependent upon providential gifts. Man was 'always a beggar in regard to the favours bestowed by God'.[220] The giving of alms, in turn, was not merely a gift of sustenance and an acknowledgement of the humble status of the mendicant, but also a recognition of the Christian obligation to offer charity. Begging was, therefore, both a survival strategy involving intense competition over unequally shared resources and a deeply symbolic activity the meaning of which was enmeshed in a wider web of dependency and reciprocity. The exchange of alms for prayers of gratitude was a living expression of the intimate relationship between the social and the cosmic order.[221] As such, begging existed in a symbiotic relationship with hospitality, and the practices of beggars can be understood only in the context of the attitudes of the householders from whom they solicited alms, an issue to which we shall return in Chapter 2.

Enshrined as it was in the rituals and practices of Christian culture, begging was also enveloped by legal ambiguity. Sixteenth-century policy-makers seem to have been very inconsistent in their attitude to begging: it was regulated by licence in 1531; prohibited altogether in 1536, and again in 1547; condemned once again in 1552; but licensed again by the statutes of 1555 and 1563. The two great statutes which together formed the Elizabethan poor laws were contradictory. A clause in the 1598 act licensing begging was quietly dropped in 1601. *An Ease for Overseers* nevertheless went out of its way to justify the practice on the grounds that 'the impotencie and impediments' of the indigent were more likely 'to stirre up' mercy if householders were personally confronted by them, rather than informed about them by a third party. Beggars would, after all, be grateful for 'many fragments' given in alms that would otherwise 'be cast

[219] Thomas, *Religion and the Decline of Magic*, 555.

[220] W. J. Courtenay, 'Token Coinage and the Administration of Poor Relief During the Late Middle Ages', *Journal of Interdisciplinary History*, 3 (1972), 279.

[221] L. P. Wandel, 'Begging', in H. J. Hillerbrand (ed.), *The Oxford Encyclopaedia of the Reformation* (4 vols., New York, 1996), i. 137. For historical discussions of almsgiving as a form of gift exchange in early modern society, see Ben-Amos, 'Gifts and Favors'; N. Z. Davis, *The Gift in Sixteenth-Century France* (Oxford, 2000), esp. 23–35.

away'.[222] The result of these contradictions was confusion, even amongst legal authorities: Cromwell's law reformer William Sheppard thought that begging was still legal in 1675. He was not the only one under a misapprehension about the direction of policy: a Kentish man mistakenly thought (and openly lamented) that the 1598 statute had 'put down begging', although his error did not prevent him being prosecuted for seditious words.[223] These legal uncertainties helped ensure that begging remained socially acceptable long after it was supposedly prohibited in 1601.

What did the needy beg for? The more habitual mendicants, especially those who had travelled from afar (perhaps with counterfeit licences), tended to beg for cash. Whatever they were given by private householders, parish authorities were hardly generous, especially in rural communities where the gift of a penny or two from the churchwarden would likely be dispensed with a dismissive warning to move on.[224] Although the numbers of beggars passing through small communities, especially on main roads, might be very substantial, their cumulative demands representing a significant drain on parish resources, the returns for the individual mendicant were slight.[225] But the known neighbourhood poor were far more likely to beg for food, especially under the terms of licences. Phillip Stubbes wrote disparagingly in 1583 that those who begged for victuals could expect only 'refuse meat, scraps and parings'. In the 1630s, Barbara Stafford of Sileby (Leicestershire) sent her children to beg for buttermilk and whey. By the late seventeenth century, Hannah Wolley thought that the poor were fobbed off with skim milk that their prosperous neighbours usually fed to pigs, though she discouraged householders from permitting their kitchen servants to give them even this meagre fare.[226] Even at times of high prices, the charitable themselves were perhaps more inclined to give alms in kind because of the scriptural 'type' of the man of charity (described in Matthew's Gospel) as

[222] The vacillations of policy can be traced in Slack, *Poverty and Policy*, 113–37 (Ch. 6: 'The Making of the Poor Law, 1485–1610'); *An Ease for Overseers of the Poore*, 30.

[223] W. Sheppard, *A Grand Abridgment of the Common and Statute Law of England* (London, 1675), 512; *Calendar of Assize Records; Kent Indictments, Elizabeth I*, ed. J. S. Cockburn (London, 1979), 423.

[224] Beier, *Masterless Men*, 27–8, estimates (somewhat optimistically) that a beggar might regularly collect as much as 6*d*. a day, which (given the fact that mendicancy could be practised all year round) might result in an annual income of £9, or six times the value of the average parish pension.

[225] Cf. Beier, *Masterless Men*, 110–11.

[226] P. Stubbes, *The Anatomy of Abuses*, ed. F. J. Furnivall (2 vols., London, 1877–82), i. 105; Capp, 'Life, Love and Litigation', 71; H. Wolley, *The Gentlewoman's Companion; Or, A Guide to the Female Sex* (3rd edn., London, 1682), 302. By the 18th century, housemaids were sometimes dismissed for giving food to the poor. Broad, 'Parish Economies of Welfare', 1004.

he who gave of his *own* food, clothing, and time. As Ralph Josselin of Earls Colne (Essex) described one charitable act he performed in 1647, 'we gave them such old things as we any ways could spare'.[227]

Even after the Elizabethan poor laws, and especially in the light of provision of the 1598 statute, which authorized licensed begging, mendicancy was often a surrogate for parish relief. The West Riding justices famously signalled their hostility to poor rates on the grounds that the resident poor were more effectively catered for at the kitchen doors of their more prosperous neighbours: 'many are able to give relief that are not able to give money'. That such attitudes were so strongly held is unsurprising given that the introduction of formal poor relief came so soon after the widespread and generally successful campaign for co-ordinated almsgiving during the dearth of the 1590s.[228] Indeed, begging was tolerated, even actively encouraged, throughout England during the first half of the seventeenth century.[229] In Salisbury in 1626, for instance, begging in their home parishes was recommended for those who were 'totally impotent and not able to work' who had been approved and badged by the city fathers.[230] It was common even in the 1630s for poor relief and licensed begging to be considered as alternative policy options. The justices of Wirrall (Cheshire) informed the privy council in 1632 that the impotent were either relieved by weekly contributions or 'otherwise ordered' by the overseers 'to aske alms within their parishes'. In 1633 the only pauper in the Shropshire parish of Myddle was blind John Matthews, who was allowed to go round the parish doing odd jobs and begging. Elizabeth Crabbe of Seaton (Devon) similarly survived by working and running 'errands for divers people & hath sometimes meate and sometimes money for her paynes'.[231] Elsewhere, it seems, begging and the parish pension were never considered mutually exclusive. The parish officers of Tonbridge (Kent), for instance, ordered in 1682 that all aged pensioners be permitted to beg 'broken victuals' from their neighbours at mealtimes. Practices of this kind continued well into the eighteenth century, especially in the far north-west. Although the blind, 80-year-old

[227] Matthew 25: 34–40; *The Diary of Ralph Josselin, 1616–1683*, ed. A. Macfarlane (Records of Social and Economic History, NS 3, Oxford, 1976), 106. Cf. Courtenay, 'Token Coinage', 286 n. 26.

[228] *West Riding Sessions Records, 1597–1642*, ed. J. Lister (2 vols., Yorkshire Archaeological Society Record Series, 3, 54, Leeds, 1888–1915), i. 84; Hindle, 'Dearth, Fasting and Alms'.

[229] See Ch. 4 below.

[230] *Poverty in Early Stuart Salisbury*, ed. P. Slack (Wiltshire Record Society, 31, 1975), 89. Cf. Ch. 6.5 below.

[231] NA, SP16/197/19; D. Hey, *An English Rural Community: Myddle under the Tudors and Stuarts* (Leicester, 1974), 188; Sharpe, *Population and Society*, 218.

widow Mary Wildman of Burgh-by-Sands (Cumberland) had never claimed relief before 1709, the justices ordered her a weekly pension of 6*d.* and 'leave to seek more round the parish'.[232] As we have seen, begging was often carried out by family members on behalf of an indigent relative: 89-year-old Matthew Rothery of Embleton claimed that he had 'only been Sustained by [his] Aged wife going in[to] the Country to begg for him'; William Crosthwaite of Workington that he used to beg alone but was now 'lead by his wife to her very great trouble'; and Thomas Bewley of Irthington that his wife had customarily begged for them both but that she was now too old to 'walk the country'.[233] Matthew Hale thought that it was the very failure of overseers to provide either adequate pensions or sufficient employment that encouraged householders to relieve beggars: how could they dare to deny alms when they feared that without them the poor would be starved?[234] Even if parish officers grew less likely over time to acknowledge the interface of mendicancy and hospitality as an acceptable mode of organizing relief, begging persisted in rural communities well into the eighteenth century and beyond.

All those who advocated the toleration of begging were at pains to point out that only the *resident* poor were permitted to seek alms, usually under licence.[235] Apologias of this kind also derived in part from the ancient Christian notion that charity begins at home. The editor of Ezekiel Culverwell's works noted that, throughout Christian history, 'though there were many poore, and none greatly rich, yet did none of the poore begge abroad for food but were relieved at home' (i.e. in their home parish).[236] Such rhetorical defences of regular almsgiving were supplemented by more practical defences of the de facto toleration of local begging. The Somerset justices argued in 1613 that householders were only to refuse alms to '*suspected* persons coming to ther doors begging'. Their colleagues in Norfolk provided an even more direct commentary on the semi-legitimacy of begging as it was actually practised by the familiar neighbourhood poor of the parish. 'If anie do begge', they informed the privy council in 1631, 'they are but neare dwellers.'[237] Henry

[232] Barker-Read, 'Treatment of the Aged Poor', 70; CRO, Q/11/1/92/1. It was, however, generally the case in the south that pensions and begging were regarded as mutually exclusive by the late 17th century for. See Ch. 6.2(*b*) below.

[233] CRO, Q/11/1/37/11, 120/6, 128/5.

[234] M. Hale, *Discourse Touching Provision for the Poor* (London, 1683), sig. A3.

[235] For an early example of a begging licence see ERO, Q/SR46/15 (Roydon, Essex, 1573). A valuable collection of licences is reproduced in B. Clarke, 'Norfolk Licences to Beg: An Unpublished Collection', *Norfolk Archaeology*, 35 (1972), 327–34.

[236] E. Culverwell, *A Treatise of Faith* (London, 1623), sigs. 3^v–4^v.

[237] *Quarter Sessions Records for the County of Somerset*, i. 100; NA, SP16/197/13.

Best noted in 1642 that 'poore folkes' would usually come begging for wool at shearing time, and ordered his shearers to set aside a special basket for the 'worst lockes of wooll', ensuring that each of the poor had an armful, although insisting that 'more' was to be given ' to those of our owne towne then to others'.[238] The notion that begging, like charity itself, began at home and moved outward to kindred and neighbourhood is best exemplified in years of high prices, when dearth and desperation weakened the restraint on begging abroad. Thus an Essex jury complained in 1596 that 'many men, women and children' went 'a-begging' out of the town of Thaxted and that 'there is neither work nor victual, unless they beg for it, provided for them'.[239]

In the early seventeenth century, inevitably, begging was an essential supplement to a parish pension that could not, in and of itself, conceivably support an under- or unemployed labourer, let alone his family. In the more remote parts of the country where dispersed settlement patterns created acute problems for the management and policing of parish relief, licensed begging might be the preferred and semi-formalized solution into the late seventeenth and early eighteenth centuries. In 1672, for example, the vestry of Holme Cultram (Cumberland) ordered 'according to a former neighbourly rule' that a 'poor indigent feeble old man' should 'goe from house to house' to 'accept of such reliefe as shall be afforded him'.[240] The importance of licences to seek alms in the far north-west is reflected in the very large number of relief orders issued by the Cumberland justices only when they became convinced that paupers were so old or ill that they were unable to continue begging.[241] Indeed, it is particularly striking that the indigent practised mendicancy to such an advanced age in these dispersed communities; of the seventeen petitioners who insisted that they were no longer able to seek alms, eleven gave their ages: three claimed to be in their seventies, a further seven in their eighties, and one aged over 90. Narratives such as these, indeed, suggest that the aged poor actually thought of begging as just another form of work, the last phase in a life-cycle of labour, albeit one which earned them only meagre recompense.[242]

238 *Henry Best of Elmswell*, 25.

239 ERO, Q/SR135/21.

240 C. M. Bouch and G. P. Jones, *A Short Economic and Social History of the Lake Counties, 1500–1830* (Manchester, 1961), 158.

241 Cf. Ch. 6.4(*a*).

242 CRO, Q11/1/5/17, 6/16, 6/21, 6/25, 8/7, 20/33, 26/31, 34/2–3, 37/17, 59/34, 73/43, 76/28, 81/18, 87/8, 97/11, 97/22, 107/2. For petitioners in Caroline Lancashire and Norfolk claiming parish relief or increased pensions on the grounds that they could no longer beg, see G. W. Oxley, 'The Permanent Poor in South-West Lancashire under the Old Poor Law', in

Mendicancy was emphatically not, however, confined to the aged. Essex magistrates complained in 1632 that while parish pensioners drank and gambled away their allowances in alehouses, their wives and children begged in the streets. As late as 1698, Richard Dunning imagined that those men who received relief in respect of their large families 'soon spend it', leaving their children either 'to beg for their own relief or starve'.[243] Indeed, child begging seems to have been particularly prevalent. At the turn of the sixteenth century the judges of the Norfolk circuit explicitly encouraged children under the age of 7 to beg. Their advice seems to have been taken seriously, at least in the parish of Salthowse, where the overseers denied a woman relief on the grounds that 'her children be ordinarily relieved at the doors' of her neighbours. In Ipswich in 1597 the census revealed eleven cases of children younger than 7, and a further two aged between 8 and 14, begging with or without their parents. The two elder children of Michael King, aged 6 and 3, for instance, were sent out to augment a family income seriously weakened by the unemployment of their father and the meagre wages paid to their mother for spinning yarn, though whether they took their 1-year-old sibling with them is a matter of conjecture. The wife of Robert Dearing apparently begged with all four of her children, almost certainly carrying the youngest, aged 2, in her arms. (Little wonder that the parish officers noted tersely that the Dearings needed not only spinning wheels and cards but 'discipline'). Others, however, had reservations. One Warwickshire widow partly based her claim for an increase in her pension in 1626 on the grounds that her youngest child, aged 5, was not old enough to beg safely.[244]

Although, therefore, the Elizabethan statutes envisaged the replacement of licensed begging with relief based primarily on parish pensions, the transition was in practice only ever partially completed, and doubtless took place at different rates in different parts of the country. But where the practice of begging did eventually come under scrutiny, the evolution from a charitable regime based on pleading and exhortation to one based on assessment and calculation is disclosed. County-wide initiatives of this kind were, of course, always vulnerable to evasion in the parishes. Much more instructive are those instances where evolving attitudes to begging

J. R. Harris (ed.), *Liverpool and Merseyside: Essays in the Economic History of the Port and its Hinterland* (London, 1969), 22; Wales, 'Poverty, Poor Relief and the Life-Cycle', 388.

[243] Wrightson and Levine, *Poverty and Piety*, 179; R. Dunning, *Bread for the Poor* (Exeter, 1698), 6.

[244] Norfolk RO, AYL17; Fletcher, *Reform in the Provinces*, 151; *Poor Relief in Elizabethan Ipswich*, ed. J. Webb (Suffolk Records Society, 9, 1966), 130, 135, 139, 140; *Warwick County Records*, i. 25.

can be traced within an individual community. In the Essex market town of Braintree, for instance, the early months of 1623 appear to have been decisive. In February, the vestry appointed a beadle 'to gather up about diner & supper time all that beg at mens doores', though they added the caveat that the overseers should still have the power to license the seeking of alms by the resident poor. Even so, they were particularly concerned to prevent children from begging. One labourer who complained of his poverty 'for want of employment' was given a gratuity of two shillings, on condition that he refrained from 'sending his boy a begging'. Another child was removed from his father and placed in the parish almshouse 'because he goes a begging'. By May 1623, the overseer was ordered to 'talke with all the poor that doe usually goe a begging and take a course to prevent that disorder'.[245] Letting one's children beg might earn short-term rewards of sustenance but it was also hazardous, since it amounted to a public declaration that the household was no longer viable and virtually invited the intervention of the authorities which might culminate in the removal of the child. Those mothers who sent their children begging knew that they were taking an enormous risk, and had perhaps already resigned themselves to the likelihood of early separation from their offspring. The suppression of almsgiving, however, also implied that the prosperous pay a price, though the costs involved were financial rather than emotional. The collection of rates and the distribution of pensions were the inevitable consequence of the prevention of casual relief, an exchange nicely encapsulated in the North Yorkshire parish of Osmotherley in 1654 when the parishioners withdrew their charity 'which formerly they gave at their doores to Alex Swailes, a poor man', thereby forcing the bench into awarding him a pension of a shilling a week.[246]

The paradoxical combination of legal ambiguity and traditional sanctification created extraordinary opportunities for beggars to play not only on the pity, but also on the hopes and fears, of their wealthier neighbours. The superimposition of migrant vagabonds upon the local population of familiar mendicants doubtless encouraged the increasing hostility to begging that was manifest by the early years of the seventeenth century, if not before. Among those who begged, it was popularly believed, ancient Christian virtues of humility and gratitude had been supplanted by more secular habits of aggression and arrogance. Householders feared that

[245] *Early Essex Town Meetings: Braintree, 1619–1636, Finchingfield, 1626–1634*, ed. F. G. Emmison (Chichester, 1970), 19, 24, 25, 30.

[246] *North Riding Quarter Sessions Records*, ed. J. C. Atkinson (8 vols., North Riding Record Society, 1884–90), v. 156.

those who sought casual alms might easily shame, perhaps even intimidate, them into giving relief. As the city fathers of Salisbury put it in 1626, the 'words of begging' had now become the words of 'clamour'.[247] The subtle power exercised by beggars over the consciences of the propertied might, furthermore, be increased by the aura of dirt, pollution, and peril with which the destitute were enveloped, and perhaps occasionally cloaked themselves.[248] Beggars were also threatening because of the curses they might offer if alms were not readily given. When John Harte was refused alms by a gentleman in the parish church of Maldon (Essex) at Christmas 1573 he railed on him that 'this year [he] would breede a scabbe before Easter daye'. Anne Person of Stourbridge (Worcestershire) similarly threatened in 1628 to make her honest neighbours 'scrape and creep', and claimed that 'those whom she hath cursed have not prospered and those whom she shall curse shall never prosper'.[249] More often than not, however, the words of the curse lie beyond historical recovery: what, for instance, were the threats issued by the Scotsman taken begging at Helions Bumpstead (Essex) in 1638, who 'being denied an alms showed himself to be a very dangerous fellow', or the 'terrible oaths of revenge' uttered by Elizabeth Waldron of Belbroughton (Worcestershire), who would 'upon the least occasion offered by her neighbours most fearfully curse them'?[250]

The kind of situation which might give rise to these curses is epitomized by the experience of Mary Stracke, who being 'verie poore' and overburdened with three children 'spoke for her releefe' in the Norfolk village of Hempnall in 1597. Not only were her pleas ignored, she was herself presented in the church courts as 'a sower of discord betweene neighboures' and a 'breaker of Christian Charity'.[251] From this perspective, begging was little more than extortion, a point made bluntly by the Buckinghamshire justices in 1688. 'Sturdy beggars' had, they argued, 'growne so insolent and presumptious that they have oft by threats and

[247] *Poverty in Early Stuart Salisbury*, 89.

[248] For the filthiness of the poor in mid-16th-century Norwich and London, see *Tudor Economic Documents*, ii. 318; S. Brigden, 'Religion and Social Obligation in Early Sixteenth-Century London', *Past and Present*, 103 (May 1984), 108.

[249] ERO, Q/SR47/17; Worcestershire RO, Worcester, QSR/1/1/52/43. For the beggar's curse, see Thomas, *Religion and the Decline of Magic*, 505–9; Beier, *Masterless Men*, 121; and for the curses of the poor in general, J. Walter, 'Public Transcripts, Popular Agency and the Politics of Subsistence in Early Modern England', in M. Braddick and J. Walter (eds.), *Negotiating Power in Early Modern Society: Order, Hierarchy and Subordination in Britain and Ireland* (Cambridge, 2001), 131–3.

[250] ERO, Q/SR300/86; Worcester RO, QSR/1/1/64/90.

[251] *Bishop Redman's Visitation, 1597: Presentments in the Archdeaconries of Norwich, Norfolk and Suffolk*, ed. J. F. Williams (Norfolk Record Society, 18, Norwich, 1946), 105.

menaces extorted money and victuals', especially from housewives who lived in isolated dwellings 'remote from neighbours'. 'The people', they insisted, were in 'a general consternation or feare' that those seeking alms 'will fire their houses or steale their goods'.[252] Indeed, the conventional wisdom was that begging led directly to theft, an axiom epitomized by the accusation made in Essex in 1649 that Mary Taylor of Bocking was 'a notable beggar in the towns adjacent and not necessitous but under that colour doth filch and steal where she has alms'. The Shropshire magistrates bluntly but eloquently bracketed together 'begging and filching' among the 'misdemeanours arising amongst' the poor.[253]

Those begging without licences were, of course, vulnerable to prosecution under the vagrancy acts, as was William Jennetts, 'being well fitted to labour and having no land nor goods nor having any art or mystery by which he could gain a livelihood' found begging by the constable of Callow Hill (Worcestershire) 'and comporting himself as an incorrigible vagabond and mendicant' in 1614. John Wakeman confessed in 1623 that he and his 11-year-old son had been wandering and begging for the last five years and that they had 'no dwelling place'.[254] To habitual beggars like Jennets and the Wakemans might be added the desperate local poor, turned out by their landlords when they could no longer pay rent or when they threatened to become a burden. In a case which also casts interesting light on frustrations which might result when kin support was unforthcoming or exhausted, Joan Whittle had lived 'forty years and upwards' in Eldersfield (Worcestershire) as a servant to her brother 'and now that she has grown old and weak' he had thrown her out so that she was 'taken begging' within the parish in 1618.[255]

The extent and value of begging, like that of most of the expedients discussed in this chapter, are impossible to quantify. It is almost certainly the case that some, like the poor householders of early sixteenth-century Coventry, were discouraged, perhaps even prevented, from begging openly by their personal feelings of pride, shame, and self-respect, to say nothing of public attitudes of disapprobation expressed in the terms of charitable bequests and parish orders.[256] For others, sentiments of this

[252] *County of Buckingham: Calendar to the Sessions Records*, ed. W. Le Hardy and G. L. Reckitt (4 vols., Aylesbury, 1934–51), i. 258. Cf. B. Capp, 'Arson, Threats of Arson and Incivility in Early Modern England', in P. Burke *et al.* (eds.), *Civil Histories: Essays in Honour of Sir Keith Thomas* (Oxford, 2000), 197–213.

[253] ERO, Q/SR342/28 (and for other examples see Beier, *Masterless Men*, 120–1); NA, SP16/215/53 (1633).

[254] Worcester RO, QSR/1/1/43/21, 46/83.

[255] Worcester RO, QSR/1/1/28/20. Cf. Ch. 5.2 below.

[256] C. Phythian-Adams, *Desolation of a City: Coventry and the Urban Crisis of the Late Middle Ages* (Cambridge, 1979), 135.

kind were a luxury, a mere self-indulgence that served only to close off one potential way of making a living. Even so, the fact that children (whose personal sense of shame was under-developed and for whom questions of reputation had less critical purchase) figure so prominently in accounts of mendicancy suggests that the labouring poor, like many of their Continental counterparts, were shame-faced. For poor householders such as these, the 'silent and close beneficence' advocated by the Devon clergyman Thomas Foster in 1630 on the grounds that it would prevent the 'exprobation' of those who received charity was far preferable to the public humiliation of seeking alms from door to door.[257]

If the giving of alms to known beggars was one expression of neighbourliness, another—equally difficult to trace in the historical record—was the extension of credit. For the poor, this might be less a matter of elaborate networks of formal obligation inscribed on parchment and sealed in wax than of semi-formal arrangements of barter and exchange secured only, if at all, by word of mouth. The negotiations involved are imagined in the early seventeenth-century ballad in which 'a poore man' implores help from local farmers while searching for fuel in the woods: '"O lend to me", he said, | "one loafe of barley bread, | One pinte of milke for my poor wife, | in child-bed almost dead; | Thinke on my extreme need, | To lend me have no doubt— | I have no money for to pay— | But I will worke it out".[258] Transactions of this kind constituted less of a formal 'economy of obligation' than an 'economy of mutual favours'.[259] This informal economy might include both simple loans and even the toleration of goods spontaneously borrowed, a practice suggested by the remark of William Wright of Elton (Cheshire) who, when resisting magisterial pressure to prosecute William Crewe for the theft of a 'bottle of hay', affirmed that 'he and his neighbours had been used to make bould with one another' for greater matters than that.[260]

Indeed it has been argued that relationships of credit and debt were so ubiquitous in seventeenth-century England that the act of forgiving a debt was a far (perhaps as many as twenty times) more valuable source of support for the poor than that provided by formal relief and endowed

[257] T. Foster, *Plouto-mastix: The Scourge of Covetousnesse: or, An Apologie for the Publike Good, Against Privacie* (London, 1631), 25.

[258] 'A New Ballad, Shewing the Great Misery Sustained by a Poore Man in Essex, his Wife and Children, with Other Strange Doings Done by the Devil', in *The Roxburghe Ballads*, ed. W. Chappell and J. W. Ebsworth (9 vols., Ballad Society, London, 1871–99), ii. 222–8, lines 41–8.

[259] Capp, *When Gossips Meet*, 56. Cf. Muldrew, *The Economy of Obligation.*

[260] NA, STAC8/32/5, m. 2.

charity.[261] The irregular incomes and insecure circumstances of labouring households made defaulting on a debt a very real and regular possibility, especially at times of high prices when the demands of earthly necessities might undermine the ability to repay even the smallest financial obligation. Some employment was, furthermore, so seasonal or so vulnerable to periodic slump that those who relied upon it (Tyneside keelmen, for instance, or Essex clothworkers) found themselves living for protracted periods on 'trust'. In consequence the forgiveness of the debts of the poor became not only a religious obligation and an article of neighbourliness but a practical necessity. 'Although the poor were often described as being without credit, and suffered because of it', they were certainly not excluded from the culture of credit.[262] Those poor men who were described as lacking in estimation or credit were examples of moral failure in a competitive market economy, and only by the inculcation of habits of discipline and thrift amongst them could the sheer scale of redistribution through the forgiveness of debt be brought under control. Indeed, the poor laws were in part an attempt 'to come to grips with this deluge of defaults by providing a minimum predictable income in the form of a cash dole to reduce the amount of credit which needed to be extended to the poor'.[263]

Even so, some of the very poorest were ultimately driven beyond the apparently pervasive networks of credit. Few of the inhabitants of Sileby (Leicestershire), for instance, were prepared to lend John and Isabel Salter even sixpence, knowing it would never be repaid. Indeed, generic references to the poor as lacking in credit were ubiquitous: they were 'persons of idle conversation and no credit or estimation to whose sayings little credit is given'.[264] Others, once deemed creditworthy, found themselves having to default. Ten (13 per cent) of those who pleaded for support from the charity trustees of Bruton (Somerset) during the 1660s referred to the extent of their indebtedness. The frequency with which the labouring poor moved on from tenement to tenement or cottage to cottage because of their inability to pay rents was, furthermore, almost proverbial.[265]

[261] Muldrew, *The Economy of Obligation*, 304–5. The following discussion relies heavily on Muldrew's sensitive analysis of the participation of poor households in networks of credit and debt at 303–12.

[262] Muldrew, *The Economy of Obligation*, 309.

[263] Ibid. 311.

[264] Capp, 'Life, Love and Litigation', 69; Amussen, *An Ordered Society*, 154; Sharpe, *Population and Society*, 218.

[265] SARS, DD\SE/45/1/13, 26, 27, 29, 32, 43, 51, 72; 2/1, 8; Gough, *History of Myddle*, 178–9, 188–9.

The provision of credit to the poor is most visible in the historical record where it was organized, especially in the practice of pledging goods for pawn. 'I cannot comprehend', wrote one mid-eighteenth-century observer of the labouring poor, 'how they live without the pawnbroker.'[266] Pawnshops, it has recently been argued, regularly offered the poor those small sums that were 'at time essential for a family budget'.[267] Many of the poor themselves explained that pawning all their goods was one last desperate measure before they turned either to pilfering or to pleading for formal relief. Margaret Hobson told the Cheshire bench in 1629 that she had 'sould all her apparel and all that she ever hath for the relief of herself and her child and hath now nothing to maintain it and herself but only her service'. One elderly widow in Exeter explained that she had chosen to sell and pawn her belongings because she was ashamed to ask relief of the parish. Robert Thomas of Bruton (Somerset) similarly claimed that he been 'constrained to pawn and sell all' he had 'to keep alive because he would not be chargeable to the town'. The desperate condition of those who had sold what little property they had is epitomized by the sad case of 82-year-old Edward Black of Maidstone, discovered in 1692 by the parish officers in a house whose rent they paid, but whose possessions amounted only to the rags he wore and the bundle of straw on which he slept.[268]

Others sought strategic advantage in describing how they had been forced to sell their goods, since on accepting formal relief a pauper forfeited any rights over his or her property, which was usually sold on after their death.[269] Better, therefore, to sell (better still to pawn) one's accumulated belongings before seeking relief, thereby escaping the ignominy of the parish brand.[270] Even so, at least eight (10 per cent) of those who pleaded for patronage from the trustees of a charity in Bruton (Somerset) during the 1660s claimed that they had pawned their goods, and sought help from the charity to redeem them.[271] The vestrymen of Trull (Somerset), Leytonstone (Essex), and of the Kent parishes of

[266] B. Lemire, 'Peddling Fashion: Salesmen, Pawnbrokers, Tailors, Thieves and the Second-Hand Clothes Trade in England, *c.*1700–1800', *Textile History*, 22 (1991), 78.

[267] B. Lemire, 'Consumerism in Pre-Industrial and Early Industrial England: The Trade in Secondhand Clothes', *Journal of British Studies*, 27 (1988), 11.

[268] Hindle, *The State and Social Change*, 162; Slack, *Poverty and Policy*, 192; SARS, DD\SE/45/1/77; Barker-Read, 'Treatment of the Aged Poor', 83.

[269] Cf. Ch. 4.2 below.

[270] Cf. Ch. 4.3(*c*) below.

[271] For the possibility that statements of this kind had become formulaic by the mid-18th century, see R. B. Outhwaite, '"Objects of Charity": Petitions to the London Foundling Hospital, 1768–72', *Eighteenth-Century Studies*, 32 (1999), 503.

Cranbrook and Maidstone occasionally made specific payments to help parishioners redeem their goods, including crockery, tools, and even beds, from pawnbrokers.[272]

Foremost among those goods which might quickly be exchanged for cash or credit were, however, the clothes of the poor. Vital sixpences or shillings might be 'loaned' the customer in exchange for pawning a coat, a bonnet, or a shawl and it is not difficult to imagine that some garments and the pittances which they 'earned' passed back and forth between pawnshop and pauper on a regular basis. In pawning her clothes, protested one relief claimant in 1711, she was 'starved with cold to prevent being famished to death'.[273] It is even possible that the rough hempen clothing provided by the parish might itself be pledged for credit, a tendency which may go some way to explain the enthusiasm of parish officers for badging the coats they gave to the poor even before the 1697 statute.[274] Intermittent small-scale credit of this kind might be secured not only on the surrender of clothing but also on the likelihood of a future regular income. Richard Dunning thought that the poor of late seventeenth-century Devon only secured a daily sufficiency by 'living on the credit of the next [parish] pay day', which might be perhaps a fortnight or even a month away. In this, he was echoing the mid-seventeenth-century balladeer who recollected hearing an old woman begin 'to weepe, | and sadly thus complaine, | Her pention would never keepe | her till th' pay day comes againe'.[275] Other critics were convinced that alewives in particular encouraged the poor to drink on credit, which not only became the bane of poor men but also resulted in goods being pawned simply for ale. Of course, those who did petition for relief explained that they had 'pawned all to get bread' and that they needed their 'pawns loosed' to

[272] SARS, DD\SE/45/1/24, 29, 67, 68, 69, 72, 77 (though another two made reference to having sold property in their desperation: DD\SE/45/1/55, 61); Jones, 'Trull Overseers Accounts', 95; J. Rule, *Albion's People: English Society, 1714–1815* (London and New York, 1992), 125; Barker-Read, 'Treatment of the Aged Poor', 93–4. Cf. B. A. Holderness, *Pre-Industrial England: Economy and Society, 1500–1750* (London, 1976), 204.

[273] Capp, *When Gossips Meet*, 55; CRO, Q/11/1/99/28. For a Lancashire petitioner 'like to starve with cold and famish for want of sustenance' in 1699, see LRO, QSP/823/46.

[274] Lemire, 'Consumerism', 11. Cf. Hampson, *Treatment of Poverty in Cambridgeshire*, 181; Tomkins, 'Pawnbroking', 186. S. King, 'Reclothing the English Poor, 1750–1840', *Textile History*, 33 (2002), 44, believes that by the late 18th century badging was primarily designed to prevent the pawning of parish clothing. For badging, see Ch. 6.5 below. For a Leicestershire woman whipped for selling clothes provided for her by the parish officers of Lutterworth, see Lane, 'Work on the Margins', 93.

[275] Dunning, *Bread for the Poor*, 8; 'The Good Fellow's Complaint' (*c.*1647), in *Cavalier and Puritan: Ballads and Broadsides Illustrating the Period of the Great Rebellion, 1640–1660*, ed. H. E. Rollins (New York, 1923), 212 (stanza 9).

defend themselves 'against Approaching Winter'.[276] Even a magistrate's relief order might be valuable currency in the circulation of goods and credit, and the consequences could be disastrous if the parish officers did not honour it. 'Those who ventured to lend [her] anything upon the credit' of her parish pension, complained Ann Bowman of Kirkoswald, who had regularly been pawning her clothing in the first decade of the eighteenth century, were 'discouraged' from helping her any further when her pension was reduced in 1710.[277]

Pawning was itself all too often part of a cycle of debt. Goods might be pawned simply to pay off debts. One Cumbrian blacksmith had been forced to pawn all his working gear to satisfy creditors now 'urgent for his money'. Widower George Backhouse of Torpenhow had 'sold all to pay his debts' and to maintain his poor motherless children.[278] The Hertfordshire justices reported in 1637 that high prices and unemployment put such pressure on the labouring poor that they were frequently forced to pawn and sell what goods they had.[279] Whether the labouring poor of late Elizabethan Ipswich, who lacked not only fuel, clothing, and bedding but also spinning-wheels and combing cards, had also, in desperation, pawned their tools may be open to question. Cheap and circulating credit of this kind nonetheless lubricated the wheels to which the poor put their shoulders in making ends meet.[280]

Although there is little evidence of the organization of pawnbroking in the seventeenth century, it is almost certain that inns and alehouses, with their ample supplies of ready money and their custom of providing services on the slate, were the principal focus for the circulation of cheap credit.[281] Since women were so widely employed in retailing and victualling and were accustomed to providing goods for small cash sums and on credit, it is hardly surprising that they should become the acknowledged experts in the management of alehouse pawnbroking.[282] By the mid-eighteenth century, however, alehouses had been supplanted as a centre of credit by the pawnbroker's shop, of which it was reported that there was one in every village in England by 1736.[283] The running of pawn-

[276] Wrightson, 'Alehouses, Order and Reformation', 17; CRO, Q11/1/96/25, 99/28.

[277] CRO, Q11/1/97/7.

[278] Muldrew, *The Economy of Obligation*, 303–4; CRO, Q/11/1/59/3, 74/12.

[279] NA, SP16/385/43

[280] *Poor Relief in Elizabethan Ipswich*, 122–40; Slack, *Poverty and Policy*, 82.

[281] For the role of alehouses in pawnbroking, see Wrightson, 'Alehouses, Order and Reformation', 17; P. Clark, *The English Alehouse: A Social History, 1200–1830* (London, 1983), 137–8, 229.

[282] M. Roberts, 'Women and Work in Sixteenth-Century English Towns', in P. J. Corfield and Derek Keene (eds.), *Work in Towns, 850–1850* (Leicester, 1990), 95.

[283] Clark, *The English Alehouse*, 229.

shops, where it was rumoured that clients had to pay 2*d.* for every item they pawned and 6*d.* a month for every pound borrowed, nonetheless remained a largely female occupation.[284] Some of the goods which circulated in this black economy were obviously stolen, like the hatband 'layed to pawne' with William Myles of Bletchingley (Surrey) in 1608 or the brass pot pawned for 4*s.* in Somerton (Somerset) in 1657. One man's pawnbroker was to this extent another woman's receiver of stolen goods.[285]

These formal, if illicit, credit transactions notwithstanding, the essence of neighbourly support for the poor must inevitably remain concealed from us, for the trivial acts of kindness of which the culture of mutual help was constructed are elusive in the historical record. Gifts of food, water, and fuel were only the most valuable specie in the currency of neighbourliness circulating back and forth between those whose resources were often so meagre that any expectation of reciprocity might quite likely prove misguided. Those who nursed their neighbours or minded their children, or who lent them tools or gave them succour, often did so not because they expected anything in return but simply because that was what neighbours did for each other. These transactions might be the 'small change of neighbourliness' but cumulatively they reinforced the bonds of friendship and trust which were fundamentally necessary if the more celebrated (and fully documented) rituals of neighbourliness—the practices of 'social economy' or the gestures of 'general hospitality'—were to succeed in helping the poor to make ends meet.[286] The kindness of neighbours' credit was, therefore, just one expression of communal cohesion, a system of social and economic mutuality which, as we have seen, found its most sophisticated expression in the exploitation and management of common rights.

5. CRIMES OF NECESSITY

There has been considerable reluctance even among those historians who have emphasized the desperation of the labouring poor to include theft within the 'economy of makeshifts'. Indeed, Hufton's original

[284] Capp, *When Gossips Meet*, 48, 64–5. For a remarkable study of an 18th-century pawnbroker's pledge book, see Tomkins, 'Pawnbroking'.

[285] 'Notebook of a Surrey Justice', 178–9; *Quarter Sessions Records of the County of Somerset*, iii. 329. Cf. G. Walker, 'Women, Theft and the World of Stolen Goods', in J. Kermode and G. Walker (eds.), *Women, Crime and the Courts in Early Modern England* (London, 1994), 81–105; B. Lemire, 'Theft of Clothes and Popular Consumerism in Early Modern England', *Journal of Social History*, 24 (1990–1), 255–76.

[286] Capp, *When Gossips Meet*, 56. Cf. Walter, 'Social Economy of Dearth'; Hindle, 'Dearth, Fasting and Alms'.

account separated out the strictly illegal activities of theft and prostitution from the licit practices of migration and begging.[287] It is nonetheless clear that 'crime, in the sense of being on the wrong side of the law, was, for the vast number of undifferentiated working people, normal'.[288] Every community doubtless had its pilferers, like John Aston of Myddle (Shropshire), 'very idle and much given to stealing of poultry and small things', or the Marks and Nurton families of North Petherton (Somerset), who 'habitually lived on stolen mutton and poultry'.[289] Petty larceny was therefore probably endemic, perhaps even instinctive, among the labouring poor, characteristically perpetrated by those such as another family of Myddle, the Wenlockes, who apparently 'never stole any considerable goods, but were night walkers, and robbed oarchyards and gardens, and stole hey out of meadows, and corn when it was cutt in the fields, and any small thing that persons by carelessness left out of doors'.[290] Indeed, casual theft by the disorderly poor was undoubtedly widespread, and is probably under-represented in the archives of criminal justice since the goods stolen frequently did not justify the expenses of prosecution even at quarter sessions, still less at assizes. Perhaps, as the Somerset magistrate Edward Hext feared, the victims of pilfering were content to clip the offender round the ear, especially if they had secured the return of their property.[291]

More problematic still is the issue of 'social crime', a category created by a shift across the seventeenth century in the definition of those activities that were considered criminal.[292] The distinction between custom and crime was not simply a legal nicety; it was also a matter of survival. When other alternative strategies disappeared, 'theft must have become, by stages, a very real possibility'.[293] Indeed, although the relationship between economic hardship and theft was probably *indirect* in nature, it is

[287] Hufton, *The Poor of Eighteenth-Century France*, 245–84, 306–17.

[288] E. Thompson, 'Eighteenth-Century Crime, Popular Movements and Social Control', *Bulletin of the Society for the Study of Labour History*, 25 (1972), 10.

[289] Gough, *History of Myddle*, 145; *Quarter Sessions Records of the County of Somerset*, iii. 380.

[290] Gough, *History of Myddle*, 107. Cf. J. S. Cockburn, 'The Nature and Incidence of Crime in England, 1559–1625: A Preliminary Survey', in id. (ed.), *Crime in England, 1550–1800* (London, 1977), 64. For nightwalking, see P. Griffiths, 'Meanings of Nightwalking in Early Modern England', *The Seventeenth Century*, 13 (1998), 212–38.

[291] *Tudor Economic Documents*, ii. 341. Hext's views are contextualized in Sharpe, 'Social Strain and Social Dislocation, 1585–1603', 192–3.

[292] For a recent critique of the concept of 'social crime', see J. A. Sharpe, *Crime in Early Modern England, 1550–1750* (2nd edn., London and New York, 1999), 176–9, 198–202. For an impassioned plea for the recognition of the informal economy as a *regular* resource in the working lives of women, see Lane, 'Work on the Margins', 96.

[293] Lawson, 'Property Crime and Hard Times', 107.

possible to identify what those 'stages' might have been. 'For many individuals', the 'initial response to economic crisis may have been migration; theft would have come later, as a means of survival while on the road.'[294] This suggestion is confirmed by the finding that of the 1604 vagrants questioned by magistrates in a sample of examinations drawn from a number of jurisdictions in the period 1571–1641, 707 (45 per cent) were suspected of theft. The operative word here, however, was *suspicion*. Indeed, in nearly half of these cases, justices were uncertain that a crime had actually been committed and were investigating the origin of a vagrant's clothing or possessions simply because it was thought likely that they had been pilfered.[295]

So did the hungry really steal? The analysis of motivations for theft is notoriously problematic.[296] It is, of course, tempting to dismiss the very frequent narratives of distress offered to judges and juries by individuals who were pleading for mercy and even, in some cases, for their lives. Some defendants doubtless told magistrates what they wanted to hear: that their crimes were born rather of desperation than of a desire for profit. Thus William Westfeelde, apprehended in Walkern (Hertfordshire) in 1598 for stealing a piece of bread, some butter, and a meat pie, explained that he had been unable to find work since being dismissed by his master in Essex and that 'he had been driven by necessitie to search for foode'. Christiana Weekes of Cliffe Pypard (Wiltshire) was acquitted of theft in 1651 after she told the magistrates that she stole beans 'for the hunger for her children'. Thomas Hatley, a youth of Great Bardfield (Essex), confessed in 1674 that he had stolen a dish 'to get something to eat' because 'what he got from his labour his parents took from him and would not allow him wherewithal to subsist'.[297] Although such examples could be multiplied, it is by definition impossible to generalize with any confidence on the basis of fragmentary narratives constructed to play on the merciful instincts of examining magistrates and trial jurors alike.[298] But the fact that the honest poor might find apologists when they were

[294] Ibid. 113.

[295] Beier, *Masterless Men*, 126, 127, 225.

[296] For attempts to categorize motivations for theft, see C. B. Herrup, *The Common Peace: Participation and the Criminal Law in Seventeenth-Century England* (Cambridge, 1987), 147–8; L. MacKay, 'Why They Stole: Women in the Old Bailey, 1779–1789', *Journal of Social History*, 32 (1999), 623–39.

[297] Lawson, 'Property Crime and Hard Times', 122; HMC, *Reports on Manuscripts in Various Collections*, vol. i (London, 1901), 120; ERO, Q/SR428/144. For another example, see *Quarter Sessions Records for the County of Somerset*, iii. 383.

[298] For a sensible cautionary note on the recklessness of taking defences of this kind at face value, see MacKay, 'Why They Stole', 637 n. 19.

driven to steal through want is suggestive. Only 105 cases of theft of foodstuffs, accounting for less than 4 per cent of all theft indictments, found their way before the Essex courts in the period 1620–80, a surprisingly low figure that might be explained in terms of a general disinclination to prosecute the theft of small amounts of food.[299] The apparent tolerance of persons stealing food was, moreover, 'paralleled by the lenience by which they were treated by the courts'. Where it *was* prosecuted, indeed, the theft of foodstuffs was generally dealt with mercifully. Only one prosecution for the theft of food in seventeenth-century Essex resulted in a capital conviction, and that was probably an exemplary punishment in the context of rising prosecution rates. Similarly, although those who burgled houses for food were treated severely by the courts, only one grand larcenist convicted of the theft of food and poultry was sentenced to death in East Sussex between 1592 and 1640.[300]

Even so, the aggregative evidence is suggestive of an increasing tendency of even the respectable poor to turn to petty theft at times of high prices. Although it will never be possible to completely isolate the incidence of crime from the workings of the criminal justice system, the patterns of prosecution described by the records of the Elizabethan and Jacobean courts arguably 'reflect real changes in the level of property crime', changes which were 'themselves rooted in economic conditions'.[301] Thus, detailed analysis of the chronology and geography of Hertfordshire prosecutions demonstrates that theft and economic trends were indirectly related, and in particular that an 'increase' in theft became evident only after prices crossed a certain threshold, a tendency which might be taken to suggest that the 'honest' poor might exhaust all other possible expedients before extremity drove them to steal in order to survive. Furthermore, the lag between the trends of prices on the one hand, and prosecution on the other, suggests that migration, and ultimately vagrancy, mediated the relationship between hard times and property crime.[302]

These conclusions sit very comfortably with much else that is known about the vulnerability of the labouring poor. In the first place, it is clear that theft prosecutions tended to cluster in and immediately after years of high prices. The pattern of indictments for property crime on the home circuit in the period 1559–1624 reveals a concentration of theft prosecutions in specific years of harvest crisis, such as 1586–8, 1590–2,

[299] Sharpe, *Crime in Seventeenth-Century England*, 99–100
[300] Ibid. 100; Herrup, *The Common Peace*, 171.
[301] Lawson, 'Property, Crime and Hard Times', 126–7.
[302] Ibid. 112–13.

1595–9, 1600–2, 1612–17, and 1622–4. The steady increase in the indictment of crime in the 1590s in particular is almost certainly associated with economic problems caused by harvest failure, and suggests that there was an increasingly close link between high grain prices and high levels of indictment for crime, especially larceny, burglary, and robbery, particularly in Essex.[303] This pattern is even more striking in the experience of individual communities. Theft prosecutions in the Essex village of Terling, for instance, usually brought by more substantial villagers against their poorer neighbours, were rather more numerous in the 'years of economic stringency': 1597–1603, 1630–1, 1649–50. Sudden reductions in the purchasing power of those already at subsistence level, as at Rye (Sussex) in 1596–7, led to an equally sudden spate of theft prosecutions, especially of those whose occupations made them liable to seasonal unemployment.[304] In the second, foodstuffs appear to have grown increasingly preponderant among the goods stolen in rural areas in crisis years.[305] While it is emphatically not true that all hungry labourers became petty thieves, the temptation to commit crimes of necessity must have been acute. As the lawyer Robert Powell put it in 1636, 'multitudes of people not able to provide necessary victuals and cloathing for themselves, their wives and children, were so discouraged with misery and poverty that they fell dayly to theft, robbery and other inconveniences, or pitifully dyed for hunger and cold'. Without sufficient employment, wrote Matthew Hale in 1683, the poor 'must live by begging, or stealing'.[306]

One other form of theft, embezzlement, and especially false or short reeling, was equally popular among the labouring poor as a means of supplementing meagre and irregular income. *An Ease for Overseers* noted in 1601 that the working population included not only the 'willing', the 'wilfull', and the 'negligent', but also the 'fraudulent' who, although they would apply themselves to their materials, would defraud their employer by 'imbeasling or purloining some away'. By using less of the material than they were supposed to in the production of yarn and selling on the surplus, spinners might boost their earnings by as much as 6 per cent. Such activities might be encouraged both by the popular notion that the

[303] Ibid. 110, 114–15; Sharpe, 'Social Strain and Social Dislocation', 200–2. Cf. J. Samaha, *Law and Order in Historical Perspective: The Case of Elizabethan Essex* (New York, 1974), 168–9; Cockburn, 'Nature and Incidence of Crime', 67–70.

[304] Wrightson and Levine, *Poverty and Piety*, 122; G. Mayhew, *Tudor Rye* (Falmer, 1987), 212.

[305] J. Walter and K. Wrightson, 'Dearth and the Social Order in Early Modern England', *Past and Present*, 71 (1976), 25; B. Lenman and G. Parker, 'The State, the Community and the Criminal Law in Early Modern Europe', in Gatrell *et al.* (eds.), *Crime and the Law*, 37.

[306] Powell, *Depopulation Arraigned*, 37–8; Hale, *Provision for the Poor*, 6.

appropriation of working materials was not theft but a customary right and by a sense of moral outrage at the nefarious practices of employers.[307] Either way, at times of high prices, the desperation of the labouring poor was likely to be compounded by the reluctance of employers to tolerate the taking of those customary perquisites to which they might in prosperous times have turned a blind eye, with the result that the regulation of the informal economy was most intense just at the very point when more of the indigent population were likely to be drawing upon it.

Although there are few explicit references to embezzlement in the court records of the seventeenth century, those outworkers who stole the yarn they had been given to work were almost certainly dealt with as simple thieves, and it is hardly surprising that prosecutions for textile theft seem to have been concentrated in and around the cloth-working districts of the country.[308] Indeed, a particularly widespread network of embezzlement was disclosed in Essex in 1592, when Dutch wool merchants based in Colchester complained that a poor woman of Earls Colne who had been given substantial quantities of wool to spin and the cards with which to clean it had, instead of returning the thread at the appointed time, sold the raw materials to three other women of the village at less than half their value. By 1595, it had become apparent that this exchange had been only one transaction in a wider black economy of pilfering and receiving which involved as many as a dozen inhabitants of the community. Although the parish appears to have been slow in appointing overseers of the poor in accordance with the Elizabethan statutes, it was forced in 1602 to ensure that local yeomen would police cloth-working in the parish to ensure that rings of embezzlement such as that suppressed in the 1590s did not develop again.[309] The policing of embezzlement certainly did bring other cases to light well into the seventeenth century and beyond. Evelyn Mineffe was hired as a spinster and entrusted with 'a good quantity of wool' by a local yeoman's wife in Devon in 1655, only to 'very much abuse' her by withholding much of the yarn and having

[307] *An Ease for Overseers of the Poore*, 18; J. Styles, 'Embezzlement, Industry and the Law in England, 1500–1800', in M. Berg *et al.* (eds.), *Manufacture in Town and Countryside Before the Factory* (Cambridge, 1983), 176, 181, 182–4, 186. Cf. A. Randall, 'Peculiar Perquisites and Pernicious Practices: Embezzlement in the West of England Woollen Industry, *c.*1750–1840', *International Review of Social History*, 35 (1990), 193–219. For a coruscating critique of the poverty wages paid by clothiers, see P. Collinson, 'Christian Socialism in Elizabethan Suffolk: Thomas Carew and his *Caveat for Clothiers*', in C. Rawcliffe *et al.* (eds.), *Counties and Communities: Essays on East Anglian History* (Norwich, 1996), 161–79.

[308] Sharpe, *Crime in Seventeenth-Century England*, 100–1.

[309] M. Williams, '"Our Poore People in Tumults Arose": Living in Poverty in Earls Colne, Essex, 1560–1640', *Rural History*, 13 (2002), 128–9.

her family fence the surplus.[310] Embezzlement also probably occurred wherever the poor were set on work by parish officers, as they were in early seventeenth-century Layston (Hertfordshire), where any inhabitant found guilty of embezzling or wasting the 'commodities' was to be excluded from the parish work scheme. The kind of behaviour which might provoke such pre-emptive orders is revealed in a startling case from Westward (Cumberland), where it was alleged in 1697 that Jane Langrigg gave in 'false tale' [returns] for every coil of flax she had been provided with to spin.[311] The Exeter clergymen and polemicist Richard Dunning would have taken comfort from such an episode, for he was convinced that the supervision of the working practices of the poor was more easily achieved when they were set to labour on work with private masters who would ensure that embezzlers were whipped. Employers, especially those who took on parish apprentices, would not necessarily have agreed: one parish apprentice was described in 1701 as a 'vitious and thievish boy' whose master did not know 'what to do with him or how to govern him'.[312] Some of those who embezzled their master's goods apparently did so for philanthropic reasons. Elizabeth Kemer's service to a Colyton mercer in the early seventeenth century was punctuated by the pilfering of his household goods, which she then gave away to those she considered to be indigent, thereby not only redistributing his wealth but also censuring his lack of charity.[313]

Although the legal authorities of the seventeenth and eighteenth centuries might seem at first sight quite sanguine about what modern criminologists term the 'social theory of necessity' (the idea that crimes of desperation should be treated more leniently than those committed for profit), closer analysis suggests that their attitudes amount rather to a striking modification of the traditional medieval doctrine that theft was a permissible alternative to starvation.[314] The very fact that the common law had since the early fourteenth century defined the theft of any goods

310 Mendelson and Crawford, *Women in Early Modern England*, 294.

311 HALS, D/P 65/3/3, 113; CRO, Q/11/1/47/15.

312 Dunning, *Bread for the Poor*, 15; *Buckinghamshire Sessions Records*, ii. 294–5. On hostility to parish apprentices, see Ch. 3.2(*c*) below.

313 Sharpe, *Population and Society*, 218.

314 The following discussion is indebted to K. Thomas, 'The Social Origins of Hobbes's Political Thought', in K. C. Brown (ed.), *Hobbes Studies* (Oxford, 1965), esp. 225–7; T. A. Horne, *Property Rights and Poverty: Political Argument in Britain, 1605–1834* (Chapel Hill, NC, 1990), esp. 126, 131; I. Green, *The Christian's ABC: Catechisms and Catechising in England, c.1350–1740* (Oxford, 1996), 462–4; S. G. Swanson, 'The Medieval Foundations of John Locke's Theory of Natural Rights: Rights of Subsistence and the Principle of Extreme Necessity', *History of Political Thought*, 18 (1997), 399–459; and L. O. Fradenburg, 'Needful Things', in B. A. Hanawalt and D. Wallace (eds.), *Medieval Crime and Social Control* (Minneapolis, 1999), 49–69.

worth less than 12*d.* as petty larceny, a misdemeanour (and therefore punishable only by a whipping) rather than a felony (which would have been punishable by death), reflects the facts that pilfering was regarded more sympathetically than grand larceny, and that if carried out during dearth, medieval judges might even decide that it did not merit any punishment whatsoever.[315] As late as the 1590s, the circuit judges were recommending pardons for those offenders who had been convicted of thefts of 'small value' on the grounds that these were 'crimes of opportunity, weakness or need'.[316]

As we have seen, however, crimes of desperation, especially when committed in stealth, were taken ever more seriously at the turn of the seventeenth century, especially in the wake of the 1601 statute which brought pilfering within the purview of justices acting out of sessions. While it is true, therefore, that Chief Justice Matthew Hale started out from the sympathetic premise that levels of need were theoretically relevant to the question of whether theft was ever justified, he qualified this traditional view almost immediately: 'men's properties would be under a strange insecurity, being laid open to other men's necessities, whereof no man can possibly judge but the party himself'. The lenient treatment of desperate thieves would result only in the encouragement of theft by those who 'judged themselves in want of necessaries' and ultimately in the destruction of 'all the ligaments of property and civil society'.[317] If the starving had any rights to subsistence, therefore, they were rather a matter of local and contractual negotiation than of abstract moral law. Hale's relatively unsympathetic tone was, moreover, punctuated by a note of complacency. The question of whether the poor were ever justified in their petty theft was, he argued, redundant in the English case because 'by the laws of this kingdom sufficient provision is made for the supply of such necessities by collections of the poor and by the power of the civil magistrate'.[318] Almost a century later, Blackstone argued that, because charity was 'reduced to a system and interwoven in our constitu-

[315] Sharpe, *Crime in Seventeenth-Century England*, 91. For the judges, see B. Tierney, *Medieval Poor Law: A Sketch of Canonical Theory and its Appreciation in England* (Berkeley, 1959), 38, 147. This doctrine was restated by Thomas Hobbes in the mid-17th century. Thomas, 'Social Origins', 225.

[316] K. J. Kesselring, *Mercy and Authority in the Tudor State* (Cambridge, 2003), 107.

[317] M. Hale, *Historia Placitorum Coronae: The History of the Pleas of the Crown* (2 vols., ed. S. Emlyn, rev. G. Wilson, London, 1778), i. 54–5.

[318] Ibid. Cf. A. Cromartie, *Sir Matthew Hale, 1609–1676: Law, Religion and Natural Philosophy* (Cambridge, 1995), 95. By 1683, Hale was rather less optimistic about the effectiveness of statutory welfare provision in precluding either begging or theft, or even starvation. Hale, *Provison for the Poor*, 6.

tion', it was 'impossible that the most needy stranger should ever be reduced to the necessity of thieving to support nature'.[319] For both Hale and Blackstone, therefore, the very existence of the poor law meant that the dire necessity which might justify theft simply could not occur in England, and that the excuse of necessity was no longer a viable plea.

Clerical attitudes seem, similarly, to have shifted under the pressure of possessive individualism. Down to the mid-seventeenth century, some moralists and clergymen remained wedded to the traditional doctrine of that necessity might legitimize theft. In the tract *Dives and Pauper*, first published in 1493 but written at the very beginning of the fifteenth century, Pauper argued that those who stole out of 'myschiefe of hunger or of thirst or of colde' were excused 'from syn and from theft' provided that they acted 'for nede and not for covetise'. 'In the last nede', he argued, 'all thynge is common.' William Ames echoed this view that 'all things are made common in urgent necessitie' to argue that a man did not incur the sin of theft if he stole 'to succour his owne present extreame necessitie which he could not helpe by any other meanes'.[320] It was this tradition which in 1636 inspired Peter Hausted's explicit argument for the granting of mercy to those convicted of crimes of necessity. He envisaged a 'young man *compeld by hunger*' who 'steales from his neighbour, bread or other necessaries whereby to releeve and sustaine *Nature*'. Hausted proposed that not only should the youth and good character of his imagined offender be taken into account, but also his motive, for the youth did not steal 'to maintaine his riot and intemperance, but [was] driven to it *by necessity*'. While Hausted supposed that the 'strictnes of our law' implied 'that this man must *dye*', he insisted that there was room for the judge, 'weighing the circumstances of the fact', to blunt 'the edge from the rigour of the law' and afflict 'a milder punishment upon him'.[321] In 1649 Anthony Ascham, vicar of Burneston (North Yorkshire), was still prepared to argue that, even though Lazarus, 'redy to perish (not by fault but misfortune)', had taken Dives's goods contrary to his will, 'yet he had not sinned'.[322] Even into the late seventeenth century, some moralists were

[319] Blackstone, *Commentaries*, iv. 31–2.

[320] *Dives and Pauper* (London, 1536), fo. 243^{r-v}; W. Ames, *Conscience with the Power and Cases Thereof, Divided Into Five Bookes* (2nd edn., London, 1643), 260.

[321] P. Hausted, 'A Sermon Preached at the Assises at Huntingdon', in id., *Ten Sermons* (London, 1636), 272, 264. Hausted's views are set in the context of other assize sermons by Ingram, 'The Conscience of the Community', ch. 2. It is striking here that Hausted urged the restriction of this discretionary power to the judge (through benefit of clergy or petitioning for a royal pardon) rather than extending it to the jury (through partial verdicts). Cf. Hindle, *The State and Social Change*, 133–5.

[322] A. Ascham, *Of the Confusions and Revolutions of Governments* (2nd edn., London, 1649), 13.

prepared to insist that necessity remained a viable plea. For Samuel Shaw (rector of Long Whatton, Leicestershire), writing in 1682, the violation of property for the preservation of life in extreme necessity was 'no theft', or at least it was merely such theft as incurred no sin. Indeed, it actually became a *duty* to steal under such circumstances, not only because 'no man can be necessarily placed between two evils' but also because those that did not give to the hungry in such circumstances were themselves thieves. For James Lowde, as late as 1694, there were several reasons why a hungry man who helped himself to 'so much of other men's goods as are necessary to preserve his life' did not incur 'the guilt of theft': not merely because the wealthy were bound to give as much to the poor to sustain them, but also because, at the very foundation of rights in property 'at the first division of things', exceptions had always been made in cases of necessity.[323]

By the second half of the seventeenth century, however, these views were beginning to look antiquated. Some ambivalence could still be found as late as 1676, when although Gabriel Towerson conceded the general principle that it might be 'lawful to the extremely necessitous to withdraw so much from [other men] as to satisfie their necessities', he argued that it could not apply 'in any Christian nation, and much less' in England: not only did the realm abound with a 'multitude of charitable persons' (to say nothing of those parish officers who were legally obliged to relieve the poor in their wants), but most necessities arose not from misfortune but either from 'sloth and idleness' or from a thriftless instinct to live above one's station. Bare necessity could therefore 'be no warrant to us to invade our neighbours goods'.[324] As early as 1625, moreover, John Dod and Robert Cleaver had argued that poor men deluded themselves when they advanced excuses for their thefts, especially when the goods purloined were 'small things' about which victims 'should not make much ado'. On the contrary, Dod and Cleaver feared that 'he that cares not to break one commandment for a piece of bread, let him have hope of greater booty and he will break every one'. Even in his necessity, therefore, the poor man should rather put his faith in God than his light fingers in the hedges of his neighbours. Henry Hammond insisted that God would 'curse or blast' a destitute man who used 'unlawfull means' to 'relieve or secure' himself when he should rather trust and rely on the Lord. By the early 1660s, Jeremy Taylor was arguing that 'no fear of temporal evil' could be any 'excuse or warranty' for theft. To justify

[323] S. Shaw, *The True Christian's Test* (London, 1682), 51; J. Lowde, *A Discourse Concerning the Nature of Man* (London 1694), 178.

[324] G. Towerson, *An Explication of the Decalogue* (London, 1676), 444–5.

pilfering upon the basis that 'an honest man that is asham'd to beg may steal what is necessary to him' was, from this perspective, to deceive not only one's neighbour, but also to break the laws of man and God. By 1686, Thomas Comber could bluntly tell the impoverished set of catechumens whom he envisaged to be his audience that it was wrong to steal small things 'because we are poor'.[325]

By the second half of the seventeenth century therefore, the poor were being reminded both from the pulpit and in their catechisms that the idea that 'necessity knoweth no law' would not help them escape either civil or spiritual punishment. Nonetheless the fact that Peter Hausted's far more sympathetic remarks about the appropriate judicial response to crimes of necessity were openly made in an assize sermon preached at Huntingdon in 1636 before an audience which doubtless included the leading property-holders in the county, not to mention the royal judges themselves, is striking testimony to the great frequency with which the trial juries of the late sixteenth and the seventeenth centuries were confronted with gaol calendars lengthened by the cases of poor men and women, even *respectable* poor men and women, who were driven, or at least claimed that they had been driven, to commit crimes of opportunity as part of their survival strategy.[326]

Those historians who have so exhaustively analysed those property crimes which were eventually prosecuted in seventeenth- and eighteenth-century England have argued that theft was generally undertaken 'as a means of survival, as a way of supplementing inadequate wages or of supplying the most basic wants'.[327] It may, even so, be doubted whether this assessment actually holds true for most theft that was actually prosecuted in the courts. After all, once the archives of the criminal justice system permit analysis of the age of offenders (as they do by the late eighteenth century), it becomes clear that young men loom large in the profile of indicted thieves, a finding which does not sit well with the

[325] J. Dod and R. Cleaver, *A Plaine and Familiar Exposition of the Ten Commandments* (16th edn., London, 1625), 287–8; H. Hammond, *A Practical Catechisme* (Oxford, 1645), 134; J. Taylor, *Ductor Dubitantium, or The Rule of Conscience* (London, 1660), 511–12; Taylor, *A Dissuasive From Popery* (London, 1664), 263; T. Comber, *The Church-Catechism, with a Brief and Easie Explanation Thereof* (London, 1686), 21.

[326] Hausted, 'A Sermon Preached at the Assises at Huntingdon'; P. G. Lawson, 'Lawless Juries? The Composition and Behaviour of Hertfordshire Juries, 1573–1624', in J. S. Cockburn and T. A. Green (eds.), *Twelve Good Men and True: The English Criminal Trial Jury, 1200–1800* (Princeton, 1988), 117–57.

[327] J. M. Beattie, '"Hard Pressed to Make Ends Meet": Women and Crime in Augustan England', in V. Firth (ed.), *Women and History* (Toronto, 1995), 106. Cf. Beattie, 'The Pattern of Crime in England', 95.

equation of poverty and pilfering and which suggests that opportunity was at least as significant as need (if not more so) in stimulating petty theft.[328] If it were actually possible to consider all acts of pilfering, including those which went unprosecuted, the majority would almost certainly prove to have been committed by the poor, though it is doubtful whether the very wide range of offences which might be categorized as 'crimes of misappropriation' are, even in principle, quantifiable. It is nonetheless likely that, even though they would probably never attempt clear-cut larceny, many really poor people helped themselves to the goods of their employers and neighbours whenever they had the chance and thought they could get away with it.[329]

6. CONCLUSION: 'LIVING BY THE SHIFT'

Long into the seventeenth century and even beyond, therefore, a wide variety of resources—from casual labour to common rights, from the cultivation of cottage gardens to the rearing of livestock, from kin support to neighbourly credit, from petty theft to covert embezzlement—helped the poor to shift for themselves independently of the parish. Although, as we shall see, formal relief gradually became a fact of life as the seventeenth century progressed, parish pensions were never universal and never intended to be anything other than income supplements even when they were granted. Into the 1650s at least, it is probable that habits of spontaneous relief, mutual aid, and self-help discussed here remained crucial, perhaps even central, to the relief of the poor.

The foregoing discussion has, perforce, artificially separated out various components in the economy of makeshifts of the poor. The difficult thing, of course, is to assess the relative significance of these components in the survival strategies of individual paupers and their families. Generalizations are obviously difficult, though the individual case-histories recorded in quarter sessions petitions and settlement examinations provide vivid enough testimony of the complexity and diversity of the mixed resources which might enable the poor to shift for themselves. Occasionally these complex strategies might be associated with entire communities. The vicar of Prescot (Lancashire) wrote in 1640,

[328] P. King, *Crime, Justice and Discretion in England, 1740–1820* (Oxford, 2000), 169–217 (Ch. 6: 'The Offenders: Property Crime and Life-Cycle Change').

[329] J. Innes and J. Styles, 'The Crime Wave: Recent Writing on Crime and Criminal Justice in Eighteenth-Century England', repr. in A. Wilson (ed.), *Rethinking Social History: English Society 1570–1920 and its Interpretation* (Manchester, 1993), 210–11.

for example, that his parishioners were 'very pore, a great part of them living in summer tyme by digging and winding coals, in the winter time by begging'.[330] More striking still is the evidence of individual resourcefulness, as the strands of support were woven together in innumerable patterns and textures. Seventy-four-year-old Jane Brice had lived in the Cumberland parish of Cumrew for twelve years but was now destitute because she was unable to work or pay rent. Her survival strategy was seasonal, supplementing mendicancy in the summer with kin support in the winter, but she was now too lame to beg and her son-in-law could no longer afford to lodge her.[331] Blind William Cooper of Melmerby (Cumberland) and his wife, both of them in their eighties, had supported themselves with the help of their son, who not only provided them with housing and fuel but also sent their granddaughter to wait on them, and with the forbearance of their landlord, who had demanded no rent for three years.[332] The fragility of these makeshift economies is powerfully expressed in the petition of John Appleby, who had looked after his mother-in-law Mabel Grayson for the past four years, during which time both her sight and hearing had deteriorated to the point that she was no longer able to feed herself. Appleby noted that, although she was now friendless, she had always 'made part Shift as long as She had hir Sight'.[333] These survival strategies were often recounted with pride. Jane Gooden of Leyland (Lancashire), widowed with three small children, explained to the Lancashire bench in 1699 that she had 'made hard shift' with 'what goods her husband left her', but was now reduced to 'extreame poverty provisions being so deare'. Robert Brock of Bruton (Somerset) explained that, although he had always been 'a painstaker in the world' for the 'dayly livelihood' of his family, 'hard tymes cold winters and dearth' had forced them into 'many hard & narrow shifts to keep alive'. Another elderly Somerset man explained that prolonged illness meant that his family were 'lyke to be turned out of doors and to lye in the streets being very miserable poor'. His wife had, he insisted, 'made all the shift she can until she can make [shift] no more'.[334] The resonance of the phrase to 'make shift' lies in its very vagueness: contriving to get by somehow—anyhow—without actually specifying the expedients involved. Some 'shifts', as we have seen, involved 'sinister dealing', and perhaps even outright criminality. *An Ease for Overseers* even included 'shifting' in its list of

[330] *Prescot Churchwardens' Accounts*, p. xii.
[331] CRO, Q/11/1/107/2.
[332] CRO, Q/11/1/118/9.
[333] CRO, Q/11/1/117/8
[334] LRO, QSP/823/16; SARS, DD\SE/45/1/21, 56.

'unlawful courses' alongside 'picking', 'stealing', and 'begging'.[335] The very fact that these survival strategies went undefined or were euphemized perfectly embodies a subculture of survival in which 'shift' was at the same time both strongly censured and perforce practised by those who veered towards the margins of subsistence.

Some doubtless spent their entire lives at those margins. Among the most detailed account of such a career of desperation is that provided by the neighbours of John and Isabel Salter of Sileby (Leicestershire).[336] John attempted to made a living by taking a sequence of casual jobs in agriculture: droving cattle, threshing corn, tending sheep. He supplemented his meagre earnings in cash and kind by stealing wood and poultry, often at night. So desperate was he for income that it seems he was even prepared to manufacture testimony in court cases, perjuring himself to secure the patronage of his more prosperous neighbours. Isabel sometimes took harvest work for wages or payment in kind, only to be accused of theft under colour of gleaning, a light-fingeredness which allegedly extended to the household goods of her employers. She too, was apparently prepared to perjure herself for cash or favours. In sum, it was alleged, the couple were so lacking in moral and financial credit that they 'lived together rather like Roagues and rascoulds then man and wife'.[337] The popular reputation of the Salters stands in marked contrast to the epitaph provided by the clerk of Pluckley (Kent) for a parishioner who had striven as long as she could to remain independent of parish support: the burial of Jane Dan on 30 April 1605 was subscribed with the note that 'she was a pore old maide that lived partly by the parish . . . but she wrought much for her living as long as she was able spinning and carding wouls diligently for her pore lyvinge'.[338]

These examples reveal the bifurcation of attitudes between the propertied and the propertyless about the proper relationships between the planks of the economy of care. Whereas elites were naturally suspicious of survival strategies that might be constructed from a series of *overlapping* expedients, they were generally far happier when various forms of relief *interlocked*. The process of regulating the natural, familial, and neighbourly resources from which the poor might make shift, with which this chapter

[335] For the popular equation of 'living by the shift' with 'sinister dealing', see the early 17th-century ballad 'Ragged, Torne, and True: Or, The Poore Man's Resolution', *The Roxburghe Ballads*, ii. 408–13; *An Ease for Overseers of the Poore*, 18.

[336] Capp, 'Life, Love and Litigation', 69–71.

[337] For other allegations that the poor casually, perhaps even habitually, forswore themselves for financial gain, see Hindle, *The State and Social Change*, 111.

[338] Davie, 'Custom and Conflict', 237.

has principally been concerned, was at heart a matter of ensuring that independence, from the labour discipline of the workforce on the one hand and from the civil parish on the other, was no longer a realistic possibility for the indigent.

In the last analysis, therefore, tales of living by the shift are narratives not only of distress but also of despair. Time and again, those who were finally subject to a crisis of dependency vividly described the evaporation of their last best hope: 'like to have starv'd living upon meal and water since a month before Christmas . . .'; 'has lost the power of her side and where she falls there she must lye . . .'; 'an aged poor widow past all servile labour . . .'.[339] In circumstances like these, the needy turned not only to their neighbours for support, but eventually to their betters for charity and ultimately to their parish officers for relief. They were not, as we shall see, invariably successful. When the labourer Adam Rochester died in Whickham (County Durham) in 1686, for instance, the curate wondered whether his children would 'shift for themselves' or fall upon the parish. Neither for particular individuals nor for the poor as a class, therefore, was there any inevitable transition from informal to formal relief. When confronted with cases of indigence, the parson of the Buckinghamshire village of Middle Claydon noted caustically in 1672, most householders felt that the poor 'should be put to their shifts a while longer'.[340]

[339] CRO, Q/11/1/157/2, 177/14, 182/29.

[340] Levine and Wrightson, *Making of an Industrial Society*, 329; Broad, 'Parish Economies of Welfare', 995.

2
Dole

As touching how much wee shall give, we are taught that if wee have much, we should give accordingly: if we have but little, give what we can spare: S. Luke councelleth us if we have two Coates, wee must give one to him that hath not: & of meate likewise: but as touching this question, little need to be spoken, when our owne covetous heartes are readie enough to frame excuses.

Some will make a question of their almes and saie they know not what the partie is that demaundeth reliefe or beggeth almes of them: O saieth some I suspect he is an idle person, dishonest, or perhaps an unthrift and therefore refuseth to give anie reliefe at all. To this I answer they are needless doubtes, for we ought to releeve them if wee know them not for such persons: And let theyr bad deedes fall on their own necks, for if they perish for want, we are in danger of Gods wrath for them: but to give unto such as wee know of lewde behaviour, therby to continue them in their wickednesse, were verie offensive . . .

Henry Smith, *The Poore Mans Teares*[1]

If the poor *were* to shift for themselves without falling upon the parish, the most valuable of the human resources available to them was, as we have seen, the charity of their neighbours. Indeed, because even those who received regular parish relief could not expect to survive on pensions alone, especially in the first half of the seventeenth century, the kindness of neighbours in giving alms long remained central to the relief of the poor. As Henry Smith's tortured discussion of the obligations to dispense charity demonstrates, however, Elizabethan and early Stuart attitudes to the giving of alms were ambiguous. While no one in late sixteenth- or seventeenth-century England seriously doubted that there was a Christian obligation to perform charitable works, there was room for much greater debate about how and to whom alms should be given.

Indeed, the coexistence of the traditions of informal and formal relief

[1] *The Poore Mans Teares: A Sermon* (1592), 12–13.

presents almost as many problems of interpretation to the historian as it did problems of eligibility to contemporaries, problems that are (and were) exacerbated by the increasingly prominent practice of quasi-formal relief through endowed charity. Indeed, the running theme of this chapter is the endemic conflict that arose from what Keith Thomas famously described as 'the uneasy conjunction of public and private charity'.[2] Against the background of the transformation of the poor law from an emergency expedient to a regular system of relief, the following discussion traces the relative significance of three specific forms of charity: *alms* (the private, often spontaneous, giving of aid in cash and kind), *doles* (semi-formal gifts to income, usually, though not always, as a single payment arising from a testamentary bequest), and *endowments* (gifts of capital, the interest of which was administered by charitable trusts and which might take the form of perpetual doles).

Two problems of interpretation in particular must be emphasized at the outset. First, it is axiomatic that alms, most often taking the form of gifts in cash or kind—dispensed from the glow of a kitchen door or from the cobbled courtyard of an inn, in the bustle of a market square or the quiet of a church porch—are almost by definition beyond historical reconstruction. Innumerable acts of private benevolence, spontaneous or solicited, reluctant or readily given, doubtless remained characteristic of the charitable impulse in rural communities long after the Elizabethan regime had supposedly forbidden begging. Even poor strangers might be offered a night's shelter in a barn or a cow house, in a hay-loft or a servant's lodging, and were often offered victuals or even clothing before they went on their way. Perhaps such alms were given in return for services rendered: the charring of kitchens, the running of errands, the watering of horses. If hospitality of this kind might be offered even to migrants, it was doubtless (as we have seen) more forthcoming to neighbours, who might share meals, tools, and information, or lend money, food, or clothing even when there was no realistic prospect of reciprocity.[3] There were, nevertheless, occasions on which the voluntary giving of alms was actively encouraged and co-ordinated by local and central authorities and the evidence left in the wake of these campaigns

[2] K. Thomas, *Religion and the Decline of Magic: Studies in Popular Beliefs in Sixteenth- and Seventeenth-Century England* (London, 1971), 564.

[3] I. K. Ben-Amos, '"Good Works" and Social Ties: Helping the Migrant Poor in Early Modern England', in M. C. McClendon *et al.* (eds.), *Protestant Identities: Religion, Society and Self-Fashioning in Post-Reformation England* (Stanford, 1999), 125–40; Ben-Amos, 'Gifts and Favors: Informal Support in Early Modern England', *Journal of Modern History*, 72 (2000), 295–338. Cf. Ch. 1.4 above.

for 'general hospitality' discloses a great deal about habits of informal relief which would otherwise remain invisible to us.[4]

Second, historiographical understanding of the significance of doles and endowments has been seriously undermined by the influence of, and reaction to, Wilbur Kitchener Jordan's series of studies of the charities endowed in England between 1480 and 1660.[5] The weaknesses of Jordan's methodology have frequently been rehearsed: an obsession with an exaggerated and largely unsustainable secularization thesis; a failure to correct for the impact of price inflation when measuring the value of bequests; a preference for long-term aggregative analysis of trends rather than close investigation of the cultural impact of charity; a reliance on crude typological categories of 'the great charitable causes' ('the poor', 'social rehabilitation', municipal betterment', 'education', 'religion'), the boundaries of which both manifestly overlap and fail to take account of regional variation.[6] Most damaging of all, however, was his obvious admiration for charitable trusts as 'social institutions of great and abiding utility'. Jordan focused his analysis on those generous capital bequests that, he insisted, not only reflected the visionary secular aspirations of testators but also exerted a powerful and perpetual influence on English social structure.[7] Although the endowments with which he was pre-

[4] S. Hindle, 'Dearth, Fasting and Alms: The Campaign for General Hospitality in Late Elizabethan England', *Past and Present*, 172 (2001), 44–86.

[5] Jordan's contribution is organized into three central volumes: W. K. Jordan, *Philanthropy in England, 1480–1660: A Study of the Changing Pattern of English Social Aspirations* (London, 1959); Jordan, *The Charities of London, 1480–1660: The Aspirations and the Achievements of the Urban Society* (London, 1960); Jordan, *The Charities of Rural England*; and three subsidiary case-studies: Jordan, 'The Forming of the Charitable Institutions of the West of England: A Study of the Changing Pattern of Social Aspirations in Bristol and Somerset, 1480–1660', *Transactions of the American Philosophical Society*, NS 50, pt. 8 (1960); Jordan, *Social Institutions in Kent, 1480–1660: A Study of the Changing Pattern of Social Aspirations* (Kent Archaeological Society, 75, Ashford, 1961); Jordan, *The Social Institutions of Lancashire: A Study of the Changing Pattern of Aspirations in Lancashire, 1480–1660* (Chetham Society, 3rd ser., 11, 1962).

[6] See the criticisms voiced by W. G. Bittle and R. T. Lane, 'Inflation and Philanthropy in England: A Re-assessment of W. K. Jordan's Data', *Economic History Review*, 2nd ser., 31 (1976), 203–10; J. Hadwin, 'Deflating Philanthropy', *Economic History Review*, 2nd ser., 31 (1978), 105–17; D. C. Coleman, 'Philanthropy Deflated: A Comment', *Economic History Review*, 2nd ser., 31 (1978), 118–20; J. D. Gould, 'Bittle and Lane on Charity: An Uncharitable Comment', *Economic History Review*, 2nd ser., 31 (1978), 121–3; W. G. Bittle and R. T. Lane, 'A Reassessment Reiterated', *Economic History Review*, 2nd ser., 31 (1978), 124–8; M. Feingold, 'Jordan Revisited: Patterns of Charitable Giving in Sixteenth and Seventeenth Century England', *History of Education*, 8 (1979), 257–73; J. Hadwin, 'The Problem of Poverty in Early Modern England', in T. Riis (ed.), *Aspects of Poverty in Early Modern Europe* (Florence, 1981), 219–51; C. Wilson, 'Poverty and Philanthropy in Early Modern England', in Riis (ed.), *Aspects of Poverty*, 253–79; Slack, *Poverty and Policy*, 162–4, 166, 169–71.

[7] Jordan, *Philanthropy*, 119.

occupied accounted for the overwhelming bulk (82 per cent) of the *value* of charitable funds in his sample, they originated from the wills of only a small proportion (18 per cent) of the *number* of donors.[8] While Jordan was frequently at pains to emphasize the enduring significance of small gifts to income by testators of relatively humble status, his perspective primarily eulogized those wealthy benefactors who might command the legal counsel and dutiful trustees by whom endowments were managed, thereby seriously distorting his vision of 'social aspirations'. Cumulatively, therefore, Jordan's experiment in aggregation abstracts philanthropy to a plane far removed from its real manifestations in the parishes: doles, almshouses, and town lands. If his occasional caveats about the continued importance of doles relative to endowments are taken seriously, however, Jordan's corpus nonetheless remains an invaluable starting point for the study of the *texture* of semi-formal relief in the English local community, notwithstanding its notorious limitations as a source for the *scale* of philanthropy. Rather more characteristic examples of charitable behaviour lie buried beneath the crumbling masonry of Jordan's grand philanthropic edifices.

If alms, doles, and endowments were the mechanisms through which informal relief was distributed, each was undoubtedly influenced by the discourses of charity propagated from the pulpit and printing press in the century or so after 1550, and although a full-scale analysis of changing attitudes to charity is self-evidently beyond the remit of this discussion, it is with these that this chapter must begin. Preachers and propagandists were themselves concerned with the very questions which will inform the subsequent discussion. What were the obligations of the wealthy towards their poorer neighbours? To whom, how often, and how should charity be given? What were the appropriate motives of benefactors? What was the relationship between the ancient moral duty of care for the needy and the more recent legal obligations to contribute to rates for relief of the impotent? And to what extent did the poor have grounds to believe that they had a right to the charity of their neighbours and betters?

1. DISCOURSES OF CHARITY

The earliest and most ubiquitous post-Reformation statement of the 'charitable imperative' was the 'homily of alms-deeds, and mercifulness towards the poor and needy', first published in 1547 and reissued in 1563

[8] Ibid. 118.

with further editions in 1595 and 1626.[9] The 'glory of God and the declaration of the vocation of His most faithful servants', it argued, ought principally to be expressed in 'works of mercy and pity shewed upon the poor which be afflicted with any kind of misery'. In practice, however, householders were infected with such a 'slothful sluggishness' in dispensing the very charity that the homily was designed to stir in their sleepy minds. The argument proceeded in three parts. First, those who had hitherto neglected to give alms were reminded that God now required it of them and those who had been liberal were assured that their godly doings were thankfully taken at God's hands. Second, those who might be tempted to believe that the performance of charitable works would secure their salvation were warned that justification proceeded only from faith, of which charity was but one outward sign. Third, those who pleaded that giving alms to the poor would lead to their own destitution were admonished against unmerciful dealing, and encouraged to believe that God would never suffer those who relieved others men's needs to be oppressed with penury.[10]

In none of this, however, was there any mention of the distinction between the deserving and the undeserving. Like other early expositions of the Protestant vision of charity, the homilies were very reluctant to emphasize the division of the poor into the worthy and the unworthy, not only because discrimination was in practice difficult to manage but also because it might provide householders with an excuse to escape their social duty. During the second half of the sixteenth century, however, the voluntaristic tradition was gradually eroded by the double burden of Elizabethan Protestant thinking about charity: first, that donors should endeavour to distinguish between the categories of the poor; and second, that provision should be public rather than private. By the late sixteenth century, therefore, propertied elites were able to draw upon a 'common fund of ideas' about riches, idleness, and poverty, which approached the status of a moral orthodoxy.[11] Privy councillors, clergymen, and moralists performed a chorus of exhortation to charity which, for all its polyphony, was nonetheless harmonious. Churches across the land echoed with the

[9] For the publication history of the homilies, see *Certain Sermons or Homilies (1547) and a Homily Against Disobedience and Wilful Rebellion (1570): A Critical Edition*, ed. R. B. Bond (Toronto, 1987), 1–25 (Ch. 1: 'A Two-Edged Sword: The History of the Tudor Homilies'). Cf. C. Jones, *The Charitable Imperative: Hospitals and Nursing in Ancien Regime and Revolutionary France* (London, 1989), 1.

[10] 'An Homily of Almsdeeds and Mercifulness Towards the Poore and Needy, in Three Parts', in *The Two Books of Homilies Appointed to Be Read in Churches* (Oxford, 1859), 382–99.

[11] I. Breward, 'The Direction of Conscience', in *The Works of William Perkins*, ed. I. Breward (Abingdon, 1970), 75.

injunctions that the relief of the poor was an inescapable duty; that almsgiving must be discriminating in order that resources be bestowed on the deserving poor; that charity began at home and moved outward to kindred and neighbourhood; that idleness was dangerous; that the poor should behave with forbearance and patience even in the face of oppression; that covetousness was corrosive of social harmony and social order; and that man's relationship to property was one of temporary stewardship rather than absolute ownership.[12] These were the terms of the charitable imperative as contemporaries understood them. It would, however, be a serious mistake to assume either that all the components in the equation of riches and poverty were given equal weight throughout our period or that all those who participated in the discourse necessarily agreed about the result of the calculation.

There were, it must be emphasized, counter-currents within the elite discourse of charity. Controversies over eligibility for charity were, after all, of ancient standing. The arguments in favour of discrimination in particular had been prefigured in medieval thought, in the calculations of the early sixteenth-century humanists, and in the mid-Tudor polemics towards vagrants, which were rehearsed even by those commonwealth thinkers who espoused conceptions of social justice. The canonists of the twelfth century had, in fact, actively debated the very same questions to which the early seventeenth-century moralists returned. Should eligibility for relief be a simple matter of need or should there be other moral considerations? Was there a hierarchy of preference among those considered eligible? Should the criteria of selection be inflected with the principles of punishment, or perhaps even of reform, for those who were excluded?[13] A running theme of canonist discourse was that the answers to these questions necessarily differed according to economic context: when funds were sufficient, all the needy might be relieved without question; when they were not, hard choices had to be made about the limits of eligibility, which in turn revived old questions about the relative duties of

[12] This analysis owes much not only to Breward but also to J. Walter and K. Wrightson, 'Dearth and the Social Order in Early Modern England', *Past and Present*, 71 (1976), 22–44; J. Walter, 'The Social Economy of Dearth in Early Modern England', in J. Walter and R. Schofield (eds.), *Famine, Disease and the Social Order in Early Modern Society* (Cambridge, 1989), 75–128; F. Heal, *Hospitality in Early Modern England* (Oxford, 1990), 91–140; A. McRae, *God Speed the Plough: The Representation of Agrarian England, 1500–1660* (Cambridge, 1996), 23–79; Ben-Amos, '"Good Works" and Social Ties', 134–39; and P. Collinson, 'Puritanism and the Poor', in R. Horrox and S. Rees-Jones (eds.), *Pragmatic Utopias: Ideals and Communities, 1200–1630* (Cambridge, 2001), 242–58.

[13] B. Tierney, 'The Decretists and the "Deserving Poor"', *Comparative Studies in Society and History*, 1 (1958–9), 360–73.

individuals, of their families, and of the communities in which they lived, in providing for the marginally poor.[14] It is therefore arguable that the emphasis on discrimination which is so prominent in late Elizabethan and early Stuart discourses of charity owes at least as much to the hard times in which treatises were drafted and sermons were preached as to the Protestant theology from which they were constructed. The key differences were, therefore, those of emphasis. Most observers might have agreed with St Paul that those who would not work should not eat. Only a few radicals would state the issue as baldly as did John Rogers of Dedham (Essex): 'for those that can work and will not, let them starve'. Even Alexander Strange of Layston, whose views on the allocation of charity were, to say the least, exclusionary, stopped short of Rogers's 'sharp construction' of the notorious Pauline text, preferring instead 'a more mild & civill exposition': '*They that will not worke should not eate*, that is, eate so much and so freely as they doe, but bite of the bridle, and be pinched with hunger.'[15] But since the higher priority of pulpit rhetoric was the excoriation of a miserly elite that was manifestly failing to meet its charitable obligations, discrimination against the undeserving was, as we shall see, as often passed over in silence as it was rehearsed with full rigour.[16]

The popular perception that theirs was an ice age in which charity had frozen helps explain why some polemicists advocated the perpetuation of the 'voluntaristic' tradition of relief long after the demise of the mid-sixteenth-century 'commonwealthsmen' with whom it has conventionally been associated. Indeed, indiscriminate charity remained a particularly prominent theme in the homilies and other sermons preached during the harvest crises of the 1590s, on the very eve of the codification of the Elizabeth poor laws.[17] Well into the 1630s, furthermore, we find even the 'hotter sort of Protestants' arguing that charity should be given indiscriminately. As part of his rebuttal of claims that the

[14] R. M. Smith, 'The Structured Dependence of the Elderly as a Recent Development: Some Sceptical Thoughts', *Ageing and Society*, 4 (1984), 422.

[15] 2 Thessalonians 3: 10; J. Rogers, *A Treatise of Love* (London, 1632), 213–14; Inner Temple Library, London, MS Petyt, 530B, fo. 23[v]. For Alexander Strange, see S. Hindle, 'Exclusion Crises: Poverty, Migration and Parochial Responsibility in English Rural Communities, *c.*1560–1660', *Rural History*, 7 (1996), 125–49; *'This Little Commonwealth': Buntingford with Layston Parish Memorandum Book, 1607–c.1750*, ed. H. Falvey and S. Hindle (Hertfordshire Record Society, 19, Braughing, 2004); and Chs. 3.1, 5.3, and 6.1 below.

[16] Collinson, 'Puritanism and the Poor', 245; I. W. Archer, 'The Charity of Early Modern Londoners', *Transactions of the Royal Historical Society*, 6th ser., 12 (2002), 227.

[17] Hindle, 'Dearth, Fasting and Alms'. Cf. McRae, *God Speed the Plough*, 23–57 (Ch. 1: 'Covetousness in the Countryside: Agrarian Complaint and Mid-Tudor Reform').

godly were 'covetous', because 'they do not give pharasaically to every clamorous beggar', the Northamptonshire clergyman Joseph Bentham claimed that indiscriminate generosity was the true instinct of the godly: 'by their will', he insisted, '*none* shall go from their doores empty handed without reliefe'.[18] Despite the self-evident dangers of encouraging (and, perhaps worse, of being seen to encourage) a shiftless lifestyle, the godly might be moved to relieve the unworthy out of pity, for these too were 'creatures' of God. An outward show of generosity might also be necessary to 'take away all occasion of scandall from God's children and their profession'. The godly should not, therefore, be thought hard-hearted, even if the price to be paid for protecting their reputation was the relief of the unworthy. John Downame similarly argued that discrimination might all too easily become 'a vaile to hide our niggardlinesse and hardhartednesse', leading ultimately to the abrogation of the charitable ideal. 'Let not the disorder and inordinate courses of some', he warned, 'make you desist from doing the workes of mercy and pick a quarrell against almes deedes because of the unworthinesse of those who are to receive them'.[19]

Although tensions of this kind were rehearsed by preachers well into the seventeenth century, long after the distinction between the deserving and the undeserving had become enshrined in the Elizabethan poor law, discrimination did eventually become the central, though never the hegemonic, idiom of charitable discourse.[20] Thus John Rogers's 'rules for right relieving' specified that charity be given righteously ('of our own lawfully come by, not what we have gotten by oppression or wrong'); freely ('without expecting a recompense'); cheerfully ('as a freewill offering'); seasonably ('not tomorrow, if now they need'); and wisely ('not lashing it on too fast, but measuring it out as it may continue'). Alms should, above all, be given where they would be of maximum benefit. Charity should be dispensed where there is 'most neede: not the lusty to have it and the old, lame, blind, impotent and young children to want'.[21] This emphasis on discrimination, which prefigured the subsequent appropriation of discretion by the officers of the civil parish, was widely shared among early Stuart clergymen. Even Downame, who had argued

[18] J. Bentham, *The Societie of the Saints* (London, 1636), 25 (emphasis added).

[19] J. Downame, *The Plea of the Poore, or A Treatise of Beneficence and Almes-Deedes* (London, 1616), 41.

[20] Cf. the emphasis on indiscriminate giving in 18th-century discourse on charity in D. Andrew, *Philanthropy and Police: London Charity in the Eighteenth Century* (Princeton, 1989), 12–22; W. M. Jacob, *Lay People and Religion in the Early Eighteenth Century* (Cambridge, 1996), 155–6.

[21] Rogers, *A Treatise of Love*, 205, 209, 210, 211, 212. Cf. the discussion of 'in what manner and measure we must give to the poore', in *An Ease for Overseers of the Poore: Abstracted from the Statutes* (Cambridge, 1601), 34–5.

against hard-heartedness, insisted that the 'honest poore' could be 'more liberallie relieved' only if 'evil devourers did not eate up their portion', a distinction which prompted a characteristically lurid description of that 'promiscuous generation' of 'sturdy beggars and vagrant rogues' that he regarded as a 'blemish of our government and a burthen to the commonwealth'.[22] Rogers agreed, describing the dreadful abuse of resources implied by indiscriminate hospitality. 'It is a great disorder in some great mens keeping open house at Christmas that the rude idle prophane round about they come thither to meate, but the very poore indeed which cannot travell in the dirt and cold and crowd, they sit at home and want'. The discriminating dispensation of alms should not, however, altogether preclude the relief of the delinquent: 'give even the bad in their want, if they be diligent to do what they can; yet give them with instructions and admonitions to keepe their church, have a care of their soules, and to bring up their children to worke, not to pilfering, idleness or begging, rebuking them for these or any such faults'. Informal provision for the poor should, therefore, be accompanied by moral teaching.[23] Almsgiving along these lines was all the more necessary, Bentham argued, because the laws that were intended to discriminate between the idle and unfortunate poor (and therefore make life easier for benefactors by relieving them of the obligation to make hard choices about the moral worth of those who solicited alms) were 'but sleeping statutes in the execution'.[24] It therefore fell to clergymen and other householders to continue the ancient traditions of feeding the hungry, clothing the naked, and sheltering the destitute.

2. CHARITIES OF HOSPITALITY

The tradition of casual, albeit regular, almsgiving to neighbours and strangers was most closely associated with the aristocracy and gentry, who were expected to preside over the quiet of their country throughout rural England, and especially to invite their poor tenants and neighbours into their dining halls to enjoy the succour of hospitality. In some communities, however, the throwing open of one's doors was expected even of the middling sort. The 'ancients of the congregation' of Dedham (Essex) ordered in 1585 that all householders were to invite either one or two of their 'poore neighbours' to dine with them, providing them with either 'no more [food] then ordinary' or very generous fare, according to

[22] Downame, *The Plea of the Poore*, 38.

[23] Rogers, *A Treatise of Love*, 212, 213.

[24] Bentham, *Societie of the Saints*, 25.

their 'habilitie'. This early experiment in communal hospitality was emphatically not, however, indiscriminate. Only those poor inhabitants who had 'submitted themselves to the good orders of the church, and walke Christianly and honestly in their callings' were welcome, and even then only for so long 'as they shall thankfullie accepte' such charity. The godly of Dedham evidently recognized that commensality of this kind would give them a better opportunity to admonish and exhort 'the poorer and weaker sort' to the 'good workes and holy duties of Christianitye'.[25] Elsewhere, however, hospitality was predominantly the preserve of the gentry.

Landlords had long known, and wherever they forgot they were frequently reminded, that it was their Christian duty to extend their charity to the local poor during their lifetime as well as after their death. Historians have wisely been cautioned both about the reliability of the sources for 'paternalism' of this kind, and about the dangers of interpreting its scale from the perspective of donors rather than that of recipients. Despite the rich fund of prescription and nostalgia expressed in funeral sermons and family memoirs, evidence for the actual practice of gentry hospitality is rather limited, and even where it can accurately be measured it constituted only a tiny fraction of the income of the landed elite. It is nevertheless arguable that that the practice of lordly benevolence proved remarkably resilient, even in the face of 'the changing vision of hospitality'.[26] Although the impact of religious change and demographic growth over the course of the sixteenth century had fragmented and marginalized the very ideal of hospitality, the Stuart gentry occasionally did continue to take seriously their obligations to provide weekly relief to poor neighbours and tenants. The Suffolk gentleman Edward Lewkenor, for example, carefully nurtured the poor of Denham by providing a dining room at his gates in the 1610s, a practice that may have been emulated by Richard Brownlow of Belton (Lincolnshire) at about the same time. Sir Hugh Cholmley of Whitby in the North Riding of Yorkshire recorded that during the 1630s 'a certain number of old people, widows and indigent persons' were twice a week 'served at my gates with bread and good pottage made of beef'. Even in the mid-seventeenth century, the Kentish landowner Sir George Sondes apparently opened his doors to at least twenty poor people each week.[27] In the Northamptonshire parish of

[25] *Conferences and Combination Lectures in the Elizabethan Church: Dedham and Bury St Edmunds, 1582–1590*, ed. P. Collinson *et al.* (Church of England Record Society, 10, Woodbridge, 2003), 125, 129.

[26] Walter, 'Social Economy of Dearth', 108–9; Heal, *Hospitality*, 91–140.

[27] P. Collinson, 'Magistracy and Ministry: A Suffolk Miniature', in id., *Godly People: Essays in*

Weekley, Joseph Bentham proudly recorded, Sir Edward Montagu ensured that Boughton House remained a consistent source of both employment and hospitality for the poor. Montagu was said to keep his cottagers 'continualy in worke', while the poorest among them had 'bread, broth, beere, broken meate, upon theire dole-daies'.[28]

Most often, however, the characteristic pattern of gentry hospitality was seasonal. At Christmas 'many hundreds' were served with beef and bread at Boughton House as Montagu's hospitality was extended even to poor men from outside the parish. Even within this bastion of traditional charity, however, practices had to change under social and demographic pressure. Whereas poorer guests had once taken it in turns to sit at tables *within* the house, it was decided that 'onely some of the men'—presumably those considered most respectable—should be allowed inside, while the rest were 'served out of the gate' with the women and children.[29] The Christmas hospitality of both the Lowells of Harling and the Hollands of Quidenham enjoyed a famous reputation for the 'good relief' provided to the poor of south Norfolk into the second decade of the seventeenth century. Sir Thomas Pelham of Halland (Sussex) spent £35 on Christmas doles in 1626 and again in 1627. Francis, Lord Dacre continued the tradition of a Christmas distribution of beef, loaves, and cash to forty-four poor people at Herstmonceux (Sussex) throughout the 1640s.[30] Although these examples provide rather more concrete evidence of the practice, rather than the ideal, of gentry benevolence, it should be remembered both that hospitality of this kind represented a redistribution of resources whose value was only a fraction of gentry incomes, and that it was not invariably spontaneous, sometimes being coerced by the complaints, curses, and threats of the poor themselves.[31]

Over the course of the seventeenth century, moreover, the tradition of

English Protestantism and Puritanism (London, 1983), 464; Heal, *Hospitality*, 177; J. T. Cliffe, *The Yorkshire Gentry from the Reformation to the Revolution* (London, 1969), 114; C. Chalklin, *Seventeenth-Century Kent: A Social and Economic History* (London, 1965), 210.

[28] NRO, MS Montagu, 186 ('Life of Montagu' by Joseph Bentham), 25–6.

[29] NRO, MS Montagu, 186, 23–4. For the tendency to relieve the 'alien' poor at the gate see F. Heal and C. Holmes, *The Gentry in England and Wales, 1500–1700* (London and New York, 1984), 284.

[30] HMC, *Eleventh Report, Appendix, Part IV: The Manuscripts of the Marquess Townshend* (London, 1887), 19 (though Walter, 'Social Economy of Dearth', 108 n. 94, suspects that this report implies the provision of employment rather than of hospitality); A. Fletcher, *A County Community in Peace and War: Sussex, 1600–1660* (London, 1975), 155.

[31] Walter, 'Social Economy of Dearth', 109; J. Walter, 'Public Transcripts, Popular Agency and the Politics of Subsistence in Early Modern England', in M. Braddick and J. Walter (eds.), *Negotiating Power in Early Modern Society: Order, Hierarchy and Subordination in Britain and Ireland* (Cambridge, 2001), 123–48.

gentry hospitality slowly evolved into one of lordly largesse. Even in the early Stuart period, critics had bemoaned the covetousness of absentee landlords whose breach of hospitality had left the poor unrelieved, especially at those festive times of the year where charity was not so much expected as insisted upon.[32] Abrogation of the customary obligation to relieve the poor through hospitality was particularly sensitive when it occurred in years of dearth, as it did in Hunton (Kent) in 1598 or at Arbury (Warwickshire) in 1607–8.[33] Perhaps the most characteristic gentry attitude by the mid-seventeenth century was voiced by the Cheshire baronet Sir Richard Grosvenor, who argued that it was a gentleman's duty to 'bee charitable to the truly poore', to 'receive strangers [and] cloath the naked' so that their 'wretchedness' would not be exposed. On the other hand, he insisted, the deserving could be relieved only if the gentry drove from their gates 'lusty rogues and sturdy beggars that are able to earne their owne bread by their labour'. 'The stokes and howse of correction', Grosvenor insisted, 'are the alms that best befit them.'[34] After the Restoration, when royal proclamations and privy council tirades were no longer bullying the gentry to reside in the country where they were expected to live as paragons of paternalism, absenteeism became even more common and hospitality was ground under the wheels of coaches trundling towards the metropolis. There are, moreover, notorious examples of resident landlords who seem to have decided that, since hospitality was an unconscionable time a-dying, it was best to kill it off. John Verney of Middle Claydon (Buckinghamshire) decided in 1698 that if his cook kept feeding his poor tenants and neighbours he would have nothing left, and therefore ordered 'nothing given away at the door'.[35]

Even so, there were numerous gentry families who continued, if not to keep open house, then at least to exercise their traditional role as dispensers of charity.[36] Some of them even singled out particular individuals, usually retired servants, who were deserving of estate pensions, granting

[32] F. Heal, 'The Crown, The Gentry and London: The Enforcement of Proclamation, 1596–1640', in C. Cross *et al.* (eds.), *Law and Government under the Tudors: Essays Presented to Sir Geoffrey Elton on his Retirement* (Cambridge, 1988), 211–27.

[33] J. Thirsk, 'The Farming Regions of England', in id. (ed.), *The Agrarian History of England and Wales*, vol. iv: *1500–1640* (Cambridge, 1967), 63; Walter, 'Public Transcripts', 129–30.

[34] *The Papers of Sir Richard Grosvenor, 1st Bart. (1585–1645)*, ed. R. Cust (Record Society of Lancashire and Cheshire, 134, Stroud, 1996), 32.

[35] S. Whyman, *Sociability and Power in Late Stuart England: The Cultural Worlds of the Verneys, 1660–1720* (Oxford, 1999), 159. For similar policy on hospitality (and its subsequent reversal by a new landlord) at neighbouring East Claydon, see J. Broad, 'Parish Economies of Welfare, 1650–1834', *Historical Journal*, 42 (1999), 1003, 1004.

[36] This and the following paragraph are based on D. R. Hainsworth, *Stewards, Lords and People: The Estate Steward and his World in Later Stuart England* (Cambridge, 1992), 161–2.

them quarterly payments that became customary over time. In the late 1670s, Viscountess Elizabeth Cholmondley enjoyed a particularly close relationship with the elderly women she regarded as her 'pensioners'. Well into the late seventeenth or even the early eighteenth century, moreover, landlords were instructing their estate stewards to distribute annual Christmas gifts to groups of the deserving poor, who might be defined rather narrowly in terms of their status as tenants or former servants, or more generously as the impotent inhabitants of all the villages on the estate. From the 1680s, Viscountess Cholmondley supervised an annual Christmas dole worth £5 to thirty poor widows of Malpas (Cheshire), though it had to be given in cash after her husband insisted on the abandonment of the traditional distribution in kind. The Christmas bounty of Lord Fitzwilliam of Milton (Northamptonshire) in the 1690s took the form of 6*d.* to each of ninety-one poor men in five of the villages where he was landlord. Twenty shillings in bread and fuel was distributed amongst the poor of Marholme (Northamptonshire) at Christmas 1705 on the instruction of Lady Fitzwilliam. At Christmas 1707, Sir James Lowther had 40*s.* distributed on his Whitehaven estate in the form of a sixpenny loaf for every poor collier who had dependent children. Even when these gifts had become customary, stewards forbore to distribute them without explicit letters of authorization, and where these were delayed, the poor simply had to wait.

That these were evidently not indiscriminate doles is, moreover, confirmed by the gentry practice of drawing up for their stewards lists of those thought to be deserving, from which names could be (and often were) crossed out. Lowther thought a prior list of those who were entitled to his bounty essential so that there would be 'no wrangling' at its distribution. Reports of its demise notwithstanding, the tradition of gentry largesse evidently continued well after the Restoration, and was by some landlords such as the Tichbornes of Tichborne (Hampshire) strategically reinvigorated.[37] But even at Christmas—when the poor tenants of the Elizabethan and early Stuart period had once stood the greatest chance of gaining intimate access to the lord's generosity in his great hall—late seventeenth- and early eighteenth-century almsmen and women were usually relieved at a safe distance, either in their own homes or at the estate 'payhouse'.[38] Although, moreover, a landlord's own charitable giving might satisfy both his own conscience and the inherited tradition of generosity, it also became an arm of estate policy. Nowhere was this more evident than in the tendency of the gentry, either during their life-

[37] See Ch. 2.7 below.

[38] Cf. Heal, *Hospitality*, 74–7.

times or in their wills, to finance apprenticeship premiums for the children of cottagers, thereby relieving both their present and future ratepaying tenants of a liability which, by the end of the seventeenth century, they could ill afford.[39]

3. CHARITIES OF ABSTINENCE

It would be a serious mistake, however, to assume that almsgiving was expected only by the gentry or that the country seat was the only locus of hospitality. Especially at times of crisis, advocates of the reinvigoration of hospitality might insist that the poor be fed not merely occasionally by their landlords but even on a weekly, perhaps even daily, basis by their neighbours. 'General hospitality' on this model was usually exhorted from the pulpits, which were tuned by the archbishops at the insistence of the privy council, in preaching campaigns which made extensive use not only of the homily on alms-deeds but also of special prayers. Indeed, there was a long history of public prayers specified by the ecclesiastical hierarchy as 'fit for the time' of natural disaster or political crisis.[40] The nationwide encouragement of a felicitous combination of prayer, fasting, and almsgiving aimed explicitly at poor relief was, however, first attempted during the dearth of 1586–7.[41] This campaign originated with the bishops in May 1586, when preachers were instructed to 'move the people to hearty repentance, prayer, fasting, amendment of life and liberality to the poor', a policy justified by Bishop John Aylmer of London on the grounds that the people had not 'answered [God] with true repentance humiliation and obedience' but rather with 'too lavishe excessive

[39] C. Clay, 'Landlords and Estate Management in England', in J. Thirsk (ed.), *The Agrarian History of England and Wales*, vol. v: *1640–1750, Part II: Agrarian Change* (Cambridge, 1985), 241.

[40] C. J. Kitching, '"Prayers Fit for the Time": Fasting and Prayer in Response to National Crisis in the Reign Of Elizabeth I', in W. J. Sheils (ed.), *Monks, Hermits and the Ascetic Tradition* (Studies in Church History, 22, Oxford, 1985), 241–50. For the longer-term history of public prayer and fasting in England, see R. Bartel, 'The Story of Public Fast Days in England', *Anglican Theological Review*, 37 (1955), 190–200; W. S. Hudson, 'Fast Days and Civil Religion', in *Theology in Sixteenth and Seventeenth-Century England* [Papers Read at a Clark Library Seminar, 6 Feb. 1971] (William Andrews Clark Memorial Library, Los Angeles, 1971), 3–24; C. Durston, '"For the Better Humiliation of the People": Public Days of Fasting and Thanksgiving During the English Revolution', *The Seventeenth Century*, 7 (1992), 129–49.

[41] For the demographic context of 1586–7, when a very deficient harvest caused real wages to plummet 21% below trend, see A. B. Appleby, 'Disease or Famine? Mortality in Cumberland and Westmorland, 1580–1640', *Economic History Review*, 2nd ser., 26 (1973), 408–14; Appleby, *Famine in Tudor and Stuart England* (Liverpool, 1978), 95–108; E. A. Wrigley and R. S. Schofield, *The Population History of England, 1541–1871: A Reconstruction* (Cambridge, 1981), 666 n. 51, 672–3 (esp. fig. A10.4).

and riotous spending'. Since 'God hath begun to shake His fatherly rod already at us by some scarsitye and dearthe of victuals', his wrath must be appeased by 'the true preaching of his worde of peace and plentye'.[42] The bishops insisted that 'the churchwardens and other discreete men of the parish' report on any negligent clergy or disobedient congregations.[43] From the outset, therefore, the ecclesiastical hierarchy intended that the performance of 'this godlie exercise' be effectively monitored.

A second campaign of 1596 used the same form of prayer originally stipulated in 1586. Congregations were urged to 'turn unto the Lord with all your heart, with fasting, with weeping and with mourning'. Preachers were to condemn the people for their 'unthankful receiving' of 'God's exceeding benefits and blessings' and to 'exhort them to sincere and true repentance' so that 'the inward affection of their hearts' might be matched by 'the outward exercises of prayer, fasting and alms-deeds'. One of three specified homilies might equally be used 'if there be a convenient number of hearers'.[44] In 1586 their texts were abridged in the *Order for Publike Prayers*; in 1596 they were supplemented by a new set of *Three Sermons, or Homelies to Move Compassion Towards the Poor and Needy*.[45] As might be expected, the 'doctrine of judgements' figured prominently in this discourse. The *Three Sermons* interpreted dearth 'as a checke of our gluttonie' and as a 'punishment of our idleness'.[46] They insisted, moreover, on the essential brotherhood of rich and poor, strikingly representing the continued power of the commonwealth ideal in a fairly pristine form. Citing Luke 14: 13–14, they urged all householders at mealtimes to 'call the poore, the maymed, the lame and the blind'. The stipulation of catholicity in giving was, however, qualified in an unusual way. The repeated injunction to 'call them' revealingly singled out the *labouring* poor, who 'by reason of the extremity of the world' can neither 'live by

[42] *Records of the Old Archdeaconry of St Albans: A Calendar of Papers, A.D. 1575 to A.D. 1637*, ed. H. R. Wilton Hall (St Albans and Hertfordshire Architectural and Archaeological Society, St Albans, 1908), 47–8 (Bishop Aylmer to the archdeacon of St Albans, 14 May 1586). For the form of prayer itself, see *Liturgies and Occasional Forms of Prayer*, ed. W. K. Clay (Parker Society, Cambridge, 1847), 591–4.

[43] *An Order for Publike Prayers to be Used on Wednesdays and Fridays in Every Parish Church Within the Province of Canterburie* (London, 1586), sig. A3ᵛ.

[44] *Liturgies*, 592–3. The relevant homilies were those 'of good works and first of fasting', 'of alms-deeds and mercifulness towards the poor and needy', and 'of repentance and true reconciliation unto God'. *The Two Books of Homilies Appointed to be Read in Churches* (Oxford, 1859), 279–96, 382–409, 525–49.

[45] *Three Sermons, or Homelies to Move Compassion Towards the Poor and Needy* (London 1596). The second book of homilies was itself reissued in 1595 (*STC*² 13764).

[46] *Three Sermons*, sig. C1ᵛ. For the 'doctrine of judgements', see Walter and Wrightson, 'Dearth and the Social Order', 27–9.

their labour nor maintain their charge': '*call them also; nay, call them first of all*'. Charity should therefore be targeted among those who were 'fallen into decay' not through their own fault 'but through the oppression and injury of the rich'. In an even more resonant expression of the commonwealth tradition of moral economics, the homilies insisted that the predicament of the labouring poor was so desperate because 'their rents are so great, the prices of necessities so deare and the hearts of men so heardened'. Although, therefore, the relief of the impotent was a 'proper work of charity', it was less urgent than hospitality to those who, their manifest need notwithstanding, were 'ashamed to begg and crave thy charity as others doe'. The *Three Sermons* thus not only refrained from employing the conventional distinction between the deserving and undeserving, but actually inverted the usual moral order of priority by subordinating the needs of the 'poore by casualtie' to those who were ashamed that they 'cannot get their living by their labour'.[47]

In normal circumstances, the frequency and the value, let alone the demeanour, with which alms were given are almost by definition beyond historical recovery.[48] Remarkably, however, the late sixteenth-century campaigns for co-ordinated almsgiving have generated very rich evidence of how and by whom casual charity was dispensed and even in some cases to whom it was given. On Christmas Day 1596, in the bleak midwinter of a second consecutive year of harvest failure, the privy council reminded the archbishops of Canterbury and York of Queen Elizabeth's 'great and princely care' at this 'tyme of scarsety' to 'provide for the relief of the poorer sort of people'.[49] After reiterating the provisions for market regulation specified by the dearth orders last issued in October 1595, the council condemned the continuation of 'want and dearth'.[50] The 'heavie displeasure of God' had been rekindled, it argued, not by abuses in the grain market, but by dietary extravagance, 'a custome

[47] *Three Sermons*, sigs. C3–3^{v}. Discussions of the shame-faced poor are rare in England in comparison with the Continent. But this theme was picked up by the minister of Farway (Devon) in 1630, who argued that charity should ideally take the form of 'silent and close beneficence' so that 'neither themselves, who give, may doe it in Ostentation; nor they, who receive, may feare exprobation'. T. Foster, *Plouto-mastix: The Scourge of Covetousnesse: or, An Apologie for the Publike Good, Against Privacie* (London, 1631), 25.

[48] Slack, *Poverty and Policy*, 163–72.

[49] *APC*, xxvi (1596–7), 383–6. Except where noted otherwise, all subsequent quotations are from this source.

[50] *A New Charge Given by the Queenes Commandment . . . for Execution of Sundry Disorders Published the Last Yeere for Staie of Dearth of Graine* (London, 1595); P. Slack, 'Books of Orders: The Making of English Social Policy, 1577–1631', *Transactions of the Royal Historical Society*, 5th ser., 30 (1980), 3; Slack, 'Dearth and Social Policy in Early Modern England', *Social History of Medicine*, 5 (1992), 2 n. 2.

generally received throughout all partes of the realme'. The council's remedy for food shortage was not, therefore, its time-honoured legalistic prescription of the exemplary punishment of engrossers and forestallers of grain. Instead, it attempted a more sophisticated treatment, combining the spiritual palliative of repentance with the secular medicine of frugality. Clergymen throughout the realm were accordingly urged to recommend the observation of public prayer, fasting, and almsgiving on Wednesday and Friday evenings. 'All sortes of persons', the council insisted, should abstain from 'nedeless waste and riotous consumption' and 'be contented and restrained to use more moderate dyett'.

In late March and early April 1597, the churchwardens of 117 Buckinghamshire parishes submitted presentments to William Chaderton, bishop of Lincoln, reporting on their performance of the council's orders.[51] For almost two-thirds (61 per cent) of the 191 parishes falling under the jurisdiction of the archdeacon of Buckingham, therefore, there is positive evidence that the campaign was implemented.[52] This compliance rate, moreover, is almost certainly an underestimate, since some churchwardens' accounts suggest that certificates were evidently compiled even though they have failed to survive in the archdeaconry papers.[53] It is, of course, possible that in drawing up certificates parish officers deliberately perjured themselves to preclude the wrath of the ecclesiastical authorities. Indeed, fifty-two (44 per cent) of the extant presentments used a standard formula that 'we have had public prayers observed in our church and better frequented than they have been heretofore and the poor of our parish are provided for according to our

[51] LA, Ch.p/2, 3, 4 (churchwardens' presentments and certificates for the archdeaconry of Buckingham, 1597). The presentments are mapped in Hindle, 'Dearth, Fasting and Alms', 63.

[52] Of the 210 ancient parishes in the county, nineteen could not have made presentments to the archdeacon of Buckingham, eleven because they were peculiar juridictions and a further eight because they were in the archdeaconries of Bedford, Oxford, or St Albans. See Jordan, *The Charities of Rural England*, 72; *The Phillimore Atlas and Index of Parish Registers*, ed. C. R. Humphery-Smith (Chichester, 1995), 3, 116–19

[53] The expenses for the year 1596–7 of the churchwardens of Aston Abbots, one of four Buckinghamshire parishes in the archdeaconry of St Albans, include 2*d.* spent on 'the answer of the letter given us in charge at St Albans concerning fasting and releiveing the poor'. The churchwardens of Ludgershall, who the same year recorded '12d paid for a letter from the bishop and a certificate', were similarly drawn into the presentment mechanism. CBS, PR7/5/1, fo. 29^{v}; 138/5/1, unfol. In four of the parishes, moreover, churchwardens either provided a certificate for late February or made explicit reference to the previous presentment, which suggests that the bishop had successfully insisted upon monthly reports. LA, Ch.p/3/9–10 (Clifton Reynes), 3/20 (Loughton), 3/40 (Wolverton), 4/9–10 (Ludgershall). The vicar and churchwardens of Dinton referred specifically to the fact that they had actually 'from time in our church read my Lord of Canterbury his graces commandment'. LA, Ch./p/4/15.

ability and the orders for fasting are observed so far as we know'.[54] This unspecific statement of compliance might be interpreted as the slightly more elaborate equivalent of the monotonous refrain of *omnia bene* that punctuates many sets of churchwardens' presentments.[55] The temptation to interpret the standard formula as evidence of minimal compliance is, however, discouraged by the close scrutiny of the presentments from the parishes of Loughton and Ludgershall. In both these cases, a formulaic certificate was supplemented by a fuller idiosyncratic account of the provision of alms.[56] In some parishes, moreover, churchwardens evidently regarded the archiepiscopal orders as redundant, on the pretext that they repeated the requirements of a 'charge' previously issued by the justices of the shire.[57] Nonetheless, the evidence for compliance is overwhelming, with parishes large and small, open-field and wood pasture, gentry-dominated and peasant-settled, participating in the campaign. Only the larger market towns, in which the demand for market regulation was probably considered more pressing than the requirements of general hospitality and in which formal poor relief was most likely to have been introduced under the terms of the 1572 statute, are conspicuous by their absence from the sheaf of presentments.

The diverse formulations used by the majority of parish officers are uniquely revealing of the allocation of alms before the codification of the Elizabethan poor laws. They suggest that the effectiveness of exhortations depended primarily on the frequency with which parishioners could be persuaded to attend Wednesday and Friday services. While the standard formula used in a substantial minority of the certificates noted that public prayers had been 'better frequented' than usual, some churchwardens were even more upbeat. Prayers were 'duly said and frequented' at Burnham, 'well resorted to' at Chenies, and attended 'in reasonable good sort' at Chalfont St Peter.[58] Optimism was only slightly more qualified elsewhere: 'as many as might lawfully be spared from their labours' attended services at Chesham Bois, and public prayers were

[54] See e.g. LA, Ch.p/2/25 (Dorney). The heavy concentration of these standardized returns in the deanery of Buckingham, where all but one of the fifteen presentments used this formula, strongly suggests some collusion amongst parish officers.

[55] M. Ingram, *Church Courts, Sex and Marriage in England, 1570–1640* (Oxford, 1987), 325. This practice also flew directly in the face of the Lord Keeper's insistence in July 1596 that the assize judges closely scrutinize responses to articles of inquiry and 'not find *omnia bene*' but 'encourage where it is done [and] punish where it is not done'. J. Hawarde, *Les Reportes del Cases in Camera Stellata, 1593–1609*, ed. W. P. Baildon (London, 1893), 56–8.

[56] LA, Ch.p/3/21 (Loughton), 4/9–10 (Ludgershall).

[57] See e.g. LA, Ch.p/2/32 (Taplow), 48 (Slapton). The justices' charge has not survived.

[58] LA, Ch.p/2/17, 2/18–19, 2/20.

'indifferently frequented by the people' at Edlesborough.[59] Parishioners who did attend were evidently moved to be merciful. The minister of Hawridge noted simply that he had found his people 'very charitable herein'. 'Collection' was described as 'verie goode' at Beaconsfield, 'plentiful' at Chesham Bois, 'charitable' at Denham, 'convenient' at Edlesborough, 'sufficient' at Hoggeston, 'very orderly' at Tyringham, and 'large' at West Wycombe'.[60] At Fulmer, the churchwardens reported that 'both the aged and fatherless people and also other poor men which are not able of their owne worke in this harde time of dearthe to provide all things necessarie' had been provided for 'to the uttermost of our ability'.[61]

In a tiny minority of parishes, the social economy of dearth was managed largely by resident landlords. Here hospitality really did imply the gentry largesse stipulated in domestic conduct literature and in royal proclamations.[62] The poor of Hambleden, for example, were 'provided for of certain corne' by the appointment of Sir William Peryam, Lord Chief Baron of the Exchequer, and 'otherwise liberallie and charitablie releeved by his Lordship'. This was striking generosity indeed from the judge who had in February 1597 presided at Burford assizes, where the conspirators who had planned a 'rising of the people' on Enslow Hill in Oxfordshire were indicted. Perhaps the experience alerted him, as it did Sir Edward Coke, to the depths of desperation to which the poor husbandmen and artisans of the south Midlands were sinking.[63] The fact that general hospitality was also effectively provided at Chenies, the ancestral seat of the Russells, is also suggestive of elite supervision.[64] Elsewhere, clerical hospitality predominated. Besides dispensing alms 'twise every week to all that came', Dr Roger Hackett, minister of North Crawley, contributed one-fifth of the weekly collection in the parish. The

[59] LA, Ch.p/2/21, 4/16.

[60] LA, Ch.p/2/16, 2/21, 2/23, 2/39, 2/41, 2/42, 3/35, 4/28.

[61] LA, Ch.p/2/26.

[62] F. Heal, 'The Idea of Hospitality in Early Modern England', *Past and Present*, 102 (1984), 69–79; Heal, 'The Crown, the Gentry and London'.

[63] LA, Ch.p/4/20. John Walter, 'A "Rising of the People"? The Oxfordshire Rising of 1596', *Past and Present*, 107 (1985), 127, 134 n. 154. Sir William Peryam (1534–1604) had been appointed Lord Chief Baron of the Exchequer in Jan. 1593, and was among the Crown lawyers appointed to steer the bills against depopulation and conversion to pasture through parliament in October 1597. E. Foss, *A Biographical Dictionary of the Judges of England from the Conquest to the Present Time, 1066–1870* (London, 1870), 512–13. For his family estate at Hambleden, see *The Victoria History of the County of Buckinghamshire*, ed. W. Page (4 vols., London, 1925), iii. 47, 49; and for his widow's educational charity, see Jordan, *The Charities of Rural England*, 29–30, 58–9. Peryam was also active in the enforcement of conciliar policy on market regulation, serving on the Oxfordshire commission for restraint of grain. *APC*, xxv (1595–6), 112–13.

[64] LA, Ch.p/2/20.

rector of Loughton, meanwhile, bore almost a quarter of the monthly assessment.[65]

The majority of those enmeshed in the web of hospitality, however, were entertained in humbler households. Indeed the council itself assumed that all householders of 'habillitie' would participate, and churchwardens evidently endeavoured to take the interests of these middling parishioners into account.[66] In so doing, parish officers were negotiating the dilemma posed by the stipulations for the 'public distribution of alms' in the *Three Sermons*. The homilies had insisted on a delicate balance between the resources of those who gave and the needs of those who received alms: 'in the one an arithemeticall proportion is to be kept, and in the other the proportion geometrical is to be kept'. Although the ecclesiastical hierarchy implied that this meant that 'they that have much must cast in the more and they that have little may give the less', the churchwardens evidently found that the middling householders of rural parishes read the injunction rather more selectively.[67] They reported that relief had been implemented at Upton 'to the contentation of all of our parishioners *as well the givers* as the poor receivers'. At Dinton, the scale of relief had apparently been the subject of intensive negotiation: the churchwardens had 'pryvately conferred with the gentlemen and better sort' and found them 'all very willing to observe' the orders 'to the utmost of their powers'.[68]

The hospitality dispensed by these middling men was almost certainly less generous than the cornucopia dispensed by some peers and gentlemen, although it was probably not as meagre as the leftovers and offcuts condemned by Philip Stubbes in 1583.[69] As might be expected, alms were not primarily given in cash. Only one parish specified monetary disbursements, the 'inhabitants' of Iver agreeing to 'bestowe weekly unto the poor as they thinke most meete and needful' sums ranging from 16*d.* to 3*d.*

[65] LA, Ch.p/3/12 (North Crawley), 3/21 (Loughton). In his will, proved 10 Jan. 1622, Hackett not only left 40*s.* to the poor of North Crawley, but also 30*s.* to the poor in each of the two neighbouring parishes of Cranfield and Lidlington (which lay just across the Bedfordshire border); and 40*s.* to the poor of Horton [?Kirkby] (Kent). CBS, D/A/WF/23/267; *VCH Buckinghamshire*, iv. 338.

[66] *APC*, xxvi (1596–7), 38.

[67] *Three Sermons*, sig. B4. This formula foreshadows that used in the handbook for overseers of the poor issued after the 1601 statute. S. Hindle, 'Exhortation and Entitlement: Negotiating Inequality in English Rural Communities, 1550–1650', in Braddick and Walter (eds.), *Negotiating Power*, 109–10.

[68] LA, Ch.p/2/33, 4/15 (emphasis added).

[69] P. Stubbes, *Anatomy of Abuses*, ed. F. J. Furnivall (2 vols., London, 1877–82), ii. 105. Cf. Ch. 1.4 above.

'which they think sufficient'.[70] Indeed, references to formal rating (rather than charitable collection) were relatively rare.[71] The scale of these formal assessments is apparent in only three parishes, and in each the social base from which alms were given was relatively restricted. At Clifton Reynes, where there were approximately 130 inhabitants in 1603, eight (or 30 per cent) of the householders contributed 3*s.* 4*d.* weekly between them. At North Crawley, a parish of 435 inhabitants, the weekly assessment of 5*s.* was raised by contributions from only twenty-seven (or 29 per cent) of the households, six of whom bore almost half of the burden. The assessment at Loughton (174 inhabitants divided among thirty-seven households), meanwhile, was made monthly, and three of the eleven contributors provided almost 60 per cent of the total.[72] In each of these three cases, general hospitality was funded by between one-quarter and one-third of all the households. In communities like these, it seems, relatively few households could be expected to carry the burden of their resident poor.

In some parishes, it seems, churchwardens went from house to house as soon as prayer had ended on Wednesday and Friday evenings, and collected alms in cash and kind.[73] At North Crawley, the timing of the minister's hospitality suggests that, although collection was made after evening prayer on Wednesday, distribution was deferred until the following day.[74] Perhaps churchwardens learnt by experience whether a collection in church or a collection from door to door would yield a higher charitable return. On the one hand, peer pressure might encourage greater contributions to pleas made before the whole congregation; on

[70] LA, Ch.p/2/28 (Iver).

[71] There was 'a common charge of the abler sort' at Fulmer, and the 'wonted collection for the poore by statute' was 'gathered and paid orderly' at North Crawley. LA, Ch.p/2/26, 3/12. At Burnham, the churchwardens were anticipating a magistrates' order that specified 'a certain rate to be gathered weekly according to the number of those that are of ability and also that be destitute and want relief'. LA, Ch.p/2/17.

[72] LA, Ch.p/3/9–10, 3/12, 3/20–1. These calculations assume that the number of communicants listed in the 1603 diocesan survey should be multiplied by 1.5 to provide a population estimate, and that average household size was 4.75. Cf. *The Compton Census of 1676: A Critical Edition*, ed. A. Whiteman (British Academy Records of Social and Economic History, NS 10, Oxford, 1986), pp. lxvii–lxviii, 369–71.

[73] This appears to have been the mechanism of collection on specially appointed fast-days in Jacobean and Caroline Dorchester. D. Underdown, *Fire from Heaven: Life in an English Town in the Seventeenth Century* (London, 1992), 125. Cf. the arrangements in St Bartholomew Exchange, London, where it was envisaged that 'every householder every month shall send unto the churchwardens such money as they shall save by abstynence upon Wednesday suppers to the end that the same may be distrybuted to the poore and needy'. *The Vestry Minute Books of St Bartholomew Exchange in the City of London, 1567–1676*, ed. E. Freshfield (London, 1890), 37–8.

[74] LA, Ch.p/3/12 (North Crawley).

the other, it might prove more difficult to resist the face-to-face injunction of a churchwarden on the doorstep.[75] The mixed economy of relief was nicely described by the parish officers of Swanbourne, who noted that they provided for the poor 'by way of collection and otherwise according to our charge by benevolence'. 'Money and corne' was given to the 'poore people' monthly 'or as it is needful for them' at Stewkley; and collected every Sunday and 'given to the poor without delay' at Ickford. At Chalfont St Peter, the churchwardens reported that they had given 'a stocke of corne' worth £20 to 'the use of the poore'.[76] Elsewhere, donors apparently preferred subsidies to gifts. At Denham, the resident magistrates and 'the wealthier sorte' had 'made sufficient provision weekly for corne to be delivered to the poore people at a reasonable price', while the parishioners of Chenies had made 'provision of rie' to be 'soulde [to] the poorer sorte according to their abilitie'. In these instances of grain subsidy, it seems, general hospitality shaded into the kind of market regulation dictated by the dearth orders.[77]

Indeed, it was an official assumption that regular fasting would encourage the distribution not only of grain but of food ready for immediate consumption. The Buckinghamshire evidence suggests that frugality was in fact observed. Nobody at all disobeyed 'the order touching abstinence' at Burnham, and the 'wealthier sort' of Chesham were apparently happy to 'forbear supper on Wednesday nights'. 'Moderation in diet' was similarly popular at Milton Keynes, especially on 'those days that collection for the poor is made and seasonably bestowed'. At Mentmore, 'that which is saved by fasting is given to the poor', an economy which the churchwardens of Chalfont St Peter actually quantified: 'in respect of the days of abstinence' they had raised 'by leavy the sum of 9s. a week'.[78] In some communities, moreover, food was evidently distributed not indirectly through collections but directly through the exercise of hospitality. The frequency with which the poor were invited into the houses of their wealthier neighbours varied from parish to parish. The churchwardens of Burnham noted that the poor only had 'access to our houses for food *on Sunday*'. 'Diverse of the able sort' of Chenies did '*thryse* in the

[75] T. L. Auffenberg, 'Organised English Benevolence: Charity Briefs, 1625–1705' (unpublished Ph.D. thesis, Vanderbilt University, 1973), 52, 402, argues that door-to-door collections (or 'walking briefs') 'invariably produced larger returns than those limited to the confines of the church' both by augmenting the sum raised but also by increasing the number of donors, though it should be noted that house-to-house appeals were generally reserved for the most important causes.

[76] LA, Ch.p/2/18–19, 2/49, 2/50, 4/7.

[77] LA, Ch.p/2/23, 2/30.

[78] LA, Ch.p/2/17, 2/18–19, 2/22, 2/45, 3/22.

week take unto them some of the poorer sorte'. 'That which is by abstinence saved' by the parishioners of North Crawley was distributed to the poor by 'their *daily* relief at their house'.[79] Although general hospitality in these instances might at first resemble organized beggary, the invitation of the indigent into the domestic environment of the middling sort had more subtle yet nonetheless profound implications, especially at a time when the houses of the yeomanry were being expanded. As newly built (and heated) parlours enabled the yeoman and his wife to withdraw beyond the hall into more comfortable enclosed space, the reconstruction of rural relations took place in their absence, in kitchens staffed by servants.[80]

Although its landscape was undoubtedly blasted by dearth and enclosure, therefore, Buckinghamshire was emphatically not a wilderness into which the chorus of exhortation was fruitlessly cried. Despite the extraordinary difficulties of this second consecutive dearth year, the 'better sort' of the majority of these parishes strove to fulfil their Christian obligations: throwing open their doors, distributing alms in cash and kind, and sacrificing their own dietary needs for those of the distressed. In doing so, the propertied themselves not only tasted of the dearth but also suppressed their contempt for a group which was increasingly regarded as noisy, repulsive, and contaminating. 'When we admit [the poor] to eat at our table', argued Samuel Bird in 1598, 'it is a token that we do not disdaine them.'[81] The hospitality of middling householders therefore revealed the *scale* of economic inequality in late Elizabethan England, yet at the same time disguised the *meaning* of the social differentiation to which it contributed. General hospitality actively encouraged those doorstep encounters between the prosperous and the needy which disappeared after the introduction of formal poor relief. It also vindicated the paternalistic and charitable self-image of the middling sort. 'We doubt', reported the parish officers of Fulmer, that the poor 'shall have either cause to famish for want nor yet just cause of us to complain.' Although the 'wealthier sort' had striven 'to avoid all excesse so that their poor brethren may be better holpen', insisted the rector of Little Woolstone, he hoped that 'the poorer sort' would neither 'grudge against God nor envy at their rich neighbours'. In congratulating themselves on the 'succour' and 'comfort' they had provided for the distressed, the

[79] LA, Ch.p/2/17, 2/20, 3/12 (emphasis added).

[80] Cf. the suggestive comments of M. Johnson, *An Archaeology of Capitalism* (Oxford, 1996), 157–70.

[81] S. Bird, *The Lectures of Samuel Bird of Ipswich upon the 8 and 9 Chapters of the Second Epistle to the Corinthians* (London, 1598), 79 (emphasis added). Cf. S. Brigden, 'Religion and Social Obligation in Early Sixteenth Century London', *Past and Present*, 103 (1984), 108.

middling sort subscribed to a myth of community in which their smoking chimneys and groaning boards symbolized the ancient and reciprocal obligations between rich and poor upon which inequality depended in a Christian society.[82] One might speculate, therefore, whether alms were dispensed with sincere pity, with quiet self-satisfaction, with palpable tedium, with suppressed fearfulness, or even with silent disgust.

Whether general hospitality could have been sustained for long remains a matter of conjecture. Although some churchwardens expressed confidence that the initiative could be continued at least until 'God send a new harvest and withall plenty and cheapness again of grain', the compassion fatigue experienced during other prolonged crises was a real possibility.[83] There are, moreover, signs in some of the parishes that under-employment was so extensive that even an apparently generous charity of abstinence could not hide the desperation of the labouring poor. At Padbury, 'the wealthier sort' had been 'careful to make collections for the poor', but the churchwardens noted that only 'the most distressed' had been 'succoured and relieved'.[84] The churchwardens of Drayton Parslow reported that the orders were performed only 'as nere as tyme and abiltye have served'. Although the poor of Bletchley had been 'comforted' in as 'reasonable sort' as the ability of the parish could sustain, the churchwardens reported that relief was negligible in the context of 'their extreme poverty and great multitude'. Relief at North Crawley was 'smale in comparison to the multitude of the poor which amount to six score and upward which receive almes, besides other sixe score which are not able to maintain themselves'.[85] This last example provides impressive testimony of the scale of the problem of structural poverty compounded by dearth. In a parish of perhaps 435 inhabitants, the churchwardens estimated that, when those in need and not on relief were combined with existing pensioners, 'the poor' numbered approximately 240 (or well over half the population). The weekly collection of 5*s*. therefore hardly even scratched the surface of conjunctural poverty, and could never penetrate to the deep-rooted problems of the structural poor.[86] Faced with such an enormous burden, it is not difficult to see why

[82] LA, Ch.2/26 (Fulmer), 3/42 (Little Woolstone). Cf. Walter, 'The Social Economy of Dearth', 128; Heal, 'The Idea of Hospitality', 90.

[83] LA, Ch.p/2/23 (Denham), 2/33 (Upton), 2/36 (Cheddington), 2/47 (Pitstone), [quoting] 3/2 (Bletchley), 4/27 (Bishop's Woburn). Cf. Underdown, *Fire from Heaven*, 126–7.

[84] LA, Ch.p/2/10.

[85] LA, Ch.p/2/38, 3/2, 3/12.

[86] For a similar situation in Brailes (War.) in 1599, see Ch. 4.1 below. On the distinction between 'structural' (or 'background level') and 'conjunctural' (or 'crisis level') poverty, see Slack, *Poverty and Policy*, 39.

richer villagers might object to the very principle of regularized charitable giving, let alone to that of formal parish relief. Once weekly relief became understood as a legal imperative as well as a moral obligation, the implications for the twenty-seven ratepayers of North Crawley (and others like them) would be daunting indeed.

Well into the eighteenth century, however, private individuals continued to give directly to the poor 'on their doorsteps, in the streets, even distributing largesse on special occasions in the traditional way'. The pious and charitable often devoted considerable time to considering and evaluating applications for alms, some of them even retaining their own almoners to assist them in distributing bounty.[87] Lifetime contributions to the poor, moreover, began to outstrip posthumous bequests both in number and significance, as donors sought greater control over the recipients of their charity. Since almsgiving of this kind was *voluntary*, and usually spontaneous, unco-ordinated by either central or local government, it remains, for the most part invisible in the historical record. The haze of documentary obscurity should not, however, blind us to the fact that 'crowds of beggars continued to obtain some form of casual help at the door and in the street well into the eighteenth century'.[88]

4. CHARITIES OF DISCRETION

Although they might, at first sight, seem almost invisible alongside these co-ordinated campaigns of almsgiving and dwarfed by the substantial and complex provisions of institutional endowments to which our discussion will turn in due course, casual doles remain one of the most significant and least explored mechanisms for the relief of the poor. Despite Jordan's obvious enthusiasm for those charitable trusts which involved comparatively large bequests and intricate administrative procedures, almost everywhere he looked, the majority of his donors in fact left benefactions for immediate rather than for perpetual use. Although they never make up anything like even a substantial minority of the *value* of bequests to the poor in any of his sample counties, doles were almost invariably characteristic of the overwhelming majority of bequests: 76.8 per cent in Norfolk, 76 per cent in Buckinghamshire, 74 per cent in

[87] J. Innes, 'The "Mixed Economy of Welfare" in Early Modern England: Assessments of the Options from Hale to Malthus (*c.*1683–1803)', in M. Daunton (ed.), *Charity, Self-Interest and Welfare in the English Past* (London, 1996), 143–4, 171, n. 16; D. Andrew, '*Noblesse Oblige*: Female Charity in an Age of Sentiment', in J. Brewer and S. Staves (eds.), *Early Modern Conceptions of Property* (London, 1995), 290, 292–3, 296 n. 26.

[88] Ben-Amos, '"Good Works" and Social Ties', 139.

Yorkshire; 62.1 per cent in Kent.[89] Some of these bequests for the poor might be for nominal, perhaps even tiny, sums paid as a single gift of alms. Doles, then, might be insignificant in *amount*, but not in *number*.[90]

Most characteristically, doles took the form of post-mortem charity, which derived from the practice of testamentary almsgiving, one of the characteristic expressions of late medieval piety. As recent commentators have argued, provision for the poor in wills, and more specifically at funerals, is best understood as a classic form of 'gift relation', in which the Christian obligation to provide a dole in cash or kind was exchanged for the spiritual energies and social deference of those people who effectively defined themselves as poor by their very willingness to accept it. Although funeral doles and dinners were the last great worldly exercise of hospitable largesse, they were quasi-contractual in nature, since doles for the poor were given in the expectation that they would be reciprocated by prayers for the dead.[91] These doles undoubtedly enjoyed a popular appeal in the mid-sixteenth-century, when the normative expectation of charity meant that the numbers who attended funerals could be very large. With donations of 6*d.* a piece to as many of the poor who would hold up their hands to take it, they could also be formidably expensive. Although historiographical polemic that these 'rowdy picnics for the poor' were 'socially injurious' can be dismissed as confessional bile, the picture of gentry funerals thronged with 'great crowds of indigent people, old, ill maimed or handicapped, many doubtless undernourished or emaciated, ragged dirty and smelling strongly' is probably accurate.[92] Protestants were increasingly hostile to funeral doles for several reasons: they argued that they perpetuated belief in purgatory; that the emphasis on post-mortem charity discouraged benevolence during the testator's lifetime; and that they were inherently disorderly, thronged by huge crowds of people who came covetously in search of alms.[93] Indeed, parliamentary condemnation of 'commen and open doolis' had originated as early as the poor relief statute of 1536.[94]

In the late sixteenth and early seventeenth centuries, these attitudes began to have an effect on testamentary practice, with the tradition of

[89] Jordan, *Charities of Rural England*, 27, 95, 223; Jordan, *Social Institutions of Kent*, 10.

[90] Jordan, *Charities of Rural England*, 95.

[91] E. Duffy, *The Stripping of the Altars: Traditional Religion in England, 1400–1580* (New Haven, 1992), 360–1; D. Cressy, *Birth, Marriage and Death: Ritual, Religion and the Life Cycle in Tudor and Stuart England* (Oxford, 1997), 443; P. Marshall, *Beliefs and the Dead in Reformation England* (Oxford, 2002), 19.

[92] R. Houlbrooke, *Death, Religion and the Family in England, 1480–1750* (Oxford, 1998), 264. Cf. Jordan, *Charities of Rural England*, 228.

[93] Marshall, *Beliefs and the Dead*, 167.

[94] 27 Henry VIII, c. 25 (1536).

funeral commensality to all 'the poor' giving way to cash distributions to 'the poor of the parish'. This process has been most intensively studied in the Durham parish of Whickham, where testators, who in the mid-Tudor period had made donations to the poor man's box, began from the 1580s to stipulate doles of 20*s.* to 40*s.* to the poor of the parish, with explicit statements from the 1590s that the bequest was to be distributed at the funeral. Donations of this kind persisted into the 1670s but decreased thereafter, their stipulations becoming more and more specific.[95]

Although the chronology of change doubtless differed from parish to parish, the same tendencies can be identified elsewhere. Doles were reserved specifically to the poor of the parish in various Essex communities as early as the Elizabethan period, and by the turn of the seventeenth century they commonly took the form of cash payments to be distributed by executors with the assistance of overseers of the poor.[96] As parish relief spread across the country, detailed testamentary prescriptions for the distribution of charity through parish officers became more frequent. The sense of social distance between rich and poor is further emphasized by those cash bequests to the deserving which explicitly abrogated the tradition of a funeral dole. In 1624 Robert Hawes of Brandeston bequeathed 50*s.* to the poor of four Suffolk parishes to be distributed by the parish officers in order that 'there shall be no concourse of poor people at my funeral and no dole to be given then'. The same year, 20*s.* was distributed to the poor of Saxmundham between the death and burial of William Norman who had insisted that there was to be 'no common dole'.[97] When Thomas Perrott died in 1663, he bequeathed £6 to the poor of Caddington and three neighbouring Chiltern parishes. All these bequests, however, were made on the condition that the poor 'trouble not my house at my funeral'.[98] Even the gentry, among whom the tradition of funeral commensality had been strongest because of the social pressure on gentlemen to exercise charity in death as they had dispensed hospitality in life, now sought to exclude the rabble. When Edward Phelips of Montacute (Somerset) made his will in 1680 he

95 K. Wrightson and D. Levine, 'Death in Whickham', in Walter and Schofield (eds.), *Famine, Disease and the Social Order*, 164; D. Levine and K. Wrightson, *The Making of an Industrial Society: Whickham, 1560–1765* (Oxford, 1991), 341–2.

96 *Elizabethan Life: Wills of Essex Gentry and Merchants*, ed. F. G. Emmison (Chelmsford, 1978), 21, 73, 150; Cressy, *Birth, Marriage and Death*, 444.

97 *Wills of the Archdeaconry of Suffolk, 1620–24*, ed. M. Allen (Suffolk Records Society, 31, Woodbridge, 1989), 363, 423.

98 Bedford and Luton Archives and Record Service, Bedford, ABP/W/1663–4/92, fo. 1^{v}. For the context, see S. Hindle, 'Persuasion and Protest in the Caddington Common Enclosure Dispute, 1635–39', *Past and Present*, 158 (1998), 37–78.

insisted on 'no great dole or feasting', preferring instead to send a shilling to the houses of fifty-eight poor persons of Montacute and Odcombe, chosen with the advice of the ministers of those parishes.[99] By the third quarter of the seventeenth century, funeral doles to the poor were waning all over the country, falling to less than half their frequency of a generation earlier in Berkshire, Lincolnshire, and Kent, although isolated examples can be found even in the mid-eighteenth century.[100] These patterns suggest not only the increasing wealth of the propertied in rural communities but also their enhanced awareness of the predicament of the poor as a class. Changing testamentary practices and the patterns of sociability to which they gave rise are therefore valuable indices of the nascent sense of social differentiation in the neighbourhood.[101] Increasing scepticism about the power of prayer to help the souls of the departed, compounded by growing confidence in the provision of parish relief, ultimately rendered the participation of the poor in the funerals of their betters redundant. In the exchange of benefits at funerals, the poor no longer had anything to offer.[102]

Spontaneous as they often were, doles were no less subject than endowments to careful regulation. In the first place, executors who detained small bequests from their intended recipients might be presented in the ecclesiastical courts, as they were in Romford (Essex) in 1564. In Bishop Still's visitation of the diocese of Bath and Wells in 1594, the executors or administrators of at least four wills were presented for detaining legacies (mainly in the range of 15*s.* to 20*s.*) to the poor, two of them in the Somerset parish of North Perrott. In only one case, from the parish of Glastonbury St John, did the judges look sympathetically on this abuse of trust, dismissing the allegations against one executrix for 'want of proof and by reason of her poverty'.[103] In the second, it was not

[99] Houlbrooke, *Death, Religion and the Family*, 283–4.

[100] C. Gittings, *Death, Burial and the Individual in Early Modern England* (London, 1984), 241. As late as 1743, George Hooper of Rochester left £5 to be distributed among the poor who attended his funeral. M. Barker-Read, 'The Treatment of the Aged Poor in Five Selected West Kent Parishes from Settlement to Speenhamland, 1662–1797' (unpublished Ph.D. thesis, Open University, 1988), 314.

[101] K. Wrightson, *English Society, 1580–1680* (London, 1982), 223–4.

[102] Houlbrooke, *Death, Religion and the Family*, 294.

[103] M. K. McIntosh, *A Community Transformed: The Manor and Liberty of Havering, 1500–1620* (Cambridge, 1991), 281 n. 70; *Bishop Still's Visitation 1594 and The 'Smale Booke' of the Clerk of the Peace for Somerset 1593–5*, ed. D. Shorrocks (Somerset Record Society, 84, Taunton, 1998), 70 (North Perrott), 95 (Otterhampton), 106 (Glastonbury St John). For other examples, see *Bishop Redman's Visitation, 1597: Presentments in the Archdeaconries of Norwich, Norfolk and Suffolk*, ed. J. F. Williams (Norfolk Record Society, 18, Norwich, 1946), 24–5; W.M. Palmer, 'The Archdeaconry of Cambridge and Ely, 1599', *Transactions of the Cambridgeshire and Huntingdonshire Archaeological Society*, 6 (1947), 27–8.

uncommon (especially where parish officers were responsible for administering doles) for county magistrates to police the distribution of bequests. The churchwardens and overseers of Bishop Burton (East Yorkshire), for example, were ordered in 1651 to distribute Lady Gee's charity 'according to her will and not to detain the arrears'.[104] Although only the commissioners for charitable uses could investigate the misapplication of endowed funds, outright gifts to income evidently fell within the purview of the justices of the peace.[105]

Although, as we shall see, the terms of eligibility for most outright doles were rarely stipulated as explicitly as they were in the provisions of more enduring endowments, they were value-loaded in more subtle ways. Even the generic stipulation that cash or fuel be distributed only to the 'most needy' implied the exercise of fine judgement about the indigence of one recipient relative to another. Testators often stipulated that these judgements were to be made by parish officers—either churchwardens or overseers or both—and by clergymen. This was also true, moreover, of the administration of perpetual gifts, since although the *trustees* of endowments were often drawn from gentry networks of patronage and association, those who doled out weekly, quarterly, or annual distributions at parish level were usually of far humbler status. Henry Smith, for instance, stipulated that the churchwardens of each of the numerous parishes favoured by his trust were to meet monthly to consider the needs of the poor, giving public notice in advance.[106] Indeed, it was the churchwardens who were usually required either by testators or trustees to distribute charitable doles. They might act on their own, as they did, for instance, at Beckington (Somerset) from 1578, at Aylsham (Norfolk) from 1604, at Rotherham (North Yorkshire) from 1606, or at Didlington and seven other Norfolk parishes from 1616. They enlisted the help of

[104] G. C. F. Forster, *The East Riding Justices of the Peace in the Seventeenth Century* (East Yorkshire History Series, 30, 1973), 50.

[105] For other examples of magistrates policing the administration of doles, see *Quarter Sessions Records of the County of Somerset*, ed. E. H. Bates-Harbin (4 vols., Somerset Record Society, 23, 24, 28, 34, Taunton, 1907–19), i. 23, 25 (East Chinnock, 1608), 84–5 (Taunton, 1612), 89–90 (West Monckton, 1612), 217 (Sutton Mallett, 1617), 248–9 (Rympton, 1619); *Warwick County Records*, ed. S. C. Ratcliff *et al.* (9 vols., Warwick, 1935–64), i. 40 (Wilnecote, 1626), 101–2, 104 (Henley in Arden, 1630); ii. 86 (Knightcote, 1641), 133–4 (Cubbington, 1646), 172 (Balsall, 1647), 201–2 (Berkswell, 1648); iii. 266 (Swacliffe, 1655), 287 (Fillongley, Corley, and Allesley, 1655), 288–9, 306–7, 323 (Fillongley, 1655–6), 293, 296, 323 (Sawbridge, 1655–6), 316–17 (Atherstone, 1656), 351 (Swateley (Oxon.), 1657); iv. 130 (Wootton Wawen, 1660); v. 13 (Priors Hardwick, 1665), 74 (Frankton, 1667). Where magistrates did make orders on complaints about the handling of *capital* gifts, they did so illegally. T. G. Barnes, *Somerset, 1625–40: A County's Government during the Personal Rule* (Cambridge, Mass., 1961), 150.

[106] Jordan, *Charities of London*, 120.

such other 'honest parishioners' as the 'sixteen men' of Wiveton (Norfolk) from 1558 and required 'the advice and assent of the principal inhabitants' of East Sutton (Kent) from 1566. They might equally be subject to an annual audit by six 'honest inhabitants' as at Eastry (Kent) and each of four adjacent parishes from 1593. By the seventeenth century, they began to co-operate with the overseers of the poor as they did at Oxburgh (Norfolk) from 1625; in the West Yorkshire parishes of Coxwold, Fishlake, and Holbeck from 1640, and of Sharleston and Foulby from 1651; and in four parishes in the city of Norwich from 1660.[107] Even more commonly, however, churchwardens were to act in consort with the vicar of the parish in allocating funds, as at Harrietsham and Hollingbourne (Kent) from 1591; at Sandal Magna (Yorkshire) from 1607; at East Dereham and adjacent parishes in Norfolk from 1613; at East Harptry (Somerset) from 1618; at Knaresborough (West Yorkshire) from 1638; and in a host of communities in Northamptonshire, Warwickshire, and Yorkshire under the will of John, Lord Craven in 1648.[108] Rather less commonly, the vicar might be required to distribute a dole, either by himself as at Mereworth (Kent) from 1566, or with others: 'six of the most substantial men', as at Ivinghoe (Buckinghamshire) from 1576; the churchwardens and three other 'honest and sufficient persons', as at Halifax from 1608; all the parish officers as at North Raynham and four other rural parishes in Norfolk from 1618; or even the lord of the manor, as at Chilham (Kent) from 1638 or Marske (North Yorkshire) from 1648.[109] The infrequency with which overseers of the poor were to administer charitable funds in isolation from the churchwardens or other inhabitants (the endowment in Tenterden and three adjoining Kent parishes from 1654 provides a rare example) reflects the acute sensitivity of trustees to the separate status of parish collections and endowed gifts.[110]

How frequently and to whom were doles given? The parish officers of Wivenhoe (Essex) received at least a dozen 'legacies or 'gifts' to the poor, ranging between 3*s.* and £5, in the period 1576–94. Six testators left gifts totalling £24 to the overseers of Frampton (Lincolnshire) in the period

[107] Jordan, *Charitable Institutions of the West*, 50; Jordan, *Charities of Rural England*, 104, 107, 110, 112–13, 236, 243, 244, 247; Jordan, *Social Institutions of Kent*, 20, 22.

[108] Jordan, *Social Institutions of Kent*, 22; Jordan, *Charities of Rural England*, 107, 236, 242; Jordan, *Charitable Institutions of the West*, 51.

[109] Jordan, *Social Institutions of Kent*, 25–6, 27; Jordan, *Charities of Rural England*, 35, 108, 236.

[110] Jordan, *Social Institutions of Kent*, 29. See Ch. 2.5(*b*) below. Jordan, *Charitable Institutions of the West*, 47, notes that only two (2.2%) of the ninety-one documented trusts in Somerset were vested solely in the overseers of the poor.

1648–1766.[111] Unlike the generous endowments so lovingly described by Jordan, most small gifts to income of this kind made only terse stipulations about the allocation of doles. The usual testamentary formulae were 'the poore' or the 'poore of the parishe', though the latter was often considered redundant in accordance with the ancient canon law principle that any bequest to 'the poor' implied the poor *of the parish*, to whom it was assumed the testator would 'bear a great affection'.[112] In Coney Weston (Suffolk), for instance, twenty-one (46 per cent) of the forty-six testators whose wills survive for the period 1527–1660 made small bequests to 'the poore'.[113] Elsewhere, however, testators explicitly singled out the deserving objects of their charity: the 'most aged and impotent' poor people of five parishes in rural Norfolk from 1618; the 'aged impotent weak and sickly poor' of Yalding (Kent) from 1621; the 'most needy' poor of the parish of Oxburgh (Norfolk) from 1625.[114] Occasionally, indeed, the language of *need* shaded into the language of *worth*: 'the most poorest, eldest, honest and impotent poor' of Taunton from 1614; the 'poor honest, thrifty young men' of Stowey (Somerset) from 1623; the 'most religious, painful and honest poor' of Eccleston (Lancashire) from 1627; the 'worthy' poor of East Lexham and six neighbouring Norfolk parishes from 1629 and of Ormesby (Yorkshire) from 1656; the 'honest and religious poor people' of Taunton (Somerset) and Bampton (Devon) from 1646; the 'deserving poor' of Marske and of Ripon (West Riding) from 1648 and 1649 respectively; the 'laborious poor people' of four Norwich parishes from 1650; 'the most honest poor people of the parish' in six communities across Cambridgeshire, Norfolk, Suffolk, and Yorkshire under the terms of the will of Richmond Girling of Old Buckenham (Norfolk) from 1659.[115]

As early as 1607, therefore, the bequest of Luke Sprignell of Sandal Magna (Yorkshire) to 'all the indigent people in the parish' was beginning to look old-fashioned. Even here, however, the trust stipulated that the

[111] F. G. Emmison, 'The Care of the Poor in Elizabethan Essex: Recently Discovered Records', *Essex Review*, 62 (1953), 16; S. Hindle, 'Power, Poor Relief and Social Relations in Holland Fen, *c.*1600–1800', *Historical Journal*, 41 (1998), 94. For other examples of small gifts to the poor in the early 18th century, see I. F. Jones, 'Aspects of Poor Law Administration, Seventeenth to Nineteenth Centuries, from Trull Overseers' Accounts', *Somerset Archaeological and Natural History Society Proceedings*, 95 (1951), 89.

[112] G. Jones, *History of the Law of Charity, 1532–1827* (Cambridge, 1969), 5.

[113] B. Wilkinson, '"The Poore of the Parish"', *The Local Historian*, 16 (1984–5), 21. Cf. the pattern of testamentary gifts to the poor in D. Hey, *An English Rural Community: Myddle Under the Tudors and Stuarts* (Leicester, 1974), 217.

[114] Jordan, *Charities of Rural England*, 108, 110; Jordan, *Social Institutions of Kent*, 25.

[115] Jordan, *Charitable Institutions of the West*, 23, 51, 52; Jordan, *Social Institutions of Lancashire*, 17; Jordan, *Charities of Rural England*, 110, 112, 113, 246, 247.

dole was to be distributed by the churchwardens at the nomination of the vicar. By 1634 Richard Castleman's bequest to the poor of Bridgewater (Somerset) 'without partiality to any' was positively antiquated.[116] One of the last posts of indiscriminate testamentary charity was arguably sounded in 1655 by John Leigh of Cranbrook (Kent), who, at the age of 77, stipulated that a shilling each be given to seventy-seven of the most ancient poor people of the parish, with an extra beneficiary for every year he survived, a request that was ultimately to cost his estate another 3*s*.[117]

Even where doles seem quite literally to have been hand-outs, moreover, parish officers and clergymen were required to exercise discretion. At Ludgershall (Buckinghamshire) in 1593, for example, the minister and churchwardens distributed a charitable dole 'to the poorest people there at their discretion and to their most comoditie'. They accordingly divided 40*s*. amongst fourteen individuals (including five widows), each of whom received a sum varying between 1*s*. and 4*s*.[118] Indeed, where it has proved possible to penetrate the shrouded identity of those who were defined as 'the poor of the parish' by testators and their trustees, it is apparent that 'the poor' thought worthy of relief were 'the long term residents, who formed an integral and accepted part of their community' rather than 'the transient, migratory poor such as servants, tramping labourers and vagabonds'.[119] When John Brown of Flixton-by-Bungay (Suffolk) requested on 8 January 1608 that 2*s*. be left to each of ten 'households of the poore of Flixton', he took the unusual step of naming the head of each of the households to whom the intended dole should be given. Although all ten were either propertyless labourers or cottagers with at most an acre or two of land, it is striking that none were newcomers to the parish. The recipients of Brown's charity, and of thousands of others like them, were certainly *poor* but they were emphatically not *marginal*.

The cash value of a dole might, nonetheless, represent a sizeable proportion of parish expenditure on the poor and the numbers considered

116 Jordan, *Charities of Rural England*, 236; Jordan, *Charitable Institutions of the West*, 51.

117 Jordan, *Social Institutions of Kent*, 31. For other examples of doles whose value reflected the age at death of the testator, see Jordan, *Social Institutions of Lancashire*, 15 (Preston, 1606), 18 (Salford, 1635).

118 CBS, PR138/5/1, unfol. For the context, see Hindle, 'Dearth, Fasting and Alms', 76. In 1596 a testamentary dole of £3. 6*s*. 8*d*. was divided between 95 inhabitants of Eaton Socon (probably the majority of the householders), including 67 men and 28 women, 24 of whom were widows, each of them receiving sums varying between 12*d*. and 3*d*. F. G. Emmison, 'Poor Relief Accounts of Two Rural Parishes in Bedfordshire, 1563–1598', *Economic History Review*, 3 (1931–2), 114.

119 For this and what follows, see N. Evans, 'Charitable Requests and their Recipients', *The Local Historian*, 15 (1982), 225–6. Cf. Wilkinson, '"The Poore of the Parish"', 23.

eligible for casual charity of this kind could be very large. At Wellesbourne Hastings (Warwickshire) in 1639, the 9*s.* 'given amongst the poor' by way of the traditional midsummer dole amounted to 11 per cent of the annual relief budget. Doles at neighbouring Great Wolford, 6*s.* 'distributed among several poor people of the town at Christmas' and 2*s.* 6*d.* 'given to the poor at another time', were even more significant, constituting over 18 per cent of annual expenditure. The Christmas and Easter doles at Cawston (Norfolk) in 1606 represented 24 per cent, and the Christmas dole at Blyth (Nottinghamshire) in 1636 as much as 38 per cent, of annual relief expenditure. Most striking of all, however, is the record of Fenny Compton (Warwickshire), where the amount dispensed in doles (over £4. 3*s.* 0*d.*) in 1639 represented 78 per cent of the sum disbursed (over £5. 7*s.* 0*d.*) from assessed income.[120] It is occasionally possible to identify just who the recipients of these doles were, and it is unsurprising that the categories of almsmen and pensioners occasionally overlapped. Especially in those parishes where the number of collectioners was even smaller than usual, it was not uncommon for both parish pensioners and a very much wider range of the indigent to receive yearly, half-yearly, or even quarterly doles, sometimes in cash, sometimes in fuel, occasionally in food. At Eaton Socon (Bedfordshire), the thirty-three collectioners were among ninety-five parishioners, who must have constituted the majority of the population, who benefited from Gerey's dole in 1596. In Elsdon (County Durham), for instance, six of the seven parish paupers were among the thirty-seven people who received charity payments in the year 1717. In 1663 the twenty-one paupers of Heighington were joined by a further thirty-four inhabitants who benefited from parish charities. When the Watts annuity was paid in Buntingford on 8 December 1616, £2. 4*s.* 6*d.* was doled out in payments ranging from 6*d.* to 5*s.*, being divided not only among the six spinsters and widows who were already in receipt of parish pensions but also among twenty-six others, the vast majority of them women. Three of those relieved were almost certainly living together in the town's poor-house.[121]

Similarly, although there were only five individuals receiving weekly pensions at Fenny Compton in 1639, they and thirty-three other named inhabitants were recipients of small cash payments on one or, in some cases, two other occasions during the year when the parish officers

[120] SBTRO, DR3785/6/7 (Fenny Compton), 45 (Wellesbourne Hastings), 49 (Great Wolford); Norfolk RO, MC254/2/5; NA, SP16/329/63.

[121] P. Rushton, 'The Poor Law, the Parish and the Community in North-East England, 1600–1800', *Northern History*, 25 (1989), 144–5; Emmison, 'Poor Relief Accounts', 109, 114; HALS, D/P65/3/3, 28–9.

received doles from named donors. Unfortunately the two payment lists are undated, but in all probability they constitute midwinter and midsummer doles: the more extensive list recorded £2. 11*s.* 8*d.* divided in sums from 2*d.* to 2*s.* 2*d.* between thirty-eight inhabitants (only nine of them women, seven of whom were widows); the less extensive list accounts for £1. 12*s.* 0*d.* divided in similar sums between thirty-eight inhabitants (only ten of them women, six of whom were widows). At a time when there were probably only eighty households in the parish, almost half were therefore beholden to the charity of their betters in some degree.[122] At East Hoathly (Sussex), the feast of St Thomas (21 December) was the 'day that the poor of the parish go about asking charity against Christmas', and in the mid-eighteenth century (when the parish had a population of approximately 200) between twenty-nine and forty poor people received a penny and a draught of beer each from the churchwarden. In 1756, only eleven of the thirty-three relieved were women, six of them widows. Furthermore, twenty-seven poor householders had a share of 'Atkins dole' (worth £4 annually) when it was distributed in 1763.[123] The relatively high proportion of adult males on these lists suggests that the families of poor labouring men, although not in regular receipt of parish pensions, were considered by the parish officers to be the 'occasional poor'.[124]

In dispensing doles in this discretionary fashion clergymen and parish officers were, whether they knew it or not, acting in accordance with the advice on the parson's charity famously given by George Herbert in 1633.[125] Herbert identified three ways in which a parson might prevent beggary and idleness among his parishioners. First, of course, there was 'perswasion' or exhortation to charitable behaviour amongst his neighbours, a strategy which might be adopted on an individual basis but which might more usually be employed in the full face of a congregation. Moral pressure of this kind might be exerted not only from the pulpit but also at the communion table. When Richard Purdye of Mettingham (Suffolk)

[122] SBTRO, DR3785/6/7 (Fenny Compton). Twenty-five parishioners appear on both of these lists, which are reproduced in S. Hindle, *The Birthpangs of Welfare: Poor Relief and Parish Governance in Seventeenth-Century Warwickshire* (Dugdale Society Occasional Papers 40, Stratford-upon-Avon, 2000), 44–6.

[123] *The Diary of Thomas Turner, 1754–1765*, ed. D. Vaisey (Oxford, 1984), 19, 74, 127, 169, 196, 214, 241, 262, 266, 283, 310.

[124] Cf. Ch. 4.3(*a*) below.

[125] All quotations in this and the following two paragraphs are taken from G. Herbert, 'A Priest to the Temple or, The Country Parson, His Character, and Rule of Holy Life', in *The Works of George Herbert*, ed. F. E. Hutchinson (Oxford, 1941), 244–5 (Ch.12: 'The Parson's Charity') (emphases added). Herbert's ideas are placed in the broader context of the hospitality exercised by the post-Reformation clergy in Heal, *Hospitality*, 286–99.

was presented for not receiving communion at Easter 1597, for example, the churchwarden explained that the minister had turned him away on the grounds that he was 'hard to the poor'.[126] Ostracism of this kind, thought Robert Allen, minister of Culford (Suffolk), was entirely appropriate: 'the 'covetous and unmerciful man', he argued in 1600, was 'no better than a rotten or dead branch cut off and excommunicate from the holy communion of Christ and his church'. 'Faithful christians', he insisted, should not 'have any familiarity with such as withdraw themselves from holy contributions & the liberal practice of mercy and goodnes among the rest of the people of God'.[127]

Second, the minister might resort to legislative authority, 'making use of that excellent statute, which bindes all parishes to maintaine their owne'. In a rich parish, this might be a simple matter of reminding his parishioners of their legal obligations.[128] Third, however, and especially in a poorer parish, he might supplement (though not defray) the parish rates by dispensing his own 'bounty'. His personal charity must not, however, be distributed as a regular pension, 'for this in time will lose the name and effect of Charity with the poor people', who will come to 'reckon upon it, as on a debt'. Indeed, if a dole became too regular, the level of expectation among the poor would be raised to the point where 'if it be taken away' they will 'murmur and repine'. The ideal solution, Herbert insisted, was for the almsgiver to make 'a hook of his charity', instilling in the poor an awareness of their dependence rather than any notion of expectation, let alone one of right. 'Not knowing when they shall be relieved' would encourage the poor 'to praise God more, to live more religiously, and to take more paines in their vocation'. If, on the other hand, they came to reckon upon charity, they would simply 'turn to idleness'.

There were, Herbert recognized, special occasions—'great Festivals', especially Christmas, and 'Communions' (presumably at Easter in particular)—when the minister should be particularly charitable, and pressing circumstances—'hard times and dearths'—when his hospitality should include 'giving some corn outright and selling other at under rates'. He should, furthermore, encourage the practice of this social economy among his fellow parishioners, 'pressing it in the pulpit and out

[126] *Bishop Redman's Visitation*, 115. Cf. C. Haigh, 'Communion and Community: Exclusion from Communion in Post-Reformation England', *Journal of Ecclesiastical History*, 51 (2000), 699–720.

[127] R. Allen, *A Treatise of Christian Benificence* (London, 1600), 111.

[128] All this is to say nothing of the minister's own liability for poor rates as an occupier of land in the parish. For the relative standing of the clergy in poor rate assessments, see D. A. Spaeth, *The Church in an Age of Danger: Parsons and Parishioners, 1660–1740* (Cambridge, 2000), 40.

of the pulpit and never leaving them till he obtaine his desire'. In all his charity, however, 'he *distinguisheth*, giving them most, who live best, and take most paines, and are more charged'. Even his casual almsgiving to strangers should not be exercised without some testimony of the causes of their misery, and even then alms should be given only to the beggar who was able to recite 'their Prayers first, or the Creed, and ten Commandments'. Should any beggar's religious knowledge be found perfect, then the minister might reward him more generously. To 'give like a priest', then, was to make charity 'in effect a sermon'.[129]

The levels of charitable giving expected by the clergy were evidently high. As Jonathan Bryden, vicar of St John's Hereford, noted in 1637, 'he was bound by his pastorall charge to take care of the poore to his best power'. Ministers who refused their charitable obligations could, of course, be criticized by their neighbours, as was Mr More of Myddle who was 'blamed for his too much parsimony or covetousness', a 'want of charity' thrown into even greater relief because his predecessor had 'kept good hospitality and was very charitable'. They might also be censured in the ecclesiastical courts, as was the non-resident rector of Stringston (Somerset) who was presented because he 'bestows nothing upon the poor' in 1594.[130] There were, however, plenty of clergymen who did live up to Herbert's ideal. In 1639 George Verney, rector of Wellesbourne Hastings (Warwickshire), personally donated 15*s*. (about 17.5 per cent of the parish's annual income) to the fund for the poor. At neighbouring Great Wolford, the vicar gave 2*s*. 6*d*. to each of the two overseers 'for his benevolence besides his levy'. These were almost certainly snapshots of an ongoing tradition of clerical benevolence. Giles Moore of Horsted Keynes (Kent) recorded in the 1600s that he was accustomed each year to give to collections made at his door over and above his parish assessment. Giving 5*s*. or 10*s*. a year in this way might provide extra fuel or bread for the indigent.[131] Such generosity not only relieved the poor but might also be used to protect ratepayers. Edward Butterfield, minister of Middle Claydon (Buckinghamshire), personally gave an elderly widow 6*d*. a week towards her fuel bills in the winters of the early 1670s so that she would not be a charge to the overseers, and was even prepared to make up the

[129] For casual charity dispensed by clergymen, see Ben-Amos, '"Good Works" and Social Ties', 128–9.

[130] HMC, *Thirteenth Report, Appendix, Part IV: The Manuscripts of Rye and Hereford Corporations; Capt. Loder Symonds, Mr E. R. Wodehouse MP, and Others* (London, 1892), 341; Hey, *An English Rural Community*, 217; *Bishop Still's Visitation*, 97.

[131] SBTRO, DR3785/6/46 (Wellesbourne Mountford), 49 (Great Wolford); *The Journal of Giles Moore, 1656–1679*, ed. R. Bird (Sussex Record Society, Lewes, 1971), 313–36.

difference in cases where pensions were awarded but fell short of the hopes of the claimant.[132]

The charity of one particular clergyman will repay investigation in some detail. In 1579 William Sheppard, the vicar of the Essex parish of Heydon, composed a 'brigmente or a breviate Epitome of All the beneficiall good dedes' he had performed 'principally to gods glory & for the weale of the Inhabiters' over the preceding two decades.[133] Sheppard noted that he had spent very substantial sums repairing the fabric of the church and churchyard (the steeple, the roof, the windows, the pews, the gates, even a sundial) and building and maintaining bridges, roads, and pathways throughout the parish, both initiatives which would have subsidized the financial burdens on his parishioners. But he also noted repeated donations directly to the poor: gifts and doles that were made in a wide variety of forms. In the 'hard yere' of 1560, he gave 'xx nobells' to 'xx^{ti} power hussholds of this parysch'. In 1568 he gave all his glebe lands to the use of his 'power neyghbors' by allowing 'to evry power man one acre the powrest havynge the first choise wt out paying any rent therfor'. Between 1574 and 1576 he subsidized the dowries of fifteen 'power maydens' at 'ther marriage of my neyghbors children' in sums ranging from 'a quart of grayne worth x^{s} a pec' to 'one quarter of otts worth ix^{s} a quarter' to 'a nobull a pece'. In addition he was particularly generous at the marriages of his own household servants, one of whom he described as 'a power mayde of this parysche', giving almost £15 between them in 1582. He was also an occasional practitioner of the social economy of dearth. In 1574, 'beyng a very dere yere for corne', he sold his crop to his poor neighbours 'so longe as yt lasted after the rate as [he] had sold yerres before'. In 1579, moreover, he spent 20*s.* on four gowns for 'power folke of the parishe'. All this is to say nothing of his will, drawn up in 1569 during an illness which he feared would prove terminal, under the terms of which 20*s.* was to be given to each of the thirty-three households of the parish within three years of his death. In the event, Sheppard survived but carried out the intended bequest anyway, giving each householder 'a cote of blacke clothe' worth 8*s.* to 10*s.* a yard, to each housewife 'a kercheff of fine clothe' worth 5*s.* a yard and 'the Residew in money'.

Conspicuous by its absence from Sheppard's account, however, is any reference to the charitable use of money from the communion plate. That

132 Broad, 'Parish Economies of Welfare', 995.

133 ERO, D/P135/1/1, fos. 100^{r}–103^{r}. For Sheppard, see M. Byford, 'The Price of Protestantism: Assessing the Impact of Religious Change on Elizabethan Essex: The Cases of Heydon and Colchester, 1558–1594' (unpublished D.Phil. thesis, University of Oxford, 1988).

exhortation and collection were intrinsic to the rituals of communion is evident from the description of worship in Northampton in 1571, where the ministers standing together at the communion table to celebrate the eucharist 'often times do call on the people to remember the poor which is there plentifully done'.[134] At Dedham (Essex) it was ordered in 1585 that 'every communion ther be a collection for the poore by one of the Churchwardens after the cuppe be delyvered', an injunction that suggests the giving of charity to the poor was 'virtually part of the sacramental action'. It is unclear whether these collections, 'made of such as willinglie and cheerfully will geve of their own benevolence', were a surrogate for, or supplementary to, a poor rate. They were, nonetheless, to be 'bestowed' on the poor 'according to the discretion of the minister, collectors and two of the hedboroughs'.[135] Indeed, the discretionary dispensation of communion money was evidently central to the charitable strategies of some clergymen throughout our period. In Elizabethan London, it was not unusual for £2–£3 to be collected whenever a sermon was preached, though this figure might increase dramatically if a renowned clergyman such as Richard Greenham was in the pulpit. Collections made at communions, conventionally a halfpenny for each communicant every Easter, might in normal circumstances bring in a further £2–£3 a year, though Greenham's presence at Christ Church Newgate boosted this to over £5 in the early 1590s.[136] In some rural parishes, it is possible to be reasonably precise about the relative yield of collections of this kind. At Knebworth (Hertfordshire), each communion might raise between 2*s.* and 5*s.* for the poor in the early years of the seventeenth century, and communicants seem to have been particularly generous at Christmas. 'Benevolence at the communion' supplemented the annual collection in Knebworth by 14 per cent in 1600 and at least 26 per cent in 1602. At Wellesbourne Mountford (Warwickshire) some 33*s.* 2*d.* (a sum representing 39 per cent of all parish expenditure on the poor) was raised by collections from the communion plate in 1639.[137]

Unsurprisingly, ministers ensured that collections of this kind were distributed very carefully and kept detailed lists of those who received alms from the communion plate, as they did in the Essex parishes of

[134] NA, SP12/78/38, fo. 244 (article 14). The Northampton Orders are set in context in W. J. Sheils, *The Puritans in the Diocese of Peterborough, 1558–1610* (Northampton Record Society, 30, 1979), 26–32, 119–27.

[135] *Conferences and Combination Lectures in the Elizabethan Church*, 128, 138.

[136] Archer, 'Charity of Early Modern Londoners', 239.

[137] *Tudor Churchwardens' Accounts*, ed. A. Palmer (Hertfordshire Record Society, 1, Braughing, 1985), 75, 77, 82; SBTRO, DR37/85/6/46 (Wellesbourne Mountford).

Romford in the 1560s, Great Hallingbury in the 1580s, Rayne in the 1630s, and Ardleigh even into the 1720s.[138] At Bamburgh (County Durham) in 1684, thirty-eight families (approximately 10 per cent of all the households in the parish) received communion collection.[139] Some ministers were explicit about their motives for the bureaucratization of collection along these lines. John Garnett, rector of Sigglesthorne (East Yorkshire), noted in 1730 that for him it was 'a case of conscience' to encourage the poor to attend services three days a week through the 'skilful management' of his charity towards them, by 'encouraging those that more frequently attended with more of [his] charity and subtracting from the rest that do not use such diligence therein'. He tersely noted that 'the like use may be made of the charity money in the sacramental offerings'. He had made it 'a standing rule to give the sacrament money to those only that attend at the altar except any of them be sick & then they have a portion of that money constantly sent to their houses'.[140] When the payments made to the poor householders of the Sussex village of East Hoathly under the terms of Atkins dole exceeded the interest payable on the endowment in 1763, the rector 'made it up out of the money given at the sacrement'.[141]

5. CHARITIES OF SUBORDINATION

Doles were, therefore, characteristically small gifts, made by lay people and the clergy alike, for direct and immediate use, normally in the form of occasional alms, funeral bequests, or outright testamentary or lifetime payments. As such they derived from the medieval view of charity in which the prevailing view of relief did not extend beyond the immediate needs of the recipient. Gifts to income did not, as we have seen, preclude discrimination amongst the poor, since they were often administered at the discretion either of executors themselves or of those they in turn appointed to distribute the dole. The endowment, by contrast, was a capital gift, usually involving a larger sum and almost invariably administered by a group of trustees whose duty it was to project the donor's philanthropic aspirations into the historical future. The creation and

[138] ERO, T/R147/1, unfol.; D/P 27/1/2, unfol; 126/3/1, unfol.; 263/1/3, unfol. William Sampson, rector of Clayworth (Notts.), noted from 1684 that he took collection at the offertory during holy communion, but did not record what he did with the money. *Coming into Line: Local Government in Clayworth, 1674–1714*, ed. A. Rogers (Nottingham, 1979), p. xi.

[139] Rushton, 'The Poor Law, the Parish and the Community', 144.

[140] East Yorkshire Archives Service, Beverley, PE 144/T38, unfol.

[141] *Diary of Thomas Turner*, 266.

administration of endowments was actively encouraged by the Elizabethan statutes of charitable uses of 1593 and 1601, which codified a body of case law badly wanting classical statement and granted formidable protection to the aspirations of donors.[142] Jordan argued in 1959 that the conception and definition of charitable purposes advanced in the preamble was 'starkly and coldly secular', an interpretation which fitted perfectly his reading of the character of the benefactions of the age.[143] The act, Jordan argued, crystallized the worldly impulses of benefactors who had been stimulated into activity by the dissolution of the chantries and guilds under the terms of Edwardian legislation.[144] Spurred by the Reformation and encouraged by the statutes for charitable uses, testators had created at least 10,000 charitable trusts in England by 1660, nearly a fifth of which were vested in the bodies politic of parishes.[145]

The following discussion accordingly seeks to contextualize the endowed charities of early modern England in the parishes themselves, where their principal effects were felt. It takes its cue from the observation that the guiding principle of the statute of charitable uses was 'public benefit' and that its principal manifestation was the relief of poverty.[146] Indeed, the objects of philanthropy listed in the preamble of the statute bear a striking resemblance to the statutory and common law duties of the English parish. While only education, aid for decayed tradesmen, and the provision of dowries for young brides were totally beyond the obligations of the parish, the provision of houses of correction, the relief of maimed soldiers, the maintenance of prisoners, and the ransom of captives were at the very least tangential to them. Three responsibilities, moreover, were shared *both* by charitable trusts *and* by the parish: the maintenance of the parish church and other public works; national taxation; and the relief of the poor. Whereas parishes had long borne legal obligations (the maintenance of the parish church, for example, from the fourteenth century) and financial responsibilities (contribution to national taxation in the quotas of the fifteenths and tenths from the fifteenth century, and to assessments towards county militia rates from the mid-sixteenth) the new charitable trusts superimposed upon these new powers of administration and control.

[142] 39 Elizabeth I, c. 6 ('An Acte to reform Deceiptes and Breaches of Trust, towching Landes given to charitable Uses'); 43 Elizabeth I, c. 4 ('An Acte to redresse the Misemployment of Landes Goodes and Stockes of Money heretofore given to Charitable Uses').

[143] Jordan, *Philanthropy*, 114.

[144] 1 Edward VI, c. 14. For the context see Jordan, *Philanthropy*, 58, 306; Jones, *History of the Law of Charity*, 10–15.

[145] Jordan, *Philanthropy*, 29, 118–23.

[146] Jones, *History of the Law of Charity*, 27.

Even more strikingly, two of the most obvious and frequently stipulated charitable bequests, to finance the apprenticeship of pauper children and to endow almshouses, actually fell within the competence of parish overseers, who were ordered to enforce the former and empowered to facilitate the latter. This close overlap between the functions of endowed charities and of the parish is reflected in the very considerable presence of parish officers (acting with or without clergymen and/or specified numbers of substantial inhabitants) as trustees of the endowments in Jordan's samples. Although, as we have seen, parish officers in various combinations were expected to distribute the outright gifts to income of charitable doles, they were also very frequently enlisted to administer capital gifts. Of the 2,121 perpetual endowments in Jordan's sample, 397 (or 19 per cent) were vested in the parish, or more accurately, in its most respected and competent officers, which acted as a corporation on which the trust might be imposed. This is to say nothing of a further 471 (or 22 per cent) trusts which took the form of rent charges on real property out of which fixed sums were paid to agents who might include the parish officers.[147]

The powers granted to commissioners for charitable uses under the late Elizabethan statutes facilitated detailed local investigation of the administration of endowments.[148] Almost 1,400 (1,376) inquiries were conducted by charity commissioners in the years 1597–1688, and between them they resulted in some 3,860 decrees, each of them in respect of a specific charitable trust.[149] Although there was a flood of over a thousand decrees sealed in the years before 1625, it was not until the 1630s that the number of commissions increased significantly.[150] Although a commission did not invariably lead to a decree, it is nonetheless clear that chancery took any misadministration of a bequest very seriously and that inquiries reached into every county in the kingdom. Indeed, these 1,400 commissions would represent as many as one in every seven parishes in the country even on the conservative assumption that each inquiry was concerned exclusively with the charities of a single parish, which (given that commissioners were required to ask the officers of every parish in each county whether property devoted to charitable

147 Jordan, *Philanthropy*, 121–3.

148 For the mechanics of the commissions, see Jones, *History of the Law of Charity*, 39–52.

149 Ibid. 251–6.

150 NA, C90, C91, C93; *List of Proceedings of Commissioners for Charitable Uses Preserved in the Public Record Office* (Public Record Office Lists and Indexes, 10. 1892); B. W. Quintrell, 'The Making of Charles I's Book of Orders', *English Historical Review*, 95 (1980), 566 n. 1. Cf. Jones, *History of the Law of Charity*, 52.

uses had been applied according to the intent of the donors) was not usually the case.[151]

This is not, of course, to imply that every delinquent executor or administrator inevitably faced the commissioners. Many potential prosecutions of negligent or corrupt trustees must have been deterred by the not inconsiderable trouble and charge of seeking redress in chancery. In 1629, for instance, the parish officers of Frampton (Lincolnshire) spent £17, a sum roughly equivalent to the annual yield of the bequest, on obtaining a chancery decree to enforce the terms of a trust endowed by Reginald Broughton. Even where decrees were issued, furthermore, recalcitrant trustees could make life difficult for their intended beneficiaries, as did John Boosey of Witham (Essex), who offered up nine 'exceptions' to an award that the charity commissioners had made on behalf of the poor of the parish in 1638.[152] There was doubtless, therefore, a dark figure of unprosecuted corruption. Financial difficulties were often compounded by the micro-politics which might further hinder the proper allocation of resources. Two of the best examples are provided by the bread dole at Wiveton (Norfolk) and the town lands of Layston (Hertfordshire), each of which will be discussed in turn.

(*a*) The Politics of Charitable Trusts: Two Case Studies

Wiveton was a coastal community in north Norfolk with perhaps 150 inhabitants in the early seventeenth century.[153] Although it was certainly not among the most well-endowed parishes in Norfolk, its income from local or county bequests (£5. 11*s.* 0*d.*) was swollen by substantial gifts (£133. 7*s.* 0*d.* in all) from metropolitan sources.[154] George Briggs of Letheringsett had made small bequests to the poor of Wiveton and two neighbouring villages in 1598, but his doles were overshadowed by two previous substantial endowments. In 1577 the London draper John Quarles, once resident in Blakeney, Cley, and Wiveton, had left £50 'to the bridge and the poor'.[155] The most significant and controversial of the parish charities, however, was financed through a bequest by the London

[151] For the geographical distribution of commissions, see Jones, *History of the Law of Charity*, 251–2.

[152] Hindle, 'Power, Poor Relief and Social Relations', 83. For the inquisition, see NA, C93/11/9 and for the decree C90/5. For Boosey, see Leicestershire RO, DE221/13/2/16.

[153] *The Compton Census*, 227 n. 612, suggests that there were 100 communicants (and possibly a further two non-communicants) in the parish in 1603.

[154] Jordan, *Charities of Rural England*, 199 n. 2. For charity provision in Wiveton, see *Parliamentary Papers*, Charity Commissioners' Report, vol. xxvi, pp. 294 ff.

[155] *The Papers of Nathaniel Bacon of Stiffkey*, ed. A. Hassell Smith *et al.* (4 vols., Norfolk Record Society, 46, 49, 53, 64, Norwich, 1978–2000), iv. 299 n. 619; NA, PROB11/60, 25 Jan. 1578.

grocer Alderman Ralph Greenaway, a native son of the parish, who in 1558 left £7. 6*s.* 0*d.* a year arising from the purchase of the Norfolk living of Brinton. The endowment stipulated that a penny in money and a penny loaf was to be distributed to each of thirteen poor people in the parish 'on every Sunday of the year in perpetuity'.[156]

The existence of these charities did not, it should be noted, preclude the formal provision of social welfare in Wiveton, which was one of the many north Norfolk parishes to have appointed overseers of the poor by 1600.[157] In the six months to Easter 1601 the parish officers collected £3. 5*s.* 0*d.* from twenty-nine ratepayers, though they noted that their accounts were substantially (£2. 7*s.* 11*d.*) in arrears. In the same period, they spent £3. 17*s.* 2*d.* on relieving seventeen named recipients.[158] By the following year, however, the overseers' income had increased to £11. 8*s.* 7*d.*, of which they spent £9. 8*s.* 4*d.* in relieving some twenty-eight pensioners. They were, nonetheless, still over £2 in arrears, and the auditing magistrate's clerk endorsed their accounts with the terse requirement that 'a stock of £3 was to be levied & disbursed for wool and hempe'.[159] There is, therefore, a strong suggestion that Wiveton was overburdened with poor, the proportion of its population 'on the parish' rising from 11.1 to 18.3 per cent. Its ratepayers were evidently struggling, or at least reluctant, to meet the relief burden. An assessment for the Wiveton constables' rate on 2 August 1599 lists thirty ratepayers liable for £3. 16*s.* 2*d.*, but noted that only 40*s.* (53 per cent) had been collected by the following week, some twenty-one inhabitants having defaulted in part or full. The four principal ratepayers—John King, Mr Bishop, Mistress Brigg, and Robert Stileman—who represented only 13 per cent of those taxed, were liable for over 51 per cent of the assessment, and of these, one (King, liable for 17 per cent) defaulted altogether and another (Stileman, liable for 10 per cent) paid only two-thirds of his contribution.[160] When poor rates were assessed in 1600, the hierarchy of contributions would doubtless have been similar if not identical.

John King in particular seems to have been determined to reduce the scale of his contributions. When the first generation of trustees of Greenaway's charity died out, King was one of the new appointees responsible for improving the value of the rent to about £20 a year, but

[156] Jordan, *Charities of Rural England*, 103–4; NA, PROB11/40, 27 June 1558; *Bacon Papers*, iv. 271.

[157] Cf. Ch. 4.1(*c*) below.

[158] *Bacon Papers*, iv. 192.

[159] Ibid. 238.

[160] Ibid. 139.

apparently retained the profit to himself without increasing either the value of the cash dole or the number of loaves given to the poor. Although King had repeatedly been called to account both by the inhabitants and by the local gentry, he had resisted, detaining the charity archive that had once been in the town chest 'under lockes and keyes of 3 or 4 of the best inhabitants'. Sometime churchwarden of Wiveton and head constable of Holt hundred, King had a history of antagonism with his neighbours, some of whom had sued him in the Exchequer for engrossing corn in 1583, and had been imprisoned for debt in 1590.[161] In July 1602 the 'inhabitants' of Wiveton petitioned Chief Justice Popham, then the senior judge on the Norfolk circuit, complaining that theirs was 'a poor seafaringe town wonderfully much decayed, & overburthened with moore poore people farre' than could be maintained at parish expense. If its rents were fully improved to an annual value of £30 and this sum were properly accounted and bestowed, they argued, the Greenaway gift would 'furnyshe their wantes and myseries'.[162]

The comparison of those who signed this petition with those assessed for parish rates makes interesting reading. Of the twelve petitioners, four were among the ratepayers, having been assessed for almost one-third of the collection of August 1599 between them; two were among the four overseers of the poor in the parish in 1602; and one was head constable of the hundred.[163] As is common in such cases, the inhabitants who claimed to be speaking in the interests of the poor were in fact the leading ratepayers. Popham instructed JPs Nathaniel Bacon and Henry Spelman to examine the case, and King was induced to accept their adjudication. The petitioners were to be disappointed, although they enjoyed moderate success in winning an order that all the charity deeds were to be returned to the 'common towne chest'; that a full inquiry should be made into who had been granted loans out of the town stock; and that future loans 'to anie pore man of the towne' may be made 'only with the consent of the more parte of the subsidie men'. Even so, Bacon and Spelman insisted on a proper rating of all Wiveton properties so that all the inhabitants could be 'made contributory to the relief of the poor' and that the proceeds of the Brinton parsonage should be used only to make up the shortfall in, rather than to subsidize, the Wiveton poor rate.[164] The petitioners did not, however, concede defeat. Although they had (somewhat disingenuously) alleged in 1602 that their 'weake estates were unfitting to contend in lawe', the inhabitants were forced to take action in chancery in 1612, suing out a commission for charitable uses alleging that Greenaway's

[161] Ibid. ii. 253; iii. 100, 145, 294.
[162] Ibid. iv. 269–70.
[163] Ibid. iv. 192, 238, 270.
[164] Ibid. 272–3, 297–8.

bequest was worth £28 a year and that King retained over £13 in hand at the time of his death.[165] This time, the petitioners were more successful, and secured not only an increase from thirteen to nineteen in the number of recipients of bread but also a rise in the value of the cash dole from 1*d.* to 5*d.* weekly for thirteen of the almspeople and doles for another six of 2*d.* weekly. The decree therefore had the effect of diminishing the significance of the parish pension relative to Greenaway's gift. In the years before this chancery decree, the annual value of the Wiveton dole (£5. 12*s.* 6*d.* in bread and cash) had borne comparison with the sums raised and disbursed from parish poor rates. In 1601, for instance, the seventeen Wiveton parish pensioners had received cash sums ranging between 4*d.* and 16*d.* a month. From 1612, by contrast, thirteen of the nineteen almspeople were receiving 20*d.* a month, the other six 8*d.* The notion of social justice which informed the chancery commissioners' inquiries was not in this case empty rhetoric: after the Jacobean decree, the Greenaway dole dwarfed the parish pension in Wiveton.[166]

A further example of a community in which parish relief paled before more generous charitable endowments is that of Layston (Hertfordshire) where the rector Alexander Strange left a remarkable memorandum book which included, *inter alia*, detailed lists of payments made to the poor.[167] These included memoranda on alms bestowed on the poor in the years 1607–18 and a more detailed record of monthly charity payments made between October 1616 and March 1617. In recording these payments Strange was accounting not only for the resources of the relatively generous parish charities, but also of formal collections for the poor assessed by overseers. Although the overseers' own accounts do not survive, memoranda for the year 1608–9 indicate that the overseers were raising and spending approximately £12 each year. That this sum was outweighed by the doles payable under the terms of parish endowments is clear from Strange's note that the poor had received 'in moneye & moneyes worth, by ordinarye & extarordinarye Charitye' over £29.[168] By 1612, charitable endowments had further outstripped the monthly collection: formal poor relief of £12. 11*s.* 0*d.* collected in that year constituted only 32.7 per cent of all the charity bestowed on the poor.[169]

The endowments involved were numerous and varied, and Strange

[165] *Bacon Papers*, iv. 273 n. 565.

[166] NA, C93/4/14, m. 3 (decree of 18 Mar. 1612).

[167] The following analysis is based on HALS, D/P65/3/3, 24–33, 214–55, and on *Parliamentary Papers*, Charity Commissioners' Report, vol. xxix, pp. 358 ff.

[168] HALS, D/P65/3/3, 219.

[169] HALS, D/P65/3/3, 234.

himself found it necessary to make an abstract of them in preparation for a chancery commission of 1630.[170] Of the eight trusts itemized, six made provision for the poor, though the smallest of these (providing for only 2*s.* a year) was not endowed until 1628. There were therefore five endowments operating in the early years of the seventeenth century. Three of these were gifts of property: 'howses & landes' given by Thomas Skinner in 1583; one-and-a-half acres of arable donated by John Gill in 1593; and 'a howse in the towne of Buntingford' given by John Brograve in 1601. Two others were annuities: £4 arising from the gift of the London alderman John Watts in 1602 and a further £2 bequeathed by Joan Sandbach. In practical terms, the regular income of the parish from endowed charity amounted to £13. 6*s.* 8*d.* (that is, £7. 6*s.* 8*d.* from the two town houses, and sums of £4 and £2 from the rents of the property left by Watts and Sandbach respectively). To these might be added numerous casual doles provided both by the living and the dead: 40*s.* by the will of Mr Harris in January 1608; and 20*s.* from Mr Tracy's legacy at Christmas 1609.[171] A special collection was apparently made at Christmas 1608, for the 'almes distributed', including cash sums from four donors and gifts in kind ('20s in bread', '12 bushelles of barlie', and 'a quarter of miscelin') from another three, totalled £7. 10*s.* 2*d.* Others, noted Strange, also gave 'according to their goodwill and abilitye'. By 1612 Christmas doles of 20*s.* to 40*s.* provided by resident householders seem to have evolved into regular payments.[172] These were to be further augmented by weekly doles of 1*s.* and 6*d.* paid respectively out of the largesse of John Crouche (from 1632) and of Strange himself (from 1637).[173] Strange's own summary perfectly encapsulated this situation. In 1636, he wrote, 'besides a towne howse wherein two or three couple of the poore do dwell, there are other howses and landes which make up that which they call their rentes and that is 13 or 14 powndes at least by the yeare a certen revenew, besides the charity of others usually given at a good tyme'. This provision, he cautioned, was sufficiently generous not only to attract shiftless migrants from neighbouring parishes but also to tempt careless landlords into admitting them in the confidence that the town charities would maintain them in their indigence.[174]

How, then, was all this revenue distributed? Where cash was involved,

170 HALS, D/P65/3/3, 125–8. For the commission itself, see NA, C91/11/12 (1630).

171 HALS, D/P65/3/3, 215, 221.

172 HALS, D/P65/3/3, 218, 233.

173 HALS, D/P65/3/3, 35, 323.

174 HALS, D/P65/3/3, 329. For a full exposition of this critique, see Hindle, 'Exclusion Crises', and Ch. 5.3 below.

it seems that payments were made on Sundays 'in the chapel of Buntingford'. The income from at least two of these endowments nonetheless seems to have been distributed in kind, and especially in fuel, for quarterly payments (made out of specific rents) for 'fagots laid into the poor folks howses' occur regularly, especially in the first decade of the century.[175] There was undoubtedly a seasonal preference for cash, however, and the recipients themselves apparently had some say at least in this practice, for the payment of 26*s.* in November 1607 was distributed 'in fagots & money at the will of the poore'.[176] A more intimate insight into the distribution is afforded from the autumn of 1617, when payments to individuals are recorded in detail for the first time. This change in accounting procedure originated with an attempt to rationalize the relations between overseers' and charity payments. On 13 and 14 October the parish officers called before them the seven widows in receipt of parish pensions who 'did voluntarylie make choise and contented themselves with the former contribution as it was used by the overseers of the parish heretofore'.[177] Even so, the pattern of payments for the next six months was a complex tangle of disbursements from the overseers on the one hand and the vicar and churchwardens on the other. Strange was therefore probably correct in identifying a number of families which 'receyve not only the almes which ariseth out of your towne howses and annuityes, but sometymes also part of that charitye which is raised by your weekly collector'.[178] In a well-endowed parish like Layston, therefore, it was especially difficult to distinguish dole from collection.

(*b*) Endowed Charity and Parish Relief

Parish officers were, moreover, evidently tempted to use exceptionally generous endowments such as those in Wiveton or Layston to subsidize the poor rate. Overseers of the poor were, nonetheless, repeatedly enjoined not to do so, even though they were often called on to administer bequests of town lands from testators, such as John Preston of Dalton-in-Furness (Lancashire) in 1625, whose explicit intention was to free their descendants from liability for parish rates.[179] Old habits of this kind died hard, but they increasingly fell foul both of chancery commissioners' decrees and of the instructions of central and local government. Although (as we have seen) institutional charities were frequently administered by trustees who included, or might at least be required to co-operate with, the parish officers, early seventeenth-century com-

175 HALS, D/P65/3/3, 216.

176 HALS, D/P65/3/3, 214.

177 HALS, D/P65/3/3, 24.

178 HALS, D/P65/3/3, 326.

179 Jordan, *Social Institutions of Kent*, 25. For the significance of town lands see Ch. 4.4 below.

missioners for charitable uses repeatedly insisted that formal and semi-formal relief be separately administered. While endowments might be granted for 'the extraordinary reliefe of the poorer sorte of the inhabitants', they should not be used to 'free or ease any of the parishioners of or in their ordinary weekely or monethly rates for the reliefe of the poore of the parish'.[180]

These stipulations were echoed by the fifth direction of the Caroline Book of Orders of 1630–1 that, 'where any money, or stocke, hath beene, or shall be given to the reliefe of the Poore in any parish, such gift [was] to be no occasion of lessening the rates of the parish'. Even so, the Warwickshire bench had to warn all the overseers in the county as late as 1675 that 'no stock or former gift to the poor of any parish shall be a cause to lessen the levies'. The very fact that this proviso was so frequently reiterated suggests that parish officers only too often played fast and loose with parish charities. The complaint that 'old donations' were being used 'to save the pockets of the present farmers' were heard in Wadhurst (Sussex) in 1633 and in Bolnhurst (Bedfordshire) as late as 1757. These reservations notwithstanding, the parish officers of Gnosall bluntly noted the incorporation of Hencock's charity into parish poor relief funds in 1733. By 1764, the churchwarden of East Hoathly (Sussex) was quite open about the fact that, although he presumed that the poor householders who benefited from the £4 payable every February as Atkins dole should 'be such as had no monthly or even any relief at all out of the parish book', he and his fellow parish officers 'now deviate from that rule'.[181]

There is, of course, plentiful evidence of the importance of voluntary contributions to the relief of the poor long after the tradition of co-ordinated almsgiving had begun to give way to compulsory assessments. At Halford (Warwickshire) in 1639, for example, the overseers happily admitted to the fact that, in addition to the three parish pensioners maintained by levies, there were 'diverse other people in our towne the whiche we relieve without collection' who 'otherwise would be a great burden unto us'. At Hanworth (Norfolk), the poor were relieved without rates

[180] See e.g. NA, C93/15/20, 13/7. Cf. S. Birtles, 'Common Land, Poor Relief and Enclosure: The Use of Manorial Resources in Fulfilling Parish Obligation, 1601–1834', *Past and Present*, 165 (1999), 81–2; Archer, 'Charity of Early Modern Londoners', 231–2.

[181] 'The Book Of Orders', sig. G2; *Records of Rowington Being Extracts from the Deeds in the Possession of the Feoffees of the Rowington Charities*, ed. J. W. Ryland (2 vols., Birmingham, 1896–1927), i. 192; W. E. Tate, *The Parish Chest: A Study of the Records of Parochial Administration in England* (3rd edn., Cambridge, 1960), 109, 112, 117; S. A. Cutlack, 'The Gnosall Records, 1679 to 1837: Poor Law Administration', *Collections for A History of Staffordshire, Part I* (1936), 96; *Diary of Thomas Turner*, 288.

altogether in the dearth years 1647–50 at the behest of the minister. These expedients were probably arranged through billeting or general hospitality, rather than the creative (some would say nefarious) use of endowed income which occurred in Rympton (Somerset) in 1619 when the overseers detained a legacy of £3. 6*s.* 8*d.* and allegedly 'gave forth speeches that they will not allow anything out of the increase, so that the poor are not like to have the benefit but the overseers will make a gain thereof'.[182]

Such perversion of the intentions of charitable trusts only encouraged that circular tendency so astutely identified by late seventeenth-century commentators. Josiah Child explained in 1694 that the charity of our 'pious ancestors' was 'now decreased', not because the charitable imperative had lost its purchase but because testators were hostile to the idea that private gifts from the benevolent should be used to reduce the poor rates. In 1697 Dudley North agreed: 'I am certain that now care being taken by overseers publiquely chosen in every parish a great many that have compassionate hearts do not so much in that kind as they would do otherwise, for what is more natural than to think such care needless when God knows many cases are so ill supplyed by those whose duty it is to look after them that the poor creatures suffer by this meanes, many people not only thinking it needless but foolish to do that which is parish business'.[183] Just occasionally, private almsgivers can be found concurring with North's assessment. Sarah Byrd explained in 1693 that she had denied alms to a poor widow of Luppitt (Devon) because 'she designed not to give anything to such poor people as had monthly reliefe of the parishe'. Petitioners for relief certainly argued that the hearts of householders had been hardened under the weight of the tax burden. Although the inhabitants of Cronton (Lancashire) were 'able people not burdened with above five poor persons', complained Thomas Holland in 1699, they had of late 'withdrawn their alms towards him'. Later that year, another Lancashire petitioner, James Shemerdine, was even more explicit in reporting the negative response of the householders of Ardwick to his request for alms: 'they say they pay great levies and everything is so deare that they cannot keep their owne families and then they think that they shall not give [charity] to others'.[184] Whether or not the institutionalization of parish relief cumulatively served to obviate (or 'crowd out') pri-

[182] SBTRO, DR3785/6/18 (Halford); T. Wales, 'Poverty, Poor Relief and the Life-Cycle: Some Evidence from Seventeenth-Century Norfolk', in R. M. Smith (ed.), *Land, Kinship and Life-Cycle* (Cambridge, 1984), 357, 359; *Quarter Sessions Records for the County of Somerset*, i. 248–9.

[183] J. Child, *A New Discourse on Trade* (London, 1693), 84; BL, MS Additional, 32512, fo. 127^{r-v}.

[184] P. Sharpe, *Population and Society in an East Devon Parish: Reproducing Colyton, 1540–1840* (Exeter, 2002), 223; LRO, QSR/827/2; 828/25.

vate charitable initiatives in this way (and many recent commentators have been sceptical), in turn forcing the indigent to seek the alms of the parish, the ambiguous relationship between parish relief and endowed charity was to vex charity commissioners well into the nineteenth century.[185]

Some testators had very quickly become aware of these dangers. Thomas Trowbridge of Taunton (Somerset) stipulated in 1620 that his charity should under no circumstances be set off against the poor rates 'lest the benefit thereof be turned to the rich, and taken from the poor'.[186] The charity of the London merchant Henry Smith, extending as it did throughout 219 parishes in twenty-three counties, similarly stipulated in 1626 that the bequest must be regarded as a supplement to, rather than a replacement for, any sums that the overseers might raise by taxation.[187] Indeed, it was increasingly common for testators to stipulate that doles should be given only to those who were *not* already pensioners of the parish. As might be expected, Smith's trustees stipulated that parish collectioners in any of the communities favoured by his charity were to be denied his dole.[188] None of those who were on poor rates in Chilham (Kent) or Wood Dalling (Norfolk) were to benefit from bequests of 1638 and 1658 respectively.[189] It is especially striking that, in the south-east of the country, some testators were already distinguishing between doles and pensions in the Elizabethan period, a tendency which points towards the precocious institutionalization of relief in these areas. Those who had at any time during the previous year received payments from the parish of Chislet (Kent) were specifically excluded from John Taylor's charity as early as 1581, for example, and only those who declined to take relief from parish collections were to benefit from the will of Edmund Drake of Hemsby (Norfolk) in 1583. Bequests to the poor of Trull (Somerset) were

[185] Cf. the critical comments of the 19th-century charity commissioners concerning the 'injudicious' use of endowed charity 'in aid of the poor rates'. *The Report of the Commissioners . . . Concerning Charities . . . Relating to the County of Warwickshire, 1819–1837* (London, 1890), 133–4. For scepticism towards the view that 'legal charity' crowded out 'voluntary charity', see Slack, *Poverty and Policy*, 164; A. L. Beier, 'Poverty and Progress in Early Modern England', in A. L. Beier *et al* (eds.), *The First Modern Society: Essays in English History in Honour of Lawrence Stone* (Cambridge, 1989), 236; Innes, 'The "Mixed Economy of Welfare"', esp. 144; P. Slack, *From Reformation to Improvement: Public Welfare in Early Modern England* (Oxford, 1999), 163.

[186] Jordan, *Charitable Institutions of the West*, 51.

[187] Jordan, *Charities of London*, 119. For another example of a bequest extending over a wide number of parishes, see Jordan, *Charities of Rural England*, 233 (forty-four parishes endowed by the will of Thomas Wood of Kilnwick Percy, Yorkshire, in 1583).

[188] Jordan, *Charities of London*, 120. For converse examples of metropolitan testators reserving their charity exclusively for those who were *already receiving* parish pensions, see Archer, 'The Charity of Early Modern Londoners', 233.

[189] Jordan, *Charities of Rural England*, 113; Jordan, *Social Institutions of Kent*, 27.

frequently made exclusively to 'the second poor' who were not regular collectioners of the parish.[190] In the early eighteenth century, efforts were still being made to ensure that paupers received money either from charitable doles or from the parish, but not from both. The overseers of Boarstall (Buckinghamshire), for instance, were forbidden in 1710 from giving John Colley any further relief because he had 'received several considerable sums of money' from a parish charity 'sufficient to maintain him for a considerable tyme without any collection'. The charity of Alderman Mott endowed in Cambridge in 1762 bequeathed small sums to the poor of the town 'not receiving collection'.[191]

(*c*) Eligibility for Charity

It would be a mistake to assume, however, that being beholden to the parish was the only characteristic that might disqualify the needy from receiving the doles provided under the terms of endowed charities. For endowments might stipulate very restrictive codes of conduct on those identified as worthy objects of pity. Perhaps the most famous example is the very extensive charity of Henry Smith, administered in 134 Surrey parishes and another eighty-five communities—including Dorchester (Dorset), East Dereham and Thetford (Norfolk), and Terling (Essex)—across twenty-two other counties from 1626. The trust defined the deserving in terms of their sobriety, propriety, and industry: 'no poor person that takes Almes of the Parish or those that are guilty of excessive drinkinge, profane swearing, pilfering and other scandalous crimes or are Vagrants or are Idle persons or have been incorrigible when Servants or do entertain Inmates shall have any of this charity'.[192] There are numerous other instances of such restrictions, several of them predating Smith's bequest. As early as 1550, William Fordred of Selling (Kent) left lands and an annuity of £6 to the worthy poor of seven parishes, targeting the old, the lame, and those overburdened with children, but specifically excluding 'young and lusty persons who would not labour for their

[190] Jordan, *Social Institutions of Kent*, 21; Jordan, *Charities of Rural England*, 105; Jones, 'Trull Overseers' Accounts', 92. For the suggestion that clauses such as these, restricting eligibility only to those 'never having been in the receipt of parochial assistance', were rarely stipulated by the original donor and were commonly invented by parish officers, see Tate, *The Parish Chest*, 117.

[191] *County of Buckingham: Calendar to the Sessions Records*, ed. W. Le Hardy and G. L. Reckitt (4 vols., Aylesbury, 1934–5), iii. 223; E.M. Hampson, *The Treatment of Poverty in Cambridgeshire, 1597–1834* (Cambridge, 1934), 186.

[192] Underdown, *Fire from Heaven*, 109; Jordan, *Charities of Rural England*, 110; K. Wrightson and D. Levine, *Poverty and Piety in an English Village: Terling, 1525–1700* (2nd edn., 1995), 179, 222. For Smith, see Jordan, *Charities of London*, 117–22 (with the generic stipulations on entitlement to the trust at 120).

bread'. In 1585 Sir John Cheyney left £16 per annum 'in brotherly charity towards the pious poor professing the gospel' in six Buckinghamshire parishes, stipulating that the recipients should be 'good and godly in living, and had most need of relief'. In 1600 Thomas Cartwright of Brodsworth (Yorkshire) provided for thirty of the poorest men and women of twenty-five Yorkshire communities who were not 'drunkards, common swearers or of other evil demeanour'. The annuity of £5 payable to the poor under the terms of the will of Gilbert Spence of Tynemouth (County Durham) in 1607 was to be distributed neither to 'needless lewde and idol persons' nor 'drunkards, swearers or any infamous persons notoriously detected of any vice or wicked crime'. Sir Edward Hales stipulated in 1610 that men who had begged or pilfered in their youth should not be accounted among the 'most honest impotent and aged poor' of Woodchurch (Kent) who were to benefit from his charity.[193]

As time went by, endowments became progressively more restrictive. Sir Francis Cheyney's bequest of £3 per annum in perpetuity to the poor of the Buckinghamshire parishes of Drayton Beauchamp and Chesham in 1620 stipulated that 'no newe comers to the towne, nor those dwelling in newe created cottages' were to be among the almsmen. From 1631, the bequest of another Buckinghamshire gentleman, Sir Simon Bennett, provided £44. 10*s*. 0*d*. annually to provide clothing for the aged poor of Beachampton, Claverton, and Stony Stratford, but stipulated that the recipients must have resided within the parish for at least seven years, must be independent householders without inmates, and must have a personal record clear of hedge-breaking or other such depredations. In an interesting echo of George Herbert's advice on the parson's charity, the fifty poor householders who benefited from the will of Abraham Colfe, the vicar of Lewisham (Kent), in 1651 had to be able to recite the Lord's Prayer, the Creed, and the Ten Commandments. William Elmer of Beachampton (Buckinghamshire) singled out the aged poor as beneficiaries of his will in 1653, according to which £2 per annum was to go to each honest man 'worn out' by labour and half that sum to each widow of quiet temper.[194] The honest poor of Tenterden and three other Kent parishes who were to benefit from the Hales bequest of 1654 were not to include 'such as inhabit or dwell in cottages illegalie erected on wastes or in the

[193] Jordan, *Social Institutions in Kent*, 19, 29; Jordan, *Charities of Rural England*, 36, 235; *Wills and Inventories from the Registry at Durham, Part IV*, ed. H. Maxwell-Wood (Surtees Society 142, Durham, 1929), 18–19. For some metropolitan examples of restricted eligibility for testamentary charity, see Archer, 'Charity of Early Modern Londoners', 233.

[194] Jordan, *Charities of Rural England*, 37, 39, 40; Jordan, *Social Institutions of Kent*, 30. For a similar metropolitan example, see Archer, 'Charity of Early Modern Londoners', 233. For Herbert, see Ch. 2.4 above.

high waies or live idlely by freebooting begging filching or stealing'. The ten poor widows of Ripon (West Riding) who benefited from a bequest by William Underwood in 1658 were to be 'of good conversation'.[195] Some testators made explicit the numerical terms of the calculus of eligibility to be computed by their feoffees. In 1639 Samuel Rabanke stipulated that, although eighteen poor people of the parish of Danby (North Yorkshire) might be *nominated* for alms by the vicar, the churchwardens, and the overseers, the nine beneficiaries were to be selected by his principal trustees. All this is to say nothing of such confessional stipulations as the exclusion of papists, as at All Hallows York from 1629, or the preference for Quakers, as in numerous Yorkshire communities from 1649.[196]

It was not unusual for the terms of eligibility for these endowments to be displayed in church on the charity boards that commemorated the benefactors of the parish. Indeed, in 1626 Henry Smith explicitly requested that the list of characteristics of those considered deserving were to be advertised in the church of each community he endowed 'so the poor may see it'. It was, however, rather less common for the *names* of those considered eligible to be openly listed as they were in the parish church at Eccleston (Lancashire) from 1629.[197] Either way, these more enduring and generous bequests arguably came to occupy a central place in the household economy of the labouring poor, at which point they might begin to exert some influence on the behaviour, perhaps even on the demeanour, of recipients. To this extent, those who met the stringent qualifications of these charities of subordination might be more properly characterized not simply as the deserving, but as the 'honorary poor'.[198]

Whether or not endowments of this kind really did affect the spirit of independence among recipients, it might have encouraged at least outward conformity to the Anglican Church. After all many bequests stipulated that doles were to be dispensed after divine service or after an annual, bi-annual, or quarterly sermon: the bequest of Thomas Almond of Thame (Buckinghamshire) in 1653, for example, provided 6*s.* 8*d.* each for the clergymen of Cuddington and Great Missenden to preach an annual Easter sermon, and stipulated that the residue of the £24 annuity be distributed among the poor of the two parishes 'immediately after the said sermon'.[199] Even where this requirement was not explicit, the fact

[195] Jordan, *Social Institutions of Kent*, 29; Jordan, *Charities of Rural England*, 249.

[196] Jordan, *Charities of Rural England*, 240, 242.

[197] Jordan, *Charities of London*, 119–20; Jordan, *Social Institutions of Lancashire*, 17.

[198] Cf. Sharpe, *Population and Society*, 229.

[199] Jordan, *Charities of Rural England*, 38–39. For further examples, see ibid., 235, 242; Tate, *The Parish Chest*, 114.

that churchwardens and overseers were so frequently enlisted to distribute gifts at least implies that the parish church should be the locus of largesse. The churchwardens of seven Norfolk parishes, for example, were to see that £8. 3*s.* 0*d.* per annum bequeathed in 1616 by Thomas Hopes, rector of Colveston, was to be distributed only to those who attended church. In early eighteenth-century Colyton, the bell was tolled at the church when alms were about to be distributed.[200] Indeed, the church porch was traditionally the place where doles were distributed, which might account for its selection by those soliciting alms as a desirable space from which to advertise their plight, or even to harass the parish officers.[201]

(*d*) Casting Bread upon the Waters

One particularly interesting variant of this church dole model was the bread charity, usually distributed in the form of penny loaves dispensed to specified numbers of good Protestants who attended sermons weekly and were well-behaved. Bread charities of this kind were by no means unusual in early modern England. Indeed, their existence might even be said to qualify the argument, gradually gaining the status of an orthodoxy in the historiography, that 'transfer payments' had rendered relief in kind superfluous by the 1630s.[202] As we have seen, at Wiveton (Norfolk), Ralph Greenaway's endowment of 1558 stipulated that the churchwardens were to distribute a penny in money and a penny loaf to each of thirteen poor people of their parish on every Sunday of the year. At Frankton (Warwickshire), the interest on a gift of 40*s.* was 'employed for the buying of bread and was yearly upon Good Friday distributed to the poor people there'.[203] There were also bread charities in Buckingham from 1574 (six halfpenny loaves given weekly among the twelve poorest inhabitants of the borough); in Sutton-in-Holderness (East Yorkshire) from 1631 (twelve penny loaves each Sunday and an annual dinner for forty poor children after a sermon to commemorate deliverance from the gunpowder treason); in Buntingford (Hertfordshire) from 1631 (a bread dole for twelve poor persons after a weekly sermon); in Kirby Misperton (North Yorkshire) from 1637 (£5 weekly in bread and 10*s.* for a special distribution after an anniversary sermon); in Sedbergh (North Yorkshire) from 1637 ('every Sabbath day weekly 12 tenpenny loaves of the second

[200] Jordan, *Charities of Rural England*, 107; Sharpe, *Population and Society*, 234.

[201] Cf. Ch. 5.2 below.

[202] For charities distributing other types of food to the poor, especially at Christmas, see Tate, *The Parish Chest*, 113–14. Cf. Slack, 'Dearth and Social Policy', 13, 17.

[203] *Bacon Papers*, iv. 271; *Warwick County Records*, v. 74.

sort of bread and 2d apiece in money' to six poor men and six poor women); in East Greenwich (Kent) from 1653 (bread for fifteen poor widows resident in the parish); and in Colyton (Devon) from 1670 (twelve sixpenny loaves to be distributed every six weeks to twelve poor people of the parish to be selected regardless of whether they received poor relief or not and to enjoy the charity for life).[204] In several of these cases, as at Knaresborough (West Yorkshire) from 1638, the income of the trust was payable to the vicar and churchwardens who were to distribute bread to poor persons of their parish chosen at their discretion.[205] The preference for fixed numbers of recipients rather than a fixed amount of bread reflects the operation of the Assize of Bread, through which the production and marketing of bread was regulated.[206] Since the Assize governed the relationship between the weight of loaves of a specified price and the cost of grain, the quantity of bread provided to each recipient would fluctuate in accordance with the quality of the harvest. By specifying how many loaves were to be baked, benefactors at least ensured that a bare minimum number of poor people would benefit from their charity even if the amount of bread (and, accordingly, of nutrition) received by each might fall to relatively low levels. A penny wheaten loaf might, for example, vary in weight from as little as 4.25 oz when the price of wheat rose as high as 80*s*. a quarter to as much as 22¼ oz if it dropped as low as 20*s*. per quarter. The nutritional value of a charity loaf therefore varied according to the economic context, reinforcing the suggestion that the purpose of giving relief in bread was not so much practical as symbolic charity.[207]

Testators nonetheless continued to endow bread charities well into the eighteenth century. In Whickham (County Durham), an endowment by Sir James Clavering was partly used from 1702 by the overseers of the poor to distribute 'twenty foure penny loaves of wheaten bread' at twelve noon every Sunday 'to twenty foure poore people of the said parish who shalbe present at Divine service or sermon (if not hindered by age, or sicknes then to be sent to them'. At Highley (Shropshire), rents arising from cottages purchased at parish expense in 1744 were used to buy bread which was distributed to poor people who attended Sunday service and

[204] Jordan, *Charities of Rural England*, 35, 241–2; HALS, D/P 65/25/4 (Crowch Charity); Jordan, *Social Institutions of Kent*, 31. For Lancashire examples, see Jordan, *Social Institutions of Lancashire*, 17 (Eccleston, 1627).

[205] Jordan, *Charities of Rural England*, 242.

[206] A. S. C. Ross, 'The Assize of Bread', *Economic History Review*, 2nd ser., 9 (1956), 332–42; C. Petersen, *Bread and the British Economy, c.1770–1870*, ed. A. Jenkins (Aldershot, 1995), 97–124.

[207] Barker-Read, 'The Treatment of the Aged Poor', 124–6.

took the sacrament. The endowment of the bread charity in Bledow (Buckinghamshire) was sufficiently generous to provide bread for 112 persons once a year by the eighteenth century. In Gnosall 6*s*. 8*d*. was spent on wheaten bread for the poor every Lady Day.[208] Some testators, such as the Kentish clergyman Abraham Colfe who in 1651 endowed several bread doles simultaneously, seem to have had a special affection for this kind of charity.[209] Others rigorously insisted on the demeanour of recipients: those who received the loaves bequeathed by Thomas Chapman in Ashwell from 1668 were to be 'in no way licentious or guilty of any lewdness or debauchery'.[210]

One of the better-documented examples is, however, the Northamptonshire parish of Geddington, where from 1636 two dozen loaves were distributed to the poor weekly under the terms of the will of Robert Dallington.[211] Dallington was born in Geddington in 1561 'of humble yeoman stock'. A Cambridge graduate, he served as a schoolmaster in Norfolk before becoming 'travelling tutor' and 'secretary' to the earl of Rutland, in whose service the seditious libel 'the poor man's joy and the gentleman's plague' had passed through his hands after the Midland Rising of 1607. He subsequently became an intimate member of the godly circle surrounding Henry, Prince of Wales, and was appointed to the lucrative mastership of Charterhouse in 1624. He built a free school in Geddington in 1635, and by his will in 1636 endowed a charity with £300 'for the distribution of twenty-four three-penny loaves everie Sunday to twenty-four of the poor of the parish'.[212] The mechanics of the trust, like those of many such endowments, were intricate: the capital sum was used

[208] Levine and Wrightson, *Industrial Society*, 347. G. Nair, *Highley: The Development of a Community, 1550–1880* (Oxford, 1988), 135; Broad, 'Parish Economies of Welfare', 987; Cutlack, 'Gnosall Records', 36.

[209] Jordan, *Social Institutions of Kent*, 30.

[210] J. Kent and S. King, 'Changing Patterns of Poor Relief in Some English Rural Parishes, *circa* 1650–1750', *Rural History*, 14 (2003), 141.

[211] For the context of what follows, see S. Hindle, '"Not by Bread Only"? Common Right, Parish Relief and Endowed Charity in a Forest Economy, *c*.1600–1800', in S. King and A. Tomkins (eds.), *The Poor in England, 1700–1850: An Economy of Makeshifts* (Manchester, 2003), 39–75. For charitable provision in Geddington, see *Parliamentary Papers*, Charity Commissioners' Report, vol. xxiii, pp. 289 ff.

[212] For Dallington himself, see K.-J. Holtgen, 'Sir Robert Dallington (1561–1637): Author, Traveller, and Pioneer of Taste', *Huntington Library Quarterly*, 47 (1984), 147–77; Holtgen, 'The English Reformation and Some Jacobean Writers on Art', in U. Broich *et al.* (eds.), *Functions of Literature: Essays Presented to Erwin Wolff on his Sixtieth Birthday* (Tübingen, 1984), 119–46; R. Strong, *Henry Prince of Wales and England's Lost Renaissance* (London, 1986), 30–1; and S. Porter, 'Order and Disorder in the Early Modern Almshouse: The Charterhouse Example', *London Journal*, 23 (1998), 8–9. Copies of Dallington's will, dated 20 Apr. 1636, survive as NRO, 133p/158–9, 166–8. For its probate, see NA, PROB11/176, 1 Mar. 1638.

to purchase two closes, thirty-one acres in total, in the nearby parish of Loddington. The annual rents payable on these properties grew from £15 in the 1630s, to £19 in the 1670s, £23 in the 1730s, and £31 in the 1770s. After payment of land tax and tithe, and the provision of an annual dinner for the tenants, the bread was distributed weekly (at an annual cost of almost £16), and any remaining sums were divided amongst the twenty-four recipients in cash at Easter. In 1745 this Easter dole amounted to £6.[213] This type of arrangement was entirely typical of the impulse to cast bread upon the waters in scores of endowments across rural England.

The terms for entitlement to the Geddington charity set by Dallington and his trustees, publicly declared in their 'directions for the choosing and well governing of the poor', were, however, quite extraordinary.[214] Their rigour might be explained either by Dallington's own religious commitment or by his previous experience of administering discretionary charity at the great London hospital Charterhouse.[215] Local knowledge, however, almost certainly played its part. Dallington was doubtless aware of the long-standing concerns about immigration and lawlessness in this part of Northamptonshire.[216] This was an exclusive charity in every sense of the word: its compassion had a hard edge. 'Deserving' persons were to be selected by the trustees, and then to draw lots for the bread. The three basic requirements for eligibility range from the all too predictable to the very surprising: it is little wonder that 'the honest number of twenty-four shall not contain any who has made himself poor by idleness, drunkenness or disorder', or that a discriminating attitude should be applied to incomers and strangers. Such provisions, as we have seen, echo those of many a rural charity. Dallington's criteria of residence were, however, extreme: recipients must be either born in Geddington 'or have dwelt in the town in good behaviour at least fourteen years before'. This extended time period is significant because it excludes not only migrant labourers and young married couples but also servants and apprentices. The third, and most surprising, clause states that 'if any have consumed their estates by giving away their estates to their children or by buying or building houses they shall not be partakers of this charity'. The attempt to prevent the elderly from receiving charity after they have passed property to their

213 These details on the mechanics of the charity are drawn from NRO, 133p/160–4.

214 All quotations from the charity regulations in this and the subsequent paragraphs are taken from NRO, MISC Photostat 1610.

215 Porter, 'Order and Disorder in the Early Modern Almshouse', 8–9.

216 Geddington and the adjacent parishes in Rockingham Forest had been at the epicentre of the series of anti-enclosure protests known as the Midland Rising in 1607. Cf. Hindle, '"Not by Bread Only"', 39–40.

children implies that those very children should maintain their parents.[217] The willingness of the trustees to locate charitable relief in the context of the transmission of property in the parish is among the more far-reaching provisions of any endowment in this period, and supports the recent claim that 'in providing welfare payments and services, seventeenth- and eighteenth-century overseers of the poor and charity trustees were not undermining inter-generational support within the family but in certain key respects were attempting to preserve or foster it'.[218]

Preliminary eligibility was, however, only the tip of an iceberg of other stipulations, which amounted to an extensive system of penalties and forfeitures. Recipients of the dole might have their loaf indefinitely withheld if they allowed 'married folk . . . strangers or children' into their houses, or if they 'let part of their houses whereby the poor are increased and the town overcharged'. One week's provision would be forfeited by any of the twenty-four 'found begging, either at home or abroad', by any heard 'lying, scolding or slandering', and by any failing to attend church on Sunday morning. A whole month's entitlement would be withheld if any of the twenty-four or their families indulged in hedge-breaking, fence- and gate-smashing, or unauthorized gleaning, a provision whose severity explicitly reflects the immediacy of memories of the insurrection of 1607. Perhaps most significantly, concern with youth unemployment and overpopulation was manifested in the most draconian of the terms: any of the twenty-four could be permanently 'displaced and another put in their room' if they 'kept more children at home than is needful for their use'. As in other forest economies, the authorities aimed 'to prevent young people staying at home (where they had to be supported from the poor rates) and to force them to find work or service, preferably elsewhere'.[219] The Geddington case anticipates by some seventy years the drastic order of the Buckinghamshire justices that the poor parents of those children in the forest parish of Brill in Bernwood who refuse 'to go out and hire at service' should have their parish relief or collection withheld until they forced their children into apprenticeship.[220] Indeed, such orders became increasingly common throughout rural England, especially after the ambiguous apprenticeship clauses of the Elizabethan poor laws had been clarified by a statute of 1697.[221] The demeanour of

217 Cf. Ch. 1.3 above.

218 P. Horden and R. Smith, 'Introduction', in eid. (eds.), *The Locus of Care: Families, Communities, Institutions and the Provision of Welfare Since Antiquity* (London, 1998), 6.

219 J. Broad, 'The Smallholder and Cottager after Disafforestation: A Legacy of Poverty?', in J. Broad and R. Hoyle (eds.), *Bernwood: The Life and Afterlife of a Forest* (Preston, 1997), 102.

220 *Buckinghamshire Sessions Records*, ii. 398.

221 8 & 9 William III, c. 30 (1697). Cf. Chs. 3.2(*b*) and 6.2(*e*) below.

recipients was also powerfully insisted upon by the trustees. No bread was to be received at all 'if any of the twenty-four do proudly or stubbornly refuse their penalty and do not meekly make their submission for their offence until that be done'.[222]

Painted on the charity board on the chancel wall at Geddington, the 'orders and directions' both symbolized the social discipline exercised by the trustees and advertised the ethical norms to which recipients of the charity were expected to conform. The discriminatory terms of the charity were not, however, simply symbolic. The regulations imply very active networks of policing and information into which both chief inhabitants and prospective applicants would be drawn. The absence of the early administrative records of the charity regrettably renders problematic the extent to which the rhetoric of the regulations was actually carried through to rigorous enforcement. The fragmentary surviving eighteenth-century trustees' orders nonetheless suggest a sporadic pattern of social discipline imposed for exemplary purposes.[223] There were, inevitably, individual exclusions, both threatened and actual. Jonathan How, for instance, was to 'have no more benefit from the charity till he put his family into better order'. John Chapman Jr. and John Clipshoe were, furthermore, 'admonished about attending church and if it be not reformed that they be excluded' from the twenty-four. There were also general trustees' orders which actually modified the terms on which bread was to be allocated. From the 1770s, 'younger persons' were denied access to the charity 'when they have constant collection of the parish'. The trustees were also required to maximize the revenue from the endowment: investigating whether the leases to their present tenants were binding; temporarily suspending (in a subconscious echo of the charity of abstinence?) the allocation of a half-guinea for the tenants' dinner 'considering the hardness of the times'; and enquiring whether they could sell wood from the Loddington closes without injury to the farm. The fact that these restrictive orders date from the late eighteenth century in general, and from the 1790s in particular, when the parish officers were struggling to cope with rising relief expenditure, is hardly coincidental.

222 For a similarly bald statement (intriguingly, in another forest economy) of the 'deferential imperative' through which subordination was organized, see S. Hindle, 'Hierarchy and Community in the Elizabethan Parish: The Swallowfield Articles of 1596', *Historical Journal*, 42 (1999), 850 (article 15).

223 The following discussion is based upon NRO, 133p/179 (Account Book of Receipts and Expenditure of Dallington Charity, 1744–1847), unfol.

6. NARRATIVES OF DISTRESS

So much, then, for the *management* of endowments, which (as we have seen) saw the charitable imperative refracted through the discrimination of donors and the discretion of their trustees. Prospective recipients of doles might, however, be just as calculating as their 'paternalistic' betters, since for them charity was not so much an act of giving as a way of getting.[224] Indeed, when we turn from the regulations and the penalties to the predicament of those who were relieved under the terms of such trusts, the problems of evidence become notoriously acute. Surviving petitions for endowed charity in seventeenth-century England are, by comparison with appeals for formal poor relief, extremely rare.[225] The following discussion is in fact based on the archive of an almshouse, the stock of which was so generous that its trustees were able to dispense annuities and gratuities on a regular basis. The almshouse, more formally the hospital, at Bruton (Somerset) was endowed by Hugh Sexey, who had been born in the parish in 1556, rising to become Auditor of the Household for Elizabeth I and James I.[226] Sexey died in 1619, and, although his hospital was built in 1626–9, it was not formally incorporated until 1638. Residential provision was made for twelve inmates, to include seven men and five women, under the supervision of a master. There were two levels of administration in the hospital: the 'governors' or 'overseers' were the town schoolmaster, the bailiff and constables of the hundred, and the officers of the parish. In turn, both inmates and governors were subject to the authority of twelve 'visitors', principally drawn from the resident gentry of Dorset, Somerset, and Wiltshire, who were empowered to exercise 'rule and government', meeting annually at Whitsuntide to 'see good order performed and to punish or correct the master poore men and poore women who from time to time shall be found offenders either by expulsion or suspension as in the discretion of the overseers shall think fit'. Inmates were, of course, expected to conduct themselves respectably. The visitors were specifically empowered to remove 'drunkards, swearers, unquiet and disorderly persons'.[227] Even so, the rule of the almshouse was curiously vague, conspicuously lacking

[224] E. Thompson, *Customs in Common* (London, 1991), 46, 72.

[225] Cf Ch. 6.4(*a*) below. For an 18th-century archive of petitions for charitable relief, see R. B. Outhwaite, '"Objects of Charity": Petitions to the London Foundling Hospital, 1768–72', *Eighteenth-Century Studies*, 32 (1999), 497–510.

[226] Jordan, 'The Charitable Institutions of the West', 56.

[227] *The Victoria History of the County of Somerset*, ed. W. Page and R. W. Dunning (7 vols., London, 1906–97), vii. 42; NA, PROB11/134, 21 Aug. 1619; SARS, DD\SE/38/8; H. Hobhouse, *A Short History of Hugh Sexey's Hospital Bruton Somerset and its Endowments* (3rd edn., Taunton, 1951), 8–9.

the elaborate stipulations of decorum that characterized the constitutions of the Montagu Hospital at Weekley (Northamptonshire), the College of the Poor at Southwark (Surrey), or the almshouse at Studley (Oxfordshire), which were founded at about the same time.[228] To be sure, the residents were badged with the letters 'H.S.' in commemoration of the founder, but these canvas initials were not fixed to the shoulder of rough hempen coats as was the case with so many parish paupers by the turn of the century, but sewn onto gowns provided at a combined cost of almost £30 in 1652.[229] The stipends for residents were, as might be expected, very generous indeed, amounting to *2s. 6d.* a week, at an annual cost of over £75.[230] The almshouse was so well endowed that the visitors had substantial stock available, out of which they might regularly pay annuities or gratuities to those who could persuade them of their fitness for charity. In doing so, they were apparently continuing Sexey's own practice, for the founder of the hospital had frequently housed and supported the indigent of the parish by outright gifts. By the early 1680s, these payments, varying between a minimum total of £98 and a maximum of £122 annually, were themselves far in excess of the cost of stipends. In the 1650s there appear to have been seven recipients of annuities, though these made up only a relatively small proportion of what we might call 'casual expenditure', which might include one-off payments as generous as £5. From the early 1660s, moreover, the visitors were also financing the apprenticeship of poor children to local tradesmen, and had bound out at least eighty-eight boys in this way by 1750.[231]

It is, however, with the applications for gratuities with which we are principally concerned here. The waiting list for admission to the hospital was so long, and the number of places so small, in a town whose popula-

[228] NRO, MS Montagu, 186, 27–8 ('Orders for the governing and directing of the Maister & Brethren of Weekely Hospital'); J. Boulton, *Neighbourhood and Society: A London Suburb in the Seventeenth Century* (Cambridge, 1987), 143–4; Jordan, *Charities of Rural England*, 48. For 15th-century regulations on the moral conduct of almsmen taken very seriously by Elizabethan trustees, see McIntosh, *A Community Transformed*, 282.

[229] SARS, DD\SE/43/5, fo. 14. For the provision of badged gowns for almspeople elsewhere, see Jordan, *Charities of Rural England*, 43 (Stoke Poges, Bucks., 1573), 46 (Shenley, Bucks., 1615). Cf. the discussion of badges in Ch. 6.5 below.

[230] SARS, DD\SE/43/5, *passim*. This at a time when there were twenty-two regular collectioners 'on the parish' of Bruton, only two of whom received as much as *2s. 6d.* a week, the remainder being paid pensions of between *6d.* and *2s.* weekly. Annual expenditure on *regular* poor relief in Bruton in 1662 was, in fact, only 75% of the cost of the almshouse stipends. SARS, D\P\brut/13/2/1, unfol. The Bruton annuities of £6. *10s. 0d.* were towards the upper limit of the range of almshouse stipends discussed in Jordan, *Charities of Rural England*, 48–9.

[231] Jordan, 'The Charitable Institutions of the West', 56; SARS, DD\SE/43/5, fos. 12–16; SE/44; SE46/1–7.

tion probably lay somewhere in the range 1,200–1,500 in the middle of the seventeenth century, that the indigent were far more likely to have their needs met by casual payments than by a stipendiary residence: the 'respectable, gowned, Trollopian worthies' who lived in the almshouse might be a long time a-dying.[232] There are 105 extant petitions for relief in the charity archive for the 1660s, only two of which sought admission to the almshouse itself.[233] An applicant typically pleaded for the support of the 'hand of charity', without specifying the relief they sought. There were seventy-nine separate petitioners, fourteen of whom applied for relief on two occasions, and a further six made three requests. The profile of these applicants is unsurprising. Twenty-seven (34 per cent) were women, at least twenty-three of whom were widowed and only one was married (writing on behalf of her sick husband). Of the fifty men, at least forty-one were married (only three describing themselves as widowers). Only two were submitted on behalf of children, both of them orphans

There are, of course, very great dangers involved in taking these petitions at face value. They, like appeals for formal poor relief, were designed to make a case. Even though they might deploy a subtle blend of deference, exaggeration, and distortion, the effectiveness of the petitions depended on the credibility of the claims they made, claims that might more easily have been checked by contemporaries at the time than by historians at a distance of over 300 years.[234] Indeed, only the most painstaking record linkage with the parish registers, and overseers' accounts would now verify the applicants' claims made about age, about the burden of children, about disease, or about their previous independence of support.[235] More interesting for our purpose here is the rhetorical mode of these claims on charity. For the most part, the petitions were personalized. They were not usually written in the applicant's own hand and almost invariably went unsigned and unmarked. Like the applicants

232 Slack, *From Reformation to Improvement*, 25. For the population estimates, see *VCH Somerset*, vii. 23 n. 92 (based on a report of 252 families in the parish in 1650); D. Underdown, *Revel, Riot and Rebellion: Popular Politics and Culture in England, 1603–1660* (Oxford, 1985), 294 (based on an analysis of the parish registers).

233 The following discussion is based on SARS DD\SE/45/1–2. The two exceptions are DD\SE/45/1/38, 1/47

234 For useful discussions of the interpretative problems surrounding petitions of this kind, see J. S. Taylor, 'Voices in the Crowd: The Kirkby Lonsdale Township Letters, 1809–36', in T. Hitchcock *et al.* (eds.), *Chronicling Poverty: The Voices and Strategies of the English Poor, 1640–1840* (London and New York, 1997), 112–14; D. Andrew, 'To the Charitable and Humane: Appeals for Assistance in the Eighteenth-Century London Press', in H. Cunningham and J. Innes (eds.), *Charity, Philanthropy and Reform* (London and New York, 1998), 91–3.

235 Cf. the correlation of overseers' accounts and parish registers in Hedenham (Norfolk) in the period 1662–1709 in Wales, 'Poverty, Poor Relief and the Life-Cycle', 360–7.

for formal poor relief, therefore, claimants for Sexey's dole relied upon 'epistolatory advocates'.[236] Petitions were, however, far from standardized, and the scrivener or clerk who drew them up seems to have done so with the claimant at his elbow, perhaps inflecting his or her language to bolster the case where appropriate. Although it is possible that the influence of sermons and prayers was reflected in the idiom deployed in the petitions, a more plausible source of inspiration for their sophisticated charitable rhetoric are the charity briefs that were so frequently read in parish churches by the late seventeenth century, and especially in the early 1660s.[237] Briefs might refer to the inability of the poor to buy bread, to the destitution of trade, even to the transformation of towns from thriving monuments to posterity to ruined graveyards mourning in silence. They might also play on the previous good reputation of the populace. In a brief provided for the parish of Eynsham (Oxfordshire) in 1634, for instance, the inhabitants were said to have previously 'lived well, & maynteyned their charge & were helpful to others in their necessitie', a claim which, as we shall see, resonates with those made in several of the applications for Sexey's charity.[238]

Thirty-three (42 per cent) of the Bruton petitioners made some reference to their age: although nineteen were unspecific, describing themselves as 'ancient' or 'elderly', four claimed to be in their sixties, three in their seventies, and seven in their eighties. Another sizeable constituency was that of poor families over-burdened with children: thirty-three (42 per cent) mentioned the burden of their families. In objective terms, the desperation of the claimants is self-evident. Ten referred to their own blindness or failing sight, another four to that of their dependants. They were ravaged by diseases (referring variously to the symptoms of lung disorders, probably typhus rather than the usually fatal tuberculosis, of epilepsy, of scrofula, and of ulcers), and even where the nature of their illness went unspecified, their narratives were hobbled with lameness and sickness. They chose to embroider their accounts of their personal circumstances with references to the wider economic context. Four

[236] T. Sokoll, 'Old Age in Poverty: The Record of Essex Pauper Letters, 1780–1834', in Hitchcock *et al.* (eds.), *Chronicling Poverty*, 135. Cf. Ch. 6.4(*a*) below.

[237] Auffenberg, 'Organised English Benevolence', 387–8, notes the comparatively large number of briefs issued in the early 1660s. Some indication of the number of briefs heard in mid-17th-century Somerset can be gleaned from E. H. Bates-Harbin, 'Briefs for Cucklington, Somerset', *Notes and Queries for Somerset and Dorset*, 5 (1896–7), 280–3. For the suggestion that the rhetoric of sermons was quoted back to the authorities, especially at times of dearth, see Walter, 'Public Transcripts', 276 n. 65.

[238] *Oxfordshire Justices of the Peace in the Seventeenth Century*, ed. M. S. Gretton (Oxfordshire Record Society, 16, Oxford, 1934), pp. xl–xli.

referred specifically to dearth, another ten to cold winters, and sixteen more generically to the 'hardness of the tymes'. In these respects, 1662–3 seems to have been a particularly problematic year: almost one-quarter of the extant petitions can be dated to the visitors' meeting of Whitsun 1663, and these contain a significant proportion of the references to the 'hard cold winter and extreame tymes' or to the 'late extremity of the tymes'. A few, mainly from those working in the cloth industry, referred to the 'dulnes of trading' or to 'deadness of clothing' by which 'work is very scarce and wages so meane'. 'Weaving', pleaded Edward Carrier, 'is a dead trade.' There is 'little or no work to be gotten', lamented Thomas Higham, 'in 'these miserable hard tymes'.[239] Most applicants, however, were unable to work by virtue of age, sickness, or the burdens of child-care, and theirs were desperate tales of rent arrears, of debts unforgiven, and of goods pledged to the pawnbroker.

The language of the petitions is highly revealing of what the applicants, or their scribes, thought (or, more accurately, of what they wanted their prospective benefactors to think) they were pleading for. Variations on the same phrases recur throughout this archive: 'pity'; 'comfort and supply'; 'favour and allowance'; 'charitable benevolence'.[240] Petitioners frequently expressed their wish to be 'commiserated' or 'compassionated' and fulsomely played upon the charitable self-image of the visitors, whose 'bounteous inclinations' and 'pious dispositions' came in for considerable praise.[241] At least two of the applicants evidently sensed that they were appealing to a body whose decisions carried considerable weight, perhaps feeling that they were in some respects being judged, referring to the annual meeting of trustees as 'the court of lords knights and gentlemen'.[242]

How did petitioners characterize themselves as fitting recipients of benevolence? Some cases were relatively straightforward. Those who had been entrusted with the care of the two orphaned children of Florence Collens, for example, simply described them as 'the greatest object of charity that can be'. Other petitioners' statements of the peculiar severity of their own plight were more controversial. William Gossen proudly, perhaps naively, claimed to be 'as poor a man as the town doth yeeld'.[243] The remaining claimants were rather more circumspect, relying to some extent on vivid, if somewhat generic, statements of misery: 'sad and

[239] SARS, DD\SE/45/1/27, 1/48.
[240] SARS, DD\SE/45/1/9, 1/14, 1/34, 1/78.
[241] SARS, DD\SE/45/1/15, 1/34, 1/78, 1/85.
[242] SARS, DD\SE/45/1/56, 2/16.
[243] SARS, DD\SE/45/1/25, 1/40.

deplorable condition'; 'a piteous decrepit creature'; 'condition sad and mean'; 'extremely necessitous and indigent'; 'the insupportable burden of extreme indigency and misery' ; 'grown almost blind through hard labour and toyle'; 'nothing scarcely at all left for to keep alive'; 'very old blind and bedrid having very little or nothing for a dayly subsistence but what charity affords'; 'not enough to buy bread'.[244] These narratives of distress are perhaps best exemplified by the case of Joan Young, who described herself as 'a very indigent disconsolate widow full of years and necessities almost blind and impotent unable to get a penny towards her subsistence widowed with nothing but misery and sadness [who] unless supported by the hand of charity will necessarily perish'.[245]

Descriptions of despair were only one idiom in this popular discourse of pity, of which several other features stand out. In the first place, petitioners were keen to emphasize they had never required support before, especially from the poor rates. They pleaded that they had taken 'excessive paines' to maintain their families 'without being chargeable to any'; that their labour had 'afforded them a being in the world without charging any yet' or 'without being anyway chargeable to the town'; that they 'strove hard to get their maintenance without the charging of any'; and even that they had been 'constrained to pawn and sell all' they had 'to keep alive because [they] would not be chargeable to the town'.[246] They were, furthermore, reluctant to appeal even now: only the 'sad truthes' of her age and weakness, claimed Elizabeth Harptry, had 'forced her to make this address' for relief.[247] These petitioners, then, sought to portray themselves as 'shamefaced', reluctant to pose a burden, determined to shift for themselves as long as they could. In the minority (only 11 per cent) of cases where applicants referred to the support they had previously been afforded by Sexey's trustees, they were always fulsome in their platitudes of gratitude and keen to express their 'thankfulness for former relief'.

In beseeching the charity of the trust, moreover, several petitioners chose to remind the visitors of their own past habits of generosity. One applicant noted that 'his condition was such that he was [once] willing and able to relieve others'; another that he had 'heretofore supplied the indigency of others'; a third that he had always lived 'with a charitable disposition towards the relief of others'.[248] The relief implied here was purely philanthropic, though some petitioners explained that they had

[244] SARS, DD\SE/45/1/30, 1/31, 1/32, 1/33, 1/34, 1/42, 1/44, 1/65, 2/11.
[245] SARS, DD\SE/45/1/85.
[246] SARS, DD\SE/45/1/6, 1/21, 1/37, 1/50, 1/69.
[247] SARS, DD\SE/45/1/43.
[248] SARS, DD\SE/45/1/8, 1/9, 1/34.

been significant employers in Bruton. One described himself as 'an ancient tradesman who kept many people to work in the town'; another referred to the fact that he had formerly 'kept a great number of poor' employed. Rather more common was the proud assertion of a lifetime of labour. A 72-year-old tailor claimed that he had been regularly employed by men of good repute, 'but now being old and younger men stepping in' he was 'turned aside'.[249] They were nonetheless at pains to demonstrate their awareness that, without the workings of providence, their labours would have been in vain. Several applicants explicitly represented themselves as God-fearing: one had only 'by Gods assistance hitherto bin refreshed'; another had 'by Gods blessing on her honest endeavour maintained herself'; a third 'endeavoured as much as in him lyeth in the feare of God to work out a poor living'.[250] Providence had been all the more significant to these men and women because their resources of kinship were so meagre: they had 'no father or mother or any friend to rely on'; their parents were 'poor and are not able to supply what may be wanting'; they had only 'the smale assistance of friends'.[251]

Their petitions also spoke more directly to questions of character, and the most valuable currency in the charitable exchange was that of honesty. Applicants argued that they had consistently 'endeavoured for [their] dayly livelihood in all honesty'. They were, they insisted, 'known to be painfull in the world and of honest life and conversation'. Allied to the notion of honesty was that of credit: 'by his industrie in his calling', pleaded one applicant, he had 'lived in very good fashion and credit among his neighbours'. Others had 'heretofore lived in good credit' or 'maintained themselves in a good and decent manner'.[252] Overwhelmingly, it seems, good reputation was constructed from widely recognized habits of industry and of the proper maintenance of one's children. One petitioner was 'painful for the breeding up of her ten children'; another was 'a painstaking man in the world for the breeding up of his family'; a third was 'a laborious person in his calling and hath a great charge of children who he hath endeavoured by his labour to maintain and breed up'; a fourth was 'a painstaker in the world for [his] dayly livelihood'.[253] In all four of these cases (and in several others), public knowledge of this carefulness was emphasized: 'well known in the town' and 'as is well known' are idioms that recur throughout the petitions. Robert Thomas

[249] SARS, DD\SE/45/1/8, 1/11, 1/76.
[250] SARS, DD\SE/45/1/28, 1/53, 2/11.
[251] SARS, DD\SE/45/1/7, 1/30, 2/10.
[252] SARS, DD\SE/45/1/10, 1/11, 1/41, 2/18.
[253] SARS, DD\SE/45/1/12, 1/16, 1/21, 1/50.

put it most bluntly of all. He was, he argued, 'well known in the town [to be] a great paynes taker and noe waster'.[254]

These rhetorical strategies are not entirely dissimilar from those which, as we shall see, might be deployed by applicants for parish relief.[255] There are, however, two significant departures in the Bruton archive which suggest that popular discourses of charity might be inflected with local concerns, some of them intrinsic to the nature of the endowment itself. In the first place, a significant minority (21 per cent) of the applicants for gratuities or annuities bolstered their claim for the visitors' favour by rehearsing their links of kinship or patronage to the founder of the hospital. This also had the incidental effect of drawing in a range of applicants from outside the parish itself, for Sexey had long lived in London. Only rarely did petitioners specify the exact nature of the relationship with the founder. Elinor Haines of Wyke Champflower stated that she was the daughter of one Thomas Shorley of Cloford who was 'nearly allied' to Sexey ('they were brothers and sisters children').[256] For the remainder, it was enough to state that they were related in some way, though it helped if the length and proximity of the relationship could be demonstrated. Thus one petitioner claimed that her father had been 'one of the ancientest of nearest kin' to Sexey.[257] Even more desirable was the rehearsal of favours that they and their kin had extended to Sexey himself, especially in his youth, which now cried out for reciprocity. Thus one elderly shoemaker explained that his grandfather 'was the only supportance of Sexey in the time of his youth to bring him preferment'.[258] One particularly acute statement of these kinship claims came from the petitioner who argued that because of her affinity with Sexey she would prefer to receive charity from his trust rather than 'from those that are further off and stranger'. In this respect, the social and political networks which secured the favour of the Bruton trustees resonate with those at play in the hospitals of European cities.[259]

The second striking departure in our Somerset sample is the frequency with which petitioners stressed their own or their family's unswerving royalism in 'the late unhappy warre'. Nine of the petitioners explained that were 'very well known to be faithful and loyal' to the Crown: some, like James Flinger, had fought for Charles I; others had been wounded

[254] SARS, DD\SE/45/1/77.

[255] See Ch. 6.2(*e*) below.

[256] SARS, DD\SE/45/1/46.

[257] SARS, DD\SE/45/1/64.

[258] SARS, DD\SE/45/1/81.

[259] SARS, DD\SE/45/1/46. Cf. S. Cavallo, *Charity and Power in Early Modern Italy: Benefactors and their Motives in Turin, 1541–1789* (Cambridge, 1995), 40–6.

more recently in the Dutch wars. Others still were widows of loyal soldiers.[260] Although there were no formal political or religious restrictions on eligibility on the trust (dissenters were in fact only excluded from 1842), applicants were well aware of both the town's formidable reputation for staunch royalism and the political complexion of the board of visitors. Bruton was a town reputed to be 'at the heart of all the malignancy of Somerset'; the scene of a minor royalist uprising in 1643 and of clubmen disturbances in 1645; a place where the congregation proudly sang malignant psalms, and not necessarily because local landlords told them to do so. Royalism and its rituals were part of the cultural matrix of the region, and they were unsurprisingly represented very strongly among the trustees of the almshouse. Prominent among the visitors were members of the pre-eminent aristocratic family of the area, the Berkeleys, which provided no less than three of the original twelve visitors.[261] As we shall see, one of the most significant features of the Bruton petitions are the annotations by both the governors and trustees, but it is especially striking that the Berkeleys reserved their greatest praise for the widow of a royalist soldier: the petition of Elizabeth Stroud was subscribed by all three members of the Berkeley family, one of whom explained that he supported the application not because her late husband had been a servant of his, 'but because I have been credibly informed he deserved as much for his loyalty as any of his quality could do'. 'To my knowledge', he affirmed, 'he was very honest and she a very proper object of charity.'[262]

Observations of this kind bring us to perhaps the most valuable of all the characteristics of the Bruton charity archive. Although there are no extant minutes of the annual visitors' meetings (and even if there were, they would doubtless omit the most interesting and controversial elements of the discussion), a significant proportion of the petitions are subscribed with notes or even with certificates provided either by the overseers or by the visitors themselves. The most frequent signatory is John Randall, the vicar and schoolmaster, whose ministry in Bruton extended for forty-three years ending only in 1679.[263] Usually Randall's name was followed by that of his fellow overseers, but it was in his own clear hand that the decisive notations were made: the petitioner had 'lived

[260] SARS, DD\SE/45/1/35, 1/69, 1/74, 1/75, 1/81, 1/84, 1/85, 2/23.

[261] Hobhouse, *Hugh Sexey's Hospital*, 9; Underdown, *Revel, Riot and Rebellion*, 168, 180–1, 215–16.

[262] SARS, DD\SE/45/1/74.

[263] Randall was himself a staunch royalist and had fallen under the suspicion of the Major Generals. *VCH Somerset*, vii, 38.

a very honest and industrious life, was ever of good repute and is now old poor and a fit object of charity'; is 'very aged and hath ever had the repute of an honest and industrious man'; was 'ever a very laborious man and now poor and aged'; had always been 'a very laborious poore man but now he is very aged, uncloathed and every way comfortless his labour done'; is 'a very poor woman aged and lame poore and in necessitie her labour neere spent'.[264] It is especially striking that Randall and his fellow officers frequently used the language of civility, an idiom that was used in only two of the petitions themselves and never by the visitors: 'always lived civilly and industriously is now become necessitous and more than an ordinary object of charity'; 'a very poor woman of civill life and conversation much the object of charity'; 'a man of civill life and conversation but now fallen into povertie and want'; 'a very poor woman who since her coming to town hath behaved herself civilly and is now very much the object of charity'.[265] In the light of these glowing endorsements it is striking whenever Randall was less forthcoming in his approbation: one petitioner was noted simply to be 'a poore man'; another to be 'a very poore man and much indebted'; a third as 'somewhat aged and a poor man'; yet a fourth 'to be a very poore woman'.[266] Perhaps unsurprisingly, it was those whose testimonials from Randall were either absent altogether or were laconic and might therefore be construed as lukewarm who were less likely to earn the visitors' favour, their applications lacking the notation 'to have 5s' which characterizes some two-thirds of the petitions. In such hastily scrawled orders for payment, postures of humility found their reward.

7. CONCLUSION: THE POLITICS OF THE GIFT RELATION

The parish charities of seventeenth-century England were, therefore, anything but indiscriminate. This was, as we have seen, especially true of those endowments which provided specified numbers of loaves to the respectable poor who heard sermons, took communion, and lived lives of honesty and civil conversation. The exception that proves this rule is, ironically, the most well-known of all seventeenth-century charities, the bread dole in the Hampshire parish of Tichborne which was dispensed, indiscriminately, to all the poor of Tichborne, Cheriton, and Lane End who came to Tichborne House on Lady Day to claim it. Indeed, there can

[264] SARS, DD\SE/45/1/8, 1/22, 142, 1/53, 1/82.
[265] SARS, DD\SE/45/1/9, 1/43, 1/66, 1/85.
[266] SARS, DD\SE/45/1/47, 1/51, 1/70, 1/79.

be few more idealized representations of charity in early modern England than Gillis van Tilborch's celebrated *Tichborne Dole*, painted in 1670.[267] Sir Henry Tichborne, Lieutenant of the New Forest and of the Ordinance, prominent recusant and loyal supporter of the Stuarts, is depicted as he is about to distribute the annual bread dole in the garden of his estate at Tichborne. Accompanied by members of his household who variously carry loaves in their aprons and indicate the cornucopia that they are about to dispense, Tichborne is portrayed as the epitome of hospitality both to domestic staff, grouped on the left of the composition, and to tenants and villagers alike, grouped on the right. The painting is saturated with notions of honour, lineage, and hierarchy. The magnanimity of the baronet himself, the splendour of his Tudor manor house, and the visible gratitude and deference of his guests all serve to emphasize the authority of landed wealth, the obligations that perforce accompanied it, and the respect in which it was held. It is also arguable that the painting sanitizes what must have been a rather rowdy gathering, for it became customary for the Tichborne kitchens to bake 1,440 loaves for the Dole, and to give 2*d.* to any applicant if these did not go far enough.

The Tichbornes had owned land in this part of Hampshire since the early twelfth century, and their association with a tradition of good house-keeping was almost as antiquated. The dole originated in the thirteenth century with the deathbed plea of Lady Mabella Tichborne that her husband endow a charity for the poor. He grudgingly agreed that the corn from the land around which his dying wife was capable of crawling while a brand was burning would be annually provided as bread for the poor. The twenty-three-acre field around which Lady Mabella perambulated is still known as 'The Crawls'. Van Tilborch's painting is not therefore simply a valuable document of social history, in which architecture, dress, and posture are vividly recorded; it is also a portrait of the self-image of a late seventeenth-century gentleman, redolent not only of power and patriarchy, but also of the ancient and reciprocal obligations between rich and poor in an unchanging social order.

As a pictorial representation of the paternalism of the Stuart gentry,

[267] The painting is conveniently reproduced on the dust-jackets of A. M. Coleby, *Central Government and the Localities: Hampshire, 1649–1689* (Cambridge, 1987); P. Slack, *The English Poor Law, 1531–1782* (London and New York, 1990); S. D. Amussen, *An Ordered Society: Gender and Class in Early Modern England* (Oxford, 1988); and J. T. Cliffe, *The World of the Country House in Seventeenth-Century England* (New Haven, 1999); and in Heal, *Hospitality*, pl. 4 (between 226 and 227). The following discussion is based on *The Victoria History of the County of Hampshire*, ed. W. Page (5 vols., London, 1900–12), iii. 336–8; J. Harris, *The Artist and the Country House* (London, 1979), 9, 37, 40, 43, 52; G. Jackson-Stops (ed.), *The Treasure Houses of Britain* (New Haven, 1985), 147; and Coleby, *Central Government*, 151, 173, 180, 197–9, 226.

The Tichborne Dole is virtually unique. As we have seen, the tradition of indiscriminate hospitality portrayed by van Tilborch had almost certainly faded long before the Restoration. The noxious aura that had become associated with the poor as a class by the early years of the seventeenth century encouraged the separation of hospitality to the prosperous and alms to the needy that had always been latent in English culture.[268] The fact that Sir Henry Tichborne did not merely reinvigorate the Lady Day dole in the 1660s, but also saw fit to have it painted for posterity at a time when his estate was heavily encumbered by debt, therefore reveals a great deal about the perceived need to reconstitute traditional social relationships in the aftermath of the English Revolution. A similar impulse probably motivated Sir Thomas Pelham to endow the Halland dole in East Hoathly (Sussex) in 1654, under the terms of which beer, bread, and cash (4*d.* for each adult, 2*d.* for each child) was to be distributed annually on St Thomas day (21 December).[269] It would be foolish to underestimate the longevity or significance of these gestures of paternalism, for they became principal co-ordinates in the field of force through which the social equilibrium of eighteenth-century England was maintained.[270] Indeed, the mid-eighteenth-century churchwarden Thomas Turner recounted that it was his job to enumerate the recipients who were paid the Halland dole by the estate steward. This was a very considerable undertaking, for he reckoned that the numbers relieved were 'between 5 and 6 hundred' (at a cost of 'upwards of £7') in 1761; 'between 7 and 8 hundred, of all ages and sexes' (costing 'near £9') in 1759; and as many as '9 hundred' (costing £11) in 1762. In 1763 costs fell back to £8. 6*s.* 0*d.*, but Turner noted even so that four bushels of wheat had been baked into bread and imagined that 'not less than 100 gallons of beer' had been consumed. Turner was so concerned with numbers because it was his responsibility to 'take down the names' of the recipients, a practice which suggests that the behaviour and demeanour of the recipients could be monitored.[271]

By dispensing these charities of consumption, gentry families like the Pelhams and the Tichbornes not only propagated a myth of community which helped to disguise the nature of expanding economic inequalities,

[268] Heal, *Hospitality*, 91–140. Cf. Slack, *Poverty and Policy*, 91–112.

[269] Coincidentally, this was also the day on which the poor of East Hoathly were licensed to beg the parishioners' charity. See Ch. 2.4 above.

[270] Cf. Thompson, *Customs in Common*, 73.

[271] *Diary of Thomas Turner*, 195–6, 241, 262, 283. There is a sophisticated discussion of the language Turner uses to describe these expressions of Pelham's 'patriarchal patronage' in N. Tadmor, *Family and Friends in Eighteenth-Century England: Household, Kinship and Patronage* (Cambridge, 2001), 85–9.

they also attempted to restore the terms on which social relationships had been conducted before the world was turned upside-down.[272] These gestures and postures were well rehearsed and ritualized, perhaps even cynical.[273] The plebs, however, did not necessarily interpret them as patricians might have wished. In so far as there was conflict between donors and recipients, it turned on the question of whether the poor had a right to the charity of their betters. The social implications of endowments like the Tichborne and Halland doles were, to be sure, implicit rather than explicit. It is nonetheless arguable that the beneficiaries of paternalistic doles felt a stronger sense of entitlement to the charity of their betters than did parish pensioners. After all, although the recipient of a dole was marked out as a member of a separate and dependent social group, he or she was simultaneously recognized to be an integral participant in the local community. Doles were undoubtedly of economic significance, contributing an important, perhaps even a decisive, seasonal supplement to the incomes of the poor, but they were also of immense cultural value, symbolizing the incorporation of the poor into the parish community as they received their due in the church or the church porch during the major festivals of the church calendar. The implications of social and cultural recognition along these lines were profound. Since charitable relief was perceived by the poor themselves to be a moral obligation, almsmen and women came to believe they had a strong ethical claim on the hospitality and charity of their betters, a register of entitlement that was in many respects less vulnerable to challenge than the notion of legal right to which parish pensioners, at least by the eighteenth century, so often (and so misguidedly) clung. Some early eighteenth-century observers certainly thought so. William Sampson, rector of Clayworth (Nottinghamshire), argued in 1701 that, although charity had begun to 'wax cold', it still rested on the shoulders of the clergy, especially at rogationtide, and 'was expected as a right'.[274]

It was thinking along these lines that led to the protest voiced on behalf of the poor of the Buckinghamshire parish of Westbury in 1601. For 'the space of almost thirty yeares' until her death at Christmas 1596, Mary Cornwall had apparently distributed 'settled usual and continual almes' to the poor of a number of Buckinghamshire communities, including 10*s.* a year in Westbury. When her executor Ferdinand Pulton sent but two-thirds of that amount in the three years after her death, the vicar reported

[272] Cf. Walter, 'Social Economy of Dearth', 128.

[273] Thompson, *Customs in Common*, 46, 72.

[274] *The Rector's Book: Clayworth, Nottinghamshire*, ed. H. Gill and E. L. Guildford (Nottingham, 1910), 143.

that 'he hath heard dyvers of the poor of the said parish complain and find fault' that he 'did not send so great a some of money to be distributed to them as she did in her lifetime'.[275] Pulton allegedly answered 'that it was at his curtesy whether they should have any more or not', and went on to argue that her almsgiving had always been irregular. He was, he explained, simply continuing her practice: he had 'sent money sometimes to be distributed to the poor of some towns, and sometimes to other towns, to some towns at one time more, and at another tyme less, and sometimes to special persons of some towns'. Most of his charity, however, had been dispensed at his own discretion, 'with his own hands upon the poore of the same towns when they came unto him upon every of them as he then thought in his conscience the said poor persons need required'. He gave only, he insisted, 'to whom he thought good, when he thought good, and how much he thought good'.[276]

Faced with such a robust defence of the discriminatory principles of almsgiving, popular notions of entitlement to charity were difficult to defend. In their complaints to the commissioners for charitable uses, petitioners might actually play upon this sense of powerlessness. The recipients of the dole in Attleborough (Norfolk), paid sometimes as 'a shilling in mony' and sometimes in beef, funded from a £3 annuity arising from College Close, were fully sensitive of rights denied them when Sir Francis Bickley sold the close in 1604. When popular hopes of continued largesse were frustrated, Anne Kensey, a 73-year-old widow, recounted that she and a dozen or so of her poor neighbours had gone to Attleborough Hall only to be told that Bickley was not at home and that there was nothing for them either in hospitality or in alms. The cards were, inevitably, stacked in the interests of the rich and powerful. There was some hot talk among the frustrated petitioners about close-breaking in protest at the non-payment of the rent, but because Bickley was a magistrate and 'a person of great power in the Town', the poor, 'being afraid to disoblige him', 'desisted from doing anything further'.[277]

Doles, then, were a function rather of expectation than of eligibility, still less of entitlement. Expectations might nonetheless develop very quickly. In 1686 Viscountess Cholmondley's steward informed her that 'several of the poor have been at Cholmondley *expecting* their Christmas dole', though their hopes derived from an invented tradition of only nine years' standing.[278] When regular lifetime almsgiving was practised on the

[275] NA, C93/1/9, m. 40 (deposition of Richard Crockett of Westbury, clerk, 1599).

[276] NA, C93/1/9, m. 4 (deposition of Ferdinand Pulton of Boughton, esq., 1599).

[277] NA, C91/20/2 (1604), m. 5 (deposition of Anne Kensey of Harpham, widow).

[278] Hainsworth, *Stewards, Lords and People*, 162 (emphasis added).

very substantial scale of the marchioness of Winchester and her daughter, who each gave over £40 a year to the poor of the parish of St Margaret's Westminster in the 1580s and 1590s, it is easy to imagine that both the poor (and the parish officers who made such creative use of their philanthropy) might be profoundly disappointed when their expectations were frustrated.[279] The depth and power of popular expectations of largesse helps to explain why some benefactors were so very sensitive to the dangers of creating a precedent. When a controversy blew up in Lichfield (Staffordshire) in 1685 about a bequest which the parish officers claimed to have customarily received from the lord of the manor of Drayton Basset, the estate steward Captain Powell reminded them that anything given to the poor derived rather from the earl of Weymouth's 'bounty or kindness' than from any legal obligation. In private, moreover, Powell warned Weymouth that 'charity is near to chancery', a comparison that emphasized the perpetuity and expense of those gifts which became legal dues rather than spontaneous bounties. Weymouth concluded that precisely *because* the parish officers had had 'the impudence to send for it', the donation should be refused that summer.[280]

More drastic, perhaps even permanent, curtailment of customary doles might be the result of periodic bouts of aristocratic retrenchment. Although bread and beer had been distributed weekly to twenty parishioners of the Sussex villages of East Hoathly and Laughton for as long as anybody could remember, the appointment of a new estate steward in September 1764 saw at least a century of tradition abrogated by Michaelmas, at an estimated annual cost to the parish officers of £50. 'At first sight', thought Thomas Turner, 'it should appear that we have an undoubted right to it, as it has been continued without any alteration that I ever could find in the same manner that now is (and has been looked upon as our right) for time immemorial, and I should think we could trace it back upwards of hundred years.' Turner had the Pelham archives searched in an attempt to defend the 'rights' of ratepayers and almspeople alike, only to discover that the custom was inscribed only in oral tradition rather than in 'any deed or writing'. Whether the steward's decision really was born of 'economy and frugality', or, as Turner suspected, rather of 'niggardliness' and a desire to 'gain self applause', he expressed little hope that they might enforce the payment when their claim was only 'prescriptive'.[281]

Negotiations over alms, doles, and endowments therefore disclose a

279 Archer, 'Charity of Early Modern Londoners', 240.

280 Hainsworth, *Stewards, Lords and People*, 163–4.

281 *Diary of Thomas Turner*, 305–6, 317.

micro-politics in which contested visions of social obligation are the most prominent theme. As we have seen, these conflicts took different forms in different chronological and geographical contexts, and were doubtless inflected with highly localized assumptions and expectations. Cumulatively, however, they were of profound, ultimately even of national, significance in a society so keenly attuned to the rhythms of clientage and dependence. Nowhere is this significance more vividly articulated than in the records of the General Council of the Army at Putney, where in 1647 the rights of free-born Englishman were debated. One of the civilian spokesmen, Maximilian Petty, recommended that those that take alms, by which, it should be emphasized, he meant not simply all those who had ever received poor relief but every poor villager who 'received alms from door to door', be denied the franchise. Although this line of argument is abhorrent to the world-view of twenty-first-century liberal democracy, it provides an invaluable contemporary perspective on the political realities of charitable relief in seventeenth-century England. Petty advocated the exclusion of the poor not because of their poverty but because of their dependency. As objects of charity, almsmen had no freedom for independent action: they must inevitably be dependent 'upon the will of others and should be afraid to displease them'.[282]

Almsgiving therefore functioned as a quasi-contractual mechanism in which charity was exchanged for prestige and recognition.[283] On the one hand, the charity informally and semi-formally organised through alms, doles, and endowments raised and reinforced expectations about the proper conduct of propertied elites, expectations which might in turn be used by applicants for relief as a lever for continued largesse. On the other, semi-formal relief fostered a mentality of deference and gratitude amongst those who received it, a mentality which might be expressed in gestures of humility and respect whenever rich and poor came face to face. Indeed, by its very personalized nature, the giving of alms created numerous points of contact across a gulf of social distance which the poor law not only failed to bridge, but actually came to symbolize.[284]

[282] *The Clarke Papers*, ed. C. H. Firth (4 vols., Camden Society, London, 1891–1901), i. 342. Cf. A. Woolrych, *Soldiers and Statesmen: The General Council of the Army and its Debates, 1647–1648* (Oxford, 1987), 241.

[283] A. W. Coats, 'The Relief of Poverty, Attitudes to Labour, and Economic Change in England, 1660–1782', *International Review of Social History*, 21 (1976), 104.

[284] Cf. the emphasis on the explicit recognition of obligations and rights arising from the day-to-day administration of the poor laws in Levine and Wrightson, *Industrial Society*, 353.

3
Work

[Objection:]
But there are a sort of idle People that will rather beg than work, though they may be employed, and so that Trade of Begging and Idleness would be still continued.

[Answer:]
1. That we do surmise a compulsary Law to inforce Idle Persions to work; which would prevent it.

2. By this means, the benefit of Working would exceed the benefit of Begging, which would cause Persons to leave it.

3. By the educating of Children in a way of industry there would be gradually a Disaccustomedness to that way, which would in time quite remove it.

But 4. When men were once assured by a clear Evidence, that the poor might have Work on reasonable terms, no man would give; the Laws against Wanderers that were able to work, and against the relievers of such, would be cheerfully put in Execution, which now men even upon the account of common Charity cannot bring themselves to.

Sir Matthew Hale (1683)[1]

Chief Justice Matthew Hale's justification of labour discipline as a means of transforming the habits and attitudes not only of the idle poor but also of the householders who were tempted to relieve them with alms is a valuable reminder that the leitmotiv of the great Elizabethan statute 'for the relief of the poore' (39 Eliz. I, c. 3) was work. Its very first clause stipulated the duties of overseers of the poor, and first among those duties was the assessment of taxation for the provision of a parish stock. The first call on that stock, it should be emphasized, was not 'the necessary reliefe of the lame ympotent olde and blynde' but the setting to work of those who were under- and unemployed. That clause was also explicit in its identification of who was to be set to work: first, 'the

[1] *Discourse Touching Provision for the Poor* (London, 1683), 20.

Children of all such whose Parents' who were not thought by the overseers 'able to kepe and mayntaine their Children'; and, second, 'such persons maryed or unmaryed as having no means to mayntayne them, use no ordinary and dayly Trade of life to gett their lyvinge by'. It also specified what labour they should be made to perform: they were to be set to work on 'a convenient Stocke of Flaxe Hempe Wooll Threed Iron and other necessary Ware and Stuffe'.[2] The statutory requirements of 1598, reiterated in 1601, were supplemented by a series of resolutions and readings by the judiciary, acting both individually and in consort, and by the first of the 'directions' of the 'Book of Orders' of January 1631 'that the Lords of the manours and townes take care that their tenants, and the parishioners of every towne, may be releeved *by worke*, or otherwise at home, and not suffered to straggle, and beg up and downe their parish'.[3]

In both legislation and proclamation, therefore, labour discipline loomed larger than the parish pension in the prevention of beggary. These initiatives were born of the recognition that the poor constituted a 'pool of badly managed labour' from whom more productive endeavour could be coaxed.[4] As the projector Walter Morrell put it in 1617, those 'persons whoe now live in idleness for want of ymployment' were not only 'a great burthen to the Inhaubitantes amongst whom they live' but were also 'unprofitable to the Common Weale'.[5] It is all the more striking, therefore, that the setting of the labouring poor on work has generally been regarded as the least successful of all the terms of the Elizabethan statutes, indeed virtually as a dead letter almost from the very outset. The 'directions, such as they were, about organising work for the poor were the most impractical aspect of the whole corpus of Tudor legislation', argued Anthony Fletcher, and 'were generally undertaken only during the harsh conditions of dearth'.[6] The nature of these 'impracticalities' was, by the middle of the seventeenth century, apparent to contemporaries. Matthew Hale, the pre-eminent apologist of the employment of the idle, was quick to point out that, although four of the five duties of overseers were intimately concerned with work, the statute made no explicit reference to the payment of those paupers employed. Although there was a general clause empowering parish officers to ensure the disposition of the

[2] 39 Elizabeth I, c. 3 (1598), sect. i.

[3] 'The Book of Orders', sig. F4 (emphasis added).

[4] A. Fletcher, *Reform in the Provinces: The Government of Stuart England* (New Haven, 1986), 214. Cf. J. Appleby, *Economic Thought and Ideology in Seventeenth-Century England* (Princeton, 1978), 129–57.

[5] NA, C66/2112/6. For the context, see M. L. Zell, '"Setting the Poor on Work": Walter Morrell and the New Draperies Project, c.1603–31', *Historical Journal*, 44 (2001), 651–75.

[6] Fletcher, *Reform*, 213.

stock, the act provided 'no means at first before the return of the manufacture' to pay the poor any wages.[7]

Indeed, by the time his *Discourse on the Provision of the Poor* was written (probably around 1650, though it was published posthumously in 1683) Hale felt able to offer a rigorous critique of this aspect of poor law policy, supplying four reasons for the failure of parish employment schemes. First, he argued, ratepayers were unwilling to contribute the large sums necessary to finance a stock. Despite his estimate that a one-off payment of perhaps three times the normal assessment might reduce contributions over the next seven years by as much as a half or even two-thirds, ratepayers preferred to pay their usual rates 'year after year though it exhaust them in time and make the poor nothing the better at the year's end'. Second, tradesmen were keen to avoid paying rates for stocks out of their own capital, and jealously guarded their own interests as employers and merchants. Third, overseers were reluctant to incur the wrath of their fellow ratepayers by instituting work schemes that were regarded as expensive and inefficient. Fourth, the parish was simply too small a unit to make such schemes effective, a weakness compounded by the magistrates' lack of legal authority to supervise them even where the overseers seemed timorous or negligent.[8] Thus it was that 'a charity of greater extent'—the employment of the poor—was subverted to a 'charity of more immediate exigence'—the relief of the impotent.[9]

This chapter begins by briefly testing Hale's claims against the records of county and parish administration of work for the poor across the seventeenth century. While it emphasizes the complexities of the fragmentary evidence available for employment schemes, it nonetheless broadly concurs with the assessments of both contemporaries and historians: setting the poor on work was a relative, though by no means a complete, failure. Although there are several exceptionally well-documented cases which illustrate the harnessing of the productive capacities of the poor, and especially of elderly women, to yokes provided by parish officers, the overall impression is of experiments aborted after a couple of years of frustration and waste. Failures of this kind are, however, thrown into even starker relief by plentiful evidence of the relative success of another, and less frequently noticed aspect of the Elizabethan poor laws: the apprenticeship of pauper children. In part, of course, the survival of richer sources—indentures sealed, premiums accounted for, runaways disciplined, masters coerced—creates a more optimistic

[7] Hale, *Provision for the Poor*, 3.

[8] Ibid. 7–8.

[9] Ibid. 3.

impression of this aspect of poor law policy. The very survival of those sources, however, is itself testament to the sheer political will of ratepayers, overseers, and magistrates in enforcing labour discipline on the young, sometimes in the face of considerable resistance from parents and employers alike.

1. THE EMPLOYMENT OF THE POOR

The most detailed rehearsal of Elizabethan policy towards the labouring poor was offered by *An Ease for Overseers* in 1601. The overseers' handbook characteristically divided the constituency into categories, who should be differentiated above all by their place of work. While the 'wilfull', the 'negligent', and the 'fraudulent' should be constrained to labour and punishment in the house of correction, the 'willing and tractable' should be employed in their own homes, since it would be an 'indiscretion to offer them any place of discredit when they are pliable in their business at home'.[10] The most appropriate work was the production of material that 'may be easily learned and readily sold'. Thus 'spinning of flaxe into thread for linnen', 'carding and spinning of wooll into yarn for woollen', and 'bunching of hempe' were tasks 'soon compassed by any that are capable of wit'.[11] Jobs were to be allocated according to the 'education' and to the 'constitution' of the indigent. To set them to unfamiliar tasks would mean that 'the losse will be greater in learning than the gain will be in working'. Overseers were to differentiate the work expected of the poor by sex, by age, and by physical strength, ensuring that they 'tender the poore and lay no more upon them than they are able to bear.[12] There must, however, be labour discipline: the poor must be held to work; they must be enumerated in terms of their number, their capacity, their productivity, and their likely earnings; and the goods they produced must be sold both to augment the capital and to ensure that the poor were paid. To this latter end, overseers should persuade local tradesmen to buy the commodities produced by the poor on the grounds that it was 'for the benefit of the towne'.[13]

Parish work schemes, it should be emphasized at the outset, were not necessarily doomed to failure. In some areas at least, parish responsibility for setting the poor on work chimed both with burgeoning consumer

[10] *An Ease for Overseers of the Poore: Abstracted from the Statutes* (Cambridge, 1601), 18–19.
[11] Ibid. 21.
[12] Ibid. 19–20.
[13] Ibid. 20–1.

demand and with the ambitions of local projectors and entrepreneurs.[14] Tudor government had long shown an interest in stimulating the production of industrial crops, partly for the oil that could be derived from crushed seeds, but more especially to encourage the making of thread, linen, and canvas from flax and hemp. Even when parliamentary support for the economic logic of growing hemp died away in the 1560s, stocks of hemp usually dominated the working materials on which the poor were to be employed, both under Elizabethan relief statutes and in the charitable bequests of testators for the next century.[15] Projectors from John Stratford in the 1620s to Walter Blith in the 1650s and Carew Reynel in the 1670s advocated the importance of hemp for the production of thread, which might be used to sew the very wide range of linen goods (aprons, petticoats, shirts, sheets, and napkins) which were becoming commonplace even in the homes of husbandmen. Since 'not a single family in the kingdom could dispense entirely with thread', the production of the hemp from which it was made diffused outwards from its earlier centres such as the Orwell estuary in Suffolk so that 'in scattered villages all over England hemp and flax growing were pursued on a scale sufficient to support a local industry' that Gregory King thought worth approximately £1 million a year to the English economy by the 1690s.[16]

Parish officers and projectors might conceivably, therefore, have much to offer each other, as they did at Milcote (Warwickshire), where Lionel Cranfield's woad-growing enterprise employed almost 250 field workers, some of them doubtless sent there by the officers of the parishes of Kineton hundred, every day throughout the summers of the 1620s and 1630s. The coincidence of the 'project' for the growing of hemp devised by John Stratford of Winchcombe (Gloucestershire) in 1624 and the spread of hemp-dressing in the parish work schemes of the 1620s is, similarly, interesting.[17] Even so, it is striking, though perhaps not entirely surprising, that the most ambitious co-ordinated work scheme of all, Walter Morrell's project to reinvigorate the moribund Hertfordshire textile industry by the employment of the labouring poor in eight colleges

[14] J. Thirsk, 'Projects for Gentlemen, Jobs for the Poor: Mutual Aid in the Vale of Tewkesbury, 1600–1630', repr. in id., *The Rural Economy of England: Collected Essays* (London, 1984), 287–307.

[15] e.g. 18 Elizabeth I, c. 3 (1576). In the Guildford workhouse founded by Archbishop Abbot, spinning flax and hemp into cloth was regarded as a 'great comfort to many poore workefolke men, women and children'. NA, SP16/191/42.

[16] J. Thirsk, *Economic Policy and Projects: The Development of a Consumer Society in Early Modern England* (Oxford, 1978), index, s.v. 'hemp', quotations at 48, 73.

[17] Ibid. 5, 102–5. Cf. Thirsk, 'Projects for Gentlemen, Jobs for the Poor'. Cf. Ch. 4.1(*d*) below.

for the manufacture of the new draperies, proved to be an outright, if protracted, failure. It was, moreover, hostility among those very magistrates who were responsible for implementing the scheme to the idea of creating a wage-dependent class of clothworkers in a county renowned for agricultural specialization that killed Morrell's project off.[18]

The Stuart regime also took seriously the possibility that the poor might be employed in agriculture. In 1617, for instance, the justices of the Norfolk circuit proposed that 'gardening for rootes and other thinges be used amongest the poorer sort', and ordered that 'the poore that dooe worke in his owne garden have 2d for one day in the weeke so as it may appeare to the overseere that there groweth good to the partie and the commonwealth therebie'.[19] There is, however, little evidence that parish officers ever encouraged such cultivation of cottage gardens or indeed of any agricultural work, though the comparative silence of overseers' accounts on this issue should not necessarily be taken to imply that the poor were never set to work on the fields of their more prosperous neighbours. It may well be that the vestries of many rural parishes functioned in effect as job-creation services, with parish officers using a rota system to farm out the able-bodied poor as agricultural labourers among local employers whether they actually required them or not. Richard Dunning's observation of 1698 that poor men in husbandry should be offered work around the parish is less of a report than a recommendation, though his note that the poor tended to be averse to going about with lists in this way (an attitude he applauded because it kept them off the rates) suggests that it was one coloured by experience.[20] Arrangements of this kind were organized without any direct financial contribution from the overseers, and have therefore left no trace in their account books. It seems likely, therefore, that collaborative and reciprocal schemes for the provision of agricultural work were far more common than the evidence of parish archives suggests, and, in turn, that the conventional picture of parish employment based predominantly around textile production is a serious distortion of the experience of labour under the Elizabethan poor laws.

It is certainly true that the best-documented experiments in employing the poor, even in agricultural parishes, were those in which paupers were set to work on stocks of raw materials provided by the parish officers. The employment of the poor in this way might at first sight seem to have been sporadic, especially since there are so few extant accounts from the early

[18] Zell, '"Setting the Poor on Work"', 674–5.

[19] Bodl., MS Tanner, 243, fo. 13^{v}.

[20] R. Dunning, *Bread for the Poor* (Exeter, 1698), 11.

seventeenth century, the very period in which the imperative to set the poor on work was so stridently rehearsed by privy council and county magistrates alike. Terse summaries of the practice of hemp-spinning, flax-winding and lace-working do, very occasionally, survive in the few parish accounts extant from the period before 1630, but the impression they create is of short-lived and often ill-managed experiments. In 1596–7, for example, the overseers of Eaton Socon (Bedfordshire) were paying one Goodwife Clarke 2*d.* weekly to teach the poor children of the parish to work bone lace, and their colleagues at Cowden (Kent) recorded that the poor had woven, washed, and whitened some 74 ells of canvas which had been sold for over £3.[21] Generally, however, even fragmentary evidence of this kind is absent in the years down to 1603. Although the hundredal juries of Essex suggested in January 1599 that stocks had been provided in every parish in the county, not one of five Essex parishes with extant Elizabethan overseers' accounts was making payments for the provision of wool, flax, or hemp.[22] At Shorne (Kent), where the earliest surviving overseers' papers survive from April 1598, 'the articles given in charge' to the parish officers included a request for information about 'the employment of the assessment & of the stock', but 'there is nothing in the accounts suggesting any attempt to put the able bodied to work'.[23] Of the 117 Buckinghamshire parishes which reported to the bishop of Lincoln on their performance of general hospitality in April 1597, only two (2 per cent) certified that the poor were set on work, although in neither case did the churchwardens specify the nature of the employment. The record of the south Warwickshire communities in the early Stuart period is marginally better. Four (5 per cent) of the eighty-six Warwickshire parishes whose officers submitted returns on how the poor were relieved in 1606 referred explicitly to employment: the poor of Ettington were 'kept in work and sufficiently relieved', of Fenny Compton 'sufficiently relieved and set on work', and of Stretford Burges 'set on work and the stock maintained'. At Abbots Salford, 'such of the poor as are able have been kept to work' while the 'old and ympotent' were relieved.[24]

The evidence from west Essex and north Norfolk is, however, slightly more optimistic, and suggests that the influence of the late Elizabethan

[21] F. G. Emmison, 'Poor Relief Accounts of Two Rural Parishes in Bedfordshire, 1563–1598', *Economic History Review*, 3 (1931–2), 111–12; E. Turner, 'Ancient Parochial Account Book of Cowden', *Sussex Archaeological Collections*, 20 (1882), 96–7.

[22] F. G. Emmison, 'The Care of the Poor in Elizabethan Essex: Recently Discovered Records', *Essex Review*, 62 (1953), 25–6.

[23] A. F. Allen, 'An Early Poor Law Account', *Archaeologia Cantiana*, 64 (1951), 75, 80.

[24] LA, Ch.p/2/27 (Hitcham), 4/27 (Bishops Woburn); WCRO, CR1618/W19/3, unfol.

legislation might have been, if not decisive, then at least gently persuasive. Two of the four Essex parishes whose accounts survive for 1599 were evidently using a stock to set the poor on work, a third thought one necessary, and a fourth was directly purchasing spinning-wheels for them.[25] Of the twenty-six parishes whose accounts Nathaniel Bacon audited in April 1601, two (8 per cent) itemized expenditure for setting the poor on work. While the overseers of Holt Market spent 41*s.* 6*d.* (or 26 per cent of their annual income) on wool and hemp, their colleagues at Houghton-next-Marpley disbursed 21*s.* 4*d.* (or 61 per cent, though they used a large proportion of their old stock to do so).[26] At Cawston (Norfolk), the parish officers were optimistic in 1606 that 'tuching the setting of pore on work the aged have as much works as they ar hable to do', but noted that there were ten 'pore mens children which might be set to learn to spinne or knit'. The first attempt to employ the poor of Buntingford (Hertfordshire) in November 1607 was funded by 'a voluntary contrubution' which raised 43*s.*, 'all wch was layde out in wheeles & cardes for the use of the poore'.[27]

The sporadic nature of these references almost certainly reflects the difficulties experienced by parish officers in managing such schemes, or at least in running them at a profit. Overseers were, in fact, told to anticipate that work schemes might make a loss, especially at the outset: every scheme 'must have a beginning and where theyre are many learners there will be muche losse'. The 'untowardnesse and unaptnesse of many to work' also made longer-term deficits inevitable, and the only solution was to augment the capital. Although schemes were, therefore, never intended to be profitable in and of themselves, wastage was tolerable on the grounds that it was preferable 'to sustain some losse in learning [the poore] to worke then to keep them idle to induce them to evil'. And losses there certainly were. At Cowden in 1602, the cloth woven by the poor was sold at a loss of 7*s.* 8*d.*, or over 8 per cent of what it cost to produce. At Kempston (Bedfordshire) in 1631, for example, the overseers sum-

[25] ERO, D/DBa/O8/1–5.

[26] Sadly, neither of these two parishes was among the thirteen whose papers survive in Bacon's archive for the following year (1601–2), none of which made explicit reference to employment schemes. Many of these communities did, of course, have a parish stock which *might* be used set the poor on work. *The Papers of Nathaniel Bacon of Stiffkey*, ed. A. Hassell Smith *et al.* (4 vols., Norfolk Record Society, 46, 49, 53, 64, Norwich, 1978–2000), iv. 187–92, 237–8.

[27] Norfolk RO, MC148/17–18; HALS, D/P65/3/3, 212. The timing of the Buntingford initiative was not entirely coincidental, for it followed relatively quickly on the arrival of the new vicar Alexander Strange, whose views on idleness, that the workshy should be pinched with hunger, had received full expression in an assize sermon preached at Hertford earlier in the year. Cf. Ch. 2.1 above.

marized a year's worth of effort by noting that they had sold the cloth for £1. 11*s.* 1*d.* less than the original investment, a deficit of almost 26 per cent. Since no further evidence of parish-organized cloth manufacture survives in Kempston, the logical assumption is that the experiment was aborted.[28] Only very occasionally did parishes, Cranbrook (Kent) providing a good example, take initiatives to set the poor on work which were sustained across the seventeenth and eighteenth centuries as a whole.[29]

It would, nonetheless, be a mistake to underestimate either the spread or the rigour of initiatives to set the poor on work in this period, however unsuccessful they might ultimately prove. Some systematic attempts were made to co-ordinate parish work schemes well before the Book of Orders of 1630–1. The north Norfolk justices insisted in December 1622, for example, that 'poore children be put to schoole to knitting and spinninge dames', the parish officers being ordered to pay the schooldames' wages if the their parents were not able to do so. Far more specific, however, was the charge 'given to the overseers in every towne' in December 1623, which explained how those fit for work should be identified and how they might be employed.[30] Every Saturday night or Sunday morning, it insisted, the overseers were to enquire what work was available in the parish for the following week in order that the unemployed might meet the demand. Even in the early 1620s, however, subtle distinctions were made between the various candidates for work. While able-bodied labourers were incorporated into a primitive version of the 'roundsman' system working for the employers in the parish, the old, the infirm, and the young were provided with parish stocks on which they would be set to work directly by the overseers themselves.[31] Thus the parish officers were 'to provide materials for the men that are olde and weake and for the women and children'. In particular, the children of poor labouring families who had been neither apprenticed nor employed were 'to be taught to knit and to spin by some honest women in the Towne that are fitt to teach them'. Any who remained untaught were to be allowed a penny a week 'till they shalbe able to earne something towards their living'. Those who are so 'oulde and weake as they are not able or fitt for

[28] *An Ease for Overseers of the Poore*, 22; Turner, 'Ancient Parochial Account Book of Cowden', 98; Bedfordshire and Luton Archives and Record Service, Bedford, P60/12/1, unfol.

[29] M. Barker-Read, 'The Treatment of the Aged Poor in Five Selected West Kent Parishes from Settlement to Speenhamland, 1662–1797' (unpublished Ph.D. thesis, Open University, 1988), 199.

[30] BL, MS Additional, 12496, fo. 222; Bodl., MS Tanner, 73, fo. 390. For the origin of this latter charge, see Ch. 1.2(*b*) above.

[31] E. M. Leonard, *The Early History of English Poor Relief* (Cambridge, 1900), 232.

any other worke' were to be provided with a stock of hemp 'in the pillinge whereof they may be employed'. Indeed, the charge insisted that 'every man who is an occupier of land shall sewe hemp according to the statute'.[32]

In the absence of the parish accounts which would enable the measurement of the effectiveness of this policy, some impression can be derived from the certificates surviving in the state papers from the early 1630s. The deliberate vagueness with which many magistrates couched their reports inhibits precise analysis, as it was perhaps designed to.[33] It is nonetheless striking that a cluster of certificates submitted in April and May 1631 suggest, at the very least, that taxation had been ordered to provide a stock to employ the poor, or rather more specifically that funds had either been directly disbursed for the purchase of raw materials (as at Beverley) or transferred to the clothiers who might organize the work (as in Winchester).[34] A small number of certificates were, however, rather more specific than the usual bland statements of compliance with the orders. The JPs of Hertford hundred reported in April 1631 that they had 'caused all the poore people that are of any abillitie of bodie' to be set to work in every parish', noting that 'the townes most populous having stockes' had 'already provided for their poore'. There were, they insisted, 'stokes raised for the poore in most townes', and only 'where the parish by meanes of the povertie thereof is not able to raise a stock' were the parish officers falling back on rates and 'weekelie collection in money' for the relief of the poor ('by corne & otherwise as their present necessitie require') rather than on the provision of work.[35] In the Leicestershire hundred of Sparkenhoe, the magistrates noted in June 1631 that they had 'given order for the buying of hemp flaxe & wool for the setting of work of such as are not able to sett themselves to worke and for the ymployinge of little children not yet able to be putt to apprentizes or to service'.[36]

Only where parish accounts survive for a large number of neighbouring parishes is it possible to offer a more systematic assessment. Two certificates from the JPs of Bassetlaw hundred (Nottinghamshire) are particularly useful in this regard, and might give sceptics pause before rehearsing the usual platitudes about the impracticality of parish work schemes. The officers of eleven of the twenty parishes for which evidence

[32] Bodl., MS Tanner, 73, fo. 390.

[33] For examples of stereotypical or generic statements on setting the poor on work, see NA, SP16/188/45, 191/40/2, 192/59, 193/53, 201/13/1, 220/14, 250/11/4, 271/85, 294/33, 329/87, 390/131, 395/32.

[34] Leonard, *Early History of English Poor Relief*, 255–6.

[35] NA, SP 16/189/79.

[36] NA, SP 16/193/89.

was provided in July 1636 claimed that they had stocks of certain values ranging between 50*s*. and £11 to set the poor on work. By March 1637, a much fuller certificate suggests that in forty-five of the sixty parishes the officers were providing employment for those who could work, and that in most of the parishes which feature in both returns, the value of the stock had increased in the intervening nine months.[37] These reports might be compared to the picture in the fielden areas of Warwickshire, where sheep-corn husbandry predominated. The parish officers of at least four of the thirty-nine rural communities in Kineton hundred for which overseers' accounts survive in 1639 claimed to be setting the poor on work: at Pillerton Hersey, the overseers noted that 'we do employ all our poor labourers with constant work whereby they may be able to maintain their families'; at Pillerton Priors, those poor who were not parish pensioners were 'kept in work'; at Ratley, the town stock was used 'to set the poor on work as need requireth'; while at Priors Hardwick, levies were made 'for the relief of the poor and setting them on work'.[38] Although the employment of the labouring poor is usually dismissed as the least successful of the provisions of the Elizabethan poor laws, a compliance rate of one parish in ten even in a region dominated by arable agriculture belies the pessimism of most recent commentators.[39]

There is some evidence that even the absence of a parish stock—a capital sum to be loaned out at interest or a sum to be invested in working materials—did not preclude the employment of the poor. In the parishes of the half-hundred of Chatham (Kent), for instance, it was reported in 1653 that there was 'no parish stock, but many poor employed picking oakum'.[40] More commonly, however, the adequate provision and successful management of stock was crucial to the employment of the poor. The stock itself might be derived from taxation, from rents on town lands, or from endowments. Some testators, such as Henry Gurnay of Great Ellingham (Norfolk), who left £10 to be administered as a stock for the poor by the parish officers in 1624, made elaborate stipulations. Gurnay's stock was to be lent out to 'the poor' on security but only in portions of 20*s*. and for periods of less than twelve months, any forfeitures being added to the capital sum. Although the churchwardens were to nominate the most appropriate candidates, subject to moderation and composition by the minister in cases of dispute, Gurnay was at pains to indicate that, by 'the poor', he intended only those who either 'take

[37] NA, SP16/329/63, 349/86. Cf. Leonard, *Early History of English Poor Relief*, 256–8.
[38] SBTRO, DR37/85/6/32, 33, 35, 43, 48, 52.
[39] Cf. Fletcher, *Reform in the Provinces*, 213.
[40] Kent Archives Office, Maidstone, Q/SB/4/90.

releife of the parish or through disabillitie give notheinge thereto'.[41] Elsewhere, it seems, money from the parish stock might be loaned not only to paupers, usually widows, but also to able-bodied men for whom the money might be an invaluable aid in maintaining a degree of self-sufficiency by their labour. By 1602, for instance, at least twenty individuals were indebted to the stock of the Norfolk parish of Wiveton, most of them in sums of 20*s.* or 30*s.*[42] It usually fell to the parish officers to set the maximum proportion of the stock that might be let to any one parishioner. At Wivenhoe in the late 1570s, for instance, parishioners borrowed sums varying between £1 and £6 from the parish stock. At Great Bentley in 1575, meanwhile, the entire 'collection money' of 12*s.* was lent out in one go. The interest rate in these cases seems to have been a flat 5 per cent. At Clayworth (Nottinghamshire) by the 1670s, 6 per cent was being levied on money held on bond by several parishioners in various amounts ranging between £1 and £20, and the proceeds provided the overseers with approximately 15 per cent of all their income in the period 1674–1702. At Winston (Durham), where the stock was lent out from 1633, however, there was no hint of an interest charge. Indeed, the stock system seems to have thrived in the north-east into the early eighteenth century, with the overseers recording both payments and loans from the 'interest money'.[43]

Evidence for the allocation and control of resources in parish work schemes is difficult to find. Perhaps unsurprisingly, the better-documented schemes are those that operated in towns, especially corporate boroughs such as Dorchester or Salisbury.[44] Even so, there is interesting evidence that smaller-scale work schemes were at least attempted in rural communities. Occasionally, overseers made arrangements with individual paupers, providing a widow in early seventeenth-century Hornchurch (Essex), for example, with flax that she might spin and sell 'for her better relief'.[45] Just occasionally, however, parish

[41] Norfolk RO, Norwich, NCC Will of Henry Gurnay of Great Ellingham, esq., 1 May 1624 fo. 151^{v}.

[42] P. Rushton, 'The Poor Law, the Parish and the Community in North-East England 1600–1800', *Northern History*, 25 (1989), 138; *Bacon Papers*, iv. 298–300.

[43] Emmison, 'The Care of the Poor in Elizabethan Essex', 13, 16; *Coming into Line: Loca[l] Government in Clayworth, 1674–1714*, ed. A. Rogers (Nottingham, 1979), *passim*; Rushton, 'The Poo[r] Law, the Parish and the Community', 138–9.

[44] P. Slack, 'Poverty and Politics in Salisbury, 1597–1666', in P. Clark and P. Slack (eds.), *Cris[is] and Order in English Towns, 1500–1700: Essays in Urban History* (London, 1972), 164–203; D[.] Underdown, *Fire from Heaven: The Life of an English Town in the Seventeenth Century* (London, 1992), 113–15.

[45] M. K. McIntosh, *A Community Transformed: The Manor and Liberty of Havering, 1500–162[0]* (Cambridge, 1991), 285.

archives furnish some detail on the economics of more ambitious parish employment projects in rural parishes and market towns. On 15 February 1624, for example, twenty chief inhabitants of Buntingford (Hertfordshire) met to agree the terms on which the poor of the neighbouring parishes should be employed.[46] One Richard Gossen of London had donated a stock of £20 value to set the poor on work, a gift which the chief inhabitants decided should be applied towards 'spyyninge hempe and Flaxe & not otherwise'.[47] The scheme was to be administered by one of their number, John Brand, who was to be paid 40*s.* a year from the funds of the neighbouring parishes of Layston, Wyddial, and Aspenden for his pains. Brand was to guarantee to repay the capital sum to the parish officers but to use it in the interim to employ forty inhabitants of the three parishes. The parish officers were required to inculcate the work ethic. The overseers were to ensure that any of the poor who embezzled or wasted either the raw material or the goods produced were excluded from the scheme. The vicar and churchwardens, 'for the better encoraginge of such as shall worke paynfullie in this worke', were to distribute the quarterly doles at their disposal only 'unto such as doe most worke & best' and to ignore those 'able persons as will not work in this or in some honest vocation'. If any of those employed disagreed with Brand about the value of their work, they were to be allowed to purchase the raw materials at a penny below the cost price. Because a register of those employed was to be kept in the town book, it is possible to analyse the social and gender composition of those required to spin flax and beat hemp at the will of the parish. Unsurprisingly, women predominated: thirty-nine of the forty-four persons listed in March 1624 were women, seven of them widows. In several cases parish labour evidently penetrated right to the heart of the household economy: six of those employed were to be set on work with their daughters.[48]

The Lincolnshire parish of Frampton provides another striking example of an employment scheme that operated for as long as two decades in the early seventeenth century.[49] In the early 1620s, the overseers recorded that their income derived from 'stock', 'sessment', and 'town rent'. The capital seems to have been invested in hemp, 3 stone of which was in

[46] The following details are taken from HALS, D/P65/3/3, 111–15.

[47] Gossen's will specified that the parish officers of Layston and of Hatfield Broad Oak (Essex) were each to have received £20, with which they should buy flax 'to sett the poore on worke'. NA, PROB11/141, 25 Feb. 1623

[48] HALS D/P65/3/3, 111–15, 274–5.

[49] The following paragraph is based on the entries for the years 1620–40 in LA, Frampton PAR, 10/1, unfol. For the context, see S. Hindle, 'Power, Poor Relief and Social Relations in Holland Fen, *c.*1600–1800', *Historical Journal*, 41 (1998), 67–96.

hand by 1625. Dressing hemp—a process which included 'bunching, hickling, spinyng and weaving'—for yarn and cloth was in full swing by 1631 when the overseers provided a fitting workplace for the labouring poor, spending almost £5 on a 'workhouse with stuffe and other implements and hemp and flax drest and undrest'. The inventory of this workshop, which should be distinguished from the residential parish workhouses of the early eighteenth century, included 67 lb of hemp and flax, 3 stone of undressed femble, and 9 lb of 'dressed flax teare'. At Easter 1633, the overseers passed on to their successors some 163 lb of teare hemp, 20 lb of which was already spun into yarn. Only very small sums (as little as 12*s.* 3*d.* in 1636) were, however, raised by the sale of the finished materials, and the capital sum on which the scheme was based accordingly diminished over time, from £10 in 1626 to £7 in 1639 and £4 in 1644. As at Wisbech (Cambridgeshire), the Frampton overseers recognized that the rough hempen cloth produced by the paupers, who were characteristically aged with failing sight and arthritic limbs, was of such poor quality that it could only be used (if it could be used at all) to clothe the very people who had woven it, and spent £5 in 1631 for 'clothing the poor and other charges' in making coats.[50] By the end of the 1640s, the scheme appears to have collapsed, and there are no further references to a workhouse in the Frampton parish archive until the mid-eighteenth century.[51]

Rural workshops of this kind were, however, rare, and it was far more usual for cloth to be spun, whitened, wound, woven, and warped in paupers' own homes, as it was in Wisbech in the 1620s and Goldington (Bedfordshire) in the 1650s. Such schemes were, ultimately, no more successful than that at Frampton. In Goldington, a parish of perhaps 350 inhabitants in the mid-seventeenth century, the paupers worked up almost three-quarters of a tonne of hemp and flax into approximately 500 metres of cloth in the five years 1649–54. Making it was one thing, however, selling it quite another. The Wisbech scheme was making a loss of 18 per cent a year in the 1620s and the deficits at Goldington proved so catastrophic that the parish officers could only comment sadly of the poor they had set on work that 'all is lost by their labour'.[52] There is, of course, the possibility that the poor deliberately sabotaged the scheme by

[50] E. M. Hampson, *The Treatment of Poverty in Cambridgeshire, 1597–1834* (Cambridge, 1934), 36; Hindle, 'Power, Poor Relief and Social Relations', 86.

[51] By the 18th century, however, the poor both lived and worked in the Frampton workhouse. When it burnt to the ground in 1753 the churchwardens had to reimburse John Hudson both for 'getting the goods out of the poor house and lodging the poor people' while it was rebuilt. LA, Frampton PAR ,7/3, unfol.

[52] Bedfordshire and Luton Archives and Record Service, P78/12/1, unfol.

embezzling the materials that they had been loaned. Indeed, the fears of embezzlement, described so bluntly at Layston, were entirely characteristic of schemes that allowed the poor to take raw materials into their own homes.[53] When the Cumberland justices ordered the officers of Westward parish to provide hemp or flax for Jane Langrigg to spin in 1698, she first complained that 'she could not live upon spinning hemp' at 5*d.* a hank, and subsequently exaggerated the number of coils of 'good Heckled Lyne' (flax) she had spun. If an accusation of embezzlement could be made to stick, the consequences for the pauper could be devastating. One Norfolk woman apparently had a fatal seizure when one of her neighbours accused her of keeping back hemp for herself.[54]

Although, therefore, the initiatives of the 1630s probably represent the high-water mark for the setting of the poor on work, sporadic campaigns took place in some parishes into the later seventeenth century. The parish officers of Pluckley (Kent) regularly provided stockards, stockard stools, and spinning-wheels for the poor in the period 1650–63, and did so occasionally even later in the century. In 1666 they purchased stockards for Widow Marten 'to encourage her in her work', an instance which anticipated the widespread eighteenth-century practice of providing 'encouragement money'—nominal sums paid on the value of the goods produced—to workhouse inmates. The overseers of Cranbrook provided 'cards' for some widows even when they were well into their seventies. Elsewhere, work might be provided to meet seasonal need, as it was in Wisbech in 1660 when William Scotred was given 2 stone of hemp 'for his relief this winter'. It remains true, therefore, that parish officers long recognized their obligation to provide work for individual paupers: as the parson of Middle Claydon (Buckinghamshire) wrote in 1674 of an elderly widow, 'if she want the overseers of the parish must find her *work*'.[55]

[53] J. Styles, 'Embezzlement, Industry and the Law in England, 1500–1800', in M. Berg *et al.* (eds.), *Manufacture in Town and Countryside before the Factory* (Cambridge, 1983), 173–210. Cf. Ch. 1.5 above.

[54] CRO, Q/11/1/47/15; Norfolk RO, C/S3/28.

[55] N. Davie, 'Custom and Conflict in a Wealden Village: Pluckley, 1550–1700' (unpublished D.Phil. thesis, University of Oxford, 1988), 238; Barker-Read, 'Treatment of the Aged Poor', 66–7; Hampson, *Treatment of Poverty in Cambridgeshire*, 37; J. Broad, 'Parish Economies of Welfare, 1650–1834', *Historical Journal*, 42 (1999), 994–5 (emphasis added). For parish officers similarly encouraging the purchase of wheels and cards for individual paupers to spin, and even of earthenware for them to sell, in late 17th-century Staffordshire, see S. R. Broadbridge, 'The Old Poor Law in the Parish of Stone', *North Staffordshire Journal of Field Studies*, 13 (1973), 13–14. Stockards ('stock cardes') were 'large cards fastened to a stock or support used for separating and combing out fibres of wool, hemp etc'. 'Cardes' were implements similar to a wire brush' used for the same purpose. R. Milward, *A Glossary of Household, Farming and Trade Terms from Probate Inventories* (Derbyshire Record Society, Occasional Paper 1, 3rd edn., Chesterfield, 1986), 14, 52.

Larger-scale initiatives than these, such as the 'scaleraking' undertaken by thirty widows and infants of late seventeenth-century Hexham, were, by then, unusual.[56] In 1681 the high constable of Blackburn hundred (Lancashire) sarcastically noted the latest responses to his usual requests that parish officers inform him of how poor were provided for, 'which were generally to this effect viz: "the poore within our parish are sufficiently provided for by money taxed upon the inhabitants for their reliefe. We have no other stock of money to imploy or set them to worke."'[57] Providing the material, checking the stock, and selling the product of the poor's labours was, quite simply, too much bother. It is especially striking, therefore, that even in such well-documented parishes as Gnosall (Staffordshire), Lacock (Wiltshire), or Trull (Somerset), references to the employment of the parish poor *as a group* are conspicuous by their absence.[58]

By the late seventeenth century, therefore, frustration with the inefficient management of parish labour schemes led polemicists, projectors, and policy-makers alike to explore alternative strategies through which habits of industry might be inculcated among the poor. The Societies for the Reformation of Manners of the 1690s were particularly influential in the establishment of the Corporations of the Poor, sanctioned by statute in fifteen cities including London in the period 1696–1711, which were intended both to centralize relief across large numbers of urban parishes and to establish municipal workhouses.[59] As might be expected, ideas and initiatives of this kind took longer to penetrate the countryside, though from the mid-1710s onwards, workhouses were being established and publicized with the encouragement of the Society for the Propagation of Christian Knowledge (SPCK) in hundreds of communities, including not only market towns but also larger rural parishes, up and down the country. This 'parochial workhouse movement' received belated statutory recognition in 1723 under the terms of Knatchbull's Act, which permitted parishes to hire or erect workhouses and to contract for the employment of the poor within them, combining

[56] Rushton. 'The Poor Law, the Parish and the Community', 139.

[57] R. S. France, 'A High Constable's Register, 1681', *Transactions of the Historic Society of Lancashire and Cheshire*, 107 (1956), 70.

[58] S. A. Cutlack, 'The Gnosall Records, 1679 to 1837: Poor Law Administration', *Collections for a History of Staffordshire, Part I* (1936), 37; F. H. Hinton, 'Notes on the Administration of the Relief of the Poor of Lacock 1583–1834', *Wiltshire Archaeological Magazine*, 49 (1940–2), 187–8; I. F. Jones, 'Aspects of Poor Law Administration, Seventeenth to Nineteenth Centuries, from Trull Overseers' Accounts', *Somerset Archaeological and Natural History Society Proceedings*, 95 (1951), 90.

[59] P. Slack, *From Reformation to Improvement: Public Welfare in Early Modern England* (Oxford, 1999), 102–14, 127–33.

if necessary for either of these purposes, and authorized the 'workhouse test', which empowered vestries to withhold relief from those who were unwilling to enter.[60] The earliest foundations, which were almost always the result of highly localized initiatives, were established in Essex and the East Midlands: by 1725, for instance, at least ten rural parishes in Bedfordshire had introduced workhouses.[61] The number of parish workhouses continued to rise throughout the 1720s and 1730s, falling off only in the 1740s. By the middle of the eighteenth century, it has been estimated, there were at least 600 of these institutions, in which almost 30,000 people were being housed and set to work, at an average of forty-seven inmates per workhouse. By 1777, there were almost 2,000 workhouses in England.[62]

Like the parish apprenticeships and the paupers' badges enforced by legislation of 1697, parochial workhouses operated on the principle of deterrence, and were intended to give pause to those who contemplated an application for parish relief. As Richard Cocks argued in the House of Commons in 1695, workhouses were designed 'not only to employ the impotent in some measure' but also 'to terrify those of ability'.[63] Whereas outdoor relief had functioned as part of the 'mixed economy of welfare' in which the parish pension was easily combined with the support derived from kin or neighbours, the workhouse test presented paupers with a stark choice between total and institutionalized dependence on the one hand and complete reliance on their own resources on the other. Although workhouses were undoubtedly undermined to some extent by magistrates' continued insistence on issuing orders for outdoor relief, their success lay in bolstering the powers of parish officers who might succeed in deterring applications for relief by establishing a regime so austere and disciplinarian that to the pensioner it would resemble nothing so much as a house of correction.[64] The role of the SPCK, which propa-

[60] 9 George I, c. 7. For the genesis of the act, see T. Hitchcock, 'Paupers and Preachers: The SPCK and the Parochial Workhouse Movement', in L. Davison *et al.* (eds.), *Stilling the Grumbling Hive: The Response to Social and Economic Problems in England, 1689–1750* (Gloucester, 1992), esp. 158–9; Slack, *From Reformation to Improvement*, 133–5.

[61] J. Simon, 'From Charity School to Workhouse in the 1720s: The SPCK and Mr Marriott's Solution', *History of Education*, 17 (1988), 113–29; F. G. Emmison, 'The Relief of the Poor at Eaton Socon, 1706–1834', *Publications of the Bedfordshire Historical Record Society*, 15 (1933), 23 n. 69

[62] Hitchcock, 'Paupers and Preachers', 144, 160.

[63] Bodl., MS Eng. Hist., b.209, fo. 81^{v} (reverse foliation). See Chs. 3.2, 6.2(*e*), and 6.5 below.

[64] J. Innes, 'The "Mixed Economy of Welfare" in Early Modern England: Assessments of the Options from Hale to Malthus (*c.*1683–1803)', in Daunton (ed.), *Charity, Self-Interest and Welfare*, 139–80; cf. Innes, 'Prisons for the Poor: English Bridewells, 1555–1800', in F. Snyder and D. Hay (eds.), *Labour, Law and Crime: An Historical Perspective* (London, 1987), 42–122.

gated the ideology which drove the movement, ensured, however, that industry went hand in hand with piety. As their manifesto put it in 1732, in the well-regulated workhouse, 'the children of the poor instead of being bred up in irreligion and vice, to an idle, beggarly and vagabond life, will have the fear of God before their eyes, get habits of virtue, be inured to labour, and thus become useful to their country'.[65]

Like the parish work schemes of the early seventeenth century, moreover, workhouses were never intended to produce an absolute profit from the labour of the poor: the spinning, knitting, baking, and brewing practised there was more for the good of the inmates' souls than for the benefit of the overseers' ledgers. Their contribution to parish finances lay rather in alleviating the relief burden on ratepayers by reducing, and preferably by altogether eliminating, the number of pensioners. In some cases, as at Romford (Essex) in 1719 or Strood (Kent) in 1729, the intention to provoke paupers 'to maintain themselves rather than come into the house' was explicitly stated, although it should be emphasized that the 1723 act did not actually penalize overseers who continued to provide outdoor relief in special cases.[66] In this respect, they were often very successful, at least in the short to medium term, in driving down the numbers of people on relief in most parishes by over 50 per cent. At Eaton Socon (Bedfordshire), for example, the numbers relieved by pensions had fallen from thirty-eight to just three within six months of the establishment of the workhouse in May 1719. At Tavistock (Devon), only fourteen of the thirty-one parish pensioners chose to enter the workhouse when the test was introduced in 1747.[67] Whether workhouses really did restrict the growth of relief expenditure is, however, open to question. At Wisbech (Cambridgeshire), the vestry was able to reduce the poor rate assessment by some 38 per cent in the wake of the erection of the workhouse in 1720. At Tavistock in the period 1736–61, not only did the number of pension payments fall (from 109 to 64), but the average value of each payment also dropped from 1*s.* 3*d.* to 1*s.* 0*d.*, suggesting that the workhouse had accommodated many individuals who would have represented a significant charge to overseers, especially in their old age. The workhouse test emphatically did not, however, entirely eliminate outdoor relief even in those parishes where it was introduced. At Pattingham (Staffordshire), for instance, where annual relief expenditure

[65] Hitchcock, 'Paupers and Preachers', 152–3; Anon., *Account of Workhouses in Great Britain in the Year 1732* (London, 1732), pp. viii–ix.

[66] Slack, *From Reformation to Improvement*, 134.

[67] Emmison, 'The Relief of the Poor at Eaton Socon', 21; Hitchcock, 'Paupers and Preachers', 163 n. 3.

had more than doubled in the two decades before the workhouse was established there in 1734, the institutionalization of the poor does not seem to have saved the parish much money.[68]

The regime envisaged for the workhouse at Ashwell (Hertfordshire) under a vestry resolution of February 1728 explains why so few paupers were willing to take the test. All parish pensioners were given five days' notice to have their goods inventoried and enter the workhouse or forfeit their relief. All able-bodied inmates were to labour under the authority of a master and mistress, either within the house or, if they might find work ploughing or washing for local householders, outside it, but then only with the permission of the parish officers. Weekly church attendance and a daily round of religious observances were mandatory, and both cleanliness and good conduct were insisted upon, with a system of regulatory procedures established so that the house 'would not fail to answer the end for which it was established, to be a house of good manners, piety, charity and industry'. Both vestrymen and inmates alike were to live 'calmly and sedately without wrangling or malice', to be 'in exact harmony', and to behave like 'good neighbours and pious Christians'.[69] As the vestry of South Mimms (Middlesex) put it in 1724, if the poor were to be prevented from 'following idle and vagrant courses', it was necessary only to 'instruct them in the knowledge of their duty towards God'.[70] The potential for abuse must nonetheless have been significant. Although the master of the workhouse shared between the Staffordshire parishes of Gnosall and Penkridge was empowered in 1764 to feed and clothe all the poor 'who shall choose or be obliged' to enter, he was also required to indemnify the parish against any litigation which might result from his 'cruelty, barbarity or negligence'. Regimes like these suggest that parish workhouses had less and less in common with the houses of noble

[68] Hampson, *Treatment of the Poor in Cambridgeshire*, 75; R. M. Smith, 'Ageing and Well-Being in Early Modern England: Pension Trends and Gender Preferences under the English Old Poor Law, *c.*1650–1800', in P. Johnson and P. Thane (eds.), *Old Age from Antiquity to Post-Modernity* (London, 1998), 89; J.R. Kent, 'The Centre and the Localities: State Formation and Parish Government in England, *c.*1640–1740', *Historical Journal*, 38 (1995), 398–9; Kent, 'The Rural "Middling Sort" in Early Modern England, *circa* 1640–1740: Some Economic, Political and Socio-Cultural Characteristics', *Rural History*, 10 (1999), 34–5. It may well be that the existence of a workhouse in Frampton (Lincs.) helped drive down relief expenditure in the 1740s. Hindle, 'Power, Poor Relief and Social Relations', 81, 86. At Shipston on Stour (Worcs.), expenditure on pensions had been running at almost £60 a year until the poor were 'forced into the workhouse' in August 1735. WCRO, DR446/22, unfol. (3 Aug. 1735).

[69] Broad, 'Parish Economies of Welfare', 997–8; Kent, 'The Rural "Middling Sort"', 34–35; . Kent and S. King, 'Changing Patterns of Poor Relief in Some English Rural Parishes, *circa* 650–1750', *Rural History*, 14 (2003), 141.

[70] London Metropolitan Archives, London, DRO/5/c2/2 (8 July 1724).

poverty of the fifteenth century than they did with the model industrial villages of the nineteenth.[71]

These good intentions notwithstanding, workhouse regimes (like parish work schemes) might function only intermittently. At Ashwell there was a vestry coup less than twelve months after the 1728 resolution that reversed the decision to incarcerate the deserving poor and reintroduced a regime of outdoor relief. At Eaton Socon (Bedfordshire), parish policy was similarly overturned, apparently on the initiative of the vicar after a workhouse experiment lasting less than a decade, though the grounds for this decision probably had more to do with dissatisfaction at the failure of the workhouse scheme to stem the gradual rise in relief expenditure than with any sympathy on the part of the ratepayers for the plight of the elderly women made to work lace within its walls.[72] Within seven years of its foundation in 1733, the workhouse at Gnosall (Staffordshire) had become the subject of protracted litigation between a Uttoxeter clothier and the inhabitants, almost certainly because the governor had failed 'to see that nothing goes to loss' as the terms of his contract had required.[73]

Even though there were undoubtedly numerous rural parishes in which these initiatives enjoyed prolonged success, however, the parochial workhouse movement never affected more than a tiny proportion of the indigent population. In most rural communities, therefore, the employment of the poor remained a matter of providing occasional tasks to individual paupers: trenching the fields of Priors Hardwick (Warwickshire) in 1639, whipping dogs from the streets of Winston (Durham) in the 1690s, stone-picking and lace-making in mid-eighteenth-century Chalfont St Peter.[74] Despite the enthusiasm of contemporaries, therefore, historians have probably been correct to judge the provision of

[71] Cutlack, 'Gnosall Records', 100. Cf. the characterization of Higham Ferrers, where the Chichele almshouse was founded in 1427, as 'a virtual Chicheleville', in P. Morgan, 'Of Worms and War: 1380–1558', in P. C. Jupp and C. Gittings (eds.), *Death in England: An Illustrated History* (Manchester, 1999), 138; and of the daily grind of devotion expected of the bedesmen of Ewelme (*c.*1437–50) as 'more Victorian than Plantagenet', in C. Richmond, 'Victorian Values in Fifteenth-Century England: The Ewelme Almshouse Statutes', in R. Horrox and S. Rees-Jones (eds.), *Pragmatic Utopias: Ideals and Communities, 1200–1630* (Cambridge, 2001), 233.

[72] Broad, 'Parish Economies of Welfare', 997–8; Emmison, 'Relief of the Poor at Eaton Socon', 26–7. Drastic reversals of policy of this kind were apparently even more common in the urban context, with the workhouse test being abandoned after experiments of varying duration in Hull, Canterbury, Liverpool, and Leeds. Slack, *From Reformation to Improvement*, 134–5 n. 35.

[73] Cutlack, 'Gnosall Records', 95–8.

[74] SBTRO, DR37/85/6/52; Rushton, 'The Poor Law, the Parish and the Community', 139; G.C. Edmonds, 'Accounts of Eighteenth-Century Overseers of the Poor of Chalfont St Peter', *Records of Buckinghamshire*, 18 (1966), 20.

employment for the labouring poor as the 'least practical' of the clauses of the Elizabethan poor laws. Work for the under-employed evidently proved to be a weaker pillar of policy than either doles for the deserving or whipstocks for the wandering: parochial work schemes appear to have been successful only intermittently, if at all. To argue that late seventeenth-century overseers largely neglected their obligation to set the poor on work is not, however, to imply that labour was unimportant to them. On the contrary, parish officers and magistrates alike almost invariably insisted that relief was to be denied to those who were able to work towards their own support, and pensions were adjusted in line not only with the seasonality of the labour market but also with the productive capacities of individual paupers.[75] The work ethic was not, moreover, simply reinforced among adults: it was also inculcated amongst their offspring.

2. THE APPRENTICESHIP OF PAUPER CHILDREN

The 'best way of providing for the poor', argued Sir Simon Harcourt in 1705, was to apprentice their children.[76] The fate of this provision of the welfare regime—the enforcement of pauper apprenticeship at the expense of the parish—has, however, received little attention in the recent scholarship on seventeenth-century social welfare.[77] Most studies of the binding out of poor children have tended to focus on the

[75] See Chs. 6.2(*b*) and 6.2(*e*) below.

[76] BL, MS Harley, 5137, fo. 178.

[77] The seminal account is still O. J. Dunlop and R. D. Denman, *English Apprenticeship and Child Labour: A History* (London, 1912), 248–60 (Ch. 16: 'Apprenticeship as a Device of Poor Relief') and there is, of course, much of value in Leonard, *Early History of English Poor Relief*, 374 (index s.v. 'apprentices, poor children placed as'). More recent discussions, almost all of them extremely brief, include E. Lipson, 'The Relief of the Poor', in id., *The Economic History of England*, vol. iii: *The Age of Mercantilism* (6th edn., London, 1956), 435–9; I. Pinchbeck and M. Hewitt, *Children in English Society*, vol. i: *From Tudor Times to the Eighteenth Century* (London, 1969), 223–59 (Ch. 9: 'The Twin Disciplines of Work and Worship, I: Apprenticeship'), esp. 234 ff.; G. J. Ashworth, 'Some Uses of Apprenticeship Returns in Local Studies', *The Local Historian*, 8 (1969), 232–6; E. G. Thomas, 'The Old Poor Law and Maritime Apprenticeship', *Mariner's Mirror*, 63 (1977), 153–61; E. G. Thomas, 'Pauper Apprenticeship', *The Local Historian*, 14 (1981), 400–6; J. Lane, *Apprenticeship in England, 1600–1914* (London, 1996), 81–94; and M. K. McIntosh, 'Networks of Care in Elizabethan English Towns: The Example of Hadleigh, Suffolk', in P. Horden and R. M. Smith (eds.), *The Locus of Care: Families, Communities, Institutions and the Provision of Welfare Since Antiquity* (London, 1998), 83–5. M. G. Davies, *The Enforcement of English Apprenticeship, 1563–1642: A Study in Applied Mercantilism* (Cambridge, Mass., 1956), 12–13, eschewed discussion of parish apprenticeship because of its limited bearing on the enforcement of service contracts under the statute of artificers of 1563. More surprisingly, detailed treatments of pauper apprenticeship are conspicuous by their absence from both Slack, *Poverty and Policy* and P. Griffiths, *Youth and Authority: Formative Experiences in England, 1560–1640* (Oxford, 1996).

eighteenth century, partly because of the increased survival rate of indentures for that period and partly because of the enduring historiographical interest in the settlement laws, with which parish apprenticeship became closely intertwined.[78] Historians of the seventeenth century have generally been concerned with pauper apprenticeship only as an index of the efficiency of local government.[79] Indeed, so fragmentary is the existing scholarship that the current historiographical orthodoxy is bound to be impressionistic: in the early seventeenth century, it has been suggested, pauper apprenticeship 'may have made some modest contribution to dealing with the unemployed bulge in a relatively youthful population'.[80]

The following discussion investigates the problems and opportunities presented by the compulsory binding out as apprentices of the children of the labouring poor, focusing not only on the notorious difficulties experienced in coercing recalcitrant masters to accept them but also on the less familiar problem of persuading reluctant parents to let their young go into service. In part, it will be argued, these tensions arose from the legal ambiguities of the statutes themselves. Although the poor laws had not *explicitly* obliged either masters to receive apprentices or parents to give up their children, rulings by the Jacobean and Caroline judiciary emphasized that the statutes *implied* compulsion. Despite repeated challenges to the prerogative basis of the policy, the certificates returned to the privy council by county benches under the terms of the Caroline Book of Orders nonetheless suggest that by the 1630s magistrates and

[78] For studies based on apprenticeship indentures surviving in parish archives, see E. M. Hampson, 'Settlement and Removal in Cambridgeshire, 1662–1834', *Cambridge Historical Journal*, 2 (1926–8), 282–4; Emmison, 'The Relief of the Poor at Eaton Socon', 66–71; Cutlack, 'The Gnosall Records', 53–62; Hinton, 'Relief of the Poor of Lacock', 182–7; Jones, 'Trull Overseers' Accounts', 96–9; H. Fearn, 'The Apprenticing of Pauper Children in the Incorporated Hundreds of Suffolk', *Proceedings of the Suffolk Institute of Archaeology*, 26 (1955), 85–97; P. Anderson, 'The Leeds Workhouse under the Old Poor Law, 1726–1834', *The Thoresby Miscellany: Volume 17* (Thoresby Society 56, 1981), 99–104; M. B. Rose, 'Social Policy and Business: Parish Apprenticeship and the Early Factory System, 1750–1834', *Business History*, 31 (1989), 5–32; and P. Sharpe, 'Poor Children as Apprentices in Colyton, 1598–1830', *Continuity and Change*, 6 (1991), 253–70. For the relationship with the settlement laws, see K. D. M. Snell, *Annals of the Labouring Poor: Social Change and Agrarian England, 1660–1900* (Cambridge, 1985), 277–93; Snell, 'Settlement, Poor Law and the Rural Historian: New Approaches and Opportunities', *Rural History*, 3 (1992), 157–60.

[79] Fletcher, *Reform*, 215–17, provides a convenient summary. For the view that the obligation to apprentice poor children was widely forgotten, see G. W. Oxley, *Poor Relief in England and Wales, 1601–1834* (Newton Abbot, 1974), 74.

[80] Slack, *From Reformation to Improvement*, 66. For the youthful age-structure of early 17-century English society, see E. A. Wrigley and R. S. Schofield, *The Population History of England, 1541–1871: A Reconstruction* (Cambridge, 1981), 216 (fig. 7.4).

parish officers, if not employers, parents, or children, had been gradually persuaded of the merits of the policy. By placing these early seventeenth-century initiatives in the context of the enforcement of service contracts and wage regulation in the later Stuart period, the following discussion illuminates an under-explored area of early modern social policy. It reassesses the nature of social relations not only between parents and children, but also between employers, parish officers, magistrates, and the labouring poor; and restores work to its appropriate place at the heart of any consideration of the historical provision of welfare. As we shall see, the work stipulated by the statutes was 'husbandry and huswifery', the very occupations that Gervase Markham, writing in 1613, thought most fitting for 'Boyes and Girles, or other waste persons'.[81]

(*a*) Pauper Households and Labour Discipline

It has become axiomatic in recent historical scholarship that the household was the foundation stone of the early modern political nation, the institution through which the most fundamental cultural values of obedience, deference, and discipline were socially reproduced. The patriarchal language used by contemporaries to describe families has been reconstructed and the implications of its central idiom, that the household was the little commonwealth in which the authority of the father and husband was analogous to that of the monarch, more fully appreciated.[82] Indeed, the family is now understood as only the smallest of a series of concentric spheres of authority that expanded outwards from the household, to the parish, to the county (or 'country'), and ultimately to the realm itself.[83] It was by no means unusual for each of these concentric spheres to be described as a 'commonwealth' in its own right. The Hertfordshire clergyman Alexander Strange, for instance, described his own community as the 'little commonwealth of Layston' in 1636; the vestrymen of a Cornish parish similarly described themselves as the 'principal members of the commonwealth of Constantine' in 1596.[84]

[81] G. Markham, *The English Husbandman. The First Part* (London, 1613), sig. D4[b]. As A. McRae, *God Speed the Plough: The Representation of Agrarian England, 1500–1660* (Cambridge, 1996), 168, points out, this was a relatively novel use of 'waste' in the sense of 'offscourings, dregs, worthless people'.

[82] S. D. Amussen, *An Ordered Society: Gender and Class in Early Modern England* (Oxford, 1988), 34–66.

[83] K. Wrightson, 'The Politics of the Parish in Early Modern England', in P. Griffiths *et al.* (eds.), *The Experience of Authority in Early Modern England* (London and New York, 1996), 13–18 ('The Politics of Patriarchy').

[84] S. Hindle, 'A Sense of Place? Becoming and Belonging in the Rural Parish, 1550–1650', in A. Shepard and P. Withington (eds.), *Communities in Early Modern England* (Manchester, 2000), 98.

Ideally, these spheres of authority should have been perfectly congruent, the interests of fathers, parish officers, magistrates, and monarch working together in the interests of order and harmony.

The household was also, however, 'a well organized operational unit geared for work'.[85] Its resources were directed towards the satisfaction of the household's needs as a unit not only of consumption and reproduction but also of production.[86] The survival of households, especially among the labouring poor, depended upon contributions by all their members, contributions that were organized on the principle of hierarchical differentiation.[87] Roles were allocated according to prevailing assumptions about gender, age, and place. For the women of the labouring poor, whose responsibility it was to provision the family through the exploitation of tiny holdings and common rights, the opportunities for participation in household-based productive activity were rarer than they might be in manor house, farmyard, or workshop. For them, the flexibility and adaptability of the female role were principally conditioned by the rhythms of pregnancy, childbearing, and childrearing, which in turn ensured that they became the principal carers of the household. In such a context, it was expected that children too should play their role in the household economy. Although work skills were acquired early, the extent to which child labour was exploited should not be exaggerated. Even so, from the age of 7 or 8 most children had become part of the productive life of their families, and therefore contributed to, although they were unlikely to earn in full, their own keep. Until that age, the children of the poor in particular were 'likely to have been a charge on, rather than a significant asset to, the family economy'.[88]

In practice, however, the circuits of social authority and household production overlapped and intersected in curious ways. Indeed, pauper apprenticeship is of particular interest to students of social and economic relations precisely because it is earthed to one of those points of contact, indeed to a node of friction, in the local community. Under the terms of the Elizabethan poor laws, magistrates and parish officers were effectively empowered to *reconstitute* households by binding out not only orphans, but also pauper children, as apprentices, thereby reducing relief

[85] N. Tadmor, 'Concepts of the Family in Five Eighteenth-Century Texts' (unpublished Ph.D. diss., Cambridge University, 2002), 278.

[86] K. Wrightson, *Earthly Necessities: Economic Lives in Early Modern Britain* (New Haven, 2000), 30. The following paragraph draws heavily on Wrightson's vivid account of roles in the domestic economy.

[87] Tadmor, 'Concepts of the Family', 269.

[88] Wrightson, *Earthly Necessities*, 50.

expenditure by redistributing the burden of children from the less well-off to the more prosperous households within and beyond the parish. The relevant clause of the Elizabethan statute was laconic, referring only to the binding of children apprentice 'where they shall be convenient', but its implications became clear as the statute was subsequently glossed by privy councillors, judges, and magistrates.[89]

Compulsory pauper apprenticeship, it was argued, would inculcate those very virtues of industry and thrift that were all too frequently corrupted by the widespread practice of sending small children out begging. If begging was 'a school of idleness' as the puritan divine William Perkins thought, then parish apprenticeship was a school of industry in which the children of the poor in particular must be educated.[90] The anonymous author of the parish officers' handbook, *An Ease for Overseers of the Poore* (1601), provided the most coherent rationale for this policy. He noted that the world was becoming so 'populous and poore' precisely because 'in this age, the poorer sort of men are straight inclined to marry without any respect howe to live' and 'commonly the poor do most of all multiply children'.[91] The percipience of the Elizabethan poor laws therefore lay in the recognition that, 'although [children] bee blessings', they 'are a burden to many poore men'. The statutes accordingly provided that pauper children 'should be trained up to some honest trade of life, when their parents for povertie cannot performe it'.[92] Michael Dalton provided an even more idealized vision of the social function of pauper apprenticeship in 1635, when he argued in the authoritative magistrates' handbook, *The Country Justice*, that the binding out of the children of the poor was 'a seminarie of mercie'.[93] How, then, did judges, magistrates, and parish officers set about convincing the labouring poor and the prospective masters of their children of the desirability of the policy?

(*b*) Judicial Interpretations

From the very outset, the binding out of pauper children was arguably the most controversial issue in the judicial interpretation of the Elizabethan poor laws. Indeed, only the vexed question of settlement proved anything

[89] 39 Elizabeth I, c. 3 (1598), sect. iv.

[90] W. Perkins, 'An Instruction Touching Religious or Divine Worship', in *The Works of William Perkins*, ed. I. Breward (Abingdon, 1970), 319.

[91] *An Ease for Overseers of the Poore*, 26. For the wider resonance of these views, see S. Hindle, 'The Problem of Pauper Marriage in Seventeenth-Century England', *Transactions of the Royal Historical Society*, 6th ser., 8 (1998), 71–89, and Ch. 5.4 below.

[92] *An Ease for Overseers of the Poore*, 26.

[93] M. Dalton, *The Country Justice* (London, 1635 edn.), 94. This gloss on pauper apprenticeship is conspicuous by its absence from the 1618 edition.

like as problematic in this regard.[94] So much courtroom oratory was necessary not only because of the centrality of work and training to Elizabethan welfare provision, but also because the wording of the apprenticeship clauses of the 1598 act, confirmed in this respect as in so many others in 1601, was ambiguous: the children of those parents which '*shall not . . . be thought* able to kepe and mayntaine' them were to apprenticed until they reached specified ages (24 for men, 21 for women).[95] These clauses were not, it should be emphasized, principally concerned with orphans, since they assumed that at least one of the parents of poor children was still alive. The discretionary power of parish officers and magistrates therefore lay in determining whether the parents themselves were 'thought able' to bring up their children, either for the present or in the future. Overseers were advised to be circumspect both in choosing which children to apprentice, and to whom they should be bound. Parish officers were to distinguish between the child who 'by his labour' was 'able to keep himselfe and yeelde some releefe to his parents', who must be allowed to remain at home, and the child who was 'a burden and charge', who should be bound out. They should also have a keen eye to the 'facultie, honestie and abilitie' of the masters, lest they either provoke the apprentices to abscond or fail to provide adequate training and discipline.[96]

In interpreting the legislation, the judges initially trod carefully. Chief Justice Popham insisted that 'it is most convenient' for children between the ages of 7 and 16 to 'be put to apprentis and especially to husbandrye and huswifery'. This would by definition relieve those families who were 'overburthened through charge of children'. The parents of any poor

[94] P. Styles, 'The Evolution of the Law of Settlement', repr. in id., *Studies in Seventeenth-Century West Midlands History* (Kineton, 1978), 175–204. Cf. Chs. 5.2 and 5.3 below.

[95] 39 Elizabeth I, c. 3 (1598), sects. i, iv (emphasis added). An amendment in 1601 permitted poor girls to leave apprenticeship early in order to get married: 43 Elizabeth I, c. 2 (1601). When the act was continued in 1604, it was modified slightly to empower those who were given the custody of children by the overseers of the poor to take them on as apprentices, thereby formalizing the relationship between boarding and binding out. D. M. Dean, *Law-Making and Society in Late Elizabethan England: The Parliament of England, 1584–1601* (Cambridge, 1996), 280. The origins of the policy lie not in the statute of artificers (5 Elizabeth I, c. 4, 1563) but in the earliest poor relief legislation of the Reformation Parliament, which stipulated that children between the ages of 5 and 14 'that live in idleness who may be taken begging may be put to service': 27 Henry VIII, c. 25 (1535). Under 14 Elizabeth I, c. 5 (1572), beggars' children aged between 5 and 14 were to be bound out to farmers and others until the boys were 24 and the girls 18. In Scotland, parish apprenticeships under the terms of an act of 1574 were of even longer duration, being mandatory until the ages of 24 for boys and 28 for girls. Leonard, *Early History of English Poor Relief*, 279 n. 2.

[96] *An Ease for Overseers of the Poore*, 27.

children who remained at home unbound, he implied, were to be denied parish relief: 'for the rest of the children they must laye *at the charge of their parentes* to be relieved by the labour of their parents' rather than by the parish.[97] The eighth of the judges' 'resolutions' of 1599 concurred: 'if the parents be able and cannot gett worke they are to keepe their children by their owne labour and *nott* [*by*] *the parishe*, but if they be over burthened with children it shallbe a very good waye to procure some of them to be apprentices according to the statute'.[98] Under the terms of both rulings, it seems, poor parents were not legally compelled to comply with the apprenticeship of their children, but could easily be coerced into doing so. Persuasion of this kind was the corollary of the powerful discretionary impulse that lay at the heart of all seventeenth-century social policy. Perhaps its most extreme manifestation is revealed in the dynamics of the transportation of vagrant children to the American colonies in the period 1618–22. Any parents in the City of London who, being 'overcharged and burdened with poor children', refused to send them to Virginia were to be told that they would not receive any further poor relief from the parish until they complied.[99] By the late 1610s, then, Popham's doctrine of 'implied compulsion' was becoming something of a mantra, and was rehearsed verbatim by Chief Justice Montagu in 1617.[100]

The judges were, however, concerned to demonstrate that the discretionary binding out of pauper apprentices was not merely a matter of expediency, but also one of conscience. In the first place, it was in the putative interests of the child him- or herself. As the Lancashire bench put it in 1618, pauper apprenticeship was appropriate for all those poor children 'whose parents are not able to breed them wooll [*sic*: ?well]'.[101] In the second, parish officers had a moral obligation to protect ratepayers from the unnecessary inflation of welfare costs. Montagu recognized as much in 1617 when he justified parish apprenticeships on the grounds that the tax base could not otherwise cope with the demands of children: 'there are a multitude of poor through idleness in all places which if they should be relieved whollie by charritie would be more burthensome than

[97] HMC, *Report on the Manuscripts of the Marquess of Lothian Preserved at Blickling* (London, 1905), 76 (emphasis added). For the genesis of this reading see Ch. 6.4(*b*) below.

[98] W. Lambarde, *Eirenarcha* (London, 1599), 206 ff. (here quoting resolution no. 9, emphasis added). For these resolutions, see Ch. 6.4(*b*) below.

[99] R. C. Johnson, 'The Transportation of Vagrant Children from London to Virginia, 1618–1622', in H. S. Reinmuth (ed.), *Early Stuart Studies: Essays in Honour of David Harris Willson* (Minneapolis, 1970), 142.

[100] Bodl., MS Tanner, 243, fo. 14.

[101] *Proceedings of the Lancashire Justices of the Peace at the Sheriff's Table during Assize Week, 1578–1694*, ed. B. W. Quintrell (Record Society of Lancashire and Cheshire, 121, Chester, 1981), 176.

the better sort are well able to bear'.[102] Characteristically, Lord Keeper Bacon chose to emphasize the economic advantages of the policy to the commonwealth in general, and to the textile industry in particular, when he urged the judges to monitor the binding out of poor children as parish apprentices to 'cherish manufactures, old and new, especially draperies'.[103] These apologies notwithstanding, pauper apprenticeship remained a profoundly controversial item on the agenda of governors of county and parish alike, especially after the Caroline Book of Orders emphasized its centrality to the operation of the Elizabethan poor laws.

The Book of Orders was issued on 31 January 1631. Its third 'direction', significantly ranking pauper apprenticeship ahead of the enforcement of both the statute of artificers and the relief of the poor by rates, stipulated that 'the poore children in every parish' were to 'be put forth apprentices to husbandry, and other handy-crafts'; that 'money [was] to be raised in the parishes for placing them'; and that 'if any party shall refuse to take the said apprentice, being put out according to the law', he was to 'be bound over to the next quarter sessions, or assizes, and there to be bound to his good behaviour, or otherwise ordered, as shall be found fit'.[104] The intention was clearly to reduce the burden on rates by alleviating life-cycle poverty. Ratepayers, however, came to feel that they were doubly charged, financing both pensions and premiums. As early as June 1631 the Hertfordshire yeoman John Dards of Knebworth was hauled before the privy council and committed to the Fleet prison for having publicly challenged the legality of pauper apprenticeship. He had argued in open sessions that ratepayers had 'sufficiently provided for their poore and therefore for them to take or put forth theire Prentizes was more than they were compellable to by lawe and that the direccions of the Lords of the Councell could not impose any such thing upon them'.[105] By April 1632 the council was becoming suspicious of passive resistance among the justices, whose silence, it argued, would henceforth be construed as an admission of negligence. By 1633, the binding out of pauper children had proved so controversial that Lord Keeper Coventry's charge to the judges began with the injunction that a 'strict course be taken against

[102] Bodl., MS Tanner, 243, fo. 14. Montague then went on to reiterate verbatim Popham's order of 1598. The parish officers of Marke rehearsed the formula back to the Somerset bench when they sought to compel recalcitrant masters to co-operate with an enforcement drive on pauper apprenticeship in 1621. *Quarter Sessions Records of the County of Somerset*, ed. E. H. Bates-Harbin (4 vols., Somerset Record Society, 23, 24, 28, 34, Taunton, 1907–19), i. 300.

[103] *The Works of Francis Bacon*, ed. J. Spedding *et al.* (14 vols., London, 1857–74), xiii. 302–6.

[104] 'The Book of Orders', sigs. G–G^{v}.

[105] *APC*, xlvi (1630–1), 386, 388, 401–2; NA, PC2/42, 410–11.

them that oppose' it.[106] The first serious attempt to settle the controversy occurred in 1633, when Chief Justice Heath was asked to rule on a number of controversies which had arisen in the parishes on the Norfolk circuit.[107] The first seven of the thirty-eight questions turned on the legality of compulsory pauper apprenticeship. By now, magistrates and parish officers were wondering whether they had authority to force not only poor parents to allow their children to be bound, but also whether they might compel reluctant employers to take them on. As far as Heath was concerned, both masters and parents could be compelled: the act of 1601, he insisted, 'necessarily implyeth that such as are fit must receive apprentices' (resolution 1). Indeed, no social rank was exempt from accepting pauper children (resolution 3), and any ratepayer could be taxed to finance the expense of the premium (if any), the value of which was left to the discretion of the parish officers and if necessary arbitrated by the JPs (resolution 2). Those who refused to accept such apprentices should be bound over and, failing that, committed to gaol (resolutions 6 and 7). Further recalcitrance should result in indictment for contempt or ultimately even a summons for personal appearance before the privy council. Any parents refusing to have their children bound 'or being bound intise them away' were not only to be denied relief but also sent to the house of correction (resolution 7).[108]

There was also, moreover, an important spatial dimension to the 1633 resolutions, since Heath argued that apprentices could be placed not only within the parish, but also beyond its borders in other parishes in the county (resolution 5). It is often argued that, in stipulating that legal apprenticeship actually *created* a settlement, the 1662 and 1691 settlement laws encouraged the policy of binding out apprentices to foreign parishes in order to remove a potential liability from the resident ratepayers. It is, however, clear that judicial interpretation of the Elizabethan statutes had tended in this direction for almost thirty years. Indeed, Heath explicitly argued that 'servants and apprentices are by law settled' in the parish where they were in service (resolution 25).[109] In one respect, this policy amounted to an indirect means by which neighbouring parishes provided a form of 'rate-in-aid' for a particularly overburdened community, since the weight of the poor in one parish could be distributed more evenly on a number of her neighbours.

[106] NA, PC2/41, 545; NA, SP16/232/42.

[107] For the resolutions and their impact, see Ch.6.4(*b*) below.

[108] NA, SP16/255/46, printed in *Somerset Assize Orders, 1629–1640*, ed. T. G. Barnes (Somerset Record Society, 65, Taunton, 1959), 63–70 (no.186).

[109] Ibid. 68.

In some respects, Heath's decisions created more problems than they solved. Their authority was not always accepted unquestioningly. Although popularly known as the 'resolutions of all the judges', Heath's brethren in the Exchequer Chamber apparently refused to subscribe to them, and Justice Twisden denied their validity in King's Bench in 1676, brusquely dismissing a barrister who had cited Heath in support of compulsory apprenticeship with the retort, 'Why do you use that as an authority which all the judges disclaimed?'[110] They were certainly subject to legal challenge. In one case, at least, Heath dashed the hopes of the recalcitrant. The Somerset attorney Thomas Trevellian of Langport argued that as 'a wealthy man keeping few or noe servants' he was liable only to contribute towards costs of binding out apprentices rather than actually to receive one himself, and he referred, unsuccessfully as it turned out, to the recently issued resolutions for a final settlement of the matter.[111] Much more serious were those reservations expressed by those same local officers who were responsible for enforcing the policy. The resistance of John Potkins, churchwarden of Pluckley (Kent), who refused to take an apprentice even when offered a premium in 1633, undermined the whole enterprise in a parish riven by factional strife between a 'busy' magistrate on the one hand and a parish elite (including the clergyman) that he regarded as complacent on the other.[112] Perhaps the most serious objections, however, arose among magistrates themselves. The Hertfordshire JP Thomas Coningsby was dismissed from his commission in January 1633 and subsequently fined £1,000 in Star Chamber for publicly declaring his opinion that enforced apprenticeship was illegal. Coningsby's were precisely the kind of objections that George Cock had in mind in 1651 when he condemned 'the pettish wilfulness or niggardliness of some men in authority' who construed the imposition of a pauper child on a reluctant master to be 'against the libertie of the subject'.[113]

[110] *Somerset Assize Orders, 1629–1640*, p. xxviii; Dalton, *The Country Justice* (1727 edn.), 231.

[111] NA, SP16/239/6; PC2/43, 71. Trevellian's position turned on the distinction made in Heath's third and fourth resolutions between those whose callings required them to hire other servants (who could therefore be compelled to take parish children) and those who had no personal use for servants (who could only be taxed towards binding parish children out). Since Heath did not explicitly include attorneys in the latter category, Trevellian was forced to submit. T. G. Barnes, *Somerset, 1625–40: A County's Government during the Personal Rule* (Cambridge, Mass., 1961), 185–6.

[112] NA, SP16/240/35; PC2/43, 98. The tensions in Pluckley, where at least three parishioners (including Potkins and the minister John Copley) refused to take apprentices in 1633, are reconstructed in Davie, 'Custom and Conflict', 267–70, 331–47. Cf. P. Clark, *English Provincial Society from the Reformation to the Revolution: Religion, Politics and Society in Kent, 1500–1640* (Hassocks, 1977), 352.

[113] Coningsby compounded his original offence of alleging that 'his fellow justices did more

The increased assiduity with which magistrates applied the apprenticeship policy in the years 1633–5 almost certainly owes something to Heath, though arguably also to Archbishop Laud, 'a well-known sponsor of charities for poor children'.[114] Heath himself certainly reiterated the message to the Somerset assizes at Chard in 1638: 'for prevention of charge that cometh upon parishes by children which live idely and be fitting to be bound forth apprentices', any recalcitrant parents were to be committed to the house of correction whether or not they were actually in receipt of the 'almes of the parish'. For the next three decades, the judges upheld the compulsive spirit (if not the letter) of the law as interpreted by Heath. Sergeant Wilde exemplified this stance in a decision at the Salisbury summer assizes in 1648, when one recalcitrant master was actually committed to gaol.[115] By 1651, however, George Cock was arguing that the usual procedure of binding recalcitrant masters to answer for their contempt at quarter sessions had little or no effect, since magistrates felt themselves 'plagued and maliciously vexed with attendance' and 'lawyers make such work for their clients as they go home without fine or any other punishment'.[116]

The first judicial decision against compulsion came after the Restoration, perhaps as part of the backlash against the prerogative basis of much early Stuart social policy, the arbitrary nature of which tainted pauper apprenticeship by association.[117] From 1679, the judges at the Staffordshire assizes were discharging employers of the apprentices which they had reluctantly taken on, citing as their justification a declaration 'by all the Judges that no employer ought by law to be so enforced'. Even so, judicial opinion on the issue was still divided into the very late seventeenth century. Dalton's *Country Justice* had to concede in 1682 that the compulsive powers that lay behind pauper apprenticeship were 'never judicially & solemnly resolved'. Matthew Hale noted in 1683 that the act

than they could justifie' by showing contempt for the threat of Star Chamber process: he was not, he affirmed, 'the sonne of feare'. NA, PC2/42, 410; Barnes, *Somerset*, 186 n. 30; G. C. Cock, *English-Law; or, a Summary Survey of the Household of God on Earth* (London, 1651), 50.

[114] Leonard, *Early History of English Poor Relief*, 216–17, 295. For criticism of Leonard's view that the 'orders and directions' were originally *formulated* by Laud (and by Wentworth), however, see B. W. Quintrell, 'The Making of Charles I's Book of Orders', *English Historical Review*, 95 (1980), 556–7.

[115] *Western Circuit Assize Orders, 1629–1648: A Calendar*, ed. J. S. Cockburn (Camden Society, 4th ser., 17, London, 1976), 144–5, 286 (nos. 613, 1198). For the subsequent decisions in favour of compulsion, see Parish of Henton (Kent) *vs.* Steers (1654) and Rex *vs.* Gislifer (1663) in E. Bott, *A Collection of Decisions of the Court of King's Bench upon the Poor's Laws* (2 vols., London, 1793 edn.), i. 540–1.

[116] Cock, *English-Law*, 50.

[117] Slack, *Reformation to Improvement*, 53–76 (Ch. 3: 'Absolute Power').

did not explicitly compel masters to take parish apprentices.[118] The upshot was that various county benches reached conflicting decisions. In 1688 Sir Edward Lutwyche charged the Lancashire bench that, although 'some judges have been of contrary opinion', the 1601 act 'undoubtedly *by implicacion*' (note Heath's formulation here) empowered JPs to compel recalcitrant masters. After further consultation with Lutwyche and his fellow judge Sir Edward Powell, the JPs satisfied themselves that compulsory pauper apprenticeship would 'much tend to lessen the numbers of the poor and conduce greatly to the ease and benefit of the Country', and accordingly resolved to recommend Lutwyche's opinion to all the other justices in the county. 'Their care', Lutwyche insisted, 'should be to have the poor provided for that they should not need nor be permitted to wander and beg abroad as they now doe to the great reproach of the Country.' Instead, the JPs should reform or punish not only 'the vagabond that will not be reclaymed' but also the 'remiss overseers' who refused to enforce pauper apprenticeship. At the Aylesbury sessions of January 1690, by contrast, 'upon the complaint of several parishioners of High Wycombe', the opinion of the Buckinghamshire JPs was given that 'no persons ought to be burthened with parish children as apprentices against their consents'.[119]

The practical difficulties created by these inconsistencies are nicely revealed in the protracted dispute over the legality of forcing masters to take apprentices in the Warwickshire parish of Solihull. The parish officers and ratepayers of Solihull had their differences about the principle of enforced pauper apprenticeship as early as 1662, but they resurfaced in earnest whenever attempts were made to bind out large numbers of parish children simultaneously: nine in 1677, a further five in 1679, and another eight in 1685. During these decades the parish officers repeatedly updated lists of the most suitable masters, and regularly had to withstand appeals to the justices that they were acting illegally. Even the vicar Henry Greswold was subject to a justices' order of this kind in 1679.[120]

[118] NA, ASSI2/1, fo. 306; Dalton, *Country Justice* (1682 edn.), 151; Hale, *Provision for the Poor*, 4.

[119] *Proceedings of the Lancashire Justices of the Peace*, 154 (emphasis added); *County of Buckingham: Calendar to the Sessions Records*, ed. W. Le Hardy and G. L. Reckitt (4 vols., Aylesbury, 1934–51), i. 322.

[120] The dispute can be traced in *Warwick County Records*, ed. S. C. Ratcliff *et al.* (9 vols., Warwick, 1935–64), iv. 193; vii. 76, 107, 149; viii. 63, 65, 126, 128, 138, 166, 174, 200, 240, 245, 253, 261, 269; ix. 3, 14. For a similarly hard-fought campaign in a late 17th-century Buckinghamshire parish, see J. Broad, 'The Smallholder and Cottager after Disafforestation: A Legacy of Poverty?', in J. Broad and R. Hoyle (eds.), *Bernwood: The Life and Afterlife of a Forest* (Preston, 1997), 102–3. On clerical desire for exemption from compulsory apprenticeship even

The legal basis of pauper apprenticeship was finally resolved only in the parliamentary session of 1696–7, when 8 & 9 William III, c. 30 stipulated that local masters and mistresses might be forced to take quotas of parish apprentices, and fined heavily if they refused to do so.[121] By the time the compulsory obligation of ratepayers to receive parish apprentices was abolished in 1844, moreover, a very extensive body of legislation afforded what may have been greater legal protection to parish apprentices than to their private counterparts, a corpus which was created partly because of the widely recognized tensions consequent upon the export of the children of the poor into the houses of their wealthier neighbours.[122] For a century, the Stuart regime had wrestled with the ambiguities of the Elizabethan legislation, creating space for local negotiation of a policy which was as controversial in rural vestries and in the cottages of the labouring poor as it was in the court of King's Bench.

(*c*) Popular Responses

Despite the ambiguous legal basis of pauper apprenticeship, there is some patchy evidence of precocious enthusiasm for the policy, with parishes such as Elmstead (Essex), Lacock (Wiltshire), and Shorne (Kent), which each bound out three children in 1598, complying almost immediately. By 1606, the overseers of Cawston were able to list twenty-two prospective apprentices, though they could identify only three masters prepared to take any of them on.[123] In some communities, such as Great Bentley and Wivenhoe (both Essex), where the earliest pauper apprenticeship indentures survive from 1577 and 1578 respectively; Colyton (Devon), where the parish officers had bound out fifty-five children by the turn of the seventeenth century; or Eaton Socon (Bedfordshire), where the equivalent of a year's poor relief expenditure was spent 'for putting forthe of the childrinn' in 1595, pauper apprenticeship evidently predated the 1598 statute. In these parishes, perhaps (as at Walsham le Willows, Suffolk or Great Berkhamsted, Hertfordshire),

after the act of 1697, see HMC, *Twelfth Report, Appendix, Part II: The Manuscripts of the Earl Cowper, K.G., Preserved at Melbourne Hall, Derbyshire*, vol. ii (London, 1888), 387 (Revd John Ward to Thomas Coke, 15 Mar. 1699).

[121] 8 & 9 William III, c. 30 (1697). In 18th-century Leeds, these fines generated income of at least £8,340 in the years 1730–1808. Anderson, 'The Leeds Workhouse under the Old Poor Law', 112 (appendix 1).

[122] Snell, *Annals*, 284–5 n. 32; Snell, 'The Apprenticeship System in British History: The Fragmentation of a Cultural Institution', *History of Education*, 25 (1996), 312 n. 24.

[123] Emmison, 'The Care of the Poor in Elizabethan Essex', 22–3; Hinton, 'The Relief of the Poor of Lacock', 182–3; Allen, 'An Early Poor Law Account', 83; Norfolk RO, MC148/17–18.

it evolved from the 'boarding out' system which was widely practised (primarily for orphans) in the Suffolk parishes of Hadleigh, Sudbury, or Wattisfield in the Elizabethan period.[124]

The policy was evidently far easier to enforce in those parishes, such as Henley (Oxfordshire), where a local charity endowed for the specific purpose of financing pauper apprenticeship provided funds to induce reluctant masters to undertake the commitment, sometimes by offering premiums twice or three times as generous as the nominal sums that would otherwise have been paid by overseers.[125] Indeed, it was not uncommon for those with experience of administering parish relief to endow charities specifically for the purposes of apprenticing pauper children. When Thomas Alcock, vestryman, churchwarden, and overseer of Prescot (Lancashire), died in 1653, he left £50 to the parish for the apprenticing of poor boys.[126] Particularly influential charities of this kind were endowed at Low and High Ham (Somerset), in Myddle (Shropshire), and in Denham (Suffolk) in 1672.[127] Indeed the Gough charity was responsible for the binding out of twenty-seven children in the years 1672–1701. One of the most influential charities of all, that endowed by Henry Smith in 1626, seems to have been administered with the discipline of children particularly in mind. In Kingston-upon-Thames (Surrey), for example, the churchwardens used Smith's endowment for 'the maintenance and setting on work of the poor of the said town and for the

[124] Emmison, 'The Care of the Poor in Elizabethan Essex', 13, 14; Sharpe, 'Poor Children', 259; Emmison, 'Poor Relief Accounts', 110; M. K. McIntosh, 'Local Responses to the Poor in Late Medieval and Tudor England', *Continuity and Change*, 3 (1988), 232, 244 n. 95; McIntosh, 'Networks of Care in Elizabethan English Towns', 84. Cf. Ch. 1.4 above. Parish officers within the Landrich hundred of Norfolk were empowered to bind out poor children from 1595. W. B. H. Chandler, 'Directions to Overseers of the Poor, 1595', *Norfolk Archaeology*, 32 (1961), 230–1.

[125] Thomas, 'Pauper Apprenticeship', 400. For discussion of several Yorkshire charities endowed for subsidizing the costs of parish apprenticeship, see W. K. Jordan, *The Charities of Rural England, 1480–1640: The Aspirations and Achievements of the Rural Society* (London, 1961), 288. Jordan notes, however, that only one-quarter of the value of benefactions for the support of apprenticeship schemes in his sample was vested in parish officers to provide premiums for pauper children, the remainder being donated to secure footholds for poor boys in the named and recognized companies and guilds. W. K. Jordan, *Philanthropy in England, 1480–1660: A Study of the Changing Pattern of English Social Aspirations* (London, 1959), 268.

[126] *Prescot Churchwardens' Accounts, 1635–1663*, ed. T. Steele (Record Society of Lancashire and Cheshire, 137, Stroud, 2002), 71 n.

[127] SARS, Q\SPET/1/51; P. Collinson, 'Magistracy and Ministry: A Suffolk Miniature', repr. in id., *Godly People: Essays in English Protestantism and Puritanism* (London, 1983), 463; D. Hey, *An English Rural Community: Myddle under the Tudors and Stuarts* (Leicester, 1974), 217. For other examples see W. E. Tate, *The Parish Chest: A Study of the Records of Parochial Administration in England* (3rd edn., Cambridge, 1960), 116–17; Jordan, *Charities of Rural England*, 50, 60, 130–1, 287–8, 433.

education and bringing up of poor people in some good Christian course and trade of life'.[128]

Irrespective of such endowments, the judges certainly maintained the pressure on overseers across the country. Parish relief of the poor by apprenticing children was included in articles to JPs from the second decade of the seventeenth century: in Norfolk and Suffolk in 1617, for example, and in the West Riding and Lancashire in 1618.[129] There is some evidence of an attempt at systematic, if patchy, enforcement. While the Norfolk justices claimed in response to have placed 500 children out, the Suffolk bench had been almost entirely negligent.[130] Occasionally, individual parishes themselves sought to sweep the households of the labouring poor clean of their wasting assets irrespective of the existence of a county-wide campaign. At Marke (Somerset) in 1621, the parish officers appointed five masters 'to take as many children into their service whereof the masters were content'. In 1628 the two resident magistrates of the sprawling Lancashire parish of Rochdale bound out 180 apprentices who had previously been 'chargeable to the countrey by beging'.[131] Even so, it is difficult to be sure how sustained these initiatives were. Although the Hertfordshire bench, for example, apprenticed over 1,500 poor children when moved to do so by the judges in 1619, the grand jury complained in 1624 that most of them had left their masters and 'now live idly at home with their friends to the hurt of the common wealthe'.[132] Even if the policy had succeeded, however, the Hertfordshire bench had evidently co-operated only because they saw parish apprenticeship as a lesser evil than the 'verry troublesome and chargeable' new draperies scheme envisaged by Walter Morrell. Indeed, the deputy lieutenants of Hertfordshire informed the council in 1620 that they had 'founde the Cuntrey the rather willing to take the said children apprentices to husbandry, for that they did hope in soe doinge they should be eased' of Morrell's project.[133] Even this early initiative suggests that magistrates were prepared to enforce the policy only when they could see no realistic alternative. By the early 1620s, the stand-off between the council and the

[128] Hey, *An English Rural Community*, 178; *Kingston-upon-Thames Register of Apprentices, 1563–1713*, ed. A. Daly (Surrey Record Society, 28, Guildford, 1974), pp. xi. 141 (no.1488).

[129] BL, MS Additional, 39245, fo. 4 (reverse foliation); *West Riding Sessions Records, 1597–1642*, ed. J. Lister (2 vols., Yorkshire Archaeological Society Record Series, 3, 54, Leeds, 1888–1915), i. 397; *Proceedings of the Lancashire Justices of the Peace*, 176.

[130] BL, MS Additional, 39245, fo. 4.

[131] *Quarter Sessions Records of the County of Somerset*, i. 300; NA, SP16/273/56.

[132] *Calendar of Assize Records: Hertfordshire Indictments, James I*, ed. J. S. Cockburn (London, 1975), 275 (no. 1369).

[133] NA, SP14/115/13. Cf. Zell, '"Setting the Poor on Work"'.

county benches had reached stalemate. Sir Julius Caesar, Master of the Rolls, was informed in 1624 that the vagrancy problem was so acute in Norfolk precisely because overseers had failed to enforce the apprenticeship clauses of the Elizabethan statutes, with the result that the young were 'so tainted and infected with idleness as with a leprosie which is almost incurable'.[134]

It was, however, the Book of Orders and more particularly the acute social problems of the years 1629–31 to which it was a response, that most effectively galvanized the magistrates into activity, especially in the two or three years after Heath had reiterated the compulsory logic of the legislation. Apprenticing parish children was generally a feature of hard times.[135] This impression is confirmed by systematic analysis of the magistrates' reports to the privy council in the 1630s, which provide the clearest, though by no means unambiguous, evidence of popular response to the policy.[136] The certificates are, sadly, highly inconsistent on the numbers of children bound. When the privy council collated sixty-three certificates from eighteen counties which had been submitted in 1633, only eighteen (29 per cent) gave explicit statistical detail on the enforcement of the policy. Although caution should be used in the aggregation of figures which are sometimes suspiciously rounded, the scale of the achievement is nonetheless impressive. These eighteen certificates (drawn, remarkably from only five counties) give a combined total of 2,292 pauper children bound apprentice—74 in Kent, 106 in Sussex, 200 in Rutland, 285 in Surrey, and 1,627 in Yorkshire—within the space of

[134] BL, MS Additional, 12496, fo. 258 (Francis Williamson to Sir Julius Caesar, 26 Aug. 1624).

[135] J. Lane, *The Administration of an Eighteenth-Century Warwickshire Parish: Butlers Marston* (Dugdale Society Occasional Papers, 21, Stratford-upon-Avon, 1973), 17, notes that after 1760 the apprenticing of poor children was generally a feature of years of disaster.

[136] The magistrates' certificates in NA, SP16 provide the basis of the following discussion. For very brief preliminary work on apprenticeship as revealed by the certificates for individual counties, see J. Hurstfield, 'County Government: Wiltshire, *c.*1530–1660', repr. in id., *Freedom, Corruption and Government in Elizabethan England* (London, 1973), 272–4; Barnes, *Somerset*, 185–7; A. Fletcher, *A County Community in Peace and War: Sussex, 1600–1660* (London, 1975), 157–8; Clark, *English Provincial Society*, 350–3; C. Holmes, *Seventeenth-Century Lincolnshire* (Lincoln, 1980), 109–12; S. K. Roberts, *Recovery and Restoration in an English County: Devon Local Administration, 1646–1670* (Exeter, 1985), 183; A. Hughes, *Politics, Society and Civil War in Warwickshire, 1620–1660* (Cambridge, 1987), 57–8; A. Duffin, *Faith and Faction: Politics and Religion of the Cornish Gentry before the Civil War* (Exeter, 1996), 114–17. The best survey of local response to the requirements of the book of orders is H. Langelüddecke, '"Patchy and Spasmodic": The Response of Justices of the Peace to Charles I's Book of Orders', *English Historical Review*, 113 (1998), 1231–48; and the best introductions to the genesis of the orders themselves is Quintrell, 'The Making of Charles I's Book of Orders'. For the pre-history of the orders, see P. Slack, 'Books of Orders: The Making of English Social Policy, 1577–1631', *Transactions of the Royal Historical Society*, 5th ser., 30 (1980), 1–22.

one calendar year.[137] Numerous other statistical reports are scattered around the certificates, some of them bearing striking testimony to the zeal of parish officers and magistrates alike.[138] In other cases, silences are eloquent. Of the twenty-seven parishes in the Ashendon hundred of Buckinghamshire which reported in 1636, for instance, not a single one had bound out a poor child.[139]

Nonetheless, the evidence of parish papers suggests that the Caroline enforcement drive really did have a marked effect in local communities. Nineteen (over 6 per cent) of all the pauper children documented as apprenticed in seventeenth-century Colyton were bound out in the year 1631 alone, and over half of the surviving indentures for Eaton Socon date from the 1630s. The parish constables of Gissing made at least three appearances before the Norfolk justices concerning apprentices in 1631.[140] *Forty* boys and girls from Cuckfield (Sussex) were bound out at a single sitting of the vestry there in January 1634. Indeed, assuming that the parish of Cuckfield had a population of approximately 1,200 in the early 1630s, then perhaps 17 per cent of all children aged 7–16 were bound out in one go on 21 January 1634, and another 11 per cent on 6 March 1699.[141] The cumulative significance of these figures is striking. The (significantly precise) figure of 1,526 pauper apprentices bound out in Hertfordshire in 1619 might represent as many as 30 per cent of all the boys and girls in the county aged between 7 and 16.[142]

Although there is, therefore, abundant evidence that magistrates and parish officers might be persuaded to seek masters for poor children, it is nonetheless clear that employers resisted the policy, sometimes actively. The objections of masters were predictable and exceed even their chorus

[137] NA, SP16/259/88. Twenty-two others referred to unspecified numbers of children bound (although one of these to 'a great number'). The remaining twenty-three made no reference at all to pauper apprenticeship.

[138] For what it is worth, in a sample of fifty certificates from various counties which included (usually, of course, suspiciously rounded) numbers bound in the period 1634–7, the binding out of some 3,924 children is itemized. NA, SP16/267–363.

[139] NA, SP16/328/6.

[140] Sharpe, 'Poor Children', 259–60; Emmison, 'Poor Relief Accounts', 67 n. 157; J. Kent, *The English Village Constable 1580–1642: A Social and Administrative Study* (Oxford, 1986), 192–3.

[141] *Mid-Sussex Poor Law Records, 1601–1835*, ed. N. Pilbeam and I. Nelson (Sussex Record Society, 83, Lewes, 2000), 101, 128–9, 136–7.

[142] *Calendar of Assize Records: Hertfordshire Indictments, James I*, 275. This approximate calculation assumes that no more than 20% of the population was aged between 7 and 16. Wrigley and Schofield, *Population History*, 528 (table A3.1), suggests that the proportion aged between 5 and 14 in 1621 was 20.74%. It also assumes that the population of Hertfordshire was approximately 25,000 in the early 17th century. L. Munby, *Hertfordshire Population Statistics, 1563–1801* (Hitchin, 1964), 21, suggests that there were 5,526 'families' in the county in 1603. *Mid-Sussex Poor Law Records*, 101, 128–9, 136–7.

of disapproval with respect to the 1563 statute of artificers.[143] Employers were both resentful of zealous magistrates and suspicious of idle children. 'Most men', reported the Yorkshire justices in May 1631, were 'desirous to free themselves of the burden'.[144] Accordingly, it was especially difficult to find sufficient numbers of employers for pauper children. By June 1631 the JPs of Norfolk had 'bound out apprentice [only] soe manie poore children as wee can find masters fitt to be charged with such', implying that the supply of masters had been exhausted.[145] In 1637 the vicar of St John's Hereford urged the mayor and magistrates there 'to command' compliance with the statute by those known 'to be able men and fitt to take' as apprentices the 'many poore children whose parents are no wayes able to bring them up'.[146]

The situation was exacerbated in years of high prices. In May 1631, the justices of Fawsley (Northamptonshire) found pauper apprenticeship 'somewhat difficult in respect of the hardness of the tymes'. 'Those masters who should take apprentices', they reported, 'seeme somewhat unwilling to increase their charges as feeling the burthen of their own familyes already.' The Devon bench, which had combined the apprenticeship of children with the billeting (i.e. boarding) of those too young to work, despaired of enforcing the policy, 'considering the great burthens of the persons of every quality and deadness of the time'. These protests chime with the common assumption that servants were dismissed in years of high prices.[147] Even when prices fell, there were problems securing apprenticeship contracts in an agrarian economy in which the demand for labour fluctuated markedly over the course of the year. The Norfolk bench acknowledged in the summer of 1634 that pauper apprenticeship had to be accommodated with the seasonal demands of the local labour market. Although they noted that a few children had recently been apprenticed, they could fulfil their intention 'to putt forth as many as we can find masters for' only after 'the end of harvest'.[148]

Even after indentures were signed, however, there were abuses on

[143] Davies, *The Enforcement of English Apprenticeship*, pt. II, *passim*.

[144] NA, SP16/190/56.

[145] NA, SP16/193/40. This formula is repeated in three other Norfolk certificates SP16/310/104, 329/23–4.

[146] HMC, *Thirteenth Report, Appendix, Part IV: The Manuscripts of Rye and Hereford Corporations Capt. Loder Symonds, Mr E. R. Wodehouse MP, and Others* (London, 1892), 341.

[147] NA, SP16/191/67, 189/5. H. Arthington, *Provision for the Poore, Now in Penurie* (London 1597), sig. C2; A. Standish, *New Directions of Experience to the Commons Complaint by the Incouragement of the Kings Most Excellent Maiesty, As May Appeare for the Planting of Timber and Fire-wood* (London 1611), 16; J. Cook, *Unum Necessarium: Or, The Poor Man's Case: Being An Expedient to Make Provision for all Poore People in the Kingdome* (London, 1647), 5.

[148] NA, SP16/272/44.

both sides. Disputes were ubiquitous and were most commonly adjudicated at quarter sessions, where parish apprenticeship seems to have been much more controversial than its non-parochial equivalent in the 1630s.[149] Outwardly compliant masters might subsequently prove themselves to be devious and fraudulent, abusing or maltreating unwanted children to the extent that they would abscond, and some employers were doubtless serial offenders in this respect.[150] As early as May 1631, Norfolk JPs were concerned about 'such poor children as departed from service unlawfully or are by their masters cast off least any by such ways should be inforced to become rogues'.[151] By July 1632, the Cambridgeshire JPs had been forced to take action against those who had taken apprentices but 'had putt them away' by this kind of stratagem, and had 'settled them againe with their said masters where they remayne quietly'.[152] The Nottinghamshire justices adopted a similar policy of forcing masters to take back those children they had unlawfully discharged, and backed it up with a fine of a shilling a week for those who were reluctant to comply.[153] That reluctance was almost certainly encouraged by the increasing association of the poor with dirt, pollution, and peril, and of their offspring with inherited traits of idleness and disobedience. The clothiers and other tradesmen of Wiltshire were particularly unwilling to take pauper apprentices on the grounds that the children of the poor were 'for the most part untrustye and theevishe and therefore daungerous for them to keepe'. Fears that parish apprentices might not simply undermine the credit, but also perhaps even embezzle the goods, of their masters doubtless lie behind statements of this kind.[154]

The concomitant fear that employers might be particularly severe on the children of the poor explains the passive resistance of parents to the removal of their offspring. The parish officers of Buckland St Mary (Somerset) had no option but to finance the prosecution of 'parents which did keep their children from their masters' in 1638. The Wiltshire JPs complained of 'the unwillingness of the foolishe poore parents to depart with their children', a statement redolent of magistrates' patronizing disdain for the affective bonds within poor labouring families.[155]

149 Davies, *The Enforcement of English Apprenticeship*, 211; Barnes, *Somerset*, 186; Roberts, *Recovery and Restoration*, 35.

150 For a notorious example, see Barnes, *Somerset*, 186. Cf. Hampson, *Treatment of Poverty in Cambridgeshire*, 160.

151 NA, SP16/197/13.

152 NA, SP16/216/45.

153 *Nottinghamshire County Records*, ed. H. H. Copnall (Nottingham, 1915), 129.

154 NA, SP16/250/10. Cf. Ch. 1.5 above.

155 SARS, D/P/b.my.13/2/1, unfol. (31 May 1638); NA, SP16/250/10.

Their colleagues in Leicestershire were only slightly more sympathetic, accommodating the request of those parents who had 'prayed a short tyme to provide masters for their children, desiringe rather that they might comende maisters to their children than to be appointed by the overseers'.[156] The Nottinghamshire JPs complained that even though parish apprenticeship had left them with 'little rest either at home or abroad' they still found 'manie difficulties to contente poore people'.[157] Given that over 90 per cent of those poor children bound out in the first half of the seventeenth century had at least one parent surviving, and that over 25 per cent were apprenticed from households where both the mother and father were still alive, it is hardly surprising that parents should be so concerned about the fate of their children.[158] In Nottinghamshire, parents apparently adopted desperate measures, encouraging their children to behave badly so as to get themselves dismissed from apprenticeships.[159] The parental sense of emotional deprivation that fuelled such reactions was arguably also infused with a sense of indignation that parish officers and magistrates did not trust them to bring up their own offspring effectively. After all, to insist on the apprenticeship of a poor child was by implication to impugn the capacity of its parents to inculcate the habits of diligence and deference upon which labour discipline and social order depended.

To these emotional reservations might be added the economic rationale of the utility of children in the domestic workforce. Historians are becoming increasingly sensitive to the significant contribution child labour might make in the cottages of the labouring poor. The labour power of the whole household might be significantly increased by the 'substitution effect', whereby young children took over useful but unpaid tasks from their elder siblings and parents, thereby releasing more productive hands to be turned to paid work. Up to the age of 8, a child's work might include fuel-gathering, water-fetching, food preparation, cleaning, sweeping, errand-running, and care, or at least oversight, of their younger siblings. Between the ages of 9 and 12, children might be encouraged to spin, knit, mend clothes, tend fires, and tend livestock and poultry.[160] The

[156] NA, SP16/193/89. Even the foster-parents of a parish child in Aylesbury (Bucks.) refused to part with her when the parish officers ordered her bound out in 1697, and claimed that she had already voluntarily entered service with them. *Buckinghamshire Sessions Records*, ii. 141–2.

[157] NA, SP16/189/12.

[158] Of 165 poor children apprenticed in Colyton 1598–1649, only 16 (9.7%) were orphans and 42 (25.4%) had both parents alive. Sharpe, 'Poor Children', 263.

[159] NA, SP16/272/40.

[160] D. Levine, *Reproducing Families: The Political Economy of English Population History* (Cambridge, 1987), 112–14.

large number of runaways suggests that the children were themselves reluctant. Mary Science refused point blank to be bound out by the overseers of Weston Turville (Buckinghamshire) in 1698 and even when hauled before the county bench 'offered nothing materiall in her excuse and only expressed an unwillingness to labour'. The bench thought this 'an ill example to lazy and thriftless people' and committed her to Bridewell.[161]

Almost everywhere, therefore, the policy sapped the energy and enthusiasm of the magistrates: it was 'difficult' in Northamptonshire, 'troublesome and difficult' in Wiltshire, a 'labour' in Monmouthshire, a 'matter of no small difficultie' and even of 'continuall trouble' in Nottinghamshire. The East Riding justices complied with it only 'with a great deale of reluctation'.[162] In one part of Norfolk the magistrates had been forced to meet 'severall tymes touching the service'; in another it required 'care and diligence'; and in a third it had taken up 'some extraordinary time' at meetings.[163] In Cambridgeshire the 'putting forth of apprentices' had 'imployed soe much of [the magistrates'] time' that they had 'perfected nothing' with respect to the enforcement of the 1563 statute of artificers.[164] By the mid-1630s, however, some benches were striking a more optimistic note. The JPs of Usk (Monmouthshire) reported that they had 'laboured with all sorts of men, with whom we found great conformitye', even to the extent of exhausting the labour supply among those 'whoe are not settled and imployed to gett their maintenance'.[165] In Lancashire in 1635 the magistrates were at least rewarded by the feeling that, although they had spent 'much labour and paynes' in the business, it had 'yeelded such satisfaction' that it made their 'burdens seeme less'.[166] By 1638, the Norfolk magistrates' efforts had apparently resulted in fewer refusals or complaints over the binding out of parish children.[167]

A number of county benches nonetheless dared to elaborate on the shortcomings of a policy that they regarded as patently unenforceable. In May 1631, the justices of Fawsley (Northamptonshire) pleaded that it was far better to relieve poor children by collection than by coercing recalcitrant employers, who also, of course, paid poor rates.[168] Wiltshire JPs

[161] *Buckinghamshire Sessions Records*, ii. 184.
[162] NA, SP16/190/56, 191/67, 250/10, 270/40, 270/74.
[163] NA, SP16/329/9, 329/10, 385/27.
[164] NA, SP16/216/45.
[165] NA, SP16/270/74.
[166] NA, SP16/535/115.
[167] NA, SP16/385/27.
[168] NA, SP16/191/67.

argued that the fault lay with parish officers, who were apparently either negligent (preferring to tax ratepayers for the relief of poor families than to organize parish apprenticeship) or malicious ('imposinge apprentices upon such as are not of abilitye to keepe them').[169] In the summer of 1637, the Lancashire bench reported the converse problem, that the extensive participation of poor labouring families in 'the great trading of fustians and woollen cloth' meant that the 'inhabitants have contynuell ymployment for their children in spinning and other necessary labour'. Even if it was poorly paid and vulnerable to cyclical slump, domestic employment in the cloth industry was infinitely preferable to apprenticeship with a reluctant and potentially abusive master.[170]

It would, however, be a mistake to assume that parish officers abandoned the policy when they were no longer under conciliar or magisterial pressure. In the Cornish parish of Constantine the apprenticeship drive continued long after the abandonment of prerogative paternalism, with the vestry insisting in October 1650 that 'all such as have children and have not an estate able to maintain them but are likely to be chargeable be publiquely warned' to bind them out. Thirty-three children from seventeen families were listed as eligible, and masters were persuaded to take them without premiums. Even so, within two years they had been forced to sweeten the pill, conceding that any master who took an apprentice should not be required to take another before the first child had reached the age of 18, and that the sum of 10*s.* should be allowed from parish funds to defray the costs of clothing the child. The parish officers of Colne, who had complacently certified to the Lancashire justices in 1681 that there were no poor children fit to be put forth and no masters fit to receive them in any case, were brusquely told to 'goe forth and bethink themselves of some'.[171]

(*d*) Gender, Age, and Trade

Although the Caroline privy council was clearly more interested in the numbers rather than the gender of those apprenticed, the occasional certificate provides names of pauper children, from which the sex of the child can be deduced. Indeed, in 1635 the judges of the western circuit required magistrates to 'expresse the particular names of all those apprentices formerly bound', information that had not previously been required by the Orders themselves.[172] The county benches of Cornwall, Dorset

[169] NA, SP16/250/10.

[170] NA, SP/364/122.

[171] Cornwall RO, Truro, DDP39/8/1, unfol. (resolutions of 10 Oct. 1650, (?)1652); France 'A High Constable's Register', 74.

[172] NA, SP16/289/14

Somerset, and Wiltshire immediately complied, and their reports, combined with five others submitted throughout the country in the period 1634–6, provide a sample of thirteen certificates in which the gender of some 802 pauper apprentices is apparent. A very consistent pattern emerges. Boys were very significantly over-represented, almost invariably comprising at least two-thirds of those bound out. The proportion of male apprentices ranged from a maximum of 83.9 per cent in the Dorchester division of Dorset to 62.5 per cent in the Lincolnshire wolds and averaged 69.6 per cent across the country.[173] This sex ratio of 229 boys for every 100 girls is much higher than that for seventeenth-century Colyton, even despite the rise which occurred in that community from 156.8 in the period 1600–49 to 197.0 in the period 1650–99.[174] The high and rising proportion of poor boys apprenticed in Colyton has been explained in terms of the increasing home employment opportunities for girls in domestic lace-making. The very high male ratios in our Caroline sample might, however, suggest that the gender preferences of *employers* were less significant than those of *parents*. The regional differentials are slight, but they suggest that poor girls may have formed a higher proportion of children apprenticed in areas where the textile industry required spinners, as in the North Riding of Yorkshire where girls comprised 34.4 per cent of those bound. The under-representation of girls may also reflect greater unwillingness on the part of parents to send their daughters away, even though the fragmentary evidence suggests that girls were bound out when slightly younger than boys.[175]

Indeed, the advantages of apprenticing children 'timely', when they were pedagogically malleable, were frequently stressed. *An Ease for Overseers* urged that poor children, like 'a twigge that will best bende when it is greene', were 'fittest to be bound when they are young'. William Lambarde advised overseers in 1602 to put the poor in service 'while they be young and tractable, and before they be corrupted with vice and idle-

[173] NA, SP16/272/23, 272/43, 281/84, 289/14, 289/20/1, 289/29/1, 289/43, 289/48, 289/57, 289/64, 289/73, 329/9, 310/65. The Wiltshire figure of 76.4% male is very close to 18th-century figures in the county. In the Wiltshire parish of Lacock, 74.4% of the parish apprentices bound in the period 1667–1832 were male. Hinton, 'The Relief of the Poor of Lacock', 186. In the years down to 1750, boys constituted 68.9% of all parish children bound out in eleven mid-Sussex parishes and 67% of those in five Berkshire parishes. *Mid-Sussex Poor Law Records, passim*; *Berkshire Overseers Papers, 1654–1834*, ed. P. Durrant (Berkshire Record Society 3, Reading, 1997), 68–70 (Burghfield), 141–4 (Englefield), 150 (Sulhamstead Abbots), 224–33 (Thatcham), 253 (Woolhampton).

[174] Sharpe, 'Poor Children', 259.

[175] NA, SP16/310/65. In 17th-century Colyton, by contrast, the girls' average age (12 years) was slightly higher than the boys' (11.7 years). Sharpe, 'Poor Children', 256.

ness'.[176] As we have seen, moreover, the judges repeatedly emphasized that children might be apprenticed from the age of 7. Indeed, although the modal age of the 38 boys and girls of known years who were bound out in the West Riding in the mid-1630s was 11, the average was less than 10, with the mean age of the girls (9 years and 3 months) being slightly lower than that of the boys (9 years and 9 months).[177] It is nonetheless striking that only three children as young as 7 occur in this sample. Despite the suggestion that 'the most common age for apprenticing children was when they reached their eighth birthday', most parishes seem to have waited at least a year, and possibly two, longer.[178] In Shorne (Kent) and Hadleigh (Suffolk) 9 and 10 respectively seem to have been the minimum ages at which parish children were apprenticed in the Elizabethan period.[179] Indeed, when the Hampshire justices sought likely apprentices among the poor of the Fawley division in 1631, they enquired only after those aged 10 and over, and the Leicestershire bench similarly referred only to 'children and youthes between *ten* and sixteen as fitt for apprenticeship'.[180] A similar minimum was judged appropriate in Cambridgeshire, where, although girls were frequently apprenticed at the early age of nine, the 'boys not usually till twelve, or even fourteen or fifteen'.[181] The forty-nine children bound out in mid-Sussex before 1750 whose ages are given in indentures were just over 11 years old on average.[182] As we have seen, the age at which children were bound out had important implications for the activities they might reasonably be asked to perform.

Several benches made explicit provision for children who were regarded as too young to be apprenticed, although they are seldom as explicit on what they considered to be the minimum age. The JPs of the Arundel rape of Sussex took a note 'of all children above the age of *eight* years, which are yet unfit to be put forth', although the reasons for their unsuitability are unspecified. They nonetheless made ready a list of the names of 'the ablest inhabitants in every parish which are fitt to receive them'.[183] The Hertfordshire JPs noted in 1631 that those poor children

176 *An Ease for Overseers of the Poore*, 27; W. Lambarde, *The Duties of Constables* (London, 1602) 129.

177 NA, SP16/310/65.

178 Sharpe, 'Poor Children', 254.

179 Allen, 'An Early Poor Law Account', 77; McIntosh, 'Networks of Care in Elizabethan English Towns', 85.

180 NA, SP16/188/85, 193/89 (emphasis added).

181 Hampson, *Treatment of Poverty in Cambridgeshire*, 49–50; Hampson, 'Settlement and Removal', 283.

182 *Mid-Sussex Poor Law Records, passim.*

183 NA, SP16/263/82 (emphasis added).

who were 'not yet of fitt yeares to be putt forth they had caused to be sett to spinning or such small worke as is moste meete for them according to the tendernesse of their age that idlenesse may not fasten in them'. The Leicestershire JPs had similarly ordered the purchase of hemp, flax, and wool 'for the imployinge of little children not yet able to be putt apprentice or to service'. Other expedients were used elsewhere. For example, Widow Hodgson and two young children 'not fitt to be bound apprentice' had a house provided her by the parish officers of Kirkham (Lancashire) in 1636 and was accordingly able to maintain herself without a pension.[184]

The magistrates only very occasionally referred to the trades to which pauper children were bound. The generic reference, however, was to the trades of 'husbandrie and huswiferie', as in Norfolk in 1634.[185] Although this was the kind of profile envisaged by those who drafted the statute, it was by no means universal. Even in such an agricultural county as Cambridgeshire, less than 4 per cent of the parish apprentices bound between 1631 and 1830 were apprenticed to husbandry, a strikingly low proportion which demonstrates the extraordinary reluctance of farmers to take on such a long-standing commitment. For boys, the most common occupation was cordwaining, the remainder being set to other village craftsmen or shopkeepers. Elsewhere, there are the merest hints of occupational specialization: children were bound to 'husbandmen and artificers' in Norfolk in 1631, for example; to 'handicrafts' in Guildford (Surrey) in 1631; or to 'several trades and husbandryes' in Monmouthshire in 1634.[186] Of the ten masters who accepted pauper apprentices in the half-hundred of Hitchin (Hertfordshire) in 1638, the occupations of eight can be determined: five yeomen, two maltsters, and one weaver.[187] The craftsmen who agreed to take parish apprentices in early seventeenth-century Worth (Sussex) included two ironworkers, two blacksmiths, a mason, a warrender, a thatcher, a silkweaver, and a tanner. Even so, twenty-one (70 per cent) of the thirty children bound out in Worth between 1615 and 1660 were destined for husbandry and housewifery.[188] The overwhelming majority of girls were bound to the 'art and mystery of huswifery'. Indeed, all the girls who were apprenticed from Rye (Sussex) between 1602 and 1645 were bound to housewifery. Only two of the 170 children bound out in Trull were apprenticed to trades

[184] NA, SP16/189/79, 193/89, 330/64.
[185] NA, SP16/281/84.
[186] NA, SP16/190/20, 191/78, 191/42, 270/74.
[187] NA, SP16/385/43.
[188] Thomas, 'Pauper Apprenticeship', 401.

other than husbandry or huswifery.[189] On balance, it seems, parish apprenticeship was easier to enforce in arable parishes where there were limited opportunities for children to earn an independent living, or at least to contribute regularly to the productive capacity of the household, in a seasonal agricultural economy. Indeed, the ubiquity of the apprenticeship of pauper children in husbandry belies recent scepticism about the frequency of child employment in agriculture.[190]

Evidence of the premiums paid to masters is relatively scarce, since they were usually itemized only where a more specialized trade was involved. Two paupers were apprenticed from the Lancashire parish of Kirkham in 1636, for example, Jane Fletcher to the wife of a local bonelace worker with a premium of £8. 6*s*. 8*d*., and William Barnes to a weaver with a premium of £5.[191] But 'considerations' of this kind were the exception rather than the rule. In a sample of 344 apprenticeship indentures drawn up in the parishes of mid-Sussex between 1589 and 1750, only sixty-two (18 per cent) specified that any premium at all was to be paid to the master. The sums involved ranged from £1 to £10 and were very occasionally supplemented by clothing or shoes. The average cash value was £5. 1*s*. 0*d*., though the fluctuations either side of this mean owe more to the length of the apprenticeship (and, therefore, ultimately to the age of the child) than to the particular trade involved. Cumulatively, of course, these expenses might be very substantial in a particular parish. In St Giles Cripplegate, the expenditure on premiums and clothing for the nineteen parish apprentices bound out in the years 1630–2 totalled almost £34, just less than half the annual income from the poor rate.[192] A similar situation prevailed in Kenilworth (Warwickshire), where the overseers spent almost £25 (46 per cent) of their outgoings for the accounting year 1670 on apprenticing five parish children. Expenditure on this scale might easily be justified in a context where the maintenance of just two parish orphans represented a recurrent drain of £10 annually on parish finances.[193] On the whole, however, the nominal premiums on offer were usually only attractive to householders who were themselves indigent, a tendency reflected in complaints that 'poor inhabitants' had taken on

[189] Hampson, 'Settlement and Removal', 283; Thomas, 'Pauper Apprenticeship', 401; Jones 'Trull Overseers' Accounts', 97.

[190] Cf. H. Cunningham, 'The Employment and Unemployment of Children in England *c*.1680–1851', *Past and Present*, 126 (1990), 115, 146–7; Cunningham, *Children and Childhood in Western Society Since 1500* (London, 1995), 82–3.

[191] NA, SP16/330/64.

[192] NA, SP16/226/78.

[193] T. Arkell, 'The Incidence of Poverty in England in the Later Seventeenth Century', *Social History*, 12 (1987), 41.

apprentices 'for the lucre of gain' only for their households in turn to fall upon the parish.[194] Indeed it was not uncommon for masters to be forced to enter into penal bonds for substantial sums which would be forfeited to the parish if they breached the terms of the agreement: twenty-six (8 per cent) of the mid-Sussex masters were bound in this way, some of them in recognizances of £100.[195] Other inducements were therefore occasionally used to persuade reluctant masters, some of whom evidently drove a hard bargain. Edward Sewer not only received a premium of £5 for taking a parish child of Henfield (Sussex) in 1600 but also secured an agreement that he should not contribute to poor rates for the following six years. Michael Harmes persuaded the parish officers of Bolney (Sussex) to supplement his consideration of £2 with a promise that he would not be obliged to take any other child while James Terry was apprenticed to him.[196]

Financial considerations aside, magistrates were blunt about the desirability of removing children from the pernicious influence of their parents. For the JPs of Leicestershire, for instance, pauper apprenticeship was simply a matter of taking children from their parents so that 'young people and children may receive imployment and fitting education and soe avoide idleness and lewdenes of life'. In doing so, they distilled the fears of *An Ease for Overseers*, which had argued in 1601 that poor children, 'by reason of their idle and base educations', would 'hardly hold service'. Because they had 'wavering and straying mindes', it had argued, 'their wandering and unstaied bodies' would 'sooner be disposed to vagrancie than activitie, to idlenesse then to worke'.[197] Norfolk JPs adopted a rather more sympathetic tone in 1636 when they noted that they had bound forth such children 'whose *friends* were not able otherwise to provide for them'.[198] This laconic reference to the attenuated nature of kin support helps explain the relatively large proportion of apprentices who were bound out to foreign parishes, even in the 1630s. Of twenty-six paupers apprenticed in the Norfolk hundreds of South Erpingham and Eynsford in 1634, seven (27 per cent) were bound out to masters outside their own parish, a proportion which bears comparison with those for many rural parishes *after* the late seventeenth-century settlement acts had supposedly perverted parish apprenticeship into a mechanism for ridding ratepayers

[194] *Buckinghamshire Sessions Records*, ii. 256, 265. One master from Lorton (Cumberland) taunted his parish apprentice in 1702 with the threat of dismissal because 'he could have a better lad with more money'. CRO, Q/11/1/62/9.

[195] *Mid-Sussex Poor Law Records, passim*. Cf. Hampson, *Treatment of Poverty in Cambridgeshire*, 162.

[196] *Mid-Sussex Poor Law Records*, 68, 242.

[197] NA, SP16/193/89, 216/103; *An Ease for Overseers of the Poore*, 27.

[198] NA, SP16/193/89, 216/103, 329/10, 329/11 (emphasis added).

of the liability of a pauper child.[199] Even so, the disciplinary agenda of the policy is nicely encapsulated in Michael Dalton's reminder of the very limited ambitions of the scheme: the apprenticeship clauses of the poor laws were intended 'not for the education of boys in arts but for charity to keep them and relieve them from turning to roguery and idleness'.[200]

(*e*) From Persuasion to Compulsion

Pauper apprenticeship generally seems to have fallen into abeyance in the late seventeenth century, partly because the use of the prerogative to enforce social policy was so politically sensitive and partly because of the changing demographic circumstances of the Restoration period.[201] Magistrates apparently turned their attention from apprenticing parish children to enforcing compulsory service for young adults under the terms of the statute of artificers. General initiatives of this kind were taken in the West Riding of Yorkshire in 1641, in Wiltshire in 1656, in Cambridgeshire in 1661, in the North Riding in 1670, in Hertfordshire in 1675 and 1687, in Essex in 1677 and again in 1684, and in Buckinghamshire repeatedly in the late 1680s.[202] As the late seventeenth-century cycle

[199] NA, SP16/281/84. In the 18th century, the proportions bound out beyond the parish boundary ranged from 17.6% in Gnosall (1691–1816), 22.2% in Eaton Socon (1693–1731), 24.4% in Doveridge (Derby., 1699–1818), 68.2% in Maulden (Beds., 1658–1788). Cutlack, 'Gnosall Records', 34–5; Emmison, 'The Relief of the Poor at Eaton Socon', 70; Tate, *The Parish Chest*, 221. The study which shows the most striking change in policy between the 17th and 18th centuries is Hampson, 'Settlement and Removal', 282–3, which demonstrates that the proportion bound out 'abroad' rose from 15.3% (1631–91) to 69.3% (1691–1830), although the proportion sent to 'distant' rather than 'neighbouring' parishes dropped from 7.7% to 0.7%. The equivalent figures for Henfield (Sussex) are 13% before the 1691 statute, nearly 60% afterwards. More continuity (a nominal increase from 20% to 25% in the Sussex parish of Worth, even a constant proportion across the whole period 1638 to 1840 at Yealmpton in Devon) is evident elsewhere. Thomas, 'Pauper Apprenticeship', 403. The vestrymen of Frampton, Lincolnshire repeatedly changed their policy on binding apprentices in the early 18th century. Hindle, 'Power, Poor Relief and Social Relations', 86–7. In 18th-century Stone (Staffs.), full use was made of the opportunity to apprentice pauper children to distant masters in the Potteries and the Black Country. Broadbridge, 'The Old Poor Law in the Parish of Stone', 14. The temptation to apprentice out of parish was greatest in heavily burdened areas such as London, where proportions in excess of 90% were not uncommon at the turn of the 19th century. Rose, 'Social Policy and Business', 9. The classic statement of the damaging consequences of the settlement laws for the operation of parish apprenticeship is Dorothy Marshall, *The English Poor in the Eighteenth Century. A Study in Social and Administrative History* (London, 1926), 183.

[200] Dalton's gloss on the judges resolutions of 1633, cited in R. E. Leader, *History of the Company of Cutlers in Hallamshire in the County of York* (2 vols., Sheffield, 1906), i. 57 n.

[201] Slack, *From Reformation to Improvement*, 53–76; S. Hindle, 'The Growth of Social Stability in Restoration England', *The European Legacy*, 5 (2000), 563–76.

[202] *West Riding Sessions Records*, ii. 11, 33; 'The Records of Quarter Sessions in the County of Wilts.', in HMC, *Reports on Manuscripts in Various Collections*, vol. i (London, 1901), 132; Hampson

of demographic stagnation, modest price deflation, and rising wages reduced the bargaining power of employers, magistrates seem to have devoted more of their energies to the labour discipline of a slightly older age group.

It was only, it seems, after 1697 that parish apprenticeship once again rose up the agenda of local government. It certainly kept Kent JPs busy in the early eighteenth century: magistrates at the Sevenoaks petty sessions signed thirty-one sets of indentures in the period 1716–19, and their colleagues at Blackheath forty sets in the period 1745–8.[203] More contracts inevitably entailed more disputes, and it is hardly surprising that at least ninety Kent apprentices had their indentures cancelled at quarter sessions between 1705 and 1754.[204] Even so, parish apprenticeship became ubiquitous in the eighteenth century, at least if the large numbers of extant indentures are anything to go by. It is important to recognize, however, that the survival of parish indentures of this kind is somewhat erratic. Although there is clear evidence from household listings that the children of the poor left home at an early age, this is not always reflected in the archive of parish apprenticeship. The fact that only twenty-five pauper apprenticeship indentures survive for the parish of Ardleigh (Essex) in the entire period 1719 to 1834 suggests that much of the migration and employment of poor children went altogether unrecorded.[205] It is quite conceivable that even in those communities for which apparently very large numbers of parish indentures survive, a substantial minority (perhaps even a majority) of poor children may have been farmed out in various ways within the parish in ways that have left little trace within the records, especially because neither premiums were paid nor indentures engrossed. The fact that only ten apprenticeship premiums, for instance, are accounted for in the overseers accounts of thirty-nine south Warwickshire parishes in the year 1638–9 suggests that parish children were almost certainly bound out to native employers by informal agreements among the ratepayers, without the need for 'the parish' to consent to the kind of premium necessary in the case of one 'Beard's son' of

Treatment of Poverty in Cambridgeshire, 55; *North Riding Quarter Sessions Records*, ed. J. C. Atkinson (9 vols., North Riding Record Society, 1–9, London, 1884–92), vi. 220; *Hertford County Records*, ed. W. Le Hardy (9 vols., Hertford, 1905–39), i. 254; vi. 405–8; J. A. Sharpe, *Crime in Seventeenth-Century England: A County Study* (Cambridge, 1983), 45; *Buckinghamshire Sessions Records*, i. 176–7, 234, 322, 336.

203 N. Landau, *The Justices of the Peace, 1679–1760* (Berkeley, 1984), 216–17.

204 Ibid. 250–1.

205 T. Sokoll, *Household and Family among the Poor: The Case of Two Essex Communities in the Late Eighteenth and Early Nineteenth Centuries* (Bochum, 1993), 166–7.

Tanworth.[206] Between 1710 and 1728, the vestrymen of Frampton similarly embarked on a policy of simple agreements with prominent farmers or graziers, many of whom had recently sat (or were shortly to sit) on the vestry, and no money changed hands between overseers and masters. Fifty (52 per cent) of the extant pauper apprenticeship contracts for the parish were made in this eighteen-year period.[207] Even less formal—and historically altogether invisible—arrangements might well have been made as a part of rotational systems of reciprocal apprenticeships among local households, perhaps lubricated by the inducement of a remission in rates.

It is therefore difficult to find a suitable yardstick to judge the seemingly impressive numbers of extant indentures in parishes with substantial archives. The average annual number of extant indentures in parish archives ranges from 0.60 in Doveridge (Derbyshire) 1669–1818; 0.89 in Trull (Somerset), 1618–1809; 0.96 in Frampton (Lincolnshire), 1678–1772; 1.18 in Lacock (Wiltshire), 1667–1832; 1.73 in Gnosall (Staffordshire), 1691–1816; to 2.95 in Colyton (Devon), 1650–1837. If these figures are calculated as a proportion of the population in each parish aged 7–16, it is probable that between 0.5 and 1 per cent of all eligible children were apprenticed each year. Over the lifetime of each cohort, therefore, between 5.85 and 8.73 per cent of boys and girls in these parishes seem to have been bound out, although the differentials in these figures may owe as much to the vicissitudes of record survival as they do to the varying burden of poverty across the parishes.[208]

Calculations of this kind must be read in the light of scattered criticisms of pauper apprenticeship as it was practised in the later seventeenth and

[206] The ten formal apprenticeships were at Lapworth (3), Packwood (2), Pillerton Priors, Lower Shuckburgh, Tanworth, Tysoe, and Little Wolford. SBTRO, DR37/85/6/23, 30, 33, 37, 39–40, 42, 50. While the Gaydon overseers paid expenses to return an apprentice to her master in London, their colleagues at Idlicote and Pillerton Priors noted that they had no further children fit for service. SBTRO, DR37/85/6/15, 20, 33.

[207] Hindle, 'Power, Poor Relief and Social Relations', 86–7. Cf. Edmonds, 'Overseers of the Poor of Chalfont St Peter', 9. Whether the Frampton experiment of apprenticeship without premiums was ended by the kind of vestry coup which overturned this policy in Stone (Staffs.) in 1777 is unclear. Broadbridge, 'The Old Poor Law in the Parish of Stone', 14.

[208] Tate, *The Parish Chest*, 221; Jones, 'Trull Overseers' Accounts', 97; Hindle, 'Power, Poor Relief and Social Relations', 86; Hinton, 'The Relief of the Poor of Lacock', 184; Cutlack, 'Gnosall Records', 53–4; Sharpe, 'Poor Children', 259. These calculations assume that approximately 20% of the population was aged between 7 and 16. These rural rates of apprenticeship were dwarfed by those in the industrializing towns. In Leeds, the parish bound out almost 1,800 apprentices in the years 1730–99, at an annual average of almost twenty-six. In the capital, 2,794 children were apprenticed by the parishes within the London Bills of Mortality in the years 1767–78. Anderson, 'The Leeds Workhouse', 112 (appendix A); Rose, 'Social Policy and Business', 9.

early eighteenth centuries. Indeed, several commentators provide particularly revealing anecdotal evidence of the limitations of the policy. Samuel Pepys noted on 20 August 1663 that he had returned home for lunch to 'find a little girle, which she told my wife herself her name was Jinny; by which name we shall call her—I think a good likely girl and a parish-child of St Bride's, of honest parentage and recommended by the church-warden'. That evening, however, having been deloused and clothed by Mrs Pepys, 'she run away from Goody Taylor that was showing her the way to the bakehouse, and we heard no more of her'. The following day, Jinny was brought back by 'a beadle of St Bride's parish', only to be stripped and sent away by her master and mistress. Pepys laconically noted that a new parish child came, also at the recommendation of churchwarden Griffings, 'which I think will prove a pretty girl—her name, Susan'.[209] For Jinny, and others like her, parish apprenticeship was little more than an endless sequence of revolving doors, an experience nicely, if a little sardonically, described by Richard Dunning in 1685 as a 'masterless method', whereby 'many serve more masters in a week than they spend sober nights'.[210]

The Quaker tradesman William Stout of Lancaster had a different, though no less problematic, encounter with a parish apprentice at the turn of the eighteenth century. Stout remembered that he 'had a parish apprintice put upon' him in 1706. John Robinson was about 10 years of age, and Stout not only 'sent him to the free schoole for at least fower years', where 'he learned well to the entring into Greek and could write well', but also bound him in turn apprentice with a premium of £4 and clothing to a worsted weaver. Robinson 'served his time and then begun trade for himselfe, but was not so industrious or carfull as he ought, fell to drinking and broke; then went to London, got a wife and portion, which he spent, and left her, and went to America'. 'He cost me', Stout lamented, 'at least forty pounds.'[211] That Stout's frustrations are far from unique is demonstrated by the comprehensive critique of pauper apprenticeship launched by the Norfolk magistrate Robert Doughty. In a remarkable memorandum drawn up in the early 1660s, Doughty located the difficulties of administering parish apprenticeship in the wider context of the desirability of enforcing the labour laws, especially the statute

[209] *The Diary of Samuel Pepys: A New and Complete Transcription*, ed. R. Latham and W. Matthews (11 vols., London, 1971), vi. 282, 283–4.

[210] R. Dunning, *A Plain and Easie Method Shewing How the Office of Overseer of the Poor May be Managed* (London, 1685), 'The Prefatory Dedication', unfol.

[211] *The Autobiography of William Stout of Lancaster, 1665–1752*, ed. J. D. Marshall (Chetham Society, 3rd ser., 14, Manchester, 1967), 154.

of artificers.[212] Doughty noted the obvious structural problem that, because children were apprenticed young, the seven years which was the maximum which most masters were prepared to tolerate would expire well before they had reached the age of 24. Others were still bound by antedated indentures which meant that they 'really serve but three, foure or five of the seaven'. Whether indentures were correctly drawn up or not, they were seldom enrolled, which created acute difficulties in enforcing the penalties stipulated by the statute. Worse still, few employers wanted these children after their apprenticeship expired, so that they were forced to live at their own hands and haunt alehouses, tending not only to 'the loss of their tyme and money' but also to the 'corrupting, depraving and debauching of all youth'. Even more significantly, Doughty pointed to the gender-specific difficulties of enforcing parish apprenticeship: those 'wenches (or maydes) as are ablest' for housewifery abandoned apprenticeship because they could make far better earnings 'by spinning and knitting, gleaning & stealing in harvest, & perhaps by secret whoredoms all the yeare'. To this prurient fantasy Doughty added another, hardly more sympathetic, image of lads who had abandoned service only to 'play smoake & slaver away' their summer earnings in the winter murk of the alehouse. For Caleb Parfect, incumbent of Strood (Kent), however, parish apprenticeship was disastrous not because it did not work, but precisely because it was widely enforced: to bind small children to wretched masters in pauperized trades, he argued in a polemic designed to advertise the virtues of parish workhouses, was 'as good as murdering them'.[213]

And what of the reactions of the poor and their parents? As might be expected, the sources are altogether less forthcoming about the sentiments that magistrates and vestrymen were only too willing to dismiss as 'fond and foolish pity'. One anonymous woman of the parish of Whickham (County Durham) might, however, speak for all. When she was told in 1775 that she would be relieved only if she entered the parish workhouse and agreed to have her children 'bound out or put into reputable families', she replied, 'What, would you sell my chil-

[212] Norfolk RO, AYL304 (undated memorandum headed '5 Eliz c.4'). Unless otherwise noted, all subsequent quotations are taken from this source, which is *not* among those in *The Notebook of Robert Doughty, 1662–1665*, ed. J. M. Rosenheim (Norfolk Record Society, 54, Norwich, 1989). For Doughty himself, see J. M. Rosenheim, 'Robert Doughty of Hanworth: A Restoration Magistrate', *Norfolk Archaeology*, 38 (1983), 296–312; Rosenheim, 'Documenting Authority: Texts and Magistracy in Restoration Society', *Albion*, 25 (1993), 591–604. Doughty also figures prominently in Fletcher, *Reform in the Provinces*, *passim*.

[213] Simon, 'From Charity School to Workhouse', 127.

dren?'[214] At its best, then, pauper apprenticeship had 'all the advantages of boarding out plus technical training'.[215] At its worst, it amounted to little more than the exploitation of cheap labour on the land and in domestic drudgery. For the majority, the experience must have lain somewhere between the two.

3. CONCLUSION: INDUSTRY AND IDLENESS AMONG THE LABOURING POOR

Economic historians have recently disagreed over the essential purpose of parish apprenticeship as it was practised in the late eighteenth and the nineteenth centuries. From one perspective, the policy seems little more than 'a method of transmitting child labour into the low skilled trades rather than an investment in the human capital of poor children'.[216] More optimistically, it has been regarded as a direct means of 'shoring up the health and human capital formation of children in poor households'.[217] Although the two assessments share a common lack of historical perspective about the difficulties of enforcing the policy, their different emphases reflect the divergent agenda of studies aimed at the historiographies of early factory production on the one hand and of the 'standard of living debate' on the other. They also grow out of the long-standing reluctance of welfare historians to take seriously the apprenticeship and employment clauses of the Elizabethan poor laws. The plentiful evidence of the provision of parish pensions has itself obscured the leading role of work and labour discipline in early modern welfare policy. From its very outset, it should be emphasized, Elizabethan poor relief was a form of governmental intervention 'intended to break the cycle of deprivation and ensure that poor children grew up to become productive members of the community'.[218]

It is nonetheless dangerous to underestimate the acute tensions created by a policy that strained the political and economic, and arguably even the emotional, sinews of households and communities all over the country. All the evidence suggests that the enforcement of parish apprenticeship was deeply problematic for judges, magistrates, and

214 D. Levine and K. Wrightson, *The Making of an Industrial Society: Whickham, 1560–1765* (Oxford, 1991), 381.

215 Pinchbeck and Hewitt, *Children in English Society*, vol. i. 242.

216 Rose, 'Social Policy and Business', 9.

217 S. Horrell *et al.*, 'Destined for Deprivation: Human Capital Formation and Intergenerational Poverty in Nineteenth-Century England', *Explorations in Economic History*, 38 (2001), 358.

218 Ibid. 356.

parish officers; for parents, employers, and ratepayers; and, not least, for the children themselves. Indeed, the conflicts created by judicial interpretation of, and popular responses to, parish apprenticeship reveal the extraordinarily ambiguous role of children in the makeshift economies of the labouring poor. Children's hands might equally be busied in spinning in the family home or outstretched in a gesture of importunacy at the kitchen doors of their neighbours. From one perspective, then, children represented an invaluable supply of cheap labour, contributing in numerous ways to the operation of the household economy. From another, however, they represented a potential drain on the charitable resources of wealthier neighbours, either through the dispensation of casual alms or the provision of formal relief, and were therefore a group in particular need of social discipline. Contemporaries actually made creative use of this paradox, for it helped them discriminate between the 'deserving' and the 'undeserving' at the very time when that age-old binary distinction was being distorted by the 'discovery' of the labouring poor in the urban censuses of the late sixteenth century.[219] Of course, the deserving might be characterized, and (as we have seen) might indeed seek to characterize themselves, in numerous ways: by their industry, their thrift, their sobriety, their deference, their 'credit', and their fear of God. But it was arguably in their relations with their children that the deserving poor were most easily identified, and identified themselves.

The result was the elaboration of the very frequently employed social stereotypes of the 'worthy', who took pains for their children's education and maintenance, and the 'unworthy', who allowed, arguably even encouraged, their children to develop habits of idleness. Among the most frequent references in the testimonials provided by chief inhabitants in support of those considered deserving is that they took pains through their labour for the maintenance of their family. Magistrates were informed that John Weaver of Danbury (Essex) was 'an honest poor man and a painful labourer', for instance, and that Thomas Oakley of Tollesbury (Essex) was 'a poor man and having many children is very painful in his calling'. When the parishioners of Stoke St Gregory (Somerset) provided a certificate in support of John Kent in the early 1650s, they reported that he had always behaved himself, 'educating and maintaining his wife and four small children by his industry'.[220] 'The poore' *as a class* might conversely be characterized by the indiscipline and disorder that they transmitted to their young. Matthew Hale made

[219] Slack, *Poverty and Policy*, 27–32.

[220] SARS, Q\SPET/1/109; ERO, Q/SR122/67–8, 448/128. For the deployment of this idiom in applications for endowed charity, see Ch. 2.6 above.

precisely this point in 1683. 'Poor families', he wrote, 'daily multiply in the Kingdom for want of a due order for their employment in an honest course of life.' As a result they 'do unavoidably bring up their children either in a trade of begging or stealing or such other idle course which again they propagate to their children, and so there is a successive multiplication of hurtful or at least unprofitable people, neither capable of discipline nor beneficial imployment'. He was echoed in 1683 by Joseph Keble, who argued that 'children brought up in idleness might be so rooted in it, that hardly they may be brought after to good thrift and labour'. The minister of the Northamptonshire parish of Geddington noted in the parish register that fifteen of the children he baptized in the year 1701–2 were 'poor', though he maintained a politic silence about the economic morality of the parents whose poverty they had inherited. Others were less discreet. Richard Gough complained in the early eighteenth century that Mother Gittins of Myddle had 'brought up her children in idleness and favoured them in their bad courses'. 'It was noe marvell', he went on, 'that shee was noe better, for her mother Sina Davis and her children have for many yeares been a charge to us' and 'was a crafty, idle dissembling woman'.[221]

'Life-cycle' poverty, then, was the unfortunate condition of the deserving poor, an inevitable consequence of universal human processes of reproduction and ageing.[222] 'Inherited' poverty, however, was a far less sympathetic state, most often understood by contemporaries rather as the consequence of imprudent parental behaviour than of the deteriorating real-wage levels identified by historians.[223] This concern extended even to the regulation of family formation. As we shall see, parish officers not infrequently inhibited the marriages of the poor on the grounds that they would 'breed up a charge' on the poor rate.[224] Perhaps for these reasons, it was the parents of young families who were most vulnerable to the discretionary punishments of the civil parish. Where the poor were disorderly, parish officers were actively enjoined to suspend or abate

[221] Hale, *Provision for the Poor*, sig. A2^{v}; J. Keble, *An Assistance to Justices of the Peace* (London, 1683), 479; S. Hindle, '"Not by Bread Only"? Common Right, Parish Relief and Endowed Charity in a Forest Economy, *c.*1600–1800', in S. King and A. Tomkins (eds.), *The Poor in England, 1700–1850: An Economy of Makeshifts* (Manchester, 2003), 55–6; R. Gough, *The History of Myddle*, ed. D. G. Hey (Harmondsworth, 1981), 257–8. For another clergyman noting the poverty of individual parishioners in his parish register in the same period, see Edmonds, 'Overseers of the Poor of Chalfont St Peter', 6.

[222] Wales, 'Poverty, Poor Relief and the Life-Cycle'.

[223] B. Stapleton, 'Inherited Poverty and Life-Cycle Poverty: Odiham, Hampshire, 1650–1850', *Social History*, 18 (1993), 339–55.

[224] Hindle, 'The Problem of Pauper Marriage', 79. Cf. Ch. 5.4 below.

pensions. Such threats were most difficult to carry out in the cases of the elderly, amongst whom all too evident human need occasionally militated against anything other than the temporary withdrawal of parish pensions and for whom the notion of a customary 'right' to relief was most difficult to challenge.[225] Parents who kept their children at home, by contrast, might plausibly be accused of encouraging idleness. Alexander Strange, vicar of Layston (Hertfordshire), was eloquent on this issue in 1636, when he complained about the poor families who had flooded his parish over the previous generation. 'The young people in these familyes are brought up so idlye', he argued, that 'no honest man will willingly take such ill condicioned people into their howse for servants, hardly upon any termes or conditions, because they have bynne so ill and unprofitably brought up'.[226] In the context of such attitudes, it was little wonder that parish officers took very seriously the advice of the judges and actually did withhold pensions from parents who refused to bind out their children and kept them at home. Having more children at home 'than was needful' for them, therefore, evidently rendered the poor vulnerable to the disciplinary sanctions of the civil parish.[227] It is, therefore, arguable that the compulsory binding out of poor children came to be seen, no less than the parish badge or the workhouse test, as a deterrent, designed to discourage applicants for relief from approaching the parish officers.

These sanctions demonstrate the operation of legal power of the early modern state to intervene in the processes through which poor households were constituted and social and moral values inculcated. If labouring parents overburdened with young children were among the more frequent recipients of the carrots dispensed by the overseers of the poor, it was precisely this group, and their 'waste' children, who were most commonly beaten with their sticks. In their attitudes to childrearing and parish apprenticeship, therefore, the labouring poor opted themselves, and were placed into, the mental categories of the authorities—to be seen as worthy or unworthy; painful or careless; industrious or idle.

[225] Smith, 'Ageing and Well-Being', 82. See Ch. 6.2 below.

[226] HALS, D/P65/3/3, 327.

[227] See Ch. 6.2(*e*) below. Parish charities also employed similar tactics. See Ch. 2.5(*d*) above.

4
Collection

> In this obdurate age of ours, neither godly persuasions of the pastors nor pitifull exclamations of the poore can move any to mercie unless there were a law made to compel them: whereby it appeareth that most give to the poor rather by compulsion than by compassion.
>
> *An Ease for Overseers of the Poore* (1601)[1]

The Elizabethan poor relief statutes defined the deserving—the 'lame ympotent olde blynde and such other amonge them being poore and not able to worke'—as a residual category in terms of their inability (as opposed to their unwillingness) to support themselves through their labour. The very phrase 'not able to worke', overseers were reminded, was merely 'an exposition' of the defects of age, blindness, and lameness, which were not in and of themselves grounds for parish relief.[2] This criterion of deservingness was emphatically not new, having been developed and refined by medieval canon lawyers.[3] The novelty of the late sixteenth-century legislation lay rather in the incorporation of ancient principles of charity into a rate-funded administrative system that placed a legal obligation on each parish to supplement the incomes of those whose idleness was involuntary. Under the terms of the first clause of the 1598 act, the 'impotent' were to be relieved at home in cash and/or kind on the basis of assessments taxed 'wekely or otherwise' on all the householders of ability.[4] Collection of this kind was, as the contemporary handbook for parish officers *An Ease for Overseers of the Poore* emphasized, compulsory by law, and therefore represented a departure from the voluntaristic traditions that had long been central to the relief of the poor in England.

The introduction of the Elizabethan statutes marks a watershed in the history of welfare provision, beyond which perceptions of social

[1] *An Ease for Overseers of the Poore: Abstracted From the Statutes* (Cambridge, 1601), 22.

[2] 39 Elizabeth I, c. 3, sect. i; *An Ease for Overseers of the Poore*, 23.

[3] See Ch. 2.1 above.

[4] 39 Elizabeth I, c. 3, sect. i.

obligation were decisively transformed. The most significant innovation was the appointment of unpaid officers, initially known (from 1572) as *collectors* for the poor but subsequently (after the statutes of 1598 and 1601) to become central to the welfare process in the more familiar guise of *overseers* of the poor, two of whom were to be responsible in each parish for the estimation of need, the making of rates, the collection of assessments, the distribution of payments, and the casting up of accounts. Whereas the propertied and the indigent had previously come face to face in the gift exchange of charity, they were now separated by a gulf of social distance across which only the overseer might regularly step, in visiting the households of the poor to assess the level of need, and in disbursing 'collections' (or 'allowances' or 'pensions' as they gradually came to be called), usually in the church porch after the Sunday morning sermon, to those deemed deserving. The social relations expressed in parish relief were therefore relatively impersonal, more formal, and arguably colder, than those that had prevailed under the traditional regime of casual (though sometimes regular) almsgiving inspired by the theology of 'works-righteousness' in which donor and recipient were enmeshed in a complex web of dependency and reciprocity.[5] Formal poor relief was, above all, *bureaucratic*, involving systematic processes of decision-making about how the resources of the parish should be marshalled and to whom they ought to be distributed.[6]

This characterization of the social and political impact of the Elizabethan statutes assumes, of course, both that the laws were effectively administered and that formal welfare provision came to monopolize practices of relief at the expense of informal and semi-formal arrangements. But these assumptions in themselves beg two questions which are fundamental to the analysis of the micro-politics of parish relief: How effectively were the pension provisions of the poor laws enforced in the parishes? And to what extent did formal collection obviate or preclude other systems of relief? In turn, the answers to these questions raise others. To whom were pensions in fact disbursed? Did the social profile of 'collectioners' change over time? What contribution might 'collection' make not only to the survival of the impotent but also to the economy of makeshifts of the labouring poor, whose idleness might have been involuntary but was nonetheless emphatically not a consequence of their physical defects? What proportion of the population of a rural com-

[5] L. P. Wandel, 'Social Welfare', in H. J. Hillerbrand (ed.), *The Oxford Encyclopaedia of the Reformation* (4 vols., Oxford, 1996), iv. 81.

[6] Slack, *Poverty and Policy*, 191; S. Hindle, *The State and Social Change in Early Modern England, c.1550–1640* (London and New York, 2000), 204–30.

munity might regularly receive relief, and how did this constituency of pensioners relate to the much larger social groups who were only occasionally relieved, or who were in need and were never relieved at all? Perhaps most significantly of all, how strong was the tax base of parish communities on which the burden of poverty was placing significantly greater weight, especially in years of dearth?

The following discussion addresses these issues first by exploring in detail just how quickly formal welfare provision spread across rural England in the years after the Elizabethan statutes. It then discusses the mechanics of collection in those parishes where assessments, rates, and pensions *were* introduced, before moving on to investigate the nature and scale of parish provision, and especially the balance between cash pensions, payments in kind, and occasional relief. This chapter is also, however, concerned to investigate the possibility that there was a distinctive *ecology* of poor relief, in which the nature of the problem of poverty, and of the responses adopted to ameliorate it, varied across different social and economic settings. Indeed, there is an urgent need for an analysis of this kind, not least because the numerous local studies of poor relief administration, which proliferated until the 1960s, tended to be distressingly innocent of any references to the peculiarities of context. Although a full-scale historical geography of English welfare provision obviously lies beyond the scope of this analysis, the discussion of local ecologies of relief offered here is intended to go some way to reconciling the paradox of a nationally co-ordinated system that was administered on a parish-by-parish basis in widely divergent economic contexts. If the legislation of the Elizabethan relief statutes was a political achievement at Westminster, its implementation in the countryside was no less remarkable, especially in the extent to which local office-holders, and the ratepayers they represented, successfully accommodated and frequently adapted the requirements of the statutes to the prevailing, and often highly localized, patterns of social and economic relations in the parishes.[7]

1. THE SPREAD OF PARISH RELIEF

As welfare historians have long recognized, the early history of parish relief remains frustratingly obscure. Some regimes of formal relief were apparently precocious, especially in the towns. Poor rates had been introduced in Norwich and York by 1550; in Exeter, Colchester, Ipswich, King's Lynn, and Worcester by 1560; in Chester and Salisbury by 1570; in

[7] Slack, *Poverty and Policy*, 114.

Gloucester, Hull, Leicester, and Oxford by 1580; in Lincoln by 1600; and in Bristol and Reading by 1610.[8] Implementation in rural communities seems to have been much patchier. The task of mapping the spread of parish relief across the countryside of Elizabethan England is rendered particularly difficult because the fragmentary calculations carried out by collectors for the poor were usually scrawled haphazardly in the margins of lengthy lists of churchwardens' expenditure. It is further complicated by the ambiguous language deployed by churchwardens, collectors, and overseers alike to describe the mechanics of fund-raising. Their preferred idiom was 'collection', the meaning of which migrated over the course of the early modern period. 'Collection' originally implied the giving of alms inspired by clerical exhortation and only gradually came to mean the paying of parish rates under the compulsion of law. By the second half of the seventeenth century, moreover, the term was commonly used to describe not only the collection of money for a charitable purpose but also the money so collected. 'To take collection' or 'to be in collection' was, by then, to be in receipt of parish relief, and it is arguable that the use of the idiom in this sense in parish accounts is as reliable an indicator as any of the spread of formal rating and distribution for the poor.[9] In the late sixteenth century, however, the practices implied by 'collection' might be altogether less uniform.

It is, nonetheless, true that the few extant sixteenth-century accounts —surviving variously in books kept by churchwardens, vicars, and rectors, as well as overseers and vestrymen—suggest that collection of some kind was being practised in Clare (Suffolk) from as early as 1552; in the three Essex parishes of Ingatestone, Stock, and Buttsbury from 1555; in Hadleigh (Suffolk) from 1558; in Heydon (Essex) and Northill (Bedfordshire) from 1563; in Great Bentley (Essex) from 1572; in Wivenhoe (Essex) from 1576; in Great Easton (Essex) from 1577; in Boreham (Essex) from 1585; in Lacock (Wiltshire) from 1589; in Eaton Socon (Bedfordshire) from 1591; in Elmstead (Essex) and Shorne (Kent) from 1598; and in Cowden (Kent) from 1599.[10] The parish officers who

[8] P. Slack, 'Great and Good Towns, 1540–1700', in id. (ed.), *The Cambridge Urban History of Britain*, vol. ii: *1540–1840* (Cambridge, 2000), 367.

[9] *OED*, s.v. 'collection'. The scriptural source for collection in this sense appears to have been 2 Chronicles 24: 9 ('That they shulde bring in to the Lorde the colleccion which Moses appointed'). For the suggestion that collection as an idiom for charity was derived from 'collation', i.e., the provision of food or meals, and therefore implied relief in kind, see *Coming into Line: Local Government in Clayworth, 1674–1714*, ed. A. Rogers (Nottingham, 1979), 116.

[10] M. K. McIntosh, 'Local Responses to the Poor in Late Medieval and Tudor England', *Continuity and Change*, 3 (1988), 229, 243 n. 81; F. G. Emmison, 'The Care of the Poor in Elizabethan Essex: Recently Discovered Records', *Essex Review*, 62 (1953), 7–8, 13, 14, 18, 22–3,

drew up these accounts, however, often made only the haziest of distinctions between payments disbursed by churchwardens on the basis of collections at communion and other times, and those made by collectors for the poor out of funds raised by assessments. Indeed, churchwardens had, since the mid-fifteenth century, been required to keep a parish 'poor box', usually kept in the church, into which donations might be made and from which alms were distributed at their discretion, a policy which (briefly) received statutory backing in 1536.[11] These arrangements prevailed in many parishes throughout the sixteenth century, even though legislation of 1572 introduced the principle of compulsory poor rates assessed and distributed by 'collectors' in each parish.[12] The Elizabethan accounts both disclose a wide variety of fund-raising mechanisms and remind welfare historians of the importance of extreme sensitivity to the terminology overseers employed to describe their revenue. To take only the Essex parishes, for instance, income was derived from 'semi-voluntary, semi-compulsory' contributions in Heydon; from weekly collections which corresponded directly with disbursements in Boreham; from weekly and quarterly assessments in Wivenhoe and Great Easton respectively; and from annual rates in Elmstead.[13]

The traditional voluntaristic arrangement of donations to the poor box is clearly discernible in a small sample of five Hertfordshire parishes with extant sixteenth-century churchwardens' accounts. The 'poor men's boxes' of Baldock and of St Albans St Peters, for example, were repaired in 1548 and 1594 respectively, suggesting that they had previously been used to store collections before these dates.[14] The pattern of disbursement in these parishes was extremely varied. At Baldock, where the churchwardens' income was primarily derived from rent payments, an annual payment of 20*s.* seems to have been made to the poor on Good Friday, a ritual which expresses the other-worldly impulse that often

28; Emmison, 'Poor Relief Accounts of Two Rural Parishes in Bedfordshire, 1563–1598', *Economic History Review*, 3 (1931–2), 104, 108; F. H. Hinton, 'Notes on the Administration of the Relief of the Poor of Lacock 1583–1834', *Wiltshire Archaeological Magazine*, 49 (1940–2), 169; A. F. Allen, 'An Early Poor Law Account', *Archaeologia Cantiana*, 64 (1951), 74–84; E. Turner, 'Ancient Parochial Account Book of Cowden', *Sussex Archaeological Collections*, 20 (1882), 95. The most effective summary of the early history of parish relief in the years before 1598, concentrating mainly on south-eastern England, is McIntosh, 'Local Responses to the Poor', 230–4.

[11] C. Dyer, *Standards of Living in the Later Middle Ages: Social Change in England, c.1200–1520* (Cambridge, 1989), 248; 27 Henry VIII, c. 25.

[12] 14 Elizabeth I, c. 5 (1572); Slack, *Poverty and Policy*, 124–5.

[13] Emmison, 'The Care of the Poor in Elizabethan Essex', 12, 15, 19, 22.

[14] *Tudor Churchwardens' Accounts*, ed. A. Palmer (Hertfordshire Record Society, 1, Braughing, 1985), 66, 151.

characterized medieval charity.[15] At Ashwell, the churchwardens were annually receiving sums from 'collectors for the poor' in the late 1560s, though the fact that the amounts varied significantly from year to year suggest that the fund-raising mechanism was as yet lubricated by exhortation and donation rather than assessment and compulsion. The standardized sums collected in Knebworth in the late 1590s, conversely, suggest that formal rating had been introduced by then, though they were evidently being supplemented by benevolence at the communion.[16]

Neither of these parishes, however, seems to have developed the elaborate system of disbursement that came to characterize the provision of relief in St Peter's over the closing decades of the century. The sums spent by churchwardens on their poor parishioners increased from 8*s.* 8*d.* (18 per cent of their total expenditure) in 1574, to 15*s.* 6*d.* (12 per cent) in 1587, to £2. 15*s.* 3*d.* (22 per cent) in 1592. The rather more detailed accounts of the late 1590s suggest that the welfare regime was coming under strain. In 1597 the costs of poor relief, including sums spent on the maintenance of orphans, the care and burial of the sick, the apprenticeship of poor children, and a weekly pension of 4*d.* to an aged widow, amounted to just over £11, well over half the churchwardens' total expenditure.[17] In Knebworth, by contrast, 'collectors' were still disbursing relief from the 'poor box' in 1605–6, and expenditure was being described as 'almes to the poor' as late as 1609. Distribution seems to have been rare: the only disbursements for which the churchwardens accounted in 1599 were Christmas payments of a shilling to each of nine parishioners. In 1602, however, they recorded that much more varied sums had been given to named parishioners, some of whom had been helped at two or three times during the year.[18] In addition, of course, the churchwardens of these parishes might disburse casual payments of a penny or two to anonymous poor men and women, usually migrants whom they encouraged to pass through, and sometimes even more generous sums of a shilling or two to those who begged under licence.[19] Significantly, however, the officers of one of the Hertfordshire parishes for which churchwardens' accounts survive (Stevenage) recorded no provision of any kind to the poor. In this case, it is just possible that accounts were rendered orally, perhaps describing payments made from

[15] *Tudor Churchwardens' Accounts*, 66.

[16] Ibid. 8, 10, 11, 74, 75, 77. Cf. Ch. 2.4 above.

[17] Ibid. 96, 130, 143, 161.

[18] Ibid. 76, 77, 82, 85. For a Staffordshire parish paying for a new 'poor box' as late as the early *eighteenth* century, see J. Kent and S. King, 'Changing Patterns of Poor Relief in Some English Rural Parishes, *circa* 1650–1750', *Rural History*, 14 (2003), 127.

[19] *Tudor Churchwardens' Accounts*, 78, 96, 161, 163.

bequests or communion gifts, or more likely (given that Stevenage was a market town) that collectors for the poor kept a separate account book which has not survived. It is nonetheless clear that in Bedfordshire, Essex, Hertfordshire, and Kent (and also, as we shall see, in Buckinghamshire), the closing years of the sixteenth century witnessed the growing sophistication and bureaucratization of poor relief under the authority of collectors for the poor, especially in the market towns and large villages, where need was more urgent, where networks of informal relief were more loose, and where the administrative and fiscal systems of the parish were more sophisticated.[20] The success of these localized experiments in formal relief in the years before 1598 doubtless promoted the expansion of the system even into small rural parishes in the years after the late Elizabethan statutes.

The early history of parish relief in many English regions might be described in similar ways on the basis of extant churchwardens', collectors', or overseers' accounts.[21] The problems involved in extrapolating from isolated records of this kind are, however, worth rehearsing. On the one hand, although it may seem reasonable to assume that, 'if in Northill, then why not also in every other Bedfordshire parish?', it is dangerous to generalize a county-wide or regional pattern on the basis of what might either be an unusually precocious account generated under the auspices of an assiduous collector, overseer, or magistrate, or an atypically sophisticated initiative rendered necessary by peculiar economic circumstances (or, indeed, a combination of both). On the other, it is even more problematic to assume that where there are no extant parish records, there can have been no rates or pensions, not only because archives might have been damaged, lost, or destroyed, but also because accounts might have been cast informally, perhaps even orally. Each of these interpretative difficulties is compounded in those numerous cases where a series of overseers' accounts is interrupted, sometimes for several years at a time.

It is, nonetheless, worth sketching the pattern of record survival. A search of the archives of ten Midland counties suggests that, of approximately 2,000 ancient parishes, only 46 (2.3 per cent) have extant overseers' accounts (however fragmentary or interrupted) predating 1650, and only another 113 (5.5 per cent) have those originating between

[20] See Ch. 4.1(*a*) below.

[21] Cf. the analysis of the process by which the old system of voluntary almsgiving was by degrees giving way to the compulsory system as it is revealed in the churchwardens' accounts of the Bedfordshire parishes of Clifton, Northill, and Shillington. *Elizabethan Churchwardens' Accounts*, ed. J. E. Farmiloe and R. Nixseaman (Publications of the Bedfordshire Historical Record Society, 33, Luton, 1953), pp. xxix–xxxii.

1650 and 1689. All in all, therefore, only one in every thirteen Midland parishes has a surviving set of overseers' papers that include accounts for the period before 1690.[22] In Warwickshire, indeed, only nineteen parishes have surviving overseers' accounts for the period before 1760, and only two (Fillongley from 1623, Kenilworth from 1629) predate 1650.[23] To judge from extant parish archives, then, the parish pension was almost unheard of in rural England until after the Restoration, and relatively uncommon even then.

Indeed, the poor survival rate of overseers' accounts for the period before 1650 has encouraged a rather pessimistic reading of the scale of parish relief in the late sixteenth and early seventeenth centuries. At its most extreme, this has led some commentators into serious under-estimates of the significance of formal welfare provision in early Stuart England. W. K. Jordan notoriously suggested that 'in no year prior to 1660 was more than 7 per cent of all the vast sums expended on the care of the poor derived from taxation'.[24] In part, of course, this calculation was distorted both by his rose-tinted perspective on the nature and scale of philanthropy and by his confidence that charitable funds were successfully channelled to the purposes for which they were intended, but it was also the product of a fundamentally flawed assumption that the absence of an extant overseers' account book implies that rates went uncollected and pensions undisbursed.

Even so, recent commentators have been only slightly more optimistic than Jordan. Paul Slack, for instance, is 'not persuaded that annual rating

[22] This research was conducted in 1986–7 by Kate Birch on behalf of Joanna Innes, to whom I am grateful for making its results available. The counties are Bedfordshire, Buckinghamshire, Cambridgeshire, Huntingdonshire, Leicestershire, Northamptonshire, Oxfordshire, Rutland, and Warwickshire, and the consistency of the pattern of record survival across the sample is striking: for the period before 1650, between 5.3% (Beds.) and 1.3% (Bucks. and War.); for the period 1650–89, between a further 8.6% (Cambs.) and a further 1.8% (Hunts.).

[23] The growth of relief expenditure in sixteen of these parishes is charted in S. Hindle, *The Birthpangs of Welfare: Poor Relief and Parish Governance in Seventeenth-Century Warwickshire* (Dugdale Society Occasional Papers, 40, Stratford-upon-Avon, 2000), fig. 4. The relevant overseers' accounts for these sixteen parishes, all held in the WCRO (except where noted), are Alcester 1658–89 (DR360/63); Astley 1656–1741 (DR19/251–322); Atherstone-on-Stour 1702–1873 (DR240/58); Bidford 1665–82 (HR71/11 (Box 2)), 1682–1740 (SBTRO, DR203); Brailes 1710–62 (DR308/50–53); Claverdon 1709–52 (DR166/19, 23–4); Farnborough 1665–98, 1717–1813 (DR 30B/1–2); Fillongley 1623–1713 (DR 404/86–91); Grandborough 1704–71 (DR111/26); Ilmington 1709–57 (DR20/21–22); Kenilworth 1629–75 (DR296/43); Knowle 1705–65 (DRB56/135–6); Leamington-Hastings 1655–1735 (DR43A/19–22); Napton 1663–1736 (NI/1–19); Sowe 1667–1728 (DR104/63); and Tysoe 1727–38 (DR467/1), 1749–68 (DR288/41).

[24] W. K. Jordan, *Philanthropy in England, 1480–1660* (London, 1959), 140.

was practised in the majority of country parishes before 1650'.[25] This sceptical reading of the significance of the *survival pattern* of overseers' accounts intriguingly coincides with much the most sophisticated analysis of their *content*, conducted on the parish archives of the county of Norfolk. Tim Wales suggested that it was not until the years of political, religious, and economic crisis in the years 1647–50, a full half-century after the decisive legislation, that the maximum parish pension doubled, the share of formal rose disproportionately above that of informal relief, and the poor law was finally institutionalized where it was not already a fact of life.[26]

Less obvious sources than overseers' account books are, however, available to give at least a plausible reading of the spread of parish pensions across rural England before 1650, and taken together they suggest that the now orthodox 'slow-track' interpretation of the implementation of the poor laws is unduly pessimistic. The following discussion is based on five of them: the churchwardens' presentments of the archdeaconry of Buckingham for Easter 1597; the returns of expenditure on poor relief surviving in the papers of the Barrington family of Hatfield Broad Oak (Essex) in 1599; the administrative papers kept by the Norfolk magistrate Nathaniel Bacon of Stiffkey in the years 1600–2; the reports by the churchwardens of the parishes in the Warwickshire hundreds of Kineton and Barlichway in 1605–6; and the certificates drawn up by the parish officers of south Warwickshire at Easter 1639. Each of these sources has the advantage of covering a number of contiguous local communities, enabling the historian of welfare to overhear dialogue, some of it only faintly audible above the white noise generated by archival attrition, about the organization of parish relief.

25 P. Slack, *From Reformation to Improvement: Public Welfare in Early Modern England* (Oxford, 1999), 67 n. 55. For his earlier assessment that perhaps one-third of English parishes were accustomed to raising taxes for the poor by 1660, see Slack, *Poverty and Policy*, 170 n. 37. Cf. the view that even in 'much-governed' Essex the introduction of poor rates 'proceeded only slowly and steadily from 1570 down to the civil war'. W. Hunt, *The Puritan Moment: The Coming of Revolution in an English County* (Cambridge, Mass., 1983), 248.

26 T. Wales, 'Poverty, Poor Relief and the Life-Cycle: Some Evidence from Seventeenth-Century Norfolk', in R. M. Smith (ed.), *Land, Kinship and Life-Cycle* (Cambridge, 1984), 354, 357, 359–60. For the influence of this view, chiming as it does with evidence drawn from Cheshire, Devon, and Lancashire, see A. Fletcher, *Reform in the Provinces: The Government of Stuart England* (New Haven, 1986), 187. Cf. the more speculative remarks of A. L. Beier, 'Poverty and Progress in Early Modern England', in A. L. Beier *et al.* (eds.), *The First Modern Society: Essays in English History in Honour of Lawrence Stone* (Cambridge, 1989), 234–6; and Hindle, *The State and Social Change*, 153–62.

(*a*) Buckinghamshire, 1596–7

At Christmas 1596, as we have seen, the privy council enjoined the archbishops of Canterbury and York to require the bishops and, in turn, the churchwardens of every parish in the country to co-ordinate the giving of alms to the poor.[27] This campaign provides fascinating insights into both elite and popular thinking about the nature of charitable obligations, but because it exploited a machinery of presentment through which the churchwardens would inform their archdeacons and, in turn, their bishops, the archbishops, and ultimately the privy council, of the nature and scale of local co-operation, it also generated remarkable, indeed unique, evidence of the practice of formal relief across the parishes of late Elizabethan England. Since the council's orders required that collections for the poor under the terms of the 1572 statute be 'carefully gathered and charitably increased', the surviving presentments offer an unrivalled glimpse into the provision of welfare on the eve of the introduction of the great poor laws of 1598 and 1601.

In late March and early April 1597, the churchwardens of 117 Buckinghamshire parishes submitted presentments to William Chaderton, bishop of Lincoln, reporting on their performance of the council's orders.[28] The standard formula of response, used in fifty-two of the certificates, represents particularly problematic evidence of the organization of parish relief. When churchwardens reported that 'the poor of our parish are provided for according to our ability' they (perhaps deliberately) revealed nothing about the mechanics of welfare, making no reference to collectors or overseers, let alone rates or pensions. Although these formulaic presentments might conceivably conceal a far wider range of practices, these parishes were probably running 'collection' schemes that remained firmly based on voluntary contributions, co-ordinated (however regularly) by the churchwardens and inspired (however conscientiously) by the exhortation of the parish minister. Indeed, the ambiguous nature of revenue-raising of this kind is perhaps best described in the terms used by Henry Arthington in 1597, who thought 'collection' was a matter of 'general ceassement voluntarie'.[29] This supposition is borne out by a comparison of the 1597 returns with

[27] For the context, see S. Hindle, 'Dearth, Fasting and Alms: The Campaign for General Hospitality in Late Elizabethan England', *Past and Present*, 172 (2001), 44–86; and cf. Ch. 2.2 above.

[28] LA, Ch.p/2, 3, 4 (churchwardens' presentments and certificates for the archdeaconry of Buckingham, 1597).

[29] H. Arthington, *Provision for the Poore Now in Penurie* (London, 1597), sig. C1^{r}.

other evidence of the early development of social welfare provision in Buckinghamshire.

The Buckinghamshire justices had reported to the privy council in February 1587 that 'divers honest and discreet persons' had been appointed overseers 'in every market towne, as in other townes needful'.[30] The collection of rates was, therefore, initially focused in particular parishes, and especially market towns, rather than being generally applied. When, after the enactment of the 1598 statute, Chief Justice Popham issued a set of twenty articles stipulating the enforcement of the new statutes, at least one Buckinghamshire parish (Swanbourne) can be shown to have received and kept them.[31] The lack of evidence of enforcement of either the 1587 order or the 1599 articles is nonetheless striking. Not a single Buckinghamshire parish has an extant overseers' account book which predates 1600, and the chronology of their survival over the course of the following century is patchy to say the least. Of the twenty-six Buckinghamshire parishes with extant seventeenth-century accounts, only four (Amersham from 1611, High Wycombe from 1630, Stoke Poges from 1639, Great Marlow from 1646) predate 1650.[32] It is, admittedly, unwise to assume that the absence of overseers' account books proves that rates went uncollected, not least because (as we have seen) the very small sums that were involved in late sixteenth-century poor relief probably rendered separate formal accounting unnecessary. Nevertheless, in only two of the Buckinghamshire parishes for which certificates survive is there unequivocal evidence that emergency relief required in 1597 was supplementary to *existing* collections for the poor: the churchwardens of Langley Marish referred to 'ordinary collections' and those of North Crawley to the 'wonted collection'.[33] On balance, it is likely that these two parishes were not raising money by rates.

Similarly, at least three of the five surviving volumes of Elizabethan churchwardens' accounts for Buckinghamshire parishes include refer-

[30] NA, SP12/199/43/1–2, 4–5. The 'other townes needful' were almost certainly those in which there were no resident magistrates, or at least those with no gentlemen. This formula was also used in the certificates from Bedfordshire (NA, SP12/191/6, 200/10), a county in which only two sets of overseers accounts from rural parishes survive from the reign of Elizabeth. Emmison, 'Poor Relief Accounts', 102 n. 4. Of the Buckinghamshire certificates, only that from Ashendon hundred (NA, SP12/199/43/3) failed to refer explicitly to the appointment of overseers.

[31] W. Lambarde, *Eirenarcha* (London, 1599), 206 ff.; '[Articles] To the Constables of Swanbourne, 10 Dec. 1599', in *Papers from an Iron Chest at Doddershall, Bucks.*, ed. G. Eland (Aylesbury, 1937), 39–43 (no. 16).

[32] CBS, PR4/12/2; 249/12/1; 198/12/1; 140/12/1–2.

[33] LA, Ch.p/2/30, 3/12.

ences to payments for the poor. At Wing, collectors for the poor were first appointed in 1567, and disbursements 'out of the [poor man's] box', ranging between 4*d.* and 3*s.* in total, were being made annually to the poor on All Souls' Day until 1583. By the late 1570s, the balance of the fund varied between £4 and £5, and accounts were rendered 'before the vicar, the churchwardens and other of the parish'. This system appears to have fallen into abeyance in the mid-1580s, however, since the churchwardens' accounts for the 1590s lack any reference to poor relief.[34] At Ludgershall, collectors for the poor were first nominated by the churchwardens in 1592, and the records of their appointment become regular thereafter. The parishioners agreed at the same time that a poor rate of a penny a yardland should be collected each month.[35] Arrangements were much less formal at Aston Abbots, where the accounts record only very sporadic payments to individual 'poor foulkes'. Here too, however, there was an interesting change of register during the course of the 1590s. Occasional payments were generally described as having been made to those 'that gathered' (i.e. begged) until 1598, when the language of accounting came to reflect novel statutory provisions, recording payments to those 'with a lycense' (i.e. to beg).[36] The churchwardens of neither Great Marlow nor Amersham, the only other parishes with extant Elizabethan accounts, by contrast, concerned themselves with the poor, the former not appointing collectors for the poor until 1609, the latter purchasing an overseers' account book only in 1611.[37] In only one Buckinghamshire parish (Ludgershall), therefore, is the evidence unequivocal that poor relief was being funded out of formally assessed rates at any time before 1598.[38] Indeed, Ludgershall is the one unambiguous case of a parish whose poor were provided with both parish relief under the terms of the 1572 statute and the co-ordinated almsgiving specified in 1596. This was a peasant-settled, forest-edge parish in which cottages, doubtless originally erected by squatters engaged in woodland

[34] CBS, PR234/5/1, fos. 64–86. The charitable practices of the parishioners of Elizabethan Wing may have been inflected with religious conservatism, for All Souls' was by the 1560s an abrogated feast. *The Book of Common Prayer, 1559*, ed. J. E. Booty (Washington, DC, 1976), 46.

[35] CBS, PR138/5/1, unfol.

[36] CBS, PR7/5/1, *passim.*

[37] CBS, PR140/5/1, fo. 24; 4/5/1, *passim*; 4/12/2.

[38] The meagre provision of formal relief in Elizabethan Buckinghamshire was almost certainly outstripped by the provision of private charity in the county. Indeed, Jordan believed that 'a substantially larger proportion of charitable wealth was devoted to the succour of the poor' in Buckinghamshire 'than in any of the other ten counties in his study, or, for that matter, there is reason to believe, any other county in England'. W. K. Jordan, *The Charities of Rural England 1480–1660: The Aspirations and Achievements of the Rural Society* (London, 1961), 33.

clearance, were clustered almost randomly around either side of the high street leading to a large village green.[39]

Comparison of the Buckinghamshire certificates of 1597 with the evidence of churchwardens' accounts therefore suggests that, although emergency relief might have been supplementary to existing *collections*, it was emphatically not augmenting a system of *rates*, whatever the 1572 statute and the *Three Sermons or Homilies* of 1596 might suggest. The *Three Sermons*, significantly, conceded that the day-to-day management of parish assessments was beyond the capacity of the county justices themselves: 'how well would it beseeme the godly care of our magistrates to see some order taken for the provision and relief of the poore and to choose out in everie parish men of conscience fearing God and hating covetousness into whose hands they might comit the trust of the business'.[40] The reality of charitable provision in Buckinghamshire reflects this sober assessment, for compulsory rating seems to have been virtually unknown in the county before the harvest failures of the late 1590s. The collective charity of Elizabethan householders seems to have been embodied less in the rate book than in the communion collection; less in the parish pension than in the Easter dole; less in discretionary relief than in general hospitality.

(*b*) Essex, 1599

There is some evidence in parish archives of precocious relief experiments in Essex, not only (as we have seen) in the scattered parish accounts which survive from the 1560s onwards, but also in the minutes of the Dedham conference, where a complaint of 1584 that householders were oppressed with the begging of strangers notwithstanding the fact that they 'paid money besides' hints that the communities of north Essex were already rated for poor relief.[41] The poor relief returns kept by Sir Thomas Barrington of Hatfield Broad Oak (Essex) in 1599 are, nonetheless, particularly useful evidence of the nature of parish relief in the immediate aftermath of the 1598 statute, especially since they were drawn up before its provisions were slightly amended in 1601. The Essex bench had, in fact, almost immediately complied with the earlier of the two

[39] Cf. the Elizabethan map of Ludgershall reproduced in Hindle, 'Dearth, Fasting and Alms', 79. For Ludgershall, see *The Victoria History of the County of Buckinghamshire*, ed. W. Page (4 vols., London, 1925), iv. 68–73.

[40] *Three Sermons, or Homelies, to Move Compassion Towards the Poor and Needy* (London, 1596), sig. G2.

[41] *Conferences and Combination Lectures in the Elizabethan Church: Dedham and Bury St Edmunds, 1582–1590*, ed. P. Collinson *et al.* (Church of England Record Society, 10, Woodbridge, 2003), 10. See the introductory section to this chapter.

statutes, commanding in April 1598 the appointment of overseers where none had yet been named. The five certificates relate only to four parishes, in two of which relief was administered by overseers, in a third by churchwardens, and in a fourth by unspecified officers. They are nonetheless extremely revealing of the potentially rapid progress of, but also of the chronic problems inherent within, parish relief.[42] At Latton, there were fifty poor people, including five 'aged and impotent', sixteen who were 'able to worke and neede to be releved', and twenty-three children, four of whom were old enough to be set to work. The impotent, the overseers reported, were relieved 'by the collection and other helpes raised amongst th'inhabitants' and the able-bodied were employed 'in such sorte as not any one of them hath or shall have cause to complaine through want'. No householders, they insisted, refused to contribute 'as they are assessed'.[43] At Roydon, the overseers had spent over £14 on the impotent poor, of whom they calculated there were twelve, and further £7. 10*s.* 0*d.* in providing a stock for the thirty-eight indigents who were 'in sorte able to take paynes & to labour'.[44] At Harlow, relief expenditure on the poor totalled over £13, 13.5 per cent of which was spent on the purchase of 'sartyn apparyll' and 'wheles for the poar', and the officers noted that they were overspent on their income by some 6 per cent.[45] Relief expenditure at Sheering was almost £24, but here too the overseers were struggling to make ends meet, not least because the parish was 'greatly charged with young children', two of whom were boarded out and a further four of whom had been apprenticed. The officers complained both of the necessity of a stock of between £5 and £6 to maintain the employment of ten poor labourers and of the insufficiency of the pensions of 4*d.* weekly allocated to five aged paupers who had perforce been 'much favoured and relieved otherwise'.[46]

It is apparent from these accounts that the overseers of western Essex had implemented assessments for the poor almost as soon, if not before, the 1598 statute had required them to do so. Although parish officers might be prepared to comply quickly with the legislation, however, they were immediately confronted with significant problems which were to

[42] BL, MS Harley, 7020, fo. 267 (28 Apr. 1598) misdated to 3 Apr. 1598 in *Tudor Economic Documents*, ed. R. H. Tawney and E. Power (3 vols., London, 1924), ii. 362–4; ERO, D/DBa/O8/1–5. For another county bench responding almost immediately to the statute with general orders for the relief of the poor in June 1598, see *West Riding Sessions Records, 1597–1642*, ed. J. Lister (2 vols., Yorkshire Archaeological Society Record Series, 3, 54, Leeds, 1888–1915), i. 84–7.

[43] ERO, D/DBa/O8/1 (Latton).

[44] ERO, D/DBa/O8/5 (Roydon).

[45] ERO, D/DBa/O8/4 (Harlow).

[46] ERO, D/DBa/O8/2–3 (Sheering).

recur across rural England over the next century: the relative preponderance of able-bodied over impotent paupers; the necessity of substantial investment in parish stocks to prevent the needs of the aged being swallowed up by those of the labouring poor; and the extraordinarily heavy demands placed on parish budgets by the very young, a constituency which included not only orphans but also the children of the indigent. Indeed, the situation in these parishes almost perfectly embodied Chief Justice Montagu's worst fear, expressed in 1618, that the tax base of most parishes simply could not cope if ratepayers were expected to meet all the needs of the idle (and their children), as well as those of the impotent.[47] Little wonder that two of the parishes should refer explicitly to other 'helps' and 'favours' upon which pensioners had been forced to draw in addition to their collection. The precocious introduction of parish relief had emphatically not obviated informal aid in late sixteenth-century Essex, and it would be several decades before it came anywhere close to doing so.

(*c*) Norfolk, 1600–2

The papers of the Norfolk magistrate Nathaniel Bacon of Stiffkey contain two sheaves of overseers' accounts which Bacon appears to have audited at Easter 1601 and Easter 1602. The first, and fuller, set (for the accounting year 1600–1) is for twenty-six contiguous parishes in the north-east of the county, at least twenty-five of which were assessing and collecting contributions from ratepayers, and eighteen of which were distributing relief to named parishioners, at least three of them doing so on a weekly basis.[48] A second set of thirteen accounts for the year 1601–2 suggests that rating was practised and pensions disbursed in ten parishes, at least two of them weekly.[49] That references to 'old stock' (in twelve of the parishes audited at Easter 1601 and six of those at Easter 1602) and to 'arrears' (twice in 1601, and on a further two occasions in 1602) are common throughout these accounts suggests that formal relief was probably not an innovation in these years, and that the momentum of bureaucracy had been building in these communities since, and possibly even in some cases before, the 1598 statute.

Accounts of the kind kept by Bacon and Barrington can never tell us exactly how and when parish relief was first introduced in north-east

[47] Bodl., MS Tanner, 243, fo. 14.

[48] The following discussion is based upon *The Papers of Nathaniel Bacon of Stiffkey*, ed. A. Hassell Smith *et al.* (4 vols., Norfolk Record Society, 46, 49, 53, 64, Norwich, 1978–2000), iv, 187–92.

[49] Ibid. 237–8. Since ten parishes are common to both sets of accounts, reconciliation of the evidence for the twenty-nine parishes suggests that twenty-seven raised a rate and twenty-two distributed pensions in either or both of the accounting years.

Norfolk or western Essex, but they are very revealing of its spread across a number of communities under the supervision of an energetic magistrate. Indeed, it is highly likely that the very requirement to have overseers' accounts audited by a JP itself stimulated the transition from oral accounting or marginalia by churchwardens to the keeping of a separate formal record of income and expenditure by overseers. In this respect, the late Elizabethan legislation represented a significant change in the character of welfare. Throughout the sixteenth century, poor relief statutes had made vague, and sometimes contradictory, stipulations about the hierarchy of responsibility within the parish relief system. From 1552, the bishops might admonish those who refused to contribute to collections, a responsibility transferred in 1563 to the magistrates, who might coerce the recalcitrant by threats of imprisonment. From 1572, JPs were responsible for surveying the poor in their county divisions, a requirement that only complicated the ambiguous division of labour with overseers, who were to restrict the administration of relief in the parishes only to those individuals listed. Latitude of this kind is perhaps to be expected in a system which, in all its essentials, remained voluntary until at least 1572.[50] The 1598 statute therefore marked the first attempt to bind parishes into a county-wide system supervised and audited by magistrates, and ensured that overseers recognized the importance not only of casting, but also of keeping, formal accounts. They could, after all, be fined 20*s.* for failing to do so.[51] The accounts surviving in the archives of Thomas Barrington and Nathaniel Bacon are, in themselves, testimony to the bureaucratic imperative implied by the legislation, for overseers must have been far more assiduous in keeping accurate records once they knew that they would be inspected by magistrates. The requirement for annual audit also, by definition, increased the chances of record survival, for even if original account books might perish in, or disappear from, insecure chests in damp parish vestries, copies could more safely be kept in the libraries and muniment rooms of the magistracy.[52] As we shall see,

[50] For the ambiguities of these statutes, see Slack, *Poverty and Policy*, 124–5; McIntosh, 'Local Responses to the Poor', 229, 233–4.

[51] 39 Elizabeth I, c. 3 sect. i, stipulated that overseers should have their accounts audited by two justices within four days of the end of their year of office.

[52] On habits of archive management in Elizabethan and early Stuart parishes, see J. S. Craig 'Co-operation and Initiatives: Elizabethan Churchwardens and the Parish Accounts of Mildenhall', *Social History*, 18 (1993), 357–80; P. Griffiths, 'Secrecy and Authority in Late Sixteenth- and Early-Seventeenth Century London', *Historical Journal*, 40 (1997), 925–51. For the muniment rooms and libraries of the landed elite, see F. Heal and C. Holmes, *The Gentry in England and Wales, 1500–1700* (London and New York, 1994), 278–82; and J. T. Cliffe, *The World of the Country House in Seventeenth-Century England* (New Haven, 1999), 163–76.

a Warwickshire magistrate with even more enthusiasm for the collection and storage of archives retained a set of parish accounts in the late 1630s that provide an invaluable supplement to those kept by Barrington and Bacon.

(*d*) Warwickshire, 1605–6

Where magistrates were not so dedicated, however, it might be some considerable time before overseers were ever appointed, let alone before they submitted formal accounts. When the parish officers of Barlichway and Kineton hundreds in Warwickshire were asked in the autumn of 1605 to report on the social and moral condition of their parishioners, and especially about levels of recusancy, drunkenness, alehouse-haunting, and vagrancy, it was, significantly, the churchwardens rather than the overseers of the poor who were expected to reply. Almost as an afterthought, they were also required to describe the provision they had made for the relief of the poor.[53] Eighty-six parishes responded: thirty one (36 per cent) commented merely that the poor were 'relieved' or 'provided for'; a further fifteen (17 per cent) that such relief took place 'within the parish'; and another twenty-four (28 per cent) that relief was sufficiently well organized that the poor were no longer 'wandering [i.e. begging] abroad'.

These anodyne formulae might well obscure a range of provision that had been fine-tuned to accommodate local circumstances. Relief 'within the parish' perhaps suggests that the poor were boarded or billeted, and relief without 'wandering abroad' might well have been organized through general hospitality and localized door-to-door begging. Only six parishes (7 per cent), after all, made explicit reference to provision 'according to the statute', a phrase which might be taken to imply that rates were being raised and pensions distributed, and only one (Chadshunt and Gaydon) mentioned 'collection'. On the other hand, only ten (12 per cent) of the presentments confessed that there was no provision for the poor at all. On the very rare occasions when parish officers supplemented their formulaic certificates with more precise details, the strengths and weaknesses of these early stages of formal welfare provision become slightly more apparent. In Newbold Pacy, it was reported, the poor were provided for 'in good sort'; at Ullenhall and Ippesley they were 'well relieved'. At Alcester, where there were perhaps c.120 households, the parish officers quantified their achievement, commenting that 'the poor people being twenty in number are relieved in the

53 WCRO, CR1618/W19/3, unfol.

parish without wandering'. In Moreton Morell, however, the officers reported that, although the poor were generally provided for, one 'John Wilson a poor blind man wanteth relief', a failure that they did not see fit to explain. In only one parish, however, does the apparatus of relief seem to have been seriously unstable. In Brailes, it was reported, 'the poore have been releyved, but the number beinge greate and inhabitantes abilities small, they can no longer releive them without helpe of the hundred or Countie'.

The fact that other contemporary comment elaborates on this laconic plea for a rate-in-aid to be raised in adjacent parishes suggests that the realities of relief in these south Warwickshire villages were far more precarious than the euphemistic language of the presentments suggests. The situation in Brailes was evidently desperate. At least thirty of its inhabitants, explained Barnabas Bishop in January 1599, were utterly unable to 'gett any parte of their living', and were therefore forced either to beg or to solicit somebody to beg for them, 'they not being able'. At least another seventy inhabitants were 'old people and children that are not able to gett the one half of their lyvinge', even 'if they have worke fytt for them'. A further ninety residents were labourers, the majority of whom 'for wante of worke' were 'compelled to begge, and yf they should not have good helpe now, they must steale or starve'. In a parish of perhaps 130 households, therefore, almost 200 individuals were victims of under- and unemployment.[54] Worse still, the tax base could not support the burden. There were too few men of means in the parish to supply the demands of the indigent out of an assessment for the poor: 'there is not any man within our parish', Bishop insisted, 'that we thinke able to spare a penny a weeke, but he is at a weekely paiment'. Bishop therefore feared that 'diverse of our poore must be suffered to begg amongst us until more forraine help be had'.[55] In at least one parish, therefore, the logical flaw of the Elizabethan statutes, the presupposition that there was both a constituency of poor people who were in need of relief and a pool of ratepayers who might not only be willing but actually *able* to relieve them, was already apparent.[56]

[54] See Henry E. Huntington Library, San Marino, California, MS Temple of Stowe, 110 (Barnabas Bishop to John Temple, 23 Jan. 1599). For the context, see E. F. Gay, 'The Rise of an English Country Family: Peter and John Temple to 1603', *Huntington Library Quarterly*, 4 (1938), 389–90; J. E. Martin, *Feudalism to Capitalism: Peasant and Landlord in English Agrarian Development* (London and New York, 1983), 207–13. There were 115 households in Brailes in 1563, and 18[illegible] in 1664. See Hindle, *The Birthpangs of Welfare*, appendix I.

[55] Henry E. Huntington Library, MS STT, 110.

[56] Beier, 'Poverty and Progress', 239.

(*e*) Warwickshire, 1639

Much the most comprehensive of the early seventeenth-century sources for the nature and scale of formal welfare provision, however, is the series of overseers accounts and papers for thirty-nine south Warwickshire parishes for the accounting year 1638–9.[57] They appear to have been presented to a meeting of the justices of Kineton hundred at Wellesbourne in April 1639, almost certainly in preparation for a report to the privy council under the terms of the *Orders and Directions* of January 1631, popularly known as the 'Book of Orders', and were preserved for posterity by the antiquarian and magistrate Sir Simon Archer.[58] Although the *Orders* restated existing legislation with respect to the relief of the poor, the employment of the idle, the apprenticeship of children, the punishment of vagrancy, the construction of houses of correction, and the closing of alehouses, they also stipulated new administrative procedures in the localities, not the least significant of which were quarterly reports on the enforcement of the orders to the privy council by magistrates in each division of each county.[59] While the origins, nature, and significance of the *Orders* have generated historiographical controversy too complex to rehearse here, the dangers of using the numbers of magistrates' certificates surviving among the state papers as an index of the enthusiasm of county benches for the prerogative paternalism of the Caroline regime have recently been emphasized. Certificates were often sent and never received, or even received and never filed.[60] There is no extant return to the privy council on the basis of the 1639 Kineton hundred accounts, for example, although, given magistrates' capacity for economy with the truth, it would doubtless have made interesting reading.

[57] SBTRO, DR37/85/6/1–53. The returns, which survive among the miscellaneous official and legal manuscripts of the magistrate and antiquarian Sir Simon Archer, are transcribed in Hindle, *The Birthpangs of Welfare*, 37–74 (appendix II). These documents are very briefly noticed in A. Hughes, *Politics, Society and Civil War in Warwickshire, 1620–1660* (Cambridge, 1987), 57–8 n. 31. For Archer himself, see P. Styles, 'Sir Simon Archer: "A Lover of Antiquity and the Lovers Thereof"', repr. in id., *Studies in Seventeenth-Century West Midlands History* (Kineton, 1978), 1–41.

[58] 'The Book of Orders'. Sir Simon Archer's antiquarian notebook contains a note (dated 19 July 1639) of the amounts due from nine parishes in Kineton hundred towards five different county expenses, suggesting that Archer was frequently in receipt of parish papers as part of his work as a JP. SBTRO, DR473/293, fo. 50.

[59] For the origins of the *Orders and Directions* of 1631, see B. W. Quintrell, 'The Making of Charles I's Book of Orders', *English Historical Review*, 95 (1980), 553–72. This 'Book of Orders' is set in the context of pre-existing plague and dearth orders by P. Slack, 'Books of Orders: The Making of English Social Policy, 1577–1631', *Transactions of the Royal Historical Society*, 5th ser., 30 (1980), 1–22; and Slack, *From Reformation to Improvement*, 53–76.

[60] H. Langelüddecke, '"Patchy and Spasmodic": The Response of Justices of the Peace to Charles I's Book of Orders', *English Historical Review*, 113 (1998), 1231–48.

For the record, the nine extant certificates submitted by Warwickshire JPs in the 1630s convey an overwhelming sense of complacency.[61] Only one of these was drawn up by the justices of Kineton hundred, again meeting at Wellesbourne in August 1631, and its contents vividly convey the manner in which magistrates might gloss the reports they had themselves received from parish governors. Rehearsing both their own achievements ('the reformation wrought by the longe continuance of our monthly meetings') and the negligible scale of social problems ('the paucity of alehouses within our division, which are the true nurseries of almost all the disorders pointed at in the Book of Orders'), the justices informed the council that they had 'so little to certify you as in truth deserveth not the mention'. Their long postscript on the subterfuges practised by local recusants nevertheless conceded that their inability to distrain the goods of Catholics had provoked the 'disapoyntment of the needy poor from that good relyfe' that should have been 'afforded unto them very seasonably in the time of the late hard and pinching dearth'.[62] This casual reference to the deteriorating economic context ought to have given the privy council pause to wonder whether the certificate concealed as much as it revealed. It is certainly very significant that this 1631 report makes no mention at all of parish rates, referring only to the relief of the deserving poor out of fines on those who would not accommodate themselves to the services of the Established Church.

Although, as we have seen, welfare initiatives had probably been undertaken in at least one south Warwickshire parish (Brailes) as early as 1599, formal rating long remained the exception rather than the rule in this part of the Midlands.[63] The county magistrates generally stipulated that parish rates should be raised only 'in aid' for adjacent parishes whose householders could not relieve their own poor informally through parochial 'collections'.[64] The 'grevaunces' of those who protested about the evils of depopulating enclosures in Warwickshire in 1607 similarly betray the popular expectation that relief was rather a matter of gentry paternalism than of ratepayers' assessments.[65] Indeed, in one of the few

[61] The certificates are NA, SP16/198/48 (19 Aug. 1631), 199/65 (17 Sept. 1631), 200/40 (28 Sept. 1631), 293/44 (5 July 1635), 293/65 (5 July 1635), 305/75 (31 Dec. 1635), 314/116 (29 Feb. 1636).

[62] NA, SP16/198/48.

[63] As at Brailes in 1599. See HEHL, MS STT, 1444 (three Warwickshire justices to John Temple, 9 Jan. 1599).

[64] Cf. the policy of the Somerset justices revealed in HMC, *Report on the Manuscripts of the Marquis of Lothian Preserved at Blickling* (London, 1905), 77–8.

[65] NA, SP16/307/2, fo. 2. This petition was apparently submitted after the 'pacifacon' of the 'troubles' of 1607, but is inaccurately dated to (?)1635 by *Calendar of State Papers, Domestic, 1635–36*, 22.

Warwickshire grand jury charges to survive from the early seventeenth century, Sir John Newdigate's 1608 list of 'the statutes that now being executed will best relieve the poore' placed less emphasis on the Elizabethan poor laws than on the fining of alehouse keepers and drunkards to the benefit of the impotent, and on 'pernicious' and 'unchristian' breaches of hospitality.[66]

By the later 1630s, however, all this had changed. The privy council itself was all too aware of the dangers of dearth, openly admitting in January 1638 that 'the poor of the counties of Gloucester, Worcester and Warwick without some present relief are not able to subsist'.[67] Indeed, whether the privy council eventually heard about it or not, the parish returns collated at Wellesbourne in April 1639 suggest that institutionalized poor relief was very widespread by that date. The interest of the 1639 accounts lies in the fact that not a single one of the thirty-nine parishes that made returns has an extant overseers' account book for any period before the civil war. The accounts therefore illuminate several important aspects of early seventeenth-century welfare provision that would otherwise be invisible. Because these parishes were virtually contiguous, the nature and scale of relief across a large number of welfare republics can be compared and contrasted, and the notion of generalizing on the basis of the returns becomes all the more plausible. There are, inevitably, limitations. Little can be said about change in the provision of parish relief over time, for the returns constitute a broad cross-section rather than a narrow time series. Caution must also be exercised about the typicality of this particular accounting year, which (it should be emphasized) was one of relatively high prices. Nonetheless, the returns bring the early history of parish relief into clearer focus.

Although the thirty-nine parishes that submitted returns ranged in population from Wasperton (approximately seventy-seven inhabitants) to Tanworth (approximately 1,270 inhabitants), the vast majority contained between twenty-five and fifty households.[68] All were in Kineton

[66] WCRO, CR136/B711 (2 Oct. 1608). For the context, see V. M. Larminie, *The Godly Magistrate: The Private Philosophy and Public Life of Sir John Newdigate, 1571–1610* (Dugdale Society Occasional Papers, 28, Stratford-upon-Avon, 1982). For the role of penal forfeitures in relieving the poor, see Ch. 6.1 below.

[67] NA, PC2/48, 506. For the context, see R. B. Outhwaite, 'Dearth and Government Intervention in English Grain Markets, 1590–1700', *Economic History Review*, 2nd ser., 33 (1981), 398 n. 67. The harvests of 1637 and 1638 are classified as 'deficient' and 'average' respectively in W. G. Hoskins, 'Harvest Fluctuations and English Economic History, 1620–1759', *Agricultural History Review*, 16 (1968), 16.

[68] See Hindle, *The Birthpangs of Welfare*, appendix I. These rough population estimates are derived from the numbers of households listed in the hearth tax return of Michaelmas 1664: NA, E179/259/10. I am grateful to Professor Ann Hughes for making her analysis of the

hundred, and all (except the three detached Arden parishes of Lapworth, Packwood, and Tanworth) lay in the felden area of mixed farming. The scene of the great depopulating enclosures of the sixteenth century and of the Midland Rising of the early seventeenth, this south-eastern part of the county was dominated by rich yeomen and gentry, the latter standing at the 'pinnacle of a tightly-knit hierarchical society'.[69] Here 'people attended the same parish church and the same manorial court as their neighbours and were in intimate contact with their leading local landlords'.[70] The majority of these thirty-nine parishes were closed, highly manorialized communities able to discourage immigration. They nonetheless had sufficiently productive agriculture to accommodate demographic growth, effectively a recovery after a protracted period of depopulation, of almost 102 per cent between 1563 and 1664. It should be noted, however, that only eighteen of the parishes exceeded this average, and that the populations of at least two (Barford and Wasperton) shrank significantly over the same period.

There were similar variations in the population densities of the parishes. Overall, there were 24.5 households per thousand acres in the region, but Halford and Fenny Compton had rates of forty households per thousand, and above. Although the area is therefore easily characterized as one in which economic change had been relatively slow, 'leaving a society where traditional landmarks remained intact', it was nonetheless relatively heterogeneous in terms of its experience of population growth, immigration, and enclosure.[71] To judge by the hearth tax return of 1664, and more particularly by the proportion of householders exempted from

Warwickshire hearth tax available to me: A. Hughes, 'Politics, Society and Civil War in Warwickshire, 1620–1650 (unpublished Ph.D. thesis, University of Liverpool, 1980), 457–66. The multiplier used here is 4.3, as suggested in T. Arkell, 'Multiplying Factors for Estimating Population Totals From the Hearth Tax', *Local Population Studies*, 28 (1982), 57. The significance of the Warwickshire hearth tax returns is elaborated in P. Styles, 'Introduction to the Warwickshire Hearth Tax Records', in *Warwick County Records: Hearth Tax Returns*, vol. i *Hemlingford Hundred, Tamworth and Atherstone Divisions*, ed. M. Walker (Warwick, 1957), pp. xi–xcviii. Cf. T. Arkell, 'Assessing the Reliability of the Warwickshire Hearth Tax Returns of 1662–74', *Warwickshire History*, 6 (1986–87), 183–97.

[69] Hughes, *Politics, Society and Civil War*, 5. For the economic context, see M. Beresford, 'The Deserted Villages of Warwickshire', *Transactions of the Birmingham Archaeological Society*, 66 (1945–6), 49–106; Beresford, *The Lost Villages of England* (London, 1954), *passim*, but esp. 435; N. W. Alcock, 'Enclosure and Depopulation in Burton Dassett: A Sixteenth Century View', *Warwickshire History*, 3 (1977), 180–4; C. Dyer, *Warwickshire Farming, 1349–c.1520: Preparations for Agricultural Revolution* (Dugdale Society Occasional Papers, 27, Stratford-upon-Avon, 1981); C. Dyer, 'Deserted Medieval Villages in the West Midlands', *Economic History Review*, 2nd ser., 3[illegible] (1982), 19–34; Martin, *Feudalism to Capitalism*, 161–215, esp. 188–92, 204.

[70] Hughes, *Politics, Society and Civil War*, 6.

[71] Ibid. 6. See Hindle, *The Birthpangs of Welfare*, appendix I.

payment of the tax, the social distribution of wealth in Kineton hundred was unexceptional by the standards of rural England, although, as will become clear, there were substantial deviations from the mean exemption rate of 34.4 per cent, reinforcing the perception that some parishes in this region were notoriously poor.[72] Indeed, proverbial wisdom on the condition of some of these south Warwickshire communities was unmerciful: 'Whatcote Downderry, Beggarly Oxhill, Lousy Fulready, Yawning Yettington [Ettington], Peeping Pillarton [Pillerton] and one-eyed Marston'.[73]

Some of them, moreover, were growing poorer. The parish of Brailes, for instance, contained large pools of under-employed labour fruitlessly seeking work in an overwhelmingly pastoral economy. Where the generic problems of open communities like Brailes were compounded by enclosure, the results were explosive, as the participation of the poor husbandmen of Fenny Compton, Harbury, Napton-on-the-hill, and Tysoe in the insurrection of 1607 suggests.[74] Long after the bloody suppression of the rising, the poverty of these parishes provoked the attention of the county bench, which repeatedly ordered rates-in-aid for them, usually at the expense of the graziers of the substantial neighbouring pastures (at Fenny Compton in 1638 and 1648, at Harbury in 1638, and at Napton-on-the-hill in 1638, 1639, 1651, 1653, and 1661). Harbury was so poor, and its ratepayers so recalcitrant, that in 1648 there were insufficient welfare resources to sustain a pension even for an elderly couple who had lived in the parish forty years, surely as deserving a case as can be imagined.[75] By 1664, 91 (49.7 per cent) of the 185 households in Brailes were excused payment of the hearth tax. Some parishes fared even worse: the exemption rate in Fenny Compton was 50 per cent, that in Packwood 53.8 per cent. These differentiated patterns were reflected in the highly localized nature of social welfare provision as it is revealed in the 1639 returns.[76]

That provision, however, was almost universal. While only one of the thirty-nine returns (that for Ettington) was not signed by an overseer of

[72] NA, E179/259/10. Cf. the findings of Tom Arkell reported in D. Levine and K. Wrightson, *The Making of an Industrial Society: Whickham, 1560–1765* (Oxford, 1991), 157. The dangers of using the hearth tax as an index of poverty in isolation from other sources are emphasized in T. Arkell, 'The Incidence of Poverty in England in the Later Seventeenth Century', *Social History*, 12 (1987), 23–47.

[73] K. D. M. Snell, 'The Culture of Local Xenophobia', *Social History*, 28 (2003), 11.

[74] Martin, *Feudalism to Capitalism*, 211–13; R. B. Manning, *Village Revolts: Social Protest and Popular Disturbances in England, 1509–1640* (Oxford, 1988), 245.

[75] *Warwick County Records*, ed. S. C. Ratcliff *et al.* (9 vols., Warwick, 1935–64), i. 88; ii. 8, 17, 19, 78, 82, 193–4, 206, 216; iii. 50, 71, 194, 304; iv. 138–9.

[76] NA, E179/259/10. Cf. Ch. 4.5 below.

the poor, thirty-three itemized relief expenditures for the preceding year and twenty-three actually listed disbursements—including both weekly sums to named pensioners and casual payments—in detail.[77] In five cases, overseers provided summary certificates rather than expenditure totals, though even some of these suggest that the poor were being relieved on a regular, weekly basis. Thus the poor of Honington were both 'relieved weekly' and provided with an annual collection in Easter week; at Moreton Morrell, they were 'duly and sufficiently provided [for]' and maintained 'weekly as they had need'; and at Ratley, they had 'weekly collection'.[78] Rather more ambiguous were the cases of Charlecote, where the overseers declared simply that 'we do maintain and keepe all our poore within our towne that none of them travel [i.e. work] not'; and Wasperton, where the poor were relieved 'at the charge of the parish' when 'they are in necessity and want'.[79] In a sixth case, that of Priors Hardwick, the overseers provided both a laconic testimonial that 'our poor are provided for' and a full set of poor relief disbursements and receipts.[80] Although it should be emphasized that pensions were not invariably funded out of parish rates, it is therefore probable that thirty-six (or 90 per cent) of these parishes were providing regular—in most cases weekly (but in Wasperton and Whichford almost certainly monthly)—pensions or collections for the poor.

There was also a wide range of fund-raising practices, many of them euphemized under the anodyne terminology of 'collection', a term whose ambiguity is well conveyed in its usages in the 1639 accounts. Thus, the parish officers at Fenny Compton described themselves as 'collectors and overseers', and those at Lower Shuckburgh and Whichford simply as 'collectors'. While 'collection' was used to describe *revenue* at Halford, it evidently implied weekly and/or monthly *disbursements* both at Whichford and Priors Hardwick. At Warmington, the overseers inconsistently referred to pensions as both 'collection' and 'pay', while their colleagues at Ratley employed the term to describe both income and expenditure.[81] Nonetheless, although twelve of the thirty-nine parishes entirely failed to provide any details at all of their income, and a further five simply stated

[77] SBTRO, DR37/85/6/13 (Ettington). The Ettington certificate, referring only to the good conduct of an alehousekeeper, is signed by the churchwardens and constable. A partially completed list of new parish officers nonetheless suggests that the parish had in fact appointed overseers of the poor by the following year (1639–40). SBTRO, DR37/85/6/1.

[78] SBTRO, DR37/85/6/19 (Honington), 27 (Moreton Morrell), 35 (Ratley).

[79] SBTRO, DR37/85/6/6 (Charlecote), 44 (Wasperton).

[80] SBTRO, DR37/85/6/17 (Priors Hardwick).

[81] SBTRO, DR37/85/6/7 (Fenny Compton), 18 (Halford), 35 (Ratley), 37 (Lower Shuckburgh), 43 (Warmington), 48 (Whichford), 52 (Priors Hardwick).

their revenue without specifying its origin, the Kineton hundred evidence is nonetheless extremely suggestive. Two sets of parish officers were undeniably ambiguous on their sources of income: the Ratley overseers referred both to 'town stock' and to 'weekly collection'; and those at Wasperton to 'the charge of the parish'.[82] In only one case, in fact, is it certain that overseers were not resorting to compulsory rating: the quarterly receipts of the overseer of Wellesbourne Hastings were sufficiently irregular in size to imply that they were informally collected rather than formally assessed, a suggestion borne out by more precise references made by his colleague at Wellesbourne Mountford to sums collected at communion four times during the year. Even in this latter case, however, 'collections' were supplemented by a parish assessment at the rate of 6*d.* per yardland.[83]

This remarkable, almost unique, archive therefore portrays the efficient and conscientious management of an extensive scheme of parish relief, in which weekly pensions were almost universal and monthly rating extremely common, across virtually the whole of south-east Warwickshire.[84] It must, of course, be remembered that parish officers might deliberately perjure themselves in order to keep 'busy' magistrates off their backs. Indeed, their references to the employment of the labouring poor are suspiciously superficial, detailed inventories of work-stocks or accounts of sums raised being conspicuous by their absence.[85] Nonetheless, the bureaucratic thoroughness with which the officers of the overwhelming majority of these thirty-nine parishes listed their disbursements in particular is plausible evidence that, even before the civil war, the rating and pension provisions of the late Elizabethan poor laws were very effectively enforced in the Midlands, and arguably across rural England as a whole.

(*f*) The Early Chronology of Innovation

All of this leaves unresolved the central question of the precise chronology of innovation during the early seventeenth century. After all, some Warwickshire parishes may well have administered formal relief long before 1639. At Atherstone-on-Stour, it was claimed in 1649, poor relief had been administered 'time out of mind', and at Newbold-on-Avon, in

[82] SBTRO, DR37/85/6/35 (Ratley), 44 (Wasperton).

[83] SBTRO, DR37/85/6/45–6 (Wellesbourne).

[84] Only one of the hundreds of justices' certificates actually filed by the Clerk of the Privy Council, that for the Nottinghamshire hundreds of North and South Clay and Bassetlaw in July 1636, named individual paupers and indicated the size of their doles. NA, SP16/329/63.

[85] Cf. Ch. 3.1 above.

1655, for a period 'beyond the memory of man'.[86] Although these assertions of customary practice may well have been 'invented traditions', exaggerated for rhetorical effect, they nonetheless hint at a hidden history of welfare practice, the archival traces of which have long disappeared. In its absence, historians have explored the records of the Caroline privy council for evidence of central initiatives to stimulate enforcement in the localities (and, of course, of responses to them);[87] and of the county magistracies, for indications of justices' work in co-ordinating parish relief, especially in settling disputes over rating and assessment and in hearing appeals arising from the denial of relief.[88] Between them, these approaches have contributed to the development of a consensus that, subject to significant regional variation, with the far north lagging well behind the south, the 1630s were a significant period in galvanizing parishes into appointing overseers.

In part, this consensus reflects the much fuller documentation surviving in privy council certificates and quarter sessions order books during a decade when the Book of Orders was keeping magistrates on their toes. It has also been reinforced by a growing sense that the emphasis of government policy towards the poor shifted as the harvest failures of the 1620s and 1630s demonstrated that market regulation was far less effective than transfer payments as the principal means of responding to dearth.[89] Finally, some contemporary complaint literature has been taken at face value to suggest that the 1610s in particular were a moribund decade for the implementation of formal relief. Michael Sparke famously complained in 1621 that there had been 'no collection' for the poor in many parishes, especially county towns, for the past seven years.[90] Some commentators have even been tempted to link the chronology of this pessimistic assessment to the fact that the 1614 parliament had failed to continue the 1601 statute, rendering the rating of the poor vulnerable to the same legalistic objections (often, of course, merely cloaking more self-interested motives) that undermined the regulation of the grain

[86] *Warwick County Records*, ii. 248; iii. 274–5.

[87] The classic treatment is E. M. Leonard, *The Early History of English Poor Relief* (Cambridge, 1900), 171–8, 246–66. For an even more thoroughgoing recent analysis of the parish relief practices revealed in the reports to the privy council in the 1630s, see H. A. Langelüddecke, 'Secular Policy Enforcement during the Personal Rule of Charles I: The Administrative Work of Parish Officers in the 1630s' (unpublished D.Phil. thesis, University of Oxford, 1995), 78–104.

[88] The findings of the numerous county studies which have adopted this approach are synthesized in Fletcher, *Reform in the Provinces*, 183–201. Cf. the micro-political approach to these issues in Ch. 6 below.

[89] Slack, *From Reformation to Improvement*, 65–6.

[90] M. Sparke, *Greevous Grones for the Poor* (London, 1621), 14.

market. However paternalistic early Stuart social policy might appear, without statutory backing it was easily portrayed as arbitrary, perhaps even absolutist. It is nonetheless clear that the circuit judges consistently publicized and promoted the implementation of the poor law after 1614, and especially in the late 1610s. Surviving orders by Justice Chamberlain on the Chester and North Wales circuit in July 1616, Justices Montagu and Dodderidge on the Norfolk circuit in November 1617, and Justices Winch and Denham in Lancashire in 1618 called for the collection of poor rates, though significantly all three emphasized the imperative of raising a stock to apprentice pauper children rather than to finance pensions.[91]

All in all, whether rating actually predated or was merely becoming more widespread much before the crisis of 1629–31 remains unclear. Even in the 1630s, few magistrates were prepared to reveal exactly when parish relief had finally been introduced. In the exception that proves this rule, however, two Lancashire JPs informed the privy council in August 1634 that rates had been collected in the parish of Rochdale only since 1628.[92] In those parishes which had already appointed overseers and drawn up assessments in the first two decades of the century, relief expenditure was rising significantly by the 1630s. The cost of parish relief in Cowden (Kent), for example, increased from £9 in 1617, to £28 in 1620, to £43 in 1627; in Pluckley (Kent) from £19 in 1623, to £39 in 1630, to £60 in 1649; and in Frampton (Lincolnshire) from an annual average of £19 in the 1610s to £42 in the 1630s.[93] It is, however, clear that only the crisis of the late 1640s ratcheted up relief costs to levels from which they were not subsequently to fall.[94]

(*g*) The Civil War and Beyond

The chronological concentration of quarter sessions orders in respect of poor law provision in the 1640s and 1650s has generally been taken as an indication that magistrates continued to co-ordinate social welfare

[91] NA, CHES21/3, fo. 368^{v}; Bodl., MS Tanner, 243, fos. 13^{v}–14, 14^{v}–15; *Proceedings of the Lancashire Justices of the Peace at the Sheriff's Table during Assize Week, 1578–1694*, ed. B. W. Quintrell (Record Society of Lancashire and Cheshire, 121, Chester, 1981), 175. The Norfolk orders were reconfirmed in 1621, and they were of sufficient utility to the Norfolk JPs in the 1660s that Robert Doughty retained and used several copies of them. Norfolk RO, AYL304. For judicial interpretation of the poor laws, see Ch. 6.4(*b*) below.

[92] NA, SP16/273/56.

[93] Turner, 'Ancient Parochial Account Book of Cowden', 100; N. Davie, 'Custom and Conflict in a Wealden Village: Pluckley, 1550–1700' (unpublished D.Phil. thesis, University of Oxford, 1988), 227; Hindle, 'Power, Poor Relief, and Social Relations', 81.

[94] Wales, 'Poverty, Poor Relief and the Life-Cycle', 354, 357, 359–60.

despite the dislocating effects of civil war. Indeed, it has been argued that the revolutionary period even saw 'increased provision of relief for the impotent and disabled poor'.[95] But a rather closer reading of the evidence suggests that the effects of military conflict and wartime taxation on the administration of the poor laws were particularly disruptive, even in those areas where magistrates proved themselves most assiduous.[96] In Warwickshire, for instance, the 'distractions' of civil war meant that poor rates had been uncollected at Napton-on-the-Hill 'of late' by 1641; at Priors Marston for the four years to 1647; at Atherstone-on-Stour for the six years to 1649; at Henley-in-Arden for the nine years to 1649; at Temple Balsall for the ten years to 1652; and at Newbold-on-Avon for an unspecified period before 1655. The Warwickshire bench complained of a general failure to enforce the laws in 1651. The absence of overseers, churchwardens, and constables became a regular criticism by petitioners to the Lancashire bench in the late 1640s. So inefficient had the administration of parish relief become in Bolton (Lancashire) by 1648 that the county bench sent the overseers a copy of the whole statute of 1601 with a reminder to 'take especiall care to provyde' for the impotent poor.[97] Although the arrival of Major-General Edward Whalley injected 'religious zeal into the civic arena' and provoked the Warwickshire magistracy in particular to increase substantially the number of poor relief orders it issued in 1656, the remodelled local government of the 1650s seems to have had virtually no impact on the plight of the deserving poor elsewhere. In Flintshire, for example, Major-General Berry had failed to galvanize the local magistracy to the extent that the 'good laws' for the provision of the poor remained 'in great part unexecuted'.[98] There is, indeed, some evidence to suggest that, during the 1650s, overseers were generally reluctant to provide pensions for the impotent until they had been required to do so by the county justices, thereby prefiguring the requirements of a statute of 1692, which insisted that pensions could be

[95] A. L. Beier, 'Poor Relief in Warwickshire, 1630–1660', *Past and Present*, 35 (1966), 81 (esp. tables I and II). Cf. J. S. Morrill, *Cheshire 1630–1660: County Government and Society during the 'English Revolution'* (Oxford, 1974), 247.

[96] P. Tennant, *Edgehill and Beyond: The People's War in the South Midlands, 1642–1645* (Gloucester, 1992), 140–5; and Tennant, *The Civil War in Stratford-upon-Avon: Conflict and Community in South Warwickshire, 1642–1646* (Gloucester, 1996), 141–4. For the growing burden of national taxation in the 1640s and 1650s, see M. J. Braddick, *The Nerves of State: Taxation and the Financing of the English State, 1558–1714* (Manchester, 1996), 95–9.

[97] *Warwick County Records*, ii. 82, 176–7, 248–9; iii. 78–9, 107, 274; A. Fessler, 'The Official Attitude toward the Sick Poor in Seventeenth-Century Lancashire', *Transactions of the Historic Society of Lancashire and Cheshire*, 102 (1951), 92.

[98] Beier, 'Poor Relief in Warwickshire', 81, 97–8; C. Durston, *Cromwell's Major Generals: Godly Government during the English Revolution* (Manchester, 2001), 79.

allocated only with the prior consent of a magistrate. Thus the overseers of Salford (Lancashire) explained in 1659 that they would 'very willingly' provide relief for Alice Hornby but only if she first obtained a relief order from the bench.[99] Perhaps the dubious legality of the commonwealth regime rendered overseers especially sensitive to the dangers of setting precedents without official sanction.

It is the closing decades of the seventeenth century, however, which have become most closely associated with a significant real-terms increase in the cost of poor relief, a finding which is all the more striking since these were years of demographic stagnation and price deflation. Although this was true particularly in the towns, the burden of rising expenditure was also felt in rural parishes.[100] The overseers of Crondall (Hampshire) were spending £25 annually in the early 1690s, a sum that more than doubled to £55 in the period 1693–7. At Frampton (Lincolnshire), annual relief expenditure jumped from £57 in the 1690s, to £84 in the 1700s, to £104 in the 1730s. At Stone (Staffordshire) relief costs increased from £111 in 1691 to £191 in 1708; at Gnosall from £32 in 1681 to £110 in 1731. At Clayworth (Nottinghamshire) expenditure on the poor doubled between 1674 and 1694 and had tripled by 1709.[101] In some cases, it has been argued, the increase was due to a rise in the value of the average level of pensions, but there is also some evidence that the numbers on relief were also increasing as they did in Crondall (from eight pensioners to seventeen over the course of the 1690s) and in Stone (from ninety-six to 114) in the two decades after 1691.[102] It also seems likely, however, that the retrenchment initiatives of the late seventeenth and the eighteenth centuries (especially the parish badge, the augmented statutory powers to bind out pauper children, and the workhouse test) may have succeeded by the 1720s and 1730s in driving down expenditure, as was the case in Stone, where expenditure had fallen to only 31 per cent of its 1708 level by 1735.[103]

[99] Fessler, 'The Sick Poor in Seventeenth-Century Lancashire', 106. Cf. Ch. 6.4(*a*) below.

[100] Kent and King, 'Changing Patterns of Poor Relief', 123–6.

[101] Beier, 'Poverty and Progress', 223–4; S. Hindle, 'Power, Poor Relief and Social Relations in Holland Fen, *c.*1600–1800', *Historical Journal*, 41 (1998), 81; S. R. Broadbridge, 'The Old Poor Law in the Parish of Stone', *North Staffordshire Journal of Field Studies*, 13 (1973), 12; S. A. Cutlack, 'The Gnosall Records, 1679 to 1837: Poor Law Administration', *Collections for A History of Staffordshire, Part I* (1936), 16. *Coming into Line: Local Government in Clayworth, 1674–1714*, ed. A. Rogers (Nottingham, 1979), p. x. For more general comments, see J. Broad, 'Parish Economies of Welfare, 1650–1834', *Historical Journal*, 42 (1999), 1002.

[102] Beier, 'Poverty and Progress', 223. For the suggestion that the increase in relief expenditure was driven in part by the proliferation of habitation orders, see Ch. 4.3(*c*) below.

[103] Broadbridge, 'Old Poor Law', 12.

In some parishes, of course, the poor went unrelieved altogether, even into the late seventeenth century. This might not be unusual in the 1620s or 1630s, when poor relief was still in the process of institutionalization. The plight of the poor of the tithing of Sturminster Marshall (Dorset), who were 'turned out of their houses' in 1635 so that 'divers of them are enforced to lodge under hedges and are like to perishe for want of succour', is a characteristic 'birthpang' of social welfare provision.[104] But for the overseers of Kenilworth (Warwickshire) to be presented 'for neglecting their office in not relieving the poor' in 1672 is rather more surprising.[105] As late as 1691, a Buckinghamshire JP was 'desired to hear the complaint of the inhabitants of Great Missenden that the officers there are very remiss in takeinge due care of the poor'.[106] Overseers might evidently prove themselves 'negligent and refractory' in failing to rate the parish for poor relief long after Justice Robert Foster criticized the parish officers of Gatcombe (Hampshire) in such terms in 1641. When the officers of Yorkshire parishes shirked their legal responsibilities in the late seventeenth century, sometimes in defiance of relief orders from the county bench, their recalcitrance could be remedied only by the clumsy process of indictment.[107] But by the 1690s, it seems, virtually every parish in the country was part of a nationally co-ordinated relief system—their overseers raising money through rates, their accounts annually audited by JPs—which was unified by magistrates' administration of the settlement laws and their appellate jurisdiction over pension disputes.[108]

2. OVERSEERS, INDIGENTS, AND THE IDENTIFICATION OF NEED

When William Harrison described provision made for the poor under the first compulsory assessments specified by the statute of 1572, he described the allocation of relief to the deserving as 'courteous refreshing

[104] *Western Circuit Assize Orders, 1629–1648: A Calendar*, ed. J. S. Cockburn (Camden, 4th ser., 17, London, 1976), no. 396.

[105] *Warwick County Records*, vi. 192.

[106] *County of Buckingham: Calendar to the Sessions Records*, ed. W. Le Hardy and G. L. Reckitt (4 vols., Aylesbury, 1934–51), i. 394. There is a nice irony in the fact that the magistrate appointed, Sergeant John Thurbane, was himself simultaneously appealing the basis of his poor rates in Ellesborough between 1688 and 1691: Ibid. i, 258, 366, 392, 411

[107] *Western Circuit Assize Orders*, no. 915; J. S. Cockburn, 'The North Riding Justices, 1690–1750: A Study in Local Administration', *Yorkshire Archaeological Journal*, 41 (1963–6), 507 n. 1.

[108] Slack, *Poverty and Policy*, 170–1; J. Innes, 'The "Mixed Economy of Welfare" in Early Modern England: Assessments of the Options from Hale to Malthus (*c.*1683–1803)', in M Daunton (ed.), *Charity, Self-Interest and Welfare in the English Past* (London, 1996), 144.

at home'. By the mid-eighteenth century, Richard Burn construed parish relief in rather different terms: the responsibilities of overseers included the obligations 'to maintain their poor as cheap as possibly they can' and 'to depopulate the parish in order to lessen the poor rate'.[109] Early seventeenth-century overseers' powers were, in fact, both more wide-ranging and more inclusive than Burn's sarcasm suggests. Indeed, it fell to overseers (and to the ratepayers and vestrymen who elected them) to construct the calculus of eligibility according to which the entitlements of the poor were computed. As the parish officers' handbook, *An Ease for Overseers of the Poore*, argued in 1601, overseers were responsible for 'employing by worke, releeving by money, and ordering by discretion the defects of the poore' and only men who had 'competencie of wealth and wisdom and care of a good conscience' were therefore fit for the 'honour of the office'.[110] Overseers should ideally be 'subsidie men', or (failing that) men of 'substantiall' standing who would embody the qualities and attributes—'grace and majestie', 'circumspection', 'diligence' (and the leisure time that made it possible), 'respectability', independence, and integrity, 'countenance to controll'—that fitted them to exercise the role responsibly. It is, however, significant that neither literacy nor numeracy was specifically required of overseers.[111] The magistrates who appointed overseers might identify suitable candidates for the office by their 'credible, charitable and conscionable' behaviour and especially by their 'willing speeches and paiments'.[112] As Justice Warburton reminded the Cheshire bench in 1610, moreover, the financial standing of parish officers was also a matter of more practical concern. Only the 'most substantial' parishioners were to be chosen overseers, he insisted, 'and none of the meaner sort who are not fitt to be trusted with the stock of the poor nor are able to pay the penalties of the lawe for their negligence and default'.[113] The primary characteristics, however, were discretion and conscientiousness. A foolish overseer would be scorned, but a discreet one would be feared and regarded for his 'crueltie', 'sanctitie', 'strength', and 'wisdom'. A careless overseer would 'oversee all but doe nothing at all, he will looke like a lyon and domineer like a devil over the poor', but a dutiful one would have 'an eye into his office to performe it with all

[109] W. Harrison, *The Description of England*, ed. G. Edelen (Ithaca, 1968), 181; R. Burn, *The History of the Poor Laws* (1764), 211–12.

[110] *An Ease for Overseers of the Poore*, 8, 9.

[111] Ibid. 9–10.

[112] Ibid. 12.

[113] Eaton Hall, MS Grosvenor, 2/33.

diligence'. Ultimately, therefore, overseers had a 'political' role: 'to be governors of the poore'.[114]

So how, then, should overseers conduct themselves? This was a fundamental question, for the 'office of overseer extendeth farre but it consisteth specially in taxing contributions for the relief of the poore and in the discrete dispensation and ordering thereof'. It was also a temporary office held 'not by patent but as tenants at will for a year', and its holders should remember that 'as they oversee others, so shall they be overseene themselves'.[115] The definitive overseers' handbook was stringent about the most suitable demeanour of parish officers. On the one hand, overseers were not to tyrannize over the poor, and should seek to exercise 'discrete government' rather than 'rigorous dealing'. Those officers who were 'to[o] busy', who had 'no felicite but in taunting, reviling and abusing the poor', were to be condemned in the words of Solomon: 'a busy body is hated'. After all, it was bad enough that the poor were punished by God with poverty without them also being crossed by man with severity. On the other, mildness in an overseer was 'a means to animate the idle: for where the officer hath not a countenance mixt with some austeritie the poor will presume too much of libertie'.[116]

For some commentators, the resolution of this dilemma lay in the requirement that parish officers themselves visit the houses of the poor to inspect their conduct and condition. They were, after all, *overseers*. Surprisingly, however, *An Ease for Overseers* was unenthusiastic about household visits. 'To inquire after poore', it insisted, 'is the next way to procure poore: for such is the impudency of this age that many will dissemble their estates to have relief' and 'if you but examine their estates to see if they want relief, some will sue to be recorded in the booke for the poore when they are better able to contribute to the poore'.[117] Although the handbook feared that household surveillance might unnecessarily inflate relief expenditure, others, especially the hotter sort of Protestant, were more sanguine. All too frequently, John Rogers warned, parish officers 'goe by hearsay which is oft uncertain', or (worse) 'by the wordes of the poore themselves', or even (worst of all) by the words of the 'most bold and importunate, when others that have more neede, and are better to be regarded, cannot so well speak for themselves'.[118] Although household visits were therefore essential, the inspection of the behaviour of the

[114] *An Ease for Overseers of the Poore*, 8, 10–11.

[115] Ibid. 14.

[116] Ibid. 28. The biblical allusion is to Proverbs 20: 3, 26:17.

[117] *An Ease for Overseers of the Poore*, 29.

[118] J. Rogers, *A Treatise of Love* (London, 1632), 225.

poor ought not to be excessive. John Downame warned that 'too much care and scrupulosity' turned overseers into magistrates who were 'so busy examining the poore about their estate and desert that they can find no leisure to open their purse or relieve their wantes'.[119]

Visits of the kind envisaged by these commentators were evidently practised as early as 1585 in Rogers's home town of Dedham (Essex), where the clergymen and ancients of the town were required to make quarterly inspection of the households of the poor to distinguish between 'the miserable estate of those that wante' and 'the naughtie disposition of disordered persons' and to make provision accordingly. When the Dedham orders were revised later that year, the inspections were to be carried out monthly and were to be made by the minister, constables, and collectors. In part, such visits served the practical purpose of searching houses suspected as venues of 'whordome, dronknnes and robbery', but they also, as Downame noted, gave the propertied the excuse to deny hospitality to the poor: if the poor were visited in their own homes, he argued, 'they would not so often have occasion to visit us at ours'. But Downame was under no illusions about the 'hungrie fare, thinne cloathes and hard lodging' that parish officers might expect to find in these hovels and cottages. His vision of 'the children crying for hunger and the parents outcrying them because they have no food to give them; some lying in straw for wante of beddes, others drinking water in stead of drinke' was doubtless designed to exhort householders to charity, yet it surely bears the hallmark of personal experience. It would have been familiar enough to the overseers of the Lancashire township of Little Hilton who reported on the condition of Thomas Gerard and his family in 1699: Gerard 'hath lain sick in bed theis five weeks his wife is now in childbed and was almost recovered but now relapsed . . . the husband wife and one small child lye in one poor bed three of the children scarce recovered of sicknes . . . there is neither meate nor fire in the house'.[120] Although household visits of this kind continued long into the eighteenth century, Georgian parish officers preferred to euphemize the desperation of the poor, as did the

[119] J. Downame, *The Plea of the Poore, or A Treatise of Beneficence and Almes-Deedes* (London, 1616), 41.

[120] *Conferences and Combination Lectures in the Elizabethan Church*, 129, 126, 140; Downame, *The Plea of the Poore*, 59–60; LRO, QSP/823/53. Downame's ideas are set in context in S. Hindle, 'Exhortation and Entitlement: Negotiating Inequality in English Rural Communities, 1550–1650', in M. Braddick and J. Walter (eds.), *Negotiating Power in Early Modern Society: Order, Hierarchy and Subordination in Britain and Ireland* (Cambridge, 2001), 102–22; P. Collinson, 'Puritanism and the Poor', in R. Horrox and S. Rees-Jones (eds.), *Pragmatic Utopias: Ideals and Communities, 1200–1630* (Cambridge, 2001), 242–58. For the requirement that parish officers search the houses of the poor for stolen goods, see Ch. 6.2 below.

overseer of Colyton (Devon) in 1748, when he claimed expenses 'for a journey to old Baker's to see what was wanting'.[121]

The process by which need was identified nonetheless remains almost completely hidden from historical observation. Overseers heard oral complaints that have left little trace in the archive unless payments were accounted for or appeals to the justices made. Sometimes, however, parish officers drew up censuses or listings of the poor which indicated the level of local need, though these were often, as we shall see, supplemented by listings of inmates, immigrants, and other strangers whose infiltration of the parish was regarded as prejudicial to the interests of the ancient settled poor.[122] *An Ease for Overseers* actually provided a model for such a listing, in which parish officers were to record for each poor household the following details: names and ages of the occupants; state of health; usual employment; weekly earnings; employer; those unemployed; those fit for apprenticeship; those who boarded orphans and others; weekly allowance; and those licensed to beg.[123] Once the level of need had been calculated pensions were to be distributed according to the two vital criteria of 'impediments' and 'seasons'. In the first place, the poor were to have a 'proportionall allowance according to the continuance and measure of their maladies and miseries'. In the second, some revenue must be 'retained and reserved in summer' in order that 'releefe may be more liberall in winter'.[124] The heart of the matter was the identification of the impotent, defined not simply by their age, their lameness, or their blindness but by their inability, either temporarily or permanently, to support themselves through their labour. Pensions were, therefore, 'a secondary meanes to ease such as be unable to worke' rather than the primary mechanism of relief, and much effort was expended by overseers in determining which of the indigent had any 'natural and necessary meanes left to live' and therefore had to survive without 'the helpe of the lawe'.[125]

Beyond these general requirements, the practices through which need was identified and relief distributed remain beyond historical reconstruction. Only where relief was denied, and an appeal to magistrates made, are the interactions between the indigent and their parish officers revealed.[126] More usually, the activities of overseers are disclosed only in the laconic

[121] P. Sharpe, *Population and Society in an East Devon Parish: Reproducing Colyton, 1540–1840* (Exeter, 2002), 234.

[122] Cf. Ch. 5.2 below.

[123] *An Ease for Overseers of the Poore*, 4.

[124] Ibid. 15.

[125] Ibid. 24–6.

[126] Cf. Ch. 6.4(*a*) below.

record of their disbursements, which were only the final stage in a protracted process of negotiation. At times of crisis, however, the welfare process becomes slightly more transparent. The harvest failures of 1629–30, for instance, provoked extraordinary measures, with the magistrates of several counties, including Sussex, Northamptonshire, Somerset, and Gloucestershire, to double the rate at which taxpayers were assessed.[127] So acute was the pressure on resources, however, that overseers were forced to make adjustments not only to the scale of their income, but also to the distribution of their expenditure. Indeed, anodyne statements about the doubling of levies for the poor might conceal far more elaborate measures for the targeting of relief payments.

In the Hertfordshire parish of Berkhamsted, for instance, the harvest failure of 1629 meant that dearth had been 'sensibly knowne and tasted by the moste, but especiallye by the poore, who therefore are compelled and doe make complaint daylye unto the overseers for reliefe'. The overseers, however, were in a quandary, confessing that 'although they pittye their wantes' they 'cannote well tell how and in which manner and measure to supplye [the poor] without further and better advice then their own'. The result was an extraordinary meeting at which the overseers 'called together the parish to praye their advice and direction'.[128]

'Discreet and charitable consideration' of the circumstances resulted in six parish orders which the officers hoped would secure the support of the local justices. First, since grain prices were twice their usual rate, the monthly pensions distributed to 'every old, lame sick or impotent person' were to be doubled from the level of their 'largest allowance'. Second, the allowances given to those children whose parents were not thought able to maintain them, provided the children were under the age of 6 and were therefore unable to work or be apprenticed, were to be raised to the same level as that of any other impotent person. Third, although children between the ages of 6 and 12 were to be 'set to some honest labour and diligently holden to it because they are hardly able as yet to supply their own wantes' and the parish desired to 'incorage them in that commendable course', they were to be allowed 8*d.* a month to supplement their

[127] NA, SP16/189/6 (Sussex), 194/9 (Northants.), 11 (Som.), 19 (Glos.). In other communities, the burden of assessment might be increased by retaining the customary level of assessment, but collecting rates more frequently, as was the case in Trull (Som.), where the standard rate remained 2*d.* in the £ into the 18th century. I. F. Jones, 'Aspects of Poor Law Administration, Seventeenth to Nineteenth Centuries, from Trull Overseers' Accounts', *Somerset Archaeological and Natural History Society Proceedings*, 95 (1951), 80.

[128] The following account is based on BL, MS Additional, 18773, fo. 105^{v}. For the context, see H. Falvey, 'Crown Policy and Local Economic Context in the Berkhamsted Common Enclosure Dispute, 1618–42', *Rural History*, 12 (2001), 123–58.

earnings 'during these hard tymes', the rate to be 'altered as cheapnesse or other reason shall require'. Fourth, because both the second and third of these orders had eased the circumstances of the 'poore people admittable to collection' in respect of their children, and since 'nature intended aswell as God and law of man that they who have bodyes of yeares and healthe may and ought to provide for ther selves necessaries', the parish officers were to deny altogether all collection to any able-bodied women or children above the age of 12. Fifth, although it would not be 'convenyent' to admit those who were 'lame or sick or in greate distress' into 'ordinarye [i.e. weekly?] collection', the parish officers were instructed 'to take notice of all such and to viset and relieve them according to the meanes they have in their power by monthly collection'. They were not, however, to diminish 'the stocke of the poore without publique and generall consent'. Sixth, in order to finance this more generous, yet targeted, welfare regime, the parish officers were instructed to distrain without hesitation anybody who defaulted upon their assessment.

Although these arrangements were born of dearth, they represent only a more elaborate, not to say stringent, form of the mechanics of poor law administration as they were to be practised with increasing efficiency and enthusiasm across thousands of rural parishes as the seventeenth century progressed: increasing the purchasing power of the totally impotent; subsidizing the incomes of those overburdened with children; insisting that even the very young and the elderly attempt to support themselves by work; restricting relief of the sick to occasional payments; and policing the distribution of casual relief through household surveillance and inspection. How, then, did parish relief intersect with the lives of the labouring poor?

3. THE NATURE OF PARISH RELIEF

(*a*) Casual Relief

In numerical terms (that is, expressed as a proportion of parishioners who benefited from parish relief), the most significant aspect of the Elizabethan poor law was not the overseers' statutory obligation to provide regular payments, but their more flexible capacity to authorize irregular ones. Because these payments were occasional or 'casual', those who received them have often been described as the 'casual poor'. Significantly, however, this term is very rarely used in contemporary sources: allowances given irregularly or in exceptional circumstances were described as 'extraordinaries' or 'extremes' in Lacock (Wiltshire);

as 'extraordinaries given as need requires' in Chalfont St Peter (Buckinghamshire); as 'accidentals' in Stone (Staffordshire); and as payments 'above book' in Bury (Lancashire). Those who received occasional payments in Trull (Somerset) were known as the 'second poor'.[129] The vagueness of many early seventeenth-century references to casual relief, which were in any case frequently paid in kind to groups of poor parishioners or to the indigent in general, makes it very difficult to estimate the numerical proportion of parish populations who were occasionally relieved in this way. In Tysoe (Warwickshire) in 1639, however, a fully itemized listing of all payments suggests that, in addition to the twenty-one pensioners (3.5 per cent of the population), a further nineteen (3 per cent) were casually relieved. At Gnosall in 1682, there were five collectioners and another six parishioners who were given occasional relief 'in their want'.[130] There is some evidence to suggest that women were the more significant beneficiaries of occasional relief and that this tendency grew more marked over time: although females accounted for 51 per cent of casual expenditure in Colyton in 1683, this proportion had risen to almost two-thirds by 1743.[131]

It is nonetheless striking that, although occasional payments were frequent, their cumulative value was relatively small, at least in the early years of the seventeenth century. Occasional relief constituted less than 5 per cent of the costs of weekly pensions in Holt Market (Norfolk) in 1601, and less than 10 per cent of all welfare expenditure across thirty-nine Warwickshire parishes in 1638–9.[132] By the late seventeenth century, however, overseers were making casual payments so regularly that parliament determined to restrict them. A statute of 1692 insisted that occasional payments could henceforth be made only with the consent of a magistrate.[133] Parish officers accordingly became much more assiduous in accounting for them separately, and it is therefore possible from the very late seventeenth century to identify patterns in the provisions in casual relief. Although the 1692 statute seems initially to have restricted the scale of casual relief, the number of occasional payments increased rapidly, to the extent that there were scores authorized every week in

[129] Hinton, 'Relief of the Poor of Lacock', 174; G. C. Edmonds, 'Accounts of Eighteenth-Century Overseers of the Poor of Chalfont St Peter', *Records of Buckinghamshire*, 18 (1966), 8; Broadbridge, 'Old Poor Law', 12; Fessler, 'The Official Attitude toward the Sick Poor', 89; Jones, 'Trull Overseers' Accounts', 84. Cf. J. Innes, 'Who Were the Casual Poor?' (unpublished paper, 2001).

[130] SBTRO, DR37/85/6/42 (Tysoe); Cutlack, 'Gnosall Records', 25–6.

[131] Sharpe, *Population and Society*, 227.

[132] *Bacon Papers*, iv. 189–90; SBTRO, DR37/85/6.

[133] 3 William & Mary, c. 2, sect. xi.

Lacock (Wiltshire) by the middle of the eighteenth century. In Brigstock (Northamptonshire), casual disbursements accounted for over 39 per cent of poor relief expenditure in the period 1741–68, though in one year (1743), they outweighed regular payments, amounting to 55 per cent of the total. A similar pattern is evident in Shipton under Wychwood (Oxfordshire) where casual relief accounted for 36.7 per cent of expenditure in the period 1740–62. In some parishes, occasional relief grew to the extent that it actually came to dwarf the pension bill. In the 1690s, at a time when annual expenditure on pensions was running at £110, the overseers of Stone (Staffordshire) were dispensing between £80 and £90 in occasional payments. By the 1730s, however, when retrenchment had driven pension payments down to £60 per annum, 'accidentals' had risen to approximately £120 each year. By the early 1780s, 'extremes' exceeded 'monthly pays' in Lacock by almost 26 per cent.[134] Although it is tempting to postulate potential conflict between the two separate constituencies of poor—the pensioners in receipt of regular collection, and the occasional poor who received 'extraordinaries'—it is important to remember that there was considerable fluidity between the two groups. Those who received extraordinary relief would frequently in time fall entirely upon the parish, and when they did so they might even then remain a significant drain on casual expenditure. Goodwife Wells, for instance, received over £230 in cash payments from the overseers of Cowden (Kent) between 1658 and 1694, but her occasional relief was probably worth another £60, or 20.7 per cent of her total income from the parish. The overseers of Whitchurch (Oxfordshire) spent almost £88 in relieving Widow Ann Foster in the period 1668–93, but almost 11 per cent of this expenditure was accounted for by causal payments: mending her house, buying her medicine, paying for her nursing, providing and repairing her clothing and shoes, and finally organizing her burial.[135]

As Widow Foster's experience suggests, occasional payments were most commonly made in kind rather than cash. This tendency was driven by overseers' desire to target resources at specific needs, but from the point of view of the indigent it might well have introduced unhelpful rigidities into a household budget whose most attractive characteristic

[134] Hinton, 'Relief of the Poor of Lacock', 174; S. Hindle, '"Not by Bread Only"? Common Right, Parish Relief and Endowed Charity in a Forest Economy, *c.*1600–1800', in S. King and A. Tomkins (eds.), *The Poor In England, 1700–1850: An Economy of Makeshifts* (Manchester, 2003), 56; R. M. Smith, 'Ageing and Well-Being in Early Modern England: Pension Trends and Gender Preferences under the English Old Poor Law, *c.*1650–1800', in P. Johnson and P. Thane (eds.), *Old Age from Antiquity to Post-Modernity* (London, 1998), 72–3; Broadbridge, 'Old Poor Law', 12.

[135] Turner, 'Ancient Parochial Account Book of Cowden', 114; Smith, 'Ageing and Well-Being', 80–1.

was its very flexibility. When a widow of Ottery St Mary (Devon) took a justice's relief order for 6*d.* a month to one of the overseers in 1681, for instance, she was frustrated to find that he was unwilling to give her money, but offered her instead small wares, including wheat, bacon, and other commodities, from his shop.[136] Although this experience may be suggestive of corruption or self-interest among overseers, it also reflects the problems created by the shortage of specie, which might strength parish officers' preference for payment in kind as a way of bolstering the local credit networks in which they and ratepayers were already deeply enmeshed.[137] Payment in kind, moreover, was also symptomatic of more discriminating relief systems, for, where resources were targeted in this way, overseers could be sure that cash sums would not be frittered away on non-essentials, especially in the alehouse.

Even so, the very wide range of goods and services—food, clothes, shoes, fuel, rent, medical care—provided as occasional relief betrays the extraordinary sensitivity of the old poor law to the specific needs of poor householders and their families. In mid-seventeenth-century Warwickshire, for example, casual payments included 4*s.* to Thomas Harris of Ilmington for 'a woman to attend him in his sickness'; 2*s.* 8*d.* to Mary Garrett the elder of Lower Shuckburgh for 'a smock and its making'; 2*s.* to William Chambers of Tanworth 'for a s[h]roud or sheete to laye about a poor man'; and 14*s.* to Nicholas Hunt of Great Wolford 'for keeping of a poor child whose father is gone away from the town'.[138]

Systematic work on the distribution of occasional payments in specific parishes has indicated both the range and the hierarchy of casual relief. Most striking, however, is the difference in practice between parishes. Although some parish officers were happy to dole out casual relief in cash, others were sensitive to the potential abuse of such generosity. In the period 1625–1700, for instance, the overseers of Cratfield (Suffolk) made 689 casual payments of cash to their pensioners, while those of Poslingford made only thirteen in the period 1663–1700, preferring instead to provide goods and services directly to the poor. There is, nonetheless, a relatively clear hierarchy of relief in kind in terms both of

[136] Sharpe, *Population and Society*, 221.

[137] C. Muldrew, '"Hard Food for Midas": Cash and its Social Value in Early Modern England', *Past and Present*, 170 (2001), esp. 99–108; C. Muldrew and S. King, 'Cash, Wages and the Economy of Makeshifts in England, 1650–1800', in P. Scholliers and L. Schwarz (eds.), *Experiencing Wages: Social and Cultural Aspects of Wage Forms in Europe Since 1500* (New York, 2003), 170–1.

[138] SBTRO, DR37/85/6/21 (Ilmington), 37 (Lower Shuckburgh), 39 (Tanworth Clayside), 49 (Great Wolford). The range of casual relief offered elsewhere is revealed, for example, in Hinton, 'Relief of the Poor of Lacock', 174–5; Emmison, 'Poor Relief Accounts', 112–13.

cost and of frequency of distribution as it is revealed in the pattern of casual disbursements made by the overseers of these two Suffolk parishes and of those of Shipton under Wychwood in the period 1740–62. In descending order of significance, casual relief primarily consisted of medical care, fuel provision, rent payments, fuel, and clothing.[139]

The significance of medical relief in kind can only be properly understood if the definition of medical treatment is expanded to include a wide range of nursing and residential care, and if it is remembered that both subsidies for rents and fuel and dietary supplements were most frequently prompted where a parishioner (perhaps a collectioner, perhaps merely a recipient of occasional relief) was suffering from temporary or chronic illness. To be sure, overseers' accounts often include references to the payment of surgeons' bills and even occasionally refer to the nature of the treatment given, but the most conspicuous characteristic of medical provision is the interpenetration of the activities of professional and amateur healers. From this perspective, it has been suggested, in excess of 20 per cent of casual expenditure was directed 'to servicing the health needs of the parish population'.[140] More striking still is the tendency for parish officers to pay the poor to look after the poor; it has even been suggested that there was a three-tier hierarchy of carers upon whom parish officers might draw in tending the sick: full-time employees of the parish, whose experience fitted them for the nursing of the sick when a major outbreak of disease occurred; 'carers', who were compensated for looking after their neighbours or even their parents on an intermittent or short-term basis; and ancillaries, who were employed only irregularly, perhaps to assist full-time nurses or to watch the dying.[141] A sick parishioner might come into contact with all three types of care as old age withdrew her into dependency and terminal illness, their last entries in overseers accounts being punctuated by references to apothecaries' visits, medicines, and dressings, culminating in payments for shrouding and laying out, and for bread and beer at the burial.

Overseers' policies on the provision of fuel were even more varied, and

[139] The following discussion is based on L. Botelho, 'Aged and Impotent: Parish Relief of the Aged Poor in Early Modern Suffolk', in Daunton (ed.), *Charity, Self-Interest and Welfare*, 99 (table 5.1), and Smith, 'Ageing and Well-Being', 73 (table 4.4(b)).

[140] Smith, 'Ageing and Well-Being', 82. Cf. the more traditional approach of Fessler, 'The Sick Poor in Seventeenth-Century Lancashire'; E. G. Thomas, 'The Old Poor Law and Medicine', *Medical History* 24 (1980), 1–19.

[141] M. Barker-Read, 'The Treatment of the Aged Poor in Five Selected West Kent Parishes from Settlement to Speenhamland, 1662–1797' (unpublished Ph.D. thesis, Open University, 1988), 99–104.

reflected the politics of access to natural resources in the parish and on its common land. Where parish vestries decided in favour of supplying firewood for fuel, they were doubtless motivated partly by fears of hedge-breaking and idleness on the wastes. As *An Ease for Overseers* insisted, the provision of 'wood, coles and other necessaries at a reasonable price for the benefit of the poore' would 'restraine them from straying to woodes, breaking of hedges and many other abuses'.[142] Among the most comprehensive schemes of this kind was that envisaged in the 'charge' issued to the overseers of every parish in north-east Norfolk in December 1623. The overseers were instructed to inspect the homes of the labouring poor on the last day of August each year to identify which households had not yet made provision for winter fuel. The purpose of this inspection was twofold, partly to inform the justices which families might be suspected of stealing firewood from their neighbours' hedges, partly to enable overseers to calculate what proportion of their expenditure they must devote to providing a stock of fuel.[143] Firewood was then to be distributed amongst the poor as need required, 'the Laborers and such others as live not upon the Collection' paying for it either 'in ready mony or giving assurance for payment within twenty dayes', and 'such others as live upon the Collection either paieng in like sort or allowing for it out of the weekly sumes that they are to receave' in pensions.[144] In this scheme, the provision of fuel by the parish depended upon the overseers' willingness to extend short-term credit and pensioners' willingness to mortgage their collection.

Some parishes actually did try to provide fuel for the poor in bulk. In 1635 the parish officers of Shipstone on Stour were buying 'seacoal' at 'the best and cheapest rate' and selling it to the poor. In 1639 the overseers of Tysoe (Warwickshire) spent 12*s*. (over 2 per cent of their annual relief bill) on 'fewell for poor foulkes'. In mid-seventeenth-century Ashwell (Hertfordshire), the north porch of the church was used to store coal purchased for the poor. Whether these were extraordinary payments remains unclear, although it is more likely that overseers would make general provision of fuel in particularly cold winters. The overseers of Trull experimented with buying wood for the poor in the late 1620s, but did not provide fuel again until the 'hard weather' of 1691. Chalfont St

[142] *An Ease for Overseers of the Poore*, 29–30.

[143] It may also have derived from 16th-century manorial practice. For manorial orders requiring tenants to prove that they had sufficient fuel for the winter, see A. J. L. Winchester, *The Harvest of the Hills: Rural Life in Northern England and the Scottish Borders, 1400–1700* (Edinburgh, 2000), 125.

[144] Bodl., MS Tanner, 73, fo. 390. For the provenance of this document, see Ch. 1.2(*b*) above.

Peter was another parish where fuel payments were sufficiently rare to be conspicuous when they were actually made, as in 1744 when the overseers spent 7*s.* on faggots.[145] By the eighteenth century, it was common for overseers either to provide winter fuel for individual pensioners or to grant them cash allowances for its purchase. Where faggots or coal were provided in kind to an individual pensioner, it might be some indication that the recipient was no longer able, perhaps through age or infirmity, to gather it for herself.[146]

In every case, where the general provision of wood was considered, parish officers had to decide whether it was in the financial interest of the ratepayers to encourage the plebeian exploitation of woodland, thereby keeping down the poor rates, or to eliminate it, leaving cottagers' fuel needs to be met by the parish. At Stockland (Devon) in 1755, for instance, the overseers agreed to defend the customary rights of the poor against the landlord who had prosecuted them for wood theft. The fact that they taxed the inhabitants to finance the necessary legal action suggests that the long-term provision of fuel for all the parish pensioners would have been an even greater liability than an immediate burst of expenditure on litigation.[147]

Most parishes enjoyed a stock of rent-free housing which might be used to shelter the poor. Accommodation of this kind might be the result of a charitable bequest; of the willingness of property-owners to let the parish use it (often in lieu of paying rates or in return for an agreement that the overseers pay for repairs); or of demographic misfortune, where the owner had died without kin to claim their inheritance. It might also be augmented either where the magistracy licensed the building of cottages with less than four acres of land attached under the terms of the 1589 statute, or where the parish officers themselves ordered the building of flimsy cottages, often little more than 'hovels of sticks and dirt' on the wastes, as the late Elizabethan statutes had provided.[148] The existence of such inherited assets notwithstanding, the lists of rents paid on behalf of pensioners, which form part of virtually all extant overseers' accounts, are eloquent testimony to the pressing demand for accommodation, which evidently outstripped the available housing stock in most parishes. Such

[145] WCRO, DR446/21, unfol.; SBTRO, DR37/85/6/42 (Tysoe); Broad, 'Parish Economies of Welfare', 996; Jones, 'Trull Overseers Accounts', 94–5; Edmonds, 'Overseers of the Poor of Chalfont St Peter', 22. Cf. Kent and King, 'Changing Patterns of Poor Relief', 132–3.

[146] For a sophisticated discussion of the use of faggots to heat the houses of the poor, see Barker-Read, 'Treatment of the Aged Poor', 90–1.

[147] Sharpe, *Population and Society*, 148.

[148] A. Everitt, 'Farm Labourers', in J. Thirsk (ed.), *The Agrarian History of England and Wales*, vol. iv: *1500–1640* (Cambridge, 1967), 442. Cf. Ch. 5.1 below.

was the fiscal drain of housing the poor at market rates that it became imperative for overseers to move those who would most likely prove a burden to the parish for the foreseeable future, especially the elderly, to what little rent-free accommodation there was.

The growth in the provision of rental accommodation for the poor was partly driven by the magistracy, who by the late seventeenth century were not only retrospectively legitimizing cottages that had been built on the wastes, but also very regularly insisting that overseers provide cottages and tenements and maintain them when they fell into disrepair, not infrequently specifying the dimensions and living arrangements they thought appropriate for the needs of the individual or family concerned.[149] Under the terms of these 'habitation orders', the poor occupants enjoyed security of tenure, almost invariably for life, and paid little or no rent, the accommodation being provided sometimes in addition to but more usually in lieu of collection in cash. The 'widows' rents' in Colyton (Devon), for instance, were worth more than half as much again to the three dozen recipients as the actual rental value of their lodging.[150] Magistrates were perfectly prepared to bully recalcitrant overseers by insisting on punitive weekly pensions until housing was provided.[151] Although such orders might initially meet with the opposition of parish officers, overseers soon came to see the merits of a system that both restricted the physical mobility of the indigent and, if they could exploit what 'public' accommodation already existed in the parish, might actually reduce their expenditure. If the parish had built up sufficient housing stock, it was almost certainly cheaper to house the poor than to pay them cash pensions. Provided their rent was paid, moreover, even the elderly might support themselves through casual labour. It is nonetheless clear that parish officers sometimes vehemently resisted habitation orders, especially those made in favour of those who were not impotent but who had been denied housing by landlords despite their ability to pay cash rent in advance. After a half-century or so of judicial sympathy for housing the poor, the tide of opinion seems to have turned around 1725 and the efflorescence of habitation orders which had occurred since the 1670s subsequently died away.[152]

[149] Cf. Chs. 5.1 and 5.2 below.

[150] Sharpe, *Population and Society*, 223–3.

[151] P. Clark, 'Migration in England during the Late Seventeenth and Early Eighteenth Centuries', in P. Clark and D. Souden (eds.), *Migration and Society in Early Modern England* (London, 1987), 240–1; J. Broad, 'Housing the Rural Poor in England, 1650–1850', *Agricultural History Review*, 48 (2000), 160–1.

[152] Broad, 'Housing the Rural Poor', 161. For Warwickshire examples, see, among very many others, *Warwick County Records*, vii. 21–2 (Joseph Whitehead at Offchurch, 1674), 90 (John Bird

They have certainly left their traces in parish archives. The overseers of Ashwell (Hertfordshire), for example, paid rents for two parishioners in 1677 but for as many as twelve by 1716.[153] This is not to say that the poor, even the aged poor, were necessarily kept in the same accommodation for the duration of their time on the parish. Paupers might be moved to cheaper housing if overseers were paying a market rent on their behalf, rotated into a local almshouse as rooms became available there, or relocated to parts of the parish which rendered them more accessible to oversight by parish officers and neighbours alike. Elsewhere, the overseers might insist on complex patterns of co-residence, renting rooms for the poor in the houses of other poor people, especially for elderly paupers who would be expected to care for one another, yet further evidence of the interpenetration of formal and informal relief.[154]

Clothing was always in demand for paupers, not least because it was so expensive relative to their income from the parish. The indigent wore what few garments they had until they either fell apart, or until they were sold off in direst need or after death.[155] It was nonetheless unusual for parish officers to provide a claimant with a complete set of clothes at any one time, unless they were either about to be apprenticed, or their destitution was so abject that they were virtually naked by the time the overseer visited them. One wonders, for instance, what provoked the parish officers of Cowden (Kent) to purchase five calf skins to have them made up into a full leathern suit for Edward Still in 1637 at a total cost of 10*s.* 6*d.* Much more typical was the treatment of Elizabeth Skinner, on whom the Cowden overseers spent 8*d.* for mending her clothes and 6*d.* for hobnails for her boots the very same year.[156] The inconsistencies of accounting practices, sometimes identifying specified items of clothing to be provided for a particular named claimant, sometimes subsuming expenditure on clothing under quarterly bills paid to tradesmen, make it extremely difficult to calculate how much clothing an individual might receive from the overseers either as occasional relief or during a pension career. Parish officers nonetheless occasionally provided coats for all the poor of the parish, as they did at Frampton (Lincolnshire) in 1631 and

and his family at Willey, 1677), 106 (Constance Hanson at Burton Dassett, 1678); viii. 259 (John Ball, his wife and five children at Tysoe, 1689), 263 (Thomas Heyward at Over Whitacre, 1689) 270 (Richard Mercer and his wife at Wolfhamcote, 1690).

153 Broad, 'Parish Economies of Welfare', 997.

154 Cf. Ch. 1.4 above.

155 For discussion of the provision of clothing to the poor in the later years of the old poor law, see S. King, 'Reclothing the English Poor, 1750–1840', *Textile History*, 33 (2002), 37–47.

156 Turner, 'Ancient Parochial Account Book of Cowden', 104, 111.

Tonbridge (Kent) in 1705, a policy which probably chimes both with the employment of the labouring poor in making clothes and with the identification of the deserving by the wearing of badged coats.[157]

Casual payments, therefore, disclose the extraordinary sensitivity of parish officers to the nature and scale of local misery. They also imply the effective flow of information between the indigent and the overseers, and perhaps even the degree of surveillance that was practised over the households of the poor. They suggest that overseers were prepared to go to very great lengths in satisfaction of the physical and material needs of the poor, providing a range of services which had expanded way beyond the simple concept of 'relief' envisaged by Elizabethan policy-makers. In fine-tuning provision in this way, overseers proved that the administration of the poor laws might be 'largely benevolent and sympathetic in operation'.[158]

(*b*) Collectioners

But it was in their allocation of weekly pensions that overseers met their most fundamental obligation, and it is in this respect that the impact of parish relief on the lives of the impotent and labouring poor must be judged. Measuring the proportion of the population in regular receipt of relief is rather more complicated than might at first be imagined. Although individual pensioners or collectioners are relatively easily identified in surviving relief rolls, there is always the possibility that they had dependants whose numbers, let alone whose age, gender, or circumstances, have gone unrecorded. Even so, it is abundantly clear that the proportion of parish populations who were regularly in receipt of relief was extremely small. In nineteen north Norfolk parishes in 1600–2, it averaged only 5.5 per cent; in twenty-seven south Warwickshire parishes in 1638–9, it was as little as 2.3 per cent; in twenty-one Durham parishes over the seventeenth and eighteenth centuries as a whole it was still lower, at 2 per cent. At Chalfont St Peter (Buckinghamshire) in 1721, 4 per cent of the population received regular monthly pay. The rather higher proportion, 7 per cent, calculated for eight rural parishes in Kent, Norfolk, and North Yorkshire for the period 1582–1630, is probably to be explained by the fact that the sample of accounts is heavily weighted towards years of dearth, especially 1598 and 1629. Indeed, levels of dependency might reach particularly striking levels in years of high prices,

[157] Hindle, 'Power, Poor Relief and Social Relations', 86; Barker-Read, 'Treatment of the Aged Poor', 97.

[158] W. Newman-Brown, 'The Receipt of Poor Relief and Family Situation: Aldenham, Hertfordshire 1630–90', in Smith (ed.), *Land, Kinship and Life-Cycle*, 420.

as they did in the township of Killington (Westmorland) where one-third of the householders listed in the parish survey of 1695 were in regular receipt of relief.[159]

These figures support the recent calculation that pensioners constituted between 0.8 and 4.2 per cent of parish populations in the seventeenth and eighteenth centuries and that these proportions might be doubled to take account of their dependants.[160] All in all, then, it seems clear that rarely if ever were more than about 5–6 per cent of the population 'on the parish' in the early modern rural community. It is striking, however, that, low as these proportions were, they fluctuated markedly over time: at Whitchurch (Oxfordshire) the proportion fell from 3.5 per cent in 1673–8, to 2.1 per cent in 1701–20, to 1.3 per cent in 1731–40, only to rise once more to 4.1 per cent in the 1750s and 1760s. In Terling (Essex) the trend was slightly different, with the proportion rising from 1.2 to 2.2 per cent over the second quarter of the eighteenth century, only to fall away to 1 per cent in the 1770s. In Tavistock (Devon) this latter pattern was still more pronounced, rising from 3.7 to 4.2 per cent of the population between 1710 and 1735, before falling away to 2.6 per cent in the early 1760s.[161] By the early eighteenth century, however, the retrenchment characterized by the parish badge and the workhouse test had begun to restrict the number of paupers who were regularly relieved by the parish. The proportions relieved in County Durham, for instance, were 'higher before 1700 than in the half-century after' only rising again at the end of the eighteenth century.[162] At Geddington, where there were 135 households in the 1720s, only seven (5.2 per cent) received regular collection. Less than 1 per cent of the populations of the Durham

[159] *Bacon Papers*, iv. 187–92; SBTRO, DR37/85/6; P. Rushton, 'The Poor Law, the Parish and the Community in North-East England, 1600–1800', *Northern History*, 25 (1989), 143; Edmonds, 'Overseers of the Poor of Chalfont St Peter', 6; Beier, 'Poverty and Progress', 207 (excluding St Mary's Warwick from the sample in table 6.2); A. Macfarlane, *The Origins of English Individualism: The Family, Property and Social Transition* (Oxford, 1978), 77.

[160] Smith, 'Ageing and Well-Being', 71. The 'normal' scale of provision becomes even more striking if calculations are made not of the proportion of *individuals* but of the number of *households* relieved. In the south Warwickshire sample, the proportion of households relieved averaged 10.1%, though it stood as high as 33.3% in Ratley. In Long Newton (County Durham), well over a fifth of households were regularly relived in the 1660s. In Aldenham (Hertfordshire) 26.9% of all households were on average regularly relieved across the 17th century, though this proportion varied from as little as 16.5% in the 1690s to 36.4% in the 1680s. SBTRO DR37/85/6; Rushton, 'The Poor Law, the Parish, and the Community', 144; Newman-Brown 'Poor Relief and Family Situation', 410.

[161] Smith, 'Ageing and Well-Being', 71 (table 4.3).

[162] Rushton, 'The Poor Law, the Parish, and the Community', 144.

parishes of Elsdon in 1717 and Houghton-le-Spring in 1751 were regularly relived.[163]

In each of the samples of groups of parishes, however, there were very substantial deviations from the mean. These might be expected in the geographically and chronologically diverse sample, in which the proportion of 'pensioners' ranged from 1.8 per cent in Strood (Kent) in 1598 to 14.3 per cent in Carlton Miniott (North Yorkshire) in 1629. They are, however, altogether more surprising in the samples constructed from the overseers' accounts of contiguous communities: from a minimum of 2.5 per cent (in Holt Market) to a maximum of 14.7 per cent (in Wiveton) in early seventeenth-century Norfolk, for example, or between parishes as 'miserly' (or 'prosperous') as Radway (0.5 per cent) and as 'generous' (or 'poor') as Wasperton (7.8 per cent) in Caroline Warwickshire. The Durham parishes of Long Newton in the 1660s and Bothal in the 1690s were regularly relieving 5 per cent of their populations, well over twice the county average.[164] That such differentials might occur even between adjacent parishes is quite remarkable and legitimizes contemporary fears that the poor might seek to infiltrate neighbouring parishes with more generous welfare regimes.[165]

As we have seen, the overwhelming bulk of parish expenditure was disbursed to the 'poor by casualtie', most often the ancient settled poor, who were deemed to deserve parish pensions. Across the Warwickshire parishes that recorded relief expenditure in 1639, approximately 90 per cent of relief funds were targeted on pensioners, or 'collectioners', as they became known.[166] This constituency was predominantly female. In mid-seventeenth-century Warwickshire, 51 per cent of pensioners were women, 38 per cent were adult males, and 11 per cent children, although the difficult circumstances of the late 1630s might account for what appears to have been a relatively high proportion of men. The average proportion of pensioners who were female across fourteen villages in seventeenth-century Norfolk was 62.8 per cent. Of the thirty-one pensioners in Chalfont St Peter in 1722, only six (19.4 per cent) of whom were adult males, twenty-two (71 per cent) were women (sixteen of them widows), and three were children.[167] The prominence of widows

163 Hindle, '"Not by Bread Only"?', 56; Rushton, 'The Poor Law, the Parish and the Community', 143.

164 Beier, 'Poverty and Progress', 207; *Bacon Papers*, iv. 189–90, 192, 238; SBTRO, DR37/85/6/34 (Radway), 44 (Wasperton); Rushton, 'The Poor Law, the Parish, and the Community', 143.

165 Cf. Ch. 5.3 below.

166 SBTRO, DR37/85/6.

167 SBTRO, DR37/85/6; Wales, 'Poverty, Poor Relief and the Life-Cycle', 360 (calculated from table 11.3); Edmonds, 'Overseers of the Poor of Chalfont St Peter', 4, 7.

amongst those relieved has been emphasized in numerous studies of parish relief: on average 50.1 per cent of the collectioners of seventeenth-century Norfolk were widowed, though the proportion might be as high as 70 per cent as it was in Wighton in 1614–15. Although they constituted only 20 per cent of the household heads in seventeenth-century Aldenham (Hertfordshire), widows constituted almost 60 per cent of the parish pensioners.[168] These women were not, it should be emphasized, necessarily elderly, for many of them would have been bereaved while their children were still young.

The demands of the life-cycle also ensured that a significant number of those on relief were young married couples overburdened with children, a constituency at which the campaign for pauper apprenticeship was principally targeted.[169] Indeed, the prominence of this group cautions against the assumption that widowhood was invariably the most significant point of entry to the relief rolls. Of the fifty-four women relieved in late seventeenth-century Odiham (Hampshire), only sixteen (29.7 per cent) first received pensions after the death of their husbands; the remaining thirty-eight had been relieved in pauper households even while their husbands were alive.[170] The suggestion that there was a continuing (and ever deepening) poverty trap is bolstered by the finding that collection was increasingly being allocated to men by the early eighteenth century, though they never came to constitute a majority. In three late-seventeenth-century communities the average proportion of those on regular relief who were male was 22.9 per cent, rising to 29.3 per cent in the early eighteenth century. This pattern might be particularly marked in specific communities, such as Whitchurch (Oxfordshire), where the proportion of pensioners who were male rose from 9.9 per cent in the period 1672–1700 to 28.6 per cent in the years 1700–30.[171]

So what exactly did it mean to be a collectioner? In Northill (Bedfordshire) in the 1560s, the average payment seems to have been 8*d.* per quarter or less than 1*d.* a week. In two north Norfolk parishes whose accounts from 1600–1 survive, the mean weekly pension was just over 4*d.*

[168] Wales, 'Poverty, Poor Relief and the Life-Cycle, 360 (calculated from table 11.3) Newman-Brown, 'Poor Relief and Family Situation', 412.

[169] R. M. Smith, 'Some Issues Concerning Families and their Property in Rural England 1250–1800', in id. (ed.), *Land, Kinship and Life-Cycle*, 68–85; Wales, 'Poverty, Poor Relief and the Life-Cycle'. Cf. Ch. 3.2 above.

[170] B. Stapleton, 'Inherited Poverty and Life-Cycle Poverty: Odiham, Hampshire 1650–1850', *Social History*, 18 (1993), 354.

[171] Forty per cent in Whitkirk (West Riding of Yorkshire) 1663–87; 16.2% in Lowestof (Suffolk) 1670–90; 9.9% in Whitchurch (Oxon.). Smith, 'Ageing and Well-Being', 76 (figure calculated from table 4.6).

a week, thought pensions of 6*d.* were not unknown.[172] By the 1630s, however, provision appears to have become slightly more generous, at least if the Warwickshire evidence is anything to go by. In twenty-three south Warwickshire parishes whose accounts survive, in 1638–9, weekly pensions ranged between a minimum of a halfpenny and a maximum of 2*s.* By far the most common collection was 6*d.* a week, although the mean, at almost 7*d.* weekly, was slightly higher than the mode, a finding 'consistent with a situation in which a small basic sum was paid to most pensioners with a relatively small number of pensioners in greater need or with fewer means of support needing more than this'.[173]

This picture of a gradual increase in the average Warwickshire pension, from roughly 4*d.* to 6*d.* a week in the first few decades of the seventeenth century, resembles that which emerges from the parish accounts of early seventeenth-century Norfolk, where pensions of between 4*d.* and 6*d.* were the norm by the 1630s.[174] Even by the middle of the seventeenth century, however, some significant regional differentials may have developed. The average pension in Whitkirk (Yorkshire, West Riding) was less than 2*d.* a week in the 1660s; that in the communities of the East Riding of Yorkshire reached 3*d.* a week in the early 1660s and 4*d.* in the 1680s. In Gnosall (Staffordshire), only one of the nine collectioners was receiving more than 6*d.* a week in 1681. Pensions of 6*d.* a week were not common in Cumberland, Westmorland, or County Durham until the later seventeenth century, and even in 1700 the typical pensioner in Woodplumpton (Lancashire) was receiving only 6*d.* a week.[175] It was already the case long before 1700, therefore, that more generous pensions were being paid in the south of England than in the north. In general, however, pension levels apparently rose across the second half of the seventeenth century to the extent that the average weekly collection in parishes as geographically dispersed as North Walsham (Norfolk), Troutbeck (Westmorland), and Winston, Eglingham, or Heighington (Durham) had reached 1*s.* by 1700.[176] These findings chime with the analysis of pension levels in

[172] Emmison, 'Poor Relief Accounts', 105; *Bacon Papers*, iv, 187–8 (Glandford and Briningham).

[173] SBTRO, DR37/85/6; Smith, 'Ageing and Well-Being', 76.

[174] Wales, 'Poverty, Poor Relief and the Life-Cycle', 355.

[175] Smith 'Ageing and Well-Being', 76–7; Cutlack, 'Gnosall Records', 37; M. A. Parsons, 'Poor Relief in Troutbeck, 1640–1836', *Transactions of the Westmorland and Cumberland Antiquarian and Archaeological Society*, 95 (1995), 179; F. W. Grainger, 'Poor Relief in Cumberland in the Seventeenth and Eighteenth Centuries', *Transactions of the Cumberland and Westmorland Antiquarian and Archaeological Society*, NS 15 (1915), 93; Rushton, 'The Poor Law, the Parish and the Community', 142.

[176] Wales, 'Poverty, Poor Relief and the Life-Cycle', 356 (table 11.1); Parsons, 'Poor Relief in Troutbeck', 179; Rushton, 'The Poor Law, the Parish and the Community', 142. Newman-

towns, where the going rate was higher in the south of England than in the north, but was increasing everywhere over the course of the seventeenth century.[177] There is, however, some sketchy evidence that rural pension levels were reduced during the second quarter of the eighteenth century. Indeed relief bills as a whole seem to have shrunk under the pressure of the workhouse test and the parish badge. At Lacock (Wiltshire), weekly pensions averaged less than 1*s.* even in the 1720s, and seem to have been no higher than 6*d.* in Troutbeck in the 1750s.[178]

The rate of growth of the value of the parish pensions across the seventeenth century seems to have been at its most rapid in East Anglia. In North Walsham (Norfolk), the most significant increases pivoted around the dearth years of the late 1640s; in Lowestoft (Suffolk) the modal weekly pension quadrupled between the late 1650s and the early 1680s. Growth elsewhere in the south was a little slower: pension levels in Cowden (Kent) rose from 8*d.* a week in the 1620s to 10*d.* a week 1660s, though here too the late 1640s seem to have been the decisive period.[179] Even in the south, however, there was at best a lagging relationship between poor relief and price trends, a tendency which was (as we have seen) even more marked further north.

The upshot is that, although a late seventeenth-century parish pauper might have been able to survive on his weekly collection, and might arguably have attained a standard of living comparable to that of a day labourer and his family, his early seventeenth-century forebears were not treated so generously, even in the south and east, let alone the far north.[180] Parish relief only gradually came to constitute a significant, let alone a sufficient, proportion of the needs of the pensioner, and in the early years of the seventeenth century it simply cannot have been enough to support a poor labouring man, let alone his wife and children.[181] Indeed it was never intended to. Overseers had been reminded in 1601 that 'reliefe' meant 'an ease or lightening of the burden' and even 'a little thing will ease where there is want or oppression'.[182] By reading the archive of pensions

Brown, 'Poor Relief and Family Situation', 410–11, demonstrates an increase in the 'burden of relief' across the 17th century in Aldenham (Hertfordshire) but does not discuss pension levels in detail.

[177] Slack, *Poverty and Policy*, 179.

[178] Smith, 'Ageing and Well-Being', 87; Hinton, 'Relief of the Poor of Lacock', 172.

[179] Wales, 'Poverty, Poor Relief and the Life-Cycle', 354; Smith, 'Ageing and Well-Being', 76; Turner, 'Ancient Parochial Account Book of Cowden', 102, 107, 111.

[180] For favourable comparisons of pension levels and wage rates in the late 17th and early 18th centuries, see Hinton, 'Relief of the Poor of Lacock', 172.

[181] Wales, 'Poverty, Poor Relief and the Life-Cycle', 354, 356–7.

[182] *An Ease for Overseers of the Poore*, 22.

payments against itself, it becomes apparent that, for the first half of the seventeenth century at least, informal relief must have remained very significant to the budgets even of those families who secured regular collection. This suggestion that the parish pension was only one asset in the economy of diversified resources is confirmed by the suggestive comments of the Hertfordshire bench in 1638 that formal and informal relief were of symmetrical significance both to the householders who paid rates and to the deserving poor who received pensions. The magistrates' attempt to raise the level of assessments in support of the labouring poor simply meant that ratepayers 'withdrew theyr charitie to the impotent poore who dayly repaire to theyr houses for relief'.[183] This picture of a core of formal provision supplemented by a penumbra of informal neighbourly support arguably characterized the dual experience of relief into the second half of the seventeenth century, perhaps even beyond.

Indeed, the relatively under-developed nature of parish relief in the years before 1630 found expression in the ambiguous language used to describe the provision made for the poor. The Somerset justices ordered, in the early seventeenth century, that the sick and children under the age of 7 should 'fetch relief' at some 'house near and certain' at hours appointed by the overseers. Begging within the parish was therefore encouraged, although begging abroad was prohibited altogether. When Justice Peter Warburton sought to galvanize the Cheshire bench into enforcing the poor laws in 1610, he similarly exploited the loophole in the 1598 legislation which permitted overseers to license begging rather than raise rates. He insisted only that the impotent poor were to 'aske relief [i.e. beg] within their parish and if that will not suffice, then to be further relieved *if there be cause* by the churchwardens and overseers of the poor'.[184] If the judges were prepared to use such language, it is little wonder that parish officers should be tempted to respond in kind. The overseers of Holkham told the Norfolk justices in 1602 that besides the twelve recipients of relief in cash or rents, there were 'dyverse alsoe within the said parishe which have no contribucion of money by reason they have *by order* daily relieffe at the houses of the inhabitantes'. In Carlton (Nottinghamshire), there were two widows receiving pensions and a further three who had 'relief at the houses of the inhabitants'. The overseers of Ratley (Warwickshire) noted in 1639 that besides those who had weekly collection the 'poore children' of the parish 'have reliefe daily at our houses'.[185]

183 NA, SP16/342/93.

184 HMC, *Lothian*, 77–8; Eaton Hall, MS Grosvenor, 2/33 (emphasis added).

185 *Bacon Papers*, iv. 237 (emphasis added); NA, SP16/329/63; SBTRO, DR37/85/6/35.

Especially in small communities, such as the Nottinghamshire parishes of Hablesthorpe and Elkesley, there were no pensions paid at all, even in the mid-1630s, the needy being provided for simply by compulsory direct relief in kind 'at the houses' of the inhabitants, a model which implied a programme of co-ordinated almsgiving to named beggars passing from household to household, especially at mealtimes.[186] To this extent, the late Elizabethan system of welfare inherited, and was in several respects decisively shaped by, the hybrid relief arrangements, especially the interpenetration of congregational charity and formal rating, that had been practised in the years before 1598.

There was evidently, therefore, a precarious balance between formal and informal arrangements, and striking it proved very difficult not only for paupers but also for the overseers who provided for them. Collectioners themselves must have found the management of their household budgets even more difficult whenever parish officers chose to adjust weekly pension levels during the course of the accounting year. In Cawston (Norfolk) in 1602, for instance, Edmund Patterson's wife received 4*d.* weekly for seventeen weeks, 3*d.* for one week, and 2*d.* for thirty-one weeks, although the overseers also paid her rent and gave her 4*s.* worth of fuel. In 1682 Margaret Davies of Gnosall (Staffordshire) received 4*d.* a week for forty-four weeks and 6*d.* for seven weeks. At Tysoe (Warwickshire) in 1639, Elizabeth Homon's weekly pension was repeatedly adjusted: 10*d.* for three weeks, 6*d.* for thirty-seven weeks, 4*d.* for thirteen weeks, and 2*d.* for one week.[187] In such cases, the pattern of regular disbursements was probably adjusted according to a number of variables: changing employment opportunities and fluctuating grain prices over the course of the harvest year; the seasonal demands of the household economy, especially for fuel; the individual needs of the pauper; and, not least, the financial priorities of the parish.

The careers of some pensioners could be extremely long: five of those admitted to pensions in Gnosall in the 1670s and 1680s remained on the parish for between eleven and sixteen years. Ann Foster's career in receipt of a pension in Whitchurch (Oxfordshire) lasted twenty-one years. Three widows of Hedenham (Norfolk) who were on the relief rolls in 1662 continued to receive collection for thirty years. In cases of chronic illness or mental incapacity, the period of dependency could be even longer. Goodwife Wells spent thirty-six years on the parish at Cowden

[186] NA, SP16/329/63, 349/86.

[187] Wales, 'Poverty, Poor Relief and the Life-Cycle', 377; Cutlack, 'Gnosall Records', 21 SBTRO, DR37/85/6/42 (Tysoe).

Cicely Badger forty-eight years on the parish of Gnosall.[188] The typical collectioner, however, was probably receiving a pension for between five and twelve years and she usually remained beholden to the parish even for her funeral.[189]

With the institutionalization of poor relief, the burials of the poor, which had once been of significance only to a small and self-contained circle of kin, were transformed into pauper funerals, rituals that raised profound and wide-ranging questions about the nature and extent of communal obligation. Burial at parish expense might be interpreted as the ultimate expression of social failure, perhaps even as a sign of exclusion from the social body, a prospect which was both terrifying to the pauper and degrading to those who survived her. It is for this reason that parish officers occasionally attempted to ensure that these occasions symbolized not worthlessness, failure, and anonymity, but the social recognition and personal respectability of the deceased.[190] Even so, the vast majority of overseers' accounts record payments only for the barest necessities of a decent burial. In the early seventeenth century, these might amount to a shilling or two for making and winding a shroud round the body, two or three pence for the digging of the grave, and sixpence or a shilling for bearing the deceased to church and churchyard. The costs even of these basics, swelled by the provision of the coffins that became increasingly common and of affidavits to certify that the deceased had been buried in woollen cloth, rose over the seventeenth century to the extent that overseers might spend between 10*s.* and 20*s.* on a pauper funeral by the early eighteenth century. Burying paupers became not only a more expensive, but also an increasingly frequent, responsibility for parish officers. The overseers of Cratfield (Suffolk) paid for the funerals of thirty pensioners in the period 1625–1700, and those of Poslingford (Suffolk) for fourteen in the period 1663–1700. In rural communities such as these, it seems, parish officers would be organizing pauper funerals at the rate of one every two or three years. Even so, burial costs only ever constituted a tiny fraction of overseers' expenditure: in Ashburton (Devon), pauper funerals accounted for 1.5 per cent of overseers' expenditure in 1691 and only 2 per cent even by 1730.[191]

[188] Turner, 'Ancient Parochial Account Book of Cowden', 114; Smith, 'Ageing and Well-Being', 80–1; Wales, 'Poverty, Poor Relief and the Life-Cycle', 364; Cutlack, 'Gnosall Records', 8.

[189] Wales, 'Poverty, Poor Relief and the Life-Cycle', 364.

[190] T. Laqueur, 'Bodies, Death and Pauper Funerals', *Representations*, 1 (1983), 109, 112.

[191] D. Cressy, *Birth, Marriage and Death: Ritual, Religion and the Life Cycle in Tudor and Stuart England* (Oxford, 1997), 429; R. Houlbrooke, *Death, Religion and the Family in England, 1480–1750* (Oxford, 1998), 277, 288–9; Botelho, 'Aged and Impotent', 99. Cf. Kent and King, 'Changing Patterns of Poor Relief', 130.

Where overseers provided more or less lavish hospitality at pauper funerals, therefore, their decisions were probably less a function of budgetary exigency than a comment on the perceived moral worth of the deceased. Commensality after the burials of pensioners was clearly not unknown, although it varied in frequency, scale, and spread. In the majority of parishes, beer was offered only at the burial of particular individuals. At Lacock (Wiltshire) in 1726, however, provision seems to have been universal, since the overseers accounted for 13*s.* 10*d.* as a lump sum 'for beer at the buryings'.[192] The range of food and drink might vary too, from as little as a groat of ale at Hennock (Devon) in 1618 to 5*s.* in bread and beer at Whitchurch (Oxfordshire) in 1693. In the parishes of early eighteenth-century Buckinghamshire and Somerset, payments for 2*s.* or 3*s.* worth of beer were not unusual, and there were similar sums spent on cakes and ale at pauper funerals in Gnosall down to the 1750s, and on ale in Stone as late as 1780.[193] It is also clear that the overseers might stipulate restrictions on who was to partake of their hospitality, occasionally providing drink only to those who laid out the body, dug the grave, or bore the coffin, rather than for the mourners who were left unrefreshed. The lack of consistency with which overseers accounted for pauper funerals makes it difficult to identify patterns of provision. What kind of arrangements, for instance, did the overseers of Pluckley (Kent) have in mind in 1679 when they ordered that Old Robert Kerison be given 'a decent burial having been a charge for a long tyme passed'? The fact that Kerison had been a collectioner only since 1670 might even qualify the interpretative temptation to equate respectability with longevity of dependence. Even so, the social meaning of these rites of passage arguably found its most decisive expression in the decision over whether or not to ring the parish bells. 'Old Huntwick' of Ashby de la Zouch (Leicestershire) was sufficiently respected in the community to merit a 'passing peal' at a cost of 2*d.* in 1631, and few of the inhabitants of Worth (Sussex) could have objected to the parish paying for a child's 'grave and knell' in 1638, but others were not so fortunate. Little wonder that, by the eighteenth century, the pauper funeral became 'the locus of enormous anxiety about dying bereft of the final signs of communal membership'.[194]

[192] Hinton, 'Relief of the Poor of Lacock', 178.

[193] Houlbrooke, *Death, Religion and the Family*, 277, 288; Smith, 'Ageing and Well-Being', 81 Jones, 'Trull Overseers' Accounts', 96; Edmonds, 'Overseers of the Poor of Chalfont St Peter' 20; Cutlack, 'Gnosall Records', 44; Broadbridge, 'Old Poor Law', 13.

[194] Houlbrooke, *Death, Religion and the Family*, 289; Davie, 'Custom and Conflict', 236; Cressy *Birth, Marriage and Death*, 429; A. Fletcher, *A County Community in Peace and War: Sussex, 1600–166* (London, 1975), 157; Laqueur, 'Bodies, Death and Pauper Funerals', 117.

The recognition of social inclusion that might be symbolized by a parish funeral did, however, have its price. Although they appear to have done so without any statutory authority, it was not unusual for overseers to seize paupers' goods at their death in order that they might be sold off to reimburse parochial expenditure on their maintenance and burial. At Trull (Somerset) in the 1650s, the overseers accounted for sums 'paid towards burial', a formulation that suggests that funeral expenses were fully satisfied only after the value of the pensioner's goods and chattels had been realized. Some parishes ensured that inventories were taken immediately after collectioners were admitted to the relief rolls, and even paid brokers 4*d.* or 6*d.* a time for 'crying a sale' of their goods after they had died. The goods themselves might be of meagre value. The property of the four pensioners that was sold off by the overseers of Chalfont St Peter (Buckinghamshire) in the early 1720s was collectively worth less than £2. The assets of the forty paupers whose property was liquidated by the parish officers of Frampton (Lincolnshire) in the period 1648–1766 had a combined value of only £127, at an average of £3. 3*s.* 6*d.* The pauper inventories drawn up by the overseers of Great Staughton (Huntingdonshire) had an average value of only 43*s.* Those inventories valued at as little as 2*s.*, as was that of Widow Ashby of Tonbridge (Kent) in 1690, may indicate not only that old or worn goods had little or no second-hand value but also that a pauper's other property had been pawned, or sold and never replaced, in hard times. The longer inventories nonetheless constituted invaluable currency in the campaign against unnecessary expenditure. At Eaton Socon, the property of John Cooper, the pensioner with the most furniture when all the paupers' goods were inventoried in 1733, was worth only £2. 18*s.* 2*d.* at his death. Even so, this sum represented 16 per cent of the relief he had received over the preceding six years. It was less rewarding for the overseers to go the trouble and expense of selling the goods of Widow Alderman, however, since they represented only 6 per cent of the cost of her care between 1731 and 1736.[195] In the Devon parishes of Colyton and Sidbury it was usual in

[195] Jones, 'Trull Overseers Accounts', 95; Edmonds, 'Overseers of the Poor of Chalfont St Peter', 7; Hindle, 'Power, Poor Relief and Social Relations', 94; Kent and King, 'Changing Patterns of Poor Relief', 137–8; Barker-Read, 'Treatment of the Aged Poor', 93; F. G. Emmison, 'The Relief of the Poor at Eaton Socon, 1706–1834', *Publications of the Bedfordshire Historical Record Society*, 15 (1933), 33; and cf. Ch.1.4 above. For other references to the practice see W. E. Tate, *The Parish Chest: A Study of the Records of Parochial Administration in England* (3rd edn., Cambridge, 1960), 205–6; Emmison, 'The Care of the Poor in Elizabethan Essex', 16 (Wivenhoe, 1576–94); Cutlack, 'Gnosall Records', 35; E. M. Hampson, *The Treatment of Poverty in Cambridgeshire, 1597–1834* (Cambridge, 1934), 182–3 (Linton, 1731); J. Boulton, 'Going on the Parish: The Parish Pension and its Meaning in the London Suburbs, 1640–1724', in T. Hitchcock *et al.* (eds.), *Chronicling*

the early eighteenth century for the goods of deceased pensioners to be recycled rather than sold, their bedding, tools, shoes, and clothing being given as relief in kind to those who took their place in the pension lists.[196] Even so, the fact that worldly goods of such meagre value might be clapped with the parish brand suggests that collection was not entirely unconditional even in the early years of formal welfare provision. By the late seventeenth century, moreover, the parish brand was only one symbol of the culture of deterrence that coloured communal attitudes to collection, since from 1697 (and in some cases even before then) pensioners were also required to 'take the patch'.[197]

4. LOCAL ECOLOGIES OF RELIEF

From the late sixteenth century, therefore, parish relief was administered by overseers of the poor and co-ordinated by justices of the peace in a national system created by parliamentary statute.[198] It has recently been argued, however, that significant regional differences had emerged in the administration of welfare by the early eighteenth century. In particular, it has been suggested that the relief policies adopted by the vestries of northern and western parishes were harsh by the standards of their southern and eastern counterparts, and that the constituency of collectioners in the north-west was comparatively small and the pensions they received less 'generous' than in the south-east. Indeed, when measured by the yardstick of the basic male wage, the package of benefits (the pension and its supplements) offered by the southern and eastern poor law was benevolent, and its administration flexible and sensitive to local need, in a way that was simply not the case in the north and west.[199]

Poverty: The Voices and Strategies of the English Poor, 1640–1840 (London and New York, 1997), 35–6; A. Tomkins, 'Pawnbroking and the Survival Strategies of the Urban Poor in 1770s York', in King and Tomkins (eds.), *The Poor in England*, 186. For the wider context of these policies, see P. King, 'Pauper Inventories and the Material Lives of the Poor in the Eighteenth and Early Nineteenth Centuries', in Hitchcock *et al.* (eds.), *Chronicling Poverty*, esp. 157–61. For other examples of extant inventories, see B. Cornford, 'Inventories of the Poor', *Norfolk Archaeology*, 35 (1970), 118–25.

196 Sharpe, *Population and Society*, 235.

197 Cf. Ch. 6.5 below.

198 The high level of coherence and integration offered by the English poor law in contrast to the more multifarious practices prevailing in the welfare regimes of Continental Europe is very effectively emphasized in P. M. Solar, 'Poor Relief and English Economic Development before the Industrial Revolution', *Economic History Review*, 2nd ser., 48 (1995), 1–22.

199 For the development of this thesis, see S. A. King, 'Poor Relief and English Economic Development Reappraised', *Economic History Review*, 2nd ser., 50 (1997), 360–8; King, 'Reconstructing Lives: The Poor, the Poor Law and Welfare in Calverley, 1650–1820', *Social History*, 22 (1997), 318–38; King, *Poverty and Welfare in England, 1700–1850: A Regional Perspective* (Manchester

This argument deserves to be taken seriously, not least because (although it is largely based on evidence dating from after 1750) it is, as we have seen, clear that there were already significant differentials in the level of pensions between northern and southern parishes by the mid-seventeenth century. The following discussion will suggest, however, that the picture of regionally differentiated poor law administration is significantly over-drawn (not to say exaggerated), especially for the period before 1750. Indeed, the micro-politics of poor relief as they have been discussed in this chapter suggest that the fundamental issue for overseers was balancing the extent of pauperization against the strength of the local tax base. To be sure, that equilibrium was struck in different ways in different economic and demographic contexts. In aggregate, on average, of course, the parochial tax base in northern parishes was so much weaker that the parish relief system must to a certain extent have been regionally skewed both in the sense of what, given regional differences in the cost of living, it was, or was not, *required* to provide, and what it could, or could not, *afford* to provide. Shortfalls in the resources of northern ratepayers doubtless forced the indigent into greater reliance on the human resources of kin and neighbours and on the natural resources of the landscape. Even so, the thrust of the following discussion is that variations in levels both of need and of relief *within* regions were at least as, if not more, significant than those *between* them. This was a national system in which the principal differentials were mosaics of local variation rather than a major regional schism.

In the first place, there were very significant variations in the nature and extent of the very poverty that the Elizabethan poor laws were designed to ameliorate. The best way of measuring these is to employ the most widespread and standardized index of poverty as it was understood in the late seventeenth century: a 'pauper' was defined not by his receipt of regular parish relief but by his inability to contribute to parish rates for the maintenance of the poor and of the church fabric, a status indicated in exemption from liability to make hearth tax payments.[200] Analysis of the geographical distribution of hearth tax exemption suggests that the most significant pattern is not a dichotomy between a highly pauperized pastoral north-west with and a more prosperous arable south-east, but a more complex mosaic of pauperized populations clustered according to

2000), 141–226; King, 'Making the Most of Opportunity: The Economy of Makeshifts in the Early Modern North', in King and Tomkins (eds.), *The Poor in England*, 228–57.

[200] The most sophisticated discussions of the relationship between poverty and hearth tax exemption are Arkell, 'The Incidence of Poverty'; and Arkell, 'Identifying Regional Variations from the Hearth Tax: An Alternative Approach', *The Local Historian*, 33 (2003), esp. 150–2.

the economic circumstances of the communities in which they lived. Thus the Essex cloth-working parish of Coggeshall had a hearth tax exemption rate of 59.8 per cent, some 77 per cent higher than that of the parishes of rural Essex. Indeed, the degree of pauperization in Coggeshall resembled that of the parishes of the Warwickshire coalfield rather more closely than that of its south-eastern neighbours. The relatively pauperized coalmining communities of north-east Warwickshire (with a hearth tax exemption rate of 49.8 per cent), in turn, had more in common with the desperately poor parishes of the Durham coalfield than they did with the felden parishes of southern Warwickshire, whose exemption rate (34.4 per cent) they outstripped by some 45 per cent.[201] Hearth tax exemption may be a very poor indicator of absolute levels of need, but its real significance lies in its capacity to reveal relative patterns of deprivation: thus the north Warwickshire parishes whose population had grown relatively quickly (by 125 per cent between 1560 and 1670) exempted 41 per cent of their inhabitants from hearth tax payments, the more slowly growing southern parishes (experiencing only a 97 per cent increase after a period of depopulation caused by enclosure and engrossing) exempted only 29 per cent. The open-field parishes of Northamptonshire had grown by only 43 per cent in the period 1524 to 1670, and had a much higher proportion of taxpayers (only 35 per cent exempted) than the forest communities (44 per cent), whose population had increased by 126 per cent over the same period. The social landscape of the countryside was not dichotomized between 'two Englands', but was a much more complex patchwork of prosperous and pauperized regions and sub-regions.[202]

Topographical and economic differences of this kind are, however, only half the story. More striking still is the range of variation of hearth tax exemption even between contiguous parishes which enjoyed relatively similar economic experiences. Thus, although the degree of pauperization as suggested by exemption from hearth tax payments across the parishes of Kineton hundred of Warwickshire was 34.4 per cent, this figure conceals very significant variations from a maximum of 53.8 per cent in Packwood to a minimum of 7.7 per cent in Gaydon.[203] These Warwickshire parishes were relatively small, and it is tempting to dismiss these differentials as mirages created by the presence of one or two more

[201] These are the findings of T. Arkell reported in Levine and Wrightson, *Making of an Industrial Society*, 157. Cf. Ch. 4.1(*d*) above.

[202] Beier, 'Poverty and Progress', 216–17; P. A. J. Pettit, *The Royal Forests of Northamptonshire: A Study in their Economy, 1558–1714* (Northamptonshire Record Society, 23, Gateshead, 1968), 142.

[203] Hindle, *The Birthpangs of Welfare*, 34–5 (appendix I).

paupers than the average. The fact remains, however, that variations of this kind mattered a great deal, precisely because the system of formal relief operated on a parish-by-parish basis. Minor variations in liability for poor rates might combine with the differential demands placed on the relief system by the structural poverty of social groups and the life-cycle experiences of individual households to create vastly different welfare regimes. In part, therefore, the demand for parish relief was a function of prevailing patterns of employment and remuneration, but it was also influenced by the distribution of landed wealth, and in turn of ancient (though evolving) patterns of settlement and immigration.

So much then for the demand side of the welfare equation. In turning to supply, it is clear that all these factors in turn might be reflected in the burden of poor rate assessments. Of twenty-three Warwickshire parishes for which evidence survives in 1638–9, at least twenty (87 per cent) were definitely raising money by parish rates. Of these, six provided no evidence for the basis of the assessment, but for the remaining fourteen the mechanics of rating can be analysed. Nine parishes made levies by the yardland at an average rate of 3*s.* each, but it is nonetheless striking that there was considerable variation, between 1*s.* 8*d.* the yardland in Radway and 5*s.* 6*d.* in Priors Hardwick, in the weight of the assessment.[204] The most complex situation was at Fenny Compton, where a levy of 1*s.* the yardland raised over £4, but was supplemented by two annual payments, totalling £3, from the graziers of the substantial enclosed pastures lying beyond the parish boundary.[205] By 1639, however, at least five of the Kineton hundred parishes were conducting their assessments on the basis of the value, rather than the acreage, of property held. At Bishop's Tachbrook, for example, the overseers made three levies, each of 3*d.* in the £, thus representing an annual assessment of 3.8 per cent of rateable value. Although the annual cost of poor relief was significantly lower in Ilmington (0.5 per cent) and Tanworth (1 per cent), the ratepayers of Warmington (12.5 per cent) and of the depopulated village of Lower Shuckburgh (20 per cent) were subject to a much heavier burden.[206]

It is clear that variations in the patterns of settlement and wealth also led to considerable variations in the social spread of liability for rates. The

[204] These in part reflected the fact that the Warwickshire yardland varied in size from manor to manor, usually between sixteen and thirty-six acres, with a median figure of below thirty acres. Dyer, *Warwickshire Farming*, 5.

[205] SBTRO, DR37/85/6/34 (Radway), 52 (Priors Hardwick). For Fenny Compton, see SBTRO, DR37/85/6/7; *Warwick County Records*, ii. 19; and P. Styles, 'A Census of a Warwickshire Village in 1698', repr. in id., *Studies in Seventeenth-Century West Midlands History*, 90–107.

[206] SBTRO, DR37/85/6/21 (Ilmington), 37 (Lower Shuckburgh), 38 (Bishop's Tachbrook), 39–40 (Tanworth), 43 (Warmington).

evidence of the hearth tax is much more reliable as an indicator of the breadth of the tax base than it is of the burden of poverty itself. Analysis of the geographical distribution of households with more than three hearths demonstrates a concentration of wealth in the south and east, receding outwards through the Midlands to the north and the west.[207] There was nonetheless marked variation even within regions, probably a function of patterns of social differentiation themselves created by localized histories of settlement, immigration, and economic development. In Hampshire, for instance, there was a clear divide between the eastern half of the county, where 32.6 per cent of the households had three or more hearths, and the west, where the corresponding figure was only 18.8 per cent. In Suffolk the situation was even more complex, with the parishes of the county falling into six distinct sub-regions, each of them with a different distribution of wealthier households.[208] These differentials are even reflected in the assessment lists of individual parishes. In twelve north Norfolk parishes for which early seventeenth-century poor relief assessments survive, for example, the proportion of adults who contributed to parish rates averaged 38.3 per cent. Much more significant, however, was the range of variation within this sample of contiguous communities in a region of sheep-corn husbandry, from a minimum of 12.9 per cent in Snoring Magna to a high of 60 per cent in Morston.[209] It is possible to analyse the hierarchy of ratepayers in only two of the parishes in our Warwickshire sample. Of the thirty-nine householders in Halford, fifteen (38 per cent) were assessed for the poor rate. The leading seven of them (including the vicar) carried almost 77 per cent, the smallest five a mere 7 per cent, of the burden of parish rates between them. The tax base at Ilmington was slightly narrower, with twenty-five (or 31 per cent) of the households paying poor rates. The gradient of assessment was correspondingly steeper: the seven leading ratepayers similarly met over 77 per cent of the levy, the smallest five as little 2 per cent.[210] In these villages, evidently, the farms had been engrossed to a small number of occupiers who formed the elite and paid most of the rate bill. Whether there were other parishes in which, although elites were doubtless evident, they paid a relatively small proportion of the total rate raised must remain a matter of conjecture, especially in the context of polarized, fielden Warwickshire. The fragmentary nature of these two itemized assessments, lying at the heart of a corpus of detailed disburse-

207 Arkell, 'Identifying Regional Variations from the Hearth Tax', 157.

208 Ibid. 160.

209 *Bacon Papers*, iv. 187–92.

210 SBTRO, DR37/85/6/18 (Halford), 21 (Ilmington).

ments, is nonetheless a powerful reminder that the social distribution of wealth amongst ratepayers is one of the great unexplored issues of seventeenth-century poor law history.

There is, moreover, some evidence to suggest that informal relief may well have proved more resilient in smaller rural parishes than in larger pastoral ones or market towns. Analysis of the proportion of the poor exempt from the hearth tax who did not actually receive regular pensions is indicative of a community's willingness to meet the needs of its indigent population without troubling the overseers. In the rural villages of north-east Norfolk, the proportion of the exempt who received collection was very low, varying only between 6 and 13 per cent. In the market towns of the region, by contrast, the equivalent proportions were as high as 24 to 25 per cent. In Colyton (Devon), as many as 20 per cent of 'paupers' were relieved by the parish. The larger rural parishes of south Warwickshire, such as Brailes and Tanworth, had relatively high ratios of approximately 18 per cent and the sprawling parish of Tysoe as much as 36 per cent.[211] In smaller parishes, it seems, the claims that poor householders might make on the households of their neighbours might prove more difficult to deny. From this perspective, the greater numbers on collection in large rural parishes and market towns may be less symptomatic of 'generous' welfare regimes than an index of the changing preferences of householders. The inhabitants of those larger parishes in which the burden of poverty was swollen by large numbers of poor migrants may well have chosen to meet their charitable obligations rather through the impersonal mechanism of formal relief than through traditional habits of almsgiving. In a small parish such as Hanworth (Norfolk), by contrast, where there were perhaps only forty households in the mid-seventeenth century, it really was quite plausible for the vicar to argue, as he did in 1647, that it was 'fitter' to provide for the poor 'by voluntary contributions than by rates and collections'.[212] Once again, however, it is the intense local variation in these arrangements that should be emphasized.

They are reflected in extraordinary differentials in the generosity of relief even between adjacent parishes. Between them, the thirty-three south Warwickshire parishes for which expenditure totals can be calculated spent almost £320 on their poor in the year 1638–9. Expenditure per head of population, however, diverged widely from the average of just over 8*d.* The most 'generous' parish was Lapworth (2*s.* per head), the least

[211] Wales, 'Poverty, Poor Relief and the Life-Cycle', 357–8; Sharpe, *Population and Society*, 225; Hindle, *The Birthpangs of Welfare*, 24–5 (appendix 1 and calculations based on the data there).

[212] Wales, 'Poverty, Poor Relief and the Life-Cycle', 359.

'generous' Lighthorne (3*d*.).[213] Such variations might, as we have seen, partly reflect the different patterns of neighbourliness prevailing in larger as opposed to smaller parishes: Lapworth was, after all, three times as populous as Lighthorne. Per capita expenditure also varied significantly across the parishes of Devon after the Restoration, though here the evidence suggests that the larger communities enjoyed no monopoly on 'generosity'. In a sample of twenty-seven overseers' accounts, the most 'generous' parish was Halberton (spending 6*s*. 1*d*. for every inhabitant on the poor in 1685), the least generous Stoke in Teignhead (only 4*d*. per head in 1668). Of the fourteen parishes that spent more than 2*s*. per head on the poor, ten had fewer than 500 inhabitants, and some larger settlements (Cullompton, Ashburton, and Bovey Tracey, each with populations exceeding 1,500) were noticeably less generous even than this.[214]

There were, therefore, other, highly localized, factors than the quality of neighbourly relations that might influence the supply of parish relief. Among the most significant variables that might affect the supply of resources to the poor was the presence of a gentry seat; or, more precisely, of a resident gentleman who might provide a sufficiently consistent charitable presence to provide regular hospitality and/or employment to the poor. In half of the parishes in the Warwickshire hundred of Kineton, there was a single manor with a resident lord, whose exercise of his charitable obligations may well have significantly reduced the demand for poor relief. In some communities, indeed, gentry largesse was sufficient to obviate the need for taxation altogether. In the Northamptonshire parish of Weekley, for example, 'there was never any taxe for the poore' because Sir Edward Montagu and others 'gave [collections] at Communions and fast dayes', which were 'distributed amongst the poorest of the parish'.[215] By the early seventeenth century, however, the seasonal flight of the gentry to London was undermining the alternatives to parish relief. 'The decaye of hospitalitie' caused by those in the country 'flocking to London & other places', it was complained in 1607, was such that 'the poorer sorte loose their reliefe and have the lesse worke for the daylie labour to be done about those houses'.[216] As the gentry deserted the

[213] SBTRO, DR37/85/6/23 (Lapworth) (£39. 10*s*. 8*d*. among a population of approximately 400), 25 (Lighthorne) (£1. 9*s*. 6*d*. among a population of approximately 130). These figures are artificial to the extent that they compare expenditure figures for 1639 with population estimates for 1664. They nonetheless plausibly indicate the range of variation in per capita poor relief expenditure.

[214] Sharpe, *Population and Society*, 226.

[215] NRO, MS Montagu, 186 ('Life of Montagu' by Joseph Bentham), 25–6.

[216] NA, SP16/307/2.

countryside, they might assuage their charitable consciences by authorizing their stewards to distribute seasonal doles, of the kind offered every Christmas by Lord Fitzwilliam of Milton (Northamptonshire) in the 1690s.[217]

Even where the gentry were absent, however, charity might be sufficiently well co-ordinated by middling parishioners to allow them to diminish or perhaps even to dispense with rating and assessment. One of the favourite methods of raising parochial funds was the organization of church ales, which had first become popular in the mid-fifteenth century, and in some villages had even supplanted a pre-existing tradition of parochial levies.[218] They were often held in church houses specifically built for the purpose, and sometimes, as at Elham (Kent) in 1511, even in the church itself.[219] By the early sixteenth century they had come to occupy a central place in parochial finance, as the largest single source of revenue of country parishes.[220] Their subsequent fate is chronologically and geographically uneven. Although ales seem to have been abrogated almost entirely in the south and east by the Edwardian Reformation, they proved more resilient in the Thames valley and the west, where they experienced a spectacular resurgence in the 1550s and 1560s. Their reappearance was much less marked in south-eastern England, however, and by the 1570s church ales seem to have vanished altogether from East Anglia, Kent, and Sussex, bringing full circle a century-long cycle of cultural development in which parishes had experimented with communal festivity as a means of generating funds only to fall back eventually on levies and rents. The ales of the south-west and north-west, however, proved much more resilient, even under attrition from the circuit judges and the local Protestant gentry. Official hostility may have been motivated by godly zeal and fear of disorder, but it was tempered with recognition that churchwardens drew very significant income from parish revels. Sir Francis Hastings's late Elizabethan attack on the church ales of five Somerset villages, for instance, was accompanied by his bequest of

[217] D. R. Hainsworth, *Stewards, Lords and People: The Estate Steward and his World in Later Stuart England* (Cambridge, 1992), 159. Cf. Ch. 2.2 above.

[218] R. Hutton, *The Rise and Fall of Merry England: The Ritual Year in England, 1400–1700* (Oxford, 1994), 59.

[219] Hutton, *The Rise and Fall of Merry England*, 70; G. A. Copeland, 'Devonshire Church Houses', *Reports and Transactions of the Devonshire Association*, 92 (1960), 116–41; P. Cowley, *The Church Houses: Their Religious and Social Significance* (London, 1970). For the chronology of church house-building, see Hutton, *The Rise and Fall of Merry England*, 309 n. 51. The church house in Lacock (Wilts.) was used for ales between 1583 and 1628. Hinton, 'Relief of the Poor of Lacock', 193.

[220] B. Kümin, *The Shaping of a Community: The Rise and Reformation of the English Parish, 1400–1560* (Aldershot, 1996), 118; Hutton, *The Rise and Fall of Merry England*, 28.

funds to augment the parish stock in compensation for the revenue that would be lost in these communities.[221] Campaigns of this kind were still under way in early seventeenth-century Devon, Somerset, and Lancashire when they fell foul of the controversies over Sunday sports in 1618 and 1633.[222] Although, therefore, church ales had almost entirely disappeared in the south-east by the turn of the seventeenth century, they were to survive a generation, perhaps even two, longer in the West Country. Richard Carew was happy to note the extent to which Cornish church ales defrayed 'any extraordinary charges arising in the parish or imposed on them for the good of the country' as late as 1602. John Aubrey remembered that the charitable funds raised by Whitsuntide revels had once been sufficiently extensive that they 'did the business' of poor rates, obviating the need for assessment altogether, as was the case in Kingston St Michael (Dorset) well into the seventeenth century.[223]

One reason why church ales died out so quietly in East Anglia in particular in the mid- to late sixteenth century was the existence of significant landed resources which might form an alternative basis of parish revenues and therefore supplement, perhaps even defray, poor relief expenditure, therefore rendering communal festivity if not an entirely redundant then at least a relatively problematic source of income. Town lands, property bequeathed by will to finance the administrative functions of the parish, seem to have been particularly significant in pastoral parishes. By 1660, it has been estimated, some eighty-eight Norfolk villages (about 15 per cent of all the parishes in the county) and forty in Buckinghamshire (19 per cent) enjoyed capital endowments of between £100 and £400, which might yield between £5 and £20 a year and therefore make a valuable contribution to parish finances.[224] In many cases, these bequests were linked to the fund from which village tax payments were paid, as they were in Thornham Magna (Suffolk) from 1434, Holme (Nottinghamshire) from 1490, and Fersfield and Tibenham (Norfolk) from 1493.[225] The chronology of these endowments is interesting, for they most often originated in late fifteenth- and early sixteenth-century bequests to defray the burden of parliamentary taxation or other

[221] Hutton, *The Rise and Fall of Merry England*, 87–9, 99–100, 113–14, 119, 138–42.

[222] Ibid. 190–2.

[223] R. Carew, *The Survey of Cornwall*, ed. F. E. Halliday (London, 1953), 141; J. Aubrey, *Wiltshire: The Topographical Collections of John Aubrey*, ed. J. E. Jackson (Devizes, 1862), 10–11.

[224] Jordan, *The Charities of Rural England*, 195.

[225] Ibid. 144–5, C. Dyer, 'The English Medieval Village Community and its Decline', *Journal of British Studies*, 33 (1994), 415; Dyer, 'Taxation and Communities in Late Medieval England', in R. Britnell and J. Hatcher (eds.), *Progress and Problems in Medieval England: Essays in Honour of Edward Miller* (Cambridge, 1996), 185.

common charges of the parish.[226] Their timing is to this extent paradoxical, since they embodied a secularized vision of collective charity long before the formal assessment of rates in relief of the poor had been dreamt of by Elizabethan parliamentarians. Although they mainly predated the Reformation, they express a trend towards that this-worldly conception of charity, defined in terms of what was of use to the parish, that is also increasingly found in testamentary bequests to the poor of this period.[227] Endowments of this kind therefore owed as little to the redefinition of charity consequent on the Reformation as they did to the increasing demands made by the early modern state. They nonetheless provided a firm financial footing from which parish officers might meet the novel financial obligations of the late Elizabethan period.

By the very late sixteenth and early seventeenth centuries, bequests of this kind were increasingly designed to relieve the heightened financial pressures on the parish created by compulsory poor relief, though by law they could be used to finance only doles and other casual payments rather than regular pensions. The town lands of Bergh Apton (Norfolk), for example, were created in 1599 by a bequest of sixty acres to the parish fund by a local yeoman, who stipulated that 20*s.* a year be given to the churchwardens for the relief of the poor. Those of Grimston (Norfolk), although founded in 1394, were increasingly being used to subsidize poor relief, and in 1640 a specific proportion of the income was set aside to apprentice pauper children. The town lands of Ashwell (Hertfordshire) originated in a bequest of 1618 which was subsequently augmented so that by 1727 the annual yield of the forty-two acres was £17. This money was divided between the financing of pauper apprenticeships (which would otherwise have had to be paid out of rates) and providing a bread dole for the poor. At Clayworth (Nottinghamshire) almost a quarter (23.3 per cent) of the overseers' income was derived from the rents on town lands by the fourth quarter of the seventeenth century, and their yield was sufficient to help the parish avoid rating altogether until 1681–2. A similar situation prevailed in Frampton (Lincolnshire), where town lands were first recorded in 1589, though they probably originated even earlier. By the 1630s, they were generating an annual income of £22, sufficient to account for 46 per cent of poor relief expenditure in the second half of the seventeenth century. It was the significant yield of the town lands that

[226] For the chronology of endowments for general municipal purposes and tax relief in Norfolk, with particular peaks in the 1490s, 1500s, and 1530s, see Jordan, *Charities of Rural England*, 144.

[227] M. McIntosh, *Autonomy and Community: The Royal Manor of Havering, 1200–1500* (Cambridge, 1986), 238–40; McIntosh, 'Local Responses to the Poor', 217–25.

enabled the Frampton overseers to restrict poor rates to 4*d.* per acre until the early 1700s. When relief expenditure rose dramatically in the first decade of the eighteenth century, moreover, the vestry's solution was not a commitment to raising ever heavier rates but the augmentation of the charity lands by the enclosure of ten acres of waste, with the result that the annual yield of the landed assets of the parish more than doubled, and was able to finance well over half of all relief expenditure in the period 1720–79.[228]

The creation of what was effectively a parish allotment in Frampton in 1717 reflects the complexity of the role played by common land, technically under the control of the manor rather than the parish, which was increasingly pressed into the parochial effort to meet the financial obligations created by the 1601 statute. This strategy benefited both those commoners who paid poor rates, for whom the burden of taxation was lowered, and those who did not, since their poverty was, in any case, the most frequent justification for the use of common land. At least one in three Norfolk parishes were using common lands to relieve the poor, either directly through using them as a site on which to build parish housing, as at Blickling before 1729, or indirectly through enclosing parcels of waste, as at Broome in 1664.[229] When combined with the vestry's tendency to sanction the poor's access to common rights (by 'privilege' or 'indulgence' rather than by right) in order to defray rates, it becomes clear both that the existence of common lands might be a very significant variable in the financing and management of parochial relief schemes and that enclosure (especially where it was carried out without adequate compensation for the poor in the form of an allotment) might fatally undermine a welfare system whose very effectiveness had lain in its ability to combine the financial assets of ratepayers with the natural resources of unenclosed land to the satisfaction of both those who funded poor relief and those who depended upon it.[230]

In the absence of either church ales or parish property, the imperative for charitable endowments became all the greater. Endowments generally seem to have played a relatively larger role than rate-based relief in urban centres and relatively small market towns than they did in rural communities, though some larger rural parishes may also have had significant charities.[231] In Devon, it seems, only fifty (13 per cent) of the

228 Jordan, *The Charities of Rural England*, 148, 163; Broad, 'Parochial Economies of Welfare', 997; *Coming into Line*, *passim*; Hindle. 'Power, Poor Relief and Social Relations', 83–4.

229 S. Birtles, 'Common Land, Poor Relief and Enclosure: The Use of Manorial Resources in Fulfilling Parish Obligation, 1601–1834', *Past and Present*, 165 (1999), 86–91.

230 Ibid. 91–106.

231 Barker-Read, 'The Treatment of the Aged Poor', 287.

parishes in the county lacked endowments, most of these being tiny villages.[232] Where they existed, parish charities might make a very considerable difference to the development, nature, and scale of parish relief. It is especially striking, for instance, that so few of the Warwickshire parishes whose precocious welfare regimes were so well documented in 1638–9 possessed generous endowments. Only seven (18 per cent) of the communities of Kineton hundred enjoyed the benefit of parish charities in the mid-seventeenth century, an absence that might well account for the sophistication of the welfare regime in the region.[233] Those larger endowments which did provide for the poor of south Warwickshire were generally confined to the more populous parishes, where habits of spontaneous neighbourliness were more difficult to sustain. Only the large detached Arden parishes of Lapworth and Tanworth enjoyed what might be regarded as very significant endowments, their charity boards packed with benefactions dating back to the medieval period, though some of the larger rural parishes in the south of the county also had endowments. The poor parishioners of both Brailes and Tysoe, for instance, were beneficiaries of £4 per annum under the terms of 'Willington's dole', bequeathed in 1555 and financed partly from rents on property in the deserted village of Compton Wynyates. This sum represented about 16 per cent of relief expenditure in Tysoe and 12 per cent of that in Brailes.[234] It similarly fell to the discretion of the constables and churchwardens (but not, significantly, the overseers) to distribute 11*s*. 4*d*. annually (about 6 per cent of annual relief expenditure) to twenty of the poorest parishioners or householders of Fenny Compton under the terms of a bequest of 1611.[235] In a less populous parish, however, even a relatively small endowment might make a very significant contribution indeed. The 'most needy poor' of Avon Dassett received 20*s*. annually from the bequest made by their vicar, John James, in 1617, a sum which was equivalent to over 22 per cent of annual relief expenditure.[236] The provision of endowed charity might, in practice, allow overseers to cut

[232] W. G. Hoskins, *Devon* (London, 1954), 244.

[233] For what follows, see SBTRO, DR37/85/6; and cf. the relevant sections of *The Victoria History of the County of Warwick*, ed. W. Page *et al.* (8 vols., London, 1904–69), vol. v.

[234] SBTRO, DR37/85/6/3 (Brailes), 42 (Tysoe). The legatee was William Willington, sometime bailiff of Brailes and Merchant of the Staple, depopulator of the Oxfordshire parishes of Barcheston and Whitchurch, and sheep-master of flocks numbering 15,000 which grazed across early 16th-century Warwickshire. Beresford, *Lost Villages*, 62, 108, 126–8, 192–3; SBTRO, DR308/101. The parish officers of Alrewas (Staffs.) paid for a charity board in 1699. Kent and King, 'Changing Patterns of Poor Relief', 127.

[235] SBTRO, DR37/85/6/7 (Fenny Compton).

[236] SBTRO, DR37/85/6/11 (Avon Dassett).

back on pensions. They were repeatedly enjoined not do so, thought it is clearly the case that this requirement was more frequently honoured in the breach than in the observance.[237]

With respect to the patterns in the *disbursement* of poor relief, however, local variations of practice are much more difficult to identify. There are obvious factors inherent in the provisions of the Elizabethan relief statutes, for example the willingness of the ratepayers to invest in work schemes or in parish apprenticeships, which might offset the rates and keep regular relief expenditure down. In those parishes where overseers co-ordinated work for the able-bodied, there might be immediate reductions in payments to the labouring poor, although these schemes often proved to be short-lived and were frequently aborted as they proved to be a drain on parish finances. As we have seen, however, it was much more likely that labour discipline would be more effectively applied to the young, especially in the 1630s, and the binding out of significant numbers of pauper children would certainly have had the effect of driving down the level of pensions paid to their parents.[238]

The overwhelming sense generated by the study of contiguous parish welfare regimes is that of intense local variation. Differentials of this kind have long been familiar to historians of nineteenth-century poor relief, but to find them represented so starkly in seventeenth-century evidence is especially striking. They reflect not only significant variations in social structure, wealth distribution, and demographic experience even between adjacent parishes, but also the realities of labour mobility in an economy characterized by chronic under-employment. The fact that labourers did not necessarily live and work in the same parish almost certainly influenced the apparent differences in welfare provision between these communities. Short-distance migration to places of work is very difficult to reconstruct, but it would be surprising, for example, if the parishes of Kineton hundred were not among those supplying migrant labour to Lionel Cranfield's woad-growing enterprise at nearby Milcote, which employed almost 250 field workers every day throughout the summers of the 1620s and 1630s.[239] It is, therefore, little wonder that subsistence migration between parishes was perceived to be an even greater danger than casual begging within them, and the injunctions that 'none begg upp and down the parish nor bee suffered to straggle, but that the parishioners of every towne be releeved by worke or otherwise at

[237] Cf. Ch. 2.5(*c*) above.

[238] Cf. Chs. 3.1 and 3.2 above.

[239] J. Thirsk, *Economic Policy and Projects: The Development of a Consumer Society in Early Modern England* (Oxford, 1978), 5.

home' was to recur throughout seventeenth-century quarter sessions orders across the country. In 1652 the Warwickshire justices even minuted their 'dislike' of the 'humour' of those who were allegedly inclined 'to remove from place to place'.[240] Given the obvious danger that the poor might wander abroad in search of more substantial welfare provision, it is little wonder that parish overseers were at pains to argue that they catered adequately for local need. The Gaydon overseers noted that, in addition to the three widows in receipt of weekly pensions, 'the rest of our poor we help according to theire several necessities so that we have none that are forced to wander abroad for their living'. Their colleagues at Priors Hardwick similarly noted that 'our poor are provided for without any wandering abroad'.[241] The combination of parochial responsibility for the poor with highly localized patterns of prosperity and indigence ensured that parish boundaries had to be well defended.[242]

5. CONCLUSION: THE CHARITY OF THE PARISH

The role of collection in the lives of the impotent poor was, therefore, transformed across the seventeenth century. To judge by the parish accounts of Buckinghamshire, Hertfordshire, and Essex, late Elizabethan parish relief was relatively small-scale and generally unsystematic, practised largely in market towns and larger rural parishes.[243] Until the crisis of the 1590s provoked the archiepiscopal inquiry into the effectiveness of parish collections, churchwardens and collectors of the poor were subject to very little supervision or monitoring by the authorities of either church or state.[244] Where formal relief did exist, moreover, its significance was generally dwarfed by other forms of charity, not only the more visible collective charity embodied in the poor box, the communion collection, and the Easter dole, but also the more spontaneous habits of mutual aid practised among individual householders.[245] The almsgiving disclosed during the campaign for general hospitality of 1596–7 is almost certainly indicative of a tradition of

[240] *Records of Rowington Being Extracts from the Deeds in the Possession of the Feoffees of the Rowington Charities*, ed. J. W. Ryland (2 vols., Birmingham, 1896–1927), 92–3 (undated, *c.*1675); *Warwick County Records*, iii. 119.

[241] SBTRO, DR37/85/6/15 (Gaydon), 17 (Priors Hardwick).

[242] Cf. Ch. 5 below.

[243] *Tudor Churchwardens' Accounts*; Emmison, 'The Relief of the Poor of Elizabethan Essex'; Hindle, 'Dearth, Fasting and Alms'.

[244] Hindle, 'Dearth, Fasting and Alms'.

[245] Cf. Ch. 2 above.

informal relief which long ensured that the victuals begged from neighbours were far more significant than cash payments provided by overseers not merely to the survival of the indigent, but even to collectioners themselves.

By the late 1630s, however, the evidence suggests that the overwhelming majority of parishes over most of the country, even small rural communities, had been incorporated into a bureaucratic national system in which income was generated by rating and assessment; relief was disbursed in cash pensions and targeted occasional payments; and audit was exercised by county magistrates. Only the furthest reaches of the north, especially Northumberland, seem to have relieved the poor without any recourse at all to rates before 1640. Even in Westmorland, however, returns made by the county magistrates in April 1638 suggest that overseers had been appointed in at least thirty-nine townships, and many of them were disbursing regular sums to named pensioners.[246] Elsewhere, rating was by then almost ubiquitous, and traditional forms of charity were increasingly, but by no means completely, confined to a residual role. Individual neighbourly aid had been diminished, especially in the form of regularized almsgiving, though it probably proved more resilient in smaller parishes where the claims of neighbourhood were both easier to assert and more difficult to deny. Indeed, neighbourly support was sometimes encouraged by (and occasionally even integrated into) the formal relief system in campaigns of boarding, billeting, and apprenticeship. Testamentary charity endured long into the seventeenth century, though bequests were increasingly targeted at specific groups of poor people, especially those who were not regularly 'on the parish'. The maintenance of a consistent charitable presence by the gentry had, together with the hospitality and employment it implied, given way to seasonal doles given at the discretion of estate stewards. Insofar as it was embodied in church ales, collective charity was dying even in those places where it was not already extinct. The redefinition of these traditions of charity was in part caused by, but in turn actually came to promote, the introduction of a system of formal welfare provision. By 1700, a Shropshire magistrate was even prepared to argue that 'what money was given [to the poor] by one, two or a few persons might be accompted charity, but what was given out of the parish leawan [i.e. levy] that hee did not accompt charity; for it was what ought by law to bee done'.[247]

[246] For Northumberland, see S. J. Watts, *From Border to Middle Shire: Northumberland, 1586–1625* (Leicester, 1975), 202. For the Westmorland certificates, many of which are too badly damaged to permit detailed analysis, see NA, SP16/388/7/1–41.

[247] R. Gough, *The History of Myddle*, ed. D. Hey (Harmondsworth, 1981), 260.

By the mid-seventeenth century, the parish relief system embodied principles of eligibility that in some respects echoed, but in others intensified, those created by medieval theologians. In particular, parish relief came to function as a system of income maintenance for well-defined groups of poor people, especially the young, the recently married, and the elderly. Correlation of the rites of passage recorded in parish registers with the payments listed in overseers' accounts suggests that there was a close, if not entirely systematic, relationship between the allocation of relief and the life-cycle needs of the poor.[248] In terms of both the numbers and type of poor people relieved and the relationship between parish relief and other forms of charity, the system created in 1598 only gradually transformed the logic of medieval charity. The formal sanctions of law had, however, succeeding in combining the age-old principles of neighbourliness, the traditions of relief variously practised across thousands of communities, and the bureaucratic sophistication of local government to create a 'charity of the parish'.

It is, however, axiomatic that only a minority of those defined as poor in the cultural sense, that is, by themselves and by their neighbours and betters, were regularly 'on the parish'. As a guide to the extent of poverty, indeed, the names of the collectioners in overseers' account books are perhaps of less use than the much more rarely surviving lists of recipients of doles and other parish charities. Indeed, record linkage seems to suggest that recipients of doles correspond much more closely to those defined as paupers by virtue of their exemption from hearth tax payments than do collectioners. In Alburgh (Norfolk) in 1674, those exempted from the hearth tax were actually described as 'such as take alms from the town'. Of the sixty-three inhabitants of the Hampshire market town of Odiham who received donations from one or more of the six parish charities in 1673, only three were listed amongst the hearth tax contributors.[249]

The most sensitive issue in the micro-politics of collection was, therefore, the fate of those in need and not on regular relief, who were forced to rely on the semi-formal charity of doles and the informal support of their kin and neighbours. Some of these individuals, as we shall see, engaged in protracted negotiations with overseers and magistrates to have themselves admitted to the relief rolls. These campaigns to secure collection were so bitterly contested precisely because the predicament

[248] Wales, 'Poverty, Poor Relief and the Life-Cycle'.

[249] Ibid. 358; Stapleton, 'Inherited Poverty', 342. For the rarity of exemption certificates indicating the presence of those receiving alms, see Arkell, 'Identifying Regional Variations from the Hearth Tax', 151.

of those at the margins of the formal relief system was so precarious by the more comfortable standards of those who were 'on the parish'. The pension undoubtedly had its social and cultural costs but it was nonetheless considered to be a prize worth fighting for.

Parish relief was, then, entirely characteristic of the nature of English governance, both because it might gradually be adapted in the light of experience, and because it was sensitive to external influences, especially those of demographic and economic change and of shifting attitudes to charity and hospitality. The rate at which parish relief came to supplant (though never of course to entirely displace) informal charitable arrangements varied not only across the country but also perhaps more significantly within regions, even between adjacent parishes, and was principally determined by the relationship between the burden of pauperism and the strength of the tax base in the parish economy of welfare. The striking of the appropriate balance between these factors was, however, overwhelmingly a function of wider processes of demographic and economic change. Crisis years such as 1596–7, 1629–31, and 1647–50 are therefore particularly significant in the history of the development of parish relief because they exposed the limitations of a system which long remained at the very least partially dependent on traditions of informal relief. This is not to say that the changing balance between informal and formal methods of relief can be explained without reference to ideals of charity, but rather to suggest that these fundamental values were not so much diminished as part of a general decline of neighbourliness as redefined in the light of difficult decisions about the appropriate allocation of resources in changing economic and social circumstances. Householders, ratepayers, and parish officers, perhaps even the indigent themselves, frequently had to make difficult choices between differing strategies of relief. Even so, it is abundantly clear that, especially in the first half of the seventeenth century, the giving of alms or other informal support by householders and the disbursement of pensions by parish officers were neither mutually exclusive nor dichotomous.

Nor could they be taken for granted, for access to both systems of relief 'presupposed membership of a community', and communities were constituted as much by processes of exclusion as by those of inclusion.[250]

[250] J. Walter, 'The Social Economy of Dearth in Early Modern England', in J. Walter and R. Schofield (eds.), *Famine Disease and the Social Order in Early Modern Society* (Cambridge, 1989), 125; K. Wrightson, 'The Politics of the Parish in Early Modern England', in P. Griffiths *et al.* (eds.), *The Experience of Authority in Early Modern England* (London, 1996), 18–22; S. Hindle, 'A Sense of Place? Becoming and Belonging in the Rural Parish, 1550–1650', in A. Shepard and P. Withington (eds.), *Communities in Early Modern England* (Manchester, 2000), 96–114.

The very existence of formal welfare provision, as we shall see, posed in a particularly acute form the questions perennially asked by those of whom both personal and parish charity was expected: 'Who is my neighbour?'[251]

[251] See e.g. Alexander Nowell, *A Catechism; or, First Instruction and Learning of Christian Religion* (London, 1571), sig. Bii ('How far extendeth the name of neighbour?'). For the subsequent catechetical emphasis on this question, see Ian Green, *The Christian's ABC: Catechisms and Catechising in England, c.1530–1740* (Oxford, 1996), 463–4.

5
Exclusion

> The statute also made for the provicion of the poore is greatlie defrawded, and in effect made utterlie voyd, for that the howses to sett the poore people in everie limitte are not buylded nor provided according to the statute, whereby ther is no place to remove them unto, neyther are the parishes dyrectlie chardged for the keeping of them, for the wordes are *yf the parishe within the which they shall be found shall not or will not provide for them etc. eyther those howses would be repared or ells the townes wherein they were borne or had their last abode etc. dyrectlie chardged*, and that if striken out as it nowe standeth the poore are greatlie disapoynted both of releif and habitacion, and in short time are like to perish for that verie manye townes doe make bylawes in their lordes courtes that none shall under a great payne take in or house anie that alreadye are not onlie poore, but that maye be poore and so to prejudicate Godes ordynaunce, so as in the end they shall be driven from all townes to lye in the highe wayes and feildes without habitacion. Such ungodly private lawes would be overruled by a generall lawe of greater aucthoritie, the cruell lordes and unmercyfull tenauntes will ells bring Godes curse and plages upon the whole land.
>
> The statute against inmates also a verie great ponishment to the poore and great trouble to the townes, it would be in diverse poyntes eyther greatlie reformed, or altogether made voyd. The poore must be still amongest us, Christ said so.
>
> Anonymous parliamentary commentator on the statute of 39 Elizabeth, *c*.3 (1598)[1]

The introduction of parish relief posed a profound challenge to traditional notions of neighbourliness, solidarity, and belonging. If ratepayers were legally obliged to contribute to the communal relief fund, they had a vested interest in ensuring that its assets would be distributed only to

[1] *The Papers of Nathaniel Bacon of Stiffkey*, ed. A. Hassell Smith *et al.* (4 vols., Norfolk Record Society, 46, 49, 53, 64, Norwich, 1978–2000), iv, 35 (emphasis added). The italicized words did not, in the end, find their way into the 1598 statute.

those genuinely impotent inhabitants whom they recognized as their own. The definition and identification of 'the poor of the parish' was, however, problematic. Were all the residents to be considered eligible for relief, or only those who had been settled in the parish for a specified period? What guarantees might be asked of immigrants that they would not at some future time claim relief? How might the thresholds of belonging and eligibility be policed without forcing the indigent into destitution and vagrancy? The charity of the parish, like all charity, might begin at home, but how far should its responsibilities extend?

The remarkable memorandum surviving in the private papers of Nathaniel Bacon, the MP for the Norfolk borough of King's Lynn in the parliament of 1597–8, poses these questions in particularly resonant language, suggesting that parish relief in some respects actually compromised, rather than reinforced, ancient Christian traditions of charity. It suggests that the ambiguous construction of belonging or 'settlement', which was only vaguely defined in the provisions of the 1598 relief statutes, and in particular the tensions between that legislation and the 1589 act against the taking of lodgers and inmates, was recognized from the very outset. Landlords who also paid poor rates might find it in their interests to evict their tenants, especially those who were recent immigrants, when they became chargeable to the parish, leaving the overseers impaled on the horns of a dilemma: to provide work, accommodation, or relief for the indigent at parish expense; or to drive the destitute across the parish boundary, thereby forcing them into vagrancy. The fundamental issue, therefore, was not how the indigent should be treated once they were evicted, but how landlords could be prevented from evicting (and perhaps even from accommodating) them in the first place. Until the adaptation of the settlement laws (originally passed in 1662) in the late eighteenth century made it possible for a pensioner to reside in one parish and receive relief from another, his or her parish of 'settlement', the accommodation of poor migrants was a particularly sensitive issue.[2] In the days before such 'non-resident' relief became common, overseers were required to police the parish boundaries in order to protect the interests not only of their fellow ratepayers but also of the resident

[2] The best introduction to the settlement laws is K. Snell, 'Settlement, Poor Law and the Rural Historian: New Approaches and Opportunities', *Rural History*, 3 (1992), 145–72. For studies of the implications of 'non-resident' or 'out-parish' relief, see, P. Sharpe, '"The Bowels of Compa-sion": A Labouring Family and the Law, *c.*1790–1834', J. S. Taylor, 'Voices in the Crowd: The Kirkby Lonsdale Township Letters, 1809–36', and T. Sokoll, 'Old Age in Poverty: The Record of Essex Pauper Letters, 1780–1834', all in T. Hitchcock *et al.* (eds.), *Chronicling Poverty: The Voices and Strategies of the English Poor, 1640–1840* (London and New York, 1997), 87–108, 109–26, 127–54.

poor whose collection might be diminished by the increased burden of 'poor strangers crept amongst them'.[3]

In the years before 1662 in particular, the two statutes of 1589 and 1598 effectively constituted the keystone of early modern policies on migration, settlement, and belonging, yet the fit between them was not always as close as its parliamentary architects would have hoped. The Bacon memorandum helpfully emphasizes the importance in the provisions of the 1598 act of the requirement that parish officers provide *housing* for the poor. Clause V of the 1598 statute had provided that parish officers, with the consent of local landlords and at the charge of the ratepayers, might accommodate the impotent poor not only by building 'convenyent Howses of dwelling' on those manorial wastes and commons which fell within the parish but also by placing 'inmates or more families than one in one cottage or howse'.[4] Those who drafted the 1598 legislation themselves conceded that the 1589 statute 'againste the erectinge and mayntayninge of Cotages' was in some respects prejudicial to this campaign to provide 'necessary places of Habitation'. The 1589 act had, after all, not only forbidden the erection of cottages with less than four acres of associated land but also insisted that 'there shall not be any inmate or more families or households than one dwelling . . . in any one cottage'. This stipulation, backed up by a fine of 10*s.* per month per inmate, constituted the real teeth of the legislation, since it closed the loophole through which landless families might seek refuge, however temporarily, with their better-off neighbours. That the 1589 statute has received relatively little attention from historians is especially surprising given its longevity, for it was repealed only in 1775, and therefore endured almost as long as the old poor law itself.[5] The Bacon memorandum noted, however, that the 1598 obligation to provide habitation was more likely to be honoured in the breach than the observance, leaving parish officers with little or no housing stock to accommodate those who had been evicted by private landlords. The destitute would, therefore, be forced to seek accommodation with settled members of the community, only in turn to fall foul of the by-laws which had (in the wake of the 1589 act) sought to restrict the taking of inmates and lodgers in rural and urban

[3] For this idiom, see S. Hindle, 'Power, Poor Relief and Social Relations in Holland Fen, *c.*1600–1800', *Historical Journal*, 41 (1998), 91.

[4] 39 Elizabeth I, c. 3 (1598), sect. v; J. Broad, 'Housing the Rural Poor in England, 1650–1850', *Agricultural History Review*, 48 (2000), 156–7, notes that this clause was significantly expanded in 1601: 43 Elizabeth I, c. 2, sects. iv and v. Cf. Ch. 4.3(*c*) above.

[5] 31 Elizabeth I, c. 7 (1589), sect. vi; cf. 39 Elizabeth I, c. 3 (1598), sect. v. For the context of the 1589 legislation, see Slack, *Poverty and Policy*, 63. The act of repeal is 15 George III, c. 32 (1775)

parishes alike. This whole sorry cycle would only be prevented, the author of the memorandum feared, by the pre-emptive removal, perhaps even the expulsion, of those who were thought likely to become chargeable to the parish. In the idiom which provoked the ire of both judges and magistrates over the next half-century, the destitute, and perhaps even the merely indigent, would be forced 'to turn vagrant'.

This parliamentary jeremiad bemoaning the structural defects of the 1598 legislation was not, moreover, a desperate cry in the wilderness. It found its echo in Secretary of State Robert Cecil's famous speech on enclosures to the parliament of 1601: 'yf the poore beinge thruste out of their howses goe to dwell with others, streight we ketche them with the statute of inmates; yf they wander abroad and be stubborne, they are within the danger of roagues; yf they be more humble and vagrant baggars, then are they within this statute of the poore to be whipte and tormented'.[6] Without either permanent habitation or temporary lodging, the poor would migrate only to fall under the provisions of the 1598 vagrancy act.[7] Both these parliamentary commentators, therefore, recognized that if parish officers failed to honour their obligation to house the impotent, the destitute would be confronted with expulsion, and with the whipstocks and branding irons to which it might ultimately lead. These warnings were to be vindicated as early as 1615, when the Somerset bench conceded that it had been overwhelmed with petitions from householders who had accommodated poor migrants at the request of magistrates only to be prosecuted under the 1589 statute and ordered to remove them under the terms of orders made by manorial courts.[8]

There was, therefore, a tension between the benevolent aims of the relief statutes (to cater for the needs of the settled impotent poor) and the exclusionary powers exercised by parochial and manorial institutions either by discretion or under the terms of by-laws inspired by the 1589 statute on cottages and inmates. This tension was, in turn, reflected both in the inconsistency and ambiguity of judicial interpretation of the meaning of settlement under the terms of the 1598 statutes and in the flexibility and variability of local practice towards the unsettled poor as revealed both in parish papers and in petitions to county quarter sessions. Indeed, the nature of the relationship between the Tudor poor

[6] *Proceedings in the Parliaments of Elizabeth I*, ed. T. E. Hartley (3 vols., Leicester, 1981–95), iii. 452. For the context, see A. McRae, *God Speed the Plough: The Representation of Agrarian England, 1500–1660* (Cambridge, 1996), 7–12.

[7] 39 Elizabeth I, c. 4 (1598). For the context, see Slack, *Poverty and Policy*, 126–7.

[8] *Quarter Sessions Records of the County of Somerset*, ed. E. H. Bates-Harbin (4 vols., Somerset Record Society, 23, 24, 28, 34, Taunton, 1907–19), i, 137.

laws and the late Stuart settlement laws has been assumed rather than explored by historians. In an important (though, sadly, largely ignored) essay, however, Philip Styles drew attention to the 'Elizabethan' tone in which the rubric of the 1662 settlement act was couched.[9] The preamble complained that

> poor people are not restrained from going from one Parish to another and therefore doe endeavour to settle themselves in those Parishes where there is the best Stocke, the largest Commons or wastes to build cottages and the most Woods for them to burn and destroy and when they have consumed it then to another Parish and att last become Rogues and Vagabonds to the great discouragement of Parishes to provide Stocks where it is lyable to be devoured by strangers.[10]

Although these comments have been dismissed by both contemporaries and historians as 'specious' and 'mendacious', they deserve to be subjected to more systematic analysis.[11] Such analysis is, however, complicated by the two conflicting images of the early modern rural community, each of them refracted through differing sources and methodologies, with which students of migration, settlement, and belonging are confronted. On the one hand, demographic analysis has revealed the extraordinarily high rates of population turnover in seventeenth-century English parishes. It has been demonstrated that 62 per cent of the population of Clayworth (Nottinghamshire) disappeared in the twelve years between 1676 and 1688, almost two-thirds of this turnover being due to migration. In Cogenhoe (Northamptonshire), the turnover rate was 42 per cent in the decade 1618–28. In late sixteenth-century towns, it has been estimated, population turnover might have been twice as rapid, especially among the poor. These case-studies, made possible by the quality of surviving censuses, have been supplemented by family reconstitutions and by analyses of surname persistence and settlement examinations which suggest that steady turnover of population (especially of servants and apprentices), with villages in perpetual and mutually beneficial exchange with their neighbours, was a significant structural characteristic of seventeenth-century rural society.[12] On the other hand,

[9] P. Styles, 'The Evolution of the Law of Settlement', repr. in id., *Studies in Seventeenth-Century West Midlands History* (Kineton, 1978), 190. Cf. D. Rollison, 'Exploding England: The Dialectics of Mobility and Settlement in Early Modern England', *Social History*, 24 (1999), 1–16.

[10] 13 & 14 Charles II, c. 12 (1662), sect. i.

[11] M. Dalton, *The Country Justice* (London, 1682 edn.), 161; S. and B. Webb, *English Local Government*, vol. vii: *English Poor Law History, Part I: The Old Poor Law* (London, 1927), 325.

[12] J. Cornwall, 'Evidence of Population Mobility in the Seventeenth Century', *Bulletin of the Institute of Historical Research*, 40 (1967), 143–52; P. Spufford, 'Population Movement in Seventeenth Century England', *Local Population Studies*, 4 (1970), 41–50; P. Laslett, *Family Life and Illicit Love in Earlier Generations* (Cambridge, 1977), 50–101; A. Kussmaul, *Servants in Husbandry in*

however, social and cultural historians have used various sources to reconstruct the intense localism, even the parochial xenophobia, of village communities. Suspicion of strangers was manifested in various ways: in ridings and rough music to which 'others' might be subjected; in intensely localized proverbs and folklore; in the particular willingness of property-holders to prosecute outsiders for crimes where settled residents might be treated more leniently; in the notorious fifty-one-week hirings designed to preclude 'foreigners' from achieving settlement; and, above all, in the retaliatory networks of dispute between parish officers under the terms of the settlement laws.[13] It was symbolized above all in the remarkable appendix to Richard Gough's *History of Myddle* (Shropshire) which listed 'certaine [settlement] cases and controversies' between Myddle and other parishes in the period 1668–99, the first of which was lost 'but thanks be to God' (and, one is tempted to add, expensive legal counsel) Myddle 'never lost any afterwards'.[14] Even if the majority of the population did not permanently reside in their parishes of birth, therefore, suspicion of outsiders seems to have been deep-seated and ubiquitous.

Although a solution to this methodological conundrum is beyond the scope of this chapter, the following discussion attempts to reconcile these contradictory images by reconstructing both the decision-making processes which justified, and the techniques which were used to carry out, those exclusions and removals which became a structural characteristic of the micro-politics of parish relief. First, it analyses the developing statutory and judicial interpretation of settlement; second, it discusses the way in which those interpretations were played out in rural parishes; third, it offers a case-study of the attempts made in one particular community to exclude those likely to become chargeable to the parish; and fourth, it emphasizes the significance of marriage as a threshold across which the

Early Modern England (Cambridge, 1981), 49–69; D. Souden, 'Movers and Stayers in Family Reconstitution Populations', *Local Population Studies*, 33 (1984), 11–28; and the essays collected in P. Clark and D. Souden (eds.), *Migration and Society in Early Modern England* (London, 1987). A. L. Beier, 'The Social Problems of an Elizabethan Country Town: Warwick, 1580–90', in P. Clark (ed.), *Country Towns in Pre-Industrial England* (Leicester, 1981), 60, demonstrates a 'turnover of almost 50% of Warwick's poor in a matter of five years' (1582–7).

[13] E. Thompson, *Customs in Common* (London, 1991), 467–533; D. Rollison, *The Local Origins of Modern Society: Gloucestershire, 1500–1800* (London, 1992), 67–83; C. B. Herrup, *The Common Peace: Participation and the Criminal Law in Seventeenth-Century England* (Cambridge, 1987), 178–9, 183; K. D. M. Snell, *Annals of the Labouring Poor: Social Change and Agrarian England, 1660–1900* (Cambridge, 1984), 75–82. For an outstanding analysis of these themes for the period after 1750, see K. Snell, 'The Culture of Local Xenophobia', *Social History*, 28 (2003), 1–30.

[14] R. Gough, *The History of Myddle*, ed. D. G. Hey (Harmondsworth, 1981), 251–64.

indigent had to step as they sought membership of the community of the parish. Finally, it assesses the implications of the rise of parish relief for the processes of becoming and belonging in English rural communities.

1. THE JUDICIAL INTERPRETATION OF SETTLEMENT

Until 1662, the only statutes that stipulated minimum periods of residence for a migrant to secure settlement, and by implication eligibility for collection, were those against vagrancy. It is, accordingly, dangerous to read these clauses, intended as they were for the eyes of parish officers, as indices of the minimum periods for which a migrant had to dwell in a parish before they could be regarded as 'assimilated into the parish community'. Even so, some contemporaries evidently thought that the poor were perfectly well aware of settlement requirements in the vagrancy legislation. The privy council itself argued in 1598 that 'poor folks' would 'make shifts' even to pay exorbitant rents 'knowing that if they can but hold out for three years, then the parish where they remain are tied to find and relieve them ever after'.[15]

In principle, the objective of all sixteenth-century vagrancy legislation was invariably to resettle vagrants in the parish of their birth. There were, nonetheless, various statutory experiments in identifying the parishes to which they should be sent should it prove impossible to discover their birthplace. Under the act of 1504, for instance, vagrants were to be removed either to their place of birth or 'to the place where they last made their abode above the space of three years'.[16] The act of 1547, however short-lived, marked an important departure in principle by mentioning only settlement by birth, a feature that almost certainly exacerbated the contemporary sense that it was unenforceable.[17] Although the relatively lenient (and more practical from the constable's point of view) alternative of settlement in the last parish of three years' residence was restored in 1572, it was further reduced in the parish officers' favour to one year in 1598.[18] Over the course of the seventeenth century, the minimum period required to achieve a settlement shrank even further, ultimately to forty

[15] *APC*, xxviii (1597–8), 435–6.

[16] 19 Henry VII, c. 12 (1504).

[17] 1 Edward VI, c. 3 (1547). For the context, see C. S. L. Davies, 'Slavery and Protector Somerset: The Vagrancy Act of 1547', *Economic History Review*, 2nd ser., 19 (1966), 533–49. The 1547 act was repealed by 3 & 4 Edward VI, c. 16 (1550).

[18] 18 Elizabeth I, c. 5 (1572), sect. xvi. For the context, see P. Roberts, 'Elizabethan Players and Minstrels and the Legislation of 1572 against Retainers and Vagabonds', in A. Fletcher and P. Roberts (eds.), *Religion, Culture and Society in Early Modern Britain: Essays in Honour of Patrick Collinson* (Cambridge, 1994), 29–55. Cf. 39 Elizabeth I, c. 3 (1598).

days. Even so, the most significant feature of sixteenth-century statutory definitions of settlement is their lack of applicability to the circumstances of most poor migrants, who were not, after all, vagrants.[19]

When compulsory poor rates were finally stipulated in the legislation of 1598, the absence of any definition of settlement for anybody other than vagrants was sufficiently conspicuous to attract the attention of county magistrates almost immediately. As early as April 1598, the Essex bench indicated their understanding that the 1598 statute implied that 'no persons (other than Roages or Vagabonds) shalbe removed from their presente habitacions', but resolved to consult the judiciary about whether such expulsions, especially those of single mothers and children under the age of 7, might still be justified by the earlier legislation of 1572.[20] The West Yorkshire justices were similarly perplexed, for their orders for relief of the poor drawn up at Knaresborough in June 1598 noted the need for 'better consideration' of the recent statute, which had already resulted in widespread campaigns of exclusion in the parishes. In the meantime, they adhered to the settlement provisions of the 1572 legislation: nobody was to be removed 'so longe as they contynue within the p[ar]ishe where they are now or have been inhabiting by the space of three yeares'. Those poor people who had been mistakenly expelled, some of whom had 'bene inhabitinge & dwellinge in those places and townes from whence they are sent by the space of twentie yeares, some more, some lesse', were not, they insisted, 'Rooges nor wanderinge beggars within the meaning of the Statute, but ought to be relieved as the poore of the p[ar]ishe wher they so inhabited and wher they wrought when they were able to work'.[21] Almost immediately therefore, the 1598 statute had provoked the shunting of the indigent back and forth across parish boundaries, as the Bacon memorandum had envisaged.

When the judges did offer an interpretation of the 1598 statute, they refused to confront the issue of what actually constituted a settlement, confining their comments to a reiteration of the twin principles that only the impotent should be relieved and only the vagrant should be removed: 'Noe man is to be putt out of the Towne where hee dwelleth, nor to be sent to the place of byrthe or Laste dwellinge, but a rogue, nor to be kepte by the parishe excepte the partie be Imputent'.[22] This reading became the

[19] For this distinction, see J. R. Kent, 'Population Mobility and Alms: Poor Migrants in the Midlands during the Early Seventeenth Century', *Local Population Studies*, 27 (1981), 35–51.

[20] *Tudor Economic Documents*, ed. R. H. Tawney and E. Power (3 vols., London, 1924), ii, 363.

[21] *West Riding Sessions Records, 1597–1642*, ed. J. Lister (2 vols., Yorkshire Archaeological Society Record Series, 3, 54, Leeds, 1888–1915), i, 85–6 (orders 4, 5, and 6).

[22] Bodl., MS Tanner, 91, fo. 163^{v}.

standard one, not least because it was widely publicized, first in Willian Lambarde's handbook for magistrates in 1599 and subsequently in th numerous editions of Michael Dalton's *Country Justice*.[23] Further 'resolu cons and advise upon a Statute touchinge the Relief of the Poore an vagabon by the Lord Chiefe Justice of England' in 1607 effectively agree with the article reprinted in *Eirenarcha*, that is: 'none ought to be sente t the places of their birthe or habitations but such onlie as are vagrante o wanderinge and not any that hath any dwellinge in any parishe or b settled with their parents or any other in the parishe'.[24] This negative (o 'residual') definition of settlement, that the settled were all those wh were not vagrant, was a mantra repeated by judges throughout the earl seventeenth century. At the Cambridge summer assizes in 1629, fo instance, Sergeant Francis Harvey ruled that the JPs, especially thos acting out of their sessions, were 'not to meddle either with the removin or settling of any poore, but only of Rogues' (i.e. vagrants).[25] At th Dorchester assizes in July 1632, moreover, Baron John Denhan emphatically ruled that the 'JPs have no power to settle [those who are neither vagrant nor impotent'. The destitute were to be relieved wit shelter, work, or collection where they were last resident, and if th inhabitants there allowed them to become vagrant by failing to provid for them, then they were to be allocated a settlement there.[26] By 163 Dalton's *Country Justice* stipulated a fine of £5 for anybody who 'sha remove or put any out of their parish' any person who was 'not to be pu out', but was uncertain of its legal basis, arguing only that 'it seemeth to b by force of the statute of 1598'.[27] All this, of course, is to say nothing o the notoriously vague terms—'wandering', 'loytering', 'refusing to wor for . . . reasonable wages'—in which the 1598 statute for the punishmen of rogues, vagabonds, and sturdy beggars actually defined vagranc itself.[28]

Even the thirty-eight 'resolutions of all the judges', the most compre hensive attempt to 'settle the recurrently troublesome questions of inter

[23] W. Lambarde, *Eirenarcha* (London, 1599), 206 ff. (here quoting resolution no. 9).

[24] HMC, *Report on the Manuscripts of the Marquess of Lothian Preserved at Blickling* (London, 1905 76.

[25] Dalton, *Country Justice* (1635 edn.), 99.

[26] NA, ASSI24/20, I, fo. 57r, printed in *Western Circuit Assize Orders, 1629–1648: A Calendar*, ec J. S. Cockburn (Camden, 4th ser., 17, London, 1976), 51 (no. 214).

[27] Dalton, *Country Justice* (1635 edn.), 100. Dalton here seems to be alluding specifically to th eleventh of the judges' resolutions of 1599 rather than to the statute itself.

[28] 39 Elizabeth I, c. 4, sect. ii; A. Fletcher, *Reform in the Provinces: The Government of Stuart Englan* (New Haven, 1986), 207; Slack, *Poverty and Policy*, 91–3; S. Hindle, *The State and Social Change* *Early Modern England, c.1550–1640* (London and New York), 168.

pretation of the Elizabethan poor laws', issued when the magistrates of the Norfolk circuit sought the advice of Chief Justice Robert Heath in 1633, created more problems than they solved.[29] Heath apparently regarded the question of 'What is accounted a lawful setling in a parish and what not?' as unanswerable.

This is too generall a question to receive a perfect answer to every particular case which may happen. But generally this is to be observed, that the law unsetleth none who are lawfully settled nor permits it to be done by practice or compulsion; and every one who is settled is a native householder, [and a] sojourner, an apprentice, or servant for a moneth at least without a just complaint made to remove him or her shall be held to be setled.[30]

For the first half of the seventeenth century at least, therefore, the prevailing judicial interpretation of the relationship between settlement and eligibility for relief was that no one must be *compelled* to turn vagrant: although settlement itself went undefined, neither magistrates nor parish officers were legally entitled to remove the poor from any parish simply on the grounds of their destitution, still less if they were merely likely to become chargeable.

There were, however, significant cross-currents in the orthodox judicial interpretation of settlement, the full force of which became apparent only at mid-century. The logic of Heath's resolution of 1633 was itself circular, and proved controversial amongst his fellow judges, who 'differed in opinion from him in many things'.[31] In 1656, moreover, William Sheppard interpreted the 1629 Cambridge decision differently, arguing that Sergeant Harvey's reading had turned only on magistrates' *summary* powers: justices were, he insisted, empowered to deal with issues of settlement at quarter sessions, but not out of sessions where their competence extended only to rogues.[32] Sheppard also emphasized the significance of a judgment made by Chief Justice Whitelocke at the Hereford assizes in 1622, which by 1669 he was able to argue prefigured several clauses of the 1662 settlement laws. The case turned on a dispute between the Herefordshire parishes of Laysters and Kimbolton, in which the JPs held the parish officers of Kimbolton in contempt for ignoring magistrates' instructions to provide a house for one Winde and his family. Whitelocke ruled that the Herefordshire bench had itself acted

[29] *Somerset Assize Orders, 1629–1640*, ed. T. G. Barnes (Somerset Record Society, 65, Taunton, 1959), p. xxviii.

[30] NA, SP16/255/46, printed in *Somerset Assize Orders, 1629–40*, 68 (no. 26).

[31] Dalton, *Country Justice* (1682 edn.), 161. For the authority of Heath's resolutions, see Ch.6.4(*b*) below.

[32] W. Sheppard, *The Whole Office of the Country Justice of Peace* (3rd edn., London, 1656), 115.

unlawfully because 'Winde was not a poor or impotent person within 43 Eliz 2 and the justices had no power by that law to compel and to provide a house for him, for he might provide one himself'. For Sheppard, this implied that 'none but the poor and impotent are thus to be ordered and setled'.[33]

In practice, as we shall see, these legal ambiguities were reflected in variations in local practice across thousands of rural communities. Questions of settlement and belonging ultimately turned on the discretion of parish officers, and by and large they seem to have ignored the advice of the judges. Indeed, overseers seem to have become more and more prepared over time to risk the wrath of the bench by removing the impotent as well as the vagrant. The notorious clauses of the 1662 settlement laws which empowered parish officers to remove pre-emptively any indigent person likely to become chargeable amounted, therefore, not to a continuation of the advice of the judges but to a codification of the practices which had become increasingly prevalent in the parishes by the 1640s and 1650s. Parliamentary critics had foreseen as early as 1598 that settlement might be denied not only to those that 'alreadye are . . . poore', but also to those 'that maye be poore'. In 1661 Henry Townshend noted that the removal of 'those likely to be chargeable' was the 'generall present practice' in Worcestershire, and could trace precedents back to at last 1649.[34] Nor was Dalton's editor blind to the implications of this trend, criticizing in 1682 the discretion implied by the words 'likely to be chargeable' as 'prejudicial to the commonwealth' on five grounds: that it unreasonably empowered excessive 'inspection and determination of another man's livelihood and condition'; that it might even on a remote possibility deprive a man of 'the company of friends and relations, choice of air and place of trade'; that it discouraged ingenuity and industry; that it restricted labour mobility; and that it encouraged depopulation, the 'greatest inconvenience an island can undergo'.[35] Although it is couched less in the idiom of Christian charity than of political economy, this remarkably liberal defence of the rights of the poor against the powers of investigation and surveillance claimed by the authorities vindicates the fears expressed by the author of the Bacon memorandum as early as 1598.

[33] W. Sheppard, *A Sure Guide for His Majesties Justice of Peace* (2nd edn., London, 1669), 223 Dalton, *Country Justice* (1682 edn.), 57–8, provides a summary of the case, which is more fully reported in *The Reports of Edward Bulstrode of the Inner Temple, Esquire* (2nd edn., London, 1688) pt. I, 341–58 ('Certain cases and resolutions upon the statutes of 18 Eliz c.3 touching bastard children and 43 Eliz. c.2 concerning the poor and provision for them'), at 347–8.

[34] *Bacon Papers*, iv. 35; 'Henry Townshend's "Notes of the Office of a Justice of the Peace"' ed. R. D. Hunt, *Worcestershire Historical Record Society: Miscellany II* (Leeds, 1967), 106, 108.

[35] Dalton, *Country Justice* (1682 edn.), 161.

2. LOCAL INTERPRETATIONS OF SETTLEMENT

Although the practical implications of the settlement laws have been the subject of extraordinary historiographical controversy, rather less attention has been paid to the parochial interpretation of migration, settlement, and belonging in the years before 1662.[36] The task of reconstructing the parish politics involved in the policing of early seventeenth-century settlement is, however, complicated by a definitional problem: who exactly was an inmate? Historians of household structure use the term in the general sense of sojourners ('individuals [temporarily] contained within another person's household who were neither identifiable kin, servants or [paying] lodgers') rather than in the narrower legal sense of those who fell foul of the 1589 statute.[37] Contemporaries seem to have interpreted the term to mean 'poor migrants', either single persons, or perhaps even whole families, given houseroom with and renting property from existing inhabitants, and that is the sense in which the term is used in the following discussion.[38]

There can be little question that parish officers and ratepayers alike were alarmed by the impact of unchecked immigration on the burden of poverty in rural communities. As early as 1569, the inhabitants of Stambourne (Essex) complained that a non-resident landlord of half a dozen cottages had not only accommodated 'such men theyr wyves and children as cannot els where have any dwellynge but are shifted from other townes and places' at the point where they were about to be a charge

[36] Two influential early studies, E.M. Hampson, 'Settlement and Removal in Cambridgeshire, 1662–1834', *Cambridge Historical Journal*, 2 (1926–8), 273–89, and J. S. Taylor, 'The Impact of Pauper Settlement, 1691–1834', *Past and Present*, 73 (1976), 42–74, failed to anticipate the subsequent controversy over the relationship between the settlement laws and the poor laws. For Norma Landau, the regulation of settlement operated independently of concerns about poverty: N. Landau, 'The Laws of Settlement and the Surveillance of Immigration in Eighteenth-Century Kent', *Continuity and Change*, 3 (1988), 391–420; Landau, 'The Regulation of Immigration, Economic Structures and Definitions of the Poor in Eighteenth-Century England', *Historical Journal*, 33 (1990), 541–72; Landau, 'Who Was Subjected to the Laws of Settlement? Procedure under the Settlement Laws in Eighteenth-Century England', *Agricultural History Review*, 43 (1995), 139–59. For Keith Snell, by contrast, the significance of settlement can be understood only in the context of the poor laws: K. D. M. Snell, 'Pauper Settlement and the Right to Poor Relief in England and Wales', *Continuity and Change*, 6 (1991), 375–415; and Snell, 'Settlement, Poor Law and the Rural Historian'.

[37] J. Boulton, *Neighbourhood and Society: A London Suburb in the Seventeenth Century* (Cambridge, 1987), 36; N. Goose, 'Household Size and Structure in Early Stuart Cambridge', repr. in J. Barry (ed.), *The Tudor and Stuart Town: A Reader in English Urban History, 1530–1688* (London and New York, 1990), 93, 112–13.

[38] H. Raine, 'Christopher Fawcett against the Inmates', *Surrey Archaeological Collections* (1969), 80.

on the rates, but also racked the rents so that they 'are brought to playne beggary' in a town already overburdened with poor. The overseers of Emborough (Somerset) protested in 1619 that 'sundry strangers from remote parts' had lodged in the house of James and Margaret Haiball, a traffic which had led in turn to the birth of numerous legitimate and illegitimate children who had fallen to the charge of the parish. In 1737 the parish officers of Troutbeck (Westmorland) complained that the subdivision of tenements tended 'to fill the town with poor and with ill members to the impoverishment and vexation' of the ratepayers; and that the erection of cottages brought 'a great charge of poor on the tenants and inhabitants' by 'settling children and servants'.[39]

The micro-politics of settlement therefore turned on the identification of the most suitable strategy for preventing the accommodation of poor migrants. In practice, parochial disputes over settlement were less often a matter of conflict between the judges and the magistrates, who broadly shared the same objective of preventing those removals which might exacerbate already troublesome problems of population mobility and vagrancy, than between the officers of the county and those of the parish (and the ratepayers they represented), who saw the solution to the threat of increased poor relief expenditure rather differently. The magistracy, anticipating the advice of Chief Justice Heath, generally preferred to force overseers to increase the poor rate assessments of those landlords who took inmates, 'according to the damage and danger' they brought to the parish by their 'folly'.[40] The Somerset bench, for instance, insisted early in the century that 'no pore person' was to be removed from any parish as long as they 'can take any howse for theire money and doe live without charging the parish', and that 'no extraordinary course be taken either to remove them, or to inhibit them to take a howse'. Instead, they ordered that any householder who took a lodger should be taxed 'to the reliefe of the poore as much as he receiveth of that inmate'.[41] But unanimity could not be assumed even among magistrates, and the Somerset bench had to concede in 1623 that, because 'diversity of opinion' about policy on inmates had arisen amongst the JPs, they needed further advice from the assize judges.[42]

Parish officers, by contrast, sought rather more directly to defray increased costs by expelling those poor migrants who they feared might

[39] ERO, Q/SR28/1; *Quarter Sessions Records for the County of Somerset*, i, 254; M. A. Parsons, 'Poor Relief in Troutbeck, 1640–1836', *Transactions of the Westmorland and Cumberland Antiquarian and Archaeological Society*, 95 (1995), 172.

[40] NA, SP16/255/46, printed in *Somerset Assize Orders, 1629–40*, 69 (no. 35).

[41] HMC, *Lothian*, 77.

[42] *Quarter Sessions Records for the County of Somerset*, i. 329–30.

become chargeable, thereby turning the impotent vagrant. Their logic was spelled out by the anonymous author of *An Ease for Overseers of the Poore* in 1601. 'The multitude of the poore', he insisted, 'must be reduced in number for in some places they be very few and in many places they swarme.'[43] Parish officers evidently took this advice extremely seriously, and their archives reek of a desire to reinforce the geographical thresholds of eligibility. They were not invariably successful. Magistrates frequently reined in the desire of the vestry to expel inmates, and instead persuaded them to seek financial restitution from the improvident landlords who had accommodated them.[44] Despite their enthusiasm for ridding themselves of inmates, for instance, the parish vestries of Elizabethan Essex were restrained both by employers and by magistrates from excluding poor migrants who might, on the one hand, satisfy the demand for labour and, on the other, turn to vagrancy and theft if they were evicted. The result was the piecemeal, marginal accommodation of poor migrants, whose chances of survival in 'suspended outlawry' varied according to the demands of the labour market, the tolerance levels of householders, and the attitudes of parish officers and magistrates.[45] Tensions of this kind very frequently resulted in those campaigns of exclusion which have left numerous trails smeared across the archives of county and parish alike.

The techniques of exclusion were various. A favourite strategy was to draw up a census of all the householders, in which poor migrants were identified as potential burdens. When the vestrymen of North Nibley (Gloucestershire) drew up resolutions for the poor in September 1614, for instance, they began with the problems associated with infiltration, requiring that the constables draw up a listing of strangers, cottagers, and inmates.[46] The vestrymen of Paddington (Middlesex) were even more explicit, prefacing their orders 'for the better mayntenance and relief of the poore' of August 1623 with instructions for the identification of potential burdens in order that the parish 'be not from henceforth overcharged with too great a number' of strangers.[47] Some indication of the

[43] *An Ease for Overseers of the Poore: Abstracted from the Statutes* (Cambridge, 1601), 17.

[44] For another example of a parish vestry persuaded to use Heath's formula, see the case of Constantine (Cornwall): Cornwall RO, Truro, DDP39/8/1, unfol. (resolutions of 20 Oct. 1650), discussed in Hindle, *The State and Social Change*, 221. It was employed as late as 1713 in Ardeley (Hants.): W. E. Tate, *The Parish Chest: A Study of the Records of Parochial Administration in England* (3rd edn., Cambridge, 1960), 163.

[45] W. Hunt, *The Puritan Moment: The Coming of Revolution in an English County* (Cambridge, Mass., 1983), 71. Cf. the brief discussion in Fletcher, *Reform*, 202–12.

[46] Gloucestershire RO, Gloucester, D8887/3, fo. 99. Cf. Ch. 6.2 below.

[47] Bodl., MS Eng. lett. c.589, fo. 52.

likely findings of such a census is conveyed by the list drawn up in 1606 by George Sawer, surveyor of the Norfolk parish of Cawston. Sawer identified thirteen houses whose lands had been let out and were now inhabited by forty-two inmates, and a further thirteen smaller dwellings which were now occupied by thirty-two lodgers, making an influx of some seventy-four inmates in all. Even more revealing is the listing of 'divers poor people' who were 'a great charge' to the parish of Eldersfield (Worcestershire) in 1618. In a parish containing between forty and fifty households, the influx of migrants and strangers had stretched the patience of the settled inhabitants to breaking point. They identified six 'grievances of the parish', in each of which they were at pains to point out that the cause of the potential charge, although currently resident in the parish, was not native to the community: a poor stranger being harboured by his mother-in-law, herself a poor widow; an elderly servant of forty years' residence whose brother evicted her, leaving her to relieve herself by begging; a stranger once harboured by his mother-in-law who had since his wife's death abandoned his two children to the care of the parish; a stranger having abandoned his wife with two children and pregnant with a third; a poor couple who had been let a cottage by a non-resident landlord, 'their state being very poor'; the children of a runaway father who had left them to the care of his brother and sister. Altogether, their 'census' revealed twenty-six individuals of whom the parishioners wished to discharge themselves.[48]

A second strategy was to prevent the building of those cottages in which poor migrants might squat, or to pull them down after they had become burdensome. The 'most sufficientest' men of Trull, for example, sought in 1622 to stop the parish officers building two cottages for the poor on the grounds that 'there are enough cottages there already' and 'that the site was unfitting'. The magistrates nonetheless found that all the ratepayers 'doubts, objections and grievances do proceed more out of a wilful and forward disposition than any just cause of complaint' and concluded that the cottages were necessary, 'there being a great number of poor people there, and the place very fitting'.[49] The chief inhabitants of Yeovil were more successful, persuading the Somerset bench that 'all erecting of cottages' was to cease in 1623 on the grounds that the number of impotent poor was now 'far surmounting the liability' of the ratepayers, and that 'these strangers once settled do tear and spoil other men's hedges'.[50]

[48] Norfolk RO, Norwich, MC254/1/7; Worcestershire RO, Worcester, QSR/1/1/28/20.

[49] *Quarter Sessions Records for the County of Somerset*, i, 297, 314, 323.

[50] Ibid. 331. Cf. Ch. 1.2(*b*) above.

The destruction of such cottages was not, however, straightforward. As the 1598 Bacon memorandum had predicted, the inability or reluctance of parish officers to provide sufficient housing stock meant that there was, quite simply, nowhere for poor migrants to go if their cottages were destroyed. The judges of the Norfolk circuit were confronted with the realities of the situation at the Bury assizes in March 1634. They were well aware of 'the great increase of cottagers and inmates' and knew that under the terms of the 1589 statute 'the cottages ought to be pulled down'. The Suffolk bench nonetheless informed them that 'if the extremity of the law be used against them, these poor people would be exposed to misery and become a burthen to the parishes where they are settled'. Although Sir John Walter accordingly ordered that any cottages recently erected without licence were to be prevented, the parish officers having power to 'disturb & hinder the building and finishing thereof and destroy the same before any inhabitants be placed therein', he was nonetheless forced to concede that some cottages just had to be tolerated. He ordered a survey of 'what cottages and inmates there are in every parish, who are the inhabitants and who the reputed owners, and how long the cottages have been erected'. The judges and magistrates might then retrospectively license those cottages that were 'agreeable to the country'.[51]

There was an increasing recognition, therefore, that to pull down cottages and expel inmates was, after all, to turn the marginal poor vagrant. The justices of south-eastern Norfolk argued in 1635 that all the cottages in their division should be permitted 'or otherwise the poore people will be destitute of habitations'. This comment was amplified in the case of the three inmates who lodged with Thomas Waters in the Norfolk parish of Acle: 'all are poore labourers and have wives and severall children and if they be put out cannot be provided in this town and by reason of ther charge and poverty are not likely to be entertained elsewhere'.[52] The plight of Henry Wright and the two very poor widows who lodged with him in his cottage at Hainford (Norfolk) provoked similar concerns in 1634: none of the three would have anywhere to live 'if they be turned away'.[53] In some circumstances, the justices were actually encouraging householders to take lodgers for whom shelter could not otherwise be found. 'Most parishes,' wrote the JPs of south-eastern Norfolk in 1636, are so 'fraighted with poore people destitute of habitations, as the number of cottages will not conteine them', and 'we are enforced not onely to admit of them, but even to presse divers others to

[51] BL, MS Additional, 39245, fo. 5 (reverse foliation).
[52] NA, SP16/310/104.
[53] NA, SP16/272/44.

receive som inmates, whoe were otherwise altogether unwilling'.[54] The Warwickshire bench similarly suppressed indictments for the illegal erection of cottages at Harbury in 1629 'in respect of the poverty and disability' of the parish to provide legitimate habitations for the poor, and considered doing so again at Napton in 1656.[55]

A more imaginative policy on cottages was adopted by the Worcestershire grand jury in 1663. Although they recognized that the lack of regulation of cottage-building had caused the county 'to abound with poor more than any county in England that we know of', they nonetheless pleaded with the bench to suspend the prosecution of those who had erected them. Since the indiscriminate suppression of cottages would simply flood the countryside with vagrants, far better for the clergymen, officers, and chief inhabitants of each parish to list all the cottages and indicate 'what persons they desire the cottages may be continued for'. The grand jury even argued that those cottagers who were to be tolerated should be allowed to live rent-free for life, presumably in an attempt to insulate the ratepayers from their demands for parish relief. The advantage for the overseers was that they should, on the death of the current tenants, be permitted either to pull the cottages down or to absorb them into the parish housing stock, thereby augmenting those resources which might be used to defray poor rates.[56]

If cottages could neither be prevented nor pulled down, parish officers at least attempted to ensure that those who built and lived in them would not be chargeable to the ratepayers. Their preferred technique was to require poor migrants to post 'indemnity bonds' (usually with sureties, more often than not provided by the landlord who had accommodated them) guaranteeing that they would never claim relief. Examples of this practice could be cited from as far afield as St Saviour's Southwark (Surrey), Woodford (Essex), Nantwich (Cheshire), Frampton (Lincolnshire), and Whickham (County Durham), though the largest extant collection of 'indemnity bonds' apparently survives in the borough archives of Stratford-upon-Avon (Warwickshire).[57] As the authorities

[54] NA, SP16/329/10.

[55] *Warwick County Records*, ed. S. C. Ratcliff *et al.* (9 vols., Warwick, 1935–64), i, 88; iii, 304.

[56] HMC, *Reports on the Manuscripts in Various Collections*, vol. i (London, 1901), 323–4.

[57] Although there is as yet no comprehensive study of this practice, Styles, 'Evolution of the Law of Settlement', 180–3, discusses 139 'harmless bonds' for Stratford in the years 1613–1714, 81 (or 58%) of them predating the 1662 act. For the other examples, see Raine, 'Christopher Fawcett against the Inmates', 81 (Southwark); Hunt, *Puritan Moment*, 72 (Woodford); NA, SP16/195/31 (Nantwich); Hindle, 'Power, Poor Relief and Social Relations', 88–9 (Frampton); D. Levine and K. Wrightson, *The Making of an Industrial Society: Whickham, 1560–1765* (Oxford, 1991), 346 (Whickham).

well knew, the imperative to indemnify the parish might deter both landlords and migrants from coming to a rental agreement. Indeed, it was not unknown for labouring families to argue that their honesty and diligence were sufficient guarantee of their independence without the need to incur the risk and expense of an indemnity bond. James Hurde told the Somerset bench in 1612 that he had rented a house in West Crenmore for two years and that he had taken 'great pains to maintain himself and his wife and two children wherewith he never yet charged the parish nor hopeth ever to do'. The parish officers were threatening him with eviction and removal unless he provided an indemnity bond 'which he cannot by reason he is a poor labourer'.[58] Failure to provide a bond with sufficient sureties might render the indigent vulnerable to eviction, as it did for five inmates of East Cottingwith (Yorkshire) in 1649, and for twenty-six others excluded in a sweep of other East Riding parishes, fourteen of them from the two communities of Beeford and Market Weighton, in 1651.[59]

Those who took inmates without indemnity bonds might, equally, be formally prosecuted at county quarter sessions: there were twenty-four such cases in Worcestershire (1591–1643), twenty-nine in Wiltshire (1615–24), 167 in Essex (1626–66), and 188 in three of the Lancashire hundreds (1626–66).[60] These cases were evidently exemplary and, however numerous, must merely have been the tip of an iceberg, since most initiatives for dealing with the problem were taken by parish vestries or manorial leets, only the more controversial cases reaching the quarter sessions. The court leet of Prescot (Lancashire) issued a stream of orders prohibiting inmates and expelling illegal under-tenants beginning as early as 1557, repeatedly issuing fines against offending landlords. Similarly, in 1596, the Swallowfield (Wiltshire) town meeting ordered that 'every man shalbe forbydden to keepe inmates', and that 'whosoever dothe keep any inmates' be denied poor relief.[61] By the 1630s, the privy council was

[58] *Quarter Sessions Records for the County of Somerset*, i. 94.

[59] G. C. F. Forster, *The East Riding Justices of the Peace in the Seventeenth Century* (East Yorkshire History Series, 30, Leeds, 1973), 48.

[60] *Worcestershire County Records: Calendar of the Quarter Sessions Papers*, vol. i: *1591–1643*, ed. J. W. Wills-Bund (Worcester, 1900), p. clxxxvi; M. Ingram, 'Communities and Courts: Law and Disorder in Early-Seventeenth-Century Wiltshire', in J. S. Cockburn (ed.), *Crime in England, 1550–1800* (London, 1977), 112; K. Wrightson, 'Two Concepts of Order: Justices, Constables and Jurymen in Seventeenth-Century England', in J. Brewer and J. Styles (eds.), *An Ungovernable People: The English and their Law in the Seventeenth and Eighteenth Centuries* (London, 1980), 300–3 (appendix).

[61] *A Selection from the Prescot Court Leet and Other Records, 1447–1600*, ed. F. A. Bailey (Record Society of Lancashire and Cheshire, 89, Chester, 1937), 139, 151, 181, 191, 201, 215, 234, 240, 250, 265, 270, 273; S. Hindle, 'Hierarchy and Community in the Elizabethan Parish: The Swallowfield Articles of 1596', *Historical Journal*, 42 (1999), 850 (article 21).

sufficiently concerned about the problem to include 'builders of cottages and takers in of inmates' among the targets for investigation by manorial stewards and in those articles of instruction that reminded parish constables of their duties.[62] Although the usual problems of corruption, discretion, and exemplary presentment ensured that prosecution would only be sporadic, it is nonetheless striking that listings of inmates crop up so frequently in the certificates presented to the privy council in the 1630s.

These, then, were the techniques of exclusion which might be pursued by parish officers in defending the boundaries of belonging. They were not always carried out in isolation. Systematic programmes to police immigration were not unusual, especially in years when there was particularly high pressure on parish resources. The dearth of 1623 provoked desperate measures in the Lancashire communities of Lowick and Rishton, where fines were ordered not only for those who took inmates but also for casual almsgivers, and even for millers who permitted the indigent to linger in hope of sustenance.[63] At Paddington (Middlesex), the vestrymen insisted in 1623 on the expulsion of inmates, the provision of indemnity bonds, the aggressive taxation of landlords, the restriction of new building, and the prevention of the subdivision of tenements. The local labour market was to be secured against 'strangers and unknown persons' who 'take awaye (by theire gettinge of worke into their handes) the meanes of mayntenance and reliefe which otherwise the poore of this parishe should have for their help and sustenance'. Above all, the 'setlinge' of 'ympotent and indigent persons likelie to bring a charge unto this parishe' was to be prevented.[64]

In the light of all this scrutiny of the likelihood that they may become chargeable and of the evictions that often followed, it is unsurprising that the destitute should so frequently claim that they really had been forced to turn vagrant. Agnes Powe claimed in 1614 that, although she had been born and had ever lived at Worle (Somerset), 'the parishioners will not suffer her there to abide'. Nicholas Webb alleged in 1615 that, although he and his wife had lodged with his mother-in-law in Wolverton for four years, the lord of the manor had ordered their eviction. John Mountyer complained in 1619 that, despite two years residence as a married man in

[62] 'The Book of Orders', sig. F4^{v}; J. R. Kent, *The English Village Constable: A Social and Administrative Study, 1580–1642* (Oxford, 1988), 37–8, 147.

[63] A. J. L. Winchester, 'Responses to the 1623 Famine in Two Lancashire Manors', *Local Population Studies*, 36 (1986), 47–8.

[64] Bodl., MS Eng. lett. c.589, fos. 52^{r-v}. All this is to say nothing of the scrutiny of the lifestyle of the settled poor, on which the Paddington vestrymen also insisted. See Ch. 6.2 below.

Milton Clevedon, the 'inhabitants there now go about to put him out of his house'.[65] In 1617, the Somerset justices investigated whether Hugh Kerle and his wife had become vagrant '*after* he was put from' the parish of Pawlett or whether '*by the means of the parishioners* there he became as a rogue and vagrant'. Margery Sybley, a native of Isle Brewers (Somerset), complained in 1621 that she had recently been evicted from a house provided for her at parish expense for the last seven years, 'whereby she is utterly destitute'.[66]

As early as 1625, indeed, the Hertfordshire magistrates were complaining that 'the conveying of cripples, diseased and impotent persons by cart and horse from one county or parish to another' had 'become common and is a great and unnecessary charge to the county'. This practice was not only offensive on financial grounds, they argued, but also because those involved were self-evidently the deserving poor 'who should long since have been settled and therefore not sent as vagrants'. They ordered that 'from henceforth no constable shall receive or take charge of conveying any such person as shall be brought to them out of another county'. Any 'bringer' attempting to remove inhabitants who ought to be settled was, they insisted, to be prosecuted under the 1598 vagrancy act.[67] Little surprise then that by 1635 Dalton could argue that 'for want of charity', poor people were 'much sent and tossed up and down from towne to towne and from countrey to countrey'.[68]

Dalton's assessment is vindicated by some genuinely shocking evidence of destitution, especially in those sad cases where poor families were forced to sleep in church porches. Vagrants, of course, frequently occupied church property to solicit alms or take shelter, as did a Lincolnshire vagabond in Norwich at Christmas 1553 and 'two beggar women' in Crowle (Worcestershire) in 1633.[69] The church porch was not only a very public space, 'where the beggars do usually lie', it was also a liminal one, the symbolic threshold of belonging to the parish, the place at which (during the marriage service) young men and women were admitted into

65 *Quarter Sessions Records for the County of Somerset*, i. 105, 122, 262.

66 Ibid. 197–8, 302 (emphasis added).

67 *Hertford County Records*, ed. W. Le Hardy (9 vols., Hertford, 1905–39), v. 47.

68 Dalton, *Country Justice* (1635 edn.), 99.

69 'Depositions Taken before the Mayor and Aldermen of Norwich, 1549–1567', ed. W. Rye, *Norfolk Archaeology*, 1 (1905), 54; Worcestershire RO, QSR1/1/58/71 (Crowle, Worcs., 1633); A. L. Beier, *Masterless Men: The Vagrancy Problem in England, 1560–1640* (London, 1985), 83, 223. Church porches were among the numerous lodging places associated with beggary by the Norwich city fathers in their 'orders for the poor' of 1571. *Tudor Economic Documents*, ii. 317. For the notion that the poor had a customary right 'to sleep in the church if they had no other accommodation', see K. Thomas, *Religion and the Decline of Magic: Studies in Popular Belief in Sixteenth- and Seventeenth-Century England* (London, 1971), 562.

full adult membership of the local community. It is nonetheless surprising to find the destitute, sometimes even whole families, lodging in church porches in order to publicize their plight: Old Scott in King's Sutton (Northamptonshire) in 1612; James Clarke, his wife and child at Kineton (Warwickshire) in 1634; Sarah Woodfall and her five children at Napton-on-the-Hill (Warwickshire) in 1650; William Round at Avon Dassett (Warwickshire) in 1655; Daniel Smith and his heavily pregnant wife at Frankton (Warwickshire) in 1655: John Woods, his wife and 7-week-old child in Ingworth (Norfolk) in 1665; John Rivett and his family at Sisland (Norfolk) in 1672; Susannah Russell at Southam (Warwickshire) in 1674; William Titmouse, his wife and two children at Wallington (Hertfordshire) in 1682—all of them sleeping in church porches, soliciting habitation orders from the county bench.[70] One woman and her four children camped out in the church porch of Sprowston (Norfolk) in 1631 after they had been ejected from her brother's house as unlawful inmates, and thereby succeeded in getting 'some provision for hir elsewhere'. The overseers of another Norfolk parish told one magistrate that they had been instructed by one of his colleagues on the bench to let one poor couple 'lie in the church porch' rather than relieve them.[71]

Families such as these were taking considerable risks, for it was not unknown for the destitute to die in church porches.[72] Some clergymen were evidently sensitive to the possibility that squatters in the church porch might exert some leverage on the charity of the householders, perhaps even of parish officers or magistrates. The vicar of Womburne (Staffordshire) had the church porch gated and railed in 1639 so that 'idle

[70] *Churchwardens' Presentments in the Oxfordshire Peculiars of Dorchester, Thame and Banbury*, ed. S. A. Peyton (Oxfordshire Record Society, 10, Oxford, 1928), 290; *Warwick County Records*, i. 190–1; iii. 38, 258, 261; vii. 21; *The Notebook of Robert Doughty, 1662–1665*, ed. J. M. Rosenheim (Norfolk Record Society, 54, Norwich, 1989), 61; Norfolk RO, C/S2/3, unfol. (October 1676); *Hertford County Records*, vi. 355. For other examples, see Leicestershire RO, Leicester, 1D/41/13/64, fo. 258^{v} (Kettleby, Leics., 1637); B. Capp, 'Life, Love and Litigation: Sileby in the 1630s', *Past and Present*, 104 (2004), 69.

[71] NA, SP16/272/44; *The Notebook of Robert Doughty*, 61.

[72] For vagrants and paupers found dead in church porches, see J. Bruce, 'Extracts from the Accounts of the Churchwardens of Minchinhampton in the County of Gloucester', *Archaeologia*, 35 (1853), 437 (Minchinhampton, Glos., 1598); D. M. Palliser, 'Dearth and Disease in Staffordshire, 1540–1670', in C. W. Chalklin and M. A. Havinden (eds.), *Rural Change and Urban Growth 1500–1800* (London, 1974), 64 (Brewood, Staffs., 1621). It is equally possible that a high proportion of the occasional 'poor strangers' for whom parish officers provided burials had also perished in the church porch. See e.g. the half-dozen cases recorded for Cowden (Kent) 1611–46, in E. Turner, 'Ancient Parochial Account Book of Cowden', *Sussex Archaeological Collections*, 20 (1882), 99, 101, 103, 106.

and impotent people might not lodge therein as in former times'.[73] These paupers nonetheless chose well, for in each case magistrates ultimately compelled parish officers to find them somewhere to live. Indeed, the increasing frequency of habitation orders during the late seventeenth century may well have been a critical factor in the dramatic rise of poor relief expenditure during the 1680s and 1690s, for parish officers were thereby required not only to subsidize the rents of the destitute but sometimes to pay them cash pensions as well.[74]

The accommodation of the poor, and especially of poor migrants, therefore tested the thresholds of tolerance of the communities in which they sought to settle. Indeed, county benches were sufficiently well aware of the sensitivity of habitation orders that they occasionally made efforts to accommodate parish opinion. In 1697, for instance, the Buckinghamshire magistrates ordered that the parish officers of Thornborough should hold a public vestry so that a vote could be taken on whether to build cottages for 'two poor inhabitants with large families'.[75] Votes like these turned on fundamental questions of entitlement and responsibility which might be answered in different ways according to the merits of the case. The experience of Mary Dickens of Brailes (Warwickshire) is particularly suggestive of the conflicting visions of social obligation which might be at play in disputes over pre-emptive removal. Dickens returned to her home parish from Whatcote in 1631. Within four months, however, her pregnancy had become apparent, and the 'inhabitants' of Brailes expelled her to ensure that her bastard was born in Whatcote. During the next year, responsibility for Dickens and her child was contested between the two parishes, each of them offering conflicting versions of the circumstances of her original removal, for the parishioners of Whatcote an act conducted 'with violence' and without any authority, for those of Brailes, one carried out only by virtue of a warrant from the justices of Kineton hundred.[76]

In such cases, it seems, both overseers and paupers sought tactical advantage by playing on the distinction between 'legitimate' public actions and 'illegitimate' private ones. At Brailes in 1642, when the over-

[73] S. Shaw, *The History and Antiquities of Staffordshire* (2 vols., London, 1798–1801), ii. 217. For churchwardens colluding with a beggar by giving him the key to the church porch in Warborough (Oxon.), see *Churchwardens' Presentments in the Oxfordshire Peculiars*, 96. On the architecture and significance of the church porch, see N. J. G. Pounds, *A History of the English Parish: The Culture of Religion from Augustine to Victoria* (Cambridge, 2000), 387–8.

[74] Cf. Ch. 4.3(*c*) above.

[75] *County of Buckingham: Calendar to the Sessions Records*, ed. W. Le Hardy and G. L. Reckitt (4 vols., Aylesbury, 1934–51), ii. 131.

[76] *Warwick County Records*, i. 115–16, 120–1, 128–9.

seers actively sought the removal of individuals who merely *might* become a burden to the parish, they emphasized the subterfuge of shiftless migrants who sought to infiltrate the parish. The pregnant maidservant, Ellen Philkins, they alleged, had 'privately' returned from Tredington (Worcestershire) to live with her father in Brailes 'in a very private manner unknown to most of the inhabitants'. Their description of the conduct of Joan Cooke was very similar: having been married for eighteen months, Joan had fled Crimscott and 'privately' come to Brailes and 'there lurked up and down in private places unknown to most of the inhabitants there'.[77] The inhabitants of Barrington (Somerset) similarly claimed in 1654 that Roger Collins, his wife and two children lay 'lurking in and about the parish' and pleaded with the county bench that their residence should not grant them rights of settlement.[78]

The questions of which poor migrants might be 'agreeable' to the country, and which cottages might be 'continued', were, therefore, highly controversial. Some indication of how they might be answered is evident in an intriguing petition from the parishioners of Chewton to the Somerset bench in 1608. A 60-year-old lead miner named Richard Feare had been born in Chew Magna and after many years working in the Mendip ore fields had 'become almost blind and was likely to become chargeable to the parishioners of Chewton except speedy redress be had therein'. The parishioners pleaded that he ought to be relieved in the parish of his birth because 'he had never any settled abiding place in any sort with us at Chewton nor was ever taken as a parishioner there by receiving the Communion or performing any other duty belonging to a subject'. The definition of settlement offered by the parish officers of Chewton therefore augmented a simple residence requirement not only with an indication of social worth (the performance of 'duty', presumably in holding office or paying rates) but also with a symbol of belonging (being in charity with his neighbours). The magistrates initially agreed, noting that, because Feare had 'only lodged in a grove house during such time as he wrought' in the parish of Chewton, he was to be sent back to Chew Magna. When they were informed that Feare had not been living in the parish of his birth 'this twenty and odd years', however, they changed their tune, and required the overseers of Chewton to relieve him.[79] As early as 1608, poor labouring men like Richard Feare were being shuttled back and forth across parish boundaries as ratepayers debated the geographical extent of their charitable obligations.

77 *Warwick County Records*, ii. 125.

78 *Quarter Sessions Records for the County of Somerset*, iii. 238.

79 Ibid. i. 4–5, 11, 13.

The quantification of cottage licences and indemnity bonds therefore only partially illuminates the nature and scale of the early seventeenth-century controversy over settlement, and is entirely unhelpful for the analysis of the social, economic, and political negotiations that underpinned multi-familial co-residence from the point of view of the landless, the illegal harbouring of the destitute by the propertied, and the prosecution of both by the authorities. The following discussion attempts a more qualitative approach to the testing of the limits of parochial responsibility by locating the problem of pre-emptive removal in the narrower context of Hertfordshire, a county whose proximity to the metropolis placed extraordinary demands on its economic and demographic resources. Elizabethan Hertfordshire was a famously agricultural county.[80] Despite the existence of a few enclaves of pastoral farming, the greater part of the county was under the plough, specializing in mixed farming and growing corn. Long enclosed, its surviving common fields were not strictly regulated. Like other rural economies in the hinterland of the metropolis, it responded vigorously to the growing commercial opportunities of the period. The impact of agrarian proletarianization, subsistence migration, and the general increase in the extent and intensity of poverty may therefore have been particularly marked in the county. While yeomen prospered, husbandmen's farm valuations appear to have collapsed in the aftermath of several poor harvests in the late 1580s and 1590s, their cumulative indebtedness driving them out of the land market. Although population growth played its part in these processes, it cannot provide a complete explanation of social and economic change. Between 1563 and 1603, it has been estimated, the population of seventy-four Hertfordshire parishes increased by 58 per cent, a far more dramatic rise than that for

[80] Except where noted, the following discussion is based on L. Munby, *Hertfordshire Population Statistics, 1563–1801* (Hertford, 1963); J. Thirsk, 'The Farming Regions of England', in id. (ed.), *The Agrarian History of England and Wales*, vol. iv: *1500–1640* (Cambridge, 1967), 50–2; W. Newman-Brown, 'The Receipt of Poor Relief and Family Situation: Aldenham, Hertfordshire 1630–90', in R. M. Smith (ed.), *Land, Kinship and Life-Cycle* (Cambridge, 1984), 405–22; P. G. Lawson, 'Property Crime and Hard Times in England, 1559–1624', *Law and History Review*, 4 (1986), 120–6; P. Glennie, 'Continuity and Change in Hertfordshire Agriculture, 1550–1700, I: Patterns of Agricultural Production', *Agricultural History Review*, 36 (1988), esp. 59–60; Glennie, 'Continuity and Change in Hertfordshire Agriculture, 1550–1700, II: Trends in Crop Yields and their Determinants', *Agricultural History Review*, 36 (1988), 145–61; Glennie, 'In Search of Agrarian Capitalism: Manorial Land Markets and the Acquisition of Land in the Lea Valley, *c.*1450–1560', *Continuity and Change*, 3 (1988), 11–40; Glennie, 'Life and Death in Elizabethan Cheshunt', in D. Jones-Baker (ed.), *Hertfordshire in History: Papers Presented to Lionel Munby* (Hertford, 1991), 65–91; and F. Newall, 'Social Mobility in the Population of Aldenham, Hertfordshire, 1600–1800', in Jones-Baker (ed.), *Hertfordshire in History*, 109–26.

the country as a whole.[81] Immigration, one of the few survival strategies open to wage labourers in such a competitive labour market, was therefore particularly significant in this context. From the 1580s, Hertfordshire court records reveal an increase in prosecution levels for squatting and vagrancy. The numbers prosecuted under the 1589 statute, for example, increased from four (1598–1608) to fifty-five (1609–18), suggesting that attitudes towards migration had hardened among parish officers.[82] Although these trends reflect the desire of local officials to discipline the idle, they also confirm independent comment that the county's roads were carrying heavy migrant traffic, a problem that the Hertfordshire justices sought to police with no fewer than seven houses of correction and a provost-marshall.[83]

Nonetheless, the difficulties created by immigration were experienced locally, in the context of the community of the parish rather than of the county. The population of King's Langley, for example, grew from less than 250 in 1563 to over 400 by 1603, an increase which could be accommodated only by the subdivision of tenancies, the total number of which increased from fifty-nine in 1591 to eighty-seven in 1619. Even more remarkably, the number of holdings of eight acres or less increased by 160 per cent in sixty years.[84] In Hinxworth, the rector reported in 1614 that 'the number of communicants in our parish are of late almost doubled, by reason of many cottages within few years erected: at Easter last, seventy-eight'.[85] In the manor of Hoddesdon, the sub-tenant problem proved enduring, and gradually forced tighter restrictions on immigration. The residential qualification for the frankpledge had once been a year and a day; by the 1570s the townsmen were insisting on three years' residence as a minimum requirement merely for migrants to remain in the manor. Even so, the major tenants were 'still troubled with the increase of inhabitants wanting a share of the grazing', and in 1573 required landlords under penalty of 6*s.* 8*d.* to ensure that each sub-tenant had 'two cartloads

[81] E. A. Wrigley and R. S. Schofield, *The Population History of England, 1541–1871: A Reconstruction* (Cambridge, 1981), 531–2, suggest that English population grew by 36.3% in the same period.

[82] P. G. Lawson, 'Crime and the Administration of Criminal Justice in Hertfordshire, *c.*1580–1625' (unpublished D.Phil. thesis, Oxford University, 1982), 181.

[83] *Hertford County Records*, v. 47–8, 398; *Calendar of Assize Records: Hertfordshire Indictments, James I*, 275.

[84] L. Munby (ed.), *The History of King's Langley* (London, 1963), 48–9, 52.

[85] W. Urwick, *Nonconformity in Hertfordshire* (London, 1884), 792. The diocesan census of 1603 had discovered eighty-seven communicants and one recusant in 1603; and the Compton Census eighty-nine conformists and twelve non-conformists in 1676. *The Compton Census of 1676: A Critical Edition*, ed. A. Whiteman (British Academy, Records of Social and Economic History, NS 10, Oxford, 1986), 322 n. 140.

of fuel wood of his own to burn'. Fears of hedge-breaking and wood-stealing, increasingly common activities amongst the poor deprived of common rights by enclosure, were evidently widespread by the 1590s.[86] By 1594, the chief tenants of Hoddesdon were being castigated for their 'covetousness' in taking inmates. Landlords had allegedly erected fifty-eight cottages 'out of Barnes Stables Kytchynes & such lyke out houses'. The inmates they had lodged there were 'for the most parte people enforced from other places and ther fynde harbor, ther being no order observed to the contrarie'. A further eighteen cottages had been built 'uppon [the] wastes and other very smale parcells of grounde in and about the towne, where never any were beforetyme' and were unfit 'for any honest man to dwell in, but onlie for beggars'.[87] In a town which reputedly contained only 130 ancient tenements, the influx of so many migrant poor placed enormous pressure on scant resources, and the increasing anger with which imputations of greed, theft, damage, and general waste were made reveals the fracturing of local social and political order.

The chronology of social change in the manor of Much Hadham was broadly similar, provoking a manorial by-law of 1579 which laid the basis for pre-emptive removal. Landlords and other householders had accommodated 'certen persons not born in this parish nor yet havinge byn resyante there by the space of three yeres' who were 'verye like themselves and also their wyves and Children to be a chardge and Burdon to the parechinars there'. The taking of inmates and sub-tenants was, accordingly, entirely prohibited, and those landlords who had without the consent of the 'moste honest & discrete' inhabitants let properties to 'maryed persons, wydowers or widowes whos husband' had either been born elsewhere or who had not been resident for three years were fined 40*s*. for each offence.[88] When the problems of ancient settled families were compounded by the immigration of the under-employed in such communities, the parameters of parochial tolerance were stretched to breaking point.

[86] J. A. Tregelles, *A History of Hoddesdon in the County of Hertfordshire* (Hertford, 1908), 334–6, 354–61. Unfortunately, the 1603 diocesan return for Broxbourne parish (of which Hoddesdon chapelry was part) has not survived, probably because it was a peculiar. *The Compton Census*, 40.

[87] Tregelles, *Hoddesdon*, 358. The farmers attempted to demonstrate the greed of the wealthier inhabitants by listing by name 29 'vyctuallers', 29 persons 'worth 100 li at the lest', and 15 'men of trade well able to lyve by the stock and the trade' who had encouraged immigration.

[88] L. L. Rickman, 'Brief Studies in the Manorial and Economic History of Much Hadham', *East Hertfordshire Archaeological Society Transactions*, 9 (1928–33), 290–1. For the simultaneous and not coincidental campaigns against hedge-breaking in Much Hadham, see Ch. 1.2(*b*) above.

3. A PAROCHIAL EXCLUSION CRISIS

The enormous implications of the failure to police the migrant poor are nowhere more vividly apparent than in the experience of the Hertfordshire parish of Layston.[89] The older settlement of Layston, the site of St Bartholomew's church, lay half a mile east of Ermine Street, but the bulk of its population was concentrated across the River Rib in the small market town of Buntingford, at the junction of Ermine Street and the road from Great Hormead heading to join the Great North Road at Baldock. Buntingford was of considerable administrative importance, being not only the site of a house of correction, but also the meeting-place of the Hertfordshire justices in the 1630s. Because of its market, Buntingford had complex economic relationships with its rural hinterland, which were further complicated for the purposes of social welfare provision by the fact that Layston was only one of four parishes into which its population extended, the others being Aspenden, Wyddial, and the deserted medieval village of Throcking. The impact of demographic pressure in these parishes was far from uniform. Although the total number of households across the four parishes grew by approximately 85 per cent in the interval between the 1524 lay subsidy and the 1673 hearth tax, disaggregation of their demographic experience suggests that Layston itself grew much faster than, and probably at the expense of, its entirely rural neighbours. While the population of Throcking probably remained unchanged, or perhaps even experienced a shrinkage in its (already tiny) number of households over this period, the rate of demographic increase in Wyddial (36 per cent) and Aspenden (65 per cent) was dwarfed by that of Layston itself (147 per cent). By 1673, at a time when its population probably stood somewhere between 450 and 500, 40.1 per cent of the households of Layston were exempt from the hearth tax.[90] As we have seen, Layston itself was extremely well endowed with charitable provision for the poor.[91]

[89] The following account is based on *The Victoria History of the County of Hertfordshire*, ed. W. Page (4 vols., London, 1902–14), iv. 85–8.

[90] Population growth rates calculated by comparing the number of households implied by the number of taxpayers in the 1524–5 lay subsidy with the number of householders assessed and exempted in the hearth tax of 1673. NA, E179/120/120 (Edwinstree Hundred Assessment Subsidy, 16 Henry VIII); E179/375/31 (hearth tax, Lady Day 1673), perforce incorporating estimates for Aspenden extrapolated from E179/248/23 (hearth tax, Lady Day 1663) because its return for 1673 is damaged. These figures substantially revise the dubious estimates in S. Hindle, 'Exclusion Crises: Poverty, Migration and Parochial Responsibility in English Rural Communities, c.1560–1660', *Rural History*, 7 (1996), 132 n. 39, and I am extremely grateful to Tom Arkell for pointing out the errors in my original calculations.

[91] See Ch. 2.5(*a*) above.

The rectory of Layston was worth £50 annually, and its vicar from 1604 to 1650 was Alexander Strange, the son of an Elizabethan Master in Chancery.[92] Strange was well connected among the squirearchy of Stuart Hertfordshire, and he enjoyed the patronage of the Leventhorpe family of Shingle Hall, Sawbridgeworth, one of the most well-established affinities on the county bench, and renowned 'favourers of Godly religion'. The advowson itself descended with the manor of Corneybury in Wyddial, and lay from 1583 to 1690 in the hands of the Crowch family of Alswick, who had purchased it from the Howards. Strange's patron at his appointment in 1604 had been John Crowch, fellow of King's College, Cambridge, 1585–98, 'an excellent scholar and worthy man who lived on his estates in Hertfordshire'. Whatever the confessional identity of the Crowch family, and although he was a graduate of Peterhouse (Cambridge), a college hardly renowned for its radical leanings, Strange's own puritan credentials were impeccable. In 1646 he subscribed to the petition of sixty-three Hertfordshire ministers to the House of Lords in support of the Directory and the Covenant. At his death in 1650, the Commonwealth Church Commissioners were informed that Strange had 'diligently served the cure with constant and frequent preaching' into his late seventies. He had also helped finance the building (at a cost of almost £420) of St Peter's chapel in Buntingford. His charity extended further, not only to an acre left for reading of divine service and the annual preaching of a Michaelmas sermon in 1625, but also to eight and a half acres donated towards the maintenance of the chapel in 1642. As early as 1620, a brass plate commemorating his contribution had been erected, representing 'Alexander, little of stature, but eminently great in strength and mind' in the pulpit, a bible in his right hand and a large hourglass at his left. After the foundation stone had been laid in 1614, Strange chose as his

[92] The following account is based on J. and J. A. Venn, *Alumni Cantabrigienses* (Cambridge, 1922), pt. I, vol. i, p. 427; vol. iv, p. 173; Urwick, *Nonconformity in Hertfordshire*, 756–8; *VCH Hertfordshire*, iv. 85–8, 117; *Journal of the House of Lords*, viii. 445 (24 July 1646); Lambeth Palace Library, London, COMM.XIIa/10/392–93, 403 (Commonwealth Church Survey, 1650); R. Clutterbuck, *A History of Hertfordshire* (3 vols., London, 1815–27), iii. 208; and J. B. Calnan, 'County Society and Local Government in the County of Hertford, *c.*1580–*c.*1630, with Special Reference to the Commission of the Peace' (unpublished Ph.D. diss., Cambridge University, 1979), 64, and appendices 1a and 1b. The deeds of the Strange Charity lands survive as HALS, D/P 65/25/3 (annual sermon, 1625) and D/P 65/25/5 (chapel maintenance, 1642). The arrangement of the communion table in St Peter's Buntingford has been described as unusual in itself (Urwick, *Nonconformity*, 756), but see G. Yule, 'James VI and I: Furnishing the Churches in his Two Kingdoms', in Fletcher and Roberts (eds.), *Religion, Culture and Society*, 182–208. For Peterhouse in the 1570s and 1580s, see P. Collinson, *The Elizabethan Puritan Movement* (London, 1967), 124–5.

motto the phrase 'Begg hard or beggar'd', words which take on a deeply ambiguous meaning in the context of Strange's surviving writings.

As we have seen, Strange's memorandum book, begun in 1607, contains abstracts of charity deeds and wills, notes of subscriptions, lists of the industrious poor, disbursements of charity money and poor rates, and, most remarkably, the draft of an address to his 'good neighbours and loving parishioners' dated 15 February 1636.[93] The text of this 'advice', some 2,750 words in length, poses considerable problems of interpretation, especially because it cannot readily be identified with a literary genre. Its informal rhetorical style, compounded by the absence of a biblical text, suggests that this was not a finished sermon, though perhaps it was a draft to which scriptural references might subsequently have been added. Internal evidence might, however, be taken to suggest that the text was intended for a more select audience. Despite the fact that Strange was intimately concerned with the 'misery' of his parishioners, it is surprising that he omitted to address the native poor directly. He made none of the conventional pleas for the patience and forbearance of the multitude, which implies that if the text were ever actually delivered, the poor themselves might well not have been present to hear him. The intended audience of the address might well, therefore, have been a vestry meeting.[94] If these words ever publicly circulated, moreover, they would have stung the landlords of Layston very sharply, for Strange's criticisms were both thoroughgoing and saturated with moral outrage. Whether the text is read as a draft sermon or as an open letter to his parishioners, it represents a full-blown exegesis of the micro-politics of settlement and belonging, touching almost every aspect of the social and economic life of the parish and her neighbours.

Strange commenced gently, accepting that although his analysis of the 'misery' into which his 'good neighbours and loving parishioners' had fallen might not remedy the present crisis, it might 'prevent the like for the tyme to come'.[95] At the very least, he hoped, his audience would be quickened and made sensible of their plight. He then boldly identified

[93] See Chs. 2.4(*a*) and 3.1 above. Layston with Buntingford Parish Memorandum Book 1607–*c*.1750 survives as HALS D/P65/3/3, of which an edition is available as *'This Little Commonwealth': Buntingford with Layston Parish Memorandum Book, 1607–c.1750*, ed. H. Falvey and S. Hindle (Hertfordshire Record Society, 19, Braughing, 2004). The text of Strange's 'advice' is at 326–38. Strange heavily emended the text, reorganizing the later paragraphs and reordering his five remedial proposals.

[94] J. Walter and K. Wrightson, 'Dearth and the Social Order in Early Modern England', *Past and Present*, 71 (1976), 22–42. The HALS catalogue of parish papers nonetheless describes the text as 'a sermon delivered in 1635' (*sic*).

[95] HALS, D/P65/3/3, 326.

parochial misery with the overburdening of poor rates, of which he perceived four causes. First, he argued, the last twenty years had seen the immigration from neighbouring parishes of 'no lesse than twentye familyes', the majority of which now received 'not only the almes which ariseth out of your towne howses and annuityes, but sometymes also part of that charitye which is raised by your weekly collector'. Second, he suggested, these twenty families contained about eighty children, some of them 'so little as that they scarce know their right hand from their left', others 'so bigge that they can doe you much service both in your corne in the tyme of harvest and in your hedges all the yeare after'. The sarcasm of these references to illicit gleaning and hedge-breaking is underlined by his observation that 'but few of them' were 'able or willing to gett their owne living'.[96] Third, these young idlers were supported only by one or two productive members of each household who, 'should they be sicke or lame or die, their children must of necessity be kept by the parish'. Finally, the moral failings of the young in these families were so acute as to make them unemployable. They were accustomed to live so 'idlye' and 'unprofitably', 'getting their living more by begging and by stealing than by any honest labor', that no householder or employer would take them into service whatever inducement they were offered.[97] The immigration of the idle poor had therefore produced a long-term liability for poor-rate payers.

Stark as this situation was, Strange did not rest there, since the social and political dynamics of such immigration required explanation. The cause, he reminded his neighbours, was 'partlye in yourselves and partlye in others'. The parishioners themselves had fallen victim to 'the roote of all evill, covetousness', greedily renting their property to 'whosoever will give most, notwithstanding they be such as in all probability will prove a charge to the parish'. These concerns echo those of the privy council in 1598 that landlords were deliberately converting their properties into tenements so that they could be filled with poor people.[98] Strange even imagined the rationale with which ratepayers might justify such self-interest: 'What though these my tenantes shall come to be burdensome to the parish? Yet my part in the rate will not be much the greater and in the mean tyme I shall make a great rent of my howse which will easyly beare out that charge whensoever it shall come.' Strange acidly criticized the self-delusion of such calculations, pointing out that when these poor tenants succumbed to the inevitable cycle of rent arrears and eviction,

96 Ibid.

97 HALS, D/P65/3/3, 326–7.

98 *APC*, xxviii (1597–8), 435–6.

ratepayers would be left both to maintain and house them. In these circumstances, the parish was theoretically empowered to increase the individual householder's rates in accordance with the burden his 'folly' had created rather than spreading the burden among the ratepayers as a whole.[99] If this sanction was actually deployed, then the landlord would be left to repent the accommodation of poor migrants 'contrary to the good liking' of their neighbours and 'to the visible hurt and prejudice of that little commonwealth' of which the ratepayers were the 'principall members'.[100] The moral failings and special pleading of landlords therefore destroyed the health of local body politic.

The pathology of the parish, however, also had exogenous causes. The poor of neighbouring communities, well enough aware that the charitable assets of Layston included a townhouse for the poor and lands worth almost £14 in annual revenue, speculated that 'if we can thrust ourselves into that parish, we shall have three or four shillings a yeare at the least to helpe pay our rent, and, it may be, in time gett a roome in the townehouse and so sitt rent free alltogether'.[101] Strange therefore identified the paradox that charity lands originally given either 'as a present helpe to the poore' or 'to enable the rest of the parishioners to relieve them in their extremitye' inevitably became 'the readyest meanes to impoverish a towne and make it at length unable to releeve their poore because of the multitude of such persons as dayly presse into the parish'. Indeed, he described a similar situation in nearby Braughing, where a house left for the rent-free use of the poor by William Bonest had shared this fate. Although originally intended for the elderly poor, it was not long before 'yonge and disordered poore crept into' it and even 'some maryed yonge folke with this hope, to have a roome' there. The ratepayers of Braughing had ultimately prevailed upon Bonest either to take the house back for his own use or to let it only to a respectable member of the community whose rent might defray poor relief expenditure.[102] Strange drew the moral: donation of property to the parish was simply 'a visible meanes to increase the poore', unless the tenancy was used 'to support the common charge' and the rent disposed by the overseers of the poor along with the ordinary parish rates.[103]

But neighbouring landlords, overseers, and ratepayers also bore their

[99] This was Chief Justice Heath's thirty-fifth resolution of 1633. Cf. Ch. 5.2 above.

[100] HALS, D/P65/3/3, 328.

[101] HALS, D/P65/3/3, 329.

[102] William Bonest of Braughing devised his tenement in Overbury to the churchwardens in 1612 on condition that not more than four widows should dwell there rent-free. *VCH Hertfordshire*, iii. 316.

[103] HALS, D/P65/3/3, 329–31.

share of the blame. 'Carefull' overseers discovering a householder with five or six children 'which may in tyme be chargeable unto them', often 'forsee the storme that is comming and therfore wisely goe aboute to prevent the damage'. Strange envisaged a meeting of the vestry in the fictional parish of Kingstone, at which some parish 'patriote' warned his fellow ratepayers about the precarious household economies of the poor and arranged a pre-emptive removal:

> You see, neighbours, how the poore man Thomas Barebones howsehold doth increase; his wife is able to doe little, they all depend of his labour; if he should die or be sicke at any tyme, the keeping of his famyly must fall on the parish and it is no small collection will keepe those children. By this occasion our rates will be enhanced and ourselves impoverished. What thinke you of the matter, neighbours?[104]

Strange's imaginary vestrymen responded with alacrity, one 'Richard Stole' enthusiastically offering a salve for the sore. Stole suggested the accommodation of Barebones's family in one of his properties in the parish of Mountsorrel so that 'we shalbe ridde of them all at a clappe and our parish free of an unprofitable burthen'. His colleagues, reported Strange, would not only applaud this motion but even consider illicitly subsidizing Barebones's rent until he 'be settled so longe in Mountsorrel that there is no more removing of him from thence.' Charity forbade Strange from accusing specific landlords of such 'projectes', but he did not fight shy of naming Aspenden and Wyddial as the parishes of origin of at least twelve of the twenty migrant families in Layston.[105]

The Buntingford case so vividly described by Strange is exceptionally well documented, but it is far from unique as an example of intra-parochial rivalry. Similar tensions were evident, for example, in the Cumberland constablewicks of Lazonby and Plumpton in the early eighteenth century. The inhabitants of Lazonby argued in 1710 that they had only one pauper, 'haveing been all along carefull in keeping out Strangers and idle Persons' who might gain settlement 'by farming Cottages and peices of Land' let from local owners at more than market value. They complained that, although neighbouring Plumpton lay on 'the decent rood' from Carlisle to Penrith and was 'filled' with the poor, the parishioners there paid less than half the total rate. The Plumpton folk allegedly declared 'openly and frequently' that 'they need not [car]e what Poor are setled with them Since they have the township [of] Lazonby, Which pays the Weight and burthen of the Poor-tax'.[106] Doubtless such

[104] HALS, D/P65/3/3, 331.

[105] HALS, D/P65/3/3, 332.

[106] CRO, Q/11/1/97/36.

examples could be multiplied, revealing the parochial xenophobia which created such acute tensions between and within communities long into the eighteenth century.

How might such tensions be resolved? Strange's analysis pointed unerringly in the direction of bolstering the defences of the little commonwealth of Layston. Parishioners must not be tempted to put short-term rental income before the long-term objective of low poor rates. He proposed five remedies, acknowledging that they might be less than popular, but arguing nonetheless that any of them might prove 'profitable' to the parishioners.[107] First, he advised, the ratepayers should bind themselves into a combination under penalty of £10 payable to Sir John Caesar 'or some other man of good name and quality' not to take inmates without the prior written consent of the parish officers. Only those migrants who were 'honest men, good labourers and such as with Gods blessing will be able to support and maintayne therselves and famlys without being a charge to the parish' would be admitted.[108] Unanimity in this matter, however, must be followed by speedy execution of forfeitures for default. Strange had apparently made a similar order with a £5 penalty clause almost twenty years previously which, although well observed for a time, was soon breached 'and, the gap being open, others rushed into the parish without exception, no man going about to levie the forfiture, and so all came to nought', the parish being flooded with 'unruly and unnecessary poor'.[109] The rigorous enforcement of such a policy would therefore preclude Layston landlords from taking inmates.

Strange's second proposal, however, was more radical still. He urged the parishioners to purchase all those dwellings which, because they were owned by residents of other parishes, fell beyond the control of Layston ratepayers. Since it was common enough practice for private gentlemen to 'buy in such howses and pull them downe to avoyd unnecessary poverty in their parish', why should not 'a whole parish lay their purses together and doe such a thinge as well'? Furthermore, if dwellings could be promptly demolished, expenses could be rapidly recouped by renting out the land on which they had stood for the use of the poor.[110] Strange sensed that this compulsory purchase scheme, effectively amounting to the nationalization of foreign property in the parish state, would be

[107] HALS, D/P65/3/3, 332.

[108] HALS, D/P65/3/3, 337. This section is struck through in the MS. Such covenants had been successfully attempted elsewhere, as at Nantwich (Ches.) in 1631. NA, SP16/195/31.

[109] HALS, D/P65/3/3, 336–8.

[110] HALS, D/P65/3/3, 332–3.

expensive and difficult to execute, hence his third proposal.[111] The parish, he argued, could easily arrange to lease all the 'foreign' tenancies in the parish, guaranteeing the landlords a secure rent, and ensuring that only those who 'must acknowledge [Layston ratepayers] for their meddiat landlords' were accepted as tenants.[112] Either by purchase or lease therefore, parish ratepayers might monopolize the allocation of Layston tenancies, stopping up the cracks in the communal defences.

Failing these first three options, Strange proposed a fourth. Where non-resident landlords planned to evict Layston tenants, rendering the parish vulnerable to a magistrates' habitation or relief order to maintain the newly destitute family, could not the ratepayers negotiate with the landlord to 'have the disposing of his howse upon the ordinary rent'? Strange was optimistic about this scheme, since he claimed that even those Layston ratepayers who had refused the covenant against taking inmates had already promised overseers first refusal of tenancies at a 'convenient and reasonable rent'. Given the financial pressures operating on Layston landlords, Strange recognized that this was 'as much as can be expected at theyr handes and enough for us to keepe out rude and disordered poor which may hereafter be a charge to our parishe'.[113]

All four of these proposals necessarily involved immediate financial sacrifices by Layston ratepayers. If none proved acceptable, Strange had a fifth, compromise, position. The ratepayers could at the very least deny the benefits of town houses or charity lands to poor immigrants. This would both inhibit the 'greedy desire' of the poor in neighbouring parishes to creep into Layston, and enable the parish to care more effectively for its 'antient poore'. Adoption of such a policy twenty years previously would have reduced the number of poor migrants chargeable to Layston ratepayers from eighty to thirty at most, 'the rest being of a later standing and such as have by yourselves or otheres, contrary to the liking of the parish, bynne brought into it'. Strange tempted his audience with a vision of a well-ordered poor relief regime: 'how much good the revenews of your howses and landes would doe amonge so few', he explained, 'you are well able to judg'.[114]

The micro-politics of migration, settlement, and belonging were particularly controversial in Layston because of the peculiar configuration of

[111] On the parish state, see Hindle, 'Power, Poor Relief and Social Relations', 94–6; and cf. Ch. 6.6 below.

[112] HALS, D/P65/3/3, 334.

[113] HALS, D/P65/3/3, 334–5. For an instance of a similar policy in Much Hadham in 1646 when an 'ancient glover' being 'warned out' of his dwelling was housed by the overseers at 'a reasonable rent', see *Hertford County Records*, v. 382.

[114] HALS, D/P65/3/3, 335–6.

its parish boundaries. So complex was the arrangement of Buntingford within Layston and its three contiguous parishes that adjacent properties in the high street might fall under the jurisdiction of the parish officers of Layston, Aspenden, or Wyddial (or even perhaps of Throcking).[115] From this perspective, Alexander Strange's address merely crystallizes suspended fears about the thresholds of belonging in the market town of Buntingford. Analysis of early seventeenth-century Hertfordshire quarter sessions papers reveals long-standing grand jury concerns about poor migrants in the parish. The abuses encouraged by the John Stansfield, alehousekeeper of 'The Eagle and Child', for example, included 'swearing, gaming, drunkenness, quarrelling and great suspicion of whoring', all of which 'brought iddle peeple to the parish'.[116] The results included prosecutions for parochial breaches of the 1589 act, a long-running parish dispute over poor law assessments, and distraints for defaulters.[117] As we have seen, moreover, taxation records confirm Strange's analysis of the shifting demographic relationship between Layston and her neighbours.

Despite the evident accuracy of his analysis, Strange's far-sighted proposals had little practical significance. Nonetheless, they had meaning enough for Strange himself. Once his parishioners had heard his diagnosis, the remedy lay in their hands alone. Whether they applied the salve or not was hardly his problem, since his conscience was satisfied: 'if upon this motion you shall doe nothinge, I shall content myselfe with mine owne desines and endevoures in that I have showne you somethinge that was profitable for the better ordering of this little commonwealth'.[118] Even so, the rhetorical strategies adopted in the address are themselves significant. Strange's repeated reference to the 'commonwealth' of Layston harks back to the prophetic preachers and publicists of the mid-sixteenth century, and in excoriating the 'covetousness' of its principal inhabitants he echoes not only one of the more famous of Hugh Latimer's sermons before Edward VI, but also the earl of Leicester's savaging of the self-interested landlords of Elizabethan Warwick.[119] In

[115] M. Bailey, 'A Tale of Two Towns: Buntingford and Standon in the Later Middle Ages', *Journal of Medieval History*, 19 (1993), 351–71.

[116] HALS, HAT/SR10/48.

[117] *Hertford County Records*, v. 106, 152 (cottages and inmates, 1628, 1631); 203, 206, 213, 215 (rating dispute 1635–6); 191 (rescue of a distress for the poor rate, 1634). This is to say nothing of the rating dispute which Strange himself tried to mediate in the years 1617–30. See Ch. 6.1 below.

[118] HALS, D/P65/3/3, 338.

[119] McRae, *God Speed the Plough*, 23–78, and cf. Ch. 2.1 above; Beier, 'Social Problems of an Elizabethan Country Town', 77.

other respects, however, his approach is far less traditional. Whether or not they were eventually propagated from the pulpit, Strange's remarks would doubtless have been regarded as divisive and uncharitable, approximating as they did to that 'personal' style of preaching which proved so controversial in Elizabethan and Jacobean parishes, often resulting in the verbal abuse of preachers during their sermons, or their prosecution, harassment, and assault thereafter.[120] Although Strange openly identified the parishes of Aspenden and Wyddial as sources of misery, he stopped short of actually naming names (either there or in Layston). His audience would, however, almost certainly have recognized the specific offenders who were implied. In particular, the story of Thomas Barebones and Richard Stole in the fictional parish of Kingstone might be regarded as clerical brinkmanship, as Strange not only satirized the offenders, but even tested their hypocrisy, inviting them (like the Old Testament King David) to reveal ignorance of their own guilt.[121]

In addition to its radical proposals and rhetorical flair, however, Strange's address is extremely revealing of contemporary attitudes to the idle poor, especially migrants. As might be expected, he condemned the moral failings of the 'unruly', 'unnecessary', 'rude', 'yonge and disordered' poor with their 'greedy desire' to infiltrate Layston charities, distinguishing them both from the 'auntient poor . . . such as have byne a good tyme dwellers' in the parish, and from those 'honest men, good labourers and such as with Gods blessing will be able to support and maintayne therselves and famlys without being a charge to the parish' who might be welcomed. Youth was clearly a key term in the equation of thriftlessness and poverty, Strange singling out those who married 'yonge folk' for particular criticism. Like William Perkins before him, moreover, Strange attacked indiscriminate charity among the better sort as mere self-indulgence. Indeed, while the first issue in Christopher Hill's 'double

[120] See e.g. the evidence of hostility to the 'personal' preaching styles of Paul Baines (who defended the practice on the grounds that 'it would not have been so well if he had spoken . . . in private') and Richard Fletcher in P. Collinson, 'Cranbrook and the Fletchers: Popular and Unpopular Religion in the Kentish Weald', repr. in id., *Godly People: Essays in English Protestantism and Puritanism* (London, 1984), 409 n. 67, 412, 418; and similar episodes in Elizabethan Hawkhurst (Kent) and Hutton Cranswick (East Yorks.) in P. Collinson, 'Shepherds, Sheepdogs, and Hirelings: The Pastoral Ministry in Post-Reformation England', in W. J. Sheils and D. Wood (eds.), *The Ministry: Clerical and Lay* (Studies in Church History 26, Oxford, 1989), 206–7, and P. Marshall, *The Face of the Pastoral Ministry in the East Riding, 1525–1595* (University of York, Borthwick Paper 88, York, 1995), 18.

[121] Cf. the brilliant analysis of similarly daring criticisms in P. Collinson, 'Christian Socialism in Elizabethan Suffolk: Thomas Carew and his *Caveat for Clothiers*', in C. Rawcliffe *et al.* (eds.), *Counties and Communities: Essays on East Anglian History Presented to Hassell Smith* (Norwich, 1996), 161–79. For Nathan's parable attacking David, see 2 Samuel 12: 1–7.

problem' of social policy, that of making the parishioners aware of their responsibilities towards their own impotent poor, had evidently been solved in the parish, the second, that of discrimination in the application of charity, remained controversial. Hence Strange felt compelled to criticize the moral failings of idle *rentiers* who served neither God nor the commonwealth.[122] The address is, however, interesting in its omissions: there is no explicit discussion here of the desirability of setting the poor on work, nor of the benefits that might accrue from the incarceration and labour discipline of the house of correction.[123] This is especially surprising given both the recurrent criticisms of Hertfordshire petitioners and grand jurymen of the failure to enforce the statute of artificers[124] and the long-running debate over the viability of proposals to create employment in the new draperies in Hertfordshire.[125] Neither, moreover, does Strange resort to the conventional exhortations to hospitality and generosity among the better sort. Indeed, his ambivalence to charitable giving is itself evident in his own will, proved in 1651. Strange bequeathed over £42 in cash to seventeen named individuals, together with jewellery, books, music, and musical instruments to two others, but left only 40*s.* to the poor of the parish.[126] The contrast with his generosity to the godly of Buntingford could not be more marked: the charity of Alexander Strange extended principally to members of the household of faith.

Ultimately, then, Strange's address constitutes an extended critique, and even a personal admission, of failure: failure on the part of landlords to look beyond their own immediate self-interest; failure on the part of parish officers to enforce the statutes and by-laws against the taking of inmates; failure on the part of Strange himself to raise the moral conscience of his parishioners; failure on the part of the community of Layston to use the poor laws either to reform the idleness of the migrant poor or, in turn, to care adequately for their 'auntient poor'. Strange's was a voice crying in the wilderness, and its demoralized tone helps explain

[122] C Hill, 'William Perkins and the Poor', repr. in id., *Puritanism and Revolution: Studies in the English Revolution of the Seventeenth Century* (London, 1956), 222–3, 232, 235–6.

[123] Cf. J. Innes, 'Prisons for the Poor: English Bridewells, 1555–1800', in F. Snyder and D. Hay (eds.), *Labour, Law and Crime: An Historical Perspective* (London, 1987), 42–122; Slack, *Poverty and Policy*, 138–61; D. Underdown, *Fire from Heaven: Life in an English Town in the Seventeenth Century* (London, 1992), 109–15. For Strange's participation in a scheme to set the poor on work in Layston in 1623–4, see Ch. 3.1 above.

[124] HMC, *Calendar of the Manuscripts of the Most Honourable the Marquess of Salisbury, Preserved at Hatfield House, Hertfordshire, Pt. 20 (A.D. 1608)*, ed. M. S. Giuseppi and G. D. Owen (London, 1968), 288–9; NA, ASSI35/66/1, fo. 44 (Mar. 1624).

[125] M. L. Zell, '"Setting the Poor on Work": Walter Morrell and the New Draperies Project *c.*1603–31', *Historical Journal*, 44 (2001), 651–75.

[126] NA, PROB11/215, 23 Jan. 1651.

why grand juries elsewhere complained that failure to enforce the 1589 statute caused their parishes to 'abound with poor' into the late seventeenth century.[127] By the 1660s Layston itself was experiencing those settlement disputes so characteristic of late seventeenth-century communities. In 1662 John Bull, a labourer settled in Aspenden, migrated to Layston (a journey which might in fact have involved only a move to an adjacent property), and allegedly 'obscured himself in a cottage about the space of three months unknown to the inhabitants, until exigency and necessity compelled him to crave their charity and relief to the burthening of the parish of Layston'. As Strange would have wished, the assize judges decided that he should be conveyed back to Aspenden.[128] A parochial exclusion crisis such as that experienced in Layston also, moreover, explains why clergymen and parish officers might adopt a more drastic and immediate expedient to ease the burden on parish rates. If pre-emptive removals and indemnity bonds were one strategy of exclusion, the inhibition of pauper marriages was another.

4. ON THE THRESHOLD OF THE COMMUNITY

The question of potential chargeability was, inevitably, particularly sensitive where young married couples were involved. The difficulties created by immigration became acute where they were superimposed upon the problem of life-cycle poverty, especially agricultural regions where the local economy afforded so few opportunities to working wives and children. In early modern Aldenham (Hertfordshire), for example, correlation of family reconstitution and poor law records suggests that, of the sedentary families, 35 per cent were recorded as poor at some period during their marriage. Only 50 per cent of families were wealthy enough to be assessed for contributions to the parish poor rate. More significantly, different families appear to have been relieved or assessed in different phases of the life-cycle, rather than one group of families being always rich and another relatively poor. The second decade after marriage appears to have been the period of greatest vulnerability to dependency in such communities.[129] As a point of entry into full membership of the parochial community, it is therefore hardly surprising that the economics

[127] HMC, *Various*, i. 324.

[128] *Hertford County Records*, i. 149.

[129] Newall, 'Social Mobility', 115, 122. Cf. R. M. Smith, 'Some Issues Concerning Families and their Property in Rural England, 1250–1800', and T. Wales, 'Poverty, Poor Relief and the Life-Cycle: Some Evidence from Seventeenth-Century Norfolk', in Smith (ed.), *Land, Kinship and Life-Cycle*, 68–85, 351–404; and Ch. 3.2 above.

of marriage should figure so prominently in the thinking of parish officers and the ratepayers they represented.

Indeed, recently married couples with young children were a very significant proportion of those who petitioned for parish pensions in the early seventeenth century. As the justices of north Norfolk noted in 1631, parish officers frequently found themselves paying out cash doles not only to the impotent poor but also 'to the meaner sort of labourers overburdened with children'. The magistracy's preferred solution to this problem was, as we have seen, to bind the children apprentice and reduce the pensions payable to their parents.[130] But other parish officers even attempted both to discourage these couples from forming unions before they would be able to support their offspring and to punish clergymen who allowed them to marry. Indeed, the eleventh direction of the Caroline Book of Orders insisted that 'wandering persons with women and children' must 'give an account to the constable or justice of peace, where they were married, and where their children were christened'. On the one hand, then, there was the stereotypical fear of the army of mobile poor as a race apart, a people 'who live like savages' and 'neither marry, nor bury, nor christen'. On the other, there was a desire to prevent those marital unions amongst the poor which were regarded as premature, irresponsible, and unstable.[131] Little wonder, therefore, that poor labouring couples might be particularly vulnerable to the sanctions of parish authorities against immigration and settlement. Even the assize judges, who (as we have seen) were wedded to the principle that no man should be forced into vagrancy, argued that the obligation of parish officers to provide housing for the poor did not extent to 'lusty yong marryed people': Sir Robert Hyde insisted at the Worcester Assizes in 1661 that 'yf yong men marry together before they have howses ther is no law to enforce churchwardens and overseers by the Justices to find howses; but yf they cannot get any, let them lye under an oke'.[132]

Historians have generally stressed the relatively unconstrained nature of the early modern English marriage pattern. Provided a couple could accumulate the economic wherewithal to set up an independent household, kin and community would welcome their joint entry into full adult membership of the community.[133] One set of influences tending to the

[130] NA, SP16/193/40. For the context, see Wales, 'Poverty, Poor Relief and the Life-Cycle'

[131] 'The Book of Orders', sig. G4^V.

[132] 'Henry Townshend's "Notes of the Office of a Justice of the Peace"', 107.

[133] For a an extended review of the historiography of nuptiality in early modern England, see S. Hindle, 'The Problem of Pauper Marriage in Seventeenth-Century England', *Transactions of the Royal Historical Society*, 6th ser., 8 (1998), 71–5.

reduction of the rate of household formation, and which might in turn have contributed to the high celibacy rates of the mid-seventeenth century, has, however, been relatively neglected.[134] *Institutional* factors limited the extent of freedom which couples really had to act in the 'rational choice' ways so beloved of recent historical demography. The 1563 statute of artificers, for instance, was motivated partly out of a desire for 'the prevention of untimely marriages', and the minimum age of departing parish apprenticeships (24 for males and 21 for women) was intended partly to defer the entry of the young into the marriage market.[135] Other institutional pressures operated relatively crudely (though they were no less effective for all that) in actually inhibiting marriages altogether, especially among those likely to be chargeable once they had children. The role of the poor law in this context is particularly significant, and it will be explored here in the light of scattered evidence collected during the exploration of the policies and priorities of parish vestries.[136] Human reproduction, and especially the public celebration of the marriages which were its only legitimate context, were subject to social regulation. In this case, however, it is possible to develop a model of 'social control' that, exceptionally, provides us with empirical evidence of its operation.[137] The context and consequences of such social discipline will be explored here, first by discussing the evidence for the inhibition of pauper marriage; second, by analysing the role and motivation of parish officers and leading ratepayers in such activity; and third, by demonstrating the extent of contemporary concern with the policy.

On 29 May 1642, the minister and churchwardens of Frampton (Lincolnshire) subscribed to a vestry memorandum that the marriage banns of John Hayes and Ann Archer, both residents of the parish, had

[134] But see, from a general theoretical perspective, R. Lesthaeghe, 'On the Social Control of Human Reproduction', *Population and Development Review*, 6 (1980), 527–48; and, more specifically, R. M. Smith, 'Fertility, Economy and Household Formation in England over Three Centuries', *Population and Development Review*, 7 (1981), 602–11.

[135] 5 Elizabeth I, c. 4 (1563). See S. T. Bindoff, 'The Making of the Statute of Artificers', in S. T. Bindoff *et al.* (eds.), *Elizabethan Government and Society: Essays Presented to Sir John Neale* (London, 1961), 56–94. Cf. D. M. Woodward, 'The Background to the Statute of Artificers: The Genesis of Labour Policy, 1558–1563', *Economic History Review*, 2nd ser., 33 (1980), 32–44; and G. R. Elton, *The Parliament of England, 1559–1581* (Cambridge, 1986), 263–7.

[136] Cf. Hindle, 'Power, Poor Relief and Social Relations'; Hindle, *The State and Social Change*, 204–30 (Ch. 8: 'The Governance of the Parish'); Hindle, 'The Political Culture of the Middling Sort in English Rural Communities, *c.*1550–1700', in T. Harris (ed.), *The Politics of the Excluded, 1500–1850* (London and New York, 2001), 125–52.

[137] Cf. G. S. Jones, 'Class Expression versus Social Control? A Critique of Recent Trends in the Social History of "Leisure"', repr. in id., *Languages of Class: Studies in English Working Class History, 1832–1982* (Cambridge, 1983), 80.

been read on three consecutive Sundays. They had not, however, gone unchallenged. On each of the three readings, Robert Pimperton of the neighbouring parish of Kirton had objected, and had in turn been required to justify his opposition. 'It was openly desyred that [Pimperton] bring witnesses to prove there was some just cause why they might not lawfully be joined but yet he hath not done it.' The minister noted that 'we know not why wee may not lawfully proceede to marriage, except [Pimperton] presently prove an impediment or put in a caution to do it'. The objection to the banns had the effect of delaying and probably preventing altogether Hayes and Archer from celebrating their marriage in the parish.[138] This was not, however, to be the only occasion on which the Frampton vestrymen recorded an objection to a marriage. Samuel Cony, minister of Frampton, whose duty it had been to record the unspecified impediment to the Hayes marriage in 1642, noted in the parish register that, when 'the intentions of a marriage' between Edward Marten and Jane Goodwin were published in January 1654, John Ayre, Thomas Appleby, and William Eldred 'in behalf of them selves and other of the inhabitants' objected on two grounds. First, it seems, Marten's marital history was in question: although he had been in service both in neighbouring Algakirke and in Frampton, it was uncertain 'where he has lived before that time nor what hee is, either a maryed or single man'. They argued that the marriage should be deferred until such time as Marten could certify the truth of these matters. Second, however, was the question of Marten's current economic status. 'For aught they knew and as they verily believed', Cony noted, Marten 'was a very poore man' and 'had not then any house to live in'. The vestry accordingly required that Marten 'might ere he wur married gett some sufficient man to be bound with him to secure the town from any charge by him or his whom they consider they were not bound to keepe hee being till he lately crept into [the parish] a poor stranger to us'.[139] Edward Marten's plans were apparently to be held in suspended animation until he could guarantee that he and his offspring would never be a drain on parochial resources.

Ecclesiastical solemnization of these two couples' unions would have served as a ritual of inclusion, as the whole community witnessed their

[138] LA, Frampton PAR, 10/1, unfol. (29 May 1642). Pimperton's concern is probably to be explained by the fact that, although he lived in Kirton, he had property interests, and therefore paid rates, in Frampton.

[139] LA, Frampton PAR, 1/2, unfol. (Jan. 1654). For the immediate context of these decisions see Hindle, 'Power, Poor Relief and Social Relations'. It is significant that the Frampton authorities were concerned about potential costs even though Marten was not a native of the parish. Marten does not seem to have been settled elsewhere, and it may be that his period of service in Frampton had earned him settlement rights in the parish.

'liminal transformation' into the state of matrimony and therefore of adulthood.[140] 'Inclusion' into the community as a settled member naturally entailed the recognition of eligibility for maintenance in the eventuality of poverty. In the case of Hayes and Archer, the reasons for forbidding the banns are unspecified, yet the couple were nonetheless denied, perhaps only temporarily, the recognition that they belonged to the community of the parish. In the case of Marten and Goodwin, it seems, inclusion was to be deferred, and (if tolerated at all) made conditional upon his provision of an indemnity bond, a guarantee that the parishioners of Frampton would never be liable for relief of his actual or prospective family.[141] Fragmentary as these references are, the micro-politics of the decisions that generated them can be deduced by considering the circumstances of other such refusals.

The Frampton evidence can indeed be buttressed by other evidence of the quasi-formal inhibition of the marriages of the poor in seventeenth-century England. In Terling (Essex) in 1617, for instance, a labourer presented in the ecclesiastical courts for incontinence protested that he and his paramour were 'contracted in matrimonie', that 'the banes of matrimonie were asked betwene them in Terling church', and that 'the parish would not suffer them to marry else they had bin marryed ere now'.[142] Another Essex labourer, Robert Johnson, had cohabited for a year with, and had a child by, Elizabeth Whitland in the parish of Upminster only to run away to London protesting that 'he would have maryed her if the inhabitants would have suffered him'.[143] The minister of the Dorset parish of Nether Compton complained in 1628 that Anne Russed 'hath no house nor home of her own and [is] very like to bring charge on the parish, and therefore will hardly be suffered to marry in our parish'.[144] Richard Guy, a 73-year-old pensioner of North Bradley (Wiltshire), defended himself against a charge of clandestine marriage by complaining in 1618 that 'the parishioners' had been 'unwilling' that 'he should marry with his now wife being but young'.[145] In 1570 the parishioners of Adlington (Kent) 'were sore against' Alice Cheeseman's

[140] D. Cressy, *Birth, Marriage and Death: Ritual, Religion and the Life-Cycle in Tudor and Stuart England* (Oxford, 1997), 286–92, provides an elegant summary of the transformations involved in matrimony.

[141] Cf. Chs. 5.2 and 5.3 above.

[142] K. Wrightson and D. Levine, *Poverty and Piety in an English Village: Terling, 1525–1700* (2nd edn., Oxford, 1995), 135.

[143] Ibid. 80.

[144] M. Ingram, *Church Courts, Sex and Marriage in England, 1570–1640* (Oxford, 1987), 131.

[145] M. Ingram, 'The Reform of Popular Culture? Sex and Marriage in Early Modern England', in B. Reay (ed.), *Popular Culture in Seventeenth-Century England* (London, 1985), 145.

projected match and 'stayed the asking of the banns and marriage and many of the cheefest of the parish counselled her to leave him because the parishioners mislyked of [him]'.[146] Perhaps the most interesting examples come from late Caroline Lancashire, where the parish officers of Ashton-under-Lyne, in a somewhat constructive interpretation of the second and eleventh directions of the Caroline Book of Orders, presented their vicar Ralph Marsden at the Oldham petty sessions for marrying a young couple 'whom they think are like to become chargeable to their parish'. They also made a second presentment to the effect that a similarly improvident marriage had been clandestinely celebrated by one Lawrence Hinslove commonly called 'Sir Lawrence'.[147] The sanctions that might be applied in such cases are illustrated by the vestry decision at Finchingfield (Essex) in 1628 that, 'if William Byfleet shall marry Susan Crosley contrary to the mind of the townsmen', his 'collection shall be detained'; and by one Canterbury deponent's report that 'the parishioners threatened Alice [Cheeseman] to expell her out of the parish' if she defied their 'hinderance' of the marriage.[148]

These examples, of course, take no account of those occasions on which already married couples were prevented from living together in communities where one or the other, or sometimes both, were born or settled. The inhabitants of Hindolveston petitioned the Norfolk JPs in 1655 that Robert Woodes of Barney and his new wife Ann Shoot 'should be settled in Barney or elsewhere according to the lawe', despite the fact that Ann was a native of the parish. After John and Isabell Salter had been forced to do public penance for pre-marital fornication in 1638, the inhabitants of Sileby (Leicestershire) closed ranks against them because they were so 'uncivill and unhonest' that they and their offspring would inevitably be a charge on the parish.[149] In 1626 the vestry of Finchingfield (Essex) ordered that 'for the preventing of more charge of poore', no householder was to lease a cottage 'to new married couples who were not borne in the towne'. In 1618, meanwhile, Anthony Adams sought to bring his young wife to dwell with him in Stockton (Worcestershire). Despite the fact that he had been born, bred, and apprenticed there, 'his parishioners [were] not willing he should bring her into the parish saying

[146] D. O'Hara, '"Ruled By My Friends": Aspects of Marriage in the Diocese of Canterbury', *Continuity and Change*, 6 (1991), 28.

[147] NA, SP14/404/96; 'Book of Orders', sigs. F4^v, G4^v.

[148] *Early Essex Town Meetings: Braintree, 1619–1636, Finchingfield, 1626–1634*, ed. F. G. Emmison (Chichester, 1970), 117; O'Hara, '"Ruled By My Friends"', 28. For the penal withholding of relief, see Ch. 6.2 below.

[149] Norfolk RO, C/S3/42; Capp, 'Life, Love and Litigation', 69. The Salters had already been refused accommodation in John's native parish of Seagrave.

he would breed up a charge amongst them'. The couple were forced to live apart, he in Stockton, she in her home parish of Bewdley. But even this arrangement proved unsatisfactory, since 'doubt of further charge' among the parishioners there led to her expulsion from Bewdley.[150] Another married couple forced to live apart because parish officers could not agree on who should be liable for them because they were now impotent were William Busher and his wife. While he was to return to his native parish of Marksbury (Somerset), 'to live and work or be relieved by the parish', she was to remain with her parents in Compton Dando to 'be relieved by the parishioners if she become chargeable or be enforced to return to her husband'.[151] Parish officers protested that unions such as these were improvident, and their accounts of the consequences of instability are vivid. The parishioners of Chilcompton (Somerset) complained of the irresponsible behaviour of Mathias Griffin, 'who hath no certain place of abode or dwellinge to their knowledge but is a wanderer from place to place'. Griffin, they alleged, had 'married a lewd woman the daughter of a very poor man' who lived along with two or three other 'coopells' in 'a house built upon the lord's waste for the poor'. Not long afterwards, Griffin ran away 'leaving his wife whose child was born within three months of the marriage' but returned to her frequently 'allways by night' refusing to provide for her elsewhere.[152] So common did disputes over the liability of recently married couples become that the Somerset bench had to make a general order for them. Widows and their children, they insisted in 1616, were to be allowed to continue in their deceased husband's parish of settlement only if they had been co-resident there for at least a year before his death.[153]

Such inter-parochial wrangling became particularly vitriolic after the passage of the settlement laws in 1662. Restoration parishes were not above actually forcing pregnant women into marriages with 'strangers', providing that the man had a settlement elsewhere, in order to pass the financial burden of maintaining the child on to someone other than her home parish.[154] The vindictive thinking that underpinned such strategies is nicely illustrated by the response of Sir Ralph Verney when the vicar of Wasing (Berkshire) took an inmate in 1655. Verney ordered his steward to arrange for the overseers to tax the vicar an extra 5*s.* weekly in poor rates to cover any potential costs, and even sarcastically remarked that if

150 *Early Essex Town Meetings*, 107; Worcestershire RO, QSR/1/1/28/13.

151 *Quarter Sessions Records for the County of Somerset*, i. 291–2.

152 Ibid. 122.

153 Ibid. 192.

154 L. Stone, *Uncertain Unions: Marriage in England, 1660–1753* (Oxford, 1992), 83–92.

the lodger was single 'you may tell [him] he may marry and soe charge the parish with a new brood at his pleasure'.[155]

There was, of course, a long-standing tradition of providing charitable support for poor young women who would otherwise have no chance of amassing a dowry. Charities to subsidize the marriages of poor maidens were actively encouraged by the ecclesiastical hierarchy, and they were established well into the seventeenth century.[156] Sir Stephen Slaney, for instance, left £40 'for the poor and for marrying poor maidens' in the Staffordshire parish of Penkridge in 1632.[157] The vestrymen of Braughing (Hertfordshire) similarly distributed 20*s.* yearly under the terms of a bequest intended to subsidize the weddings of the poor maids of the parish. In the administration of these bequests, however, considerations of settlement began to loom large. In the years 1626–43, the Braughing trustees bestowed gifts on forty-one brides, although on at least one occasion the award was conditional on the woman not bearing a child within nine months of the wedding ceremony. This hint of discrimination is bolstered by the fact that the late Caroline gifts were granted exclusively to Braughing women who married endogamously.[158]

The examples of inhibited marriages, almost always described in the most laconic or fragmentary of documents, are remarkable in several ways. First, it must be emphasized that, the actions of the Ashton-under-Lyne parish officers notwithstanding, the poverty of bride and groom was not among the justified canonical grounds for objecting to marriage banns. Although both Henrician and late Elizabethan parliaments had flirted with the tighter regulation of marriage, neither criminal nor canon law justified the prevention of the marriage of the poor.[159] Second, the dubious legality of the informal prohibition of marriage might apparently be sidestepped by any number of expedient pretexts. Those objecting raised the possibilities that Edward Marten might be a bigamist, or remarrying with several children by a previous union; that the disparity of age between Richard Guy and his intended bride was inappropriate; or

[155] Claydon House, Buckinghamshire, MS Verney, R13 (Sir Ralph Verney to William Roades, 3 Feb. 1655).

[156] Cf. the charity of William Sheppard of Heydon (Essex) discussed in Ch. 2.4 (above).

[157] Tate, *The Parish Chest*, 116.

[158] HALS, D/P23/8/1, unfol.

[159] G. R. Elton, 'Reform by Statute: Thomas Starkey's Dialogue and Thomas Cromwell's Policy', repr. in Elton, *Studies*, ii. 252, notes a policy paper sent to Cromwell suggesting the prevention of the marriages of young men until they were of 'potent age'. D. M. Dean, *Law-Making and Society in Late Elizabethan England: The Parliament of England, 1584–1601* (Cambridge, 1996), 184–5, reports an abortive bill to prevent 'sundry great abuses by licenses for marriages without banes' in the parliamentary session of 1597–8.

even that they genuinely bore Alice Cheeseman 'goodwill and affection'. These justifications, offered where unions looked expedient, disparate in age, or likely to involve young children, were almost certainly only the disingenuous 'public transcripts' of the rationale that underlay them: the desire to ease the parish burden. Third, it seems, those accused of moral lapses might in turn criticize these actions as part of their strategy of self-justification, telling the ecclesiastical authorities just exactly what they wanted to hear: that their honourable intentions had been frustrated by the hard-nosed decisions of others. Fourth, on those rare occasions when explicit references were made to the poor, immigrant, status of prospective spouses, the archival record brings us face to face with the 'social cleavage' between those who paid the poor rate (the 'other inhabitants' in whose behalf vestrymen spoke) and those who were considered likely to be a charge upon it.[160] Fifth, there is the vexed question of the identity of those objecting: just who was responsible for these decisions? The communal language used in these orders is ambiguous: (in Finchingfield) 'the townsmen', (in Terling) 'the parish', (in Upminster and in Frampton) 'the inhabitants', (in Stockton, in North Bradley, and in Adlington) 'the parishioners' were described as the authors of the policy. Such terminology implies that these decisions were made and executed consensually by the whole or the majority of the local community. But the language conceals as much as it reveals, perhaps as it was intended to. 'The parish' almost certainly denoted the vestrymen, just as 'the inhabitants' implied 'the best (or long-established) inhabitants'. In both cases, these labels referred to 'the notables of the parish concerned, in particular the ministers and parish officers'.[161] This scepticism is borne out both by one Canterbury deponent's reference to the 'counselling' of one would-be bride by 'the cheefest of the parish' and by the fact that the three men objecting to the Marten–Goodwin marriage in Frampton in 1654 were the most experienced officeholders in the parish, having four years' service as overseer and thirteen years' service as churchwarden between them. It is most tellingly confirmed, however, by the order of the town meeting at Swallowfield (Wiltshire) in 1596 that all vestrymen 'have an especyall care to speake to the mynyster to stay the maryage of such as wolde mary before they have a convenient house to lyve in according to their callynge'.[162] The use of the terms 'the parish' and 'the inhabitants' is therefore significant precisely because they represented an exclusive

[160] Levine and Wrightson, *Industrial Society*, 352.

[161] Wrightson and Levine, *Poverty and Piety*, 133.

[162] O'Hara, '"Ruled By My Friends"', 28; Hindle, 'Power, Poor Relief and Social Relations', *passim*; Hindle, 'Hierarchy and Community', 850 (article 20).

social institution (the structure of local office-holding) as an inclusive one.

Furthermore, of course, these prohibitions entailed personal costs for the couples involved, especially in those circumstances where the poor were inclined to marry (or remarry) as a means of survival, and to avoid being left alone.[163] Worse still, the objecting individuals and groups might employ sanctions which could make life very uncomfortable for any couple wanting to defy them. Presentment for incontinence, fornication, or clandestine marriage; desertion or separation; and the threat of destitution were the immediate consequences of the desire of the respective parishes to reduce the burdens on their poor rates. Cumulatively, the effect of such decisions on those of marriageable age who faced sanctions against their full adult membership of the community could be severe. In the Wiltshire village of Keevil, for example, a clutch of clandestine marriage cases involving poor cottagers and under-tenants in 1622 was provoked by a series of measures in the local manor court to restrict immigration and control sub-letting.[164] Social exclusion of this kind could also destabilize patterns of deference and paternalism. It was, after all, the inability to marry and settle in their own secure holdings that drove the poor husbandmen and servants of Oxfordshire to foment sedition on Enslow Hill in the long wet summer of 1596.[165]

The evidence for the inhibition of pauper marriage must, therefore, be interpreted in the context of what is known about migration, courtship, and marital opportunity among the poor. Gender-specific migration patterns, themselves the consequence of a diversified labour market, helped to produce skewed sex ratios in small, rural parishes where the pool of potential marriage partners was already tiny.[166] In some parishes, this pattern was evident by the early seventeenth century. The excess of female over male migrants in the Hampshire parish of Odiham, for example, provoked a ninefold increase in the proportion of exogamous

[163] M. Pelling, *The Common Lot: Sickness, Medical Occupations and the Urban Poor in Early Modern England* (Harlow, 1998), 147.

[164] Ingram, *Church Courts*, 215.

[165] J. Walter, 'A "Rising of the People"? The Oxfordshire Rising of 1596', *Past and Present*, 107 (1985), 90–143. See the theoretical discussion of the response patterns, including not only obedience and 'deferred gratification' but also deviance and rebellion, of those who lose out in systems where reproduction is subject to social control in Lesthaeghe, 'Social Control of Human Reproduction', 533–4.

[166] Kussmaul, *Servants in Husbandry*, 24–7; D. Souden, 'Migrants and the Population Structure of Later Seventeenth-Century Provincial Cities and Market Towns', in P. Clark (ed.), *The Transformation of English Provincial Towns, 1600–1800* (London, 1984), 150–61; D. Souden, '"East, West—Home's Best"? Regional Patterns of Migration in Early Modern England', in Clark and Souden (eds.), *Migration and Society*, 292–332.

marriages from 1.2 per cent (1601–20) to 10.1 per cent (1641–60). Moreover, at least 60 per cent of those coming in to the parish to marry were from within ten kilometres, usually from adjacent parishes.[167] Exogamous marriages were, therefore, increasingly likely, indeed necessary, in seventeenth-century England. In the predominantly agrarian Leicestershire village of Bottesford only 8 per cent of the 617 marriages celebrated in the period 1610–69 were entirely endogamous.[168] In the context of ambiguities in the poor laws, these marriage and migration patterns had profound implications. Only under the settlement legislation of 1662 did it become clear that women took the place of settlement of their husbands at marriage. Until then, the Elizabethan poor laws left considerable doubt among both newly-weds and parish officers about the precise demarcation of responsibility. The migrant poor and their (prospective) spouses were almost inevitably, therefore, seeking to reside in parishes which were already acutely sensitive to the problem of unchecked migration, and the consequent application of parochial sanctions evidently extended even to the frustration of their marriage plans.

The refusal to read, or the objection to, the marriage banns of the poor by the 'parishioners' or 'townsmen' might be read as a process of exclusion in which the representatives of the community ostracized, on behalf not only of those who paid the poor rate but also those who received it, those they considered guilty of imprudent and potentially burdensome marital behaviour. Historians are familiar enough with 'rough music' being applied to marital partners whose behaviour failed in various ways to live up to communal norms.[169] The prohibition of pauper marriages might be read as an institutional surrogate for such *charivari*, arguably a more effective strategy in solidifying the exclusions on which the policy of defending local 'arenas of distinctiveness' was to be built. Parochial endogamy might therefore be a crucial component of the 'idiom of solidarity' in seventeenth-century English communities.[170]

[167] B. Stapleton, 'Marriage, Migration and Mendicancy in a Pre-Industrial Community', in id. (ed.), *Conflict and Community in Southern England: Essays in the History of Rural and Urban Labour from Medieval to Modern Times* (Gloucester, 1992), 56, 62.

[168] D. Levine, *Family Formation in an Age of Nascent Capitalism* (New York, 1977), 39.

[169] Ingram, 'Reform of Popular Culture?'; M. Ingram, 'Ridings, Rough Music and Mocking Rhymes', in Reay (ed.), *Popular Culture*, 166–97. Thompson, *Customs in Common*, 454, notes the use of rough music against exogamous marriage.

[170] A. P. Cohen, 'Belonging: The Experience of Culture', in id. (ed.), *Belonging: Identity and Social Organisation in British Rural Cultures* (Manchester, 1982), 2; S. K. Phillips, 'Natives and Incomers: The Symbolism of Belonging in Muker Parish, North Yorkshire', repr. in M. Drake (ed.), *Time, Family and Community: Perspectives on Family and Community History* (Oxford, 1994), 234.

Rigorous control of marital opportunity was clearly, therefore, one strategy through which parishes sought to inhibit entitlement to poor relief. But how common was it? By its very nature, the practice has left few traces in ecclesiastical archives, leading those few historians who have noticed it at all to minimize both its scale and its significance.[171] It has been suggested, for instance, that 'the extent of these actions is very difficult to gauge', and that historians 'allied to the social control school' have shown disproportionate interest in the 'scattering of instances' of 'socially discriminating welfare-fund managers'.[172] This perspective ignores the fact that, for the most part, objections to marriage banns would have been made either behind the scenes in the vicarage or viva voce in the chancel, leaving no imprint in the historical record. Although others have recognized that objections must have been more widespread than surviving evidence suggests, they have chosen to downplay their implications. Even those who have recognized that 'such vetoes could obviously be effective, and that cases were clearly not uncommon, especially in parishes experiencing economic stresses', nonetheless insist that 'all this has to be kept in due proportion'. From this perspective, the significance of the practice is to be measured only in aggregate terms: if the inhibition of pauper marriage cannot explain 'the broad secular and regional trends in bastardy' then it can safely be relegated to the footnotes.[173] Some commentators have even been prepared to tolerate (perhaps even to condone) them, arguing that the 'complaisance of the authorities and the apparent heartlessness of the wealthier sections of parish society' are 'readily understandable'.[174]

Not all contemporaries would have concurred. Moralists were commenting on the practice as early as the 1620s. William Whateley noted in 1623 that the absolute denial of the right to marry on grounds of poverty contravened the Christian principle that marriage was lawful for all persons 'of what calling or condition soever'.[175] By the late seventeenth

[171] Thorough, though not exhaustive, searches of church court materials do not appear to have turned up any additional instances of the practice: Cressy, *Birth, Marriage and Death*, 312.

[172] R. M. Smith, 'Marriage Processes in the English Past: Some Continuities', in L. Bonfield *et al.* (eds.), *The World We Have Gained: Histories of Population and Social Structure* (Oxford, 1986), 73 n. 101; Smith, 'Charity, Self-Interest and Welfare: Reflections from Demographic and Family History', in M. Daunton (ed.), *Charity, Self-Interest and Welfare in the English Past* (London, 1996), 24.

[173] R. Adair, *Courtship, Illegitimacy and Marriage in Early Modern England* (Manchester, 1996), 138. Cf. Smith, 'Charity, Self-Interest and Welfare', 45 n. 3.

[174] M. Ingram, 'Spousals Litigation in the English Ecclesiastical Courts, *c.*1350–1640', in R. B. Outhwaite (ed.), *Marriage and Society: Studies in the Social History of Marriage* (London, 1981), 55–6; Ingram, *Church Courts*, 131.

[175] W. Whateley, *A Bride-Bush: or a Direction for Married Persons* (London, 1623), 175.

century, parochial vetoes were sufficiently common to attract the attention of ecclesiastical lawyers and economic and social projectors alike. John Johnson, rector of Cranbrook (Kent), noted that 'some parish officers have presum'd to forbid banns, because the parties have been poor, and like to create charge to the parish, or because the man has not been made an inhabitant according to the laws made for the settlement of the poor'.[176] Carew Reynel noted the 'custom in many country parishes, where they, as much as they can, hinder poor people from marrying'.[177] Sir William Coventry was concerned that 'the laws against cottages, inmates, etc. and the method of obliging poor people to give security to save the parish from charge before they are permitted to inhabit' were 'restraints' hindering the poor from marrying.[178] Dudley North believed that officers 'in defence of their parish from charges not only employ themselves to prevent new settlers, but use great care to prevent the mareage of those that they have, hindering all they can possibly the matching of young ones together'. He even imagined the likely justification for this 'industry to hinder mareage': '"Oh", say the churchwardens, "they will have more children than they can keep, and so increase the charge of the parish".'[179]

It is very significant that most surviving seventeenth-century criticism of the inhibition of the marriages of the poor originates after the Restoration. Just occasionally, clergymen might still voice support for the policy: thus Parson Butterfield of Middle Claydon (Buckinghamshire) regretted in 1695 that 'nobody has been so kind as to forbid the banns' between Jack Butcher and Mrs Verney's dairymaid, and feared the material consequences of their improvidence should no parishioner suddenly 'interpose'.[180] For the most part, however, there was widespread and outspoken opposition to these vetoes. By this time, of course, population pressure in most rural communities had eased, and the settlement laws had begun to clarify the extent of parochial responsibilities. The late seventeenth-century polemic must therefore be set in the context of the transformation of attitudes in a period of demographic

[176] J. Johnson, *The Clergy-man's Vade Mecum* (London, 1709), 186.

[177] C. Reynel, *The True English Interest* (1674), repr. in *Seventeenth-Century Economic Documents*, ed. J. Thirsk and J. P. Cooper (Oxford, 1972), 760.

[178] W. Coventry, 'An Essay Concerning the Decay of Rents and their Remedies' (*c.*1670), repr. in *Seventeenth-Century Economic Documents*, 80.

[179] D. North, 'Some Notes Concerning the Laws for the Poor', in BL, MS Additional, 32512, fo. 128^{v}.

[180] Claydon House, Buckinghamshire, MS Verney, 4/5/48 (William Butterfield to Sir Ralph Verney, 31 Mar. 1695). For the context, see J. Broad, 'Parish Economies of Welfare, 1650–1834', *Historical Journal*, 42 (1999), 993–4.

stagnation. After all, 'the most significant change of opinion about the poor was the replacement of concern about overpopulation at the beginning of the [seventeenth] century with fears about a possible loss of people at the end'.[181] By the 1670s, it was felt that marriage should be encouraged in order to foster demographic growth and (in turn) an increase in national prosperity. Thus for Dudley North 'plenty of people is the cheefest riches of a kingdom'.[182] Sir William Coventry argued that 'encouraging our own people to marry' was a means 'to mend our domestic vent by the increasing of our people'.[183] Others identified the poor as the natural constituency from which national prosperity must emerge. John Johnson argued that 'poverty is no more an impediment of marriage than riches, and the kingdom can no more subsist without poor than without rich'.[184] Carew Reynel suggested not only that 'countenancing marriage' was 'the very origin of the well being and continuance of nations', upon which 'property, families and civil government depends, also trade, riches, populacy; and without this a nation crumbles to nothing', but that 'poor people were the stock and seminary of the kingdom', whose 'marrying apace' ought 'to get a laborious hardy generation, which is best for a nation'.[185] This mercantilist critique crystallized in the debates over the passage of the marriage duty act of 1695. Political arithmeticians and projectors alike advocated the taxing of the unmarried for their neglect of the civic responsibility of childrearing. In practice, however, although parish pensioners were exempt from the marriage tax (incidentally leading to the explicit recording of their marriages in some parish registers), the labouring poor fell within its terms, provoking Charles Davenant to observe in 1699 that 'they who look into all the different ranks of men are well satisfied that this duty on marriages and births is a very grievous burden upon the poorer sort'. Although the marriage duty act almost certainly created an incentive for unmarried men to marry, some contemporaries evidently felt that it amounted to a tax on the marital bed.[186] The mercantilist argument did not, of course, persuade

[181] J. O. Appleby, *Economic Thought and Ideology in Seventeenth-Century England* (Princeton, 1978), 135.

[182] BL, MS Additional, 32512, fo. 128v.

[183] Coventry, 'Decay of Rents', 80.

[184] Johnson, *Clergy Man's Vade Mecum*, 186.

[185] Reynel, *True English Interest*, 760.

[186] C. Brooks, 'Projecting, Political Arithmetic and the Act of 1695', *English Historical Review*, 87 (1982), 39; J. Boulton, 'The Marriage Duty Act and Parochial Registration in London, 1695–1706', in K. Schurer and T. Arkell (eds.), *Surveying the People: The Interpretation of Document Sources for the Study of Population in the Later Seventeenth Century* (Oxford, 1992), 227; C. Davenant, *Works*, ed. C. Whitworth (5 vols., London, 1771), ii. 190–1; *London Inhabitants within the Walls, 1695*, ed. D. V. Glass (London Record Society, 2, London, 1966), pp. xiv–xv. Cf. E. A. Wrigley *et al.*, *English Population History from Family Reconstitution, 1580–1837* (Cambridge, 1997), 139.

everybody, especially those who feared that they would pay the local consequences of the national encouragement of fertility. Thus Parson Butterfield of Middle Claydon wrote in 1671 that 'those that are like to multiply may do it for the King, but not for Middle Claydon'.[187]

Hostility to the prevention of the marriages of the poor was not, however, justified exclusively on mercantilist grounds. Criticism also arose where the demeanour of those objecting to the banns was particularly offensive. Clergymen in particular had to ensure that their procedure in the calling of the banns fell within the terms of canon law. That they did not always succeed is suggested by the presentment in 1636 of William Jackson, rector of North Ockenden (Essex), for departing from the canonical formula when, 'in asking the banes of a poore cupple', he 'signified to the parishe that "they would marry and goe a begging together"', and asked '"yf anie knewe lawfull cause why they might not so doe", which gave great offence to the parties and to others'.[188] Jackson had obviously failed to carry parochial opinion with him, and his open invitation to the making of an illegal objection lacked subtlety to say the very least. Only in such exceptional circumstances did the ecclesiastical courts seek to halt the practice, for there is little evidence that ministers were prosecuted.[189] Nonetheless, the Restoration commentators also drew attention to its local social implications. Reynel implied that inhibiting marriage only encouraged the poor to commit the vices of fornication or cohabitation.[190] Coventry advocated the reduction of poor rates ('easing the parish') not by regulating marriage but by building workhouses which would drive down wages by 'banishing laziness in the poor'.[191] Johnson attacked the idea that 'temporal laws relating to the poor were intended to alter the laws of the church', and insisted that 'no person has authority to forbid the minister to proceed in publishing the banns'. 'The curate', he argued, 'is not to stop his proceeding because any peevish or pragmatical person without just reason or authority pretends to forbid him.' Indeed, he saw 'no reason to doubt but that banns may be published and marriage solemnised betwixt two persons that do at present abide or sojourn within a parish, tho' they be not fixed inhabitants, according to the acts for the settling of the poor'. He was prepared

[187] Claydon House, Buckinghamshire, MS Verney, 4/5/23 (Edward Butterfield to Sir Ralph Verney, 6 Feb. 1671). See Broad, 'Parish Economies of Welfare', 993.

[188] W. J. Pressey, 'Essex Affairs Matrimonial (as Seen in the Archdeaconry Records)', *Essex Review*, 49 (1940), 86.

[189] Ingram, 'Spousals Litigation', 56; Ingram, *Church Courts*, 131.

[190] Reynel, *True English Interest*, 760.

[191] Coventry, 'Decay of Rents', 80.

to concede only that, 'for cautions sake, the minister in publishing the banns may say, *N* of this parish, sojourner'.[192] Dudley North went further, emphasizing the deviousness of officers in circumventing ecclesiastical law. Marriages were inhibited, he argued, 'by judicial meanes however the occasion is given by the law, and when the consequence toucheth the pocket means will be found out right or wrong', a practice which, in tandem with the provisions of the settlement laws, reduced 'the poor inhabitants' to a condition 'little better than slaves', rendering them vulnerable to the danger 'of being sent home with the whipp at their backs'.[193] Despite the attempts of modern historians to whitewash the practice, therefore, the peevishness and pragmatism of some parish officers is well attested in the contemporary polemic.

Marriage, then, was not merely a rite of passage subject to economic, ideological, or even cultural influences, it was also a social process vulnerable to institutional and political sanctions. The broader factors affecting vestry decisions self-evidently require further investigation. Economic fears of unregulated immigration might be crucial, but there might also be ideological and cultural factors at work in answering the question 'Who is my neighbour'? Thresholds of tolerance might differ from community to community, but in each there was not only a 'continuum' but also a 'hierarchy' of belonging.[194] The recognition of the right to belong implied decision-making by parish officers, acting on behalf not only of ratepayers, but also of the ancient poor whose interest might suffer through the overburdening of rates. These decisions must therefore be understood less in terms of impersonal forces than in terms of power and of experience. It has recently been argued that 'the local financing of poor relief gave English property owners, individually and collectively, a direct pecuniary interest in ensuring that the parish's demographic and economic development was balanced'.[195] This judgement, euphemistically expressed as it is, recognizes the significance of social welfare institutions in regulating social and economic life in early modern England, yet at the same time entirely fails to recapture the human experience, the heartbreak and the humiliation, which that regulation implied.

[192] Johnson, *Clergy-man's Vade Mecum*, 186–7.

[193] BL, MS Additional, 32512, fos. 128^{r-v}.

[194] K. Wrightson, 'The Politics of the Parish in Early Modern England', in P. Griffiths *et al.* (eds.), *The Experience of Authority in Early Modern England* (London and New York, 1996), 19.

[195] P. M. Solar, 'Poor Relief and English Economic Development before the Industrial Revolution', *Economic History Review*, 2nd ser., 48 (1995), 16.

5. CONCLUSION: THE POLITICS OF BELONGING

The sensitive nature of the micro-politics of belonging is nowhere more apparent than in the series of 'cases for the judges' drawn up in 1633.[196] As might be expected, concerns about the practical application of the poor laws with respect to vagrancy (queries 8–10), to the regulation of alehouses (query 11), and to illegitimacy (queries 12–14) loom large. Given the centrality of the binding out of pauper apprentices to Elizabethan social welfare provision, it is unsurprising that four of the queries (nos. 3–7) should turn on question of liability to take the children of the poor. Right at the top of the list, however, were two queries that vividly illustrate the tensions over migration, settlement, and belonging which had become ubiquitous in the early years of the administration of poor relief. The unidentified magistrates who composed them were obviously familiar with the exclusion crises and marriage prohibitions that had been practised by parish officers across numerous local communities in the early years of the century. In the first place, they noted 'the number of poore marryed persons increasing yearly in every town' and asked whether 'by consent of the towne they may not be placed as inmates [in other houses] there being noe auncient dwelling house to be hired?'[197] In the second, they envisaged a situation in which 'one letteth his tenement to a stranger like to burden the town' and wondered 'how the towne [may] helpe themselves?'.

The judges' answers to these queries have not, sadly, survived. But in the light of the foregoing discussion it is possible to identify several of the variables that might have influenced the decision-making process within those parishes that were confronted by these problems. The most significant of them are social relations between parishes; social relations within them; the nature of the local and regional economy; and the relative influence of ratepayers, landlords, parish officers, and clergymen. Although none of these factors can justifiably be treated independently of the others, the following discussion will deal with each of them in turn.

In one sense, exclusion crises demonstrate the extraordinary hostility of social relations between parishes. Wherever vestrymen (sometimes aided and abetted by ministers) used formal and informal means to exclude poor immigrants from full membership of rural communities,

[196] NA, SP16/255/48, printed in *Somerset Assize Orders, 1629–40*, 71 (no. 188). These queries were drawn up simultaneously with, but are not identical to, the questions which prompted the more famous 'resolutions of the judges' of 1633. Cf. Ch. 3.2(*b*) above and Ch. 6.4(*b*) below.

[197] In effect this was a reformulation of the dilemma posed in the celebrated case of Laysters *vs.* Kimbolton. Cf. Ch. 5.2 above.

they reveal the extent to which parochial responsibility for social welfare had strengthened the common interests of all the settled residents, irrespective of inequalities of wealth and status. Both ratepayers and pensioners might see the advantages of an assiduous defence of parish boundaries, regarding the rental market as an arena of conflict between residents and 'foreigners', and the policing of inmates as a perfectly desirable form of social regulation. Indeed, it is implicit in the Elizabethan legislation that the successful administration of parish relief depended upon the exclusion of outsiders. Ratepayers must show common cause against the idle families of casual thieves and beggars who sought to thrust themselves into the parish, against the nefarious vestrymen of neighbouring communities who schemed to place poor tenants in parish tenements, and especially against those who married young in order to infiltrate parish charities.

That such strategies of exclusion often failed, however, raises questions not only about relations *between* parish communities, but also about relations *within* them. Although the misery of overburdened parishioners partly originated with the poor strangers who had crept amongst them, it must also be laid at the doors of those grasping ratepayers who simply accepted tenants of any kind in the full knowledge that they would in all probability prove to be a parish charge. Such attitudes were both inimical to neighbourly relations and prejudicial to the interests not only of current and future ratepayers, but also ultimately to those of the ancient settled poor. In attempting to analyse the internal patterns of conflict over the taking of inmates, a great deal more must therefore be learned about the relative costs of the poor rate among householders and chief inhabitants. Further analysis of rating disputes might illuminate the factors at play in landlords' assessments of likely outcomes, especially their self-evident confidence in their own ability to bear increased rate charges out of augmented rental income. In turn, investigation of the social and economic profile of the hierarchy of poor-rate payers might be used to explain the apparent determination of larger landholders to exploit the opportunities for augmenting their income by taking inmates and the corresponding diversification of risk amongst those with less land and property.[198] Such research will probably serve less to resolve than to complicate questions of membership and identity in rural parishes, but in

[198] Beier, 'Social Problems of an Elizabethan Country Town', 61, suggests, conversely, that the *poorer* tenants were the most likely to take inmates in Warwick, perhaps in itself a measure of their desperation. In 1615 four Hertfordshire individuals charged with erecting illegal cottages under the 1589 act were discharged because of their poverty. HALS, HAT/SR26/217–20; 9/50; 27/151. For analysis of rating disputes, see Ch. 6.1 below.

doing so its achievement (not to say its responsibility) will be to identify the fluidity and conflict which were inherent in the workings of these 'communities', challenging the supposed solidity of the orthodox understanding of the workings of the poor law and its interaction with local society.

Foremost among the variables which must be taken into account in analysing this interaction is the nature of the local and regional economy. If the policing of inmates amounted to a failed project of social discipline, it was not simply because community constraints in England 'were less direct and less effectively imposed upon a highly differentiated population within which geographical mobility and marital exogamy among adolescents and young adults were of long standing'.[199] However valid this caution against pan-European models of the 'reform of popular culture', it surely fails to take account of the immense local and regional variations *within* the English context. In Elizabethan and early Stuart Havering (Essex), for example, the flexible conditions of employment, in which the requirement of a fixed term of service was commonly ignored, made it possible for newcomers to find work with ease.[200] Similarly, the highly specialized work in building and agriculture afforded in the multi-faceted sheep-corn economy of Stiffkey (Norfolk) encouraged labouring families into work strategies and complex patterns of co-residence unmolested by manorial or judicial authority. Substantially more than half the families in the parish, the vast majority of them landless or near-landless labourers, lived in some sort of shared or divided property, in most cases unrelated by blood or marriage to those with whom they lodged.[201] By contrast, although Layston and its adjacent parishes included both a market town and its rural hinterland, their occupational structure, like those of the vast majority of Hertfordshire parishes, remained overwhelmingly agricultural. The embryonic Hertfordshire cloth industry, which had sprung up in the landscape of hamlets and isolated farms east of Royston, Buntingford, and Ware in the fifteenth century, had 'died a mysterious death in the early sixteenth'.[202] By the 1630s, Hertfordshire was part of a corn-growing region which could secure employment for its labourers only seasonally, predominantly at

[199] Smith, 'Marriage Processes', 97.

[200] M. K. McIntosh, *A Community Transformed: The Manor and Liberty of Havering, 1500–1620* (Cambridge, 1991), 26.

[201] A. Hassell Smith, 'Labourers in Late Sixteenth-Century England: A Case Study from North Norfolk, Part I', *Continuity and Change*, 4 (1989), 373–4.

[202] J. Thirsk, 'Industries in the Countryside', in F. J. Fisher (ed.), *Essays in the Economic and Social History of Tudor and Stuart England in Honour of R. H. Tawney* (Cambridge, 1961), 72.

harvest time. This was apparent to the inhabitants themselves, who had protested to the privy council in 1618 that 'the county of Hertford doth consist for the most part of tillage, it hath better meanes to sett their poor children on worke without this new invention [the Crown's attempt to establish the New Draperies in the county] then some other counties, vizt. by imploieing the female children in picking of their wheat a great part of the yeare and the male children by strayning before their ploughes in seedtyme and other necessarye occasions of husbandrye'.[203]

Local economic circumstances were, therefore, crucial. The calculus employed by parish officers involved the striking of a balance between, on the one hand, a large supply of labour, low wages, and high poor rates and, on the other, a controlled labour supply, higher wages, and low poor rates.[204] The nature of this balance depended on the needs of the local labour market, with more tolerant, even encouraging, attitudes towards immigration prevailing with respect to blacksmiths, wheelwrights, or other artisans, or to apprentices in trades which might replenish local skills. In Rawreth (Essex) in 1615, for example, the chief inhabitants pleaded that an indictment for taking an inmate be withdrawn on the grounds that the man was 'an exceeding honest and painful labourer and that the parish (having few or none such within it) had great need of him'.[205] Indeed, the preferential (though often historically invisible) terms of settlement offered to craftsmen sit comfortably with what is known about the curiously skewed networks woven by inter-parochial strategies for apprenticing the young and relieving the old alike. Overseers might act as the roving officers of the parish, forging friendly contacts with the vestries of neighbouring parishes in the hope of arranging mutually satisfactory arrangements without incurring the expense of litigation.[206] Even largely arable parishes, therefore, could sometimes incorporate strangers in the light of demographic circumstances and perceived economic need. Inclusion, however, was likely to be much more common in the industrious cottage economies of pastoral England, dependent as they were on the contributions of women and children.

[203] NA, SP14/96/39. For the new draperies in Hertfordshire, see Zell, '"Setting the Poor on Work"'; H. Falvey, 'Crown Policy and Local Economic Context in the Berkhamsted Common Enclosure Dispute, 1618–42', *Rural History*, 12 (2001), 141.

[204] Cf. Wrightson and Levine, *Poverty and Piety*, 69–72; Levine, *Family Formation*, 121; and D. Levine, *Reproducing Families: The Political Economy of English Population History* (Cambridge, 1987), 38–93.

[205] ERO, Q/SR209/103.

[206] For examples from late 17th-century Kent, see M. Barker-Read, 'The Treatment of the Aged Poor in Five Selected West Kent Parishes from Settlement to Speenhamland, 1662–1797' (unpublished Ph.D. thesis, Open University, 1988), 64–5.

Migration was tolerated, even encouraged, in the textile areas of Leicestershire and Gloucestershire, and the policing of inmates might, at least in times of prosperity, be practically a dead letter. By the late eighteenth century, the granting of relief to those who were settled *even if they were non-resident* oiled the wheels of the labour market in industrializing areas, successfully 'negotiating the Scylla of immobility and the Charybdis of unchecked migration'. Even in heavily industrialized areas, however, the insecurities of proletarian existence might lead parish officers to guard their ratepayers against seasonal underemployment.[207]

Parish officers also, however, had to take account of the interests of their fellow ratepayers and landlords. In both arable and proto-industrial contexts, ratepayers in their capacity as landlords might add other elements, especially rental income, to the equation. While parish officers might seek low poor rates through resisting the immigration of the poor, landlords apparently decided that short-term increases in rental income, together with the additional demand for agricultural labour at harvest time, justified the taking of inmates.[208] These calculations were, crucially, complicated by the fact that the economic influence of local landlords was not necessarily coextensive with parochial jurisdiction. Neighbouring vestries might use their members' propertied interests in 'foreign communities' as secret weapons in the cold war between well-defended parishes. Some parishes could not adequately defend themselves against immigration partly because of the complex nature of the local property market.[209]

All this, of course, is to ignore the level of desperation amongst both the settled and migrant poor themselves, especially in the late sixteenth and early seventeenth centuries. In 1587, nearly a quarter of the households of parish pensioners in Warwick had inmates, and 45 per cent of those who received collection either were inmates or lived in households containing inmates.[210] Such arrangements were bound to be makeshift, and their disintegration contributed both to vagrancy and (in turn) to that

[207] Levine, *Family Formation*, 58–102; J. de Vries, 'The Industrial Revolution and the Industrious Revolution', *Journal of Economic History*, 54 (1994), 249–70; J. S. Taylor, 'A Different Kind of Speenhamland: Non-Resident Relief in the Industrial Revolution', *Journal of British Studies*, 30 (1991), 208. For seasonal unemployment in mining, see Levine and Wrightson, *Industrial Society*, 250–63.

[208] For the suggestion that rents might be an issue in attitudes towards labour mobility in the 18th century, see Thompson, *Customs in Common*, 287–8.

[209] Cf. the view that the felt need for co-operative effort in addressing mutual problems is likely to be greatest where 'all members have a stake in the village economy'. G. McNicoll, 'Institutional Determinants of Fertility Change', *Population and Development Review*, 6 (1980), 452.

[210] Beier, 'Social Problems of an Elizabethan Country Town', 61.

special willingness to prosecute migrants and outsiders which was so characteristic of rural communities.[211] The frequent inability of parish officers to exclude poor strangers therefore reveals some unresolved complexities in attitudes towards immigration. Overseers and constables can, of course, frequently be found exercising discretion with respect to outsiders. The personal disposition of the officer may have been significant here, as in the case of William Isard, constable of Thundridge (Hertfordshire) in 1623, who 'seeing John Evans, a vagrant and vagabond, relieved him and allowed him to depart with impunity'.[212] Such apparent laxity is partly to be explained by the fact that Thundridge lay on Ermine Street, a busy thoroughfare along which the constables were probably only too keen to allow (even to encourage) migrants to pass. Indeed, the payments made to the 768 travellers of various categories who travelled through Thundridge over a nineteen-month period in 1651–3 accounted for over 54 per cent of recorded village expenditure.[213] But this willingness to hurry poor strangers across the parish boundary, often with financial assistance, suggests that parish officers made systematic distinctions in their application of the laws relating to vagrants, prioritizing the protection of the parish above the logic of exemplary punishment. 'Neare dwellers' who came in search of alms, work, or shelter might be tolerated, when those from further afield were whipped home without hesitation.[214] Such discrimination subsequently found expression in the curious reciprocity between some parishes in the application of the settlement laws, and almost certainly informed attitudes towards the taking of inmates. Even where the demands of the labour market were a crucial consideration in determining attitudes to outsiders, moreover, the extraordinary seasonality of harvest work, especially in communities structured around nuclear family households, complicated rather than simplified the calculus employed by parish officers.

More generally, it seems, historians have underestimated the sheer difficulty experienced by parish constables in identifying potentially burdensome migrants, especially since the 'attributes of vagrancy were less those of a sub-culture than those of the popular culture itself'.[215] The frequent assumption that the poor were easily identified on the basis of

[211] For an analysis of these trends in Hertfordshire in the years 1559–1624, see Lawson, 'Property Crime and Hard Times', 122–6.

[212] *Hertford County Records*, v. 34.

[213] *A Nottinghamshire Village in War and Peace: The Accounts of the Constables of Upton 1640–1666*, ed. M. Bennett (Thoroton Society Record Series, 39, Nottingham, 1995), p. xxvii.

[214] NA, SP16/197/13.

[215] A point made very forcefully by R. A. Houston, 'Vagrants and Society in Early Modern England', *Cambridge Anthropology* (1980), 25.

their self-evident need is belied by the rapidly developing historiographical awareness of the life-cyclical nature of poverty.[216] Given that recently married couples with young families were highly likely to become dependent on parish support, it is unsurprising that the exclusion of those who married young should be a decisive social drama in the continuous narrative of adjustment between parochial responsibilities, community norms, popular expectations, and scant resources. From this point of view, successful judgements about potential indigence must have been extraordinarily difficult to make.

Finally, the identification of the parish minister as moral conscience of his community raises the question of the role of clergymen in the micro-politics of exclusion. Some ministers were absentees and others were doubtless preoccupied with less worldly matters. The sheer force of personality of figures like Alexander Strange in Layston, Samuel Cony in Frampton (Lincolnshire), Stephen Marshall in Finchingfield (Essex), or Thomas Weld in Terling (Essex) nonetheless suggests that clerical participation in vestries might be significant, if not always decisive.[217] Such men tried to communicate to their parishioners their vision of an ideal society. For them, the parish was a little commonwealth, a community permeated by a 'culturally determined moral economy', in which reciprocal obligations between the individual and society conditioned the attitudes and behaviour of rich and poor alike.[218] This ideal found its origins in the commonwealth thinkers of the sixteenth century and extended even to Malthus in the late eighteenth, since both Christian humanists and political economists regarded the irresponsible practices and attitudes of the poor as inimical to the interests of their fellow labourers, and thus to the communities in which they lived. Clergymen, like parish officers, stood in the mainstream of this current of English political culture, their experience (and sometimes their frustration) testifying to both the complexity of the economic problems with which they were faced and the limits of clerical charisma. Where clergymen failed to defend the interests of the poor of the parish, they feared the corrosion of communal values.

[216] Wales, 'Poverty, Poor Relief and the Life-Cycle'; and Newman-Brown, 'Poor Relief and Family Situation'.

[217] For Cony, see Hindle, 'Power, Poor Relief and Social Relations', 90–1; for Marshall, see Tom Webster, *Stephen Marshall and Finchingfield* (Studies in Essex History, 6, 1994); and for Weld, see Wrightson and Levine, *Poverty and Piety*, esp. 137–9, 159–61, 179–80.

[218] Smith, 'Fertility, Economy and Household Formation', 618. Cf. R. M. Smith, 'Transfer Incomes, Risk and Security: The Roles of the Family and the Collectivity in Recent Theories of Fertility Change', in D. Coleman and R. Schofield (eds.), *The State of Population Theory: Forward from Malthus* (Oxford, 1986), 191.

The diagnosis of the pathology of the parish offered by overseers and clergymen alike should not, of course, necessarily be accepted at face value. However much parish officers sought to portray them as such, the motives of those who took inmates were not always those of covetousness, as the philanthropic practices of those who, like Richard Haynes of the Hertfordshire parish of Much Hadham, offered succour to the migrant poor out of pity and compassion suggest.[219] Inmates might be harboured for religious or humanitarian reasons, or even out of curiosity. In some respects, the taking of inmates for income or labour might be seen as yet another expedient survival strategy in the makeshift economy of the poor. It was not coincidental that, when 'the poor shed children' under the pressure of the drive for pauper apprenticeship, they simultaneously 'took in lodgers'.[220] Parish officers and magistrates seldom, however, made reference to this impulse, and even where they did they were hardly inclined to be sympathetic, revealing their incomprehension of the attitudes the poor themselves might display towards the accommodation not only of strangers but also of their own offspring. Among the poor, therefore, knowledge of the discourses and practices of parish officers and magistrates was essential to survival; for the propertied, such genuine social understanding of the poor was a luxury, requiring insight beyond the traditional though resonant alarms about the many-headed monster.[221] Limited as their empathetic skills may have been with respect to the poor, however, it is clear that magistrates and vestrymen understood the priorities of the middling sort all too well. They knew that in the politics which governed the accommodation and exclusion of strangers their communities were being tested, at their margins, where communities are always tested (and new social identities forged), and found wanting.[222]

[219] Rickman, 'Much Hadham', 304–12. Cf. I. K. Ben-Amos, '"Good Works" and Social Ties: Helping the Migrant Poor in Early Modern England', in Muriel C. McClendon *et al.* (eds.), *Protestant Identities: Religion, Society and Self-Fashioning in Post-Reformation England* (Stanford, 1999), 125–40.

[220] Beier, 'Social Problems of an Elizabethan Country Town', 61.

[221] Cf. P. Mandler, 'Poverty and Charity in the Nineteenth-Century Metropolis: An Introduction', in id. (ed.), *The Uses of Charity: The Poor on Relief in the Nineteenth-Century Metropolis* (Philadelphia, 1990), 1; C. Hill, 'The Many Headed Monster in Late Tudor and Early Stuart Political Thinking', repr. in id., *Change and Continuity in Seventeenth-Century England* (rev. edn., New Haven, 1991), 181–204.

[222] If 'the extent of risk-sharing across social class boundaries is a good measure of the degree of social integration' within a community, the implications for the failure of parochial constraint for our understanding of early modern social relations are profound. Lesthaeghe, 'Social Control', 532.

6
Negotiation

To the Honourable Her Majestyes Justices of the Peace for the County of Cumberland

The Humble petition of Ann Bowman a pore widdowe in the parish and lordship of Kirkoswald

Sheweth that the orders and warrants you were pleased to grant for my relief have proved wholly ineffectuall through the stubbornness of the overseers who will neither give me any support nor reckon with me. But such persons as either trust or sell me anything are thretned for it and the boatman who sets me over the water is threatened and misused for it. So that as feeble as I am, yet am compelled to go by the bridges [over the River Eden]. I am reduced to the greatest extremity for those who ventured to lend me anything upon the credit of your order are discouraged from helping me anymore fearing that they will . . . My goods that I have layd to pawn for bread will not be restored to me against winter unless I have money to loose them with. In this poor desolate starving condition I humbly implore your help and assistance of your authority, and your petitioner shall ever pray . . .

To be paid 6d a week since Easter sessions last and pay her 6d weekly for the future she wearing a badge.

Petition and order at the Cumberland quarter sessions, Michaelmas 1710[1]

It is, perhaps, unsurprising that the thresholds of belonging to the community of the parish should lie between the ancient settled poor and indigent migrants. It is nonetheless clear that even long-standing residents sometimes found it difficult to secure access to the circuits of welfare. Indeed, Ann Bowman's petition, and the order of the Cumberland bench which it provoked, is a classic example of the negotiations that regularly took place over the distribution of poor relief in seventeenth-

[1] CRO, Q/11/1/97/7. The Bowman family's battle with the Kirkoswald overseers 1694–1719 can be traced in CRO, Q/11/1/26/31, 27/3, 31/2, 31/28, 73/27, 81/12, 88/9, 96/25, 97/20, 99/28, 136/11.

and early eighteenth-century rural communities. An elderly widow who might be expected to have been regarded by the parish officers as an 'object of charity' alleged not only that the overseers had stood in contempt of previous relief orders, but that they refused to 'reckon' with her and intimidated those of her neighbours who were sufficiently sympathetic to relieve her in her need. Her petition succeeded in mobilizing the support of the county magistrates, who insisted that arrears be paid and relief continued, but their 'paternalism' came at a price. Ann Bowman's victory was pyrrhic, for she won her pension only if she and her children agreed to acknowledge publicly their dependency by wearing the cloth badge, 'KP' for Kirkoswald Parish, so long as they received relief.

In exploring the significance of such negotiations, students of social welfare might learn much from those historians of rural communities who have recently begun to plumb the 'social depth of politics'.[2] Indeed, 'there was a complex local politics in the administration of the poor laws which has not yet been fully explored'.[3] In this respect, investigation of the politics of welfare has lagged well behind that of the politics of several other spheres of the local community Those who have begun to reconstruct customary consciousness in early modern England, for instance, have revealed the resonant political language with which economically marginal groups legitimated their acts of defiance.[4] The historiography of riot is also increasingly preoccupied with reconstructing not only the contours, but also the content, of popular political culture.[5] Much of this burgeoning literature, however, continues to employ—sometimes self-consciously so—traditional, bi-polar models of social, political, and (above all) economic relationships: patrician and plebeian; governors and governed; propertied and propertyless.[6] Even those historians who have, rather belatedly, (re-)discovered the existence and significance of the 'middling sort' of people tend to underestimate the extent to which eco-

[2] For the clarion call to plumb the 'social depth of politics', see P. Collinson, '*De Republica Anglorum*: Or History with the Politics Put Back', in id., *Elizabethan Essays* (London, 1994), 1–30. For an early response, attempting to conceptualize micro-politics see K. Wrightson, 'The Politics of the Parish in Early Modern England', in P. Griffiths *et al.* (eds.), *The Experience of Authority in Early Modern England* (London, 1996), 10–46.

[3] Wrightson, 'The Politics of the Parish', 22.

[4] E. Thompson, *Customs in Common* (London, 1991), 1–184; J. M. Neeson, *Commoners: Common Right, Enclosure and Social Change in England, 1700–1820* (Cambridge, 1993), 259–93; A. Wood, *The Politics of Social Conflict: The Peak Country, 1520–1770* (Cambridge, 1999), 203–325.

[5] J. Walter, *Understanding Popular Violence in the English Revolution: The Colchester Plunderers* (Cambridge, 1999), 235–330. Cf. D. Underdown, *Revel, Riot and Rebellion: Popular Politics and Culture in England, 1603–1660* (Oxford, 1985), 73–239.

[6] The classic example is Thompson, *Customs in Common*, 16–96. But similar assumptions also underpin Neeson, *Commoners*, and Wood, *The Politics of Social Conflict*.

nomic inequality was relative rather than absolute.[7] Although the social order contained recognisable 'clusters', it was nonetheless relatively finely graded.[8] This insight is of fundamental significance for the reconstruction of the local politics of welfare, for it suggests, that although contemporaries often applied the blanket labels of the 'language of sorts' to subordinate or marginal groups, they invariably did so in defiance of the complex realities of economic differentiation.[9]

This chapter reconstructs the micro-politics at play in the assessment and disbursement of parish relief. In doing so, it both emphasizes the complexity and ambiguity of the relationships between the various participants—the labouring poor, the parish officers, the county magistrates, the itinerant judiciary—in the 'welfare process' and argues that this process involved protracted and often antagonistic negotiations between and among the sectional interests who had a stake in the allocation of resources in the local community. It also critiques two of the most popular paradigms in the current historiography of social welfare, which has recently (and somewhat artificially) become polarized between emphases on entitlement on the one hand and subordination on the other. Those who have been optimistic about the popular acculturation of the 'right' to poor relief have generally followed Richard Smith and Tim Wales in emphasizing the life-cyclical character of poverty and poor relief in the seventeenth century and William Newman-Brown in characterizing the moral ethos of poor law administration as 'benevolent and sympathetic'.[10] These interpretations became influential in the mid-1980s partly

[7] For the 18th-century perspective, see P. King, 'Edward Thompson's Contribution to Eighteenth-Century Studies: The Patrician–Plebeian Model Re-examined', *Social History*, 21 (1996), 215–28. The literature on the middling sort in early modern urban society is proliferating. Useful introductions are provided by the essays in J. Barry and C. Brooks (eds.), *The Middling Sort of People: Culture, Society and Politics in England, 1550–1800* (London and New York, 1994). For middling groups in rural society, see J. R. Kent, 'The Rural "Middling Sort" in Early Modern England, *circa* 1640–1740: Some Economic, Political and Socio-Cultural Characteristics', *Rural History*, 10 (1999), 19–54; H. R. French, '"Ingenious and Learned Gentlemen": Social Perceptions and Self-Fashioning among Parish Elites in Essex, 1680–1740', *Social History*, 25 (2000), 44–66; French, 'Social Status, Localism and the "Middle Sort of People" in England, 1620–1750', *Past and Present*, 166 (2000), 66–99; and S. Hindle, *The State and Social Change in Early Modern England, c.1550–1640* (London and New York, 2000), 204–30.

[8] K. Wrightson, 'The Social Order of Early Modern England: Three Approaches', in L. Bonfield *et al.* (eds.), *The World We Have Gained: Histories of Population and Social Structure* (Oxford, 1986), esp. 190–1.

[9] K. Wrightson, 'Estates, Degrees and Sorts: Changing Perceptions of Society in Tudor and Stuart England', in P. J. Corfield (ed.), *Language, History and Class* (Oxford, 1991), 30–52.

[10] R. M. Smith, 'Some Issues Concerning Families and their Property in Rural England, 1250–1800', T. Wales, 'Poverty, Poor Relief and the Life-Cycle: Some Evidence from Seventeenth-Century Norfolk', and W. Newman-Brown, 'The Receipt of Poor Relief and

as a reaction against the 'social control' paradigm that had characterized earlier approaches to the subject. Christopher Hill's reading of the relationship between 'the poor and the parish' was predicated on the notion that the 'apparent severity' of what he calls 'the new attitude towards charity' arose not merely from 'simpler economic motives', but 'directly and naturally from the central tenets of protestant theology'. Hence his suggestion that, although there had been experiments in the 'penal withholding of relief' in the period before 1640, the puritanism of the Interregnum created 'new opportunities for the exercise of this kind of control'.[11] More recent analysis of the social and political significance of relief has been at the same time more subtle and more suggestive. Keith Wrightson's oft-(mis)quoted judgement that 'the mixture of relief and control represented by the poor laws' provided in 'its balance of communal identification and social differentiation a powerful reinforcement of habits of deference and subordination' was in fact intuitive rather than empirical. Not only was it largely unsupported by contemporary evidence, it was also, it is seldom recognized, a self-conscious allusion to sociological analysis of the 'deferential dialectic'.[12] In the wake of coruscating critiques of the non-explanation and incoherence which result from the 'casual usage of "social control" metaphors', there has been since the mid-1980s almost complete radio silence on the question of the use of the Elizabethan poor laws to influence the conduct of the poor.[13]

Family Situation: Aldenham, Hertfordshire, 1630–90', all in R. M. Smith (ed.), *Land, Kinship and Life-Cycle* (Cambridge, 1984), esp. 68–85, 422. For the elaboration of the entitlement paradigm, see Ch. 6.3 below.

[11] C. Hill, *Society and Puritanism in Pre-Revolutionary England* (Harmondsworth, 1964), 277–8, 283–4.

[12] K. Wrightson, *English Society, 1580–1680* (London, 1982), 181. For the influence of H. Newby, 'The Deferential Dialectic', *Comparative Studies in Society and History*, 17 (1975), 139–64, see Wrightson, *English Society*, 57–61 and n. 29. Of the three examples of discriminating relief cited by Wrightson, it is striking that two are actually from endowed charities (those of Gilbert Spence in Tynemouth, Durham in 1607 and of Henry Smith in Terling, Essex and elsewhere from 1626, both of which are discussed in Ch. 2.5 above) rather than parish officers, and the third from the impressionistic (and unsubstantiated) summary of the 'brutal indifference' of overseers to those bastards and adulterers who claimed relief in the parishes of mid-17th-century London. V. Pearl, 'Puritans and Poor Relief: The London Workhouse, 1649–1660', in D. Pennington and K. Thomas (eds.), *Puritans and Revolutionaries: Essays in Seventeenth-Century History Presented to Christopher Hill* (Oxford, 1978), 209–10.

[13] G. S. Jones, 'Class Expression versus Social Control? A Critique of Recent Trends in the Social History of "Leisure"', repr. in id., *Languages of Class: Studies in English Working Class History, 1832–1982* (Cambridge, 1983), 80. C. Herrup, 'Crime, Law and Society: A Review Article', *Comparative Studies in Society and History*, 27 (1985), 170, identified a parallel and equally dangerous drift in the historiography of criminal justice from the 'Scylla of quantification' to the 'Charybdis of social control'. For a very recent attempt to rehabilitate the term, see C. S. Schen, *Charity and Lay Piety in Reformation London, 1500–1620* (Aldershot, 2002), 200–13.

This chapter is emphatically not intended to revivify the moribund tradition of Marxist historiography in which the faces of the poor were ground on the whetstone of social discipline. As will become clear, so many participants in the micro-politics of welfare rehearsed notions of legal obligation, Christian duty, and paternalistic care so regularly that it is quite untenable to characterize seventeenth-century poor relief primarily in terms of discipline, discrimination, and exclusion. The argument is, however, that historians need to be much more precise in their usage of terms such as 'entitlement', 'generosity', and 'paternalism' in so far as they are applied to welfare systems in general and to the experience of relief under the Elizabethan poor laws in particular.

1. RATES AND BURDENS

In the politics of assessment and disbursement, policy-makers, polemicists, and participants alike advocated the collaborative application of principled discretion by parish officers (and the ratepayers they represented) in preference to the individual exercise of caprice by almsgivers and testators. They argued that the making of rates in particular should be a collective enterprise in which the principal inhabitants of the parish should strive to achieve unanimity or (failing that) majority consensus. Overseers should ideally discuss welfare policy with their fellow parish officers and ratepayers. The anonymous author of *An Ease for Overseers* presented a somewhat exalted vision of this process of consultation at vestry meetings: 'when everyone hath delivered his opinion, let his speech be preferred which accordeth most with reason, and consisteth best in action for the benefit of the commonweal'. He also, accordingly, offered severe criticism of those parish officers who were 'so high conceited that they will hardly incline to consult with their fellowes but will bear the whole sway'.[14] Even where negotiation *was* attempted, however, the annual assessment of the parish might all too easily provoke conflict. 'What contentions' there were, bewailed John Rogers, minister of Dedham (Essex) in the 1620s, at the 'making of rates'![15]

Indeed, vestry meetings were often occasions of faction and tumult within the ratepaying community, especially where it was argued that the poorer inhabitants wielded influence disproportionate to their status and authority. Parish assemblies at Ealing (Middlesex) in the 1610s, for example, were allegedly characterized by 'much disorder' in 'taxing men

[14] *An Ease for Overseers of the Poore: Abstracted from the Statutes* (Cambridge, 1601), 28, 29. For procedure and protocol in vestry meetings, see Hindle, *The State and Social Change*, 217–19.

[15] J. Rogers, *A Treatise of Love* (London, 1632), 71.

indiscretely by the consent of the inferior sort of people'. At Chigwell (Essex), meanwhile, the admission of 'parishioners of all sorts' to church meetings had apparently created confusion and disorder, since so many of the poorer ratepayers were 'ignorant or weak in judgement' and 'were not so readie to yield to that which the better sort of the parishioners would determine'.[16] Although such complaints clearly reflect the self-interest of the leading ratepayers, *An Ease for Overseers* also warned that 'if men be not equally rated by their neighbours, they cannot agree well'. This plea for the maintenance of transparency in both assessment and audit was, ironically, made at almost exactly the same time as public accountability was being circumscribed by the oligarchic impulse of which the select vestry was the institutional expression.[17] Even so, the allegations that vestries made assessments 'not onely in private houses but sometimes in alehouses', that they failed to account to the whole parish 'how their money is bestowed', and that they devised rates which often provoked 'great contentions' were common enough. Perhaps most remarkable of all was the case of the Aylesbury vestry meeting of 1702, after which the parish officers themselves complained that not even they had been present when a group of ratepayers 'in a secret and clandestine manner' made illegal rates and assessments.[18]

A protracted dispute in Layston (Hertfordshire) conveys a vivid sense both of the controversies that arose over rates in the local community and of the efforts made by parish officers and clergymen alike to pacify them. Disagreements had arisen in the second decade of the seventeenth century about the relative proportions of the poor rates payable by those inhabitants who held property in the market town of Buntingford and by those farmers who occupied the four sprawling upland estates of Corneybury, Owles, Beauchamps, and Alswicke. At Easter 1617, twenty-eight inhabitants of Layston subscribed to a set of four 'orders conceived for the better making of rates in the parish'.[19] It was agreed that a body of

[16] London Metropolitan Archives, London, DL/C/340, fos. 47^{v}-49; DL/C/341, fos. 149^{v}-50. For the emergence of the select vestry in the second decade of the 17th century, see S. Hindle, 'The Political Culture of the Middling Sort in English Rural Communities, *c.*1550–1700', in T. Harris (ed.), *The Politics of the Excluded, 1500–1850* (London and New York, 2001), 125–52.

[17] *An Ease for Overseers of the Poore*, 14; Hindle, *The State and Social Change*, 210–13.

[18] *Vox Ruris Reverberating Vox Civitas Complaining This Year 1636 Without Cause Against the Country Taken From Her Owne Common Report and Written by Notarius Rusticus* (London, 1636), 6; *County of Buckingham: Calendar to the Sessions Records*, ed. W. Le Hardy and G. L. Reckitt (4 vols., Aylesbury, 1934–51), ii, 348–9. For vestries meeting in public houses in the late 17th and the 18th centuries, see S. A. Cutlack, 'The Gnosall Records, 1679 to 1837: Poor Law Administration', *Collections for A History of Staffordshire, Part I* (1936), 9; W. E. Tate, *The Parish Chest: A Study of the Records of Parochial Administration in England* (3rd edn., Cambridge, 1960), 172–4.

[19] HALS, D/P65/3/3, 101–3.

twelve men should have 'full power to rate all persons whatsoever which either dwell or hold Landes in the parish' and to do so 'eyther by landes or abilityes as they shall thinke fitte'. The twelve were to consist of the six usual parish officers (two churchwardens, two overseers, and two constables) together with six others, four of whom were to be 'uplande men' (farmers) with the remaining two being 'chosen out of the towne'. If rates were passed only by a majority vote, at least two of the 'upland men' had to concur. The six officers were to have full powers of collection but were to be discharged of their office only when they had accounted for their disbursements to the other six. Any litigation that might arise over non-payment was to be funded by taxation, and was to be initiated only with the consent of two of the farmers. These orders, which effectively granted the larger farmers a veto over the parish rates, were to be written up by the vicar Alexander Strange and to remain of record in the town book.

For the next seven years, then, Strange recorded the annual appointment of two townsmen to make up the number of 'the twelve'.[20] At Easter 1624, however, three of the twelve subscribed to a memorandum that the 1617 orders were 'thought to be inconvenient, as being beside Law, & preiudiciall to those whom the Law doth inable to make rates'. The townsmen had evidently had enough of gentry domination and the orders were 'disanulled and abrogated', rating powers devolving back to the officers in what amounted to a parish *coup d'état*.[21] A year later, the townsmen secured local magistrates' support 'with the consent of the better sort of the inhabitants' for a new arrangement whereby rates were to be made by the six officers joined only by four other men 'indifferently chosen'.[22] If the townsmen thought they had carried the day, however, they were to be disappointed, for the issue resurfaced in 1627 when Strange noted that he had 'mediated an agreement betweene my fower uplande parishioners towching the number of their acres and the making of rates'. Each of the four farmers volunteered an estimate of their acreage and agreed that their property should be formally surveyed if either the parishioners or the other three farmers were suspicious that they had undervalued their estates. If the sceptics were vindicated, then the farmers were to bear the costs of the survey; if the farmers' figures proved accurate, then the townsmen would pay the price. After three days of verbal negotiation, at the end of which Strange carefully minuted the commitments that each of the farmers had informally made, agree-

[20] HALS, D/P65/3/3, 104–5, 352.
[21] HALS, D/P65/3/3, 105–6
[22] HALS, D/P65/3/3, 107.

ment was reached.[23] On 2 July 1627, Strange drew up a memorandum which gave each of the farmers the right to assess the estimates given by the other three, but granted power to any three of them to judge and resolve any continued disagreement. Once a majority consensus had been reached, then the assessments were 'to stand firme and uncontroleable' and the rates were to be collected. Even then, however, Strange had to make a fruitless journey to procure one outstanding signature.[24] The dispute evidently bubbled on, since at Easter 1628 Strange pleaded with a local magistrate to intervene because his 'perswasion and authority may happily compose and take up the quarrel, which were it ended, all inferior differences would be easily accorded'.[25] In May 1630 another attempt was made to secure consensus, this time granting ratemaking power to the six parish officers provided either that two of the six be upland men or that two upland men join with the six. No power of veto was granted, however, and the fact that rates were to stand even if the farmers failed to attend a rating meeting suggests that, after thirteen years of contention, the balance had swung firmly back in the direction of the townsmen.[26]

Mediation of this kind proved less successful elsewhere. Where it failed, it might result in a paroxysm of litigation of the kind that seized the Shropshire villages of Astley, Sansall, and Clive in the wake of a new parish assessment in 1613. Three ratepayers in Astley denied their liability for rates assessed on them and together with twenty-four of their neighbours riotously resisted the distraint of their property executed in December 1615 by the parish officers, who thought it necessary to 'provide for the necessary relief of the multitude of poor people against the feast of Christmas'. The dispute was sued out not only at Shropshire assizes, but also in the Shrewsbury Guildhall and the Westminster Courts of Arches, Requests and Star Chamber. Even litigation on this scale was preferable to the bloodshed which resulted when two parishioners fell to 'justling' and scratching together after the exchange of 'severall p[ro]voaking and abasefull speeches' while 'making the Assesm[en]t' in

23 HALS, D/P65/3/3, 43–5.

24 HALS, D/P65/3/3, 46–7.

25 HALS, D/P65/3/3, 48. This aspect of the dispute nicely captures the tensions between the 'moral tradition' of conflict resolution in which the clergyman had a widely recognized role as a mediator and the more secular practice of arbitration, in which the authority of magistrates was injected into the disputing process. J. Bossy, *Peace in the Post-Reformation* (Cambridge, 1988), 73–100; cf. S. Hindle, 'The Keeping of the Public Peace', in Griffiths *et al.* (eds.), *The Experience of Authority*, 213–48.

26 HALS, D/P65/3/3, 135–6. A tenancy on the Beauchamps estate was at the centre of a further rating dispute between the parishes of Layston and Anstey in 1635–6. *Hertford County Records*, ed. W. Le Hardy (9 vols., Hertford, 1905–39), v. 203, 206, 213, 215.

the vestry at Ashby de la Zouch (Leicestershire) in 1672. Verbal rather than physical assaults were probably more typical of the 'very uncivil' behaviour which sometimes erupted at vestry meetings, as it did in the churchyard of Wraxall (Somerset) at Easter 1656. Appeals and counter-appeals against rates might often have been a matter of indignant retaliation for wrongs previously offered, as they seem to have been in Gnosall (Staffordshire) in the early 1680s.[27]

Indeed, the detailed account left by Thomas Turner of the vestry meetings at East Hoathly (Sussex) provides remarkable evidence of just how difficult vestry meetings could be. There were, inevitably, personality clashes. Turner described one of his fellow vestrymen as 'stupidly ignorant' and 'prodigiously abusive', and another as the most 'out-of-the-way quarrelsome' man he had ever met. Anyone who has ever served on a committee will be familiar with Turner's vivid depiction of the colleague who 'seldom if ever fails to oppose that which anyone else shall happen to start or give as his opinion' and who has 'the greatest skill imaginable in foretelling and judging right of things when they are past'.[28] Frustrations of this kind were compounded by over-indulgence in alcohol: at a meeting in March 1756, most of the vestrymen were 'a little in liquor' to the extent that 'they could not agree in some of their arguments'; in December 1763 Turner himself came home from a vestry meeting 'not very sober'.[29]

The combination of drunkenness and self-interest among ratepayers proved to be a potent cocktail, and the consequences were all too predictable. In the vestry of April 1760, 'several volleys of execrable oaths oftentime resounded from almost all sides of the room', which Turner thought 'a most rude and shocking thing at public meetings'. In February 1759 there were numerous 'oaths and imprecations', despite the fact that there was no business to transact. Indeed, swearing was so frequent that Turner was convinced that the fund arising from forfeitures for uttering profane oaths 'would be more than sufficient to defray all the expenses of the poor' and 'there would need no tax to be levied'.[30] Conflict was

[27] NA, STAC8/206/13, 236/6–7; Leicestershire RO, Leicester, 1D41/13/78, fo. 121; *Quarter Sessions Records of the County of Somerset*, ed. E. H. Bates-Harbin (4 vols., Somerset Record Society, 23, 24, 28, 34, Taunton, 1907–19), iii. 303; Cutlack, 'Gnosall Records', 14–15.

[28] *The Diary of Thomas Turner, 1754–1765*, ed. D. Vaisey (Oxford, 1984), 148, 308.

[29] Ibid. 35, 283. For alcohol consumption and even drunkenness in other vestry meetings, see E. Turner, 'Ancient Parochial Account Book of Cowden', *Sussex Archaeological Collections*, 20 (1882), 112; Tate, *The Parish Chest*, 171–3.

[30] *Diary of Thomas Turner*, 173, 204. This was an unconscious echo of 17th-century judicial thinking on the possibility of obviating poor rates. See the advice of Justice John Hoskyns at Ch. 5.4(*b*) below.

apparently endemic. In March 1757, for instance, a poor rate *was* agreed, but only by a majority vote. In April 1757, Turner lamented the fact that no resolution at all had been reached but noted simply that this was 'the custom with our vestries'. In April 1764, it took three meetings to agree a rate, and even then one vestryman opposed the decision on the grounds that 'it will greatly affect him'.[31]

All this was as nothing, however, compared to the vitriolic shambles of the Easter 1763 meeting, when the eight vestrymen 'stayed till near 1 o'clock quarrelling and bickering about nothing and in the end hardly did any business'. Turner blushed to recall 'what artifice and deceit, cunning and knavery there was used by some (who would think it unjust to be called dishonest) to conceal their rents, and who yet would pretend the justness of an ideal taxation was their desire'.[32] Indeed, so frequently did the 'cankerworm of self-interest' corrode the hearts of vestrymen, that Turner expressed surprise whenever a meeting passed off peacefully. The meeting of 27 March 1758, for example, was characterized by 'the most unanimity at this vestry that I ever did see at any time before'. There was 'not the least discord imaginable', and Turner was astonished that he had not 'observed above 2 oaths sworne' during the whole ten hours it took to do the business. This evidently encouraged him, for he noted the following week that 'our parish affairs' seem to move on in a better manner than formerly', there being 'now unanimity in almost all the vestries we have, when heretofore it was all noise and discord'. Within a fortnight, however, he was reporting 'a great deal of wrangling', despite the fact that the meeting passed soberly.[33] Turner's account certainly corroborates the fictional portrait of the self-interest, vanity, and ambition which dominated parish meetings in Fielding's *Tom Jones* (1749): 'schemes have indeed been laid in the vestry which would hardly disgrace the conclave. Here is a ministry and here an opposition. Here are plots and circumventions, parties and factions, equal to those which are to be found in courts.'[34]

Indeed, concealments and evasions doubtless continued long after vestry meetings were adjourned. Even if the vestry could agree on the proportion of a rate, collection itself was not always peacefully carried out, even in church. At St Andrew's Cambridge in November 1599, the collector for the poor, John Williamson, was reported for disturbing divine service. 'Whilst prayers were in reading', Williamson allegedly

[31] *Diary of Thomas Turner*, 91, 95, 289.

[32] Ibid. 267.

[33] Ibid. 143, 145, 147.

[34] H. Fielding, *The History of Tom Jones*, ed. R. P. C. Mutter (Harmondsworth, 1966), 137.

'went about the church to gather money of them to the use of the poor, by reason of which gathering there was such a noise that the minister could not be heard'. Church services were also disrupted at Whitstable (Kent), where William Cole was presented for denying 'to pay to the collection according as it is appointed by the parishioners' and for abusing 'the churchwarden and also the rest of the parishioners' one Sunday in January 1601. Perhaps disturbances such as these arose when parishioners actively begrudged their rates even after they had formally agreed to them. It is hardly surprising that the author of *An Ease for Overseers* envisaged 'sinister resistance' among ratepayers, especially their tendencies to absent themselves from meetings and to protest that 'they have no money about them' even when apprehended at church.[35] The procedures for distraining the goods of the recalcitrant were, moreover, so cumbersome that some defaulters in Cressing (Essex) bragged in 1637 that they would happily go to prison 'purposely' to ensure that the burden of the poor was 'cast upon' their neighbours.[36]

Rating disputes of this kind were ubiquitous in seventeenth-century England, though the sources that record them are almost invariably more cryptic than Alexander Strange's memorandum book or Thomas Turner's diary. The most common type of dispute arose when a single individual complained that they were rated 'more than others of their worth and ability', as did Thomas Morris of Henstridge (Somerset) in 1616.[37] By the late seventeenth century, appeals of this kind were being referred to magistrates very regularly. At least twenty-four such cases were heard by the Buckinghamshire bench in the years 1678–94, some of them requiring repeated intervention by magistrates both in and out of sessions.[38] A further twelve cases were more complex, challenging the assessments of large numbers of parishioners and calling for revision of

[35] W. M. Palmer, 'The Archdeaconry of Cambridge and Ely, 1599', *Transactions of the Cambridgeshire and Huntingdonshire Archaeological Society*, 6 (1947), 18; A. Hussey, 'Visitations of the Archdeacon of Canterbury', *Archaeologia Cantiana*, 27 (1905), 226; *An Ease for Overseers of the Poore*, 12. For assaults on elders collecting poor relief in Scotland, see M. Todd, *The Culture of Protestantism in Early Modern Scotland* (New Haven, 2002), 383.

[36] ERO, D/DEb/7/20, unfol. (Letter of Henry Nevill, 21 May 1637).

[37] *Quarter Sessions Records of the County of Somerset*, i. 167–8.

[38] For disputed individual assessments at Chalfont St Peter (1678), Great Missenden (1678), Ivinghoe (1679), Wendover (1681), Ilmore (1682), Tingwick (1682), Hambledon (1683), Marsh Gibbon (1683), Weston Turville (1685), Ickford (1686), Calverton (1687), Wendover (1687), Burnham (1688), Drayton Parslow (1688), Radnage (1687), Ellesborough (1688–92), Thornborough (1688), Stoke Hammond (1690), Aylesbury (1690–2), Aston Clinton (1690), Wendover (1693), Great Missenden (1693), Great Brickhill (1694), and Weston Turville (1694), see *Buckinghamshire Sessions Records*, i. 3, 9, 25, 65, 93, 103, 120, 128, 189, 204, 224, 233, 246, 247, 258, 261, 268, 335, 336, 343, 349, 354, 366, 379, 392, 411, 424, 451, 490, 491.

the very principles according to which rates were made.[39] Taken together, therefore, something like one in every six parishes in Buckinghamshire experienced conflict over rates in these sixteen years. The historian confronted with evidence that oscillates wildly in quality between the laconic and the arcane can easily sympathize with those magistrates who found these disputes almost impenetrable. The Somerset bench noted in 1653 that it was 'so farre unsatisfied in the trueth of the matter' at issue among the ratepayers of Over Stowey that it was reluctant to intervene. Because its priority was 'to prevent all obstructions in the way to the reliefe of the poore', however, it insisted that the existing rates should be collected, without prejudice to the outcome of the seemingly interminable litigation in the parish.[40]

Certain common features nonetheless emerge from the archive of dispute over parish assessments. In the first place there appears to have been a general seventeenth-century shift from rating parishioners by the yardland to making assessments on the basis of the rental value of the property they held. Indeed, middling ratepayers frequently protested that the traditional method of rating by the yardland failed to reflect the improved rents made possible by enhancement or enclosure, and therefore entailed levies that were 'very unequally made and taxed' to the 'great prejudice', 'discontent', and 'loss' of the less well-off inhabitants. Almost invariably, they sought to be rated 'by the pound rent according to the true value of every man's land'. Magistrates were generally sympathetic to such revisions, and repeatedly emphasized that 'a pound rate is most legall or equall'.[41] At least three of the more problematic cases in Restoration Buckinghamshire, at Wornall (1679), Ivinghoe (1680), and Chesham (1685), were resolved only by such a conversion to assessment by the pound rate.[42] Even so, the abrogation of customary rating arrangements could create tensions that festered for many years. The dispute which came to a head in Marsh Gibbon in 1683 turned on the fact that

[39] For challenges to the basis of rates in Wendover (1678–80), Waddesdon (1680), Padbury (1681), Maids Morton (1681), Walton (1682), Chesham (1685–91), Amersham (1685–91), Cuddington (1686), Calverton (1688–91), Burnham (1682), Brill (1693), and Weedon (1694), see *Buckinghamshire Sessions Records*, ii. 44, 75, 94, 170, 176, 189, 200, 270, 280, 353–4, 365, 393, 435, 462, 503.

[40] *Quarter Sessions Records for the County of Somerset*, iii. 217. The dispute can be followed over the years 1646–55 at 7, 163, 247, 276.

[41] Quoting the Cambridgeshire JP Sir Thomas Sclatter in the sixth of his rules for the making of rates in Bodl., MS Rawlinson, D1136, fo. 110. Cf. the rhetoric deployed in assessment disputes at Birdingbury and Bidford (War.) in 1648 and at Tenterden (Kent) in 1651. *Warwick County Records*, ed. S. C. Ratcliff *et al.* (9 vols., Warwick, 1935–64), ii. 192–3; *Kentish Sources, IV: The Poor* ed. E. Melling (Maidstone, 1964), 51.

[42] *Buckinghamshire Sessions Records*, i. 25, 42, 189.

'the manner of taxing in the parish was always by the yard land until the late troubles, about which tyme a pound rate there first beganne'.[43] In the second place, clergymen, especially rectors, seem to have been waging a defensive war against the poor rates imposed on their glebe and tithes, especially after enclosure had increased their value. The rectors of the Buckinghamshire parishes of Aston Clinton, Ickford, Radnage, Stoke Hammond, and Weston Turville and of the Hertfordshire parishes of Bushey, Little Berkhamsted, and Royston all took issue with their assessments during the 1670s, 1680s, and 1690s.[44] These men were doubtless amongst the wealthiest inhabitants of their parishes, perhaps second only to the squire in their liability for rates. In the third place, there were numerous occasions when parishes protested against being made to pay rates-in-aid for impoverished neighbouring communities, usually on the grounds that they were themselves overburdened with poor, as in the Somerset parishes of Long Sutton and Saltford in 1616, Stanton Drew in 1617, and Pitminster in 1622.[45]

The local grounds for disagreement over rates doubtless varied enormously. John Rogers nonetheless found it easy to identify the most common complaint about overseers' assessments: 'it is a great fault in most parishes that the meaner sort bear the most burden and not the richest'. Men of only a quarter, or even an eighth, of the substance of their wealthiest neighbours, thought Rogers, often bore a disproportionately heavy assessment, perhaps as much as a half of what the richest might pay.[46] The rector of Sigglesthorne (East Yorkshire) argued that any increase in poor rates was generally regarded as 'a burden and sensible affliction to the inhabitants, especially the petty proprietors'.[47] Although the wealthiest members of the community might justify their relative under-assessment on the grounds that they were charitable to the poor in other ways, Rogers was not deceived. What charity was it, he argued, 'for a rich man to give here twenty shillings, there forty shillings, five pounds to this good use or that?' Far better that when 'some charge is to be borne by a company of meane men', the rich man 'exempt them and bear it all himself'.[48] The author of *An Ease for Overseers* similarly lamented the

[43] Ibid. 120, 128.

[44] Ibid. 189, 204, 247, 261, 269, 335, 343; *Hertford County Records*, vi. 325, 430–1, 435. For the frequency of complaints by the clergy of Restoration Wiltshire that they had been over-rated, see D. Spaeth, *The Church in an Age of Danger: Parsons and Parishioners, 1660–1740* (Cambridge, 2000), 40.

[45] *Quarter Sessions Records for the County of Somerset*, i. 175–6, 183, 190, 195, 200, 317.

[46] Rogers, *A Treatise of Love*, 215.

[47] East Yorkshire Archive Service, Beverley, PE 144/T38, unfol.

[48] Rogers, *A Treatise of Love*, 216. Cf. the views of Thomas Carew of Bildeston (Suffolk) rehearsed in P. Collinson, 'Christian Socialism in Elizabethan Suffolk: Thomas Carew and his

'common oversight in this age that in most cases of taxation the sense of equalitie is disallowed: the poore cannot, the rich will not, but the middle sort must pay all'.[49]

The *social distribution* of liability for poor relief was, therefore, undoubtedly one issue which provoked dispute in the vestry. Even more controversial, however, was the *level* at which the assessment should be set. *An Ease for Overseers* offered conflicting advice on this point. In the first place, it repeatedly insisted that the burden of assessment should be weighed according to the *needs* of the poor. The taxing of money for a stock must be ordered according to 'the multitude of the poore', to 'the abilitie of the parish', and to 'the place of habitation'. Rates should accordingly be proportioned 'by the necessetie of the poore and not the poore by the direction of your rates'. It was therefore crucial that the overseer, like a general counting troops in preparation for a military campaign, should make a 'just computation' of the poor. He must make fine judgements about the level of need, and register them in 'a readie form for the speedie inspection of the poore'. In the second place, however, overseers should be sensitive to the possibility that the *tax burden* on ratepayers might become excessive: 'contributions are not given to make or multiplie poore but to mitigate povertie'. Just as the law gave 'libertie to taxe men always as occasion requires', it also left 'a discretion to abate something as the time serveth'. 'When things are plentiful and cheape, those rates must discontinue which were taxed in deere and extreme times.' Parish officers were therefore encouraged to reduce assessments whenever possible: 'the abilitie of the parishe must not be pretermitted, and a pitiful man will not overburden his beasts, much less his brethren'.[50]

There is, unsurprisingly, widespread evidence of reluctance to raise taxation for the relief of anybody except the deserving 'poore by casualtie'. When Richard Callow of Fulham (Middlesex) was presented for non-payment of parish rates in 1602, he argued that he was 'quitted from paying of anie such dutie by statute'. 'The constable of everie hamlet', he insisted, 'ought to keepe awaie the beggars which they do not'. The Suffolk bench hinted at a general reluctance to pay rates when they ordered in the late 1610s that the officers of every parish submit 'a bill of all the pore' that 'take or are to be relieved in charitie by the lawe' so that

Caveat for Clothiers', in C. Rawcliffe *et al.* (eds.), *Counties and Communities: Essays on East Anglian History Presented to Hassell Smith* (Norwich, 1996), 167. At Weekley (Northants.), the personal charity and hospitality of the resident landlord Sir Edward Montagu meant that there was no need for poor rates there throughout the 1620s and 1630s. See Ch. 1.2 above.

49 *An Ease for Overseers of the Poore*, 14.

50 Ibid. 7, 14, 17, 19, 22, 29.

the magistrates could give express consent to new assessments. 'Every parish', it insisted, was to be 'admonished to conceive of their newe rate for a more conformable proportion' which was 'to be generallie agreed upon with the consent of the parish or the most of the better sort that peace without complaining may be procured.' It was more explicitly reported from Essex in 1629 that there was 'a generall aversenesse in the countrie to the payment' of assessments, ratepayers 'conceivinge that they are not bound by the statute [of 1601] to contribute to the reliefe of any other people than such as are lame, impotent, blind and such others as beinge poore are not able to worke'. Indeed, many parish archives are permeated by the fear that the interests of the ancient settled poor were prejudiced by hordes of shiftless migrants.[51] Elsewhere, it seems, assessment was regarded as an undesirable basis even for the relief of the deserving. Justice John Hoskyns advised the Herefordshire bench in 1634 how 'to prevent the charge of the poore upon every parish'. Taxation could be eliminated altogether, he argued, if the native poor were bound apprentice for twenty-four years from the age of 11; if the migrant poor were whipped home; and if fines for those guilty of the statutory misdemeanours (sabbath-breaking, swearing, drunkenness, pilfering, tippling) were used as an alternative to poor rates as the basis for a parish stock.[52] The reluctance of jurors to present such offenders both wronged the poor and burdened parishes 'who might this waie be eased'. Hoskyns's lack of confidence that his advice would be heeded is implicit in his sardonic promise to 'keep all the poore of Herefordshire at his own expense' if the jurymen complied. He nonetheless believed that these 'few rules' had been used throughout England 'above these dozen years with great contentment of all degrees of persons', a view confirmed by an

[51] London Guildhall Library, MS 9064/15, fos. 189^{v}-90, 206^{v}, 213; BL, MS Additional, 39245, fos. 32^{r-v}; *Maynard Lieutenancy Book, 1608–1639*, ed. B.W. Quintrell (Chelmsford, 1993), 260. Cf. Ch. 5 above.

[52] Whether he knew it or not, Hoskyns was advocating the kind of surveillance of the morals of the population, sanctioned by fines to the poor man's box, which was so effectively practised by the kirk sessions in Scotland that poor rates were unnecessary there. Todd, *The Culture of Protestantism*, 410; R. Mitchison, *The Old Poor Law in Scotland: The Experience of Poverty, 1574–1845* (Edinburgh, 2000), 1–21. The parish officers of Wivenhoe (Essex) were collecting fines for 'offences and defaults' as early as 1583–4. In 1656 alone, the parish officers of Cowden (Sussex) raised £2. 11*s*. 10*d*. from forfeitures on swearers and sabbath-breakers. F. G. Emmison, 'The Care of the Poor in Elizabethan Essex: Recently Discovered Records', *Essex Review*, 62 (1953), 16; Turner, 'Ancient Parochial Account Book of Cowden', 109. In late 17th-century Trull, forfeitures for swearing were generally paid to the 'casual poor' rather than to regular collectioners. I. F. Jones, 'Aspects of Poor Law Administration, Seventeenth to Nineteenth Centuries, from Trull Overseers' Accounts', *Somerset Archaeological and Natural History Society Proceedings*, 95 (1951), 89.

order made by the Northamptonshire justices in 1625. Provision 'for the *necessary* relief of the poor unable to work and for setting to work all such persons as have no other means or trade of life whereby to get their living' was to be combined with the presentment of 'all such persons as shall at any time drinke or sweare or take Goddes name in vaine or shall neglect duely to observe and keepe holy the sabbath day'. Chief Justice Montagu explicitly argued in 1617 that the rewarding of informers with part of the fines for statutory misdemeanours would encourage prosecution and prevent the poor from being defrauded by the negligence of parish officers and presentment jurors. The parish officers of Pluckley (Kent) were nonetheless concerned that forfeitures under the penal statutes should be supplementary to, rather than a replacement for, poor rates. Defraying parish assessments through fines on immorality, they insisted in 1628, would only 'spare money in their purses of those who give relief and the poor who should have relief thereby are never the better'.[53]

If the vestry's preferred strategy was to reduce the rating burden by excluding those considered 'ineligible for relief', its default position was to spread the rating burden as equitably as possible. This proved to be a matter of considerable controversy, since the structure of property-holding varied from parish to parish. There were substantial local variations not only in the scale of pauperism, but also in the ability to pay poor rates. Ratepayers constituted 57 per cent of the householders in Cawston (Norfolk) in 1601, 45 per cent in Aldenham (Hertfordshire) throughout the seventeenth century, and 38 per cent and 31 per cent respectively in Halford and Ilmington (both Warwickshire) in 1639.[54] These were relatively polarized parishes in which the small number of occupiers who formed the elite and paid the rate bill exercised unrivalled authority over the allocation of communal resources. Elsewhere, however, the rating list reached far further down the social scale, including 77.7 per cent of the inhabitants of Sowerby and 81.6 per cent of those of Sand Hutton (both in North Yorkshire) in 1629.[55] It was in these parishes where the elite paid only a small proportion of the assessment that the most controversial contests over individual eligibility for relief would take place, in which (provided, of course, that they were allowed to participate at vestry meet-

[53] Herefordshire RO, Hereford, W52/2; NRO, 175p/28, unfol. (emphasis added); Bodl., MS Tanner, 243, fo. 15; N. Davie, 'Custom and Conflict in a Wealden Village: Pluckley, 1550–1700' (unpublished D.Phil. thesis, University of Oxford, 1988), 231.

[54] A. L. Beier, 'Poverty and Progress in Early Modern England', in A. L. Beier *et al.* (eds.), *The First Modern Society: Essays in English History in Honour of Lawrence Stone* (Cambridge, 1989), 207; Newman-Brown, 'Poor Relief and Family Situation', 409; SBTRO, DR37/85/6/18, 21.

[55] Beier, 'Poverty and Progress', 207.

ings) the lesser ratepayers might actively debate questions of personal reputation, alehouse popularity, and communal equity.

In part, of course, these differences reflect variations in the structure of property-holding, itself a function of the character and strength of the local economy. Indeed, although the definition of a pauper most commonly 'derived from an inability to pay parish rates', it should be remembered that pensioners were only a small sub-group of 'the poore'.[56] It was not simply, after all, a question of either paying poor rates or receiving them. At Cawston in 1601, there were two intermediate groups: 16.3 per cent of the population unable to pay rates but not needing assistance; and a further 16.5 per cent poor, but not on relief. The equivalent proportions in Shorne (Kent) in 1598 were 20.3 per cent and 5.7 per cent respectively. In Aldenham, the proportion of households neither assessed nor relieved varied between a minimum of 16.9 per cent in the 1680s and a maximum of 39.1 per cent in the 1640s.[57] The size of these intermediate groups implies that parish officers attempted to preclude the 'vicious spiral' by which the burden of poor rates might itself push households from independence into dependency by reducing the numbers not only of those *relieved* but also of those *assessed*.[58] In early seventeenth-century Norfolk, conditions were apparently favourable to such policies. At Gunthorpe, for instance, a parish of fifty-odd households, there were only five pensioners and eleven ratepayers. A similar situation prevailed in mid-seventeenth-century Warwickshire, where the three pensioners of Halford were maintained by fifteen ratepayers, and the eight at Ilmington by twenty-five. Of course, deteriorating economic circumstances might limit overseers' freedom of manoeuvre in this respect, as they did in Heydon (Essex), where the ratio of ratepayers to pensioners dropped significantly between 1564 and 1625.[59]

Overseers' judgements about the weight of the tax burden were invariably sensitive, but they became particularly controversial in years of economic dislocation. The experience of harvest crisis 'reversed the proportion of ratepayers (usually a minority) to those in need of relief'. The inevitable consequence was a significant increase in poor relief

[56] Cf. Ch. 4.3 above.

[57] Beier, 'Poverty and Progress', 207; Newman-Brown, 'Poor Relief and Family Situation', 409.

[58] J. Walter, 'The Social Economy of Dearth in Early Modern England', in J. Walter and R. Schofield (eds.), *Famine, Disease and the Social Order in Early Modern Society* (Cambridge, 1989), 117.

[59] *The Papers of Nathaniel Bacon of Stiffkey*, ed. A. Hassell Smith *et al.* (4 vols., Norfolk Record Society, 46, 49, 53, 64, Norwich, 1978–2000), iv. 189; SBTRO, DR37/85/6/18, 21; W. Hunt, *The Puritan Moment: The Coming of Revolution in an English County* (Cambridge, Mass., 1983), 43–4.

costs.[60] Even a dramatic increase in expenditure, however, did not usually result in a significant *social spread* of liability. At Aldenham, the number of households assessed remained remarkably stable, varying only between 101 and 119 over the entire period 1641–1701. Even during the notorious crisis of the 1590s, the increase in the number of those assessed at Eaton Socon (Bedfordshire) was less than might be expected, the twelve householders who were asked to contribute for the first time representing 18.2 per cent of the sixty-six regular ratepayers.[61] Placing a far more substantial burden on the shoulders of existing ratepayers was a more common solution to the problem of augmenting income, and was particularly characteristic of the dearth years 1629–31, when several county benches forced parish officers to increase, perhaps to double, triple, or even quadruple, the level at which poor rates were assessed.[62] Because such decisions were taken by magistrates who were almost certainly ignorant of the delicate balance of communal resources prevailing in the parishes, it is little wonder that overseers should so frequently defy them.

Parish officers were therefore impaled on the horns of a dilemma, the terms of which were nicely captured by the judges of the Norfolk circuit in the early 1620s. The fundamental obligation of the overseers, they insisted, was to care for the 'ould lame blind and impotent poore in every parish' so that 'none be suffered to begg but be well relieved'. And yet, they insisted, 'no parish' must be 'overcharged'. The art, as the justices of Devon recognized in 1631, was 'to raise the booke of the poore to as great a proportion' as they could, just to (but no further than) the point where 'such as are taxed' began 'to complaine on the other syde'.[63] On the one hand, then, parish officers were confronted with 'real' problems of human misery that were not simply 'constructed' by the sinfulness, idleness, and disobedience with which contemporary polemicists were obsessed. On the other, they acted as custodians of communal resources, and were therefore obliged to prevent the unnecessary inflation of welfare costs. The obvious tension between these two positions became central to the ubiquitous struggles over the calculation of eligibility that were fought out parish by parish across the seventeenth century.

[60] Walter, 'The Social Economy of Dearth', 117–18.

[61] F. G. Emmison, 'Poor Relief Accounts of Two Rural Parishes in Bedfordshire, 1563–1598', *Economic History Review*, 3 (1931–2), 114; Newman-Brown, 'Poor Relief and Family Situation', 410.

[62] NA, SP16/194/9, 11, 19; S. Hindle, 'Power, Poor Relief and Social Relations in Holland Fen, c.1600–1800', *Historical Journal*, 41 (1998), 85. Cf. Ch. 4.3 above.

[63] BL, MS Additional, 39245, fo. 1^{v} (reverse foliation); NA, SP16/189/5.

2. THE DISCRETIONARY CALCULUS OF ELIGIBILITY

But just how far did the obligations of parish officers extend within the community? To whom might they legitimately deny relief? In 1618 the most influential judicial commentator on the Elizabethan poor laws, the Cambridgeshire JP Michael Dalton, glossed the tertiary distinction enshrined in the 1601 legislation, providing a formula that was employed by several generations of magistrates to whom his *Country Justice* became an indispensable guide.[64] The 'poore by impotency and defect' including the aged, the orphaned, the disabled, and the sick, were to be provided for by parish officers according to their need. The 'poore by casualtie', including victims of injury, accident, or the life-cycle (especially those overburdened with children), were to be set on work. Dalton's third category, the 'thriftlesse poore' for whom 'the house of correction [was] fittest', included not only 'the vagabond that will abide in no service or place' but also a very much wider range of delinquents: 'the riotous and prodigall person, that consumeth all with play or drinking'; 'the dissolute person, as the strumpet, pilferer, &c'; 'the slothfull person, that refuseth to work'; and 'all such as wilfully spoile or imbesill their work'.[65] In revising this passage for his 1635 edition, however, Dalton launched a venomous attack on the granting of parish relief to these parasites. Misguided generosity, he argued, not only nourished the thriftless 'in their lewdnesse or idlenesse' and robbed more deserving causes of their relief, it also wronged the ratepayers who underwrote the parish fund and condemned the overseers who had betrayed them. From the 1630s, then, Dalton actively recommended the denial of relief to drunkards, whores, pilferers, and idlers. But what, he asked, should become of those delinquents who happened 'to prove impotent' or to experience 'manifest extremity'? Here, he was less sure: 'it seemeth', he argued, 'that they are to be releeved by the towne'.[66] By the 1643 edition, Dalton had begun to cite

[64] M. Dalton, *The Country Justice* (numerous edns.: London, 1618, 1635, 1643, 1655, 1661, 1677, 1682, 1697, 1727). This tripartite classification in fact long predates the late Elizabethan statutes, being originally drawn from the recommendations of a metropolitan committee on the relief of the poor headed by Bishop Nicholas Ridley and Lord Mayor Sir Richard Dobbes in 1551–2. Cf. P. Slack, 'Social Policy and the Constraints of Government, 1547–58', in J. Loach and R. Tittler (eds.), *The Mid-Tudor Polity, c.1540–1560* (London and New York, 1980), 94–115; S. Brigden, *London and the Reformation* (Oxford, 1989), 478–80. Dalton's source was probably R. Grafton, *A Chronicle at Large and Meere History of the Affayres of Englande and Kinges of The Same* (London, 1569), 1321–2, perhaps mediated through W. Harrison, *The Description of England*, ed. G. Edelen (Ithaca, 1968), 180–1.

[65] Dalton, *The Country Justice* (1618 edn.), 76–7.

[66] Dalton, *The Country Justice* (1635 edn.), 101.

the authority of a statute of 1495 as interpreted in an unspecified Cambridge assize charge, to the effect that the thriftless impotent were merely to be provided with 'bread and water without other sustenance'. He nonetheless insisted that 'charity wills us in cases of manifest extremity' that even the delinquent should not be left to starve.[67] He nonetheless added a caveat which empowered magistrates and parish officers to make discretionary judgements in such cases: 'I leave that to better consideration.'[68]

It is with the exercise of Dalton's 'better consideration' that we are concerned here. The following discussion artificially ignores the wider matrix of social discipline within which the granting of outdoor relief in cash and kind was located. Liability for those considered undeserving might be shifted either (as we have seen) onto other parishes (under the terms of indemnity bonds and removal orders) or even onto specific individuals (putative fathers, for instance, under the terms of paternity bonds designed to disburden the parish of bastards).[69] This is to say nothing of the whipstocks, manacles, and hemp in those houses of correction where the self-evidently delinquent were to be punished with hard labour.[70] Instead we are concerned solely with the relief of the settled poor of the parish, those for whom the granting of pensions *should* have been unambiguous. It is apparent, however, that the identification of the 'deserving poor' was problematic and that the statutory distinctions of 1601 were very difficult, if not impossible, to apply in practice. There were, inevitably, zones of transition, both between different types of relief claimant and over the life-cycle of an individual pauper. Particularly revealing in this respect are the numerous examples of relief being withheld, suspended, or even cancelled altogether according to the demeanour and conduct of the recipient. Among the canons of social respectability to which pensioners were expected to conform were church attendance, industriousness, sobriety, deference, and the duties of parenthood. The following discussion takes each of these in turn.

[67] Dalton, *The Country Justice* (1643 edn.), 122, citing 11 Henry VII, c. 2 (1495). This passage remained unchanged in all the subsequent editions down to 1727. In the early 18th century, the Buckinghamshire JP Sir Simon Harcourt took care to include this passage in his commonplace book, adding the comment 'for charity sake the town relieves'. BL, MS Harley, 5137, fo. 188.

[68] Dalton, *The Country Justice* (1618 edn.), 77; (1635 edn.), 101.

[69] Cf. Ch. 5 above. W. J. King 'Punishment for Bastardy in Early Seventeenth-Century England', *Albion*, 10 (1978), 130–51; A. Fletcher, *Reform in the Provinces: The Government of Stuart England* (New Haven, 1986), 252–62.

[70] J. Innes, 'Prisons for the Poor: English Bridewells, 1555–1800', in F. Snyder and D. Hay (eds.), *Labour, Law and Crime: An Historical Perspective* (London, 1987), 42–122.

(*a*) The 'Feare of God'

The poor were most obviously expected to demonstrate their deservingness by regular attendance at church services. In doing so, they not only participated in communal rituals of worship, but also proved that they recognized their place in the social order and that they feared God. As early as the 1590s, applicants for relief at St Bartholomew-by-the-Exchange (London) were expected not only to attend church every Sunday morning but also to satisfy parish officers of their knowledge of the Creed. From 1623, and again in 1626, no persons were to have relief in Salisbury (Wiltshire) unless they 'usually frequent his or her parish church at morning and evening prayer and at sermons on the sabbath days, unless he or shee shall be hindered by sickness or impotence of the body or other just cause'. Attendance was to be monitored by provision first of 'forms or seats for all [the poor] to sit together'; and subsequently of a bench with '*For the Poore* in great red letters' painted upon it. Similar surveillance was probably practised elsewhere, as it was in Croft (North Yorkshire), where inscriptions of this kind are still to be found. New seats had specifically been set aside for poor folk in London parishes as early as the 1570s, and 'for the poor and such as took alms' at Bardeswell (Norfolk), for example, in 1608. The poor of Oswestry (Shropshire) were made to sit on rough boards rather than pews from the first decade of the seventeenth century. In 1633 the vestrymen of Braintree (Essex) ordered the parish officers to 'do their best indeavour to fynde out such persons as absent themselves from churche', to 'take a course to force them to come', and to ensure that 'the poorer sorte that take collection shalbe abated in their collection until such time as they be reformed in it'. The parish officers of Layston (Hertfordshire) from 1613, Trull (Somerset) from 1677, Stansted Abbots (Hertfordshire) from 1678, and Linton (Cambridgeshire) from 1710 similarly insisted that 'alms people & pensioners' receive their pensions on Sunday only after first hearing the sermon.[71] Distribution in these cases almost certainly took place in the

[71] M. Berlin, 'Reordering Rituals: Ceremony and the Parish, 1520–1640', in P. Griffiths and M. Jenner (eds.), *Londinopolis: Essays in the Cultural and Social History of Early Modern London* (Manchester, 2000), 59–60; *Poverty in Early Stuart Salisbury*, ed. P. Slack (Wiltshire Record Society, 31, Devizes, 1975), 88; P. Slack, 'Poverty and Politics in Salisbury, 1597–1666', in P. Clark and P. Slack (eds.), *Crisis and Order in English Towns, 1500–1700: Essays in Urban History* (London, 1972), 185; J. C. Cox, *Bench-Ends in English Churches* (Oxford, 1916), 36; Schen, *Charity and Lay Piety*, 121; S. D. Amussen, 'Gender, Family and the Social Order, 1560–1725', in A. Fletcher and J. Stevenson (eds.), *Order and Disorder in Early Modern England* (Cambridge, 1985), 213; J. Hill, 'Poverty and Poor Relief in Shropshire, 1550–1685' (unpublished MA thesis, Liverpool University, 1973), 142; *Early Essex Town Meetings: Braintree, 1619–1636, Finchingfield, 1626–1634*, ed.

church porch, as it did at Prees (Shropshire) from 1672 and Weedon (Northamptonshire) in the 1690s, a policy which not only encouraged attendance at sermons, but also ensured transparency and publicity in the allocation of parish resources. This was a policy practised in some parishes, such as Colyton (Devon), into the eighteenth century. The vestries at Seaborough and Charmouth (Dorset) even ordered the withholding of pensions from those who failed to attend Sunday services as late as 1726 and 1784 respectively.[72]

These general injunctions to participate in communal worship were inevitably followed by the punishment of those who failed either to attend altogether or to conduct themselves with appropriate decorum when they did so. In 1641 the Warwickshire bench ordered that Roger Hodgkins of Shrewley-in-Hatton was to have his pension paid 'in the parish church there and to receive nothing if he fails to attend'. William Amarys of Salford (Warwickshire) actually had his pension halved in 1641 because the parish officers described him as a 'very disorderly fellow' who had 'behaved himself very rudely and irreligiously in the church there'. If he continued to 'demean and behave himself uncivilly and unreverently', the magistrates agreed, he was to 'have no contribution at all'.[73] All this, of course, is to say nothing of the informal prosecution of dissent through the administration of the poor laws. In February 1682, the Middlesex justices agreed that 'such poor people as shall go to any meeting house and not to their parish church shall have no benefit of the parish collections but be put out of the poor's book'. The Devon bench issued a similar general order denying relief to those who did not conform to the Anglican rites from 1684.[74] Just because pensioners were made to attend,

F. G. Emmison (Chichester, 1970), 86; HALS, D/P65/3/3, 27–8, 30, 32–4; D/P102/5/1 (19 Sept. 1678); E. M. Hampson, *The Treatment of Poverty in Cambridgeshire, 1597–1834* (Cambridge, 1934), 180, 240 n. 3; Jones, 'Trull Overseers' Accounts', 91. For similar stipulations in respect of charitable trusts, see Ch. 2.5 (*c*) above. 'Everywhere', in Scotland, 'the poor lost their place on the list of alms recipients for Sabbath breach even if they *had* come to church'. Todd, *The Culture of Protestantism*, 41 (emphasis added). For the charitable bequest of a pew specifically to the poor inhabitants of the parish of Norton-le Moors, see Tate, *The Parish Chest*, 114.

72 Hill, 'Poverty and Poor Relief in Shropshire', 125; NRO, QSR/1/176/2; P. Sharpe, *Population and Society in an East Devon Parish: Reproducing Colyton, 1540–1840* (Exeter, 2002), 234; S. Ottaway, 'The "Decline of Life": Aspects of Ageing in Eighteenth-Century England' (unpublished Ph.D. thesis, Brown University, 1998), 176; B. Kerr, *Bound to the Soil: A Social History of Dorset, 1750–1918* (London, 1968), 93.

73 *Warwick County Records*, ii. 85, 106. The sanctions were enforced in Seaborough (Dorset) as late as 1732. Ottaway, 'The "Decline of Life"', 176 n. 64.

74 NA, SP29/418/98; Sharpe, *Population and Society*, 220–1. An order at Aylesbury Sessions at Easter 1682 suggests that this policy was also enforced in Buckinghamshire. *Buckinghamshire Sessions Records*, i. 95.

moreover, should not lead us to believe that they communicated with their betters on an equal footing or even at the same time. Poor labourers and servants were often made to attend earlier services than their masters and mistresses, as was the case throughout the diocese of Peterborough in the late sixteenth century. They often received inferior communion wine, cheaper claret being substituted for more expensive malmsey at Oswestry in 1608, for example, in a distinction which, however odious to modern egalitarian instincts, accorded perfectly well with the contemporary obsession with order, hierarchy, and degree.[75]

(*b*) Industry and Thrift

Perhaps the next most obvious characteristic of communal respectability was industriousness, or at least a willingness to work. Indeed, the provision of relief seems to have been less a matter of meeting need than of preserving the incentive to wage labour. Quarter sessions records are littered with examples of pensioners forcibly being reminded of their duty to find work wherever possible. A petitioner from Salthowse (Norfolk) was denied relief by the overseers there in 1603 because 'she may have work if she will'. The vestry of Paddington (Middlesex) insisted in 1623 that any poor person able to work 'who yet neglecteth the same through idleness drunkeness or other unthriftiness, whereby he and his charge is destitute of means to be relieved', should be reported to the magistrates so that he may be 'brought to labour for his liveinge'. William Harris of Polesworth (Warwickshire) was awarded a pension in 1632 only on the condition that he would 'willingly do such work as he shall be able to perform being reasonably satisfied for the same'. If he refused, the bench insisted, his pension was to be cancelled. Two widows of the Warwickshire parish of Southam were similarly threatened with suspension of their collection in 1641 unless they undertook to 'labour at such work as they are able and according to their power'. The complex arrangements for the maintenance of the Archer family of Fillongley (Warwickshire) were confirmed in 1650 only on the condition that Archer 'do diligently follow his work'. In 1675 Mary Harper of Long Itchington (Warwickshire) had her pension reduced from 22*d.* to 12*d.* weekly on the grounds that she was 'a person able in some measure to work for her living'. Alice Parker of Bidford (Warwickshire) had her pension halved in 1676 because the overseers alleged that she was 'able

[75] Hill, 'Poverty and Poor Relief in Shropshire', 142. For numerous other examples of, and general comments on, this practice, see Hill, *Society and Puritanism*, 413–14; Wrightson, 'The Politics of the Parish', 19; J. Craig, *Reformation, Politics and Polemics: The Growth of Protestantism in East Anglian Market Towns, 1500–1610* (Aldershot, 2001), 59–60.

with her labour for the greatest part to maintain herself without any allowance'. Thomas Tilkes of West Wycombe (Buckinghamshire) actually had his pension cancelled altogether in 1680 because the overseers managed to convince the justices that 'he is a man of very able body and well able to work for his own livelihood'.[76] The magistrates of North Yorkshire ordered in 1679 that the overseers of Northallerton cancel a widow's pension and 'be no further chargeable with her than with providing her a stock' with which she might spin or weave. That even this was no guarantee of success is demonstrated by the experience of the parish officers of Westward, who pleaded with the Cumberland bench in 1698 that William and Jane Langrigg be denied further relief. Not only was William a competent shoemaker but his wife had refused to be set on work, complaining that 'she could not live upon spinning hemp' at 5*d.* a hank. Both had allegedly boasted that they could maintain themselves better than at least twenty other families of the parish, and yet they were content to receive relief.[77]

Collection was never, of course, intended to provide an adequate maintenance in and of itself, especially in the early seventeenth century. It was frequently combined with the meagre incomes which pensioners might scrape together from other sources as part of the 'economy of makeshifts'. As Robert Doughty put it in one relief order issued in 1664, a weekly allowance to a poor family should amount only to 'what *with their work* will maintain them'.[78] It is nonetheless striking that justices and parish officers should seek to adjust the value of pensions according to the seasonality of the labour market. In 1682, the overseers of Stewkely (Buckinghamshire) granted Joan Daniell a weekly pension of 1*s.* 6*d.* 'until harvest be over', but noted that the pension should be increased 'afterwards' to 3*s.* Similarly, when the Warwickshire bench allowed Elizabeth Edden of Barford, widowed with three small children, 1*s.* a week in 1684, it insisted that the sum be halved 'in harvest time' when she might supplement her income with hay-raking, straw-plaiting, or gleaning. In both cases, it seems, harvest work and its associated customary perquisites would earn a pauper at least as much as she was receiving in relief.[79]

[76] Fletcher, *Reform in the Provinces*, 151; *Warwick County Records*, i. 141; ii. 95; iii. 24–5; vii. 30, 56; Bodl., MS Eng. lett. c.589, fo. 52[v]; *Buckinghamshire Sessions Records*, i. 64. For a Cumberland order using similar language in 1708, see CRO, Q/11/1/88/11.

[77] *North Riding Quarter Sessions Records*, ed. J. C. Atkinson (9 vols., North Riding Record Society, 1–9, London, 1884–92), vii. 24; CRO, Q/11/1/47/15. A hank was the measure of yarn, which varied according to the material from which it was spun.

[78] *The Notebook of Robert Doughty, 1662–1665*, ed. J. M. Rosenheim (Norfolk Record Society, 54, Norwich, 1989), 42 (emphasis added). Cf. Ch. 4.3(*b*) above.

[79] *Buckinghamshire Sessions Records*, i. 99; *Warwick County Records*, viii. 102. For the medieval view

Overseers also took seriously the advice that pensions should be reduced when the circumstances of pensioners changed or when the general economic situation improved. The vestry of Whittingham (Lancashire) ordered in 1663 that all the parish pensions be 'mitigated, regulated and distributed' at the discretion of the overseers since maintenance was no longer necessary to several of those who had long enjoyed relief orders: 'some who are lame are able to spinne and get sumthinge towards their releefe that way'; 'others that weare infants are grown stronge and able to get for what they want amongst their neighbours as others doe'; and 'those that weare sickley doer recover their health and are better able to helpe themselves in some thinges so that less monies may well suffice'. In 1703 the overseers of Aylesbury persuaded the Buckinghamshire bench to reduce two and cancel a further one of the six pensions awarded three years previously on the grounds that the allowances had become 'very burdensome' and were made 'when corn and grayne was much dearer than now it is'.[80]

The fear that entry into the pension lists might actually *encourage* idleness was evident in the complaint of the inhabitants of Radnage (Buckinghamshire) in 1692 that, although Thomas Quainton's wife was 'well able to maintain herself', she had 'wholly given herself to an idle life' ever since she had been granted an allowance. The parish officers of Lorton (Cumberland) not only cancelled the relief of John Threlkeld in 1692 on the grounds that he was 'an idle and dissolute young man who has now recovered and is enjoying living at their expense', but also pleaded that the bench punish his 'temerity'.[81] The overseers of Aston Abbots (Buckinghamshire) similarly justified their substantial reduction of Lucy Stratford's pension on the grounds that she 'was able to work, but so indulgent to herself as to refuse work when offered her'. The pension was restored only on the condition that she 'take such work as she was offered to her and endeavour by her honest labour and industry to provide for herself'. When the overseers of Embleton (Cumberland) sought the cancellation of one relief order in 1697, they justified their application on the grounds that 'old widows and orphans' rather than those who had 'gotten a habbit of idelness' were the only legitimate 'objects of charity'.[82] Concerns that paupers and their dependants would supplement their

that alms should not be given in harvest time when work was plentiful, see C. Dyer, *Standards of Living in the Later Middle Ages: Social Change in England, c.1200–1520* (Cambridge, 1989), 237.

[80] *An Ease for Overseers of the Poore*, 29; LRO, QSP/640/5; *Buckinghamshire Sessions Records*, ii. 363–6.

[81] *Buckinghamshire Sessions Records*, i. 424; CRO, Q/11/1/20/11.

[82] Ibid. 345; CRO, Q/11/1/42/12.

pensions not through paid work but by begging are evident in the hostility to William Charter of Seaton (Devon), who had been granted 8*d.* a week in 1619 but had nonetheless 'gonne about degginge'. An order of the Buckinghamshire justices in 1680 stipulated that any resident of Aylesbury found begging at 'any inn gate or otherwise' was not only to be incarcerated in the town's house of correction but also 'expunged out of the pension roll for the relief of the poor'. In 1697 pensioners were similarly prevented from begging from door to door in Linton (Cambridgeshire) under pain of losing their regular allowance.[83] It was precisely this line of thinking that led the Devon clergyman Richard Dunning to argue in 1685 that those who were relieved by the parish could be compelled to follow their labour by forcing them to bring the parish officers certificates of 'how they have been employed and what they have done since last pay-day' and 'to receive no relief' until 'they give a good account of their diligence'.[84] All this, of course, is to say nothing of the cases when pensions were only granted as a last resort when work could not be provided.[85] Pensions might equally be discontinued when paupers were set to work by the overseers, a fate shared by the Buckinghamshire paupers Richard Fowler of Ivinghoe in 1679 and Thomas Curtis of Whitchurch in 1680.[86]

(*c*) Sobriety

Those who misspent their meagre pensions were also vulnerable to sanctions. Although Richard Jenner, a lame cooper of Havant, had been allowed a weekly pension of 2*s.* by a Sussex JP, the Havant overseers thought him well enough to offer him work at 3*s.* a week. Jenner, they alleged, not only refused but 'wastes his time and means in alehouses'. Although their attempts to have his pension cancelled in 1638 were ultimately frustrated by the judges of assize, they were only the culmination of a campaign to free themselves of their obligations towards him that stretched back to 1635. Drunkenness also probably lay behind the rather vague stipulation in 1652 that, unless Sara Woodfall of Napton-on-the-

[83] Sharpe, *Population and Society*, 218; *Buckinghamshire Sessions Records*, i, 43; Hampson, *Treatment of Poverty in Cambridgeshire*, 181.

[84] R. Dunning, *A Plain and Easie Method Shewing How the Office of Overseer of the Poor May be Managed* (London, 1685), 9. This was an argument to which he returned in 1698, by which time he was prepared to argue that a pauper's silence on this issue was to be construed as incriminating. R. Dunning, *Bread for the Poor* (Exeter, 1698), 25–6.

[85] For examples, see *Warwick County Records*, vii. 25, 48, 129, 216; *Buckinghamshire Sessions Records*, i. 110.

[86] *Buckinghamshire Sessions Records*, i. 26, 52.

Hill (Warwickshire), a 'woman most malicious against honest people' who 'misspends that which is given to her', conducted herself 'temperately', she too was to lose her pension. William Johnson of Balsall (Warwickshire), who had been awarded a weekly pension of 6*d.* in 1673, was deprived of it by the county bench the following year when the 'substantial inhabitants' of the parish informed the justices that he was a 'person of very ill behaviour and whatsoever money he gets doth spend the same in rioting and drunkenness through which ill vices he hath spent a good estate' and further that he was 'a great disturber of the whole neighbourhood there'. John Fawcett of Embleton (Cumberland) had his pension cancelled in 1697 because he continually drank away his maintenance money in Cockermouth. Pensions were also withheld from those whom the vestry regarded as 'drunken' or disorderly' at Hanwell (Middlesex) in the very late eighteenth century. The vestrymen of Braintree (Essex) were, by contrast, relatively unspecific in their insistence in February 1620 that one Browne 'being growne very filthy and troublesome shall have his collection denied him until he reform himselfe'.[87] The suspicion that sexual incontinence might also be sufficient grounds for the penal withholding of relief is borne out by the experience of the Warwickshire widow Anne Eales who, pregnant by a 'young fellow who would marry her', refused his offer and continued in her 'dissolute life', thereby forfeiting the 6*d.* she had been receiving weekly for almost three years.[88]

(*d*) Deference

In other cases the perceived moral failings of pensioners or of applicants for relief amounted to a simple lack of respect or gratitude. The parish officers of Great Easton (Essex) stated the matter very bluntly in 1603 when they argued that any poor pensioners who 'unreverently' abused any ratepayer were 'to be put from their pensions for that week'. Here are echoes of the deferential imperative so clearly stated by the vestrymen of Swallowfield in 1596 that 'suche as be poore & will malepertlye compare w[i]th their betters & sett them at nought, shalbe warned to lyve & behave them selves as becomethe them, yf suche amend not, then no man to make any other accompte of theme [but] of comon disturbers of peace

[87] *Western Circuit Assize Orders, 1629–1648: A Calendar*, ed. J. S. Cockburn (Camden Society, 4th ser., 17, London, 1976), nos. 347, 388, 695, 705; *Warwick County Records*, iii. 124–5; v. 220, 228; CRO, Q/11/1/42/1; P. Carter, 'Poor Relief Strategies: Women, Children and Enclosure in Hanwell, Middlesex, 1780–1816', *The Local Historian*, 25 (1995), 169, 171; *Early Essex Town Meetings*, 5.

[88] *Warwick County Records*, ii. 119, 200.

& quyetnes'.[89] The poor then should fear not only God but also their betters, and know their place with respect to both.

A reputation for ingratitude or truculence could be earned either by taking the charity of the parish for granted or by pleading the case for relief too aggressively. The abuses allegedly committed by Elinor Hatchett of Barton Stacey (Hampshire), a widow whose initial settlement in the parish had caused some disturbance in 1636, were ill defined, and may even have amounted only to a petition that her relief was insufficient. When she complained in 1641 that her house was in disrepair and that she was 'in great want and misery', the overseers were ordered to relieve her only 'so long as she behaved herself orderly as she ought to do' and to commit her to Bridewell if she misbehaved further. John Puxty of Buxted (Sussex) seems to have had a track-record of antagonism to employers and magistrates stretching back at least six years which culminated in the suspension of his 'weekely allowance' in January 1650. Edward Titmarsh of Harbury (Warwickshire) had his pension halved in 1658 because he 'carrieth himself insolently towards the inhabitants there'. Insolence also seems to lie behind the case of John Hansell, to whom the overseers of Hillington (Norfolk) were ordered in 1657 to pay 1*s.* 6*d.* a week until they set him to work. If he refused employment, he was to be committed to Swaffham house of correction for a month, and his weekly pay was to be stopped altogether unless he offered a personal apology to Lady Hovell, 'in the presence of the overseers and constables', to 'acknowledge that he hath done her wrong'. Although Humphrey Jones of Deriten was granted a pension of 1*s.* a week in 1692, the justices threatened him with a whipping and a spell in Bridewell 'if he troubles the court any more for further collection without just cause'. Goodwife Clapson was finally relieved by the vestry of Maidstone (Kent) in 1728, 'she promising not to be troublesome to us any more'. Due deference and subordination were also, moreover, expected of collectioners' families. A pension of 8*d.* weekly together with arrears of 5*s.* awarded to Richard Taylor of Aston-near-Birmingham in 1660 was allowed him only so long as his wife 'shall be of good behaviour to the officers there'. Occasionally, it seems that the provision of a pension was itself a stratagem of containment for those who might otherwise prove troublesome. In 1690 the overseers of Coleshill (Hertfordshire) were ordered to provide for Sarah Harwell, 'a person of very evill and bad behaviour and not of sane memory' who was

[89] Emmison, 'The Care of the Poor in Elizabethan Essex', 21; S. Hindle, 'Hierarchy and Community: The Swallowfield Articles of 1596', *Historical Journal*, 42 (1999), 850 (article 15). The Great Easton order also extended to those who were guilty of 'breaking of hedges, pulling up of stiles, breaking of gates, and carting away either rails or bars'. Cf. Ch. 1.2(*b*) above.

regularly abusive of her neighbours and destructive of their property, 'soe that she doth not for the future misbehave herself'. Well into the eighteenth century, the vestry of Wisbech (Cambridgeshire) regularly subscribed its habitation orders with the caveat that a beneficiary was to be given house room only 'during his good behaviour'.[90] Katherine Thorne's pension, awarded when she was discharged from the house of correction to return to her children in Solihull in 1696, was conditional on her wearing 'the badge', a reference to the general stigmatisation of the poor insisted on by the Warwickshire justices in 1695, two years *before* wearing the parish badge became compulsory by law.[91]

The protracted case of Widow Margaret Doughty of Salford (Warwickshire), which attracted the attention of the Warwickshire bench on at least ten occasions between 1619 and 1652, is particularly instructive of the abhorrence of parish officers and magistrates alike of those who behaved as if a parish pension was theirs by right. By 1633 Doughty had enjoyed a parish pension for fourteen years, during which time she had apparently 'grown clamorous', behaving herself 'in a very peremptory manner as if she were careless of the benefit of the said collection or at least altogether unthankful' for it. The bench accordingly instructed the overseers to withdraw her pension until she began to 'behave and demean herself peaceably and orderly' and to 'show herself thankful for the same'.[92] Mary Franklin of Great Horwood (Buckinghamshire) seems to have grown similarly reckless after being awarded a weekly pension of 5*s*. The overseers complained in 1693 that she 'hath taken the liberty to use very insolent language and threatening speeches towards the parish officers'. The justices accordingly halved her pension and ordered her to keep herself and her four children 'at hard worke and behave respectively and modestly towards her neighbours'. Franklin's dispute with the parish officers of Great Horwood dragged on for seventeen years, during which time her pension was repeatedly reduced, withdrawn, and reinstated, she even being committed to Bridewell in 1700 for having 'passionately uttered divers approbrious and threatening speeches' against the 'inhabi-

[90] *Western Circuit Assize Orders*, nos. 455, 914; *Quarter Sessions Order Book, 1642–1649*, ed. B. C. Redwood (Sussex Record Society, 54, Lewes, 1954), 201 (and cf. 55, 72, 92, 146, 193); *Warwick County Records*, iv. 46, 122; ix. 47; *Norfolk Quarter Sessions Order Book, 1650–7*, ed. D. E. H. James (Norfolk Record Society, 26, Norwich, 1955), no. 1008 (and cf. no. 839); M. Barker-Read, 'The Treatment of the Aged Poor in Five Selected West Kent Parishes from Settlement to Speenhamland, 1662–1797' (unpublished Ph.D. thesis, Open University, 1988), 75; *Hertford County Records*, vi. 447; Ottaway, 'The "Decline of Life"', 176.

[91] *Warwick County Records*, ix. 129. For further discussion of badging, see Ch. 6.5 below.

[92] *Warwick County Records*, i. 172. Doughty's case can be traced in *Warwick County Records*, i. 19, 25, 60, 162; ii. 139, 141, 199, 251; iii. 106.

tants'.[93] The parish officers of Crosthwaite persuaded the Cumberland bench in 1712 that the shilling weekly paid to Elizabeth Birkett of Keswick should be 'reduced to a more moderate allowance' not only because she had income from casual labour but also because she was 'a proud abusive woman'. The award for the least deferential conduct by a parish pensioner must arguably go to John Baldwin, of whom the overseers of Bocking (Essex) complained in 1665: 'a very refractory fellow, abusing his superiors, and coming for his allowance in so masterly manner which encourageth others in the same'. These, they argued, were sufficient grounds for withholding his relief.[94]

(*e*) Painfulness and Carefulness

The poor laws might also be used to regulate the residential arrangements and parental conduct of the poor. The 1589 statute regulating the accommodation of lodgers stipulated fines on those who accepted inmates who might subsequently prove to be a drain on parish resources, and therefore implied that those who let rooms were grasping landlords, an interpretation shared by some commentators into the 1630s.[95] The penalties stipulated by the statute were widely enforced, and in some communities, such as Swallowfield (Wiltshire) might extend even to the denying of relief to poor householders who took inmates. There is also a hint in the Swallowfield articles that householders could be punished in this way even if they gave house room to their own kin, for the chief inhabitants sought to prevent *any* householders from lodging pregnant women, whether married or not, in case their offspring proved to be a parish burden.[96] This desire to police co-residential kinship among the poor gradually became more explicit: orders prohibiting the taking of inmates were extended to preclude householders lodging their own children if they were of marriageable age in the London parishes of St Botolph Aldgate and St Michael Cornhill (London) in 1606 and 1616 respectively. In 1614, the Somerset JPs investigated the case of Agnes Burges, a widowed pensioner of Winford who gave houseroom to her unmarried daughter Joane whose illegitimate child was 'very chargeable to the parish'. One Warwickshire householder, Morris Evans, forfeited his pension in 1658 for giving houseroom 'to a kinswoman of his wife'. Another Warwickshire man, Thomas Wood of Solihull, was ordered in 1641 to expel his inmates on pain of forfeiture of 'relief of the inhabitants

[93] *Buckinghamshire Sessions Records*, i. 462, 472; ii. 29, 259, 278; iii. 59, 62, 136, 214.

[94] CRO, Q/11/1/102/27; Slack, *Poverty and Policy*, 107.

[95] Cf. Ch. 5.3 above.

[96] Hindle, 'Hierarchy and Community', 849–50 (articles 8, 21).

of Solihull as a poor [person] of the same parish'.[97] The fact that his lodgers appear to have been kin (one William Wood, his wife and child) is a valuable reminder that restrictions might extend to relations even within the nuclear family, a tendency also reflected in church court prosecutions for the harbouring of 'undesirables'. That such undesirables might include unmarried daughters is a function of both the institutionalization of poor relief and the contemporary mania about the moral and economic perils of illegitimacy.[98]

All this is to say nothing of the withholding of relief from those who resisted the overseers' pressure to have their children bound out as pauper apprentices to husbandry and huswifery, often across the parish boundary. As early as 1596, 'such pore as doe not send their children' to work bone lace were to 'receive no relief from the collection' in Eaton Socon. In 1621 Richard Frye of Street (Somerset), 'a very poor man with a great charge of six small children', could 'get no relief of the parish' because those children 'which are fit to be bound apprentice' were 'still remaining on his hands'. The justices were prepared to award him a pension only after he had agreed 'to settle and bind them forth'. At Braintree (Essex) in 1635, the overseers allowed Old Father Cleeves 10*s*. 'to relieve him in his necessity' only 'upon condicion he shall remove his son Dennis out of the towne and not receive him any more into his house'. Two residents of the Hertfordshire parish of Northaw were presented in 1637 for 'keeping their children at home without employment'. Robert Savile, a West Riding butcher, was threatened with committal to the house of correction at Wakefield in 1641 if he continued to refuse the apprenticeship of his 10-year-old son. Francis Sharpe of Bolton (Cumberland) had his pension halved in 1688 because his children were 'now grown' and might be apprenticed. The parish officers of Ireby (Cumberland) countered the 'surprise' relief order granted to Thomas and Janet Lowther in 1700 on the grounds that the couple were 'young people' and their children were fit for apprenticeship.[99]

These sanctions were deployed into the eighteenth century. In 1701 the vestry of Aldenham (Hertfordshire) ordered that, if Widow Dickenson 'doth not forthwith put her daughter to service', she was to be

[97] Schen, *Charity and Lay Piety*, 205–6; *Quarter Sessions Records for the County of Somerset*, i. 106; *Warwick County Records*, ii. 85; iv. 36.

[98] R. H. Helmholz, 'Harbouring Sexual Offenders: Ecclesiastical Courts and Controlling Misbehaviour', *Journal of British Studies*, 37 (1998), 266–7. Cf. Ch. 1.3 above.

[99] Emmison, 'Poor Relief Accounts', 111; *Quarter Sessions Records for the County of Somerset*, i. 283; *Early Essex Town Meetings*, 101; NA, SP16/344/30/3; *West Riding Sessions Records, 1597–1642*, ed. J. Lister (2 vols., Yorkshire Archaeological Society Record Series, 3, 54, Leeds, 1888–1915), ii. 26–7; CRO, Q/11/1/5/20, 57/23.

'stricken out of the monthly collection and be wholly excluded from any further relief'. In Brill (Buckinghamshire) in 1703, the parents of those children who, despite their families' inability to maintain them, yet nonetheless 'do live and cohabit' with them that thereby 'the collection is likely to be increased to the great prejudice' of the ratepayers, were 'to have no relief or collection' unless the children were swiftly bound out. The parish officers of Hayton-in-Gilsland waged a running battle with the Cumberland bench over a relief order granted in 1705 to John Schollocke, whose children were fit for apprenticeship, and did not get their way until 1711, by which time his youngest child was aged 12 and in service. Another Cumberland pensioner, Anne Hallefax of Torpenhow, refused outright to let her three children be bound and accordingly had her pension reduced in consequence. At Colyton in 1747, Widow Hannah Pitfield had her poor relief cut to a third of its original level when she refused to have her children bound out despite being destitute. The threat of the overseers of Gnosall that William Bott's 'pay be taken of[f] he refusing to let his son go out as apprentice' in 1754 certainly seems to have had an effect, for within two months his son was bound out to a Wolverhampton locksmith and his pension was restored.[100] The requirement made at the time of the parish apprenticeship of Humphrey Bernard, another poor child of Gnosall, in 1718 that his mother 'behave herself quietly and peaceably in the parish' is also suggestive of parental resistance. The desperate lengths to which reluctant parents might be driven is demonstrated by the case of Margaret Agar of Brewham (Somerset), whose curses against the parish overseer who 'made her children go to service' allegedly led to his death by witchcraft in 1665. The beggar's curse of the uncharitable, which so often gave rise to witchcraft accusations, might equally, it seems, be applied to parish officers who 'tyrannized' over their poor neighbours by sending their children away.[101]

[100] Newman-Brown, 'Poor Relief and Family Situation', 418; J. Broad, 'The Smallholder and Cottager after Disafforestation: A Legacy of Poverty?', in J. Broad and R. Hoyle (eds.), *Bernwood: The Life and Afterlife of a Forest* (Preston, 1997), 103; CRO, Q/11/1/76/19, 99/3; 96/13, 102/11, 107/15, 115/4; P. Sharpe, 'Poor Children as Apprentices in Colyton, 1598–1830', *Continuity and Change*, 6 (1991), 256–7; S. A. Cutlack, 'The Gnosall Records, 1679 to 1837: Poor Law Administration', *Collections for a History of Staffordshire, Part I* (1936), 59–60. The Cumberland bench was threatening the suspension of pensions for those who refused to be bound apprentice well into the 18th century: CRO, Q/11/1/133/8, 182/24.

[101] Cutlack, 'Gnosall Records', 58; C. L. Ewen, *Witchcraft and Demonianism: A Concise Account Derived from Sworn Depositions and Confessions Obtained in the Courts of England and Wales* (London, 1933), 33; A. Macfarlane, *Witchcraft in Tudor and Stuart England: A Regional and Comparative Study* (London, 1970), 172–6, 195–7, 205–6; K. Thomas, *Religion and the Decline of Magic: Studies in Popular Beliefs in Sixteenth- and Seventeenth-Century England* (London, 1971), 505, 506–7, 509.

Some slight latitude over the minimum age of parish apprenticeship seems, however, to have developed over time, and the age stipulations of the statutes seem to have been relaxed. By the eighteenth century any adult who applied for poor relief in Terling (Essex) and Charmouth (Dorset) was required to send only those children aged 15 and over out to service. By the 1780s, the exclusion from relief of mothers who resisted the banishment of their children to the new industrial mills encouraged the systematic traffic in pauper apprentices that was developing between many urban centres and the early cotton factories.[102] Some applicants for relief played upon their willingness to have their children bound out to strengthen their own case for a pension, as did Thomas Hall of Ware (Hertfordshire) in 1692.[103] When children *were* bound out, however, parish officers might reduce pensions accordingly. Roger Hodgkins of Shrewley-in-Hatton (Warwickshire), for example, had his weekly allowance reduced from 18*d.* to 12*d.* in 1641 because he was 'freed of some of the great charge of children', the eldest of his five sons having been bound apprentice at the insistence of the county bench. Elizabeth Rea had her allowance halved in 1660 when the Hertfordshire bench was informed that the overseers of Bayford had 'provided [apprenticeships] for two of her children'.[104]

There were also, inevitably, instances where pensions were cancelled or suspended without explanation.[105] Perhaps it was a simple a matter of economy. The inhabitants of Danby Wiske (North Yorkshire) complained in 1675 that one pensioner 'who receives 12d weekly towards his maintenance as a poor man, is not so indigent as to deserve so great a contribution', and the bench halved his allowance accordingly.[106] Elsewhere, genuine factional strife seems to have come into play, with control of the parish purse strings even figuring as an issue in the electoral politics of some small borough towns. In the parliamentary election at Honiton (Devon) in 1661, it was popularly believed that any poor person

[102] S. R. Ottaway, 'Providing for the Elderly in Eighteenth-Century England', *Continuity and Change*, 13 (1998), 406, 417 n. 47; J. Lane, 'Apprenticeship in Warwickshire Cotton Mills, 1790–1830', *Textile History*, 10 (1979), 161–74; Carter, 'Poor Relief Strategies', 170; M. B. Rose, 'Social Policy and Business: Parish Apprenticeship and the Early Factory System, 1750–1834', *Business History*, 31 (1989), 13–20.

[103] *Hertford County Records*, vi. 449.

[104] *Warwick County Records*, ii. 25, 96, 106; *Hertford County Records*, vi. 35. For a reconstruction of the progressive reduction of the pension payments made to a widow of Aldenham (Herts.) as her children were bound out, see Newman-Brown, 'Poor Relief and Family Situation', 413–14.

[105] See e.g. Mary Bayly of the Abbey Forgate (Shrewsbury) in 1654 or Mary Thunder in 1659. *Orders of the Shropshire Quarter Sessions*, vol. i: *1638–1708*, ed. R. L. Kenyon (Shrewsbury, 1901), 15, 68.

[106] *North Riding Quarter Sessions Records*, vi. 241.

who supported the royalist candidate was prejudicing their chances of obtaining parish relief, for the overseers would give them 'noe more but to keep them alive, but would not starve them'.[107]

More commonly, such decisions were often justified on the grounds that habits of 'work, learning and the feare of God' must be inculcated amongst the poor, and pensioners might easily be cajoled into at least an outward demonstration of these characteristics if they wished to earn or retain relief.[108] Threats like this, it should be noted, were an intrinsic feature of the administration of social welfare. A Norfolk justices' charge of 1623, for instance, empowered parish officers to report idle labourers to magistrates who would commit them to Bridewell; to ascertain every weekend which of the poor had work for the next week, and supply materials on which they could be employed; to ensure that pauper children be taught knitting and spinning; and to make twice-weekly search for suspected nightwalkers and stolen goods. Most significantly, however, overseers were not only to punish, but also to withhold poor relief from, pilferers and idlers. The money thus saved would be used to reward those inhabitants who informed on pauper delinquency, at the rate of 6*d.* a time.[109] The informal sanctions of the civil parish might as easily be used against thieves and malingerers as against drunkards and swearers.[110] Late into the seventeenth century, some zealous overseers seem to have regarded it as their social duty to launch parochial campaigns for the reformation of manners through the management of poor relief. The new overseer of the Devon parish of Awliscombe wrote in

[107] Sharpe, *Population and Society*, 216.

[108] This was the explicit intention behind the Norwich census of the poor of 1570: *The Records of the City of Norwich*, ed. W. Hudson and J. C. Tingey (2 vols., Norwich and London, 1906–10), ii. 344. Cf. J. Pound, 'An Elizabethan Census of the Poor: The Treatment of Vagrancy in Norwich, 1570–1580', *University of Birmingham Historical Journal*, 8 (1962), 143; and *The Norwich Census of the Poor 1570*, ed. J. F. Pound (Norfolk Record Society, 40, Norwich, 1971).

[109] Bodl., MS Tanner, 73, fo. 390. For the provenance of this document, see Ch. 1.2(*b*) above. In the three years 1630–2 the Middlesex parish of St Giles Cripplegate paid out £8. 3*s.* 0*d.* in 'rewardes to those that discovered the said forfeitures'. This amounted to about half the sum that was annually disbursed in pensions. NA, SP16/226/78.

[110] For the suggestion (usually more often conjectured than verified) that the semi-formal sanctions of the poor law might even be used to short-circuit formal prosecutions at criminal law, see P. Clark, *English Provincial Society from the Reformation to the Revolution: Religion, Politics and Society in Kent, 1500–1640* (Hassocks, 1977), 249; J. A. Sharpe, 'Enforcing the Law in the Seventeenth-Century English Village', in V. A. C. Gatrell *et al.* (eds.), *Crime and the Law: The Social History of Crime in Western Europe Since 1500* (London, 1980), 115; Sharpe, *Crime in Seventeenth-Century England: A County Study* (Cambridge, 1983), 179; Sharpe, *Crime in Early Modern England, 1550–1750* (2nd edn., London and New York, 1999), 74; P. King, 'Decision-Makers and Decision-Making in the English Criminal Law, 1750–1800', *Historical Journal*, 27 (1984), 55; Thompson, *Customs in Common*, 102; Hindle, *The State and Social Change*, 118, 174.

1662 that 'many shameful offences have been committed in this parish which have made it become odious and contemptible', and blamed those 'remyse officers' who had tolerated 'drunkenesse, fornication [and] unlicensed alehouses' among the poor. The parish, he complained, was ridden with 'masterless persons, monsters of schism and deceivers of the relief', all of whom should be punished for their idleness.[111]

The suspension of relief could only, of course, be a temporary measure. If a pauper died for want of relief in late seventeenth-century England, the sense of shock was palpable: on 22 November 1674, the parish clerk of Wednesbury (Staffordshire) recorded that 'John Russel being famished through want of food (Josiah Freeman being overseer), was buried with the solemnity of many tears'.[112] Indeed, overseers had long been warned that 'if the poore be barred of the benefit of begging' and 'you supplie not their necesseties at home you are guiltie of their deaths if they perish for want of provision'.[113] The penal administration of the poor laws was therefore designed not as a death sentence but as an exemplary sanction. As Robert Reyce argued in 1618, the poor laws were intended to 'reform the quality' of the poor as well as to diminish their number. Although there are few explicit statements of this principle in English parish sources, it certainly applied under the Irish poor law: a woman who had her relief withdrawn in Shankhill (North Armagh) in 1673 had it restored two years later she being deemed poor and having 'suffered sufficiently for her contempt'.[114]

Such practices of surveillance were to be encouraged, argued Richard Dunning in 1685, for they might in themselves deter applicants from

[111] Sharpe, *Population and Society*, 219–20.

[112] P. Laslett, *The World We Have Lost Further Explored* (London, 1983), 133.

[113] *An Ease for Overseers of the Poore*, 30. John Locke argued in 1697 'that if any person die for want of due relief in any parish in which he ought to be relieved, the said parish be fined according to the circumstances of the fact and the heinousness of the crime'. 'An Essay on the Poor Law', in *John Locke, Political Writings*, ed. M. Goldie (Cambridge, 1997), 198. Cf. T. A. Horne, *Property Rights and Poverty: Political Argument in Britain, 1605–1834* (Chapel Hill, NC, 1990), 64–5; A. L. Beier, '"Utter Strangers to Industry, Morality and Religion": John Locke on the Poor', *Eighteenth-Century Life*, 12 (1988), 34. By 1795, Arthur Young could argue that it was actually against the law to starve in England. R. Wells, *Wretched Faces: Famine in Wartime England, 1763–1803* (Gloucester, 1988), 288

[114] *Suffolk in the XVIIth Century: The Breviary of Suffolk by Robert Reyce*, ed. F. Hervey (London, 1902), 57; T. G. F. Paterson, 'A County Armagh Mendicant Badge Inscribed "Shankill Poor 1699"', *Ulster Journal of Archaeology*, 3rd ser., 10 (1947), 113. For the context, see P. Fitzgerald, 'Poverty and Vagrancy in Early Modern Ireland' (unpublished Ph.D. thesis, Queen's University, Belfast, 1994), 273–4. Cf. the case of the inhabitant of the Romford almshouse who had his stipend withheld in 1570 'for his disobedience' and was paid only after 'amendment of his faults'. M. K. McIntosh, *A Community Transformed: The Manor and Liberty of Havering, 1500–1620* (Cambridge, 1991), 282.

seeking relief. If the poor were forced 'once in a week or fortnight publicly to give an account of their demeanor' to the overseer, 'to whom they will soon give the title of bridewell keeper', he suggested, 'few or none will be willing to accept of relief from the parish on such terms'.[115] Such is 'the impudency of this age', feared the author of *An Ease for Overseers*, 'that many will dissemble their estates to have relief', perhaps even pleading 'to be recorded in the booke for the poore when they are better able to contribute to the poore'. If their households were readily inspected, however, their claims to indigence could easily be tested. Many 'whose maintenance otherwise would lie on the parish', argued Dunning, would strive to 'maintain a decrepit husband, wife or child rather than come under such weekly examination'.[116]

From the perspective of parish officers who used their discretion to withhold pensions, therefore, the poor were eligible for, rather than entitled to, parish relief. Above all, overseers were instructed to avoid the prejudice of the parish by ensuring that a pension was the very last resort. 'If you holde so many to worke as be able to worke, and ought to worke', wrote the anonymous author of *An Ease for Overseers*, 'you shall neede the less money to distribute and give away'. Those who received pensions when they might be gainfully employed were 'no better than thieves'. The 'wilfull and incorrigible', by contrast, 'must be constrained to work in the house of correction that by applying labour and punishment to their bodies, their froward natures may be bridled, their evill mindes may be bettered and others terrified by their example'. As the justices of the Norfolk circuit more tersely put it in 1617, none should be 'suffered to live meerelie upon almes' that were 'not meerelie impotent'.[117]

Parish officers evidently took this advice seriously. As we have seen, the parish officers of North Nibley (Gloucestershire) made orders for the poor in 1614. Although they began, somewhat conventionally, with the problems of infiltration, they soon passed on to the more pressing issue of idleness, personified by the presence of hedge-breakers and alehouse-haunters. Their most revealing decision, however, was

> to consider generally of the poore of the whole parish: viz. who they are that receive monethly almes, who they are that are fitt to be releeved & yet receive nothinge, howe many men or women are fitt to be bound apprentice to other men that nowe lie pilferinge and stealinge in every corner, how many and who are able to worke & nowe live idlely, what bastards there are in the parishe that nowe receive relief from the parish or from their reputed fathers, and who such reputed

[115] Dunning, *A Plain and Easie Method*, 13.

[116] *An Ease for Overseers of the Poore*, 29; Dunning, *A Plain and Easie Method*, 13.

[117] *An Ease for Overseers of the Poore*, 7, 14, 17, 19, 22, 29; Bodl., MS Tanner, 243, fo. 14.

fathers are, howe many families are in the parishe that nowe neither give nor receive contribution.

The vestrymen envisaged this census as the basis for a reallocation of communal resources: reducing the burden of assessment by the use of discretionary punishments, apprenticeship agreements, employment schemes, and paternity bonds; and balancing the demands of those in need and not on relief with the interests of those who neither paid rates nor received pensions. Precise identification of the deserving would therefore permit the more equitable allocation of entitlements. It might also, as was intended in eighteenth-century Corfe Castle (Dorset), 'enable the magistrates to form an opinion on the propriety of applications for parochial relief on the one hand and of the refusal of it by the parish officers on the other'.[118]

Just how common was the penal withholding of relief? Among the sessions rolls of the Cumberland bench for the years 1686–1749 are at least twenty-nine petitions from parish officers pleading that relief orders be revoked. Their grounds for doing so were various: that the pensioners or their children always had been, or were now sufficiently recovered from illness to be, able to work; that they had reliable networks of kin support; that, if widowed, they had remarried; that they were idle, drunk, or dissolute; that assets had in fact been bequeathed to them by will or trust.[119] Doubtless the assiduity with which parishes attempted to disburden themselves of undeserving pensioners at any particular time varied according to the personality and prejudices of the individuals who happened to be serving in parish offices, but such contingent factors were inherent in a discretionary system. Whether or not they were motivated by personal malice, overseers' petitions were heard in open sessions and doubtless served the exemplary purpose of warning other claimants of the restricted nature of their rights. Historians are now familiar with the idea that criminal justice was administered selectively in accordance with the logic of exemplary punishment, and it seems that the reduction, suspension, or cancellation of relief might be similarly effective in deterring unjustified claims.[120] Although, therefore, the discretionary punishments

[118] Gloucestershire RO, Gloucester, D8887/3, fo. 99 (and for their comments on inmates, see Ch. 5.2 above); J. Rule, *Albion's People: English Society, 1714–1815* (London and New York, 1992), 118, 122.

[119] CRO, Q/11/1/1/20, 5/20, 8/16, 8/18, 18/19, 20/11, 31/2, 42/1, 42/32, 46/23, 47/15, 47/16, 49/27, 56/26, 57/23, 62/11, 65/12, 76/19, 88/11, 88/15, 91/13, 92/25, 96/11, 99/3, 115/4, 136/2, 136/11, 137/18.

[120] P. G. Lawson, 'Lawless Juries? The Composition and Behaviour of Hertfordshire Juries, 1573–1624', in J. S. Cockburn and T. A. Green (eds.), *Twelve Good Men and True: The English Criminal Trial Jury, 1200–1800* (Princeton, 1988), 149.

carried out by parish officers are only occasionally visible in the historical record, this should not lead us to believe that they were not taken, especially when they were so actively encouraged by magistrates themselves.[121]

3. THE QUESTION OF ENTITLEMENT

Some commentators have, nonetheless, been sceptical about the possibility of withholding pensions in this way. An increasing sensitivity to relative deprivation, it has been argued, was 'a likely, if unforeseen, consequence of the poor law itself'. The operation of the law, and especially the extraordinarily ambiguous position it conferred on overseers—caught between the groans of the poor on the one hand and the threats of magistrates on the other—ensured that, in practice, 'the recognition of poverty [became] easier than its denial and the granting of relief easier than its refusal'.[122] Thus it was that notorious idlers and bastard-bearers, such as Ann Wright of Cratfield (Suffolk) or Mary Blunden of Pluckley (Kent), might be given relief well into their old age however far short they fell of expected standards of morality.[123] One other factor, it is argued, further constrained the hands of parish officers who might wish to cut back expenditure in this way. This was a face-to-face system in which the regular personal involvement of overseers in the investigation of cases created social pressures that in turn encouraged the recognition of rights and obligations.[124] In small parishes in particular, 'there was plenty of scope for custom to do what the law had not, and for an obligation on the part of the poor law administrators to become a right to relief on the part of certain categories such as the old and sick'.[125]

Indeed, these arguments have hardened into something of a consensus among historians that there was a developing sense of entitlement to relief that mitigated the discretionary powers of parish officers. 'The poor

[121] While the Essex magistrates prosecuted John Aldridge of Terling in 1632 for allowing drunkenness, swearing, and unlawful games in his alehouse, one wonders whether the parish officers in turn disciplined his clients: men 'soe poore that many of them have almes of the parishe and theire wifs and children beg'. K. Wrightson and D. Levine, *Poverty and Piety in an English Village: Terling, 1525–1700* (2nd edn., Oxford, 1995), 179. The lack of any surviving overseers' accounts for the parish makes such conjecture impossible to verify.

[122] Slack, *Poverty and Policy*, 190.

[123] P. Thane, *Old Age in English History: Past Experiences, Present Issues* (Oxford, 2000), 113; Davie, 'Custom and Conflict', 237.

[124] D. Levine and K. Wrightson, *The Making of an Industrial Society: Whickham, 1560–1765* (Oxford, 1991), 353.

[125] S. King, *Poverty and Welfare in England, 1700–1850* (Manchester, 2000), 52, 98.

man in England', Cobbett famously argued in the 1830s, 'is as secure from beggary as the King upon his throne, because when he makes known his distress to the parish officers they bestow on him not alms, but his legal dues.'[126] Although the language of rights did not surface in the contemporary polemics on the poor law until the early nineteenth century, some recent commentators have argued that seventeenth-century practice did actually embody what was later meant by a right to relief, that is to say a system in which the poor could appeal against the immediate relief grantor (the parish overseer) to a higher authority (the magistracy), and in which relief was not, and (even more significantly) was not popularly perceived to be, purely discretionary. Cobbett's assessment has, accordingly, exerted considerable influence over the generation of scholars who have done so much in recent years to revivify the historiography of early modern social welfare provision. They have suggested that the belief in the right to poor relief was widespread and deep-seated: that 'English men and women certainly believed they had a right to relief', and that 'entitlement to support from the poor laws was carefully guarded and valued by the poor'. 'The right to relief', it is argued, was 'clung to as a lifeline' and was 'a crucial weapon in the battle to avoid starvation'. Indeed, it has even been suggested that the poor 'did not even feel obliged to ask for relief', they simply claimed it 'as of right'. Even when 'the propertied increasingly attacked the notion that poor relief was a right', we are told, the poor defiantly 'continued to use a very different language', a vocabulary of wages, salaries, and pensions in which the dominant idiom was entitlement.[127]

Indeed, it is argued, so entrenched was the popular notion of the right to relief that, when both the theory and the practice of social welfare were

[126] Quoted in M. D. George, *England in Transition* (London, 1931), 198 (the context for the original quotation has proved impossible to trace). For cogent analysis of Cobbett's defence of the Elizabethan poor laws, interpreted respectively as an expression of natural rights theory and as 'the Magna Carta of the working people', see Horne, *Property Rights and Poverty*, 228–34, and I. Dyck, *William Cobbett and Rural Popular Culture* (Cambridge, 1992), 202–9.

[127] Quoting P. M. Solar, 'Poor Relief and English Economic Development before the Industrial Revolution', *Economic History Review*, 2nd ser., 48 (1995), 6; L. H. Lees, *The Solidarities of Strangers: The English Poor Laws and the People, 1700–1948* (Cambridge, 1998), 79; G. C. Smith. '"The Poor in Blindnes": Letters from Mildenhall, Wiltshire 1835–6', T. Sokoll, 'Old Age in Poverty: The Record of Essex Pauper Letters, 1780–1834', and T. Hitchcock *et al.*, 'Introduction', in T. Hitchcock *et al.* (eds.), *Chronicling Poverty: The Voices and Strategies of the English Poor, 1640–1840* (London and New York, 1997), 227–38, 140, 13. One of the few 18th-century historians to question the notion of an automatic right to relief nevertheless argues that the advent of the allowance system in 1795 confounded 'the notional distinctions between the deserving and the undeserving poor'. D. Eastwood, *Governing Rural England: Tradition and Transformation in Local Government, 1780–1840* (Oxford, 1994), 121.

transformed in the late eighteenth and early nineteenth centuries, a process which culminated in the 1834 poor law amendment act, the poor simply stood uncomprehending 'in blindness'. As 'mass poverty triggered a general revulsion against outdoor relief, and against the needy who were now told they had to labour to eat', it seems, 'the poor lost their moral entitlement to what was seen as a free lunch'. 'With the abolition of the magistrate's powers of intercession' under the terms of the 1834 act, 'the poor's right to outdoor relief was eliminated'.[128] If there was 'a right to relief', therefore, most commentators seem to agree that it was extinguished by the Whig reforms of the 1830s. The majority of these scholars, it should be noted, are generally more familiar with eighteenth- (or even nineteenth-) than seventeenth-century sources, and each is implicitly concerned to contrast the sensitive face of the old poor law with the unsympathetic countenance of the new.[129]

If it can be shown fairly clearly where the notion of a right to relief was first challenged and subsequently eliminated, what of its emergence? Tim Hitchcock, Peter King, and Pamela Sharpe have provided the fullest discussion of the origins of entitlement in their constructive introduction to a particularly fine edited collection of essays, published in 1996. Here, for the first time, the discourse of entitlement is subjected to intensive scrutiny, and its sources identified. We read here of a popular belief not simply in the right to relief, but in the 'right to a wide range of different kinds of relief in specific situations'.[130] The poor laws, it is suggested, were popularly understood to function as 'a multiple use-right', a multilateral resource analogous with the law in general and the criminal law in particular.[131] These beliefs, it is argued, grew in social depth and emotional power during the later seventeenth century as a consequence of the increasing acceptance by the propertied that the provision of parish relief in its various forms was a legal obligation. In Paul Slack's telling phrase, practice had 'taught the poor their rights under the statutes'.[132]

[128] Lees, *The Solidarities of Strangers*, 157; Smith, '"The Poor in Blindnes"', 228.

[129] King, *Poverty and Welfare*, 52–65, provides an interesting review of the historiographical debate over late 18th-century social welfare provision, in which the reading of the nature of 'entitlement' serves as one index of the differences between the 'optimistic', 'neutral', and 'pessimistic' schools.

[130] Hitchcock *et al.*, 'Introduction', 10.

[131] P. Sharpe, '"The Bowels of Compation": A Labouring Family and the Law, *c.*1790–1834', in Hitchcock *et al.* (eds.), *Chronicling Poverty*, 102. Cf. J. Innes and J. Styles, 'The Crime Wave: Recent Writing on Crime and Criminal Justice in Eighteenth-Century England', repr. in A. Wilson (ed.), *Rethinking Social History: English Society 1570–1920 and its Interpretation* (Manchester, 1993), 253.

[132] Hitchcock *et al.*, 'Introduction', 10; Slack, *Poverty and Policy*, 192.

Indeed, Hitchcock *et al.* argue that three characteristics of poor law practice were decisive in this respect. First, the putative social identification between lesser ratepayers and those who received relief contributed to the popular sense that 'poor rates represented a contribution' to what amounted to 'a state guaranteed insurance scheme at the local level'. Ratepayers paid into parish welfare funds on the expectation that they or their widows would need to draw upon them as they withdrew from work into dependency.[133] Second, popular notions of entitlement were subconsciously informed by a deep-seated deference towards a propertied class that proved itself willing to suffer a compulsory tax on property in the interests of meeting the basic needs of the poor.[134] The extent to which relief might have been a matter of *economic redistribution* is open to question, but it was at the very least one of *political exchange*, in which the legitimacy of patrician hegemony was conceded in return for recognition that 'relief was indeed a customary right'.[135] (It is worth noting here in passing that the discussion has slipped easily from the notion of a *legal* to a *customary* right, a theme to which we will return.) Third, poor law practice came to resemble a mosaic of interlocking triangles of negotiation between the labouring poor, the parish vestry, and the county magistracy, in which separate agencies of poor law administration might easily be played off against one another in the hope that a relief order might be granted.[136] The poor might not necessarily, therefore, control the system but some of them nonetheless knew how to make it work for them. These arguments add up to an extremely suggestive identification of the welfare processes through which notions of entitlement might have become internalized, a process which some have regarded not only as unique to England, but actually as 'distinctively English'. As Slack puts it, 'no other society could so easily have taken on board the notion that the poor had an entitlement to subsistence'.[137] As to the timing and geography of that process, however, the editors of *Chronicling Poverty* remain silent.

There has, meanwhile, been guarded optimism from some historians of the administration of the poor law in Stuart England. If both the comfortably off and the lower orders accepted that poor relief was an entitlement in the later eighteenth and early nineteenth centuries, 'might

[133] Hitchcock *et al.*, 'Introduction', 10. This idea is developed at length in Solar, 'Poor Relief', 7–12.

[134] Hitchcock *et al.*, 'Introduction', 11.

[135] Ibid. Cf. Solar, 'Poor Relief'.

[136] Hitchcock *et al.*, 'Introduction', 11.

[137] K. D. M. Snell, 'Pauper Settlement and the Right to Poor Relief in England and Wales', *Continuity and Change*, 6 (1991), 400–1; P. Slack, *From Reformation to Improvement: Public Welfare in Early Modern England* (Oxford, 1999), 164.

it not also have been true of the sixteenth and seventeenth centuries?' Some commentators have been even more confident, arguing that 'even in the mid-seventeenth century' Cobbett's view that relief was a legal right 'was substantially correct'.[138] Others are rather more circumspect, observing that 'whether pensions could ever be demanded as of right remains questionable since many applications for relief were probably rejected and pensions could be cancelled on grounds other than purely objective material deprivation or physical infirmity'.[139] There have, moreover, been some expressions of outright scepticism. While 'there is little sense in which the poor were able to regard relief as a right' in late sixteenth-century London, the analysis of welfare provision in some two dozen rural communities in the period after 1650 emphatically indicates that parish pensions were not 'provided as a right'.[140]

A close reading of this extensive literature reveals some slightly fuzzy thinking about the question of the 'right' to poor relief. Most fundamentally, there is no consistency among the contributors to this debate over whether the entitlement to relief had a legal, a moral, or even an intellectual basis. For intellectual historians, for instance, the notion of entitlement owed less to the Elizabethan poor laws than it did to the pervasive influence of the ideas of John Locke, for whom 'the natural right to subsistence' was 'both a primary rights claim and a theoretical presupposition underlying any . . . definition of "property"'.[141] For others, the question of statutory authority seems equally incidental, with entitlement originating in the moral imperatives of medieval charity: 'payments from the poor rate were actually called alms sometimes and their recipients called almsmen and women. Thus the obligation to secure the livelihood of the unfortunate was far older than the 1601 statute.'[142] Some

[138] Slack, *Poverty and Policy*, 6; A. L. Beier, *The Problem of the Poor in Tudor and Early Stuart England* (1983), 36; A. L. Beier, *Masterless Men: The Vagrancy Problem in England, 1560–1640* (London, 1985), 174. For another optimistic view, see Cutlack, 'Gnosall Records', 36.

[139] J. Boulton, 'Going on the Parish: The Parish Pension and its Meaning in the London Suburbs, 1640–1724', in Hitchcock *et al.* (eds.), *Chronicling Poverty*, 37.

[140] I. W. Archer, *The Pursuit of Stability: Social Relations in Elizabethan London* (Cambridge, 1991), 97; R. M. Smith, 'Charity, Self-Interest and Welfare: Reflections from Demographic and Family History', in M. Daunton (ed.), *Charity, Self-Interest and Welfare in the English Past* (London, 1996), 40. Cf. R. M. Smith, 'Ageing and Well-Being in Early Modern England: Pension Trends and Gender Preferences under the English Old Poor Law, *c.*1650–1800', in P. Johnson and P. Thane (eds.), *Old Age from Antiquity to Post-Modernity* (London, 1998), 78.

[141] R. Ashcraft, 'Lockean Ideas, Poverty, and the Development of Liberal Political Theory', in J. Brewer and S. Staves (eds.), *Early Modern Conceptions of Property* (London, 1996), 45. Cf. Horne, *Property Rights and Poverty*, 71–2. For a rather different perspective on Locke, see Beier, '"Utter Strangers to Industry, Morality and Religion"'.

[142] Laslett, *The World We Have Lost Further Explored*, 150.

commentators have, by contrast, emphasized the significance of the law, but distanced themselves from the idea that the statutes actually conferred a right to relief: 'the dole provided a modest means-tested subsistence provision which was given *not of right* like today's payments but out of the statutory obligation of the parish to provide for the indigent'.[143] For Paul Slack, however, the law *was* central to popular conceptions of social justice. Relief 'had become a legal entitlement under the Elizabethan statutes' and by its very operation 'the machinery of social welfare sharpened appreciations of deprivation and created assumptions about entitlement'.[144] Elsewhere, Slack formulates his position slightly differently, perhaps more ambiguously: participants in the welfare process 'came to view the obligation to provide for changing wants as a moral principle and to accept that poor relief was an entitlement'.[145]

These ambiguous relationships between legal entitlement, moral obligation, and customary right are, therefore, a prominent undercurrent in the discussions of late seventeenth- and eighteenth-century attitudes to parish relief, sometimes appearing as conceptual slippages, or even outright inconsistencies, within the work of a single commentator. 'In the context of the debate over the poor laws', it has been suggested, 'the assertion of the wealthy's social duty to aid the poor became . . . a conviction of the legitimacy of relief', and this observation is no less applicable to the recent historiography than to the contemporary polemic.[146] While moral obligation thus shaded (and continues to shade) into legal obligation, legal obligation itself also seems to have had its roots in customary expectations, as suggested by Hitchcock, King, and Sharpe: the 'structure of customary expectations' of relief, which 'solidified within both urban and rural plebeian culture' in the late seventeenth century, 'grew to encompass . . . a whole network of customary rights'.[147] In all of this literature, therefore, historians have been somewhat unspecific about both the *definition* and the *nature* of entitlement.

The picture is further complicated by the vexed question of pauper settlement. Keith Snell's work, for instance, is often cited in defence of the position that the poor had an unambiguous right to relief.[148] In fact,

[143] Pearl, 'Puritans and Poor Relief', 209 (emphasis added).

[144] P. Slack, *The English Poor Law, 1531–1782* (London and New York, 1990), 35; Slack, *Poverty and Policy*, 190.

[145] Slack. *Poverty and Policy*, 5–6.

[146] Lees, *The Solidarities of Strangers*, 163.

[147] Hitchcock *et al.*, 'Introduction', 11. Cf. K. D. M. Snell, *Annals of the Labouring Poor: Social Change and Agrarian England, 1660–1900* (Cambridge, 1985), 104–7.

[148] For example in Solar, 'Poor Relief', 6 n. 38; in Hitchcock *et al.*, Introduction', 10 n. 30; or in Lees, *The Solidarities of Strangers*, 79.

Snell was arguing something much more specific about the important function of pauper settlement *within* the poor law system, not as an 'imposition on freedom of movement' but as 'a guarantee of parish relief during a period of poverty': 'as a settlement was the precondition for receiving relief, it was both essential for the poor to obtain and prove their legal settlements and for parish officials to ensure that an applicant for relief was legally entitled to it in that parish'.[149] Indeed, popular knowledge of the law, gained from an all too intimate experience of its operation, 'sometimes rivalled that of lawyers consulted in parochial settlement disputes' to the extent that 'the poor themselves regarded parish settlement and the right to relief as their birthright'.[150] But, here too, it is important to distinguish between popular and elite views: 'while the poor saw poor relief as their property, the one right unambiguously conferred by settlement', the propertied recognized only that 'the poor think they have obtained a sort of right to relief or to work when work is scarce'.[151] Settlement was, therefore, not the guarantor of entitlement; it was merely the principal means through which entitlement was regulated. Settlement simply changed the terms of the calculation: not how the poor should be relieved but who should provide for them.[152] Although the 'certificate man' or settled pauper enjoyed security in his new residence under the terms of the settlement laws, he might still be denied entitlement to relief there under the terms of the poor laws.[153] It has, furthermore, been argued even more recently that 'for a far from inconsequential minority of poor relief recipients, possession of a settlement may not have been critical or a *sine qua non* regarding eligibility'. Between 30 and 40 per cent of those receiving pensions in the century after 1650 cannot be shown to have been born, married, or buried in the parish which relieved them, a fact which suggest that factors other than settlement, especially the absence of close kin, may have been more decisive in the earning of entitlement.[154] Settlement may be a blind alley, then, even for historians

[149] Snell, *Annals of the Labouring Poor*, 71.

[150] Ibid. 72, 112.

[151] T. Cooper, *Observations Upon The Vagrant Laws; Proving That The Statutes In Queen Elizabeth's Time Are The Most Proper Foundation For A Law Of That Nature, And That All Alterations That Have Been Made Since, Have Been For The Worse* (1742), 19.

[152] Snell, 'Pauper Settlement', 400–1.

[153] Slack, *The English Poor Law*, 36. Slack suggests that in the wake of the 1714 vagrancy act (13 Anne c. 26), anticipated in its most crucial provision—the levying of county rates for the expense of passing vagrants—in 11 William III, c. 18 (1700), parish officers circumvented the 'paternalistic' clauses of the 1697 settlement law by expelling the old and women as vagrants. Slack, *The English Poor Law*, 39. For examples, see J. S. Cockburn, 'The North Riding Justices, 1690–1750: A Study in Local Administration', *Yorkshire Archaeological Journal*, 41 (1963–6), 509, 512.

[154] Smith, 'Ageing and Well-Being', 74.

of notions of entitlement in the seventeenth century, let alone for those of the eighteenth. Even so, the argument that the poor were legally entitled to relief is now so widespread in the historiography that it must be taken seriously.

4. PETITIONS AND APPEALS

The following discussion seeks to investigate the extent to which the poor actually were 'entitled' to relief in seventeenth-century England. In so doing, it draws not only upon a close reading of the provisions of the Elizabethan poor laws but also on the extensive bodies of evidence of their judicial interpretation and administrative implementation. It also takes advantage of the invaluable light which has been cast into the conceptual gloom with which the entitlement paradigm is shrouded by recent attempts systematically to think through what entitlement means in the context of welfare systems and how welfare regimes might be classified according to the calculus by which entitlement was regulated. Paul Johnson, for instance, insists that rights to poor relief can only be understood in legal (as opposed to moral or customary) terms. Entitlement, he insists is 'the *legal* basis of the relationship between contribution and benefit'.[155] This is not to deny the significance of the longstanding moral obligation to relieve the poor, simply to emphasize that moral and legal entitlements were not necessarily synonymous. The charitable imperative doubtless continued to influence both attitudes and practices towards the poor throughout our period and it is no part of the intention here to devalue its significance. But the extent to which it was enshrined in the provisions and practice of the Elizabethan poor law is altogether more ambiguous.

Routine decisions about eligibility for relief were until 1692 taken by overseers of the poor who, as we have seen, were required to negotiate the conflicting priorities of charity and economy. Whenever such decisions were regarded as unjust, illegal, or even tyrannical, applicants for relief might turn for redress to the county magistrates (and ultimately even to the assize judges) who exercised powers of audit, co-ordination, and arbitration in matters arising from the poor laws. In this sense, the politics of poor relief reflected the structural characteristics of the English state in which authority was directly exercised by officeholders of middling status across thousands of local communities.[156] The initiative

[155] P. Johnson, 'Risk, Redistribution and Social Welfare in Britain from the Poor Law to Beveridge', in Daunton (ed), *Charity, Self-Interest and Welfare*, 230–1.

[156] Hindle, *The State and Social Change*, 204–30.

in seeking parish relief lay with the poor themselves, and the crucial decisions were taken initially by the parish officers with whom they had the most direct contact and only secondarily by magistrates, and perhaps subsequently even by the judiciary, when their application was rejected. The role of magistrates became even more central between 1692 and 1723 when statute transferred the power to admit new pensioners to the relief rolls exclusively to JPs. Indeed, this relatively short experiment was aborted on the grounds that justices were too generous, and had been exploited by paupers who, without the knowledge of the parish officers, 'upon untrue suggestions and sometimes upon false or frivolous pretences have obtained relief which hath greatly contributed to the increase of the parish rates'.[157]

The very large number of appeals made to justices over the heads of the parish officers might be taken as an indication that the poor were confident that the magistracy could successfully be mobilized to defend their interests. Whether popular appeals and elite responses were reflective of bilateral consciousness of the 'paternalism of the magistracy' as a class is, however, rather more problematic. As we shall see, magisterial motives were considerably more complex and less voluntaristic than this seemingly innocent phrase suggests.[158] Some paupers, like Edward Messenger of Ashwicken, who pleaded with the Norfolk justices in 1647 that 'you will not turn away yor eyes and eares from the cry of the poore', seem almost to have shamed the magistracy into redressing their grievances.[159] From the very earliest days of the Elizabethan poor law, moreover, appeals played not only on the legal obligations, but also on the Christian duty of care, not only of the gentry but also of parish officers. In 1617, for instance, John Baker and his two daughters, 'poor impotent and lame people' of the parish of Lottisham Green (Somerset), complained that Thomas Cooper the collector of the poor had not only withheld their relief but 'threatneth and raileth upon them with very unchristian like speeches'. Mary Wootton of Curland (Somerset) similarly complained in 1623 that the parishioners there, 'fearing that they will become chargeable', her husband 'having become impotent by reason of age and sick-

[157] 3 William & Mary, c. 11, sect. xi (1692); 9 George I, c. 7. (1723). Even into the 19th century, however, parish officers characterized paupers as 'those that take from our reluctant hands | What [Richard] Burn advises or the Bench Commands'. Rule, *Albion's People*, 122.

[158] The foundation text on the 'paternalistic' self-image of the gentry is Thompson, *Customs in Common*, esp. 19–24. For a more nuanced reading, see J. Walter, 'Public Transcripts, Popular Agency and the Politics of Subsistence in Early Modern England', in M. J. Braddick and J. Walter (eds.), *Negotiating Power: Order, Hierarchy and Subordination in Early Modern England and Ireland* (Cambridge, 2001), esp. 125–8.

[159] Wales, 'Poverty, Poor Relief and the Life-Cycle', 388.

ness', had summarily evicted them 'and in most unchristianlike manner suffer them to dwell under a hedge'. In a particularly poignant formulation, James Mason of Little Paxton (Huntingdonshire) complained in 1638 that his wife and six children had been turned out of the house where they had lived for fourteen years and had 'been forced to live abroad in the streets theis sixe weeks without succour or harbour'. He pleaded that 'the justices look with the eye of pittie and compassion' upon their plight, because his family were 'out of hope to receive any helpe from the frozen charitie of our towne governors other than hunger and colde to starve [them] to death'. Whether or not explicitly Christian rhetoric was strategic, it was deployed late into the seventeenth century: the Cumberland bench was confronted with one petition for relief in 1686 'for the mercy of God and the merits of Christ Jesus' and another in 1688 pleading 'for the keeping of [the petitioner's] soul and body together, till God's good time come fairly to divorce them'. In the 1690s it was not unusual for petitioners for relief in Cumberland and Lancashire to complain that their neighbours' charity was grown cold, suggesting that the stream of traditional benevolence had frozen up and that, even where it still flowed, those who came into contact with it experienced feelings of wounded self-respect and dignity.[160]

(*a*) The Magistracy and the Poor

How many such appeals actually took place? They can be traced back to at least 1594, when a widow from Clothall (Hertfordshire) sought to persuade the county bench that she and her children had not been relieved under the terms of the statute of 1572.[161] Their frequency thereafter is difficult to measure. It seems that there were 'singularly few' appeals in Jacobean Somerset, and even in the 1640s and 1650s they were apparently only sporadic, although this may be less an indication that the poor were satisfied with their lot in that county than an optical illusion

[160] *Quarter Sessions Records for the County of Somerset*, i. 204, 336–7; BL, MS Additional, 34000, fo. 265; CRO, Q/11/1/1/2, 1/20, 28/13, 37/17; A. Fessler, 'The Official Attitude toward the Sick Poor in Seventeenth-Century Lancashire', *Transactions of the Historic Society of Lancashire and Cheshire*, 102 (1951), 110. The trope of excoriating the 'cold charity' of a miserly elite was used in published sermons from as early as the 1570s. I. W. Archer, 'The Charity of Early Modern Londoners', *Transactions of the Royal Historical Society*, 6th ser., 12 (2002), 227–8. Its origins lie in the prophecy in Matthew 24: 12 that charity, which is warm almost by definition, will become cold. From the Reformation onwards, its sense was that charity was increasingly being exercised either by impersonal institutions or by individuals who gave out of duty rather than compassion.

[161] M. K. McIntosh, 'Local Responses to the Poor in Late Medieval and Tudor England', *Continuity and Change*, 3 (1988), 244 n. 109.

created by the absence of the relevant archives.[162] In other counties, however, appeals were extremely common, with some 230 complaints heard by the Lancashire bench in the years 1629–48 and over 700 by their Warwickshire colleagues between 1625 and 1680. At Easter 1682, twenty-five petitions for relief were presented to the Derbyshire quarter sessions, and a further fifteen were heard at midsummer.[163] Regional differentials in the frequency of petitioning doubtless owe much to the varying administrative practices of each county bench, and especially to the precocity and regularity of petty sessions (and, in turn, to the survival of their records). Figures such as these should be regarded, moreover, as minima, for the vast majority of appeals were, as the critics of the system suggested, made to individual justices acting out of sessions, and only systematic work in a large sample of magistrate's handbooks (whose survival rate is not high for this period) would make possible any realistic estimate of how common appeals of this kind actually were. In some respects, moreover, the significance of appeals is not to be measured in quantitative terms. The numbers who appealed were, of course, dwarfed by those who were relieved without question. Even so, the system of appeals was the mechanism by which the thresholds of eligibility for collection were policed, and its operation is therefore of profound symbolic and political importance to the experience of those who sought parish relief.

One of the finest archives of negotiation over the entitlement to relief is that of the Cumberland magistracy in the late seventeenth and early eighteenth centuries. There are some 465 petitions for poor relief surviving amongst the quarter sessions rolls of the Cumberland bench for the years 1686 to 1749.[164] Twelve of these petitions were drawn up either

[162] *Quarter Sessions Records for the County of Somerset*, i, p. xxxi. For the 1640s and 1650s, see *Quarter Sessions Records for the County of Somerset*, iii. 46 (Biddisham, Oct. 1647), 138 (Badgeworth, Jan. 1651), 145 (Crewkerne, Apr. 1651), 159–60 (Enmore, Oct. 1651), 268 (North Petherton, July 1655). There was a burst of nine appeals, from the parishes of Wellington, Bridgewater, Huntspill, and Taunton, heard at the Taunton sessions in July 1653: *Quarter Sessions Records for the County of Somerset*, iii. 212–13. At least one appeal found its way as far as the Somerset assizes: *Somerset Assize Orders, 1640–1659*, ed. J. S. Cockburn (Somerset Record Society, 71, Taunton, 1971), 31 (Mar. 1649).

[163] LRO, QSB/1/51/-301; A.L. Beier, 'Studies in Poverty and Poor Relief in Warwickshire, 1540–1680' (unpublished Ph.D. diss., Princeton University, 1969), 168–9; Beier, *Masterless Men*, 174; Fletcher, *Reform*, 189.

[164] Except where reference is made to an individual case, the following discussion is based on an analysis of the petitions for poor relief in CRO, Q/11/1/1–118, a sample which *excludes* all those petitions either from debtors and other prisoners in the county gaol or from maimed soldiers. The figures cited here should be taken as bare minima, since only those factors *explicitly* mentioned in the petitions have been counted for statistical purposes. It should also, of course,

by, or on behalf of, children or orphans. Of the 453 remaining petitions, ninety (20 per cent) were on behalf of co-resident married couples, 161 (36 per cent) from single men, and 202 (45 per cent) from single women. Of the women, eleven described themselves as spinsters, twenty-nine as abandoned wives, and a further ninety-two as widows. The remaining seventy female applicants were probably also either widows or spinsters, though they did not explicitly describe themselves as such.

As might be expected, the petitioners most often told tales of creeping old age and chronic illness. Almost 40 per cent (186) of the petitioners supported their claim by some reference to their age. Although eighty-four of these neither specified nor estimated exactly how old they were, referring to themselves simply as 'aged' or 'ancient', eight described themselves (albeit, perhaps, with poetic licence) as between 60 and 69, thirty-eight between 70 and 79, forty-two between 80 and 89, and sixteen as over 90. The aged poor, therefore, do not seem to have been socially placid, resigned to accepting their lot.[165] With age came arthritic limbs and failing sight. Leaving aside those cases where petitioners simply described themselves as 'unable to work' or 'decrepit', there were sixty-four cases of lameness, forty of blindness, and twenty-five cases of unspecified illness, the symptoms of which suggest ailments as diverse as ulcers, scrofula, typhus, and epilepsy.[166] For both married and single petitioners, the demands of families loomed large. Ninety-three (20 per cent) of the petitioners made reference to the fact that they had two or more children, and many of these emphasized the physical or mental health problems of their offspring. Then there was the under-employment experienced by the Workington weaver who told the bench in 1698 that trade 'is very dead now' and that having been 'out of work' for several months he could no longer support his wife and nine children.[167] Others linked their claims to the prices of the necessities of life: Ann Irdell of Crosthwaite sought an increase in her pension in 1735 'fireing and provision being so dear'; Alice Whitehead argued in 1738 that half her

be borne in mind that there is overlap between the various categories employed here: both widows and married women might, for example, be overburdened with children, and each might also be blind and/or sick.

[165] For examples of the elderly poor of 17th- and 18th-century Kent appealing against overseers' recalcitrance, see Barker-Read, 'Treatment of the Aged Poor', 61–2.

[166] For the profile of diseases afflicting petitioners for poor relief in 17th-century Lancashire, see Fessler, 'The Sick Poor in Seventeenth-Century Lancashire', 97–101, 106–7, where it is noted (99 n. 3) that references to scrofula in particular became especially common after the Restoration. For parish officers' responses to scrofula, see Tate, *The Parish Chest*, 156–60.

[167] CRO, Q/11/1/46/38.

weekly pension 'goes for Coals for fireing' so that 'she has the small matter as six pence to live upon'.[168]

Apart from material or physical factors, petitioners placed great emphasis on their character and their familiarity to their neighbours. Thirty-seven petitioners explicitly claimed that they were born in the parish where they sought relief, a further thirty-one to have been long resident there, and fifteen to have been lifelong residents. Twenty-one referred in various ways to their good reputation in local community, of whom eleven appended certificates from groups of 'chief inhabitants' testifying to their honest conduct and conversation. That provided by nine parishioners of Crosby-in-Eden on behalf of Mary Atkinson in 1740 may stand for all. For the seventeen years since her marriage they had known her to be free from scandal or other fault. 'Poverty', they insisted, 'was always reckoned her greatest crime.'[169] At least a dozen explicitly alluded to the fact that they had worked hard for as long as they could, one of these describing himself 'as a true labourer in time of health'.[170] Others emphasized that they had never burdened the parish before.[171] Although some, like the 80-year old Carlisle widow Mary Bell, pointed out that they had themselves always been ready to give alms to their neighbours, only four petitioners either stated or implied that they had paid rates, a surprisingly low proportion in the light of recent historiographical speculation that poor relief functioned as a form of social insurance.[172] There were, by contrast, numerous allusions to the fact that all other avenues of relief had been explored and found wanting: that kin support had disappeared or diminished; that all their remaining goods had been sold or pawned; that the charity and patience of neighbours had been exhausted. This pattern is predictable, and should probably be taken as typical of the profile of the petitions for poor relief that might be made in any seventeenth-century English county.[173] One regional peculiarity does,

[168] CRO, Q/11/1/175/20, 187/2.

[169] CRO, Q/11/1/197/41.

[170] CRO, Q/11/1/88/14.

[171] CRO, Q/11/123/2, 59/3, 96/15, 174/17. For a pensioner who had for a 'long time . . . been willing to receive' but 18*d.* weekly 'while she could doe anything for herself' but sought an increase to 2*s.* in her sickness and helplessness, see CRO, Q/11/1/165/24.

[172] CRO, Q/11/1/99/7. For the four former Cumberland ratepayers, see CRO, Q/11/1/136/2, 184/24, 197/19, 200/5. Only three (1.7%) of the 179 petitioners for relief at Lancashire quarter sessions in the years 1698–9 claimed to have been ratepayers, though a fourth pleaded that she had always assisted 'to her power the poor in almes deedes'. LRO, QSR/824/3; 828/2, 6, 37. An inhabitant of Chartham (Kent) was granted a pension in the early 1650s at least partly because his neighbours testified that he had 'always relieved the poor'. Kent Archives Office, Maidstone, Q/SB/1/26. Cf. Solar, 'Poor Relief', 7–12; Hitchcock *et al.*, 'Introduction', 10.

[173] Cf. the brief discussion of petitions to the Lancashire bench in the 1620s and 1630s in

however, stand out, serving as a potent reminder of the relatively underdeveloped nature of social welfare provision in this dark corner of the land. At least seventeen (6 per cent) of the petitioners reinforced their claim by stating not only, as might be expected, that they were unable to *work* but that they were also unable to *beg*.[174]

Where they did occur, appeals might succeed in provoking a habitation order, a warrant to provide a pension, or even a gratuity. Of all these solutions, parish officers looked most sympathetically on gratuities, which generally imposed no financial burden at all on ratepayers, the one-off payment being made from county funds. Overseers might even encourage applications of this kind (and, indeed, welcome the extension of the power to pay gratuities to justices acting out of sessions) not least because they might occasionally become semi-permanent arrangements, as was the case with the Warwickshire widow Alice Raves who was receiving a shilling a week from the county treasurer throughout the 1670s.[175] In some areas, such as the North Riding of Yorkshire, the issuing of gratuities had come to represent such a large-scale and expensive evasion of parochial responsibilities that the bench was forced to curtail it altogether by the early 1690s.[176]

More commonly, however, an appeal might result in a justices' order that the applicant be enlisted among the parish paupers, or at least be provided with housing at parish expense. Their chances of success seem to have varied. In fourteen of the fifteen cases where parish overseers were summoned before the Wiltshire magistrate William Hunt to justify their initial refusal to grant relief in the 1740s, for example, the dissatisfied paupers were eventually granted the pensions they had sought. Others were less fortunate. Only twenty-five (15 per cent) of the 168 petitions sent to the Durham magistrate Edmund Tew in the period 1750–64 resulted in orders for pensions or maintenance.[177] Even so, sympathetic

G. W. Oxley, 'The Permanent Poor in South-West Lancashire under the Old Poor Law', in J. R. Harris (ed.), *Liverpool and Merseyside: Essays in the Economic History of the Port and its Hinterland* (London, 1969), 21–4.

[174] Cf. Ch. 1.4 above.

[175] *Warwick County Records*, vii. 97, 107, 127.

[176] Cockburn, 'The North Riding Justices', 505.

[177] *The Justicing Notebook of William Hunt, 1744–1749*, ed. E. Crittall (Wiltshire Record Society, 37, Devizes, 1982), 12 and nos. 180, 214, 222, 223, 272, 340, 355, 377, 399, 436; G. Morgan and P. Rushton, 'The Magistrate, the Community and the Maintenance of an Orderly Society in Eighteenth-Century England', *Historical Research*, 76 (2003), 67. To judge by the evidence of his notebook, the Surrey JP Richard Wyatt never received any appeals from paupers against overseers. *Deposition Book of Richard Wyatt, JP, 1767–1776*, ed. E. Silverthorne (Surrey Record Society, 30, Guildford, 1978).

appeals gave magistrates like Hunt or Tew the opportunity to rehearse set-piece statements of their paternalistic self-image, often inflecting their language with that employed by the petitioner. Somerset JPs, for example, insisted in 1615 that the overseers of St George's Taunton (Somerset) 'take especial care' that Powell Day and his family 'be not constrained to lie in the streets, especially for that his wife is very sick and weak'. Robert Doughty insisted in 1665 that the overseers of Cawston (Norfolk) provide for Mary Jary, 'she lying on a lock of straw almost starved'. The rhetoric of social justice appears to have been especially characteristic of the Warwickshire bench in the 1650s, where the magistracy condemned the expulsion of a single mother from Fillongley the day before she went into labour in 1653 as 'uncivil', 'unmerciful', and 'unjustifiable'; criticized the inhabitants of Lea Marston for 'barbarously' carrying a heavily pregnant vagrant across the parish boundary of Curdworth to avoid the charge of her bastard in 1652; and 'disliked' the 'violent proceedings' of the overseers of Brailes in peremptorily raising the poor-rate assessments of employers whose servants they unjustifiably deemed likely to be chargeable to the parish in 1659. In 1654 they berated the parish officers of Ilmington for allowing William Samon and his wife to lie in the street, arguing that 'it was a great offence against God that any poor man should be so hardly dealt with as not to be suffered to have lodging within doors in this winter season'.[178] In 1671 the Norfolk bench received a complaint of the negligence of the parish officers of Haveringland, whose decision to leave a widow and her four children in the care of an incompetent parishioner had allegedly resulted in the death of one child and the nakedness, infestation, and near starvation of the other three. The resultant relief order was inflected with moral outrage, at this 'most cruel and barbarous act' which it could 'not let pass without some exemplary punishment'.[179] When informed that the parish officers of Cumrew (Cumberland) had stopped the relief due to Thomas Varty and his wife in 1694 the earl of Carlisle fulminated that 'if I heare any more complaints . . . I will have you severely punished'.[180] In 1700 the

[178] *Quarter Sessions Records for the County of Somerset*, i. 124; *Notebook of Robert Doughty*, 60; *Warwick County Records*, iii. 96, 153–4, 209; iv. 84–5. A. L. Beier, 'Poor Relief in Warwickshire, 1630–1660', *Past and Present*, 35 (1966), 99, suggests that this tone of personal sympathy for the poor was the product of the influence of puritan magistrates such as Sir Simon Archer and of Major-General Whalley. C. Durston, *Cromwell's Major Generals: Godly Government during the English Revolution* (Manchester, 2001), 169–70, reports in turn Whalley's praise for the way in which Matthew Hale had presided over Midlands assizes 'in speciall manner takeing care of poore men in their causes without which some had suffered'.

[179] Norfolk RO, Norwich, C/S2/3, unfol.

[180] CRO, Q/11/1/31/29–31.

Buckinghamshire magistrates were quick to criticize the 'inhumane' treatment of a smallpox victim whom the parish officers of Chesham had whipped, evicted, and exposed to the cold, despite her sad and languishing condition.[181]

Although the magistracy could afford to condemn publicly the conduct of vestrymen in this way, the poor were perforce more circumspect, at least in the first instance. In their historically invisible doorstep encounters with parish officers, they doubtless rehearsed platitudes of deference so conventional that overseers probably took them for granted rather than taking them seriously.[182] Rather more revealing is the language adopted in those formal petitions in which the poor sought to mobilize the intervention of the Cumberland magistracy. The question of who actually wrote these petitions on behalf of infirm and illiterate applicants for relief is a vexed one. They are generally unsigned and usually unmarked, and even where several petitions originate from a single claimant, variations in the nature and quality of the hand implies that numerous different scribes were involved. The identity of these scriveners is a mystery. Literate neighbours like Roger Lowe of Ashton-in-Makerfield or Thomas Turner of East Hoathly often wrote petitions, letters, or wills on behalf of others, and it may well be that men like them were also called upon to draw up, occasionally even to compose, applications for relief. When Thomas Gerard of Hilton (Lancashire) and his young family all lay sick in bed in 1699, for instance, he asked his neighbour Richard Tildesley 'to come to the sessions and tell their condicion', which resulted both in a petition and in Tildesley's personal appearance on their behalf.[183] It is equally possible that petitioners deliberately chose advocates who embodied particular social or moral authority, the parish clergyman, for instance, a leading ratepayer, perhaps, or even a retired parish officer. Officeholders and vestrymen were certainly favoured by applicants who sought collective subscription to testimonials of their deservingness from 'the parish'. Conversely, sympathy might be more forthcoming from disaffected householders or vestrymen who were already discontented with the direction of policy. The issues of principle or faction at play behind these arrangements will doubtless remain obscure. Either way, it is clear that the petitioners pleaded their cases in a

[181] *Buckinghamshire Sessions Records*, ii. 231–2.

[182] Boulton, 'Going on the Parish', 28, points out that applications for relief from Christ's Hospital were submitted on printed forms which included formulaic statements of deference.

[183] *The Diary of Roger Lowe of Ashton-in-Makerfield, Lancashire, 1663–74*, ed. W. L. Sachse (London, 1938), 24, 28, 42–3, 46, 48, 51, 53, 62–3; *Diary of Thomas Turner*, 79, 122, 123–4, 145, 193, 197; LRO, QSP/823/53.

wide variety of ways, and that there is little or nothing formulaic about these pitifully sad stories.

On the one hand, applicants for relief appealed to the gentry's own ancient standards of paternalism, implicitly reminding the bench of its own rhetoric. Indeed, all the petitions were by definition to some degree deferential, though the high-flown language of one or two petitioners conveyed their vivid sense of the awesome power of the magistracy. One elderly widower from Torpenhow reminded the magistrates that 'it hath pleased God to make you his vicegerents here upon earth'. A crippled orphan from Scaleby even applied subtle pressure by expressing his confidence in 'your honours, who never faile to Contrive and provide for such miserable poor creatures as he'.[184] Others described their plight vividly, occasionally even with stylistic flair: Margaret Marshall claimed that she was 'now become miserably poor, having lost her Sight and being under Great disorders both of body and mind'; and Mabel Atkinson that 'God knows [she] has no Lodging place nor no harbour to draw to'.[185] Others were more direct. John Hoe stated simply that he had become 'an object of petty' in his lameness and blindness; Sybil Latimer that she needed both 'bread and looking too' in her hungry old age.[186]

By contrast some petitioners were courageous or desperate enough to emphasize the negligence and malice of parish officers. The overseers were 'agin them', wrote two elderly inhabitants of Sebergham in 1691. I am 'plagued by the overseers' claimed another from Torpenhow in 1692. A third complained that the overseer of St Mary's, Carlisle had set aside his relief order in 1703 'using his own method'. The overseers of Westward had proved 'uncharitable and inhumane' to one petitioner, those of Kirklinton had used 'wicked language' to another. These petitioners would doubtless have agreed with the criticism offered of the parish officers of Jacobean Norfolk, who were said to 'oversee as though they did not see at all'.[187] Some went even further. Anne Bowman, a 78-year-old widow of Kirkoswald, alleged in 1710 that her feud with her 'unmerciful and savage' overseers, one of whom 'very positively saith that he will never pay her any[thing]', had left her not only destitute with all her goods in pawn but in a 'hunger-bitten condition' when 'God has blessed the land with plenty'.[188] Well into the eighteenth century, the petitions disclose a litany of threats and deceits by overseers: 'fair promises of

[184] CRO, Q/11/1/24/7, 99/18.

[185] CRO, Q/11/1/59/22, 67/11.

[186] CRO, Q/11/1/67/20, 67/21.

[187] CRO, Q/11/1/18/13, 24/7, 68/6, 137/25, 177/14. Cf. BL, MS Additional, 12496, fo. 258^{v}.

[188] CRO, Q11/1/88/9, 96/25.

civilitie and kindness' succeeded only by the abrupt suspension of relief; undertakings to comply with magistrates' orders resulting only in yet more special pleading; arrangements made for dependent children to be pressed for military service as soon as petitioners 'required an allowance out of the parish'; threats of committal to Bridewell if the applicant 'came any more for relief'.[189]

Even more striking, however, is the frequency with which such petitions referred to previous orders allocating them a pension, orders which had been ignored or condemned by vestrymen. At least 107 (or 23 per cent) of the petitions heard by the Cumberland magistracy in the period 1686–1749 were second appeals, in which 'paupers' who had already been granted pensions either from the bench or from justices acting out of sessions sought to coerce parish officers who stood in contempt of relief orders. This is to say nothing of those cases where parish officers had complied with the *letter* rather than the *spirit* of an order. Elizabeth Mushett protested to the Buckinghamshire bench in 1700 that, although the overseers of East Claydon had housed her, they had 'mixed her with so great a number of persons in one tenement' that she and her child were 'almost stifled', 'destitute of that due convenience of habitation that is necessary for the preservation of their healths and dressing, provisions of their sustenance and washing and other business'.[190] Elizabeth Miles complained that, although she was 98 and had lived in Aylesbury for sixty years, the overseers there allowed her only 15*d.* a week, 'which is little more than what she can expend in fire being old and very chilly and withal not able to make herself ready without help'. Robert Bowman protested that in implementing a habitation order the Kirkoswald overseers had housed him so far from his neighbours that his family were 'rendered destitute of all charity and assistance'.[191]

These, then, were narratives distilled from a volatile compound of frustration, desperation, and obsequiousness. Where they were ignored, the destitute might resort to the open intimidation of overseers, publicly advertising their plight by camping out in church porches. In doing so, they both placed themselves at the symbolic heart of the parish community and sought access to any doles informally distributed after communion.[192] If anything, however, the destitute and even the aged

[189] CRO, Q/11/1/157/30, 192/2, 217/9, 221/5.

[190] *Buckinghamshire Sessions Records*, ii. 234. For similar examples of petitioners claiming that they had been housed inappropriately, see J. Broad, 'Housing the Rural Poor in England, 1650–1850', *Agricultural History Review*, 48 (2000), 160–1.

[191] *Buckinghamshire Sessions Records*, iii. 183; CRO, Q/11/1/27/3.

[192] For begging in church porches, see Ch. 5.2 above. For doles distributed after communion, see Ch. 2.5(*c*) above.

self-consciously avoided the language of entitlement, since the mere suggestion that the poor thought they had a right to relief might itself alienate both vestry and magistracy who often equated assertiveness with clamour. The vestry of St Saviour's Southwark was particularly contemptuous of those indolent poor men 'well able to work' who, when 'reproved' for their 'idleness and ill-husbandry', boldly expressed their confidence that 'the parish shall keep them'. Perhaps they had sung the popular ballad, 'Hang Sorrow, cast away Care; the parish is bound to find us, &c', which eighteenth-century critics of the poor law such as Henry Fielding found such an offensive 'song of Triumph'.[193] In its earliest published form of 1671, however, the ballad was less triumphalist than fatalistic in its recognition of the realities of life on the parish: 'Hang fear, cast away care, The parish is bound to find us, | Thou and I all must dye, and leave the world behind us, | The Bells shall ring, The Clerk shall sing, And the good old wife winde us, | And John shall lay our bones in clay, where the Devil ne'er shall find us'.[194] Behind the backs of overseers, then, perhaps in alehouses or other spaces where a dissident sub-culture might thrive, pensioners created for themselves an identity as merry beggars. To their faces, however, the poor remained generally circumspect about asserting their rights long after the Restoration, one petition to the Norfolk bench in 1670 delicately referred to overseers as 'those whose office it is to provide for the wants of such as are poor and impotent and past their labours'.[195]

Indeed, whether or not they believed in an inherent right to relief, prospective paupers found it more profitable to perform due deference than to plead legal entitlement. Only one of the 465 petitioners to the Cumberland bench in the years 1686–1749 dared to use the language of entitlement. Anne Robson of Plumpton complained in 1710 that she 'cannot get her rights', but even then her emphasis lay rather on the overseers' recalcitrance in resisting a previous relief order than on the terms

[193] J. Boulton, *Neighbourhood and Society: A London Suburb in the Seventeenth Century* (Cambridge, 1987), 95; H. Fielding, 'I Hate the Mob', *The Covent Garden Journal*, 49 (20 June 1752), in id., *The Covent Garden Journal and A Plan of the Universal Register-Office*, ed. B. A. Goldgar (Oxford, 1988), 270.

[194] 'Song 267', in *The New Academy of Complements . . . With an Exact Collection of the Newest and Choicest Songs a la Mode* (London, 1671), 271–2. Different versions of the ballad between 1671 and 1752 can be traced in J. Playford, *Musical Companion, Book I* (London, 1673), 57; *Merry Drollery* (London, 1691), 217; *The Spectator*, 232 (26 Nov. 1711). A version of 1668 has been attributed to Richard Climsall. *Roxburghe Ballads*, ed. W. Chappell and J. W. Ebsworth (9 vols., London, 1869–97), i. 509. More generally, see R. Harvey, 'English Pre-Industrial Ballads on Poverty, 1500–1700', *The Historian*, 41 (1984), 539–61.

[195] Fletcher, *Reform*, 188. Cf. J. C. Scott, *Domination and the Arts of Resistance: Hidden Transcripts* (New Haven, 1990), 108–35.

of the statute itself. One other petitioner did obliquely imply a sense of injustice when pleading in 1694 that the overseers of Cumrew be made to pay the arrears on his pension: 'Wee want the Just sum of money—14s.6d.'. Much more characteristic, however, is the attitude of William Langrigg of Westward, who claimed in 1701 that, although he had some *four years* previously obtained a relief order for 9*d.* weekly for himself and his aged wife, the overseers would only pay them 6*d.* Not wishing to be 'too troublesome', they waited in hope of full payment soon, but now they were driven in desperation to petition because the parish had cut them off altogether.[196] Similar acquiescence was expressed by Elizabeth Birkett of Crosthwaite, who was allowed a pension of 1*s.* a week in 1709. Although the magistrate himself noted that the sum was 'too little', she would not refuse it because she wished to retain 'the love of her neighbours'.[197]

The frequency with which petitions were simply endorsed with directions for relief should not, however, lead us to believe that they were invariably successful. Eligibility was often contested and legal obligations were not easily mobilized. Matthew Hale doubted whether poor labouring men overburdened with children were even eligible for, let alone entitled to, relief, and observed that 'if they come for exhibitions [i.e. pensions] they are denyed, or at least have but very small and such as cannot support them and their families'.[198] Nor should the difficulties which confronted even the elderly or infirm as they sought access to the circuits of authority be underestimated. Three elderly parishioners of Walberton, for instance, were forced to spend 2*s.* in 1643 in obtaining an order from the Sussex bench compelling parish officers to fulfil their obligations, even though the relatives on whose behalf they acted fitted unambiguously into the category of the 'deserving': Ede Asuch complained that her husband's pension was 11*s.* in arrears despite the fact that 'he hath bin long bedridd' and was 'aged above a hundred years'; Martha Wilson was owed 20*s.* for maintaining 'a poore [orphan] childe of the parishe'; and Joane Page was owed 20*s.* for caring her late husband's children.[199] Although Mary Atherton of Falmer (Sussex) was 'so extreame aged and weak that she is not able to help herself nor to put on her clothes', the overseers had simply failed to provide for her 'as her age and necessity requires'. The friends of Anne Goodman complained to the Hertfordshire bench in 1693 that the parish officers of Welwyn had

[196] CRO, Q/11/1/97/10, 31/31, 59/24.

[197] CRO, Q/11/1/91/27.

[198] M. Hale, *A Discourse Touching Provision for the Poor* (London, 1683), 6.

[199] [*Sussex*] *Quarter Sessions Order Book*, 39.

refused to provide for her even though she was 'a poor lunatick distressed woman'.[200] In the early eighteenth century it could cost even very deserving cases several shillings to obtain an order to coerce recalcitrant overseers: the Buckinghamshire bench awarded James Cox, a partially sighted glover suffering from palsy, ulcers, and scrofula, 5*s*. a week and 5*s*. costs from the overseers of West Wycombe in 1711. It took widow Margaret Batey four days to hobble on her crutches from Kirklinton to the Carlisle sessions in 1735, and although she knew 'not what way to get home', the bench simply referred her case to a local magistrate.[201] There is even some evidence to suggest that, where parish officers became uncomfortable with the number of appeals made against them, they simply stopped subsidizing the expenses of the complainants, thus effectively closing off one avenue of negotiation. Faced with such tactics, it is hardly surprising that the occasional applicant for relief was tempted to give up: in 1664 widow Martha Oliver of Whitnash had been granted a relief order for 2*s*. a week in to maintain her three children, 'yet notwithstanding for her quiet she hath been content to accept 1s weekly'. Predictably, the parish officers promptly stopped paying her even that sum and had to be forced into meeting the arrears in 1667. Mary Robinson, a lame widow of Hesket, explained to the Cumberland bench in 1706 that she would have petitioned earlier had not the parish officers bought her off with a promise of 6*d*. weekly, 'which they have never yet paid'.[202] Petitions occasionally refer to an agreement, or even to a 'contract', made between pauper and the parish officers, implying that a pension had been offered only on the grounds that the petitioner would not come back for more.[203]

Even when they heard sad tales well told, it should not be assumed that the magistracy always allied themselves with the poor. When confronted in 1651 with the petition of widow Elizabeth Oughton of Allesley that maintenance be granted for her and her child, the Warwickshire bench were persuaded rather by the opinion of 'some of the inhabitants' of Allesley that her daughter was 'about eighteen years of age and although she be somewhat lame yet is able to get her own living' and that Elizabeth herself was 'an able woman' who 'doth little or nothing else but follow the justices at assizes and sessions with her petitions as she hath done for many years past'. The petition was dismissed in order that 'the inhabitants

[200] [*Sussex*] *Quarter Sessions Order Book*, 102; *Hertford County Records*, vi. 461.

[201] *Buckinghamshire Sessions Records*, iii. 265–6; CRO, Q/11/1/177/14.

[202] S. R. Broadbridge, 'The Old Poor Law in the Parish of Stone', *North Staffordshire Journal of Field Studies*, 13 (1973), 12; *Warwick County Records*, v. 72–3; CRO, Q/11/1/81/30.

[203] CRO, Q/11/1/156/4, 163/4. Cf. the case of Goody Clapson of Maidstone who accepted £4 from the overseers in 1728 'promising not to be troublesome to them any more'. Barker-Read, 'Treatment of the Aged Poor', 75.

and overseers of the poor may be freed from her clamour'.[204] The parish officers of Allesley were, in fact, engaged in a twenty-year running battle with Oughton. She was first awarded a weekly pension of 5*s*. in 1638, but nonetheless 'suffered her children to wander abroad and beg for their relief and took no course to set them to work whereby they might get their living hereafter'. Because this was likely to result in a further charge to the parish, the inhabitants offered to 'breed [the three children] up at their own charge whereby they might live in some honest vocation hereafter' but only if Oughton agreed to maintain herself. The bench accordingly ordered the overseers to cancel her pension and place all the children in service. They were nonetheless forced to grant a habitation order in her favour in 1639. Despite their frustrations with her clamour in 1651, the bench was once again confronted with Oughton in 1658, when she accused the parish of breaching an agreement to bind out her lame child at a cost of 50*s*. a year.[205] This, of course, is to say nothing of those cases where the magistracy flatly refused petitions for relief. Although extant petitions are not invariably subscribed with magistrates' decisions, it is particularly striking that the notation 'nil' or 'nothing' so frequently appears in the margins of these claims.[206]

Occasionally, however, it was the magistracy itself that actively solicited the petitions and appeals of the poor, a tendency which became particularly marked in years of high prices. When 'many poor people' complained to the Nottinghamshire bench in 1623 that they lacked 'maintenance and habitation' because of the negligence of the overseers, the magistrates ordered parish officers to make monthly inquiries into the circumstances of the poor.[207] This pressure intensified as a result of the Caroline Book of Orders of 1630–1, when the privy council itself actively encouraged inquiries into the conduct of parish officers. In 1633, the council in the north was instructed to hear 'the petition of the poorest man against the richest or against the greatest lord'.[208] County benches accordingly sought to demonstrate their assiduity in seeking out and remedying distress. The Shropshire bench informed the council in September 1631 that it had 'received [the] complaints' of the poor and taken order for them 'by collection'. Its colleagues were even more positive in March 1636, reporting that, 'when complaint was made unto us of

[204] *Warwick County Records*, iii. 58–9.

[205] Ibid. ii. 27, 35–6; iv. 64.

[206] For printed examples, see ibid. iii. 58, 59, 244.

[207] NA, SP14/160/10.

[208] 'The Book of Orders', sigs E4^{r-v}, F4^{r}–G1^{r} (order 1 and directions 2 and 5); T. Rymer, *Foedera* (20 vols., London, 1704–35), xix. 425.

the wants of any indigent poore people which were not able to [?come] unto us to make their poverty known we made orders for their present relief'.[209] But most revealing of all is the remarkable certificate from the Hampshire bench, submitted to the council in April 1631. The magistrates noted that they were aware 'that some poore are in noe small wante by reason of their greate charge in theis times of dearth and scarcity'. They nonetheless suspected that the poor 'do not make knowne their cases', a reluctance which the bench could only ascribe either to 'ignorance', to 'feare', or to 'slothfulnesse'. Accordingly, the magistrates decided 'to encourage other persons to informe' them of the 'difectes & concealments' of the poore by publishing orders in every parish church after divine service 'that by the same the whole parishe and especially the poore may take notice where to complaine and howe to be relieved by us when the case so requires'.[210] If it is more generally true that, in the early Stuart period, the poor were ignorant of the workings of the system and intimidated by those who administered it, it is probable that by the later seventeenth century they had been taught their 'rights' not so much through daily or weekly contact with parish officers but through the intervention of the magistracy acting in accordance with proclamations and orders issued under the royal prerogative.[211]

Indeed, the education of the poor in their entitlements was hardly likely to be regarded sympathetically by parish officers, who invariably sought to prevent the inflation of welfare costs. There is plenty of evidence that they often stood their ground, even after magistrates had received complaints about their negligence or complacency. When Thomas Sandes of Raynham St Mary complained to Nathaniel Bacon that he was 'greatly distressed for want of relief' in July 1602, the magistrate was initially persuaded of the merits of his case. Sandes alleged that 'he hath a wife who is in a manner impotent', that 'he hath ben forced lately to sell his cowe' to relieve his family, and that the parish officers 'yealded him but two pence a weeke for his maintenance'. Bacon fulminated that this allowance was 'verie farre shorte of that which ought to be allowed him' and threatened the overseers with prosecution for contempt if Sandes should have further ground for complaint. They responded by explaining that Sandes had 'solde his cowe to paie his sonnes dett & nott for his owne reliefe', that he had taken his son and daughter-in-law into his house 'contrary to the overseers will', and that he 'is able and will not worke'. When presented in this light, Sandes's plight

[209] NA, SP16/199/18, 316/81.

[210] NA, SP16/188/85.

[211] Cf. Slack, *Poverty and Policy*, 192.

could be made to look far less deserving, and the original relief order was quashed as soon as Bacon heard the overseers' response.[212]

Exchanges such as this were by no means unusual. The frequent granting of orders for relief by the Lancashire bench in the late 1630s, for instance, created particularly acute tensions in the parish of Prescot, where the vestrymen complained in 1641 that many pensioners had 'gotten orders' upon 'false suggestions' and accordingly undertook a full survey of the deserving poor.[213] Although the magistrates subsequently agreed that they would command no further pensions without a certificate from the churchwardens, they nonetheless confirmed fourteen of their previous relief orders at an annual cost to the parish of £18. 10*s*. 0*d*.[214] The vestrymen responded by ensuring that the parish officers always attended quarter sessions, and their accounts of the 1640s regularly record payments for travel expenses to Ormskirk or Wigan to 'prevent orders that should have been brought upon the parish'.[215] One of the reasons for this expenditure was the case of Jane Smith, against liability for whom the parish of Prescot had been defending itself for several years. Jane Smith was the widow of William Smith of Cuerdley, with whom she had been involved in breaches of the peace since at least 1633 and by whom she had a son Peter in 1637. In 1641, when Peter was 4 years old, she successfully secured an order for his relief from the justices at Wigan quarter sessions, who stipulated that the Prescot overseers should pay him 40*s*. a year. Initially, it seems, they co-operated, paying £1. 7*s*. 6*d*. to Smith's brother-in-law 'for the use of' Peter in 1642. By April 1646, however, the parish was in arrears and Smith complained that the former order lay neglected in the hands of one of the Prescot overseers. In August 1647 Justices Ireland and Brooke reiterated the original order, which the parish again resisted. The matter was eventually settled at Lancaster assizes in August 1649, where the judges found in favour of Smith, although the financial arrangements were not confirmed until Wigan sessions in October 1649 where the parish was ordered to pay him £16, raising the arrears by a special rate, and to continue annual payments of £2. Even then, a 'full and deliberate hearing' at Ormskirk sessions in

212 *Bacon Papers*, iv. 275.

213 For the importance of surveys as a means of limiting entitlement to the ancient settled poor of the parish, see Ch. 5.2 above. For another allegation that a relief order had been secured on 'false and illgrounded suggestions', see *Buckinghamshire Sessions Records*, ii. 170.

214 *Prescot Churchwardens' Accounts, 1635–1663*, ed. T. Steel (Record Society of Lancashire and Cheshire, 137, Stroud, 2002), 78 n.

215 Ibid. 45, 71, 78, 120, 121, 130, 133, 137, 145. For a nice example of a pre-emptive appeal against an application for relief of an old inhabitant of Grange (Cumberland) 'if he shall one day make one', see CRO, Q/11/1/49/27.

April 1650 was required before the parish could be persuaded to meet its obligations.[216]

Cases of this kind could be traced through many a quarter sessions archive, and their characteristically emotive pauper appeals, wilful overseers' contempts, and bombastic magisterial precepts are familiar enough to any student of the administrative work of the bench. What makes the case of Jane and Peter Smith particularly revealing is the survival of the parish officers' accounts of their expenditure during this long struggle. In all, the Prescot vestrymen spent £5. 4*s.* 0*d.* at the very least, a sum approximating to almost a third of the arrears they were seeking to deny, in resisting orders from county magistrates and judges of assize alike. To do so, they retained the services of at least one attorney, and defended themselves by obtaining writs of *certiorari* from King's Bench, by investigating Smith's parentage in local archives and by exploiting local networks of patronage and favour.[217] Among the accounts for the years during which the dispute came to a head are payments of 8*s.* 10*d.* 'spent in goeinge to Warrington with the overseers of the poore and six more of the parish to meet the justices'; of 8*d.* 'spent in goeinge to Farnworth to know the age of Peter Smith'; of 1*s.* 6*d.* 'paid for a horse hyre for a woman to ride to Ormskirke as a witness'; and of 50*s.* 'expended in going to the Lancaster assizes'.[218] All this is to say nothing of more allusive references which do not explicitly refer to the Smith case, such as 1*s.* 'spent in going to Bewsey Old Hall to acquaint Mr Ireland what charge was imposed upon the parish for releefe of the poore and to prevent any further orders'.[219] The parish archive therefore conveys a very strong sense of law- (not to say bloody-) mindedness through which vestrymen not only sought to avoid expensive precedents but also articulated local assumptions about belonging, entitlement, and justice.

The appeals and counter-appeals generated by the administration of the poor laws therefore came to involve not only overseers and magistrates but also attorneys who might be retained to plead the cause of the

[216] *Prescot Churchwardens' Accounts*, 80 n., 144 n.

[217] For the named attorney, Arthur Barron, see below. For the *certiorari*, obtained at a charge of 4*s.* in 1649, see *Prescot Churchwardens' Accounts*, 136. On the role of *certiorari* in general, see N. Landau, *The Justices of the Peace, 1679–1760* (Berkeley, 1984), 345–54; and in poor law disputes more specifically, see Ch. 6.4(*b*) below.

[218] *Prescot Churchwardens' Accounts*, 133, 134, 137, 144. That large numbers of parishioners frequently attended sessions to defend parish interests is clear from Richard Gough's account of a settlement case heard at Shrewsbury in the summer of 1701, when he noted that the two officers of Myddle represented 'a very small appearance of our parishioners to prosecute our matter', especially when their opponents from Wem were 'about thirteen in number'. R. Gough, *The History of Myddle*, ed. D. Hey (Harmondsworth, 1981), 259.

[219] *Prescot Churchwardens' Accounts*, 133.

parish. Attorneys were appearing before justices of the peace to represent towns or parishes in disputes about the disposition of vagrants or the assessment of rates from the early seventeenth century.[220] After the Restoration, when the settlement laws had institutionalized the negotiation of removal and appeal, the retention of counsel was to become even more common. At least sixteen different attorneys were practising at Warwickshire quarter sessions in the 1670s, and the bench was sufficiently concerned about their conduct to insist in 1674 that all counsel wear gowns in court.[221] Well before the 1662 statute intensified inter-parochial rivalries, however, parishes were finding it useful to draw upon legal expertise against experienced magistrates who might themselves be learned in the law. The parish of Prescot again provides a particularly well-documented example. The Prescot vestry began retaining an unnamed attorney in the late 1630s, paying him 3*s.* 4*d.* a time to plead against magistrates' orders at quarter sessions.[222] Just how useful such an advocate might be is demonstrated by his success in May 1641 in securing the justices' consent that 'noe orders should be granted for any allowance for the poore but such as the overseers and churchwardens should in their discresions thinke fitt'.[223] By the late 1640s, the parish was regularly retaining Arthur Barron, an attorney frequently employed in the palatinate courts, to solicit their business against magistrates who they regarded as trigger-happy in the issuing of relief orders. In the two years to Easter 1651, at a time when the annual relief budget in Prescot was less than £40, the vestry paid Barron almost 30*s.* in fees and expenses for his defence of the parish obligations at both county quarter sessions (at Wigan and Ormskirk) and Lancaster assizes.[224]

Poor law practice therefore came to resemble a mosaic of interlocking triangles of negotiation between magistracy, vestry, and labouring poor, which vividly depicted the image of those putatively benevolent gentlemen who frequently intervened in the welfare process in support of the interests of the applicant against the hard-heartedness of the overseers.[225] Even if such interventions can meaningfully be characterized as 'paternalistic', paternalism was often in practice, only 'a weak force exercised at

[220] C. W. Brooks, *Pettyfoggers and Vipers of the Commonwealth: The 'Lower Branch' of the Legal Profession in Early Modern England* (Cambridge, 1986), 190.

[221] *Warwick County Records*, vii. 23, 350 (index, s.v. 'counsel and attorneys, names of').

[222] *Prescot Churchwardens' Accounts,* 45. For an attorney representing the parish of Stelling (Kent) in a poor law dispute in 1660, see Kent Archives Office, Q/SB/7/66.

[223] *Prescot Churchwardens' Accounts,* 78. The attorney was paid 6*s.* 8*d.*

[224] Ibid. 136–7, 143, 145–6.

[225] King, 'The Patrician-Plebeian Model Re-Examined'; Hitchcock *et al.*, 'Introduction', 11.

distance.[226] It could nonetheless be manipulated by paupers who selected with considerable care the gentry parlours in which to make their appeals, often choosing remote magistrates with whom overseers enjoyed only difficult and sporadic contact. Robert Doughty of Hanworth received at least thirty-three poor relief petitions in Norfolk in the years 1662–5, but seems to have recorded only those cases in which he agreed with the plaintiffs to issue warrants against overseers. They originate nonetheless from parishes throughout north-east Norfolk. Edmund Tew seems to have been a particularly popular justice amongst poor appellants, being asked to intervene in some 168 poor law actions in the period 1750–64, only two of which originated in his home parish of Boldon, the remainder coming from the numerous small communities of eastern Durham. Some critics suspected that the poor knew that parish officers were less likely to challenge a justice's order if it involved a lengthy journey to a remote country seat, or (even worse) a protracted hearing at a distant quarter sessions. Richard Dunning argued in 1685 that overseers who lived far from the magistrate would 'often give the complainers far more than they need, meerly to save themselves such a journey especially when they have the wit to complaine at a busie time'. By 1698, indeed, he was arguing that the poor were successfully exploiting the poor law system by 'clamour', by 'imposing on the ignorance of some officers', by 'deceiving the charity of others', and by 'threatening the timorous sort with warrants from persons in authority'.[227] Well into the eighteenth century, parish officers like Thomas Turner felt themselves harassed by importunate paupers who had convinced magistrates that their overseers were 'hard on the poor'.[228] Even the merest threat of an appeal to the magistrate might provoke parish officers into complying with a pauper's request, as it did in East Hoathly in 1757.[229]

Parish officers might even be oblivious to the fact that a relief order had been made against them, as they were at Hayton-in-Gilsland (Cumberland) in 1706. In cases such as these it was not unknown for the overseer to withhold relief on the grounds that the magistrates had been deceived. The parish officers of Penrith refused to pay a pension in 1698

[226] P. Mandler, 'The Making of the New Poor Law *Redivivus*', *Past and Present*, 117 (1987), 137.

[227] *Notebook of Robert Doughty*, 18, 19, 21, 22, 23, 24, 27, 28, 32, 35, 40, 42, 43, 46, 51, 52, 55, 60, 61, 63; Morgan and Rushton, 'The Magistrate, the Community and the Maintenance of an Orderly Society', 68 n. 50; Dunning, *A Plain and Easie Method*, 13; Dunning, *Bread for the Poor*, 2.

[228] *Diary of Thomas Turner*, 91–2. Cf. the comments of the late 18th-century Somerset clergyman William Holland, who thought the overseers were teased by vexatious complaints from 'every scoundrel in the parish'. *Paupers and Pig Killers: The Diary of William Holland, a Somerset Parson 1799–1818*, ed. J. Ayres (Stroud, 1984), 26, 47.

[229] *Diary of Thomas Turner*, 92–3.

on the grounds that the justice's precept was 'only a night Order' and that they were not obliged to obey it.[230] Few overseers, however, were as independently minded as those of Colyton (Devon), who were contemptuous of a magistrate's relief order in 1681, insisting that 'if the justices had any more paper & inke to spare they should send it to them and if they would have the poor paid they should come and doe it themselves'. The parish officers were, they crowed, 'justices themselves in their places'.[231] Faced with such recalcitrance, it is unsurprising that some magistrates recognized the dangers of intervening in the quarrels of far-away communities between parishioners of whom they knew nothing. In 1712 the Buckinghamshire JP Francis Mardston refused to make a relief order for a petitioner from Middle Claydon on the grounds that he did 'not think it Civil to interfere' in a neighbouring magistrate's home parish. 'It has', he told John Verney, 'formerly been a resolution taken amongst the Gentlemen that another justice should not meddle where another inhabits it being supposed that every justice is the best judge who ought to be relieved in their respective parishes'.[232] Attitudes such as this were forged in the context of generic criticism that, since magistrates themselves were unlikely to be contributors to relief bills in the parishes in question, they were far too lenient in allocating pensions. Over a decade before the 1692 statute which allegedly encouraged the promiscuous provision of pensions by magistrates, for instance, the minister of Ainderby Steeple criticized the North Riding magistrates 'for easy granting orders for the relief of the poor'.[233]

The location and complexity of these negotiations over poor relief varied over time, as both case law and statutory innovation reshaped the legal processes through which relief could be solicited and awarded. As late as 1690, the House of Lords was actively debating the formalization of the role of chief inhabitants in making the discretionary decisions about eligibility long imagined and advocated by Dalton.[234] A bill of that year noted that, because 'none can better know the poor of the parish, their lives and conversations, than the parishioners of every respective parish', the 'churchwardens, overseers and parishioners or the greater part of them present in such theire assemblies and meetings' should 'have the only power and authority from time to time to determine what persons within their parish are fit to be relieved by their parish and what

[230] CRO, Q/11/1/46/36, 76/19.

[231] Sharpe, *Population and Society*, 221.

[232] J. Broad, 'Parish Economies of Welfare, 1650–1834', *Historical Journal*, 42 (1999), 989.

[233] *North Riding Quarter Sessions Records*, vii. 51.

[234] See Ch. 6.2 above.

relief from time to time to be given and to order and appoint the same'.[235] Within a couple of years, however, concern about the inflation of welfare costs provoked a rethink about the ways in which pensions should be granted. A statute of 1692 stipulated that pension lists be drawn up by vestrymen on an annual basis every Easter with a view to striking off those whom they did not 'think fit and allow to receive collection'. While this might give at least a year's security to regular pensioners, it also stipulated that new pensioners could be admitted exclusively on the authority of a magistrate. This administrative revolution, transferring the responsibility for accepting or rejecting applications directly to JPs, was justified by criticizing the 'unlimited power' of parish officers, 'who do frequently, upon frivolous pretences (but chiefly for their own private ends) give relief to what persons and number they think fit'.[236] Ratepayers frustrated by the overseers' failure to make the necessary economies had long voiced such fears. The inhabitants of West Winch (Norfolk) in 1649 and Tonbridge (Kent) in 1682 both bluntly protested that parish officers were giving relief to those who did not need it.[237]

At issue here was the problem of the 'occasional poor': indigent parishioners who were not regularly relieved by the overseers but whose needs for earthly necessities (fuel, clothing, shoes, medical care) became increasingly frequent in years of high prices.[238] The preamble to the 1692 act implied that the slack administration of relief funds had meant that these recipients of 'casual' relief 'being entered into the collection bill do become after that a great charge to the parish notwithstanding the occasion or pretence of their receiving collection sometimes ceases'. Even so, pension payments fixed months in advance in the manner envisaged by the 1692 statute seemed to preclude the consistent monitoring of levels of indigence envisaged both in the Elizabethan poor laws themselves and in manuals for magistrates and overseers alike.[239] The statute, however, had long been anticipated in many parishes and it is apparent that part of its motivation was less to guarantee the rights of pensioners than to restrict the scale of casual payments. As early as 1627, the parish officers of Braintree were attempting to restrict relief to a definitive list of pensioners to the exclusion of the occasional poor: only 'such poore as are specified' were to 'have relieffe out of such money as is to be

[235] HMC, *Twelfth Report, Appendix, Part VI: The Manuscripts of the House of Lords, 1689–1690* (London, 1889), 448–51.

[236] 3 William & Mary, c. 11 (1692).

[237] S. D. Amussen, *An Ordered Society: Gender and Class in Early Modern England* (Oxford, 1988), 161; Barker-Read, 'Treatment of the Aged Poor', 63.

[238] Cf. Ch. 4.3(*a*) above.

[239] King, *Poverty and Welfare*, 99.

distributed amongst the poore people and not any other, except there be extraordinarye cause'. Even after the 1692 act, moreover, parish oligarchies such as that of Harefield (Middlesex) sought to discourage anything other than regular monthly expenditure by ensuring that overseers were only to make casual payments on the order of the vestry.[240]

Although it has been argued that the 1692 act seems to have had little effect, there is evidence of its far-reaching implications in the archives of vestry and magistracy alike. Orders for relief on petitions to magistrates were granted not only, as we have seen, in Cumberland, but also in Gnossal (Staffordshire) in 1714; in Trull (Somerset) in 1719; and in Chalfont St Peter (Buckinghamshire) from 1721.[241] The frequency of such orders betrays the all too predictable swing from the allegedly frivolous allocation of pensions by overseers to the promiscuous granting of relief by magistrates. Although overseers had once granted relief without consulting the justices, they had usually had the interests of their fellow ratepayers at heart. Now, however, justices simply ordered relief without consulting the overseers. Even in the 1740s, a single magistrate might within the space of less than three years issue fifteen summonses requiring parish officers to justify their refusal of relief to dissatisfied paupers.[242]

The 1692 act almost certainly had the effect of enhancing the supervisory role of the magistracy in administering the poor laws, and it may even have encouraged the idea that appeals could be made to single JPs out of sessions. It is doubtful, however, that it succeeded in preventing overseers from admitting pensioners to relief rolls without a specific order from a justice. The requirements of the indigent were obviously too pressing, and the accumulated authority of the parish officers was simply too great, to permit an administrative revolution of this kind. Indeed, in granting legal recognition to the incipient division of authority between magistracy and vestry, the act resulted not, as intended, in economy, but in friction, encouraging the poor to grow ever more resourceful in their attempts to exploit the 'cracks in the wainscoting of power'.[243] The statute also had the indirect effect of institutionalizing the distinction between the regular collectioners (those allowed by the inhabitants) and the extraordinary poor whose relief was sanctioned by justices' order. Here, it seems, lie the origins of the notion that 'the poore' was in itself an

[240] *Early Essex Town Meetings*, 110; Tate, *The Parish Chest*, 164.

[241] Cutlack, 'Gnosall Records', 45; Jones, 'Trull Overseers' Accounts', 91–2; G. C. Edmonds, 'Accounts of Eighteenth-Century Overseers of the Poor of Chalfont St Peter', *Records of Buckinghamshire*, 18 (1966), 3. Cf. the scepticism of Slack, *Poverty and Policy*, 193.

[242] *The Justicing Notebook of William Hunt*, 12.

[243] Wrightson, 'The Politics of the Parish', 19.

appropriate term to describe that class of labourers who were in need but unrelieved.

(*b*) The Judiciary and the Poor

The parish vestry and the sessions chamber therefore provided two environments in which entitlements to relief were pleaded and contested. They did not, however, monopolize authority in poor law cases, for the common law judges were consistently influential both in their interpretations of the Elizabethan statutes and in their adjudication of disputes provoked by them. If, therefore, there was one triangular set of relationships between the poor, the parish, and the magistracy, there was another between the parish, the magistracy, and the central courts of common law. Indeed, the decisions of the high court judges were effectively in dialogue with legislation throughout the seventeenth and eighteenth centuries. In their role as circuit judges, moreover, judges effectively acted not only as the mediators but as the makers of policy.[244]

The first comprehensive statement of judicial opinion on the Elizabethan poor relief statute was a set of twenty resolutions drafted in 1599.[245] Their early date of formulation makes them particularly interesting, for they give an indication of the problems of implementation which the judiciary foresaw from the very outset. Indeed, Francis Moore, MP for Reading, urged the Commons in December 1601 that these resolutions should be appended to the amending statute of 1601, but Francis Bacon dissented on the grounds that the resolutions, 'done by judges, and privatelye, and perhappes in a chamber', should not be enacted 'without scanninge or viewe' by parliament.[246] They were first published in the 1599 edition of Lambarde's *Eirenarcha* and were reprinted both in subsequent editions and in Dalton's *Country Justice*. Copies occasionally survive in parish archives.[247] The majority of the resolutions, including the first seven, turn on the problem of defining and punishing vagrancy and on the related difficulties of identifying the parish of settlement and of persuading its inhabitants to accept their responsibilities. But the judges were also at pains to point out the coercive powers available to force the children of the poor into apprenticeship (no. 8); the tight restrictions on

[244] J. Innes, 'Parliament and the Shaping of Eighteenth-Century English Social Policy', *Transactions of the Royal Historical Society*, 5th ser., 40 (1990), 67, 73–4.

[245] Bodl., MS Tanner, 91, fos. 163–4.

[246] *Proceedings in the Parliaments of Elizabeth I*, ed. T. E. Hartley (3 vols., Leicester, 1981–95), iii. 440.

[247] W. Lambarde, *Eirenarcha* (London, 1599), 206–7; *Eirenarcha* (1614 edn.), 209–10; Dalton, *Country Justice* (1618 edn.), 74–6; '[Articles] To the Constables of Swanbourne, 10 Dec. 1599', in *Papers from an Iron Chest at Doddershall, Bucks.*, ed. G. Eland (Aylesbury, 1937), 39–43.

those who might legally be removed (nos. 9 and 11); the penalties for those refusing to be set on work (no. 10); and the circumstances in which paupers might be licensed to beg (no. 15). All these issues were to vex parish officers and county magistrates alike for the next century. They were also at pains to clarify the nature and extent of the obligations of kin to provide for the poor without troubling the parish (nos. 16–17) and to assert that clergymen were as liable as any other inhabitant to be assessed for poor rates (no. 18). It is especially striking that the resolutions make virtually no reference to the basis on which rates were to be levied or to the criteria according to which pensions were to be distributed.[248] As far as the late Elizabethan judiciary was concerned, these issues were made crystal-clear by the statute.

The next serious attempt to settle comprehensively the controversies arising from the operation of the poor laws occurred in 1633, when the magistrates in the counties of the Norfolk circuit put their doubts and queries to Chief Justice Heath. The result was a set of thirty-eight resolutions, not all of which were primarily focused on poor relief.[249] If vagrancy was the running theme of the 1599 resolutions, its place had been taken in 1633 by apprenticeship, which accounted for eight of the queries (nos. 1–7, 21). A far wider range of issues had now become controversial than had been anticipated a generation or so before: the discretionary powers to mitigate forfeitures to the poor under the penal statutes (no. 10); the settlement and responsibility for single mothers and their illegitimate offspring (nos. 12–13, 22–4); the financing of constables' expenses in expelling vagrants (no. 21); and the policing and punishment of those who took inmates. As might be expected, the most prominent and unbroken strand of judicial interpretation between 1599 and 1633 was the basis of the assessment of poor rates (nos. 18–20, 33). In some respects, Heath's decisions created more problems than they solved. It has been argued that the 1633 resolutions 'effected the final absorption of the Elizabethan poor laws into the routine working of the justices of the peace'. Indeed, they were first published in the 1655 edition of Dalton's *Country Justice* (where they are reproduced without prefatory comment) and subsequently appeared as an appendix to *The Complete Justice* in 1661.

[248] Bodl., MS Tanner, 91, fos. 163–4.

[249] NA, SP16/255/46, conveniently printed in Dalton, *The Country Justice* (1655 edn.), 113–19, and in *Somerset Assize Orders, 1629–1640*, ed. T. G. Barnes (Somerset Record Society, 65, Taunton, 1959), 63–70 (no. 186). Fifteen of the thirty-eight resolutions have little or no direct bearing on the poor laws. Any discussion of the resolutions is conspicuous by its absence from either P. E. Kopperman, *Sir Robert Heath 1575–1649: Window on an Age* (Woodbridge, 1989), or T. G. Barnes, 'Cropping the Heath: The Fall of a Chief Justice, 1634', *Historical Research*, 64 (1991), 331–43.

The chairman of the Worcestershire bench regarded at least six of the resolutions as authoritative in the early 1660s.[250] Even so, their authority was not always accepted unquestioningly. Although popularly known as the 'resolutions of all the judges', they failed to command the support of some of Heath's colleagues in the judiciary, and their validity, especially on the issue of pauper apprenticeship, was flatly denounced in King's Bench in 1676.[251]

All this is to say nothing of the regular adjudication of individual poor law cases by the assize judges on their circuits. The orders made on the western circuit in the 1630s and 1640s by Heath and others—providing habitations, adjudicating settlement, arbitrating rating disputes—are probably typical of the genre.[252] Or indeed of those judicial comments on the administration of the poor laws which were made during jury charges. Most often, the judges rehearsed the evils of vagabondage and the need to enforce the clauses against vagrancy and begging. Thus Justice James Whitelocke riding the North Wales circuit in the 1610s condemned 'those who have no trade to live on, wandering up and down, living upon the spoil without any lawful course'. The 'mischiefs that grow hereby', he went on, 'being now very frequent require the more care for their reformation'. The remedy was at hand, however, since 'the law hath so excellently settled it that no man ought to wander or need to beg but all be provided for either by their work if they be able or by contribution if they be impotent'.[253] Some twenty years later, an anonymous Welsh judge combined an encomium for the legislation with rather more colourful rhetoric about the consequences of the neglect in its enforcement. Although he was 'cleer of opinion that there was never law made more beneficiall to this country', he was convinced that 'the tenth man in this shire doth not use any trade or labour'. 'It is bad government', he insisted, 'that one should live by the labour of nine.' If the law were enforced for just one year, he argued, 'it would utterly extinguish all lortinge abrod,

[250] T.G. Barnes, *Somerset, 1625–40: A County's Government during the Personal Rule* (Cambridge, Mass., 1961), 189; Dalton, *The Country Justice* (1655 edn.), 113–19; *The Complete Justice* (London, 1661); 'Henry Townshend's "Notes of the Office of a Justice of the Peace"', ed. R. D. Hunt, *Worcestershire Historical Record Society: Miscellany II* (Leeds, 1967), 70, 118–20.

[251] Cf. Ch. 3.2(*b*) above.

[252] *Western Circuit Assize Orders*, *passim*. The thirteen judges who in various combinations rode the western circuit in this period were John Denham (1626–38), John Walter (1626–9), Thomas Richardson (1630–3), Humphrey Davenport (1634), John Finch (1635–9), Robert Heath (1638), Thomas Trevor (1639), Francis Crawley (1639–40), John Bramston (1640), Robert Foster (1641–2), Henry Rolle (1646), John Godbolt (1646–8), and John Wilde (1647–9). See Cockburn, *History of English Assizes*, 272–3.

[253] Longleat House, Wiltshire, MS Whitelocke, 21, fo. 111^{v}.

much filching and stealinge and redound to the perpetual relief of the poor that ought to be succored'.[254]

By the late seventeenth century, moreover, the court of King's Bench had itself come to function as a third arena of poor law negotiation as the common law judges expanded the use of the writ of *certiorari* to call justices' orders for review.[255] The relative inaccessibility of the archive of the central courts of common law has long prevented the exploration of the wide range of important decisions made there. Gradually, however, the significance of the role of the judges of King's Bench in settling conflicts arising in thousands of communities across England is being recognized.[256] Parishes which sought to annul settlement or habitation orders made in their disfavour at quarter sessions 'tended to take the matter to King's Bench as a matter of course', usually by writs of *certiorari*.[257] In the period 1690–6, for example, at least thirteen Warwickshire poor law disputes were removed from quarter sessions to King's Bench in this way, usually on the initiative of parish officers contesting decisions by JPs. Thus in April 1693, upon complaint from the overseers of Berkswell, two magistrates ordered that Edward Wale, his wife, and their four children be removed to Binley. The Binley overseers successfully appealed against this order, and Wale was returned to the care of the Berkswell overseers, who appealed in turn. By June 1693 the parish officers of Binley had successfully challenged a second removal order, and in October Wale and his family were still living in Berkswell at a charge to the parish of 3*s*. a week. The Berkswell overseers, however, had the last word in King's Bench, and in the summer of 1694, almost fifteen months after the dispute had started, the original magistrates' order was confirmed, and the Wale family were sent back to Binley.[258] Although this

[254] National Library of Wales, Aberystwyth, MS Peniarth, 377B, fo. 16^{r-v}. The rhetoric and content of this charge so closely resembles Justice John Hoskyns's advice to the Herefordshire bench in 1634 that it is tempting to identify Hoskyns as its author.

[255] Landau, *The Justices of the Peace*, 345. Cf. E. G. Henderson, *Foundations of English Administrative Law: Certiorari and Mandamus in the Seventeenth Century* (Cambridge, Mass., 1963).

[256] On King's Bench, see P. Halliday, *Dismembering the Body Politic: Partisan Politics in English Towns, 1650–1730* (Cambridge, 1998), 24–8, 67–73, 291–302, 313–22; Broad, 'Parish Economies of Welfare', 990–1; D. Hay, 'Dread of the Crown Office: The English Magistracy and King's Bench, 1740–1800', in N. Landau (ed.), *Law, Crime and English Society, 1660–1830* (Cambridge, 2002), 19–45; and C. Steedman, 'Lord Mansfield's Women', *Past and Present*, 176 (2002), 105–43. On Common Pleas, see J. C. Oldham, 'Underreported and Underrated: The Court of Common Pleas in the Eighteenth Century', in H. Hartog and W. E. Nelson (eds.), *Law as Culture and Culture as Law: Essays in Honor of John Philip Reid* (Madison, 2000), 119–46.

[257] *Warwick County Records*, vol. ix, p. xxx. For an early use of *certiorari* in a poor law dispute from Prescot (Lancs.), see above.

[258] *Warwick County Records*, vol. ix, pp. xxxii–xxxiii, 74, 78, 83.

is the best documented of the Warwickshire cases referred to King's Bench, several other disputes involved those parishes in Kineton hundred whose officers had submitted overseers' accounts in 1639.[259] While the inhabitants of Moreton Morrell and of Kineton successfully obtained writs of *certiorari* to overturn magistrates' relief orders, the parish officers of Packwood, Tanworth, and Wasperton were themselves victims of such writs. In 1692 four ratepayers even used King's Bench successfully to appeal the assessment for the poor made by the overseers of Honington.[260] When parish officers obtained a *certiorari*, the cards were heavily stacked in their favour since paupers who had been denied relief could ill afford the substantial expenses necessary to prosecute suits at Westminster. That magistrates recognized as much is suggested by their occasional agreement that the county, rather than the applicant for relief, should bear the legal costs of forcing recalcitrant overseers to enforce relief orders.[261]

Such cases are a powerful reminder that, however much discretion overseers enjoyed, their authority formed only 'the bottom line of government' in a broadly based but fully integrated hierarchy of judicial institutions which extended all the way from the vestries of rural parishes to the Hall of Pleas at Westminster. The politics of welfare, then, were as characteristic of the commonwealth of the realm as of the commonwealth of the parish.[262] All the while that parish officers were chasing each other through the thickets of the law, however, paupers were forced to shift for themselves: harried across parish boundaries, begging for bread and ale, snatching a few hours' sleep in barns and church porches, and pleading with the parish for the right to belong, the exercise of which (like all rights) was conditioned by inequalities of wealth and power.[263]

[259] Cf. Ch. 4.1 above.

[260] *Warwick County Records*, vol. ix, pp. xxxiv–xxxvi.

[261] See e.g. *Buckinghamshire Sessions Records*, ii. 65–6.

[262] Innes, 'Parliament and the Shaping of Eighteenth-Century English Social Policy'; R. Connors, '"The Grand Inquest of the Nation": Parliamentary Committees and Social Policy in Mid-Eighteenth-Century England', *Parliamentary History*, 14 (1995), 285–313; Connors, 'Parliament and Poverty in Mid-Eighteenth Century England', *Parliamentary History*, 21 (2002), 207–31.

[263] S. Hindle, 'A Sense of Place? Becoming and Belonging in the Rural Parish, 1550–1650', in A. Shepard and P. Withington (eds.), *Communities in Early Modern England* (Manchester, 2000), 96–114. Cf. Hampson, *Treatment of Poverty in Cambridgeshire*, 130. For the case of a woman denied accommodation by the overseers on the grounds that she was 'ill-conditioned' and who 'laid all summer in a barn' while the Norfolk justices debated her case, see *Notebook of Robert Doughty*, 40.

5. THE BADGE OF DEPENDENCY

As if the protraction, expense, and uncertainty of negotiations which might result from an application for relief were not a sufficient disincentive, justices and judiciary adopted other practices designed to deter the poor from claiming relief. By the closing decades of the seventeenth century, there was widespread concern among parish ratepayers about exponentially increasing relief costs. Their desire to control the welfare machine was also shared by polemicists and policy-makers, among whom there was a developing sense that outdoor relief fostered a 'dependency culture' in which the labouring poor preferred to live 'on the parish' rather than take pains for their own maintenance. Dunning argued in *Bread for the Poor* that the poor had come to recognize that 'parish pay' was 'a work of less trouble and more profit than daily labour'.[264] The MP for Gloucestershire, Sir Richard Cocks, lamented in the 1690s that, because the poor were confident that 'the parish is obliged in old age, extremities, and necessities to provide' for them, they would 'in plenty and cheap times' either 'work little, or live without saving'. The solution, he insisted, was the outright repeal of the poor laws and their replacement with harsher methods 'to affright [the poor] from their idle and negligent practices and behaviour, and force them to be as willing to work as we are to employ them'.[265] Although Cocks was to be frustrated in his desire for repeal, what piecemeal reform there was ensured that deterrence, often enforced through shaming sanctions, became a leitmotif of poor law policy. From the 1690s, in particular, ratepayers were at pains to emphasize that being 'on the parish' was a mark not only of dependency, but also of humiliation.

The shame of pauperization received its symbolic representation in the badging of the poor under a statute of 1697, which ordered that all poor persons receiving parish relief must, together with their wives and children, wear a badge with a 'P' and the initial letter of the name of their parish made of red or blue cloth on the shoulder of the right sleeve 'in an

[264] Dunning, *Bread for the Poor*, 2.

[265] Bodl., MS Eng. Hist. b. 209, fos. 81, 89–90 (reverse foliation). Cocks's views are developed and contextualized in D. W. Hayton, 'Sir Richard Cocks: The Political Anatomy of a Country Whig', *Albion*, 20 (1988), esp. 241; Hayton, 'Moral Reform and Country Politics in the Late Seventeenth-Century House of Commons', *Past and Present*, 128 (1990), 67–8; *The Parliamentary Diary of Sir Richard Cocks, 1698–1702*, ed. D. W. Hayton (Oxford, 1996), pp. xxxi–xxxii, xl, 25–6, 324; and, more generally, in S. Macfarlane, 'Social Policy and the Poor in the Later Seventeenth Century', in A. L. Beier and Roger Finlay (eds.), *The Making of the Metropolis: London, 1500–1700* (London and New York, 1986), 252–77.

open and visible manner'.[266] Any parish officer who dispensed relief to a poor person not wearing a badge could be fined 20*s.* for each disbursement, and any pensioner who refused was either to have their relief withdrawn or to be whipped and committed to Bridewell for three weeks' hard labour.[267] The Webbs famously argued that badging the poor never became general, although their assessment that 'nothing could secure compliance with the law on this point' was unduly swayed by their reading of the complaint literature of the early 1750s, which argued that the policy was 'almost universally disused'.[268] Although Dunning argued that 'the wearing of the badge or the threat of it would make the poor thrifty and industrious', he nonetheless thought that 'some [ratepayers] will be positively against it and oppose it to the utmost, and will join with the insolence of the poor and rather than hinder will lead and encourage them in their aspersions of it and otherwise oppose it'.[269]

More recent work on parish archives suggests that the visible degradation of the poor was practised far more widely than the Webbs' scepticism or Dunning's pessimism allowed. In early sixteenth-century towns, the badge had evidently been a stamp of approval, a testimonial of the 'true' status of the poor or diseased nature of those who wore them: such badges or 'tokens' were worn in London from 1517 and in York from 1515, and beggars were to be given 'signs' with which 'to ask alms weekly' in Lincoln in 1543 and 1545. In 1571 the corporation of Bristol spent over 9*s.* on tin badges for twenty poor people who were 'to go into Somerset to seek relief'.[270] These local experiments were encouraged by the formal

[266] For an extended version of the following discussion, see S. Hindle, 'Dependency, Shame and Belonging: Badging the Deserving Poor, *c.*1550–1750', *Cultural and Social History*, 1 (2004), 29–58.

[267] 8 & 9 William III, c. 30 (1697), sect. ii.

[268] S. and B. Webb, *English Local Government*, vol. vii: *English Poor Law History Part I: The Old Poor Law* (London, 1927), 161. Cf. T. Alcock, *Observations on the Defects of the Poor Laws* (London, 1752), 17; *An Impartial Examination of a Pamphlet Intituled Considerations on Several Proposals for the Better Maintenance of the Poor* (London, 1752), 19. For these debates more generally, see J. Innes, 'The "Mixed Economy of Welfare" in Early Modern England: Assessments of the Options from Hale to Malthus (*c.*1683–1803)', in Daunton (ed.), *Charity, Self-Interest and Welfare*, esp. 158–60; and Innes, 'The State and the Poor: Eighteenth-Century England in European Perspective', in J. Brewer and E. Hellmuth (eds.), *Rethinking Leviathan: The Eighteenth-Century State in Britain and Germany* (Oxford, 1999), 225–80; Connors, 'Parliament and Poverty'. More recent commentators have echoed the Webbs' interpretation. See e.g. F. H. Hinton, 'Notes on the Administration of the Relief of the Poor of Lacock 1583–1834', *Wiltshire Archaeological Magazine*, 49 (1940–2), 173; Edmonds, 'Overseers of the Poor of Chalfont St Peter', 7; Slack, *The English Poor Law*, 40.

[269] Dunning, *Bread for the Poor*, 12.

[270] 'London Orders for Restraining Vagabonds and Beggars, 1517', printed in F. Aydelotte, *Elizabethan Rogues and Vagabonds* (New York, 1913), 140–1; HMC, *Fourteenth Report, Appendix, Part VIII: The Manuscripts of Lincoln, Bury St Edmund's and Great Grimsby Corporations; and of the Deans*

licensing of beggars stipulated in Tudor legislation, especially the statutes of 1563 and 1598.[271] The officers of the parishes in the borough of Leicester were among the earliest to comply in 1577. The vestries of the metropolitan parishes of St Botolph Aldgate, St Michael Cornhill, and St Stephen Walbrook, furthermore, all badged the poor both before and after begging licences were once more explicitly authorized in 1598, and the policy was extended to all parishes in 1600. In Salisbury it was noted in 1613 that beggars had 'in times past had a certain badge sewed on their coats to the end they might be known of all people'.[272] By this time, however, the semiotics of badging had shifted. As early as 1587, John Howes had recognized that the badge might be less a sign of approval than one of odium: 'the shame of this badge', argued *Dignitie* in his 'Famyliar and Frendly Discourse Dialogue Wyse', 'will make somme kepe inn and not to goe abroad.' Such a price, responded *Dutie*, was worth paying if the streets were to be 'well cleansed of beggers'.[273] Shame had always been latent in the charitable discourse, though some clerical commentators warned explicitly of the danger that the fear of 'exprobation' amongst the recipients of charity was at least as pernicious as ostentation amongst donors.[274]

Even so, it was not uncommon for the respectable recipients of endowed charities founded in the seventeenth century to be required to wear badged coats, as in the numerous parishes provided for in the bequest of Henry Smith; at Southwark (under that of Robert Buckland); or at Llangoed and Bedgelert (that of William Wynn). The gowns worn by the almsmen of the College of the Poor in Southwark, of Hugh Sexey's Hospital in Bruton (Somerset), and of Thomas Dutton's hospital in Northleach (Gloucestershire), and the coats worn by those of Anthony Bradshaw's almshouse in Duffield, were similarly badged so that they could be easily identified. Even though the poor children lodged in the Salisbury workhouse were not permitted 'to resort home to their parents or else to wander up and down the streets', they were from 1638 to wear

and Chapters of Worcester and Lichfield andc (London, 1895), 38, 40; *York Civic Records*, ed. A. Raine (8 vols., Yorkshire Archaeological Society, 1939–53), iii. 46; [Ulster Museum, Belfast: G. Ewing?], 'Book of Information About Badges Worn By the Poor', 3.

271 5 Elizabeth I, c. 3 (1563), sect. xx; 39 Elizabeth I, c. 3 (1598), sect. x; Beier, *Masterless Men*, 154–5. Badges had also been authorized under the terms of 4 & 5 Philip & Mary, c. 9 (1557).

272 *Records of the Borough of Leicester*, ed. M. Bateson (3 vols., Cambridge, 1899–1905), vol. iii, pp. xlv, 8; Schen, *Charity and Lay Piety*, 178; *Poverty in Early Stuart Salisbury*, 83.

273 J. Howes, 'A Second "Famylar and Frendly Discourse" Dialogue Wyse', printed in *Tudor Economic Documents*, ed. R. H. Tawney and E. Power (3 vols., London, 1924), iii. 421–43.

274 T. Foster, *Plouto-mastix: The Scourge of Covetousnesse: or, An Apologie for the Publike Good, Against Privacie* (London, 1631), 25.

badges bearing the arms of the city and blue caps 'whereby they might be known the children of the workhouse and distinguished from all other children'.[275]

By the 1670s and 1680s, in an echo of the local experimentation which had a century earlier preceded the statutory requirement to collect poor rates in the first place, badging was practised in numerous parishes of the city of London and in the towns of Cambridge, Colchester, Exeter, Norwich, and Wisbech.[276] Badging was also precociously enforced in such rural parishes as Petworth (Sussex) from 1677, Romsey (Hampshire) from 1678, Tonbridge (Kent) from 1682, and Brighton (Sussex) and Cowden (Kent) from 1696. In Wem (Shropshire), 'the parishioners' had 'caused every one of their poore to weare a P. made of tin' well before the 1697 act was passed.[277] County magistrates also apparently pre-empted the 1697 statute in Hampshire, where badges of both cloth and metal were stipulated in 1685; in Middlesex, where 'pensioners refusing to wear the badge' were 'to have their pensions stopped until they conform to the order' in October 1694; and in Warwickshire in October 1695, where parish officers were to forbear from giving further relief until 'such a poor person reform himself'. In the Middlesex case, orders were motivated by the oppression of inhabitants 'by the poor begging at their doors and shops' and by the 'inconvenience' of being unable to distinguish among 'the great number of poor and the parishes to which they belong'.[278]

Other county benches, for example that of Cumberland in 1700, of the West Riding in 1716, and of West Kent in 1717 followed suit.[279] These

[275] Wrightson and Levine, *Poverty and Piety*, 179, 222–3; Boulton, *Neighbourhood and Society*, 144, 148; *Calendar of Wynn (of Gwydir) Papers*, ed. J. Ballinger (Aberystwyth, 1926), no. 2625; SARS, DD\SE/43/5, 14; [Ewing], 'Badges Worn by the Poor', 4; C. Kerry, 'Anthony Bradshaw of Duffield and the Almshouses Founded by him at that Place', *The Reliquary*, 23 (1882–3), 137–40; Slack, 'Poverty and Politics', 192.

[276] V. Pearl, 'Social Policy in Early Modern London', in H. Lloyd-Jones *et al.* (eds.), *History and Imagination: Essays in Honour of H. R. Trevor-Roper* (London, 1979), 128; Macfarlane, 'Social Policy and the Poor', 273 n. 29; Boulton, 'Going on the Parish', 34; Hampson, *Treatment of Poverty in Cambridgeshire*, 181; Slack, *Poverty and Policy*, 202 n. 27.

[277] [Ewing], 'Badges Worn By the Poor', 1; W. A. Seaby, 'Ulster Beggars' Badges', *Ulster Journal of Archaeology*, 3rd ser., 23 (1970), 97; Tate, *The Parish Chest*, 206; D. Marshall, *The English Poor in the Eighteenth Century: A Study in Social and Administrative History* (London, 1926), 103; Turner, 'Ancient Parochial Account Book of Cowden', 115; Barker-Read, 'Treatment of the Aged Poor', 70; *History of Myddle*, 260.

[278] Seaby, 'Ulster Beggars' Badges', 97 (citing a 'Hampshire Poor Letter of 1685' which has proved impossible to trace); *Middlesex County Records: Calendar of Sessions Books, 1689–1709*, ed. W. J. Hardy (London, 1905), 124; *Warwick County Records*, ix. 117. For early implementation in Harefield (Middx.), see Tate, *The Parish Chest*, 207.

[279] F. W. Grainger, 'Poor Relief in Cumberland in the Seventeenth and Eighteenth

initiatives were taken seriously in the parishes, even in small communities where they might be thought unnecessary because the dependent poor were well known and easily recognized. Early eighteenth-century overseers' accounts are replete with payments for the making of badges (a penny or two each for those made of cloth, more substantial sums for those stamped on brass) and with parish orders warning the poor of forfeiture if they failed to wear them. As Table 6.1 shows, in addition to the eleven parishes which can be shown to have badged their poor in the years immediately before the 1697 statute, a further sixty-five had done so by 1790, sixteen (25 per cent) of them by 1700, and a further sixteen by 1710.[280]

The problem with the spread of examples represented in Table 6.1, of course, is that these instances are dispersed and sporadic, making it difficult to draw more general conclusions. Even so, it should be emphasized that extant expenditure lists which do not refer to the badging of the poor in the 1690s are far less common than those that do. All four Warwickshire parishes with extant accounts for the year 1695–6 recorded outlay for cloth, thread, and craftsmanship to make and sew lettered badges on the clothes of the poor. Six of eight Somerset parishes with surviving records of expenditure for the 1690s paid for badges, two of them also providing the coats on which they were to be stitched.[281] Essex parish papers, moreover, convey a more localized sense of the nature, scale, and extent of the enterprise to badge the poor. In some of the larger parishes—St Mary's Chelmsford from 1684, Braintree from 1688,

Centuries', *Transactions of the Cumberland and Westmoreland Antiquarian and Archaeological Society*, NS 15 (1915), 93; West Yorkshire Archive Service, Wakefield, QS1/55/4; N. Landau, *The Justices of the Peace in England, 1679–1760* (Berkeley, 1984), 259. The badging of the poor also seems to have been practised in Scotland, in Wales, and in Ireland, though in these contexts it retained a much closer relationship with licensed begging. Mitchison, *The Old Poor Law in Scotland*, 98; D. W. Howell, *The Rural Poor in Eighteenth-Century Wales* (Cardiff, 2000), 99; D. Dickson, 'In Search of the Old Irish Poor Law', in R. Mitchison and P. Roebuck (eds.), *Economy and Society in Scotland and Ireland, 1500–1939* (Edinburgh, 1988), 151.

[280] See Hindle, 'Dependency, Shame and Belonging', 46–7, 55–8, and references there cited. A further five examples—Alrewas (Staffs.), Ashwell and Little Munden (both Herts.), Great Staughton (Hunts.), and Shelton (Norfolk)—have recently been discovered. J. Kent and S. King, 'Changing Patterns of Poor Relief in Some English Rural Parishes, *circa* 1650–1750', *Rural History*, 14 (2003), 136.

[281] WCRO, DR296/45, unfol. (Kenilworth, 7 Dec. 1695); DR104/63, unfol. (Sowe, 1696); DR404/67, unfol. (Fillongley, 1696); NI/17, unfol. (Napton, Apr. 1696); SARS, D/P/but/13/2/1, unfol. (Butleigh, 1698); D/Pdit/13/2/1, unfol. (Ditcheat, 1698); D/P/e.pen/13/2/1, unfol. (East Pennard, 1697); D/P/stog/13/2/2, unfol. (Stogumber, 1698); D/P/wby/13/2/1, unfol. (Westbury, 1700); D/P/wick/13/2/1, unfol. (Wick St Lawrence, 1694). The two Somerset exceptions were Hinton St George and Martock. SARS, D/P/hin/13/2/2; D/P/mart/13/2/1.

Table 6.1 Parochial initiatives to badge the poor (in chronological order, by decade)

1677	Petworth (Sussex)
1677, 1722	St Martins in the Fields (Westminster)
*c.*1677–84	Colchester (Essex)
*c.*1677–95	Norwich (Norfolk)
1678	Romsey (Hants.)
1680	St Botolph Aldgate (London)
1680	Wisbech (Cambs.)
1682	Great St Mary's (Cambs.)
1682	Tonbridge (Kent)
1684, 1705	St Mary's Chelmsford (Essex)
1685, 1697, 1700, 1704, 1707, 1711, 1715, 1719,1723, 1727, 1728, 1730	Pattingham (Staffs.)
1688	Braintree (Essex)
*c.*1688–1709	Exeter (Devon)
1692	Wivenhoe (Essex)
1693, 1694	St Martins Ludgate (London)
1694	Wick St Lawrence (Som.)
1695	Kenilworth (War.)
1696	Brighton (Sussex)
1696, 1698	Cowden (Kent)
1696	Fillongley (War.)
1696	Napton-on-the-hill (War.)
1696	Solihull (War.)
1696	Sowe (War.)
[before 1697]	Wem (Shropshire)
1697	Aylesbury (Bucks.)
1697	East Pennard (Som.)
1697	Gnosall (Staffs.)
1697	St Katherine Coleman (London)
1697	Terling (Essex)
1697	Thaxted (Essex)
1697	Whickham (Co. Durham)
1698	Butleigh (Som.)
1698, 1787	Ditcheat (Som.)
1698	Little Crosby (Lancs.)
1698	Manchester (Lancs.)
1698	Stogumber (Som.)
1698	Warton-in-Lonsdale (Lancs.)
1699	Grimsargh (Lancs.)

1699	Roxton (Beds.)
1699	Urmston (Lancs.)
1700	Westbury (Som.)
1701, 1718, 1721	Ashwell (Herts.)
1702	Burton-upon-Trent (Staffs.)
1702, 1743	Atherton (Lancs.)
1702	Prescot (Lancs.)
1703, 1720, 1740	Gnosall (Staffs.)
1703	Linton (Cambs.)
1704	Great Horwood (Bucks.)
1704, 1729	Lapworth (War.)
1705	St Andrew's Holborn (London)
1706	Bow Brickill (Bucks.)
1706	Eaton Socon (Beds.)
1708, 1714, 1717, 1720, 1723	Meldreth (Cambs.)
1708	Sevenoaks (Kent)
1708	Writtle (Essex)
1709, 1728	Trull (Som.)
1710	Kirkoswald (Cumberland)
1711	Edlesborough (Bucks.)
1712	St Botolph's Cambridge (Cambs.)
1713, 1718	Liverpool (Lancs.)
1722, 1729	Chalfont St Peter (Bucks.)
1723	Upminster (Essex)
1724	Stanford Rivers (Essex)
1727, 1730	Bottisham (Cambs.)
1729	Warrington (Lancs.)
1730s	Hackney (Middx.)
1731	Drayton (Som.)
1731	Sutton Bennington (Notts.)
1732	East Barnet (Herts.)
1733	Symondburn (Co. Durham)
1737	Frieston (Lincs.)
1737	Lambourne (Essex)
1737	Windscale (Cumberland)
1738	Whinfell (Cumberland)
1742	Shipstone on Stour (Worcs.)
1745	Puddletown (Dorset)
1745	Wimborne Minster (Dorset)
1747	Morpeth (Co. Durham)

Table 6.1 (cont.)

1755	Loxton (Som.)
1757	Marston Bagot (Som.)
1761	Highley (Shropshire)
1765	Birchanger (Essex)
1766	Fitzhead (Som.)
1767	Poulton-with-Fernhead (Lancs.)
1769	Blagdon (Som.)
1775	Long Newton (Co. Durham)
[until 1784]	Stone (Staffs.)
1790	Houghton le Spring (Co. Durham)

Wivenhoe from 1692—stigmatization predated the 1697 statute.[282] In at least one, Thaxted, compliance with the act was almost immediate.[283] In a series of others, vestries passed resolutions to badge the poor as the eighteenth century progressed: Writtle (1708), Upminster (1723), Stanford Rivers (1724), Lambourne (1737). The vestrymen of Birchanger subscribed to a badging order in 1765 with the promise that they would 'contribute to the utmost of [their] powers in all respects to see the same carried into execution'.[284] In only one case was the bitter pill sweetened: the pensioners of St Mary's Chelmsford were not only badged but clothed in blue kersey in 1705.[285] The Somerset justices also seem to have had a keen interest in badging, repeatedly insisting on the enforcement of the policy in 1731, 1755, 1757, 1769 and 1787.[286] Only very rarely did vestries grant any latitude in this matter, although the parish officers of Wimborne Minster conceded that forfeitures for not wearing the badge might be waived on occasions of 'the utmost necessity, as in cases of sickness or other accidental misfortune' in 1745.[287]

Although Richard Dunning argued that the wearing of the badge should make the poor 'submissive and orderly', deterrence was only one

282 ERO, D/P94/1/7; 264/18/5; 277/13/1.

283 ERO, D/P16/12/2.

284 ERO, D/P50/8/1; 117/8/2; 140/8/1; 181/8/2; 25/8/1.

285 ERO, D/P94/5/2.

286 SARS, D/P/dton/13/10/1; D/P/lox/13/10/1; D/P/blag/9/1/2; D/P/dit/9/1/2; D/P/fitz/13/2/2; Tate, *The Parish Chest*, 207 (Marston Bigot, Som., 1757).

287 Dorset RO, PE/WM/VE/1/1, unfol.

of the strands of thinking that had fed into the 1697 statute.[288] As we have seen, there was a long prehistory of using badges to distinguish the resident deserving poor from casual beggars, and this was a tradition on which some late seventeenth-century polemicists drew. Thomas Firmin had argued as early as 1678 that paupers should be prevented from augmenting their parish income except by labour, and suggested that those incapable of work should be badged in recognition of their inability to do anything but beg.[289] He advocated the general adoption of a policy already practised in the London parish of St Botolph-without-Aldersgate, where 'a badge with the three first letters of the parishes name upon it' was to be made up 'of blew and yellow bayes' and pinned upon 'the sleeve or breast' of all those persons who were permitted to seek alms from their neighbours. Householders, in turn, were to promise to give casual relief exclusively to those wearing badges. Firmin could not understand either 'why anybody should be offended' that 'the parishioners should invite their poor neighbours once a day to come to their houses to receive such bread and meat as they are willing to bestow' nor why those wearing badges should 'go under so dishonourable a name as beggars' when they were to all intents and purposes '*invited guests*'.[290] In turn, he argued, common beggars would either soon learn that casual alms were not to be had, or if they did not, then 'those very poor who wear the badge and are appointed to take relief' would 'soon hunt them out of the parish or provoke the beadles to do it'.[291] Despite Firmin's compassionate rationale for badging, harking back as it did to the kind of thinking that had underpinned the late Elizabethan campaign for general hospitality, there is very little evidence that badges were generally used as licences to beg, as they were in Scotland. A very few examples in support of this tendency originate, as might be expected, in the far north-west of England. The case of the 'decrepit' Eskdale widow who explained in 1732 that she had 'sought her bread up and down the parish these twentie yeares, having a badge upon her shoulder and allowed by [the parish officers] to seek' suggests that in Cumberland badges were worn both to indicate dependency and as a recognition of the right to beg long into the eighteenth century.[292]

[288] Dunning, *Bread for the Poor*, 10.

[289] T. Firmin, *Some Proposals for the Employment of the Poor, Especially in and About the City of London and for the Prevention of Begging* (London, 1678), 14. For the influence of Firmin's ideas on John Locke in particular, see Beier, '"Utter Strangers to Industry, Morality and Religion"', 37. For Locke's proposals on badging, see 'An Essay on the Poor Law', 197–8.

[290] Firmin, *Proposals for the Employment of the Poor*, 14–15 (emphasis in original).

[291] Ibid. 16.

[292] Hindle, 'Dearth, Fasting and Alms'; Mitchison, *The Old Poor Law in Scotland*, 98; CRO, Q/11/1/165/29.

That Firmin's views were not widely shared is, furthermore, made abundantly clear in a satirical critique of 'liberal' thinking on the badging of the poor which survives in the mid-eighteenth-century papers of the vestry of Wimbledon (Surrey).[293] In a searing attack on those who misguidedly regarded badging as an act of stigmatization under the terms of a tyrannical statute, its anonymous author mocked the case for repeal by postulating five putative 'reasons why the poor who are maintained by the parish should not wear a badge'. Wearing a badge would be a 'very unreasonable humiliation' of the poor and 'much beneath their dignity'. Badging would 'interrupt the poor' in their 'very agreeable method of passing the time' in 'idling begging or abusing their neighbours or benefactors'. The badge symbolized social obligation, a principle despised by the poor, who would 'scorn to wear such a deception', leaving the parish 'to lose the honour of maintaining them and only support such as are really humble and pitiful'. In order to avoid the badge, the poor would be forced to 'exert themselves to gain maintenance by their own industry' which 'would be a great hardship upon such as are not fond of working and can easily throw themselves in the poorhouse'. Finally, badging should be disregarded because it was established by act of parliament, and the common people knew that all such acts and injunctions were 'great infringements of their liberties'. Satire of this kind clearly bespoke the case in favour of badging as it was popularly understood by parish officers and ratepayers alike: that it stigmatized and deterred; that it prevented casual begging and idleness; that it encouraged gratitude and humility; that it stimulated independence and industry; and that it was underpinned by statutory authority. The Wimbledon vestrymen, and thousands of others like them, had self-evidently repudiated the commonwealth rhetoric through which badging had originally been justified as part of a programme of licensed begging.[294]

As the examples listed in Table 6.1 suggest, justices' and vestrymen's badging orders often had to be repeated. Whether repetition suggests exhaustion, negligence, or sensitivity on the part of parish officers is rather more debatable.[295] In some parishes, such as Wem, for example, it was argued that 'the wearinge of the badge was onely to save the Officers harmlesse from the penalty in the Act'.[296] Some paupers may even

[293] East Sussex RO, Lewes, SHR/1556.

[294] Under the terms of a vestry resolution of 1775, only those inmates of the Wimbledon workhouse who wore the badge were to be relieved by the parish officers, though how long (if at all) badging predated this order is unclear. *Wimbledon Vestry Minutes, 1736, 1743–88: A Calendar with an Introduction*, ed. F. M. Cowe (Surrey Record Society, 25, Guildford, 1964), 58–9.

[295] Cf. Slack, *The English Poor Law*, 40.

[296] Gough, *History of Myddle*, 260.

have seen the strategic advantages of wearing the badge, for the official recognition of respectability that it embodied might be an asset in future negotiations with overseers and justices. In persuading the Cumberland bench to increase her allowance in 1745, a 70-year-old widow from Brampton both emphasized the justice of her cause and manipulated the deferential imperative in her own interest by reminding them that she 'always wears the badge'. A willingness to wear the badge might even secure an increase in the level of the pension, as it did for the Jeffrey family of Edlesborough (Buckinghamshire) in 1711.[297] Conversely, there may even have been special dispensations for those paupers who had unchallenged reputations for honesty and propriety: among the late eighteenth-century parish papers of Cruwys Morland (Devon) is a precedent form of a justice's order to exempt paupers of good character from wearing the badge.[298] The power to badge the poor was finally repealed in 1810, though the vestry of Toddington (Bedfordshire) sought to deploy its sanctions as late as 1819.[299]

In all probability, however, the policy was most rigorously enforced when ratepayers felt particularly overburdened. After all, the efflorescence of badging orders in years of high prices, such as 1727–30 or 1741, was probably not coincidental.[300] As befitted a policy of deterrence, moreover, the logic of exemplary punishment was selectively applied to those who did not conform: to a widow from Brighton and to a single mother from Solihull (Warwickshire) in 1696; to another widow from Cowden (Kent) in 1698; to four women of Burton-upon-Trent in 1703; to a widow of St Andrew's Holborn in 1705; to three women of Chalfont St Peter in 1729; to a single mother and her bastard child in Whinfell (Cumberland) in 1738. One of the poor pensioners of East Barnet

[297] CRO, Q/11/1/221/11; *Buckinghamshire Sessions Records*, iii. 266.

[298] Devon RO, Exeter, 1092A-1/PO113. This precedent was justified by the provisions of 22 George III, c. 83 (1782), the preamble of which referred to the 'very grievous' 'sufferings and distresses of the poor' occasioned by the 'incapacity, negligence or misconduct of overseers'. As early as 1698, Dunning, *Bread for the Poor*, 11, thought that those of 'civil demeanour', the sick, children, and the aged should be exempted from wearing the badge. Henry Fielding argued in 1753 that those labourers who were 'entirely guiltless' should be distinguished from those 'guilty of some crime (idleness at least)' by the absence of badges. H. Fielding, 'A Proposal for Making an Effectual Provision for The Poor', in id., *An Enquiry into the Causes of the Late Increase of Robbers and Related Writings*, ed. M. R. Zirker (Oxford, 1988), 269.

[299] Tate, *The Parish Chest*, 207. Clause ii of the 1697 act was repealed by 50 George III, c. 52 (1810), but other parts remained in force until 1867. For other examples of late employment of the statute, see *The Oakes Diaries: Business, Politics and the Family in Bury St Edmunds, 1778–1827*, ed. J. Fiske (2 vols., Suffolk Records Society, 32–3, Woodbridge, 1990–1), i. 393 (1800); Cutlack, 'Gnosall Records', 46 (1810); Hinton, 'The Relief of the Poor of Lacock', 173 (1817).

[300] J. Innes, 'Social Problems: Poverty and Marginality in Eighteenth-Century England' (unpublished paper, 1985), 37.

(Hertfordshire) was actually committed to prison in 1732 'for insulting the churchwarden and not wearing his badge as the act of parliament directs'.[301] At least one magistrate enforced the punishment and then thought better of it. When Paul D'Aranda came across two goodwives near Sevenoaks who were not wearing the badge in 1708, he ordered the reduction of their pensions, only to rescind his order on appeal. (He nonetheless noticed that they were not wearing badges when he saw them again the following day.)[302] The laconic but resonant formula used to deprive the collectioners in the Chalfont St Peter case is, nonetheless, a powerful reminder that badging orders were not merely symbolic: 'no bodge this month no pay'.[303] Sadly, their grounds for refusal remain unspecified. Some commentators thought it a matter of pride. By the early 1720s social commentators were lamenting the touchy sensibility of the labouring poor. It was reported from Romford (Essex) in 1724, for example, that 'pride, though it does ill become poor folk, won't suffer some to wear the badge'.[304]

Indeed, paupers and their families were acutely sensitive to the stigma, and used their detailed knowledge of the law to avoid it wherever possible. Two inhabitants of Aylesbury successfully appealed against badging orders in 1697 on the grounds that, although their parents were partly dependent on the parish and wore the badge, they personally contributed to their support without a subsidy from the ratepayers and were therefore exempt under the terms of the statute.[305] The fact that badges should be refused is particularly striking in the context of inter-parochial litigation in which these stamped plates of tin or brass might even be produced in court as evidence of overseers' recognition of a settlement and the obligations that went with it.[306] In refusing to accept the public identity of dependency ascribed to them by the parish officers, these paupers forfeited whatever 'rights' they believed were conferred by the Elizabethan poor law. Perhaps they felt that entitlements of this kind were hardly

[301] Marshall, *The English Poor*, 103; Turner, 'Ancient Account Book of Cowden', 115; *Warwick County Records*, ix. 129; Webb and Webb, *Old Poor Law*, 161; *Middlesex County Records*, 291; Edmonds, 'Overseers of the Poor of Chalfont St Peter', 7; Cumbria RO, Kendal, WQ/SR/93/3; *Hertford County Records*, ii. 70.

[302] Landau, *The Justices of the Peace*, 179; *Buckingham Sessions Records*, ii. 144.

[303] Edmonds, 'Overseers of the Poor of Chalfont St Peter', 7.

[304] Anon., *Account of Workhouses in Great Britain in the Year 1732* (3rd edn., London, 1786), 110.

[305] *Buckinghamshire Sessions Records*, ii. 144.

[306] See e.g. the case of Myddle *vs.* Wem debated at three consecutive Shropshire quarter sessions in 1701, during which 'a P. made of tin' was 'shewed in Court'. Gough, *History of Myddle*, 260. This possibility probably explains why overseers sometimes travelled to distant parishes to give badges to their own non-resident paupers, as was the case in Pattingham (Staffs.) in 1729. Kent and King, 'Changing Patterns of Poor Relief', 134.

worth the irrevocable public sacrifice of their independence. Either way, they were in no position to negotiate the terms, let alone the fact, of their subordination.[307]

6. CONCLUSION: AGENCY, POWER, AND AUTHORITY IN THE PARISH STATE

The Elizabethan poor laws conferred very significant powers on those who administered them in the parishes and co-ordinated them in the counties. Overseers in particular exercised the authority to assess levels of need, to adjust the rates paid by householders, to disburse relief in cash and/or kind, and to withhold payments from those whose conduct disappointed their expectations of industry, sobriety, and deference. These powers were discretionary, in the sense that they could be exercised summarily without prior authorization by a justice of the peace and that the personal judgements of individual officeholders might exert considerable influence on the implementation of policy. They were not, however arbitrary, however much some contemporary authorities might be tempted to equate discretion with arbitrariness.[308] As we have seen, the discretionary decisions to suspend or cancel pensions were made according to a calculus of eligibility, the general principles of which were clear to all the participants in the welfare process. These decisions had to be justified not only to paupers and ratepayers but also to magistrates. Indeed, the powers of co-ordination, supervision, and audit granted to magistrates under the terms of the Elizabethan statutes ensured that overseers' decisions could be reviewed and overturned as a matter of course by the gentry. Sometimes these interventions were made on magistrates' own initiatives. More commonly, however, paupers themselves solicited the aid of magistrates as they attempted to modify or even to challenge the relief policies adopted by overseers and the vestries they represented.

As such, the politics of parish relief turned not only on issues of power and authority, but also on those of agency. The petitions that brought the magistracy into play in the welfare process are one further example of the strategies the poor might adopt as they struggled to shift for themselves,

[307] Cf. Levine and Wrightson, *Industrial Society*, 348; M. J. Braddick and J. Walter, 'Introduction. Grids of Power: Order, Hierarchy and Subordination in Early Modern Society', in eid. (eds.), *Negotiating Power*, 42.

[308] Lord Chief Justice Holt queried in the 1690s whether '*discretionary* [was] but a softer word for *arbitrary*?'. Holt KB 680, cited in *Lord Nottingham's Chancery Cases*, vol. i, ed. D. E. C. Yale (Selden Society, 73, London, 1954), p. xlvi.

and, for all their distinctiveness, appellants' voices harmonized with the chorus of complaint later to be sounded by settlement examinants and writers of pauper letters.[309] Appeals of this kind might initiate a triangular process of negotiation in which pauper, overseer, and magistrate debated issues of obligation and entitlement, and which might even become a quadrangular process in those very serious cases where the itinerant judiciary or the justices of King's Bench become involved. Petitioners for relief were often frustrated, and even on those occasions where they thought they had won, further struggle became necessary to coerce those overseers who stood in contempt of magistrates' orders. It is, however, clear that the poor were not invariably unsuccessful in these campaigns, and that in certain circumstances (provided they had sufficient energy and patience and enjoyed substantial resources of money and patronage), they might occasionally mobilize whatever rights they thought they had. The evidence nonetheless suggests that the Elizabethan statutes did not in themselves confer entitlement. The 'right to relief', rather, was negotiated in the course of local practice.

Two significant features of such negotiations require further comment. In the first instance, the fact that agency generally lay with the poor in the welfare process calls into question the view that the magistracy were motivated by considerations of 'paternalism'. Justices of the peace were often very reluctant participants in these processes. Doubtless they felt overworked and were sometimes oblivious to the precarious balance of local resources, especially in those parishes over which they exercised authority only from some considerable distance. The fact that they were nonetheless drawn in to the micro-politics of poor relief suggests that their motives were less benign than 'the myth of paternalism' might suggest. In part, the magistracy was concerned to appease the assize judges and the privy council lest their complacency provoked the usual tirades about their negligence. They also sought, moreover, to pacify the poor whose conduct in the politics of entitlement was not always as deferential as the open transcript of their public petitions and appeals suggests. Indeed, petitioning was part of a continuum of participation, and the poor might easily pass from grumbling about the conduct of vestrymen and magistrates to cursing or threatening them.[310] From this perspective, the magistracy had no choice but to negotiate, and its instincts were less those of benevolence born of paternalism towards

309 The agency of the poor is the principal theme of the essays collected in Hitchcock *et al.* (eds.), *Chronicling Poverty*.

310 Walter, 'Public Transcripts', 128–42.

the labouring poor than those of self-preservation borne of fear of the many-headed monster.[311]

At the same time, the extent of the agency that the poor might legitimately exercise in these negotiations should not be exaggerated. The granting of parish relief might have been the outcome of an 'interactive bargaining process', but the participants in that process came to the table with vastly different resources of power and influence.[312] The game was played by widely accepted rules, and one of the most easily recognized was that the poor should demonstrate their gratitude for the charity shown by ratepayers, parish officers, and magistrates alike. Deference was the lubricant that greased the machinery of welfare. It is, to this extent, unsurprising that those who clamoured for relief or took pensions for granted were singled out for exemplary punishment, and might consequently have their collection withheld, reduced, or cancelled. It is highly likely that the parish badge was most often forced upon those, like the serial petitioner of Kirkoswald (Cumberland) Ann Bowman, who harassed the parish officers or treated them with contempt. As early as the 1630s, Michael Dalton had been asking what should be done with those dissolute parishioners who happened 'to prove impotent' or to experience 'manifest extremity'. By 1697, the answer was clear: they should be forced to 'take the patch'.[313] Overall, it seems that, as the seventeenth century progressed, the labouring poor enjoyed less and less room for manoeuvre in their negotiations with parish officers and magistrates. In part, this was a function of the closing off of those numerous avenues of informal relief that they had traditionally been able to explore. As we have seen, the range of shifts that they might legitimately make was contracting across the seventeenth century.[314] But it was also inherent in the spread of parish relief that the thresholds of eligibility were defended ever more rigorously against those who might take relief for granted. The parish badge and the workhouse test were only symbols of a process of exclusion that had been in train, however episodically, since the Elizabethan statutes were passed.[315]

Even the model of negotiation sketched here does not, however, do

[311] C. Hill, 'The Many-Headed Monster in Late Tudor and Early Stuart Political Thinking', repr. in id., *Change and Continuity in Seventeenth-Century England* (rev. edn., New Haven, 1991), 181–204.

[312] Cf. M. H. D. van Leeuwen, 'Logic of Charity: Poor Relief in Pre-Industrial Europe', *Journal of Interdisciplinary History*, 24 (1994), 611.

[313] For the use of this idiom by a pauper required to wear the parish badge, see K. Wrightson, *Earthly Necessities: Economic Lives in Early Modern Britain* (New Haven, 2000), 374.

[314] Cf. Ch. 1 above.

[315] Cf. Kent and King, 'Changing Patterns of Poor Relief', 145–9.

justice to the complex realities of the decision-making process with respect to the allocation of parish resources. The archives of vestry and magistracy alike are very revealing of the attitudes of officeholders in these disputes. Indeed, it is tempting in particular to privilege the role of overseers (as representatives of the 'better sort' or of 'chief inhabitants') over against the poor, and to ignore the agency of other actors. Although this chapter has argued that the poor themselves enjoyed a degree of agency in the micro-politics of welfare, the archives on which it is based are altogether less forthcoming about the views of the lesser ratepayers, who might not hold parish office but whose collective voice might exert significant influence over issues of eligibility and entitlement. It is probable, in fact, that there was in effect a local public opinion to which the various parties in negotiation sought to appeal, and perhaps even to construct. We have seen that in some cases the oligarchical impulse which was felt even in rural parishes by the second decade of the seventeenth century might restrict the role that such lesser ratepayers might formally play in debates over assessment and disbursement. Whether it was permitted to attend vestry meetings or not, however, this constituency was particularly significant in that it was principally made up of those who might themselves be vulnerable to dependency in old age and who therefore had a vested interest in ensuring that parish policies to the poor were equitable.

Only very rarely are the views of these lesser ratepayers heard in the sources. It might be inferred from the bishops' faculties that excluded them from parish meetings that their interests were more closely aligned with the interests of those who were *on* the parish than those that *ran* it. Some contemporaries certainly thought so. Richard Dunning, for example, feared that lesser ratepayers would 'join with the insolence of the poor and rather than hinder will lead and encourage them in their aspersions' of initiatives to badge the poor. Although Dunning refused to elaborate on the motivation for such recalcitrance, it is probable that he had in mind the likelihood that those lesser ratepayers who might well become dependent on parish relief in old age would be reluctant to encourage a stigma to which they would themselves eventually become subject.[316] Evidence of this kind is, of course, notoriously difficult to interpret: is Dunning's view better characterized as that of a participant in the welfare process whose experience makes his judgements particularly

[316] Dunning, *Bread for the Poor*, 12. Cf. the emphasis on the 'considerable overlap' between lesser ratepayers and those who received relief in Hitchcock *et al.*, 'Introduction', 10, and the implication that parish relief therefore functioned as a form of social insurance across the life-cycle in Solar, 'Poor Relief and English Economic Development', 7–12.

significant, perhaps even valid, or that of a commentator whose rhetoric is constructed to influence the judgement of others? Were the lesser ratepayers really opposed to badging or did Dunning think they ought to be?

Questions of this kind become even more problematic in the light of late seventeenth-century discourses about the poor. The instincts of late sixteenth-century policy-makers, polemicists, and projectors had been to place the poor into easily recognized, and sometimes ancient, categories: deserving and undeserving, industrious and idle, worthy and unworthy.[317] Those of late seventeenth-century successors were rather the converse: to label the poor as a homogeneous group without paying any real attention to the causes of their indigence. The tripartite typology of need which had underpinned the Elizabethan poor laws—impotence, idleness, unemployment—had always been to some extent artificial: groups which exhibited these characteristics were far more easily defined on the statute book than identified in the parishes, and as early as the 1630s it was becoming very difficult to distinguish between the deserving and the idle in particular. The transparent lack of fit between the rhetoric which lumped together all the poor as idle and the identity of those who were sufficiently shamed by the experience of parish relief to refuse to wear the badge (usually women, often widows, especially those with children) is only the most obvious consequence of the late seventeenth-century tendency to homogenize 'the poor' as a class and to describe them, using terms coined by the gentry, in defiance of either the causes or the realities of their indigence.[318]

317 Slack, *Poverty and Policy*, *passim*.

318 Thompson, *Customs in Common*, 17 n. 2.

Conclusion
The Changing Experience of Poor Relief

On 25 September 1712 Martha Thompson, a widow who lived in the Lancashire township of Little Crosby, informed her landlord, Nicholas Blundell, and the overseer of the poor, Thomas Harrow, that 'she would not any longer have allowance out of the town'. Thompson had been on the parish for twenty years, the overseers having been compelled by the Lancashire justices in 1692 to pay her an annual pension of 40*s*. and to house her at a subsidized rent. The accommodation provided for her was, however, so cold and damp that it was 'nott fitt for any person to habit in', a failure compounded by the arrears that the parish officers allowed to build up on her account. She turned to her neighbours for support, borrowing 30*s*. worth of corn from one of them, without any realistic possibility of paying it back, for otherwise she might have 'famished for want of bread in the winter'. When she sought credit elsewhere, 'the best or most of the township, being roman catholics and she not of the same persuasion, was very cruel and severe with her'. In May 1698 she turned to the bench to compel the overseers to pay her arrears so that she might satisfy her creditor, and they agreed, coercing collection from the township on her behalf. The order was, however, conditional on her wearing the parish badge.[1]

Thompson's motives for seeking independence of the parish some fourteen years after she 'took the patch' can only be guessed at. Her circumstances may well have changed: her children were grown and apprenticed, perhaps; she was possibly contemplating remarriage or was maybe even contracted again (possibly after an interval of many years) in domestic service. Either way, the manner of Martha Thompson's departure from the pension lists of Little Crosby was, by the early eighteenth century, extremely unusual. Most of her contemporaries who had first received relief in the 1690s would remain in collection until they died, the parish officers paying for their funerals and recouping some of their expenditure by selling off their few remaining goods. Rarely, if ever,

[1] *The Great Diurnal of Nicholas Blundell of Little Crosby, Lancashire*, ed. J. J. Bagley (3 vols., Record Society of Lancashire and Cheshire, Manchester, 1968–72), ii. 283; LRO, QSP/811/1.

would paupers get the opportunity to shift entirely for themselves once they were on the parish, especially if they had been receiving a pension for as long as twenty years.

For most collectioners the experience of poor relief is obscured, rather than revealed, by the lists of disbursements drawn up by overseers and audited by magistrates: irregular halfpenny dribblings cumulatively building into weekly pensions which were, in turn, supplemented with increasing frequency by gratuities 'in want', by subsidies for fuel, and by payments for nursing and medical treatment, only to be terminated in terse reference to shrouds wound, coffins stuffed with wool, and bells tolled. Only very occasionally, most often where a pauper was subject to a settlement examination or made an appeal to a justice of the peace, do the lives that lie behind these calculations bleed through the overseer's scrawl. When given the opportunity, the stories prospective pensioners chose to tell were, as we have seen, narratives of struggle and courage, and sometimes of defiance and resentment, testifying to the very wide range of resources on which they might draw in making shift: goods borrowed, rent forborne, faggots gathered, food cadged. Without the parish relief system that generated these archives, evidence of survival strategies of this kind simply would not exist. In explaining how they had struggled to remain independent for so long, these petitioners surely spoke, however subconsciously, not only for the much larger constituency of those who 'lived of small wages' until age and incapacity drove them into dependency, but also for countless generations of labouring people who had lived and died before rates were ever assessed or pensions distributed. In administering parish relief, overseers and magistrates recorded for posterity the ancient traditions of mutual aid which that very system was designed first to supplement and ultimately to replace.

The tiny minority of parishioners whose experience is inscribed in overseers' accounts were, moreover, fortunate indeed, for there were many others at the margins of the relief system whose need was almost as great and who nonetheless had to wait in the long shadow cast by collection. All of them worked, many of them even begged, as long, as often, and as hard as they could. If they were lucky enough to live in a large rural community or a market town, they might receive an annual or biannual dole, sixpence at Easter perhaps, maybe a shilling at Christmas, from a parish charity bequeathed by a local worthy, though they would quite possibly be required to meet stringent tests of eligibility, especially church attendance and sobriety, to claim it. If the local squire was conscientious, he might authorize his estate steward to dispense seasonal bounty, in which case the indigent could only pray that their names were on the list of those approved for benevolence.

Otherwise they shifted for themselves, improvising a living from the pity of neighbours and the kindness of kin. If their indigence grew acute, they might make a claim on the charity of the parish, perhaps soliciting collection through an intermediary, possibly one of the relatives or neighbours who had been helping them struggle to keep a roof over their head or food on the table, maybe relying on the clergyman or another parish officer. If the overseers thought that resources would permit, an allowance might be forthcoming. If they did not, and the claimant enjoyed sufficient reserves of energy and patronage to persuade the magistracy to intervene, negotiations over eligibility for relief would begin. If the petitioner was suitably deferential, and their reputation for industry, thrift, and parental responsibility unblemished, the justices might well be moved to bring their authority to bear on the parish. The outcome of the exchanges between magistracy and vestry was, however, unpredictable: many such partitions were simply referred back to the parish officers or tersely subscribed 'nil'. Even if a payment was authorized, it was a courageous, perhaps even a reckless, pauper who counted on the parish officers complying with a relief order without the need to request the justices to intervene a second or even a third time. Although the historiography of poverty has shifted in recent years from traditional models of social control and cultural hegemony, which emphasized the degree to which the poor were ground down and struggled to get by, to more positive evaluations of agency and independence among the indigent, it is important to recognize the inequalities with which the parish relief system was saturated, and which inhibited the extent to which paupers might gain access to the circuits of authority.

Parish relief was, therefore, a *process*—indeed, an often protracted process—of which the audited overseers' disbursement is only the final record. Those historians who have characterized parish relief as generous and sensitive, and even as benevolent and sympathetic, have generally done so by reconstructing the scale of pension payments, often marrying them with the cyclical patterns of need associated with childrearing and old age. To analyse the nature of the system exclusively on the basis of those claims for relief that, by virtue of the fact that they were recorded in parish account books, were successful is, however, seriously to underestimate the complexity of the negotiations that must have been necessary before a pension was granted or an occasional payment made. The resources of the parish were not infinite, and overseers' confronted with genuine cases of human misery must have found it extremely difficult to reconcile their legal obligation to relieve the impotent with their social responsibility not to overburden their fellow ratepayers. Their solutions, as we have seen, were various: to increase the existing burden on ratepayers of ability rather than spreading it onto the shoulders of those who were not; to reduce allowances when the individual circumstances of the pensioner changed or when wider economic conditions improved; and, above all, to insist that all those who claimed relief should be incapable of supporting themselves by work.

By the late seventeenth and early eighteenth centuries, these techniques were reinforced by a number of policies of deterrence—the parish badge, the compulsory apprenticeship of children, the workhouse test—which were designed to make life on the parish as unattractive as possible. The fact that these strategies were perceived to be necessary is an index of both the success and the failure of the Elizabethan poor laws. No longer could it be argued, as it had been in the 1630s, that the indigent were ignorant of the workings of the parish relief system and intimidated by those who administered it. Over the course of the century, the magistracy, encouraged and advised by the circuit judges, had succeeded in publicizing the statutes, the provisions of which had begun to permeate plebeian consciousness. By the 1680s and 1690s, therefore, the law-mindedness that has been described as such a distinguishing feature of seventeenth-century popular culture had certainly grown to encompass the poor laws. As Matthew Hale recognized, however, the reading of the statutes which became popular in the parishes by the mid-seventeenth century was not that envisaged by Elizabethan MPs. Parish relief had become subverted from 'a charity of greater extent'—the employment of the poor—to a 'charity of more immediate exigence'—the relief of the impotent. Where the architects of the policy had envisaged labour discipline, the poor—and indeed many parish officers—only saw alms.

The parish relief system as it evolved over the course of the seventeenth century was in some respects, therefore, a modified form of the charity of householders: it began at home, and moved outward into the neighbourhood, and to some extent it inherited the medieval logic of reciprocal obligation. Ratepayers, like householders who gave alms, were, after all, acting out the Christian precept that they should do unto others as they would have others do unto them. The notion that by virtue of paying rates a householder was building up a fund of respectability which might bolster his case for relief should he fall victim to dependency in old age was arguably a secularized version of the gift exchange implied in the medieval theology of works. The radical discontinuity represented by the introduction of formal relief should not, however, be underestimated.

Although there are doubtless similarities between casual alms and parish pensions, similarities which are all the more striking in the light of the interpenetration of general hospitality and parish relief in the closing years of the sixteenth century, formal collection became over time less and less a gesture of neighbourliness and mutuality and more and more an expression of hierarchy and subordination. However much Protestants sought in the century or so after the Edwardian reformation to maintain the ideal of the parish as a social organism, the mutual interdependence of whose members was represented by the rituals of communion and other rites of passage, and however much they insisted that the pension was just another form of the collective charity of the congregation, they protested too much. By the end of the seventeenth century, and arguably by 1650, the relief of the poor in the parishes of rural England was stimulated not by the moral obligations of neighbourliness, still less by the theological imperative of works, but by the formal sanctions of law. The decisive transformation of the experience of poor relief arguably occurred, however, not in the late sixteenth century, when formal and informal relief remained so closely intertwined and pension levels were so low as to necessitate their augmentation with neighbourly charity, but in the late seventeenth, when the scale of pension payments had increased to a sufficient extent to affect the demand for, and even the supply of, the personal charity of householders.

The weekly gathering of pensioners in the church porch to receive their allowances after the Sunday sermon doubtless fostered a sense of social solidarity among the deserving poor. This nascent collective identity was surely encouraged by the requirement that paupers wear badges, which symbolized the emergence of both poverty as an inherited condition and the labouring poor as a permanent class, though doubtless one segmented by highly localized senses of place. To fall on the parish might well have been a mark of dependency and of shame, but it also implied belonging.[2] Membership of the moral community of the parish, however, could never be assumed: it had to be earned and maintained over the course of a life of labour, and even then it did not carry with it any automatic entitlement to pension payments. The experience of parish relief shared by a tiny minority was, therefore, only a small fragment of the changing experience of poor relief as a whole, and the majority of those who were in need shifted for themselves at the margins of a system in which notions of entitlement were both under-developed and contested.

[2] For a further development of this argument, see S. Hindle, 'Dependency, Shame and Belonging: Badging the Deserving Poor, *c.*1550–1750', *Cultural and Social History*, 1 (2004), 29–58.

In reconstructing the workings of that system, the evidence presented in this book provides an invaluable historical perspective for debates about the rights and obligations of the poor in twenty-first-century society, where the piecemeal dismantling of the welfare state implies that there is likely to be, once again, no right to relief from cradle to grave.

BIBLIOGRAPHY

MANUSCRIPT SOURCES

Bedfordshire and Luton Archives and Record Service, Bedford

ABP/W/1663 Wills of the Archdeaconry of Bedford (1663)
P60/12/1 Kempston parish overseers' accounts (1628–43)
P78/12/1 Goldington parish overseers' accounts (1649–82)

Bodleian Library, Oxford

Rawlinson MS

C948 Memorandum Book of the Cambridgeshire JP Sir Thomas Sclater (*c.*1660–5)
D1136 Collection of orders relating to Cambridge magistrates (*c.*1660–82)

Tanner MS

73 Letters and papers (1621–4)
91 Papers relating to the common law
243 Norfolk Lieutenancy Letter Book (*c.*1612–23)

Western MS

Eng. Hist. b.209 Writings and parliamentary diaries of Sir Richard Cocks of Dumbleton, Glos. (*c.*1681–1726)
Eng. lett. c.589 Guard book of letters (17th–20th cc.)

British Library, London

Additional MS

6223 [Francis] Taverner, 'The History and Antiquities of Hexton, in the County of Hertford' (transcribed with additions by E[dward] Steele, 1713)
12496 Miscellaneous Papers and Letters Collected by Sir Julius Caesar
18773 Berkhamsted St Peter (Herts.) parish churchwardens' accounts (1584–1748)
30278 Staplegrove (Som.) parish churchwardens' and overseers' accounts (1585–1646)
32512 Memorials of the Life and Actions of Sir Dudley North (1709)
34400–1 Huntingdonshire Petty Sessions Papers (1537–1658)
39245 Letter-Book of the Deputy-Lieutenants of Suffolk (1608–40)

Harleian MS

5137 Commonplace Book of Sir Simon Harcourt (1705)
7020 Lists of various kinds of persons, commissions etc. (16th–17th cc.).

Lansdowne MS

83 Cecil Papers

Cambridge University Library

Ee I.1

Centre for Buckinghamshire Studies, Aylesbury

D/A/WF Wills of the Archdeaconry of Buckingham
PR4/12/2 Amersham Overseers' accounts (1611–1751)
PR7/5/1 Aston Abbots parish churchwardens' accounts (1562–1630)
PR138/5/1 Ludgershall parish churchwardens' accounts (1565–1607)
PR140/5/1 Great Marlow parish churchwardens' accounts (1593–1675)
PR234/5/1 Wing parish churchwardens' accounts (1527–1723)

Claydon House, Buckinghamshire

Verney Papers

Cornwall Record Office, Truro

DD/P39/8/1 Constantine Parish Vestry Minute Book (1571–1799)

Cumbria Record Office, Carlisle

Q/11/1/1–118 Cumberland Quarter Sessions Petitions (1686–1749)

Cumbria Record Office, Kendal

WQ/SR/1–99 Westmorland Quarter Sessions Rolls (1726–38)

Devon Record Office, Exeter

67A/PW1 Farway parish churchwardens' accounts (1565–91)
1092A-1/PO105–15 Cruwys Morchard parish miscellaneous papers (1766–1838)

Dorset Record Office, Dorchester

PE/WM/VE/1/1 Wimborne Minster parish vestry minutes (1745–1808)

East Sussex Record Office, Lewes

SHR 1549–1559 Shiffner Archives, Papers relating to the poor house at Wimbledon, Surrey (1773–5)

East Yorkshire Archive Service, Beverley

PE144/T38 Notebook of John Garnett of Sigglesthorne (1710–34)

Eaton Hall, Cheshire

Grosvenor MS 2 Personal papers of Sir Richard Grosvenor (1585–1645)

Essex Record Office, Chelmsford

D/DBa Papers of the Barrington Family of Hatfield Broad Oak
D/Deb Papers of the Bramston Family
D/DU/603 Manorial Papers of Hatfield Peverel, Pebmarsh, and Hadleigh
D/P16/12/2 Thaxted parish overseers' accounts (1696–1716)
D/P25/8/1 Birchanger vestry minutes (1680–95)
D/P27/1/2 Great Hallingbury parish register (1562–93)
D/P50/8/1 Writtle parish vestry minutes (1695–1735)
D/P94/1/7 Chelmsford St Mary the Virgin parish register (1678–1812)
D/P94/5/2 Chelmsford St Mary the Virgin parish churchwardens' accounts (1724–57)
D/P117/8/2 Upminster parish vestry minutes (1721–59)
D/P135/1/1 Heydon parish register (1538–99)
D/P140/8/1 Stanford Rivers parish vestry minutes (1724–75)
D/P181/8/2 Lambourne vestry minutes (1731–64)
D/P264/18/5 Braintree parish miscellaneous papers (1619–1899)
D/P277/13/1 Wivenhoe parish overseers' accounts (1674–1816)
Q/SBa2/81 Quarter sessions depositions and petitions (Michaelmas 1652)
Q/SR28–428 Quarter Sessions rolls (1569–1678)
T/R147/1 Romford parish register (1561–1609)

Gloucester Record Office, Gloucester

D8777/3 Smyth papers, volume iii

Hatfield House, Hertfordshire

Cecil Papers

Henry E. Huntington Library, San Marino, California

STT Temple of Stowe Papers

Herefordshire Record Office, Hereford

W51–60 Papers donated by the British Records Association

Hertfordshire Archives and Local Studies

D/P23/8/1 Braughing parish vestry minutes (1626–52)
D/P65/25 Layston parish charity papers
D/P65/3/3 Memorandum Book of Alexander Strange of Layston (*c.*1607–50)
D/P102/5/1 Stansted Abbots parish churchwardens' accounts (1663–1716)
D/P105/8/2 Stevenage parish vestry minutes (1675–1723)
HAT/SR10–26 Hatfield Sessions Records, Sessions rolls (1597–1615)

Inner Temple Library, London

MS Petyt 530B Sermons Preached by Alexander Strange (*c.*1607–10)

Kent Archives Office, Maidstone

Q/SB/1–7 Quarter Sessions Papers (1649–60)

Lambeth Palace Library, London

COMM.XIIa/10 Copies of Church Surveys, Herefordshire and Hertfordshire (1647–57)

Lancashire Record Office, Preston

QSB/1/51/-301 Quarter Sessions recognizance rolls (1605–48)
QSP/640–830 Quarter Sessions petitions (1687–99)

Leicestershire Record Office, Leicester

DE221 Peake Collection
1D41/13/64–78 Archdeaconry court, act books, office causes

Lincolnshire Archives, Lincoln

Ch.p/2, 3, 4 Churchwardens' presentments and certificates for the archdeaconry of Buckingham (1596–7)

Frampton Parish Papers

PAR1/2 parish register (1558–1686)
PAR7/3 miscellaneous churchwardens' accounts and vouchers (1702–1811)
PAR10/1 parish vestry minutes (1597–1693)

London Guildhall Library, London

9064/15 Diocese of London, commissary court act book (1599–1603)

London Metropolitan Archives, London

DL/C/340–341 Vicar-Generals' books of the Diocese of London (1611–23)
DRO/5/c2/2 South Mimms parish workhouse resolution (1724)

Longleat House, Wiltshire

MS Whitelocke 21, fos. 100–65. Undated drafts of jury charges by James Whitelocke

National Archives (formerly the Public Record Office), London

ASSI2/1 Oxford Circuit Crown Book (1658–78)
ASSI24/20 Western Circuit Order Book (1629–40)
ASSI35 Home Circuit Indictments
C3 Chancery: six clerks office, pleadings series II
C66 Chancery: patent rolls
C90 Commissioners for Charitable Uses, confirmations and exonerations of decrees
C91 Commissioners for Charitable Uses, depositions
C93 Commissioners for Charitable Uses, inquisitions and decrees
CHES21/3 Palatinate of Chester Great Sessions Crown Book (1617–37)
E179 Exchequer Subsidy rolls
PC2/41–48 Privy Council registers (1631–8)
PROB Prerogative Court of Canterbury Wills
SP12 State papers, domestic, Elizabeth I
SP14 State papers, domestic, James I
SP16 State papers, domestic, Charles I
SP29 State papers, domestic, Charles II
STAC8 Star Chamber proceedings, James I

National Library of Wales, Aberystwyth

MS Peniarth

Norfolk Record Office, Norwich

Aylsham MSS

AYL17 Sir Arthur Hevingham's quarter sessions papers (late 16th–early 17th cc.)
AYL304 Miscellaneous Doughty justices' papers (late 16th–17th cc.)

Colman MSS

COL13/1–42 James Bulwer's collection of Hobart Papers

Minor Collections

MC148 Norfolk antiquarian papers (16th–18th cc.)
MC254 Papers of George Sawer of Cawston (1591–1621)

Quarter Sessions Papers

C/S2/3 Order Book (1669–81)
C/S3/13–32 Sessions Rolls (1598–1640)

NCC Wills proved of the consistory court of Norwich

PD209/187–216 North Elmham parish overseers' papers

Northamptonshire Record Office, Northampton

Geddington Parish Papers

133p/158–9, 166–8 Copies of the will of Robert Dallington
133p/160–64 Dallington charity leases (1674–1739)
133p/179 Account Book of Receipts and Expenditure of Dallington Charity (1744–1847)
MISC Photostat 1610 Directions for the choosing and well governing of the poor that receive Robert Dallington's gift

175p/28 Great Houghton parish churchwardens' accounts (1634–98)

Montagu of Boughton MS

x340 (old box no. 7.66), 5–6 Manorial court papers of Weekley (1558–1625)
x350 (old box no. 10.24) Miscellaneous papers relating to Geddington Chase and Woods (18th c.)
x350 (old box no 10.26) Geddington Chase enclosure papers (late 18th c.)
x7523 (old box no. 1330) Geddington manorial court rolls (18th c.).

Montagu MS 186 'Life of Montagu' by Joseph Bentham

QSR/1 Quarter sessions records (1658–1700)

Somerset Archives and Research Service, Taunton

Q\SPET/1 Quarter sessions petitions (mid-17th c.)

Parish Papers

D/P/blag/9/1/2 Blagdon parish vestry minutes (1765–86)
D/P/brut/13/2/1 Bruton parish overseers' accounts (1653–69)
D/P/but/13/2/1 Butleigh parish overseers' accounts (1673–1742)
D/P/b.my/13/2/1 Buckland St Mary parish overseers' accounts (1626–53)
D/P/dit/9/1/2 Ditcheat parish vestry minutes (1786–94)
D/P/dit/13/2/1 Ditcheat parish overseers' accounts (1684–1734)
D/P/dton/13/10/1 Drayton parish miscellaneous papers (1707–31)
D/P/e.pen/13/2/1 East Pennard parish overseers' accounts (1681–1760)
D/P/fitz/13/2/2 Fitzhead parish overseers' accounts (1723–86)
D/P/hin.g/13/2/2 Hinton St George parish overseers' accounts (1693–1764)
D/P/lox/13/10/1 Loxton parish miscellaneous papers (1755)
D/P/mart/13/2/1 Martock parish overseers' accounts (1676–98)
D/P/stog/13/2/2 Stogumber parish overseers' accounts (1686–98)
D/P/wby/13/2/1 Westbury parish overseers' accounts (1678–1718)
D/P/wick/13/2/1 Wick St Lawrence parish overseers' accounts (1677–1708)

Sexey MS

DD\SE/38 Documents resulting from the death and will of Hugh Sexey, and the interim administration of his feoffees
DD\SE/43 General accounts and rentals concerning the administration of the Hospital and its property
DD\SE/44 Miscellaneous papers concerning the administration of Sexey's Hospital
DD\SE/45 Petitions to the feoffees for charitable gifts
DD\SE/46 Apprenticeship papers

Shakespeare Birthplace Trust Record Office, Stratford-upon-Avon

DR203 Bidford parish overseers' accounts (1682–1740)
DR308/101 Extracts from the will of William Willington (1555)

Archer of Tanworth MS

DR473/293 Sir Simon Archer's antiquarian notebook (*c.*1640–50)

Archer of Umberslade MS

DR37/85/6 Kineton hundred parish overseers' accounts (1638–9)

Shropshire Record Office, Shrewsbury

Cressett Deeds

5460/1/1 Court Roll of the manor of Cound (1579)

Warwick County Record Office, Warwick

CR136 Newdigate Papers
CR1618/W19/3 Churchwardens' certificates for parishes in Barlichway and Kineton hundreds (1605)
DR19/251–322 Astley parish overseers' accounts (1656–1741)
DR20/21–22 Ilmington parish overseers' accounts (1709–57)
DR30B/1–2 Farnborough parish overseers' accounts (1665–98, 1717–1813)
DR43A/19–22 Leamington-Hastings parish overseers' accounts (1655–1735)
DR104/63 Sowe parish overseers' accounts (1667–1728)
DR111/26 Grandborough parish overseers' accounts (1704–71)
DR166/19, 23–4 Claverdon parish overseers' accounts (1709–52)
DR240/58 Atherstone-on-Stour parish overseers' accounts (1702–1873)
DR288/41 Tysoe parish overseers' accounts (1749–68)
DR296/43–45 Kenilworth parish overseers' accounts (1629–1712)
DR308/50–53 Brailes parish overseers' accounts (1710–62)
DR360/63 Alcester parish overseers' accounts (1658–89)
DR404/67, 86–91 Fillongley parish overseers' accounts (1623–1713)
DR446/21 Shipstone on Stour vestry minutes (1593–1693)
DR446/22 Shipstone on Stour vestry minutes (1732–8)

DR467/1 Tysoe parish overseers' accounts (1727–38)
DRB56/135–6 Knowle parish overseers' accounts (1705–65)
HR71/11 (Box 2) Bidford parish overseers' accounts (1665–82)
NI/1–19 Napton-on-the-hill parish overseers' accounts (1663–1736)

West Yorkshire Archive Service, Wakefield

QS1/35–60 Quarter Sessions Rolls (1695–1721)

Wiltshire and Swindon Record Office, Trowbridge

PR/Great Cheverell St Peter/207/27–38 Great Cheverell St Peter parish overseers' papers (1688–1836)

Worcestershire Record Office, Worcester

Quarter Sessions Records 1/1/12–58 (1604–33)

PRINTED PRIMARY SOURCES

Account of Workhouses in Great Britain in the Year 1732 (3 edns., London, 1732–86).

Acts of the Privy Council of England, 1542–1631, ed. J. R. Dasent (46 vols., London, 1890–1964).

Alcock, T., *Observations on the Defects of the Poor Laws* (London, 1752).

Allen, R., *A Treatise of Christian Beneficence* (London, 1600).

Ames, W., *Conscience with the Power and Cases Thereof, Divided Into Five Bookes* (2nd edn., London, 1643).

Arthington, H., *Provision for the Poore, Now in Penurie* (London, 1597).

Ascham, A., *Of the Confusions and Revolutions of Governments* (2nd edn., London, 1649).

Aubrey, J., *Wiltshire: The Topographical Collections of John Aubrey*, ed. J. E. Jackson (Devizes, 1862).

Bacon, F., *The Works of Francis Bacon*, ed. J. Spedding, R. Leslie, and D. D. Heath (14 vols., London, 1857–74).

Bacon, N., *The Papers of Nathaniel Bacon of Stiffkey*, ed. A. Hassell Smith, G. M. Baker, V. Morgan, J. Key, and B. Taylor (4 vols., Norfolk Record Society, 46, 49, 53, 64, Norwich, 1978–2000).

Becon, T., *Works* (Cambridge, 1844).

Bentham, J., *The Societie of the Saints* (London, 1636).

Berkshire Overseers Papers, 1654–1834, ed. P. Durrant (Berkshire Record Society 3, Reading, 1997).

Best, H., *The Farming and Memorandum Books of Henry Best of Elmswell, 1642*, ed. D. Woodward (Records of Social and Economic History, NS 8, Oxford, 1984).

Bird, S., *The Lectures of Samuel Bird of Ipswich upon the 8 and 9 Chapters of the Second Epistle to the Corinthians* (London, 1598).

Bishop Redman's Visitation, 1597: Presentments in the Archdeaconries of Norwich, Norfolk and Suffolk, ed. J. F. Williams (Norfolk Record Society, 18, Norwich, 1946).

Bishop Still's Visitation 1594 and The 'Smale Booke' of the Clerk of the Peace for Somerset 1593–5, ed. D. Shorrocks (Somerset Record Society, 84, Taunton, 1998).

Blackstone, W., *Commentaries on the Laws of England* (4th edn., 4 vols., London, 1770).

Blundell, N., *The Great Diurnal of Nicholas Blundell of Little Crosby, Lancashire*, ed. J. J. Bagley (3 vols., Record Society of Lancashire and Cheshire, Manchester, 1968–72).

The Book of Common Prayer, 1559, ed. J. E. Booty (Washington, DC, 1976).

Bott, E., *A Collection of Decisions of the Court of King's Bench upon the Poor's Laws* (2 vols., London, 1793 edn.).

Bulstrode, E., *The Reports of Edward Bulstrode of the Inner Temple, Esquire* (2nd edn., London, 1688).

Burn, R., *The History of the Poor Laws* (London, 1764).

Calendar of Assize Records, ed. J. S. Cockburn (10 vols., London, 1975–82).

Calendar of State Papers, Domestic Series, 1547–1704, ed. M. A. E. Green et al. (92 vols., London, 1856–1924).

Calendar of Wynn (of Gwydir) Papers, ed. J. Ballinger (Aberystwyth, 1926).

Carew, R., *The Survey of Cornwall*, ed. F. E. Halliday (London, 1953).

Cavalier and Puritan: Ballads and Broadsides Illustrating the Period of the Great Rebellion, 1640–1660, ed. H. E. Rollins (New York, 1923).

A Cavalier's Notebook, ed. T. E. Gibson (London, 1880).

Certain Sermons or Homilies (1547) and a Homily Against Disobedience and Wilful Rebellion (1570): A Critical Edition, ed. R. B. Bond (Toronto, 1987).

Child, J., *A New Discourse on Trade* (London, 1693).

Churchwardens' Presentments in the Oxfordshire Peculiars of Dorchester, Thame and Banbury, ed. S. A. Peyton (Oxfordshire Record Society, 10, Oxford, 1928).

The Clarke Papers, ed. C. H. Firth (4 vols., Camden Society, London, 1891–1901).

Cock, G. C., *English Law; or, a Summary Survey of the Household of God on Earth* (London, 1651).

Cocks, R., *The Parliamentary Diary of Sir Richard Cocks, 1698–1702*, ed. D. W. Hayton (Oxford, 1996).

Comber, T., *The Church-Catechism, with a Brief and Easie Explanation Thereof* (London, 1686).

Coming into Line: Local Government in Clayworth, 1674–1714, ed. A. Rogers (Nottingham, 1979).

The Committee at Stafford, 1643–1645: The 'Order Book' of the Staffordshire County Committee, ed. D. H. Pennington and I. Roots (Manchester, 1957).

The Complete Justice (London, 1661).

The Compton Census of 1676: A Critical Edition, ed. A. Whiteman (British Academy Records of Social and Economic History, NS 10, Oxford, 1986).

Conferences and Combination Lectures in the Elizabethan Church: Dedham and Bury St

Edmunds, 1582–1590, ed. P. Collinson, J. Craig, and B. Usher (Church of England Record Society, 10, Woodbridge, 2003).

Cook, J., *Unum Necessarium: Or, The Poor Man's Case: Being An Expedient to Make Provision for all Poore People in the Kingdome* (London, 1647).

Cooper, T., *Observations Upon The Vagrant Laws Proving That The Statutes In Queen Elizabeth's Time Are The Most Proper Foundation For A Law Of That Nature, And That All Alterations That Have Been Made Since, Have Been For The Worse* (1742).

Cornwall Hearth and Poll Taxes 1660–1664: Direct Taxation in Cornwall in the Reign of Charles II, ed. T. L. Stoate (Bristol, 1981).

County of Buckingham: Calendar to the Sessions Records, ed. W. Le Hardy and G. L. Reckitt (4 vols., Aylesbury, 1934–51).

Culverwell, E., *A Treatise of Faith* (London, 1623).

Dalton, M., *The Country Justice* (numerous edns.: London, 1618, 1635, 1643, 1655, 1661, 1677, 1682, 1697, 1727).

Davenant, C., *Works*, ed. C. Whitworth (5 vols., London, 1771).

'Depositions Taken Before the Mayor and Aldermen of Norwich, 1549–1567', ed. W. Rye, *Norfolk Archaeology*, 1 (1905), 1–96.

Dives and Pauper (London, 1536).

Dod, J., and Cleaver, R., *A Plaine and Familiar Exposition of the Ten Commandments* (16th edn., London, 1625).

Doughty, R., *The Notebook of Robert Doughty, 1662–1665*, ed. J. M. Rosenheim (Norfolk Record Society, 54, Norwich, 1989).

Downame, J., *The Plea of the Poore, or A Treatise of Beneficence and Almes-Deedes* (London, 1616).

Dunning, R., *A Plain and Easie Method Shewing How the Office of Overseer of the Poor May be Managed* (London, 1685).

—— *Bread for the Poor* (Exeter, 1698).

Early Essex Town Meetings: Braintree, 1619–1636, Finchingfield, 1626–1634, ed. F. G. Emmison (Chichester, 1970).

An Ease for Overseers of the Poore: Abstracted from the Statutes (Cambridge, 1601).

Elizabethan Churchwardens' Accounts, ed. J. E. Farmiloe and R. Nixseaman (Publications of the Bedfordshire Historical Record Society, 33, Luton, 1953).

Elizabethan Life: Wills of Essex Gentry and Merchants, ed. F. G. Emmison (Chelmsford, 1978).

Fielding, H., *The History of Tom Jones*, ed. R. P. C. Mutter (Harmondsworth, 1966).

—— *The Covent Garden Journal and A Plan of the Universal Register-Office*, ed. B. A. Goldgar (Oxford, 1988).

—— *An Enquiry into the Causes of the Late Increase of Robbers and Related Writings*, ed. M. R. Zirker (Oxford, 1988).

Firmin, T., *Some Proposals for the Employment of the Poor, Especially in and About the City of London and for the Prevention of Begging* (London, 1678).

Foster, T., *Plouto-mastix: The Scourge of Covetousnesse: or, An Apologie for the Publike Good, Against Privacie* (London, 1631).

GOUGH, R., *The History of Myddle*, ed. D. G. Hey (Harmondsworth, 1981).
GRAFTON, R., *A Chronicle at Large and Meere History of the Affayres of Englande and Kinges of The Same* (London, 1569).
GROSVENOR, R., *The Papers of Sir Richard Grosvenor, 1st Bart. (1585–1645)*, ed. R. Cust (Record Society of Lancashire and Cheshire, 134, Stroud, 1996).
HALE, M., *A Discourse Touching Provision for the Poor* (London, 1683).
—— *Historia Placitorum Coronae: The History of the Pleas of the Crown* (2 vols., ed. S. Emlyn, rev. G. Wilson, London, 1778).
HAMMOND, H., *A Practical Catechisme* (Oxford, 1645).
HARRISON, W., *The Description of England*, ed. G. Edelen (Ithaca, 1968).
HAUSTED, P., *Ten Sermons* (London, 1636).
HAWARDE, J., *Les Reportes del Cases in Camera Stellata, 1593–1609*, ed. W. P. Baildon (London, 1893).
HERBERT, G., *The Works of George Herbert*, ed. F. E. Hutchinson (Oxford, 1941).
Hertford County Records, ed. W. Le Hardy (9 vols., Hertford, 1905–39).
Historical Manuscripts Commission, *Eleventh Report, Appendix, Part IV: The Manuscripts of the Marquess Townshend* (London, 1887).
—— *Twelfth Report, Appendix, Part II: The Manuscripts of the Earl Cowper, K.G., Preserved at Melbourne Hall, Derbyshire*, vol. ii (London, 1888).
—— *Twelfth Report, Appendix, Part VI: The Manuscripts of the House of Lords, 1689–1690* (London, 1889).
—— *Thirteenth Report, Appendix, Part IV: The Manuscripts of Rye and Hereford Corporations, Capt. Loder Symonds, Mr E. R. Wodehouse MP, and Others* (London, 1892).
—— *Fourteenth Report, Appendix, Part VIII: The Manuscripts of Lincoln, Bury St Edmund's and Great Grimsby Corporations, and of the Deans and Chapters of Worcester and Lichfield andc* (London, 1895).
—— *Reports on Manuscripts in Various Collections*, vol. i (London, 1901).
—— *Report on the Manuscripts of the Marquis of Lothian Preserved at Blickling* (London, 1905).
—— *Calendar of the Manuscripts of the Most Honourable the Marquess of Salisbury, Preserved at Hatfield House, Hertfordshire, Pt. 20 (A.D. 1608)*, ed. M. S. Giuseppi and G. D. Owen (London, 1968).
HUNT, W., *The Justicing Notebook of William Hunt, 1744–1749*, ed. E. Crittall (Wiltshire Record Society, 37, Devizes, 1982).
An Impartial Examination of a Pamphlet Intituled Considerations on Several Proposals for the Better Maintenance of the Poor (London, 1752).
JOHNSON, J., *The Clergy-man's Vade Mecum* (London, 1709).
JOSSELIN, R., *The Diary of Ralph Josselin, 1616–1683*, ed. A. Macfarlane (Records of Social and Economic History, NS 3, Oxford, 1976).
Journals of the House of Lords.
KEBLE, J., *An Assistance to Justices of the Peace* (London, 1683).
Kentish Sources, IV: The Poor, ed. E. Melling (Maidstone, 1964).
Kingston-upon-Thames Register of Apprentices, 1563–1713, ed. A. Daly (Surrey Record Society, 28, Guildford, 1974).

LAMBARDE, W., *Eirenarcha; or, of the Office of Justices of Peace* (12 edns., London, 1581–1614).
—— *The Dueties of Constables, Borsholders, Tythingmen and Such Other Lowe and Lay Ministers of the Peace* (London, 1602).
List of Proceedings of Commissioners for Charitable Uses Preserved in the Public Record Office (Public Record Office Lists and Indexes, 10, London, 1892).
Liturgies and Occasional Forms of Prayer, ed. W. K. Clay (Parker Society, Cambridge, 1847).
LOCKE, J., *John Locke, Political Writings*, ed. M. Goldie (Cambridge, 1997).
London Inhabitants Within the Walls, 1695, ed. D. V. Glass (London Record Society, 2, London, 1966).
Lord Nottingham's Chancery Cases, vol. i, ed. D. E. C. Yale (Selden Society, 73, London, 1954).
LOWDE, J., *A Discourse Concerning the Nature of Man* (London, 1694).
LOWE, R., *The Diary of Roger Lowe of Ashton-in-Makerfield, Lancashire, 1663–74*, ed. W. L. Sachse (London, 1938).
MARKHAM, G., *The English Husbandman. The First Part* (London, 1613).
Maynard Lieutenancy Book, 1608–1639, ed. B. W. Quintrell (Chelmsford, 1993).
Merry Drollery (London, 1691).
Middlesex County Records: Calendar of Sessions Books, 1689–1709, ed. W. J. Hardy (London, 1905).
Mid-Sussex Poor Law Records, 1601–1835, ed. N. Pilbeam and I. Nelson (Sussex Record Society, 83, Lewes, 2000).
MOORE, A., *Bread for the Poor* (London, 1653).
MOORE, G., *The Journal of Giles Moore, 1656–1679*, ed. R. Bird (Sussex Record Society, Lewes, 1971).
The New Academy of Complements . . . With an Exact Collection of the Newest and Choicest Songs a la Mode (London, 1671).
A New Charge Given by the Queenes Commandment . . . for Execution of Sundry Disorders Published the Last Yeere for Staie of Dearth of Graine (London, 1595).
Norfolk Quarter Sessions Order Book, 1650–57, ed. D. E. H. James (Norfolk Record Society, 26, Norwich, 1955).
North Riding Quarter Sessions Records, ed. J. C. Atkinson (9 vols., North Riding Record Society, 1–9, London, 1884–92).
The Norwich Census of the Poor 1570, ed. J. F. Pound (Norfolk Record Society, 40, Norwich, 1971).
'Notebook of a Surrey Justice', ed. G. Leveson-Gower, *Surrey Archaeological Collections*, 9 (1885–8), 161–232.
Nottinghamshire County Records, ed. H. H. Copnall (Nottingham, 1915).
A Nottinghamshire Village in War and Peace: The Accounts of the Constables of Upton 1640–1666, ed. M. Bennett (Thoroton Society Record Series, 39, Nottingham, 1995).
NOWELL, A., *A Catechism or, First Instruction and Learning of Christian Religion* (London, 1571).

The Oakes Diaries: Business, Politics and the Family in Bury St Edmunds, 1778–1827, ed. J. Fiske (2 vols., Suffolk Records Society, 32–3, Woodbridge, 1990–1).

An Order for Publike Prayers to be Used on Wednesdays and Fridays in Every Parish Church Within the Province of Canterburie (London, 1586).

Orders and Directions, Together With a Commission for the Better Administration of Justice and More Perfect Information of His Majestie (London, 1630).

Orders of the Shropshire Quarter Sessions, vol. i: *1638–1708*, ed. R. L. Kenyon (Shrewsbury, 1901).

Oxfordshire Justices of the Peace in the Seventeenth Century, ed. M. S. Gretton (Oxfordshire Record Society, 16, Oxford, 1934).

Papers from an Iron Chest at Doddershall, Bucks., ed. G. Eland (Aylesbury, 1937).

Parliamentary Papers, Charity Commissioners' Reports.

Paupers and Pig Killers: The Diary of William Holland, A Somerset Parson 1799–1818, ed. J. Ayres (Stroud, 1984).

Pepys, S., *The Diary of Samuel Pepys: A New and Complete Transcription*, ed. R. Latham and W. Matthews (11 vols., London, 1971).

Perkins, W., *The Works of William Perkins*, ed. I. Breward (Abingdon, 1970).

The Phillimore Atlas and Index of Parish Registers, ed. C. R. Humphery-Smith (Chichester, 1995).

Playford, J., *Musical Companion, Book I* (London, 1673).

Poor Relief in Elizabethan Ipswich, ed. J. Webb (Suffolk Records Society, 9, Ipswich, 1966).

Poverty in Early Stuart Salisbury, ed. P. Slack (Wiltshire Record Society 31, Devizes, 1975).

Powell, R., *Depopulation Arraigned, Convicted and Condemned* (London, 1636).

Prescot Churchwardens' Accounts, 1635–1663, ed. T. Steel (Record Society of Lancashire and Cheshire, 137, Stroud, 2002).

Proceedings in the Parliaments of Elizabeth I, ed. T. E. Hartley (3 vols., Leicester, 1981–95).

Proceedings of the Lancashire Justices of the Peace at the Sheriff's Table during Assize Week, 1578–1694, ed. B. W. Quintrell (Record Society of Lancashire and Cheshire, 121, Chester, 1981).

Quarter Sessions Order Book, 1642–1649, ed. B. C. Redwood (Sussex Record Society, 54, Lewes, 1954).

Quarter Sessions Records of the County of Somerset, ed. E. H. Bates-Harbin (4 vols., Somerset Record Society, 23, 24, 28, 34, Taunton, 1907–19).

Records of the Borough of Leicester, ed. M. Bateson (3 vols., Cambridge, 1899–1905).

The Records of the City of Norwich, ed. W. Hudson and J. C. Tingey (2 vols., Norwich and London, 1906–10).

Records of the Old Archdeaconry of St Albans: A Calendar of Papers, A.D. 1575 to A.D. 1637, ed. H. R. Wilton Hall (St Albans and Hertfordshire Architectural and Archaeological Society, St Albans, 1908).

Records of Rowington Being Extracts from the Deeds in the Possession of the Feoffees of the Rowington Charities, ed. J. W. Ryland (2 vols., Birmingham, 1896–1927).

The Rector's Book: Clayworth, Nottinghamshire, ed. H. Gill and E. L. Guildford (Nottingham, 1910).

The Report of the Commissioners . . . Concerning Charities . . . Relating to the County of Warwickshire, 1819–1837 (London, 1890).

REYCE, R., *Suffolk in the XVIIth Century: The Breviary of Suffolk by Robert Reyce, 1618*, ed. F. Hervey (London, 1902).

ROGERS, J., *A Treatise of Love* (London, 1632).

The Roxburghe Ballads, ed. W. Chappell and J. W. Ebsworth (9 vols., Ballad Society, London, 1871–99).

RYMER, T., *Foedera* (20 vols., London, 1704–35).

A Selection from the Prescot Court Leet and Other Records, 1447–1600, ed. F. A. Bailey (Record Society of Lancashire and Cheshire, 89, Chester, 1937).

Seventeenth-Century Economic Documents, ed. J. Thirsk and J. P. Cooper (Oxford, 1972).

SHAW, S., *The True Christian's Test* (London, 1682).

SHEPPARD, W., *The Whole Office of the Country Justice of Peace* (4 edns., London, 1650–62).

—— *A Sure Guide for His Majesties Justice of Peace* (2nd edn., London, 1669).

—— *A Grand Abridgment of the Common and Statute Law of England* (London, 1675).

SMITH, H., *The Poore Mans Teares: A Sermon* (London, 1592).

Somerset Assize Orders, 1629–1640, ed. T. G. Barnes (Somerset Record Society, 65, Taunton, 1959).

Somerset Assize Orders, 1640–1659, ed. J. S. Cockburn (Somerset Record Society, 71, Taunton, 1971).

SPARKE, M., *Greevous Grones for the Poor* (London, 1621).

The Spectator, ed. D. F. Bond (5 vols., Oxford, 1965).

STANDISH, A., *New Directions of Experience to the Commons Complaint by the Incouragement of the Kings Most Excellent Maiesty, As May Appeare for the Planting of Timber and Fire-wood* (London, 1611).

STOUT, W., *The Autobiography of William Stout of Lancaster, 1665–1752*, ed. J. D. Marshall (Chetham Society, 3rd ser., 14, Manchester, 1967).

STUBBES, P., *Anatomy of Abuses*, ed. F. J. Furnivall (2 vols., London, 1877–82).

TAYLOR, J., *Ductor Dubitantium, or The Rule of Conscience* (London, 1660).

—— *A Dissuasive From Popery* (London, 1664).

'This Little Commonwealth': Buntingford with Layston Parish Memorandum Book, 1607–c.1750, ed. H. Falvey and S. Hindle (Hertfordshire Record Society, 19, Braughing, 2004).

Three Sermons, or Homelies to Move Compassion Towards the Poor and Needy (London, 1596).

TOWERSON, G., *An Explication of the Decalogue* (London, 1676).

TOWNSHEND, H., 'Henry Townshend's "Notes of the Office of a Justice of the Peace"', ed. R. D. Hunt, *Worcestershire Historical Record Society: Miscellany II* (Leeds, 1967), 68–137.

Tudor Churchwardens' Accounts, ed. A. Palmer (Hertfordshire Record Society, 1, Braughing, 1985).

Tudor Economic Documents, ed. R. H. Tawney and E. Power (3 vols., London, 1924).

Turner, T., *The Diary of Thomas Turner, 1754–1765*, ed. D. Vaisey (Oxford, 1984).

The Two Books of Homilies Appointed to be Read in Churches (Oxford, 1859).

The Vestry Minute Books of St Bartholomew Exchange in the City of London, 1567–1676, ed. E. Freshfield (London, 1890).

The Victoria History of the County of Buckinghamshire, ed. W. Page (4 vols., London, 1925).

The Victoria History of the County of Hampshire, ed. W. Page (5 vols., London, 1900–12).

The Victoria History of the County of Hertfordshire, ed. W. Page (4 vols., London, 1902–14).

The Victoria History of the County of Somerset, ed. W. Page and R. W. Dunning (7 vols., London, 1906–97).

The Victoria History of the County of Warwick, ed. W. Page *et al.* (8 vols., London, 1904–69).

Vox Ruris Reverberating Vox Civitas Complaining This Year 1636 Without Cause Against the Country Taken From Her Owne Common Report and Written by Notarius Rusticus (London, 1636).

Warwick County Records, ed. S. C. Ratcliff, H. C. Johnson, and N. J. Williams (9 vols., Warwick, 1935–64).

West Riding Sessions Records, 1597–1642, ed. J. Lister (2 vols., Yorkshire Archaeological Society Record Series, 3, 54, Leeds, 1888–1915).

Western Circuit Assize Orders, 1629–1648: A Calendar, ed. J. S. Cockburn (Camden Society, 4th ser., 17, London, 1976).

Whateley, W., *A Bride-Bush; or a Direction for Married Persons* (London, 1623).

Wills of the Archdeaconry of Suffolk, 1620–24, ed. M. Allen (Suffolk Records Society, 31, Woodbridge, 1989).

Wills and Inventories from the Registry at Durham, Part IV, ed. H. Maxwell-Wood (Surtees Society, 142, Durham, 1929).

Wimbledon Vestry Minutes, 1736, 1743–88: A Calendar with an Introduction, ed. F. M. Cowe (Surrey Record Society, 25, Guildford, 1964).

Wolley, H., *The Gentlewoman's Companion Or, A Guide to the Female Sex* (3rd edn., London, 1682).

Worcestershire County Records: Calendar of the Quarter Sessions Papers, vol. i: *1591–1643*, ed. J. W. Wills-Bund (Worcester, 1900).

Wyatt, R., *Deposition Book of Richard Wyatt, JP, 1767–1776*, ed. E. Silverthorne (Surrey Record Society, 30, Guildford, 1978).

York Civic Records, ed. A. Raine (8 vols., Yorkshire Archaeological Society, 1939–53).

SECONDARY LITERATURE

ADAIR, R., *Courtship, Illegitimacy and Marriage in Early Modern England* (Manchester, 1996).

ALCOCK, N. W., 'Enclosure and Depopulation in Burton Dassett: A Sixteenth Century View', *Warwickshire History*, 3 (1977), 180–4.

ALLEN, A. F., 'An Early Poor Law Account', *Archaeologia Cantiana*, 64 (1951), 74–84.

ALLEN, R. C., *Enclosure and the Yeoman: The Agricultural Development of the South Midlands, 1450–1850* (Oxford, 1992).

AMUSSEN, S. D., 'Gender, Family and the Social Order, 1560–1725', in A. Fletcher and J. Stevenson (eds.), *Order and Disorder in Early Modern England* (Cambridge, 1985), 196–217.

—— *An Ordered Society: Gender and Class in Early Modern England* (Oxford, 1988).

ANDERSON, P., 'The Leeds Workhouse under the Old Poor Law, 1726–1834', *The Thoresby Miscellany: Volume 17* (Thoresby Society 56, 1981), 75–113.

ANDREW, D., *Philanthropy and Police: London Charity in the Eighteenth Century* (Princeton, 1989).

—— '*Noblesse Oblige*: Female Charity in an Age of Sentiment', in Brewer and Staves (eds.), *Early Modern Conceptions of Property*, 275–300.

—— 'To the Charitable and Humane: Appeals for Assistance in the Eighteenth-Century London Press', in H. Cunningham and J. Innes (eds.), *Charity, Philanthropy and Reform* (London and New York, 1998), 87–108.

APPLEBY, A. B., 'Disease or Famine? Mortality in Cumberland and Westmorland, 1580–1640', *Economic History Review*, 2nd ser., 26 (1973), 403–31.

—— *Famine in Tudor and Stuart England* (Liverpool, 1978).

APPLEBY, J. O., *Economic Thought and Ideology in Seventeenth-Century England* (Princeton, 1978).

ARCHER, I. W., *The Pursuit of Stability: Social Relations in Elizabethan London* (Cambridge, 1991).

—— 'The Charity of Early Modern Londoners', *Transactions of the Royal Historical Society*, 6th ser., 12 (2002), 223–44.

ARKELL, T., 'Multiplying Factors for Estimating Population Totals from the Hearth Tax', *Local Population Studies*, 28 (1982), 51–7.

—— 'Assessing the Reliability of the Warwickshire Hearth Tax Returns of 1662–74', *Warwickshire History*, 6 (1986–7), 183–97.

—— 'The Incidence of Poverty in England in the Later Seventeenth Century', *Social History*, 12 (1987), 23–47.

—— 'Identifying Regional Variations from the Hearth Tax: An Alternative Approach', *The Local Historian*, 33 (2003), 148–74.

ASHCRAFT, R., 'Lockean Ideas, Poverty, and the Development of Liberal Political Theory', in Brewer and Staves (eds.), *Early Modern Conceptions of Property*, 43–61.

ASHWORTH, G. J., 'Some Uses of Apprenticeship Returns in Local Studies', *The Local Historian*, 8 (1969), 232–6.

AULT, W. O., 'By-Laws of Gleaning and the Problem of Harvest', *Economic History Review*, 2nd ser., 14 (1961), 210–17.

—— *Open-Field Farming in Medieval England* (London, 1972).

AYDELOTTE, F., *Elizabethan Rogues and Vagabonds* (New York, 1913).

BAILEY, M., 'A Tale of Two Towns: Buntingford and Standon in the Later Middle Ages', *Journal of Medieval History*, 19 (1993), 351–71.

BARNES, T. G., 'County Politics and a Puritan Cause Celebre: Somerset Church-ales, 1633', *Transactions of the Royal Historical Society*, 5th ser., 9 (1959), 103–22.

—— *Somerset, 1625–40: A County's Government during the Personal Rule* (Cambridge, Mass., 1961).

—— 'Cropping the Heath: The Fall of a Chief Justice, 1634', *Historical Research*, 64 (1991), 331–43.

BARRY, J., and BROOKS, C. (eds.), *The Middling Sort of People: Culture, Society and Politics in England, 1550–1800* (London and New York, 1994).

BARTEL, R., 'The Story of Public Fast Days in England', *Anglican Theological Review*, 37 (1955), 190–200.

BATES, E. H., 'Briefs for Cucklington, Somerset', *Notes and Queries for Somerset and Dorset*, 5 (1896–7), 280–3.

BEATTIE, J. M., 'The Pattern of Crime in England, 1660–1800', *Past and Present*, 62 (1974), 47–95.

—— '"Hard Pressed to Make Ends Meet": Women and Crime in Augustan England', in V. Frith (ed.), *Women and History* (Toronto, 1995), 103–18.

BEIER, A. L., 'Poor Relief in Warwickshire, 1630–1660', *Past and Present*, 35 (1966), 77–100.

—— 'The Social Problems of an Elizabethan Country Town: Warwick, 1580–90', in P. Clark (ed.), *Country Towns in Pre-Industrial England* (Leicester, 1981), 45–85.

—— *The Problem of the Poor in Tudor and Early Stuart England* (London, 1983).

—— *Masterless Men: The Vagrancy Problem in England, 1560–1640* (London, 1985).

—— '"Utter Strangers to Industry, Morality and Religion": John Locke on the Poor', *Eighteenth-Century Life*, 12 (1988), 28–41.

—— 'Poverty and Progress in Early Modern England', in A. L. Beier, D. Cannadine, and J. M. Rosenheim (eds.), *The First Modern Society: Essays in English History in Honour of Lawrence Stone* (Cambridge, 1989), 201–40.

BEN-AMOS, I. K., *Adolescence and Youth in Early Modern England* (New Haven, 1994).

—— '"Good Works" and Social Ties: Helping the Migrant Poor in Early Modern England', in M. C. McClendon, J. P. Ward, and M. MacDonald (eds.), *Protestant Identities: Religion, Society and Self-Fashioning in Post-Reformation England* (Stanford, 1999), 125–40.

—— 'Gifts and Favors: Informal Support in Early Modern England', *Journal of Modern History*, 72 (2000), 295–338.

BENNETT, J. M., 'Conviviality and Charity in Medieval and Early Modern England', *Past and Present*, 134 (1992), 19–41.

—— *Ale, Beer and Brewsters in England: Women's Work in a Changing World, 1300–1600* (Oxford, 1996).

Beresford, M. W., 'The Deserted Villages of Warwickshire', *Transactions of the Birmingham Archaeological Society*, 66 (1945–6), 49–106.

—— *The Lost Villages of England* (London, 1954).

Berlin, M., 'Reordering Rituals: Ceremony and the Parish, 1520–1640', in P. Griffiths and M. Jenner (eds.), *Londinopolis: Essays in the Cultural and Social History of Early Modern London* (Manchester, 2000), 47–66.

Bewes, W. A., *Church Briefs* (London, 1896).

Bindoff, S. T., 'The Making of the Statute of Artificers', in S. T. Bindoff, J. Hurstfield, and C. H. Williams (eds.), *Elizabethan Government and Society: Essays Presented to Sir John Neale* (London, 1961), 56–94.

Birtles, S., 'Common Land, Poor Relief and Enclosure: The Use of Manorial Resources in Fulfilling Parish Obligation, 1601–1834', *Past and Present*, 165 (1999), 74–106.

Bittle, W. G., and Lane, R. T., 'Inflation and Philanthropy in England: A Re-Assessment of W. K. Jordan's Data', *Economic History Review*, 2nd ser., 31 (1976), 203–10.

—— 'A Reassessment Reiterated', *Economic History Review*, 2nd ser., 31 (1978), 124–8.

Bonfield, L., Smith, R. M., and Wrightson, K. (eds.), *The World We Have Gained: Histories of Population and Social Structure* (Oxford, 1986).

Bossy, J., *Peace in the Post-Reformation* (Cambridge, 1988).

Botelho, L., 'Aged and Impotent: Parish Relief of the Aged Poor in Early Modern Suffolk', in Daunton (ed.), *Charity, Self-Interest and Welfare*, 91–112.

—— and Thane, P. (eds.), *Women and Ageing in British Society Since 1500* (London, 1991).

Bouch, C. M., and Jones, G. P., *A Short Economic and Social History of the Lake Counties, 1500–1830* (Manchester, 1961).

Boulton, J., *Neighbourhood and Society: A London Suburb in the Seventeenth Century* (Cambridge, 1987).

—— 'The Marriage Duty Act and Parochial Registration in London, 1695–1706', in K. Schurer and T. Arkell (eds.), *Surveying the People: The Interpretation of Document Sources for the Study of Population in the Later Seventeenth Century* (Oxford, 1992), 222–52.

—— 'Going on the Parish: The Parish Pension and its Meaning in the London Suburbs, 1640–1724', in Hitchcock *et al.* (eds.), *Chronicling Poverty*, 19–46.

—— '"It is extreme necessity that makes me do this": Some "Survival Strategies" of Pauper Households in London's West End during the Early Eighteenth Century', in L. Fontaine and J. Schlumbohm (eds.), *Household Strategies for Survival, 1600–2000: Fission, Faction and Cooperation* [*International Review of Social History Supplement* 8] (2000), 47–69.

Bowden, P., 'Agricultural Prices, Farm Profits and Rents', in Thirsk (ed.), *Agrarian History*, iv. 593–695.

BRADDICK, M. J., *The Nerves of State: Taxation and the Financing of the English State, 1558–1714* (Manchester, 1996).

—— and WALTER, J. (eds.), *Negotiating Power in Early Modern Society: Order, Hierarchy and Subordination in Britain and Ireland* (Cambridge, 2001).

—— —— 'Introduction: Grids of Power: Order, Hierarchy and Subordination in Early Modern Society', in eid. (eds.), *Negotiating Power*, 1–42.

BREWER, J., and STAVES, S. (eds.), *Early Modern Conceptions of Property* (London, 1995).

—— and STYLES, J. (eds.), *An Ungovernable People: The English and their Law in the Seventeenth and Eighteenth Centuries* (London, 1980).

BRIGDEN, S., 'Religion and Social Obligation in Early Sixteenth Century London', *Past and Present*, 103 (1984), 67–112.

—— *London and the Reformation* (Oxford, 1989).

BROAD, J., 'The Smallholder and Cottager after Disafforestation: A Legacy of Poverty?', in J. Broad and R. Hoyle (eds.), *Bernwood: The Life and Afterlife of a Forest* (Preston, 1997), 90–107.

—— 'Parish Economies of Welfare, 1650–1834', *Historical Journal*, 42 (1999), 985–1006.

—— 'Housing the Rural Poor in England, 1650–1850', *Agricultural History Review*, 48 (2000), 151–70.

BROADBRIDGE, S. R., 'The Old Poor Law in the Parish of Stone', *North Staffordshire Journal of Field Studies*, 13 (1973), 11–25.

BROOKS, C., 'Projecting, Political Arithmetic and the Act of 1695', *English Historical Review*, 87 (1982), 31–53.

BROOKS, C. W., *Pettyfoggers and Vipers of the Commonwealth: The 'Lower Branch' of the Legal Profession in Early Modern England* (Cambridge, 1986).

BRUCE, J., 'Extracts from the Accounts of the Churchwardens of Minchinhampton in the County of Gloucester', *Archaeologia*, 35 (1853), 409–52.

BUSHAWAY, R. W., *By Rite: Custom, Ceremony and Community in England, 1700–1800* (London, 1982).

—— 'From Custom to Crime: Wood Gathering in Eighteenth- and Early Nineteenth-Century England: A Focus for Conflict in Hampshire, Wiltshire and the South', in J. G. Rule (ed.), *Outside the Law: Studies in Crime and Order, 1650–1850* (Exeter, 1982), 65–101.

—— 'Rite, Legitimation and Community in Southern England, 1700–1850: The Ideology of Custom', in Stapleton (ed.), *Conflict and Community in Southern England*, 110–34.

CAPP, B., 'Arson, Threats of Arson and Incivility in Early Modern England', in P. Burke, B. Harrison, and P. Slack (eds.), *Civil Histories: Essays in Honour of Sir Keith Thomas* (Oxford, 2000), 197–213.

—— *When Gossips Meet: Women, Family and Neighbourhood in Early Modern England* (Oxford, 2003).

—— 'Life, Love and Litigation: Sileby in the 1630s', *Past and Present*, 104 (2004), 55–88.

Carter, P., 'Poor Relief Strategies: Women, Children and Enclosure in Hanwell, Middlesex, 1780–1816', *The Local Historian*, 25 (1995), 164–77.

Cavallo, S., *Charity and Power in Early Modern Italy: Benefactors and their Motives in Turin, 1541–1789* (Cambridge, 1995).

Chalklin, C., *Seventeenth-Century Kent: A Social and Economic History* (London, 1965).

Chandler, W. H. B., 'Directions to Overseers of the Poor, 1595', *Norfolk Archaeology*, 32 (1961), 230–1.

Chapman, J., 'The Chronology of English Enclosure', *Economic History Review*, 2nd ser., 37 (1984), 557–9.

Charles, L., and Duffin, L. (eds.), *Women and Work in Pre-Industrial England* (London, 1985).

Chaytor, M., 'Household and Kinship: Ryton in the Late Sixteenth and Early Seventeenth Centuries', *History Workshop Journal*, 10 (1980), 25–60.

Clark, P., 'The Migrant in Kentish Towns, 1580–1640', in Clark and Slack (eds.), *Crisis and Order in English Towns, 1500–1700*, 117–63.

—— *English Provincial Society from the Reformation to the Revolution: Religion, Politics and Society in Kent, 1500–1640* (Hassocks, 1977).

—— *The English Alehouse: A Social History, 1200–1830* (London, 1983).

—— 'Migration in England during the Late Seventeenth and Early Eighteenth Centuries', repr. in Clark and Souden (eds.), *Migration and Society*, 213–52.

—— and Slack, P. (eds.), *Crisis and Order in English Towns, 1500–1700: Essays in Urban History* (London, 1972).

—— and Souden, D. (eds.), *Migration and Society in Early Modern England* (London, 1987).

Clarke, B., 'Norfolk Licences to Beg: An Unpublished Collection', *Norfolk Archaeology*, 35 (1972), 327–34.

Clay, C., 'Landlords and Estate Management in England', in J. Thirsk (ed.), *The Agrarian History of England and Wales*, vol. v: *1640–1750, Part II: Agrarian Change* (Cambridge, 1985), 119–251.

Cliffe, J. T., *The Yorkshire Gentry from the Reformation to the Revolution* (London, 1969).

—— *The World of the Country House in Seventeenth-Century England* (New Haven, 1999).

Clutterbuck, R., *A History of Hertfordshire* (3 vols., London, 1815–27).

Coats, A. W., 'The Relief of Poverty, Attitudes to Labour, and Economic Change in England, 1660–1782', *International Review of Social History*, 21 (1976), 98–115.

Cockburn, J. S., 'The North Riding Justices, 1690–1750: A Study in Local Administration', *Yorkshire Archaeological Journal*, 41 (1963–6), 481–515.

—— 'The Nature and Incidence of Crime in England, 1559–1625: A Preliminary Survey', in id. (ed.), *Crime in England*, 49–71.

—— (ed.), *Crime in England, 1550–1800* (London, 1977).

Cohen, A. P., 'Belonging: The Experience of Culture', in id. (ed.), *Belonging:*

Identity and Social Organisation in British Rural Cultures (Manchester, 1982), 1–17.

Coleby, A. M., *Central Government and the Localities: Hampshire, 1649–1689* (Cambridge, 1987).

Coleman, D. C., 'Philanthropy Deflated: A Comment', *Economic History Review*, 2nd ser., 31 (1978), 118–20.

Collinson, P., *The Elizabethan Puritan Movement* (London, 1967).

—— *Godly People: Essays in English Protestantism and Puritanism* (London, 1983).

—— 'Magistracy and Ministry: A Suffolk Miniature', repr. in id., *Godly People*, 445–66.

—— 'Cranbrook and the Fletchers: Popular and Unpopular Religion in the Kentish Weald', repr. in id., *Godly People*, 399–428.

—— 'Shepherds, Sheepdogs, and Hirelings: The Pastoral Ministry in Post-Reformation England', in W. J. Sheils and D. Wood (eds.), *The Ministry: Clerical and Lay* (Studies in Church History, 26, Oxford, 1989), 185–220.

—— '*De Republica Anglorum*: Or History with the Politics Put Back', repr. in id., *Elizabethan Essays* (London, 1994), 1–30.

—— 'Christian Socialism in Elizabethan Suffolk: Thomas Carew and his *Caveat for Clothiers*', in C. Rawcliffe, R. Virgoe, and R. Wilson (eds.), *Counties and Communities: Essays on East Anglian History* (Norwich, 1996), 161–79.

—— 'Puritanism and the Poor', in Horrox and Rees Jones (eds.), *Pragmatic Utopias*, 242–58.

Connors, R., '"The Grand Inquest of the Nation": Parliamentary Committees and Social Policy in Mid-Eighteenth-Century England', *Parliamentary History*, 14 (1995), 285–313.

—— 'Parliament and Poverty in Mid-Eighteenth Century England', *Parliamentary History*, 21 (2002), 207–31.

Copeland, G. A., 'Devonshire Church Houses', *Reports and Transactions of the Devonshire Association*, 92 (1960), 116–41.

Cornford, B., 'Inventories of the Poor', *Norfolk Archaeology*, 35 (1970), 118–25.

Cornwall, J., 'Evidence of Population Mobility in the Seventeenth Century', *Bulletin of the Institute of Historical Research*, 40 (1967), 143–52.

Courtenay, W. J., 'Token Coinage and the Administration of Poor Relief during the Late Middle Ages', *Journal of Interdisciplinary History*, 3 (1972), 275–95.

Cowley, P., *The Church Houses: Their Religious and Social Significance* (London, 1970).

Cox, J. C., *Bench-Ends in English Churches* (Oxford, 1916).

Craig, J. S., 'Co-operation and Initiatives: Elizabethan Churchwardens and the Parish Accounts of Mildenhall', *Social History*, 18 (1993), 357–80.

—— *Reformation, Politics and Polemics: The Growth of Protestantism in East Anglian Market Towns, 1500–1610* (Aldershot, 2001).

Cressy, D., 'Kinship and Kin Interaction in Early Modern England', *Past and Present*, 113 (1986), 38–69.

—— *Birth, Marriage and Death: Ritual, Religion and the Life Cycle in Tudor and Stuart England* (Oxford, 1997).

CROMARTIE, A., *Sir Matthew Hale, 1609–1676: Law, Religion and Natural Philosophy* (Cambridge, 1995).

CUNNINGHAM, H., 'The Employment and Unemployment of Children in England, *c.*1680–1851', *Past and Present*, 126 (1990), 115–50.

—— *Children and Childhood in Western Society Since 1500* (London, 1995).

CUTLACK, S. A., 'The Gnosall Records, 1679 to 1837: Poor Law Administration', *Collections for a History of Staffordshire, Part I* (Stafford, 1936), 1–141.

DAUNTON, M. (ed.), *Charity, Self-Interest and Welfare in the English Past* (London, 1996).

DAVIES, C. S. L., 'Slavery and Protector Somerset: The Vagrancy Act of 1547', *Economic History Review*, 2nd ser., 19 (1966), 533–49.

DAVIES, M. G., *The Enforcement of English Apprenticeship, 1563–1642: A Study in Applied Mercantilism* (Cambridge, Mass., 1956).

DAVIS, N. Z., *The Gift in Sixteenth-Century France* (Oxford, 2000).

DEAN, D. M., *Law-Making and Society in Late Elizabethan England: The Parliament of England, 1584–1601* (Cambridge, 1996).

DICKSON, D., 'In Search of the Old Irish Poor Law', in R. Mitchison and P. Roebuck (eds.), *Economy and Society in Scotland and Ireland, 1500–1939* (Edinburgh, 1988), 148–59.

DINGES, M., 'Self Help and Reciprocity in Parish Assistance: Bordeaux in the Sixteenth and Seventeenth Centuries', in Horden and Smith (eds.), *The Locus of Care*, 111–25.

DUFFIN, A., *Faith and Faction: Politics and Religion of the Cornish Gentry before the Civil War* (Exeter, 1996).

DUFFY, E., *The Stripping of the Altars: Traditional Religion in England, 1400–1580* (New Haven, 1992).

DUNLOP, O. J., and DENMAN, R. D., *English Apprenticeship and Child Labour: A History* (London, 1912).

DURSTON, C., '"For the Better Humiliation of the People": Public Days of Fasting and Thanksgiving during the English Revolution', *The Seventeenth Century*, 7 (1992), 129–49.

—— *Cromwell's Major Generals: Godly Government during the English Revolution* (Manchester, 2001).

DYCK, I., *William Cobbett and Rural Popular Culture* (Cambridge, 1992).

DYER, C., *Warwickshire Farming, 1349–c.1520: Preparations for Agricultural Revolution* (Dugdale Society Occasional Papers 27, Stratford-upon-Avon, 1981).

—— 'Deserted Medieval Villages in the West Midlands', *Economic History Review*, 2nd ser., 35 (1982), 19–34.

—— *Standards of Living in the Later Middle Ages: Social Change in England, c.1200–1520* (Cambridge, 1989).

—— 'The English Medieval Village Community and its Decline', *Journal of British Studies*, 33 (1994), 407–29.

—— 'Taxation and Communities in Late Medieval England', in R. Britnell and J. Hatcher (eds.), *Progress and Problems in Medieval England: Essays in Honour of*

Edward Miller (Cambridge, 1996), 168–90.

Eastwood, D., *Governing Rural England: Tradition and Transformation in Local Government, 1780–1840* (Oxford, 1994).

Edmonds, G. C., 'Accounts of Eighteenth-Century Overseers of the Poor of Chalfont St Peter', *Records of Buckinghamshire*, 18 (1966), 3–23.

Elton, G. R., 'Reform by Statute: Thomas Starkey's Dialogue and Thomas Cromwell's Policy', repr. in id., *Studies in Tudor and Stuart Politics and Government* (4 vols., Cambridge, 1974–92), ii. 236–58.

—— *The Parliament of England, 1559–1581* (Cambridge, 1986).

Emmison, F. G., 'Poor Relief Accounts of Two Rural Parishes in Bedfordshire, 1563–1598', *Economic History Review*, 3 (1931–2), 102–16.

—— 'The Relief of the Poor at Eaton Socon, 1706–1834', *Publications of the Bedfordshire Historical Record Society*, 15 (1933), 1–98.

—— 'The Care of the Poor in Elizabethan Essex: Recently Discovered Records', *Essex Review*, 62 (1953), 7–28.

Evans, N., 'Charitable Requests and their Recipients', *The Local Historian*, 15 (1982), 225–6.

Everitt, A., 'Farm Labourers', in Thirsk (ed.), *Agrarian History*, iv. 396–465.

Eversley, D. E. C., 'The Home Market and Economic Growth in England, 1740–1780', in E. L. Jones and G. E. Mingay (eds.), *Land, Labour and Population in the Industrial Revolution: Essays Presented to J. D. Chambers* (London, 1967), 206–59.

Ewen, C. L., *Witchcraft and Demonianism: A Concise Account Derived from Sworn Depositions and Confessions Obtained in the Courts of England and Wales* (London, 1933).

Falvey, H., 'Crown Policy and Local Economic Context in the Berkhamsted Common Enclosure Dispute, 1618–42', *Rural History*, 12 (2001), 123–58.

Fearn, H., 'The Apprenticing of Pauper Children in the Incorporated Hundreds of Suffolk', *Proceedings of the Suffolk Institute of Archaeology*, 26 (1955), 85–97.

Feingold, M., 'Jordan Revisited: Patterns of Charitable Giving in Sixteenth- and Seventeenth-Century England', *History of Education*, 8 (1979), 257–73.

Fessler, A., 'The Official Attitude toward the Sick Poor in Seventeenth-Century Lancashire', *Transactions of the Historic Society of Lancashire and Cheshire*, 102 (1951), 85–113.

Fideler, P., 'Symposium: The Study of the Early Modern Poor and Poverty Relief. Introduction: Impressions of a Century of Historiography', *Albion*, 32 (2000), 381–407.

Fletcher, A., *A County Community in Peace and War: Sussex, 1600–1660* (London, 1975).

—— *Reform in the Provinces: The Government of Stuart England* (New Haven, 1986).

—— and Roberts, P. (eds.), *Religion, Culture and Society in Early Modern Britain: Essays in Honour of Patrick Collinson* (Cambridge, 1994).

Forster, G. C. F., *The East Riding Justices of the Peace in the Seventeenth Century* (East Yorkshire History Series, 30, 1973).

Foss, E., *A Biographical Dictionary of the Judges of England from the Conquest to the*

Present Time, 1066–1870 (London, 1870).

Fradenburg, L. O., 'Needful Things', in B. A. Hanawalt and D. Wallace (eds.), *Medieval Crime and Social Control* (Minneapolis, 1999), 49–69.

France, R. S., 'A High Constable's Register, 1681', *Transactions of the Historical Society of Lancashire and Cheshire*, 107 (1956), 55–87.

French, H. R., '"Ingenious and Learned Gentlemen": Social Perceptions and Self-Fashioning among Parish Elites in Essex, 1680–1740', *Social History*, 25 (2000), 44–66.

—— 'Social Status, Localism and the "Middle Sort of People" in England, 1620–1750', *Past and Present*, 166 (2000), 66–99.

—— 'Urban Common Rights, Enclosure and the Market: Clitheroe Town Moors, 1764–1802', *Agricultural History Review*, 51 (2003), 40–68.

Froide, A., 'Old Maids: The Life-Cycle of Single Women in Early Modern England', in Botelho and Thane (eds.), *Women and Ageing*, 89–110.

Fussell, G. E., and Fussell, K. R., *The English Countryman: His Life and Work from Tudor Times to the Victorian Age* (London, 1981 edn.).

Gatrell, V. A. C., Lenman, B., and Parker, G. (eds.), *Crime and the Law: The Social History of Crime in Western Europe Since 1500* (London, 1980).

Gay, E. F., 'The Rise of an English Country Family: Peter and John Temple to 1603', *Huntington Library Quarterly*, 4 (1938), 367–90.

George, M. D., *England in Transition* (London, 1931).

Gittings, C., *Death, Burial and the Individual in Early Modern England* (London, 1984).

Glennie, P., 'Continuity and Change in Hertfordshire Agriculture, 1550–1700, I: Patterns of Agricultural Production', *Agricultural History Review*, 36 (1988), 55–75.

——'Continuity and Change in Hertfordshire Agriculture, 1550–1700, II: Trends in Crop Yields and their Determinants', *Agricultural History Review*, 36 (1988), 145–61.

——'In Search of Agrarian Capitalism: Manorial Land Markets and the Acquisition of Land in the Lea Valley, *c.*1450–1560', *Continuity and Change*, 3 (1988), 11–40.

——'Life and Death in Elizabethan Cheshunt', in Jones-Baker (ed.), *Hertfordshire in History*, 65–91.

Goose, N., 'Household Size and Structure in Early Stuart Cambridge', repr. in J. Barry (ed.), *The Tudor and Stuart Town: A Reader in English Urban History, 1530–1688* (London and New York, 1990), 74–120.

Gould, J. D., 'Bittle and Lane on Charity: An Uncharitable Comment', *Economic History Review*, 2nd ser., 31 (1978), 121–3.

Grainger, F. W., 'Poor Relief in Cumberland in the Seventeenth and Eighteenth Centuries', *Transactions of the Cumberland and Westmorland Antiquarian and Archaeological Society*, NS 15 (1915), 90–6.

Green, I., *The Christian's ABC: Catechisms and Catechising in England, c.1530–1740* (Oxford, 1996).

Griffiths, P., *Youth and Authority: Formative Experiences in England, 1560–1640* (Oxford, 1996).

—— 'Secrecy and Authority in Late Sixteenth- and Early Seventeenth-Century London', *Historical Journal*, 40 (1997), 925–51.

—— 'Meanings of Nightwalking in Early Modern England', *The Seventeenth Century*, 13 (1998), 212–38.

—— Fox, A., and Hindle, S. (eds.), *The Experience of Authority in Early Modern England* (London and New York, 1996).

Hadwin, J., 'Deflating Philanthropy', *Economic History Review*, 2nd ser., 31 (1978), 105–17.

—— 'The Problem of Poverty in Early Modern England', in Riis (ed.), *Aspects of Poverty*, 219–51.

Haigh, C., 'Communion and Community: Exclusion from Communion in Post-Reformation England', *Journal of Ecclesiastical History*, 51 (2000), 699–720.

Hainsworth, D. R., *Stewards, Lords and People: The Estate Steward and his World in Later Stuart England* (Cambridge, 1992).

Halliday, P., *Dismembering the Body Politic: Partisan Politics in English Towns, 1650–1730* (Cambridge, 1998).

Hamilton, A. H. A., *Quarter Sessions Records from Queen Elizabeth to Queen Anne* (London, 1878).

Hampson, E. M., 'Settlement and Removal in Cambridgeshire, 1662–1834', *Cambridge Historical Journal*, 2 (1926–8), 273–89.

—— *The Treatment of Poverty in Cambridgeshire, 1597–1834* (Cambridge, 1934).

Hardin, G., 'The Tragedy of the Commons', *Science*, 162 (1968), 1243–8.

Harris, J., *The Artist and the Country House* (London, 1979).

Harris, M., '"Inky Blots and Rotten Parchment Bonds": London, Charity Briefs and the Guildhall Library', *Historical Research*, 66 (1993), 98–110.

Harvey, R., 'English Pre-Industrial Ballads on Poverty, 1500–1700', *The Historian*, 41 (1984), 539–61.

Hassell Smith, A., 'Labourers in Late Sixteenth-Century England: A Case Study from North Norfolk, Part I', *Continuity and Change*, 4 (1989), 11–52.

Hay, D., 'Dread of the Crown Office: The English Magistracy and King's Bench, 1740–1800', in N. Landau (ed.), *Law, Crime and English Society, 1660–1830* (Cambridge, 2002), 19–45.

Hayton, D. W., 'Sir Richard Cocks: The Political Anatomy of a Country Whig', *Albion*, 20 (1988), 221–46.

—— 'Moral Reform and Country Politics in the Late Seventeenth-Century House of Commons', *Past and Present*, 128 (1990), 48–91.

Heal, F., 'The Idea of Hospitality in Early Modern England', *Past and Present*, 102 (1984), 66–93.

—— 'The Crown, the Gentry and London: The Enforcement of Proclamation, 1596–1640', in C. Cross, D. M. Loades, and J. J. Scarisbrick (eds.), *Law and Government under the Tudors: Essays Presented to Sir Geoffrey Elton on his Retirement* (Cambridge, 1988), 211–27.

—— *Hospitality in Early Modern England* (Oxford, 1990).

—— and HOLMES, C., *The Gentry in England and Wales, 1500–1700* (London and New York, 1994).

HELMHOLZ, R. H., 'Harbouring Sexual Offenders: Ecclesiastical Courts and Controlling Misbehaviour', *Journal of British Studies*, 37 (1998), 258–68.

HENDERSON, E. G., *Foundations of English Administrative Law: Certiorari and Mandamus in the Seventeenth Century* (Cambridge, Mass., 1963).

HERRUP, C. B., 'New Shoes and Mutton Pies: Investigative Responses to Theft in Seventeenth-Century East Sussex', *Historical Journal*, 27 (1984), 811–30.

—— 'Crime, Law and Society: A Review Article', *Comparative Studies in Society and History*, 27 (1985), 159–70.

—— *The Common Peace: Participation and the Criminal Law in Seventeenth-Century England* (Cambridge, 1987).

HEY, D., *An English Rural Community: Myddle under the Tudors and Stuarts* (Leicester, 1974).

HILL, C., 'William Perkins and the Poor', repr. in id., *Puritanism and Revolution: Studies in the English Revolution of the Seventeenth Century* (London, 1956), 215–38.

—— *Society and Puritanism in Pre-Revolutionary England* (Harmondsworth, 1964).

—— 'The Many Headed Monster in Late Tudor and Early Stuart Political Thinking', repr. in id., *Change and Continuity in Seventeenth-Century England* (rev. edn., New Haven, 1991), 181–204.

HILLERBRAND, H. J. (ed.), *The Oxford Encyclopaedia of the Reformation* (4 vols., New York, 1996).

HINDLE, S., 'Custom, Festival and Protest in Early Modern England: The Little Budworth Wakes, St Peter's Day, 1596', *Rural History*, 6 (1995), 155–78.

—— 'Exclusion Crises: Poverty, Migration and Parochial Responsibility in English Rural Communities, *c.*1560–1660', *Rural History*, 7 (1996), 125–49.

—— 'The Keeping of the Public Peace', in Griffiths *et al.* (eds.), *The Experience of Authority*, 213–48.

—— 'Persuasion and Protest in the Caddington Common Enclosure Dispute, 1635–39', *Past and Present*, 158 (1998), 37–78.

—— 'Power, Poor Relief and Social Relations in Holland Fen, *c.*1600–1800', *Historical Journal*, 41 (1998), 67–96.

—— 'The Problem of Pauper Marriage in Seventeenth-Century England', *Transactions of the Royal Historical Society*, 6th ser., 8 (1998), 71–89.

—— 'Hierarchy and Community in the Elizabethan Parish: The Swallowfield Articles of 1596', *Historical Journal*, 42 (1999), 835–51.

—— *The Birthpangs of Welfare: Poor Relief and Parish Governance in Seventeenth-Century Warwickshire* (Dugdale Society Occasional Papers, 40, Stratford-upon-Avon, 2000).

—— 'The Growth of Social Stability in Restoration England', *The European Legacy*, 5 (2000), 563–76.

—— 'A Sense of Place? Becoming and Belonging in the Rural Parish, 1550–

1650', in A. Shepard and P. Withington (eds.), *Communities in Early Modern England* (Manchester, 2000), 96–114.

Hindle, S., *The State and Social Change in Early Modern England, c.1550–1640* (London and New York, 2000).

—— 'Dearth, Fasting and Alms: The Campaign for General Hospitality in Late Elizabethan England', *Past and Present*, 172 (2001), 44–86.

—— 'Exhortation and Entitlement: Negotiating Inequality in English Rural Communities, 1550–1650', in Braddick and Walter (eds.), *Negotiating Power*, 102–22.

—— 'The Political Culture of the Middling Sort in English Rural Communities, c.1550–1700', in T. Harris (ed.), *The Politics of the Excluded, 1500–1850* (London and New York, 2001), 125–52.

—— '"Not by Bread Only"?: Common Right, Parish Relief and Endowed Charity in a Forest Economy, c.1600–1800', in King and Tomkins (eds.), *The Poor in England*, 39–75.

—— 'Dependency, Shame and Belonging: Badging the Deserving Poor, c.1550–1750', *Cultural and Social History*, 1 (2004), 29–58.

Hinton, F. H., 'Notes on the Administration of the Relief of the Poor of Lacock 1583–1834', *Wiltshire Archaeological Magazine*, 49 (1940–42), 166–218.

Hitchcock, T., 'Paupers and Preachers: The SPCK and the Parochial Workhouse Movement', in L. Davison, T. Hitchcock, T. Keirn, and R. B. Shoemaker (eds.), *Stilling the Grumbling Hive: The Response to Social and Economic Problems in England, 1689–1750* (Gloucester, 1992), 145–66.

—— King, P., and Sharpe, P. (eds.), *Chronicling Poverty: The Voices and Strategies of the English Poor, 1640–1840* (London and New York, 1997).

—— 'Introduction', in Hitchcock *et al.* (eds.). *Chronicling Poverty*, 1–18.

Hobhouse, H., *A Short History of Hugh Sexey's Hospital Bruton Somerset and its Endowments* (3rd edn., Taunton, 1951).

Holderness, B. A., *Pre-Industrial England: Economy and Society, 1500–1750* (London, 1976).

Holmes, C., *Seventeenth-Century Lincolnshire* (Lincoln, 1980).

Höltgen, K.-J., 'The English Reformation and Some Jacobean Writers on Art', in U. Broich, T. Stemmler, and G. Stratmann (eds.), *Functions of Literature: Essays Presented to Erwin Wolff on his Sixtieth Birthday* (Tübingen, 1984), 119–46.

—— 'Sir Robert Dallington (1561–1637): Author, Traveller, and Pioneer of Taste', *Huntington Library Quarterly*, 47 (1984), 147–77.

Horden, P., 'Household Care and Informal Networks: Comparisons and Continuities from Antiquity to the Present', in Horden and Smith (eds.), *The Locus of Care*, 21–67.

—— and Smith, R. (eds.), *The Locus of Care: Families, Communities and Institutions and the Provision of Welfare Since Antiquity* (London, 1998).

—— —— 'Introduction', in eid. (eds.), *The Locus of Care*, 1–18.

Horne, T. A., *Property Rights and Poverty: Political Argument in Britain, 1605–1834* (Chapel Hill, NC, 1990).

Horrell, S., Humphries, J., and Voth, H. J., 'Destined for Deprivation: Human Capital Formation and Intergenerational Poverty in Nineteenth-Century England', *Explorations in Economic History*, 38 (2001), 339–65.

—— and Humphries, J., 'Old Questions, New Data, and Alternative Perspectives: Families' Living Standards in the Industrial Revolution', *Journal of Economic History*, 52 (1992), 849–80.

Horrox, R., and Rees-Jones, S. (eds.), *Pragmatic Utopias: Ideals and Communities, 1200–1630* (Cambridge, 2001).

Hoskins, W. G., *Devon* (London, 1954).

—— 'Harvest Fluctuations and English Economic History, 1620–1759', *Agricultural History Review*, 16 (1968), 15–31.

Houlbrooke, R., *Death, Religion and the Family in England, 1480–1750* (Oxford, 1998).

Houston, R. A., 'Vagrants and Society in Early Modern England', *Cambridge Anthropology* (1980), 18–32.

Howell, D. W., *The Rural Poor in Eighteenth-Century Wales* (Cardiff, 2000).

Hudson, W. S., 'Fast Days and Civil Religion', in *Theology in Sixteenth- and Seventeenth-Century England* [Papers Read at a Clark Library Seminar, 6 February 1971] (William Andrews Clark Memorial Library, Los Angeles, 1971), 3–24.

Hufton, O., *The Poor of Eighteenth-Century France, 1750–1789* (Oxford, 1974).

Hughes, A., *Politics, Society and Civil War in Warwickshire, 1620–1660* (Cambridge, 1987).

Humphries, J., 'Enclosures, Common Rights, and Women: The Proletarianisation of Families in the Late Eighteenth and Early Nineteenth Centuries', *Journal of Economic History*, 50 (1990), 17–42.

Hunt, W., *The Puritan Moment: The Coming of Revolution in an English County* (Cambridge, Mass., 1983).

Hurstfield, J., 'County Government: Wiltshire, *c.*1530–1660', repr. in id., *Freedom, Corruption and Government in Elizabethan England* (London, 1973), 236–93.

Hussey, A., 'Visitations of the Archdeacon of Canterbury', *Archaeologia Cantiana*, 27 (1905), 213–29.

Hutton, R., *The Rise and Fall of Merry England: The Ritual Year in England, 1400–1700* (Oxford, 1994).

—— *The Stations of the Sun: A History of the Ritual Year in Britain* (Oxford, 1996).

Ingram, M., 'Communities and Courts: Law and Disorder in Early-Seventeenth-Century Wiltshire', in Cockburn (ed.), *Crime in England*, 110–34.

—— 'Spousals Litigation in the English Ecclesiastical Courts, *c.*1350–1640', in R. B. Outhwaite (ed.), *Marriage and Society: Studies in the Social History of Marriage* (London, 1981), 35–57.

—— 'Ridings, Rough Music and Mocking Rhymes', in Reay (ed.), *Popular Culture*, 66–97.

—— 'The Reform of Popular Culture? Sex and Marriage in Early Modern England', in Reay (ed.), *Popular Culture*, 129–65.

Ingram, M. *Church Courts, Sex and Marriage in England, 1570–1640* (Cambridge, 1987).

Innes, J., 'Prisons for the Poor: English Bridewells, 1555–1800', in F. Snyder and D. Hay (eds.), *Labour, Law and Crime: An Historical Perspective* (London, 1987), 42–122.

—— 'Parliament and the Shaping of Eighteenth-Century English Social Policy', *Transactions of the Royal Historical Society*, 5th ser., 40 (1990), 63–92.

—— 'The "Mixed Economy of Welfare" in Early Modern England: Assessments of the Options from Hale to Malthus (*c.*1683–1803)', in Daunton (ed.), *Charity, Self-Interest and Welfare*, 139–80.

—— 'The State and the Poor: Eighteenth-Century England in European Perspective', in J. Brewer and E. Hellmuth (eds.), *Rethinking Leviathan: The Eighteenth-Century State in Britain and Germany* (Oxford, 1999), 225–80.

—— and Styles, J., 'The Crime Wave: Recent Writing on Crime and Criminal Justice in Eighteenth-Century England', repr. in A. Wilson (ed.), *Rethinking Social History: English Society 1570–1920 and its Interpretation* (Manchester, 1993), 201–65.

Jackson-Stops, G. (ed.), *The Treasure Houses of Britain* (New Haven, 1985).

Jacob, W. M., *Lay People and Religion in the Early Eighteenth Century* (Cambridge, 1996).

Johnson, M., *An Archaeology of Capitalism* (Oxford, 1996).

Johnson, P., 'Risk, Redistribution and Social Welfare in Britain from the Poor Law to Beveridge', in Daunton (ed.), *Charity, Self-Interest and Welfare*, 225–48.

Johnson, R. C., 'The Transportation of Vagrant Children from London to Virginia, 1618–1622', in H. S. Reinmuth (ed.), *Early Stuart Studies: Essays in Honour of David Harris Willson* (Minneapolis, 1970), 137–51.

Jones, C., *The Charitable Imperative: Hospitals and Nursing in Ancien Régime and Revolutionary France* (London, 1989).

Jones, G., *History of the Law of Charity, 1532–1827* (Cambridge, 1969).

Jones, G. S., 'Class Expression versus Social Control? A Critique of Recent Trends in the Social History of "Leisure"', repr. in id., *Languages of Class: Studies in English Working Class History, 1832–1982* (Cambridge, 1983), 76–89.

Jones, I. F., 'Aspects of Poor Law Administration, Seventeenth to Nineteenth Centuries, from Trull Overseers' Accounts', *Somerset Archaeological and Natural History Society Proceedings*, 95 (1951), 72–105.

Jones-Baker, D. (ed.), *Hertfordshire in History: Papers Presented to Lionel Munby* (Hertford, 1991).

Jordan, W. K., *Philanthropy in England, 1480–1660: A Study of the Changing Pattern of English Social Aspirations* (London, 1959).

—— *The Charities of London, 1480–1660: The Aspirations and the Achievements of the Urban Society* (London, 1960).

—— 'The Forming of the Charitable Institutions of the West of England: A Study of the Changing Pattern of Social Aspirations in Bristol and Somerset, 1480–1660', *Transactions of the American Philosophical Society*, NS 50 (1960), pt. 8.

JORDAN, W. K., *The Charities of Rural England, 1480–1660: The Aspirations and Achievements of the Rural Society* (London, 1961).

—— *Social Institutions in Kent, 1480–1660: A Study of the Changing Pattern of Social Aspirations* (Kent Archaeological Society, 75, Ashford, 1961).

—— *The Social Institutions of Lancashire: A Study of the Changing Pattern of Aspirations in Lancashire, 1480–1660* (Chetham Society, 3rd ser., 11, 1962).

KENT, J. R., 'Population Mobility and Alms: Poor Migrants in the Midlands during the Early Seventeenth Century', *Local Population Studies*, 27 (1981), 35–51.

—— *The English Village Constable 1580–1642: A Social and Administrative Study* (Oxford, 1986).

—— 'The Centre and the Localities: State Formation and Parish Government in England, *c.*1640–1740', *Historical Journal*, 38 (1995), 363–404.

—— 'The Rural "Middling Sort" in Early Modern England, *circa* 1640–1740: Some Economic, Political and Socio-Cultural Characteristics', *Rural History*, 10 (1999), 19–54.

—— and KING, S., 'Changing Patterns of Poor Relief in Some English Rural Parishes, *circa* 1650–1750', *Rural History*, 14 (2003), 119–56.

KERR, B., *Bound to the Soil: A Social History of Dorset, 1750–1918* (London, 1968).

KERRY, C., 'Anthony Bradshaw of Duffield and the Almshouses Founded by him at that Place', *The Reliquary*, 23 (1882–3), 137–40.

KESSELRING, K. J., *Mercy and Authority in the Tudor State* (Cambridge, 2003).

KING, P., 'Decision-Makers and Decision-Making in the English Criminal Law, 1750–1800', *Historical Journal*, 27 (1984), 25–58.

—— 'Gleaners, Farmers and the Failure of Legal Sanctions in England 1750–1850', *Past and Present*, 125 (1989), 116–50.

—— 'Customary Rights and Women's Earnings: The Importance of Gleaning to the Rural Labouring Poor, 1750–1850', *Economic History Review*, 2nd ser., 44 (1991), 461–76.

—— 'Legal Change, Customary Right, and Social Conflict in Late Eighteenth-Century England: The Origins of the Great Gleaning Case of 1788', *Law and History Review*, 10 (1992), 1–31.

—— 'Edward Thompson's Contribution to Eighteenth-Century Studies: The Patrician-Plebeian Model Re-examined', *Social History*, 21 (1996), 215–28.

—— 'Pauper Inventories and the Material Lives of the Poor in the Eighteenth and Early Nineteenth Centuries', in Hitchcock *et al.* (eds.), *Chronicling Poverty*, 155–91.

—— *Crime, Justice and Discretion in England, 1740–1820* (Oxford, 2000).

KING, S., 'Poor Relief and English Economic Development Reappraised', *Economic History Review*, 2nd ser., 50 (1997), 360–8.

—— 'Reconstructing Lives: The Poor, the Poor Law and Welfare in Calverly, 1650–1820', *Social History*, 22 (1997), 318–38.

—— *Poverty and Welfare in England, 1700–1850: A Regional Perspective* (Manchester, 2000).

KING, S. 'Reclothing the English Poor, 1750–1840', *Textile History*, 33 (2002), 37–47.

—— 'Making the Most of Opportunity: The Economy of Makeshifts in the Early Modern North', in King and Tomkins (eds.), *The Poor in England*, 228–57.

—— and TOMKINS, A. (eds.), *The Poor in England, 1700–1850: An Economy of Makeshifts* (Manchester, 2003).

KING, W. J., 'Punishment for Bastardy in Early Seventeenth-Century England', *Albion*, 10 (1978), 130–51.

KITCHING, C. J., '"Prayers Fit for the Time": Fasting and Prayer in Response to National Crisis in the Reign of Elizabeth I', in W. J. Sheils (ed.), *Monks, Hermits and the Ascetic Tradition* (Studies in Church History, 22, Oxford, 1985), 241–50.

KOPPERMAN, P. E., *Sir Robert Heath 1575–1649: Window on an Age* (Woodbridge, 1989).

KUMIN, B., *The Shaping of a Community: The Rise and Reformation of the English Parish, 1400–1560* (Aldershot, 1996).

KUSSMAUL, A., *Servants in Husbandry in Early Modern England* (Cambridge, 1981).

LANDAU, N., *The Justices of the Peace, 1679–1760* (Berkeley, 1984).

—— 'The Laws of Settlement and the Surveillance of Immigration in Eighteenth-Century Kent', *Continuity and Change*, 3 (1988), 391–420.

—— 'The Regulation of Immigration, Economic Structures and Definitions of the Poor in Eighteenth-Century England', *Historical Journal*, 33 (1990), 541–72.

—— 'Who Was Subjected to the Laws of Settlement? Procedure under the Settlement Laws in Eighteenth-Century England', *Agricultural History Review*, 43 (1995), 139–59.

LANE, J., *The Administration of an Eighteenth-Century Warwickshire Parish: Butlers Marston* (Dugdale Society Occasional Papers, 21, Stratford-upon-Avon, 1973).

—— 'Apprenticeship in Warwickshire Cotton Mills, 1790–1830', *Textile History*, 10 (1979), 161–74.

—— *Apprenticeship in England, 1600–1914* (London, 1996).

LANE, P., 'Work on the Margins: Poor Women and the Informal Economy of Eighteenth and Early Nineteenth-Century Leicestershire', *Midland History*, 22 (1997), 85–99.

LANGELÜDDECKE, H., '"Patchy and Spasmodic": The Response of Justices of the Peace to Charles I's Book of Orders', *English Historical Review*, 113 (1998), 1231–48.

LAQUEUR, T., 'Bodies, Death and Pauper Funerals', *Representations*, 1 (1983), 109–31.

LARMINIE, V. M., *The Godly Magistrate: The Private Philosophy and Public Life of Sir John Newdigate, 1571–1610* (Dugdale Society Occasional Papers, 28, Stratford-upon-Avon, 1982).

LASLETT, P., 'Mean Household Size in England Since the Sixteenth Century', in

P. Laslett and R. Wall (eds.), *Household and Family in Past Time* (Cambridge, 1972), 125–58.
—— *Family Life and Illicit Love in Earlier Generations: Essays in Historical Sociology* (Cambridge, 1977).
—— 'The Family and the Collectivity', *Sociology and Social Research*, 63 (1979), 432–42.
—— *The World We Have Lost Further Explored* (London, 1983).
—— 'Family, Kinship and Collectivity as Systems of Support in Pre-Industrial Europe: A Consideration of the "Nuclear-Hardship" Hypothesis', *Continuity and Change*, 3 (1988), 153–75.
LAWSON, P. G., 'Property Crime and Hard Times in England, 1559–1624', *Law and History Review*, 4 (1986), 95–127.
—— 'Lawless Juries? The Composition and Behaviour of Hertfordshire Juries, 1573–1624', in J. S. Cockburn and T. A. Green (eds.), *Twelve Good Men and True: The English Criminal Trial Jury, 1200–1800* (Princeton, 1988), 117–57.
LEADER, R. E., *History of the Company of Cutlers in Hallamshire in the County of York* (2 vols., Sheffield, 1906).
LEES, L. H., *The Solidarities of Strangers: The English Poor Laws and the People, 1700–1948* (Cambridge, 1998).
LEEUWEN, M. H. D. van, 'Logic of Charity: Poor Relief in Pre-Industrial Europe', *Journal of Interdisciplinary History*, 24 (1994), 589–613.
LEMIRE, B., 'Consumerism in Pre-Industrial and Early Industrial England: The Trade in Secondhand Clothes', *Journal of British Studies*, 27 (1988), 1–24.
—— 'Theft of Clothes and Popular Consumerism in Early Modern England', *Journal of Social History*, 24 (1990–1), 255–76.
—— 'Peddling Fashion: Salesmen, Pawnbrokers, Tailors, Thieves and the Second-Hand Clothes Trade in England, *c.*1700–1800', *Textile History*, 22 (1991), 67–82.
LENMAN, B., and PARKER, G., 'The State, the Community and the Criminal Law in Early Modern Europe', in Gatrell *et al.* (eds.), *Crime and the Law*, 11–48.
LEONARD, E. M., *The Early History of English Poor Relief* (Cambridge, 1900).
LESTHAEGHE, R., 'On the Social Control of Human Reproduction', *Population and Development Review*, 6 (1980), 527–48.
LEVINE, D. *Family Formation in an Age of Nascent Capitalism* (New York, 1977).
—— 'Production, Reproduction, and the Proletarian Family in England, 1500–1851', in D. Levine (ed.), *Proletarianization and Family History* (London, 1984), 87–127.
—— *Reproducing Families: The Political Economy of English Population History* (Cambridge, 1987).
—— and WRIGHTSON, K., *The Making of an Industrial Society: Whickham, 1560–1765* (Oxford, 1991).
LIPSON, E., *The Economic History of England*, vol. iii: *The Age of Mercantilism* (6th edn., London, 1956).
MCCAY, B. J., and ACHESON, J. M., 'Human Ecology of the Commons', in eid.

(eds.), *The Question of the Commons: The Culture and Ecology of Communal Resources* (Tucson, 1987), 1–34.

MACFARLANE, A., *Witchcraft in Tudor and Stuart England: A Regional and Comparative Study* (London, 1970).

—— *The Origins of English Individualism: The Family, Property and Social Transition* (Oxford, 1978).

MACFARLANE, S., 'Social Policy and the Poor in the Later Seventeenth Century', in A. L. Beier and R. Finlay (eds.), *The Making of the Metropolis: London, 1500–1700* (London and New York, 1986), 252–77.

MCINTOSH, M. K., *Autonomy and Community: The Royal Manor of Havering, 1200–1500* (Cambridge, 1986).

—— 'Local Responses to the Poor in Late Medieval and Tudor England', *Continuity and Change*, 3 (1988), 209–45.

—— *A Community Transformed: The Manor and Liberty of Havering, 1500–1620* (Cambridge, 1991).

—— *Controlling Misbehaviour in England, 1370–1600* (Cambridge, 1998).

—— 'Networks of Care in Elizabethan English Towns: The Example of Hadleigh, Suffolk', in Horden and Smith (eds.), *The Locus of Care*, 71–89.

MACKAY, L., 'Why They Stole: Women in the Old Bailey, 1779–1789', *Journal of Social History*, 32 (1999), 623–39.

MCNICOLL, G., 'Institutional Determinants of Fertility Change', *Population and Development Review*, 6 (1980), 441–62.

MCRAE, A., *God Speed the Plough: The Representation of Agrarian England, 1500–1660* (Cambridge, 1996).

MALCOLMSON, R. W., 'Ways of Getting a Living in Eighteenth-Century England', in R. E. Pahl (ed.), *On Work: Historical, Comparative and Theoretical Approaches* (Oxford, 1988), 48–60.

MANDLER, P., 'The Making of the New Poor Law *Redivivus*', *Past and Present*, 117 (1987), 131–57.

—— 'Poverty and Charity in the Nineteenth-Century Metropolis: An Introduction', in id. (ed.), *The Uses of Charity: The Poor on Relief in the Nineteenth-Century Metropolis* (Philadelphia, 1990), 1–37.

MANNING, B., *Village Revolts: Social Protest and Popular Disturbances in England, 1509–1640* (Oxford, 1988).

MARSHALL, D., *The English Poor in the Eighteenth Century: A Study in Social and Administrative History* (London, 1926).

MARSHALL, P., *The Face of the Pastoral Ministry in the East Riding, 1525–1595* (University of York Borthwick Paper 88, York, 1995).

—— *Beliefs and the Dead in Reformation England* (Oxford, 2002).

MARTIN, J. E., *Feudalism to Capitalism: Peasant and Landlord in English Agrarian Development* (London and New York, 1983).

MAYHEW, G., *Tudor Rye* (Falmer, 1987).

MENDELSON, S., and CRAWFORD, P., *Women in Early Modern England, 1550–1720* (Oxford, 1998).

Milward, R., *A Glossary of Household, Farming and Trade Terms from Probate Inventories* (Derbyshire Record Society, Occasional Paper 1, 3rd edn., Chesterfield, 1986).

Mitchison, R., *The Old Poor Law in Scotland: The Experience of Poverty, 1574–1845* (Edinburgh, 2000).

Moisa, M., 'Conviviality and Charity in Medieval and Early Modern England', *Past and Present*, 154 (1997), 221–34.

Morgan, G., and Rushton, P., 'The Magistrate, the Community and the Maintenance of an Orderly Society in Eighteenth-Century England', *Historical Research*, 76 (2003), 54–77.

Morgan, P., 'Of Worms and War: 1380–1558', in P. C. Jupp and C. Gittings (eds.), *Death in England: An Illustrated History* (Manchester, 1999), 119–46.

Morrill, J. S., *Cheshire 1630–1660: County Government and Society during the 'English Revolution'* (Oxford, 1974).

Muldrew, C., *The Economy of Obligation: The Culture of Credit and Social Relations in Early Modern England* (London and New York, 1998).

—— '"Hard Food for Midas": Cash and its Social Value in Early Modern England', *Past and Present*, 170 (2001), 78–120.

—— and King, S., 'Cash, Wages and the Economy of Makeshifts in England, 1650–1800', in P. Scholliers and L. Schwarz (eds.), *Experiencing Wages: Social and Cultural Aspects of Wage Forms in Europe Since 1500* (New York, 2003), 155–80.

Munby, L., *Hertfordshire Population Statistics, 1563–1801* (Hitchin, 1964).

—— (ed.), *The History of King's Langley* (London, 1963).

Nair, G., *Highley: The Development of a Community, 1550–1880* (Oxford, 1988).

Neeson, J. M., 'The Opponents of Enclosure in Eighteenth-Century Northamptonshire', *Past and Present*, 105 (1985), 114–40.

—— *Commoners: Common Right, Enclosure and Social Change in England, 1700–1820* (Cambridge, 1993).

Newall, F., 'Social Mobility in the Population of Aldenham, Hertfordshire, 1600–1800', in Jones-Baker (ed.), *Hertfordshire in History*, 109–26.

Newby, H., 'The Deferential Dialectic', *Comparative Studies in Society and History*, 17 (1975), 139–64.

Newman-Brown, W., 'The Receipt of Poor Relief and Family Situation: Aldenham, Hertfordshire 1630–90', in Smith (ed.), *Land, Kinship and Life-Cycle*, 405–22.

O'Hara, D., '"Ruled by My Friends": Aspects of Marriage in the Diocese of Canterbury', *Continuity and Change*, 6 (1991), 9–41.

Oldham, J. C., 'Underreported and Underrated: The Court of Common Pleas in the Eighteenth Century', in H. Hartog and W. E. Nelson (eds.), *Law as Culture and Culture as Law: Essays in Honor of John Philip Reid* (Madison, 2000), 119–46.

Ottaway, S. R., 'The Old Woman's Home in Eighteenth-Century England', in Botelho and Thane (eds.), *Women and Ageing*, 111–38.

—— 'Providing for the Elderly in Eighteenth-Century England', *Continuity and Change*, 13 (1998), 391–418.

OUTHWAITE, R. B., 'Dearth and Government Intervention in English Grain Markets, 1590–1700', *Economic History Review*, 2nd ser., 33 (1981), 389–406.

—— '"Objects of Charity": Petitions to the London Foundling Hospital, 1768–72', *Eighteenth-Century Studies*, 32 (1999), 497–510.

OXLEY, G. W., 'The Permanent Poor in South-West Lancashire under the Old Poor Law', in J. R. Harris (ed.), *Liverpool and Merseyside: Essays in the Economic History of the Port and its Hinterland* (London, 1969), 16–49.

—— *Poor Relief in England and Wales, 1601–1834* (Newton Abbot, 1974).

PALLISER, D. M., 'Dearth and Disease in Staffordshire, 1540–1670', in C. W. Chalklin and M. A. Havinden (eds.), *Rural Change and Urban Growth, 1500–1800* (London, 1974), 54–75.

PALMER, W. M., 'The Archdeaconry of Cambridge and Ely, 1599', *Transactions of the Cambridgeshire and Huntingdonshire Archaeological Society*, 6 (1947), 1–28.

PARSONS, M. A., 'Poor Relief in Troutbeck, 1640–1836', *Transactions of the Westmorland and Cumberland Antiquarian and Archaeological Society*, 95 (1995), 169–86.

PATERSON, T. G. F., 'A County Armagh Mendicant Badge Inscribed "Shankill Poor 1699"', *Ulster Journal of Archaeology*, 3rd ser., 10 (1947), 110–14.

PEARL, V., 'Puritans and Poor Relief: The London Workhouse, 1649–1660', in D. Pennington and K. Thomas (eds.), *Puritans and Revolutionaries: Essays in Seventeenth-Century History Presented to Christopher Hill* (Oxford, 1978), 206–32.

—— 'Social Policy in Early Modern London', in H. Lloyd-Jones, B. Worden, and V. Pearl (eds.), *History and Imagination: Essays in Honour of H. R. Trevor-Roper* (London, 1979), 115–31.

PELLING, M., *The Common Lot: Sickness, Medical Occupations and the Urban Poor in Early Modern England* (London and New York, 1998).

PETERSEN, C., *Bread and the British Economy, c.1770–1870*, ed. A. Jenkins (Aldershot, 1995).

PETTIT, P. A. J., *The Royal Forests of Northamptonshire: A Study in their Economy, 1558–1714* (Northamptonshire Record Society, 23, Gateshead, 1968).

PHILLIPS, S. K., 'Natives and Incomers: The Symbolism of Belonging in Muker Parish, North Yorkshire', repr. in M. Drake (ed.), *Time, Family and Community: Perspectives on Family and Community History* (Oxford, 1994), 225–39.

PHYTHIAN-ADAMS, C., *Desolation of a City: Coventry and the Urban Crisis of the Late Middle Ages* (Cambridge, 1979).

PINCHBECK, I., and HEWITT, M., *Children in English Society*, vol. i: *From Tudor Times to the Eighteenth Century* (London, 1969).

PORTER, S., 'Order and Disorder in the Early Modern Almshouse: The Charterhouse Example', *London Journal*, 23 (1998), 1–14.

POUND, J., 'An Elizabethan Census of the Poor: The Treatment of Vagrancy in Norwich, 1570–1580', *University of Birmingham Historical Journal*, 8 (1962), 135–61.

POUNDS, N. J. G., *A History of the English Parish: The Culture of Religion from Augustine to Victoria* (Cambridge, 2000).

Pressey, W. J., 'Essex Affairs Matrimonial (As Seen in the Archdeaconry Records)', *Essex Review*, 49 (1940), 84–93.

Quintrell, B. W., 'The Making of Charles I's Book of Orders', *English Historical Review*, 95 (1980), 553–72.

Raine, H., 'Christopher Fawcett against the Inmates', *Surrey Archaeological Collections*, 6 (1969), 79–85.

Randall, A., 'Peculiar Perquisites and Pernicious Practices: Embezzlement in the West of England Woollen Industry, *c.*1750–1840', *International Review of Social History*, 35 (1990), 193–219.

Reay, B. (ed.), *Popular Culture in Seventeenth-Century England* (London, 1985).

Richmond, C., 'Victorian Values in Fifteenth-Century England: The Ewelme Almshouse Statutes', in Horrox and Rees-Jones (eds.), *Pragmatic Utopias*, 224–41.

Rickman, L. L., 'Brief Studies in the Manorial and Economic History of Much Hadham', *East Hertfordshire Archaeological Society Transactions*, 9 (1928–33), 288–312.

Riis, T. (ed.), *Aspects of Poverty in Early Modern Europe* (Florence, 1981).

Roberts, M., '"Words They Are Women, and Deeds They Are Men": Images of Work and Gender in Early Modern England', in Charles and Duffin (eds.), *Women and Work*, 122–80.

—— 'Women and Work in Sixteenth-Century English Towns', in P. J. Corfield and Derek Keene (eds.), *Work in Towns, 850–1850* (Leicester, 1990), 86–102.

Roberts, P., 'Elizabethan Players and Minstrels and the Legislation of 1572 against Retainers and Vagabonds', in Fletcher and Roberts (eds.), *Religion, Culture and Society*, 29–55.

Roberts, S. K., *Recovery and Restoration in an English County: Devon Local Administration, 1646–1670* (Exeter, 1985).

Rollison, D., *The Local Origins of Modern Society: Gloucestershire, 1500–1800* (London, 1992).

—— 'Exploding England: The Dialectics of Mobility and Settlement in Early Modern England', *Social History*, 24 (1999), 1–16.

Rose, M. B., 'Social Policy and Business: Parish Apprenticeship and the Early Factory System, 1750–1834', *Business History*, 31 (1989), 5–32.

Rosenheim, J. M., 'Robert Doughty of Hanworth: A Restoration Magistrate', *Norfolk Archaeology*, 38 (1983), 296–312.

—— 'Documenting Authority: Texts and Magistracy in Restoration Society', *Albion*, 25 (1993), 591–604.

Ross, A. S. C., 'The Assize of Bread', *Economic History Review*, 2nd ser., 9 (1956), 332–42.

Rule, J., *Albion's People: English Society, 1714–1815* (London and New York, 1992).

Rushton, N. S., 'Monastic Charitable Provision in Tudor England: Quantifying and Qualifying Poor Relief in the Early Sixteenth Century', *Continuity and Change*, 16 (2001), 9–44.

Rushton, P., 'Lunatics and Idiots: Mental Disorder, the Community and the

Poor Law in North East England, 1600–1800', *Medical History*, 32 (1988), 34–50.

Rushton, P., 'The Poor Law, the Parish and the Community in North-East England, 1600–1800', *Northern History*, 25 (1989), 135–52.

Samaha, J., *Law and Order in Historical Perspective: The Case of Elizabethan Essex* (New York, 1974).

Schen, C. S., *Charity and Lay Piety in Reformation London, 1500–1620* (Aldershot, 2002).

Scott, J. C., *Domination and the Arts of Resistance: Hidden Transcripts* (New Haven, 1990).

Seaby, W. A., 'Ulster Beggars' Badges', *Ulster Journal of Archaeology*, 3rd ser., 23 (1970), 95–106.

Shammas, C., *The Pre-Industrial Consumer in England and America* (Oxford, 1990).

Sharp, B., *In Contempt of All Authority: Rural Artisans and Riot in the West of England, 1586–1660* (Berkeley, 1980).

Sharpe, J. A., 'Enforcing the Law in the Seventeenth-Century English Village', in Gatrell *et al.* (eds.), *Crime and the Law*, 97–119.

—— *Crime in Seventeenth-Century England: A County Study* (Cambridge, 1983).

—— 'Social Strain and Social Dislocation, 1585–1603', in J. Guy (ed.), *The Reign of Elizabeth I: Court and Culture in the Last Decade* (Cambridge, 1995), 192–211.

—— *Crime in Early Modern England, 1550–1750* (2nd edn., London and New York, 1999).

Sharpe, P., 'Literally Spinsters: A New Interpretation of Local Economy and Demography in Colyton in the Seventeenth and Eighteenth Centuries', *Economic History Review*, 2nd ser., 44 (1991), 46–65.

—— 'Poor Children as Apprentices in Colyton, 1598–1830', *Continuity and Change*, 6 (1991), 253–70.

—— '"The Bowels of Compation": A Labouring Family and the Law, *c.*1790–1834', in Hitchcock *et al.* (eds.), *Chronicling Poverty*, 87–108.

—— *Population and Society in an East Devon Parish: Reproducing Colyton, 1540–1840* (Exeter, 2002).

Shaw, S., *The History and Antiquities of Staffordshire* (2 vols., London, 1798–1801).

Shaw-Taylor, L., 'Labourers, Cows, Common Rights and Parliamentary Enclosure: The Evidence of Contemporary Comment, *c.*1760–1810', *Past and Present*, 171 (2001), 95–126.

—— 'The Management of Common Land in the Lowlands of Southern England *circa* 1500 to *circa* 1850', in M. de Moor, L. Shaw-Taylor, and P. Warde (eds.), *The Management of Common Land in North-West Europe, c.1500–1850* (Turnhout, 2002), 59–81.

Sheils, W. J., *The Puritans in the Diocese of Peterborough, 1558–1610* (Northampton Record Society, 30, 1979).

Simon, J., 'From Charity School to Workhouse in the 1720s: The SPCK and Mr Marriott's Solution', *History of Education*, 17 (1988), 113–29.

Slack, P., 'Poverty and Politics in Salisbury, 1597–1666', in Clark and Slack

(eds.), *Crisis and Order in English Towns, 1500–1700*, 164–203.
—— 'Books of Orders: The Making of English Social Policy, 1577–1631', *Transactions of the Royal Historical Society*, 5th ser., 30 (1980), 1–22.
—— 'Social Policy and the Constraints of Government, 1547–58', in J. Loach and R. Tittler (eds.), *The Mid-Tudor Polity, c.1540–1560* (London and New York, 1980), 94–115.
—— 'Vagrants and Vagrancy in England, 1598–1664', repr. in Clark and Souden (eds.), *Migration and Society*, 49–76.
—— *Poverty and Policy in Tudor and Stuart England* (London, 1988).
—— *The English Poor Law, 1531–1782* (London and New York, 1990).
—— 'Dearth and Social Policy in Early Modern England', *Social History of Medicine*, 5 (1992), 1–17.
—— *From Reformation to Improvement: Public Welfare in Early Modern England* (Oxford, 1999).
—— 'Great and Good Towns, 1540–1700', in P. Clark (ed.), *The Cambridge Urban History of Britain*, vol. ii: *1540–1840* (Cambridge, 2000), 347–76.
Smith, G. C., '"The Poor in Blindnes": Letters from Mildenhall, Wiltshire 1835–6', in Hitchcock *et al.* (eds.), *Chronicling Poverty*, 211–38.
Smith, R. M., 'Fertility, Economy and Household Formation in England over Three Centuries', *Population and Development Review*, 7 (1981), 595–622.
—— 'Some Issues Concerning Families and their Property in Rural England, 1250–1800', in id. (ed.), *Land, Kinship and Life-Cycle*, 68–85.
—— (ed.), *Land, Kinship and Life-Cycle* (Cambridge, 1984).
—— 'The Structured Dependence of the Elderly as a Recent Development: Some Sceptical Thoughts', *Ageing and Society*, 4 (1984), 409–28.
—— 'Marriage Processes in the English Past: Some Continuities', in Bonfield *et al.* (eds.), *The World We Have Gained*, 43–99.
—— 'Transfer Incomes, Risk and Security: The Roles of the Family and the Collectivity in Recent Theories of Fertility Change', in D. Coleman and R. Schofield (eds.), *The State of Population Theory: Forward from Malthus* (Oxford, 1986), 188–211.
—— 'Charity, Self-Interest and Welfare: Reflections from Demographic and Family History', in Daunton (ed.), *Charity, Self-Interest and Welfare*, 23–50.
—— 'Ageing and Well-Being in Early Modern England: Pension Trends and Gender Preferences under the English Old Poor Law, *c.*1650–1800', in P. Johnson and P. Thane (eds.), *Old Age from Antiquity to Post-Modernity* (London, 1998), 64–95.
Snell, K. D. M., *Annals of the Labouring Poor: Social Change and Agrarian England, 1660–1900* (Cambridge, 1984).
—— 'Pauper Settlement and the Right to Poor Relief in England and Wales', *Continuity and Change*, 6 (1991), 375–415.
—— 'Settlement, Poor Law and the Rural Historian: New Approaches and Opportunities', *Rural History*, 3 (1992), 145–72.
—— 'The Apprenticeship System in British History: The Fragmentation of a

Cultural Institution', *History of Education*, 25 (1996), 303–21.

SNELL, K. D. M., 'The Culture of Local Xenophobia', *Social History*, 28 (2003), 1–30.

SOKOLL, T., 'The Pauper Household Small and Simple? The Evidence from Listings and Inhabitants and Pauper Lists of Early Modern England Reassessed', *Ethnologia Europaea*, 17 (1987), 25–42.

—— *Household and Family among the Poor: The Case of Two Essex Communities in the Late Eighteenth and Early Nineteenth Centuries* (Bochum, 1993).

—— 'Old Age in Poverty: The Record of Essex Pauper Letters, 1780–1834', in Hitchcock *et al.* (eds.), *Chronicling Poverty*, 127–54.

SOLAR, P. M., 'Poor Relief and English Economic Development before the Industrial Revolution', *Economic History Review*, 2nd ser., 48 (1995), 1–22.

SOUDEN, D., 'Migrants and the Population Structure of Later Seventeenth-Century Provincial Cities and Market Towns', in P. Clark (ed.), *The Transformation of English Provincial Towns, 1600–1800* (London, 1984), 133–68.

—— 'Movers and Stayers in Family Reconstitution Populations', *Local Population Studies*, 33 (1984), 11–28.

—— '"East, West—Home's Best"? Regional Patterns of Migration in Early Modern England', in Clark and Souden (eds.), *Migration and Society*, 292–332.

SPAETH, D. A., *The Church in an Age of Danger: Parsons and Parishioners, 1660–1740* (Cambridge, 2000).

SPUFFORD, P., 'Population Movement in Seventeenth-Century England', *Local Population Studies*, 4 (1970), 41–50.

STAPLETON, B., 'Marriage, Migration and Mendicancy in a Pre-Industrial Community', in id. (ed.), *Conflict and Community*, 51–91.

—— (ed.), *Conflict and Community in Southern England: Essays in the History of Rural and Urban Labour from Medieval to Modern Times* (Gloucester, 1992).

—— 'Inherited Poverty and Life-Cycle Poverty: Odiham, Hampshire, 1650–1850', *Social History*, 18 (1993), 339–55.

STEEDMAN, C., 'Lord Mansfield's Women', *Past and Present*, 176 (2002), 105–43.

STONE, L., *Uncertain Unions: Marriage in England, 1660–1753* (Oxford, 1992).

STRONG, R., *Henry Prince of Wales and England's Lost Renaissance* (London, 1986).

STRUTT, F., and COX, C. J., 'Duffield Forest in the Sixteenth Century', *Derbyshire Archaeological Journal*, 25 (1903), 181–216.

STYLES, J., 'Embezzlement, Industry and the Law in England, 1500–1800', in M. Berg, P. Hudson, and M. Sonenscher (eds.), *Manufacture in Town and Countryside before the Factory* (Cambridge, 1983), 173–210.

STYLES, P., 'Introduction to the Warwickshire Hearth Tax Records', in *Warwick County Records: Hearth Tax Returns*, vol. i: *Hemlingford Hundred, Tamworth and Atherstone Divisions*, ed. M. Walker (Warwick, 1957), pp. xi–xcviii.

—— 'Sir Simon Archer: "A Lover of Antiquity and the Lovers Thereof"', repr. in id., *Studies in Seventeenth-Century West Midlands History*, 1–41.

—— 'A Census of a Warwickshire Village in 1698', repr. in id., *Studies in Seventeenth-Century West Midlands History*, 90–107.

—— 'The Evolution of the Law of Settlement', repr. in id., *Studies in Seventeenth-Century West Midlands History*, 175–204.
—— *Studies in Seventeenth-Century West Midlands History* (Kineton, 1978).
SUPPLE, B., *Commercial Crisis and Change in England, 1600–1642: A Study in the Instability of a Mercantile Economy* (Cambridge, 1959).
SWANSON, S. G., 'The Medieval Foundations of John Locke's Theory of Natural Rights: Rights of Subsistence and the Principle of Extreme Necessity', *History of Political Thought*, 18 (1997), 399–459.
TADMOR, N., *Family and Friends in Eighteenth-Century England: Household, Kinship and Patronage* (Cambridge, 2001).
TATE, W. E., *The Parish Chest: A Study of the Records of Parochial Administration in England* (3rd edn., Cambridge, 1960).
TAYLOR, J. S., 'The Impact of Pauper Settlement, 1691–1834', *Past and Present*, 73 (1976), 42–74.
—— 'A Different Kind of Speenhamland: Non-Resident Relief in the Industrial Revolution', *Journal of British Studies*, 30 (1991), 183–208.
—— 'Voices in the Crowd: The Kirkby Lonsdale Township Letters, 1809–36', in Hitchcock *et al.* (eds.), *Chronicling Poverty*, 109–26.
TENNANT, P., *Edgehill and Beyond: The People's War in the South Midlands, 1642–1645* (Gloucester, 1992).
—— *The Civil War in Stratford-upon-Avon: Conflict and Community in South Warwickshire, 1642–1646* (Gloucester, 1996).
THANE, P., 'Old People and their Families in the English Past', in Daunton (ed.), *Charity, Self-Interest and Welfare*, 113–38.
—— *Old Age in English History: Past Experiences, Present Issues* (Oxford, 2000).
THIRSK, J., 'Industries in the Countryside', in F. J. Fisher (ed.), *Essays in the Economic and Social History of Tudor and Stuart England in Honour of R. H. Tawney* (Cambridge, 1961), 70–88.
—— (ed.), *The Agrarian History of England and Wales*, vol. iv: *1500–1640* (Cambridge, 1967).
—— 'The Farming Regions of England', in id. (ed.), *Agrarian History*, iv. 1–112.
—— *Economic Policy and Projects: The Development of a Consumer Society in Early Modern England* (Oxford, 1978).
—— 'Projects for Gentlemen, Jobs for the Poor: Mutual Aid in the Vale of Tewkesbury, 1600–1630', repr. in id., *The Rural Economy of England: Collected Essays* (London, 1984), 287–307.
—— 'Introduction', in id. (ed.), *Chapters from the Agrarian History of England and Wales, 1500–1750*, vol. iii: *Agricultural Change, Policy and Practice 1500–1750* (Cambridge, 1990), 1–13.
THOMAS, E. G., 'The Old Poor Law and Maritime Apprenticeship', *Mariner's Mirror*, 63 (1977), 153–61.
—— 'The Old Poor Law and Medicine', *Medical History*, 24 (1980), 1–19.
—— 'Pauper Apprenticeship', *The Local Historian*, 14 (1981), 400–6.
THOMAS, K., 'The Social Origins of Hobbes' Political Thought', in K. C. Brown

(ed.), *Hobbes Studies* (Oxford, 1965), 185–236.

THOMAS, K., *Religion and the Decline of Magic: Studies in Popular Beliefs in Sixteenth- and Seventeenth-Century England* (London, 1971).

—— *Man and the Natural World: Changing Attitudes in England, 1500–1800* (London, 1983).

THOMPSON, E., 'Eighteenth-Century Crime, Popular Movements and Social Control', *Bulletin of the Society for the Study of Labour History*, 25 (1972), 9–11.

—— 'The Grid of Inheritance: A Comment', in J. Goody, J. Thirsk, and E. Thompson (eds.), *Family and Inheritance: Rural Society in Western Europe, 1200–1800* (Cambridge, 1976), 328–60.

—— *Customs in Common* (London, 1991).

THOMSON, D., '"I am not my father's keeper": Families and the Elderly in Nineteenth-Century England', *Law and History Review*, 2 (1984), 265–86.

—— 'The Welfare of the Elderly in the Past: A Family or Community Responsibility?', in M. Pelling and R. M. Smith (eds.), *Life, Death and the Elderly: Historical Perspectives* (London, 1991), 194–221.

TIERNEY, B., 'The Decretists and the "Deserving Poor"', *Comparative Studies in Society and History*, 1 (1958–9), 360–73.

—— *Medieval Poor Law: A Sketch of Canonical Theory and its Appreciation in England* (Berkeley, 1959).

TODD, M., *The Culture of Protestantism in Early Modern Scotland* (New Haven, 2002).

TOMKINS, A., 'Pawnbroking and the Survival Strategies of the Urban Poor in 1770s York', in King and Tomkins (eds.), *The Poor in England*, 166–98.

TREGELLES, J. A., *A History of Hoddesdon in the County of Hertfordshire* (Hertford, 1908).

TURNER, E., 'Ancient Parochial Account Book of Cowden', *Sussex Archaeological Collections*, 20 (1882), 91–119.

TURNER, M., and WOODWARD, D., 'Theft from the Common Man: The Loss of "Common" Use Rights in England', in T. Brotherstone and G. Pilling (eds.), *History, Economic History and Marxism: Essays in Memory of Tom Kemp* (London, 1996), 51–78.

UNDERDOWN, D., *Revel, Riot and Rebellion: Popular Politics and Culture in England, 1603–1660* (Oxford, 1985).

—— *Fire from Heaven: Life in an English Town in the Seventeenth Century* (London, 1992).

URWICK, W., *Nonconformity in Hertfordshire* (London, 1884).

VARDI, L., 'Construing the Harvest: Gleaners, Farmers and Officials in Early Modern France', *American Historical Review*, 98 (1993), 1424–47.

VENN, J., and VENN, J. A., *Alumni Cantabrigienses* (Cambridge, 1922).

VRIES, J. de, 'The Industrial Revolution and the Industrious Revolution', *Journal of Economic History*, 54 (1994), 249–70.

WALES, T., 'Poverty, Poor Relief and the Life-Cycle: Some Evidence from Seventeenth-Century Norfolk', in Smith (ed.), *Land, Kinship and Life-Cycle*, 351–404.

Walker, G., 'Women, Theft and the World of Stolen Goods', in J. Kermode and G. Walker (eds.), *Women, Crime and the Courts in Early Modern England* (London, 1994), 81–105.

Walter, J., 'Grain Riots and Popular Attitudes to the Law: Maldon and the Crisis of 1629', in Brewer and Styles (eds.), *An Ungovernable People*, 47–84.

—— 'A "Rising of the People"? The Oxfordshire Rising of 1596', *Past and Present*, 107 (1985), 90–143.

—— 'The Social Economy of Dearth in Early Modern England', in Walter and Schofield (eds.), *Famine, Disease and the Social Order*, 75–128.

—— *Understanding Popular Violence in the English Revolution: The Colchester Plunderers* (Cambridge, 1999).

—— 'Public Transcripts, Popular Agency and the Politics of Subsistence in Early Modern England', in Braddick and Walter (eds.), *Negotiating Power*, 123–48.

—— and Schofield, R. (eds.), *Famine, Disease and the Social Order in Early Modern Society* (Cambridge, 1989).

—— and Wrightson, K., 'Dearth and the Social Order in Early Modern England', *Past and Present*, 71 (1976), 22–44.

Wandel, L. P., 'Begging', in Hillerbrand (ed.), *Oxford Encyclopaedia of the Reformation*, i. 137.

—— 'Social Welfare', in Hillerbrand (ed.), *Oxford Encyclopaedia of the Reformation*, iv.77–83.

Watts, S. J., *From Border to Middle Shire: Northumberland, 1586–1625* (Leicester, 1975).

Webb, S., and Webb, B., *English Local Government*, vol. vii: *English Poor Law History Part I: The Old Poor Law* (London, 1927).

Webster, T., *Stephen Marshall and Finchingfield* (Studies in Essex History, 6, 1994).

Wells, R., *Wretched Faces: Famine in Wartime England, 1763–1803* (Gloucester, 1988).

Whetham, E. H., *The Agrarian History of England and Wales*, vol. viii: *1914–39* (Cambridge, 1978).

Whyman, S., *Sociability and Power in Late Stuart England: The Cultural Worlds of the Verneys, 1660–1720* (Oxford, 1999).

Wilkinson, B., '"The Poore of the Parish"', *The Local Historian*, 16 (1984–5), 31–3.

Williams, M., '"Our Poore People in Tumults Arose": Living in Poverty in Earls Colne, Essex, 1560–1640', *Rural History*, 13 (2002), 123–44.

Wilson, C., 'Poverty and Philanthropy in Early Modern England', in Riis (ed.), *Aspects of Poverty*, 253–79.

Winchester, A. J. L., 'Responses to the 1623 Famine in Two Lancashire Manors', *Local Population Studies*, 36 (1986), 47–8.

—— *The Harvest of the Hills: Rural Life in Northern England and the Scottish Borders, 1400–1700* (Edinburgh, 2000).

Wood, A., *The Politics of Social Conflict: The Peak Country, 1520–1770* (Cambridge, 1999).

Woodward, D., 'The Background to the Statute of Artificers: The Genesis of

Labour Policy, 1558–1563', *Economic History Review*, 2nd ser., 33 (1980), 32–44.
—— 'Straw, Bracken and the Wicklow Whale: The Exploitation of Natural Resources in England Since 1500', *Past and Present*, 159 (1998), 43–76.
—— 'Early Modern Servants in Husbandry Revisited', *Agricultural History Review*, 48 (1999), 141–50.
WOOLWRYCH, A., *Soldiers and Statesmen: The General Council of the Army and its Debates, 1647–1648* (Oxford, 1987).
WORDIE, J. R., 'The Chronology of English Enclosure, 1500–1914', *Economic History Review*, 2nd ser., 36 (1983), 483–505.
WRIGHT, S., '"Churmaids, Huswyfes and Hucksters": The Employment of Women in Tudor and Stuart Salisbury', in Charles and Duffin (eds.), *Women and Work*, 100–21.
WRIGHTSON, K., 'Two Concepts of Order: Justices, Constables and Jurymen in Seventeenth-Century England', in Brewer and Styles (eds.), *An Ungovernable People*, 21–46.
—— 'Alehouses, Order and Reformation in Rural England, 1590–1660', in E. and S. Yeo (eds.), *Popular Culture and Class Conflict, 1590–1914: Explorations in the History of Labour and Leisure* (Hassocks, 1981), 1–27.
—— 'Household and Kinship in Sixteenth-Century England', *History Workshop Journal*, 12 (1981), 151–8.
—— *English Society, 1580–1640* (London, 1982).
—— 'Kinship in an English Village: Terling, Essex 1500–1700', in Smith (ed.), *Land, Kinship and Life-Cycle*, 313–32.
—— 'The Social Order of Early Modern England: Three Approaches', in Bonfield *et al.* (eds.), *The World We Have Gained*, 177–202.
—— 'Estates, Degrees and Sorts: Changing Perceptions of Society in Tudor and Stuart England', in P. J. Corfield (ed.), *Language, History and Class* (Oxford, 1991), 30–52.
—— 'The Politics of the Parish in Early Modern England', in Griffiths *et al.* (eds.), *The Experience of Authority*, 10–46.
—— *Earthly Necessities: Economic Lives in Early Modern Britain* (New Haven, 2000).
—— and LEVINE, D., 'Death in Whickham', in Walter and Schofield (eds.), *Famine, Disease and the Social Order*, 129–65.
—— —— *Poverty and Piety in an English Village: Terling, 1525–1700* (1979; 2nd edn., Oxford, 1995).
WRIGLEY, E. A., 'Urban Growth and Agricultural Change: England and the Continent in the Early Modern Period', repr. in id., *People, Cities and Wealth: The Transformation of Traditional Society* (Oxford, 1987), 157–93.
—— DAVIES, R. S., OEPPEN, J. E., and SCHOFIELD, R. S., *English Population History from Family Reconstitution, 1580–1837* (Cambridge, 1997).
—— and SCHOFIELD, R. S., *The Population History of England, 1541–1871: A Reconstruction* (Cambridge, 1981).
YULE, G., 'James VI and I: Furnishing the Churches in his Two Kingdoms', in Fletcher and Roberts (eds.), *Religion, Culture and Society*, 182–208.

ZELL, M. *Industry in the Countryside: Wealden Society in the Sixteenth Century* (Cambridge, 1994).

—— '"Setting the Poor on Work": Walter Morrell and the New Draperies Project, *c.*1603–31', *Historical Journal*, 44 (2001), 651–75.

UNPUBLISHED DISSERTATIONS

AUFFENBERG, T. L., 'Organised English Benevolence: Charity Briefs, 1625–1705' (Ph.D. thesis, Vanderbilt University, 1973).

BARKER-READ, M., 'The Treatment of the Aged Poor in Five Selected West Kent Parishes from Settlement to Speenhamland, 1662–1797' (Ph.D. thesis, Open University, 1988).

BEIER, A. L., 'Studies in Poverty and Poor Relief in Warwickshire, 1540–1680' (Ph.D. thesis, Princeton University, 1969).

BYFORD, M., 'The Price of Protestantism. Assessing the Impact of Religious Change on Elizabethan Essex: The Cases of Heydon and Colchester, 1558–1594' (D.Phil. thesis, University of Oxford, 1988).

CALNAN, J. B., 'County Society and Local Government in the County of Hertford, *c.*1580–c.1630, with Special Reference to the Commission of the Peace' (Ph.D. diss., University of Cambridge, 1979).

DAVIE, N., 'Custom and Conflict in a Wealden Village: Pluckley, 1550–1700' (D.Phil. thesis, University of Oxford, 1988).

FITZGERALD, P., 'Poverty and Vagrancy in Early Modern Ireland' (Ph.D. thesis, Queen's University Belfast, 1994).

HILL, J., 'Poverty and Poor Relief in Shropshire, 1550–1685' (MA thesis, University of Liverpool, 1973).

HUGHES, A., 'Politics, Society and Civil War in Warwickshire, 1620–1650' (Ph.D. thesis, University of Liverpool, 1980).

INGRAM, J., 'The Conscience of the Community: Clerical Critiques of Wealth and Power in Early Modern England' (Ph.D. thesis, University of Warwick, in progress 2004).

LANGELÜDDECKE, H. A., 'Secular Policy Enforcement during the Personal Rule of Charles I: The Administrative Work of Parish Officers in the 1630s' (D.Phil. thesis, University of Oxford, 1995).

LAWSON, P. G., 'Crime and the Administration of Criminal Justice in Hertfordshire, *c.*1580–1625' (D.Phil. thesis, University of Oxford, 1982).

OTTAWAY, S., 'The "Decline of Life": Aspects of Ageing in Eighteenth-Century England' (Ph.D. thesis, Brown University, 1998).

TADMOR, N., 'Concepts of the Family in Five Eighteenth-Century Texts' (Ph.D. diss., University of Cambridge, 2002).

OTHER UNPUBLISHED PAPERS

INNES, J., 'Social Problems: Poverty and Marginality in Eighteenth-Century England' (1985).

INNES, J., 'Who Were the Casual Poor?' (2001).

Ulster Museum, Belfast [G. Ewing?], 'Book of Information about Badges Worn by the Poor'.

INDEX